Competition
and Cooperation

Competition and Cooperation

Conversations with
Nobelists about Economics
and Political Science

James E. Alt, Margaret Levi,
and Elinor Ostrom
editors

Russell Sage Foundation
New York

The Russell Sage Foundation

The Russell Sage Foundation, one of the oldest of America's general purpose foundations, was established in 1907 by Mrs. Margaret Olivia Sage for "the improvement of social and living conditions in the United States." The Foundation seeks to fulfill this mandate by fostering the development and dissemination of knowledge about the country's political, social, and economic problems. While the Foundation endeavors to assure the accuracy and objectivity of each book it publishes, the conclusions and interpretations in Russell Sage Foundation publications are those of the authors and not of the Foundation, its Trustees, or its staff. Publication by Russell Sage, therefore, does not imply Foundation endorsement.

Library of Congress Cataloging-in-Publication Data

Competition and cooperation : conversations with Nobelists about economics and political science / James Alt, Margaret Levi, and Elinor Ostrom, editors.
   p.   cm.
Includes bibliographical references and index.
ISBN 0-87154-010-X
1. Competition. 2. Cooperation. 3. Economics. 4. Political science.
I. Alt, James E.   II. Levi, Margaret.   III. Ostrom, Elinor.
HD41.C647 1999
330—dc21   99-25812
                                                                              CIP

The paper used in this publication meets the minimum requirements of American National Standard for Information Sciences—Permanence of Paper for Printed Library Materials. ANSI Z39.48-1992.

RUSSELL SAGE FOUNDATION
112 East 64th Street, New York, New York 10021
10 9 8 7 6 5 4 3 2 1

In memory of Mancur Olson and William Riker

The field of science, indeed the whole world of human society, is a cooperative one. At each moment we are competing, whether for academic honors or business success. But the background, and what makes society an engine of progress, is a whole set of successes and even failures from which we have learned.

—Kenneth Arrow, *Breit and Spencer* (1986, 57)

CONTENTS

Contributors   xi

Preface   xiii

Introduction
James E. Alt, Margaret Levi, and Elinor Ostrom   xv

Chapter 1   KENNETH J. ARROW
A Biographical Sketch   1

Kenneth J. Arrow, Welfare Aggregation, and Progress
in Political Theory
Norman Frohlich and Joe A. Oppenheimer   4

Chaos or Equilibrium in Preference and Belief Aggregation
Norman Schofield   33

Comments on the Commentaries
Kenneth J. Arrow   51

Chapter 2   HERBERT A. SIMON
A Biographical Sketch   57

Rationality Redux: Reflections on Herbert A. Simon's
Vision of Politics
Robert E. Goodin   60

Bounded Rationality, Political Institutions, and
the Analysis of Outcomes
Bryan D. Jones   85

The Potlatch Between Economics and Political Science
Herbert A. Simon   112

Chapter 3   JAMES M. BUCHANAN
A Biographical Sketch   120

Taking Constitutions Seriously: Buchanan's Challenge
to Twentieth-Century Political Science
Vincent Ostrom   123

James M. Buchanan's Contribution to Public Economics,
Political Philosophy, and Political Science
Thomas Schwartz   137

Response to Ostrom and Schwartz
James M. Buchanan   152

Chapter 4   GARY S. BECKER
A Biographical Sketch   155

Gary S. Becker: An Appreciation, Some Modest Proposals,
and a Disciplinary Self-Critique
Ronald Rogowski   158

Social Capital
Russell Hardin   170

Comments
Gary S. Becker   190

Chapter 5   DOUGLASS C. NORTH
A Biographical Sketch   197

Douglass C. North and Institutional Change in
Contemporary Developing Countries
Barbara Geddes   200

Ideology and Professionalism in International Institutions:
Insights from the Work of Douglass C. North
Robert O. Keohane   228

Response to Geddes and Keohane
Douglass C. North   247

Chapter 6   REINHARD SELTEN
A Biographical Sketch   253

Game Theory, Structure, and Sequence: The Contributions
of Reinhard Selten to Political Analysis
Kenneth A. Shepsle   256

Identity Choice Under Conditions of Uncertainty:
Reflections on Selten's Dualist Methodology
David D. Laitin   273

Response to Shepsle and Laitin
Reinhard Selten   303

Chapter 7   Discussion of Political Science and Economics:
Three Research Programs in Constitutional
Political Economy
James M. Buchanan   309

In Anticipation of the Marriage of Political
and Economic Theory
Douglass C. North   314

Comments on Remarks of James M. Buchanan
and Douglass C. North
Herbert A. Simon   318

Reflections on Political Science
Kenneth J. Arrow   321

Remarks on the Methodology of Science:
Discovery and Verification
Herbert A. Simon   326

Chapter 8   CONCLUSION
Margaret Levi, Elinor Ostrom, and James E. Alt   331

Index   339

CONTRIBUTORS

JAMES E. ALT is Frank G. Thomson Professor of Government and director of the Center for Basic Research in the Social Sciences at Harvard University.

MARGARET LEVI is professor of political science and Harry Bridges Chair in Labor Studies, University of Washington, Seattle. She-is also director of the University of Washington Center for Labor Studies.

ELINOR OSTROM is codirector of the Workshop in Political Theory and Policy Analysis and the Center for the Study of Institutions, Population, and Environmental Change at Indiana University, Bloomington. She is also Arthur F. Bentley Professor of Political Science.

KENNETH J. ARROW is Joan Kenney Professor of Economics Emeritus and professor of Operations Research Emeritus at Stanford University. He is also director of the Stanford Center on Conflict and Negotiation.

GARY S. BECKER is professor of economics and sociology at the University of Chicago.

JAMES M. BUCHANAN is advisory general director of the Center for Study of Public Choice at George Mason University.

NORMAN FROHLICH is professor of business administration at the University of Manitoba and senior researcher at the Manitoba Centre for Health Policy and Evaluation.

BARBARA GEDDES is associate professor of political science at the University of California at Los Angeles.

ROBERT E. GOODIN is professor of philosophy in the Research School of Social Sciences, Australian National University, Canberra, Australia.

RUSSELL HARDIN is professor of politics at New York University.

BRYAN D. JONES is professor of political science at the University of Washington, Seattle.

ROBERT O. KEOHANE is James B. Duke Professor of Political Science at Duke University.

DAVID D. LAITIN is William R. Kenan Jr. Professor of Political Science and director of the Center for the Study of Politics, History of Culture (Wilder House) at the University of Chicago.

DOUGLASS C. NORTH is Spencer T. Olin Professor in Arts and Sciences at Washington University.

JOE A. OPPENHEIMER is professor of political science and director of the Public Choice Center at the University of Maryland at College Park.

VINCENT OSTROM is codirector of the Workshop in Political Theory and Policy Analysis and Arthur F. Bentley Professor Emeritus of Political Science at Indiana University, Bloomington.

RONALD ROGOWSKI is professor and chair of political science at the University of California at Los Angeles.

NORMAN SCHOFIELD is William Taussig Professor and director of the Center in Political Economy at Washington University.

THOMAS SCHWARTZ is professor of political science at the University of California at Los Angeles.

REINHARD SELTEN is professor emeritus of economics at the University of Bonn, Germany.

KENNETH A. SHEPSLE is George Dickson Markham Professor of Government at Harvard University.

HERBERT A. SIMON is Richard King Mellon University Professor of Computer Science and Psychology at Carnegie Mellon University.

PREFACE

The road to this volume began when Elinor Ostrom, then the newly chosen president-elect of the American Political Science Association, invited James Alt and Margaret Levi to become co-chairs of the 1997 annual meeting program. All three of us shared an interest in the study of political institutions and in the political-economic approach to that study often referred to as "new institutionalism." We hoped to use some of the meeting to start a serious conversation between economists and political scientists about the study of institutions. But which economists to invite? An obvious strategy was to let the field of economics make its own choice of those who had done foundational work, so we turned to the list of those who had won the Nobel Prize and selected those we believed have had the greatest influence on our own work.

We chose a format that in the end proved highly productive: we invited two political scientists to write commentaries on ways in which political science has been influenced by the work of each Nobelist, circulated the papers to each Nobelist in advance, and invited each to prepare a response. Commentaries and responses were presented at a series of sessions, three at the American Political Science Association meetings in Washington, D.C., in September 1997 and three at the Russell Sage Foundation in November 1997. The commentaries and responses constitute the major part of this volume. We also recorded audience discussions that followed the presentations. In April 1998 we held one additional session at Carnegie-Mellon University, where we gained from the insights of William Keech, Jack Knight, and Gary Miller on the initial draft of the manuscript. In addition, James Buchanan and Douglass North gave public lectures on the relationship between economics and political science to a plenary session of the American Political Science Association annual meeting. We drew on these further sources in preparing the introductory and concluding parts of this volume.

We heartily thank both the American Political Science Association and the Russell Sage Foundation for their financial support of this project. We also want to acknowledge the Department of Social and Decision Sciences at Carnegie-Mellon University for its additional administrative and financial contributions. James March generously agreed to stand in for Herb Simon as a commentator in Washington, D.C., and his thoughts and remarks were very much appreciated. We thank Bill Keech for graciously agreeing to host the session in Pittsburgh. We also express our gratitude to members of the staff of the American Political Science Association, particularly Catherine Rudder and Jennifer Richards, for facilitating the sessions held at the Washington meetings; to Sharon Maccini of the Russell Sage Foundation, for undertaking the necessary arrangements for the New York sessions; and to Marian Schwarzenbach and Carole Davison, staff in the University of Washington

Department of Political Science, for helping administer the Russell Sage Foundation grant. Sara Colburn of the Workshop in Political Theory and Policy Analysis of Indiana University deserves special appreciation for her herculean transcriptions of the panel discussions. We are also especially grateful to Matt Moe and Theresa Buckley of the University of Washington for their considerable efforts in preparing the papers for publication. All three of our respective universities supported this effort at various junctures.

INTRODUCTION

James E. Alt, Margaret Levi, and Elinor Ostrom

When we originally envisaged this series of conversations—asking Nobelists to talk about what they thought they had contributed to political science, and political scientists to talk about what they thought those influences were—we hardly expected that we would without much intervention produce what has proven to be a remarkably well integrated and consistent set of contributions. Of course, our contributors are not all saying the same thing by any means, but there are clear commonalties in their thoughts, and it is easy to draw out linkages among them. One theme, often unspoken but present nevertheless, pervades their remarks: a chafing dissatisfaction with the standard neoclassical paradigm of economic analysis, particularly as a foundation for positive analysis. Although dissatisfaction with neoclassical analysis is not new (see, for example, Furubotn and Richter 1994, 11), it surprised us a little to hear it expressed with such regularity by so many who had received economics' highest award for their contributions to the field!

We have to be careful not to overstate this. There is no dissatisfaction evident with the fundamental postulate of neoclassical economics—that the unit of analysis on which all else is built is the individual choice. Indeed, it was our own shared interest in the questions of how institutions shape and yet are shaped by individual choices, beliefs, and strategies that led us to organize this series of conversations on taking economics seriously. Not only is the neoclassical paradigm worth thinking about because it has worked well in many contexts, but any one of the Nobelists might view his contributions through a lens different from the one that gives unity to our purposes here. Nevertheless, what we are looking at in these conversations are the ways in which the neoclassical paradigm, already familiar forty or fifty years ago, is being not just picked at but massively reworked by those dissatisfied with its assumptions as a basis for analyzing human behavior.

There are various ways to characterize the assumptions of the neoclassical model (see, for example, Eggertsson 1990, 3–25). Individuals make welfare-maximizing choices. Four key assumptions underlie all individual choices: no externalities, no scale economies, no decision costs (that is, full information and costless information and exchange), and preferences that are fixed and not interdependent among individuals. Each part of this structure comes under scrutiny in one or another of the essays that follow. We offer a sketch of where the contribution of each Nobelist starts and how they fit together; deliberately limited and kept simple (though we hope the outcome of our chopping and squeezing intellectual careers under headings is not too Procrustean!), the sketches foreshadow the directions we discuss further in the conclusion.

One disclaimer is in order. This volume is not intended to be a full review of the impact of economics on political science. For a superb recent example of such a review, the interested reader should see Miller (1997). If it were such a review, we would certainly have commissioned papers by Anthony Downs and the late Mancur Olson. What follows, consequently, has less to say about the economic analysis of party competition, voting, and collective action. Nor does this collection pretend to be an exhaustive list of Nobelist economists who have given something to the study of politics. Coase (1988) is already available as an example of a paper similar in spirit to the essay in this volume, representing what might have been included had resources and time been more plentiful.

Let us turn to the many contributions that we do include. In his opening remarks at one of the panels in Washington, D.C., Bob Goodin playfully commented that

> one of the amusing payoffs of being roped into this project is discovering what it takes to win a Nobel. The first thing it seems to take is to have an idea—usually one is quite sufficient—that has really wide ramifications and can be summarized in two, at most three, words. . . . The second thing . . . is a CV that would choke a horse.

Clearly, in pulling together the commentaries, comments on the commentators, and discussions, the editors discovered right away that all the Nobelists have more than one idea. Nevertheless, if we had to choose a summary phrase for the origins of the political science legacy of each Nobelist, we would assign Arrow "majority cycles," Becker "interest groups," Buchanan "externalities," North "transaction costs," Selten "backward induction," and Simon "bounded rationality." We have to qualify these assignments immediately: Simon was not an economist at all; Selten regards himself as a dualist with a behavioral contribution as large or larger than the one we mention; Buchanan also studied constitutions and ethics; and every one of the Nobelists made other contributions that have resonated in political science. But these labels gives us a place to start, a sample of the sort of contributions more fully discussed in this volume.

Several of these critiques of neoclassicism focus on the assumption that there are no decision costs. Arrow's "majority cycles," for example—under which individually transitive preferences cannot be guaranteed to aggregate up to a transitive ordering under majority rule—is at its narrowest a demonstration of the logical inconsistency of several desirable properties of a method of aggregating individual preferences. Within economics, this renders indeterminate any "social welfare function" used to evaluate the output of the economy. Within political science, however, it produced two research programs, both theoretical and empirical: one conceptualizes, describes, and measures the instability of majoritarian collective choices; the other shows how and to what extent different institutional arrangements constrain majoritarian instability and has produced a whole literature of ways to think about how cycling and other problems can be overcome in order to get to an efficient frontier when production requires social aggregation of preferences. With the possibility of endless cycling, of course, decision costs are not only positive but possibly infinite—in which case, no production at all might take place!

Buchanan's contribution is grounded in the consequences of "externalities" and decision costs. In a nutshell, he transferred the concept of gains derived from mutual exchange between individuals from the exclusive realm of economic markets to the realm of political decisionmaking. Thus, although only individuals choose, economics cannot be studied properly outside of politics. Partly this is because economics is about a game played within rules, and the choices between different rules of the game cannot be ignored. But even within a given set of rules, there are decisions about (minimally) taxes and public goods that need to be taken collectively. These decisions are made by coalitions and impose externalities on those outside the coalitions in ways that depend on the costs of decision and the size of the coalitions that form. An enduring legacy of Buchanan's work is the question of whether the rent-seeking and externalities that arise under supermajority procedures are actually better for us than the ones that arise under majoritarian procedures. Again, however, the central point is to see costly political decisions as central even to economic processes.

North's work, for our purposes here, delivers a closely related message but deals more with interpersonal interactions. His vision of the "cost of transacting" covered the difficulties and costs buyers face in observing product quality (and the costs to sellers of assuring buyers about quality), in monitoring and enforcing agreements that involve subsequent performance, and even in discerning and preparing for opportunistic behavior when contracting. From there it was a short step to beginning a theoretical program of reasoning about how institutions evolve to try to solve these costly transaction problems so that the aggregate value or volume of transactions and output can nevertheless grow. As an economic historian concerned with long-term secular change, North's research program puts transaction costs, the new economic institutionalism, and the dimension of time in the service of understanding economic performance and change. Political science applications of transaction cost analysis and the new institutionalism are growing more common, especially in the study of the design and organization of institutions like legislatures and bureaucracy and of arrangements that support political as well as economic development.

The program Herbert Simon recommends was the study of "bounded rationality" or the impact of cognitive capacity limits on rational individual choices. In his original formulation of "satisficing" (Simon 1957), actors are content with a certain level of achievement and indifferent to gains beyond that. That is, they do not attempt to optimize beyond a personal level of satisfaction. Simon's view is that we can't do economics until we have a full-blown theory of cognition to augment it, as well as enough empirical work to ground the definition of rationality in actual behavior. A minimalist response (the position of a skeptical scientist or an economist less patient than Simon) is to suppose that information is costly rather than free and universally available. Many economic and political models (including some very interesting work of Arrow's on the role and limits of organization) do just this. However, Simon's argument also depends on the characteristics of human beings as decisionmakers (our hard wiring) and of the processes under which we make our decisions.

Reinhard Selten notes that his own experimental, behavioral program is closely aligned to Simon's. But his "backward induction"—a method of analyzing how individuals form multiperiod strategies in iterated games that leads directly to the equilibrium concept of subgame perfection—was instrumental in moving formal analysis in politics from cooperative to noncooperative game theory and in bringing to the forefront the analysis of games involving reputation and incomplete information. An early application in economics was a model of predatory pricing (Kreps and Wilson 1982) subsequently extended to phenomena in international relations (Alt, Calvert, and Humes 1988). Subgame perfection, interestingly, requires players to consider counterfactuals but ignore those that are inconsistent with rational behavior by other players. The introduction of reasoning by players uncertain of each other's rationality, in contrast, has been beneficial in explaining "excessively" cooperative behavior in contribution games. Thus, the broader literature itself reflects the contrasts in Selten's own work between the abstract standard of hyperrationality represented by subgame perfection and the limited cognitive capacity evident in his behavioral models.

Even Gary Becker's work on competition between interest groups evinces the unease about the neoclassical paradigm we heard in all the Nobelists' contributions. Long interested in the study of political competition, Becker describes how the government is a major factor, one that has enormous influence on what happens in the economy, and indeed in social life. He models firms as interest groups that compete politically to create favorable market structures and conditions like patterns of ownership, regulation, and taxes. The economic basis of interest-group (firm) competition is the elasticity of demand for its product and the deadweight loss caused by the political benefits secured. Although his work says little explicitly about the political supply side, Becker raises provocative questions about how much actually is explained by differences among institutions across polities. Like many political scientists, Becker finds that interest-group competition explains a lot in areas of economic organization and public policy, including the selection of industries in which to impose tariffs, securities and banking regulation and deregulation, national airlines, and the environmental movement. Simply absent in the neoclassical paradigm, his analysis is important in giving government its due as an influence on outcomes.

There are several common elements in even this brief description of the Nobelists' legacies in political science. First, the neoclassical paradigm is too narrow to be a satisfactory model for behavior, whatever its status as a normative standard. This is obvious in the work of Simon and equally clear in Selten's (1994, 42–43) comment that although "people do have evaluative feelings about hedonic experiences . . . social norms, moral constraints, and unreflected routines are of similar importance." In conversations and discussions, Buchanan refers to the importance of the work ethic, Becker discusses endogenous preferences, North argues for the importance of appreciating cognitive complexity, and Arrow is concerned with whether we can explain how markets aggregate information into equilibria.

Second, the restrictiveness of the neoclassical paradigm produces widespread recognition of the importance of institutions. Institutions help individuals with fundamental problems of exchange, collective choice, and collective action. If nothing were ever chosen by vote, there would be no problem of cyclical instability. If there were no social dilemmas, we would have less need to deal with problems of communication, cooperation, and coordination. If information were freely available, specialization and delegation would not produce agency costs. If there were no nonsimultaneous exchange, ex post opportunism would not be a concern. However, all these problems exist, and institutions ubiquitously deal with the trade-offs they create, providing opportunities for beneficial transactions that would not take place in the absence of the institutions.

Third, many of the research agendas begun by the Nobelists call out for extensive empirical work. Consider Buchanan's externalities. There's clearly a need for an empirical program to determine whether supermajorities actually increase or decrease externalities and rent-seeking. Is it deadweight loss that leads to lobbying, fear of opportunistic behavior by others, or both? Does the structure of the political supply side really not create incentives for strategic behavior by interest groups, as Becker alleges? North has measured transaction costs (Wallis and North 1995), but in the field at large there's scarcely agreement about what constitutes a transaction cost, the size of the aggregate volume of transaction costs, and the number of forgone contracts. There could be an empirical program on the ability of institutions of different sorts (party systems, legislative organizations) to overcome cycling problems. There is no shortage of good projects to be carried out!

Finally, we are struck by the importance of cognitive science in these contributions. With the exception only of Buchanan, all the Nobelists are questioning some aspect of the rationality assumption. They are in fact carrying out the research program for which Simon won the Nobel, as is evident in North's investigation of "mental models" as a means to get at a theory of ideology and culture; Becker's new work on social capital as a means of bringing norms, trust, and the like into the neoclassical model; Arrow's long-term interest in incomplete and asymmetric information; and Selten's experimental research on the limits of rationality. This orientation may be partly attributable to the fact that the empirical program that has proceeded from Simon's work is much more advanced than anything from, say, Buchanan's, or indeed from North's work. There is nothing, for instance, that comes close to the kind of clear and convincing evidence that Kahneman (1994) presents from his experiments that people frequently use what Bryan Jones calls nonproportionate rules in processing information. Although there are many reasons for this move toward cognitive science, we take some satisfaction in seeing economists return to the agenda of a political scientist. Once joined at the hip as political economy, then separated by huge differences in subject matter and methodology, this volume suggests a new convergence of theme and approach. It demonstrates that our field, political science, is not just a learner or importer of the ideas of others; its practitioners are actively contributing to the modification of the neoclassical framework and to a new political economy.

REFERENCES

Alt, James E., Randall Calvert, and Brian Humes. 1988. "Reputation and Hegemonic Stability: A Game-Theoretic Analysis." *American Political Science Review* 82(2): 445–66.

Coase, Ronald. 1988. "The Nature of the Firm: Influence." *Journal of Law, Economics, and Organization* 4(1): 33–47.

Eggertsson, Thrainn. 1990. *Economic Behavior and Institutions.* New York: Cambridge University Press.

Furubotn, Eirik, and Rudolf Richter. 1994. "The New Institutional Economics: Bounded Rationality and the Analysis of State and Society." *Journal of Institutional and Theoretical Economics* 150(1): 11–17.

Kahneman, Daniel. 1994. "New Challenges to the Rationality Assumption." *Journal of Institutional and Theoretical Economics* 150(1): 18–36.

Kreps, David, and Robert Wilson. 1982. "Reputation and Imperfect Information." *Journal of Economic Theory* 27: 253–79.

Miller, Gary. 1997. "The Impact of Economics on Contemporary Political Science." *Journal of Economic Literature* 35(3): 1173–1204.

Selten, Reinhard. 1994. "Comment." *Journal of Institutional and Theoretical Economics* 150(1): 42–44.

Simon, Herbert. 1957. *Models of Man.* New York: Wiley.

Wallis, John Joseph, and Douglass C. North. 1995. "Measuring the Transaction Sector is the American Economy, 1870–1970." In *The Legacy of Ronald Coase in Economic Analysis,* edited by Steven G. Medema. (Aldershot, U.K.: Elgar) vol. 1, 378–444.

Chapter 1

KENNETH J. ARROW
A Biographical Sketch

Kenneth J. Arrow, Joan Kenney Professor of Economics and Professor of Operations Research at Stanford University, emeritus since 1991, is a native of New York, educated at City College. Upon graduation from there, he failed to find employment as a high school teacher and instead went on to graduate school at Columbia, where he studied under, among others, Harold Hotelling and Abraham Wald. Arrow has served on the faculties of Chicago and Harvard (and, as a visitor, at MIT and Cambridge) as well as Stanford. He holds honorary doctorates from at least fifteen universities in seven countries. He is a member of many academic societies, including the American Academy of Arts and Sciences and the American Economic Association, of which he was president in 1973. He has been a fellow of All Souls and of the Center for Advanced Study in the Behavioral Sciences, as well as a Guggenheim Fellow. He has won both the John Bates Clark Medal and the von Neumann Prize—in addition to, of course, the Nobel Prize in Economic Science in 1972.

Arrow is the author of many books and articles, including *Studies in the Mathematical Theory of Inventory and Production* (1958), *Essays in the Theory of Risk-Bearing* (1971), *The Limits of Organization* (1974), and the classic *Social Choice and Individual Values* (1951), which was originally his dissertation at Columbia. Arrow himself recalls (Breit and Spencer 1986) that economic theory was not well regarded by the faculty when he was a student, so he learned it mostly by reading. His interest in what became social choice theory was originally sparked by the question of how firms could choose among several alternative investment policies. After some false starts, his flagging interest was rekindled when he was asked how one could justify the treatment by international relations game theorists of nations as rational actors when nations are aggregations of individuals with different preference orderings. Arrow recognized that there was no assurance that aggregating the preferences of individuals by majority rule would produce a "rational actor" state. He demonstrated the minimal conditions under which individual rationality and consistency do not ensure consistent social choices.

More generally, he proved that four innocuous-seeming yet desirable properties were logically inconsistent for any social choice preference aggregation mechanism, including markets as well as majority rule. Within economics, this proof renders indeterminate any "social welfare function" used to evaluate the output of the economy. Within political science, it produced two research programs, both theoretical and empirical. One of these conceptualized, described, and measured the instability of majoritarian collective choices (see Miller 1997). The other showed how and to what extent different institutional arrangements constrain majoritarian instability, providing ways in which cycling and other problems can be overcome in order to arrive at an efficient frontier when production requires social aggregation of preferences.

Arrow's careful delineation of the meaning of preferences and his identification of desiderata for social welfare functions were among the significant contributions of a program seeking methods to aggregate citizen preferences into outcomes with normatively desirable properties. Arrow subsequently included principles of distributive justice in his analysis of social welfare functions (or constitutions, as he has come to call them). In this way, Arrow's work intersects with the agenda of modern political science and traditional political philosophy at a number of crucial junctures, much as Buchanan's work did, as Ostrom argues (this volume), though in a very different way.

Frohlich and Oppenheimer consider the implications for this part of Arrow's work—in particular, for his attempt to create a "universal set," a homogeneous preference structure for all individuals—of modern research in cognitive psychology that indicates that preferences over outcomes are determined by framing, or cues. They extend the discussion to Arrow's treatment of distributive justice and justifiable social choice mechanisms, and they consider the implications for evaluating political institutions by the moral weight of the preferences forming them.

Arrow's other contributions are too numerous to describe in any detail. Economists certainly attach great importance to his proof of the conditions under which the equations defining a general equilibrium have a solution. In a general equilibrium approach to an economy, the demand for one product depends on the prices of all products, just as the supply of a product depends on the prices of all commodities. But under what conditions will a set of prices prevail, and how does one find them? This problem had been mathematically intractable before Arrow (jointly with Gerard Debreu) offered a general answer.

Schofield notes that while some recent important theorems of social mathematics emphasize equilibrium, like Arrow's result for competitive economies, others suggest chaos, like Arrow's theorem on the inconsistency of majority rule. Schofield discusses the importance of this difference and argues that the existence of an equilibrium does not guarantee avoidance of chaos in the dynamic process by which that equilibrium is reached. He provides examples from cooperative game theory. Furthermore, he claims that even when optima in preferences exist, it is far more difficult to postulate conditions under which a "belief equilibrium" must exist; he pursues this notion to the conclusion that if activity, whether in the market or in the polity, is generated by groups, one would not expect to observe rule-governed or gradientlike behavior, at least *among* as opposed to *within* groups.

Finally, Arrow's early development of the concept of contingent contracts, as well as his many contributions to the economics of uncertainty and (especially asymmetric) information, have also been of great relevance to subsequent political and institutional analysis. Contingent contracts provide delivery of goods or money contingent on any possible state of the world; put another way, they offer insurance against any possible risk. Arrow cautions that often markets are "missing." Markets for trading goods contingent on all states of the world would be intractably numerous, and therefore some combination of financial assets and available spot markets provides the best available allocation of risk. His studies of medical insurance stress the difficulty created by the asymmetry of information between doctor and patient. Arrow generalized this in early treatments of what later became familiar theoretical concepts like moral hazard and incentive incompatibility.

REFERENCES

Arrow, Kenneth. 1951. *Social Choice and Individual Values.* New York: Wiley.

————. 1971. *Essays in the Theory of Risk-Bearing.* Chicago: Markham.

————. 1974. *The Limits of Organization.* New York: Norton.

Arrow, Kenneth, Samuel Karlin, and Herbert Scarf. 1958. *Studies in the Mathematical Theory of Inventory and Production.* Stanford, Calif.: Stanford University Press.

Breit, William, and Roger Spencer (eds.). 1986. *Lives of the Laureates: Seven Nobel Economists.* Cambridge, Mass.: MIT Press.

Miller, Gary. 1997. "The Impact of Economics on Contemporary Political Science." *Journal of Economic Literature* 35(3): 1173–1204.

KENNETH J. ARROW, WELFARE AGGREGATION, AND PROGRESS IN POLITICAL THEORY

Norman Frohlich and Joe A. Oppenheimer

*S*ocial Choice and Individual Values (1951/1963a; hereafter cited as *SCIV*) constitutes a fundamental contribution to the social sciences. It is strategically located at the intersection of economics, politics, and philosophy. Through an abstract and formal model, Arrow identifies basic problems in aggregating individual preferences. He shows that any function, algorithm, or constitution used to aggregate individual preferences to achieve a sensible and democratic group choice runs into immutable difficulties.[1] The problems assume major normative importance when one interprets the exercise, more generally, as an attempt to define a method for arriving at group welfare by aggregating the welfares of the individuals.

Although Arrow's work is often interpreted somewhat narrowly as dealing with the construction of democratic institutions to yield voting outcomes, most scholars believe that its scope is much broader. Here we focus on some implications of his work for the general justification of democratic political institutions, for policy evaluation, and for our understanding of social welfare and justice. These are, we believe, pivotal elements in Arrow's work that parallel the traditional concerns of political philosophy.

Arrow is interested in a mechanism (or at least some possible attributes of such a mechanism) for aggregating the desires (or welfares) of citizens into an outcome with desirable normative properties. The centrality of this to democratic theory should be obvious. The link between democratic theory and individual welfare is individual choice. If this choice is fixed by preferences in some stable fashion, as presumed in traditional economics, all is well and good. Arrow introduced the concept, however, of what he called the "universal set": the set of all possible alternatives, including hypothetical ones, that a person might face. In doing so, he implicitly raised the problems of the nature of preferences and their possible instability. To the degree that individual preferences are themselves unstable or ill defined, problems for democratic theory abound. With instability, the link between welfare and individual choice is broken, and with that rupture, the justifiability of the link between individual choice and social welfare is raised anew. Issues such as these lie at the heart of Arrow's concerns over the last thirty-five years. In addressing these issues, our discussion pays particular attention to a few problems at the heart of classical political philosophy: the fundamental nature of individual values, their relationship to individual choice, and the relationship between those choices and group welfare.

In 1951, when Kenneth Arrow first published *SCIV*, the discipline of political science was on a path headed toward an inductively based social science, a path with deep roots in a humanist-legalist tradition.[2] Although the normative theory of democracy was a continuation of the debate initiated by Plato in his discourses on the nature of the good state, theorists had come to realize that knowledge about institutions needed to be integrated with an understanding of political behavior to explain political choices. The methodology of the field was consistent with those antecedents and was rarely rigorous in the scientific sense. Explanation was largely the construction of convincing verbal arguments based on relatively unstructured observations.

Social Choice and Individual Values was not of the same genre. The methodology was formal and deductive and, as such, was a close cousin to mathematics. In an unnoticed irony, the demonstration of a general impossibility theorem was to help establish the possibility of formal arguments about political phenomena. Along with two other works in economics, John von Neumann and Oskar Morgenstern's *Theory of Games and Economic Behavior* (1944) and Duncan Black's *The Theory of Committees and Elections* (1958), *SCIV* demonstrated the applicability of formalized theoretical argument to the understanding of a broad range of political phenomena. In so doing, the three works set the stage for a partial reintegration of political science and economics by showing that one paradigm could perform yeoman service in two disciplines.

The three books addressed different phenomena but shared a number of characteristics. Each was methodologically individualistic: the starting point was the individual. Each posited the same behavioral assumption regarding individual choice: ordinal rationality.[3] And each used rigorous deduction from these and other contextual premises to derive conclusions about what was possible, desirable, or expectable with regard to group decisions.

As might be expected, political scientists did not immediately embrace this formal approach. Some of the reasons for their reluctance can be found in a later work of Arrow's, *The Limits of Organization* (1974, 39–40), in which he notes that "a . . . key characteristic of information costs is that they are in part capital costs; more specifically, they typically represent an irreversible investment. . . . [C]odes . . . have to be learned in order to receive messages; the technical vocabulary of any science is a case in point." At the time, only a handful of political scientists were ready to make the capital investments necessary to understand the technical vocabulary of the arguments.

Arrow, von Neumann and Morgenstern, and Black had developed theories. Fortunately, theories do not behave like money. According to Gresham's Law, bad money drives out good, but good theories drive out bad ones. Donald Green and Ian Shapiro (1994, 3), who take quite a different position on which theories are good and which are bad, note that as late as 1957 there were virtually no articles in the *American Political Science Review* relying on formalized theories posited on rational choice. By 1994 about 45 percent of all articles in that journal used this approach.

What accounted for the conversion? Why did a substantial subset of political scientists ultimately find themselves attracted to this theoretical approach? A brief look at the structure of the theoretical arguments and the substance of the findings in *Social Choice and Individual Values* can yield insight into why the approach gained converts.

SOCIAL CHOICE

Substantively, Arrow demonstrated that there is a contradiction among a minimal set of plausibly desirable properties (desiderata) of any mechanism (or rule, or constitution) for aggregating individual preferences into a social choice. That is, he showed that it is impossible to find a mechanism that can ensure the aggregation of individual preferences into a social choice that is transitive, unrestricted in domain, positively responsive to the preferences of individuals, independent of irrelevant alternatives, nondictatorial, and decisive. We can see how each of these properties is desirable.[4]

Three of the properties are directly related to what we consider to be the normative properties of democracy:

1. *Nondictatorship:* Rules out the possibility that one individual could decide all the social choices.[5]

2. *Positive responsiveness:* Requires that, as an alternative gains support from additional people relative to a second alternative, the application of the constitution does not lower the first alternative in its ranking in relation to the second.

3. *Universal domain:* Ensures that the constitution or decision rule can be applied to the full range of possible patterns of preferences held by the citizenry as input.

Three other properties help ensure that the collective decisions of the group are systematic and consistent translations of individual preferences into social choices (that is, that the similar individual preferences lead to similar collective choices):

4. *Independence of irrelevant alternatives:* Requires that the choice between two alternatives, say α and β, not depend on the preferences of the individuals over a third, not present, alternative such as γ.[6]

5. *Transitivity:* Requires that if one outcome (α) is socially preferred to a second one (β), and the latter is in turn preferred to a third one (γ), then the first outcome must be socially preferable to the third one.[7]

6. *Decisiveness:* Demands that the decision rule be able to map the preferences of the individuals into a particular collective decision without ambiguity.

Arrow's general impossibility theorem demonstrated that any reasonable mechanism for reaching a centralized social decision on the preferences of the group of affected individuals could not satisfy these properties. If the rules were democratic, they could not prevent instability or inconsistency in the group's choices.[8] In any constitution, one of or more of these desirable aspects of aggregation had to be sacrificed.

For example, if a decision rule satisfies all conditions save transitivity, one can, under specifiable conditions, expect to find voting cycles.[9] Political scientists have tended to focus on this potential intransitivity of democratic voting procedures as the crux of the "Arrow problem."[10] They have largely framed the social choice literature as a generalization of the Condorcet (voters') paradox rather than looking to the broader problem of aggregating individual preferences into social welfare.[11] This focus has led political scientists to characterize the theory as dealing primarily with voting. But voting, as an individual act involving choice, is only one sort of aggregation (even of preferences); Arrow's agenda was much broader.[12]

Since the existence of voting cycles was the prediction of a theoretical construct, political scientists had three alternatives: They could look for instances of the anticipated instability;[13] they could identify institutional mechanisms that violate one or more of the desiderata of a democratic decision process and prevent the instability;[14] or they could attack the assumptions of the model.[15] Theorists, unhappy with the dark side of democracy revealed by the general impossibility theorem, sought to find alternative assumptions and definitions that would allow for less pessimistic conclusions. On the other hand, Arrow's theoretical result cast a clear light on the function of certain institutional arrangements, and this allowed empiricists to sharpen the focus of their search. The field of social choice theory was born.[16]

Because of its severe implications regarding the impossibility of constructing democratic political systems with acceptable properties, the field of social choice has been a thorn in the side of political scientists. For political analysts, the literature defined and confined the engineering problems of voting and constitutional systems in ways that were neither expected nor welcomed. While a few political scientists and others debated the relevance of Arrow's dissertation (Coleman 1966; Dahl 1954), most continued on their way, talking about the issues of democracy as if he had never published *SCIV*. Even though this orientation has changed somewhat over the last fifty years, the implications of the original "impossibility theorem" have yet to be integrated by scholars in political philosophy, the field with the most at stake. The vast majority of political philosophers, explicitly concerned about the socially "good" and the socially "just," have integrated neither the methods nor the substance of the social choice perspective into their discourse, not only because the methodology is foreign and difficult, but also because Arrow's impossibility theorem was initially interpreted as concerned with voting.

THE NECESSITY AND CENTRALITY
OF ORGANIZATION IN HUMAN LIFE

Certainly, Aristotle was correct: We are communal animals. Our lives are very different from those of animals with meager social lives.[17] The circumstances of our survival and our limitations as individuals appear to require collective action to generate social products.[18] Collective action, however, involves problems of social and political organization. In this context, the social task of politics can be thought of as the activity required to generate collective or centralized decisions for a group of individuals in order to optimize group welfare.

This teleological definition of politics gives us a useful starting point. At least since Aristotle's *Politics*, the justification for government action has been based in part on its impact on the welfare of the ruled. Any serious attempt to evaluate government actions from this perspective requires that we be able to compare the welfare of a group of individuals in the aggregate, and in a variety of real and hypothetical situations. From a consequentialist point of view, to say that a decision leading to one state of affairs is better than an alternative decision leading to another state requires a comparison of the *aggregate* welfare of the individuals in the two outcomes. This comparison becomes a requirement whether one wishes to evaluate the outcomes of the decisions or the rules and structures used to generate those decisions.

The problem with aggregating *anything* is that any objects to be aggregated have disparate qualities. So, for example, in calculating one's net worth, one must aggregate the values of different types of assets. Luckily, there is a common measuring rod for the exercise: market values, calibrated in some monetary unit.[19] As anyone who has packed a family picnic knows, the statement that "one can't add apples and oranges" is only partially true: They can be considered as *n* pieces of fruit. But how much is the calculated total of a banana and three ounces of raisins? Is it four portions of fruit? Or (assuming about eighty raisins per ounce) is it about 241 pieces of fruit? Or is it seven ounces of fruit? And finally, retreating to the market, can we say it is sixty cents' worth of fruit? In other words, our goals, perspectives, and the cognitive tools available to us determine what we use as the basis for comparing disparate items at any given time. Our evaluations are both teleological and based on how we habitually evaluate objects. What are we interested in and accustomed to dealing with: weight, portions, or market values?

Of course, the aggregation problem can get tougher. With fruit, it is sensible to aggregate the disparate items along any of the dimensions mentioned. Weight, value, portions, or numbers of items all can be totaled using a common valuation unit. But this calculation may not always be possible using commonly available units of measure. Take a two-child family: with one child in good health and one sick with a stomach ailment, what is their aggregate state of health? Or even more complicated: what is their aggregate welfare?[20]

At a very direct level, Arrow's social choice argument asked questions about the very existence of such an aggregation: is it a sensible notion? That is, can we find reasonable ways of aggregating individual welfares, and if so, exactly what are the conditions that permit the aggregation?[21]

It is only a small intellectual leap from the evaluation of a social decision by its aggregated effect on the welfare of individuals to the normative support of democracy. This leap requires two conjectures. First, one must believe, as did Aristotle, that the affected individuals are, in general, the best judges of their own welfare, and second, that the separate judgments of the individuals can sensibly be aggregated. That is, the intellectual leap requires that some "vote-counting" process (very broadly understood) can be expected to yield a sensible indicator of aggregate group welfare. At this second, very direct level, Arrow's social choice argument demonstrated deep difficulties with the normative properties one could expect from *any* *process* that aggregates individual choices to reach a common group decision. Since one aspect of the justification for democracy is the existence of a set of sensible aggregating procedures, this difficulty is a major line in Arrow's work. Indeed, it was this aspect of his work—the problem of finding an acceptable procedure for aggregating the preferences of individuals—that was most remarked upon and followed by those who took Arrow's lead.

As indicated earlier in the example of adding up fruits, any aggregation requires an agreement on a common unit of measurement. Arrow was initially concerned with aggregating preferences that contain purely ordinal information. Such preferences allow one to answer questions such as, "Am I better off now than I was last year at this time?" They also restrict any interpretation of how much better off one is. Moreover, ordinal preferences preclude the possibility of making certain kinds of direct interpersonal welfare comparisons. Arrow considered whether one can characterize what constitutes the best outcome for society in terms of an aggregation of ordinal preferences.

CRITERIA FOR PERFORMANCE
BASED ON AGGREGATE WELFARE

The major program of the economists who deal with the welfare economics conundrum, as shaped by Arrow, has been to identify and justify institutional structures that generate acceptable outcomes based on individual welfares. In that task, economists have used the vehicle of preferences to get from individual values and welfares to social prescriptions.

The Pareto Principle

Economists have long agreed that, at the level of the individual, satisfying individual preferences is an acceptable surrogate for achieving individual welfare satisfaction.[22] In judging such satisfaction when more than one individual is involved, the economists' principle of choice has long been the Pareto principle. If, in a given state of affairs, at least one person can be made better off while no one else is hurt, one is not at a Pareto optimal point.[23] It follows that the Pareto optimal set is the set of points in which no one individual can be made better off without harming at least one other. The Pareto principle for welfare judgments, then, is that an acceptable choice must lie in the Pareto set.

This makes the Pareto principle one obvious criterion for the evaluation of institutional or organizational performance. Of course, the content of the Pareto set depends on the preferences (welfares) of the individuals. But which, if any, items in the set are *achievable* also depends on the rules by which the individuals relate. To see this, consider the following example.

> Three individuals, Messieurs *i*, *j*, and *k*, live by a stream. They would like to build a bridge across the stream, but the only feasible place to build the bridge is at a spot directly in front of the home of *i*, thereby diminishing both his view and his privacy. As a result, *i* does not support the bridge.

What does the Pareto principle tell us about the status quo? One cannot build the bridge without hurting *i*. Hence, an argument that one ought only to advocate or prescribe change that does not hurt anyone leaves one committed to advocating not building the bridge.

But other aspects of the example can be fleshed out to change this judgment. Suppose that *i*, *j*, and *k* are permitted to compensate one another (that is, make side payments) for any losses one of them may suffer from any choice that affects them jointly. Then the outcomes in the Pareto set can change. Imagine that the gain from the bridge to the other two individuals more than offsets the loss to *i* in the sense that *i* could be given something by *j* and/or *k* that *j* and *k* would gladly exchange for the bridge and that *i* would find better than the no-bridge status quo. Then they could agree to the bridge and compensation as making them all better off. If compensation is permitted (perhaps by letting *i*'s taxes be tailored to reflect his losses), building the bridge along with appropriate (and acceptable) compensation enters into the Pareto set.[24]

Whether or not compensation is possible and carried out can determine the size of the Pareto set.[25] Thus, the Pareto set must be calculated with reference to a well-defined set of alternatives, and the definition of that set will vary as either the objective of the argument or as a function of empirical constraints. As the feasible set changes, the Paretian subset of it will also change.

BEYOND THE PARETO PRINCIPLE

Of course, there are other criteria for the performance of institutions. Pareto optimality tells us nothing about distribution, legitimacy, or fairness. For example, an efficient dictator can clearly achieve Pareto optimality. If such a dictator merely ensures that the policies are optimized for her objectives, the society will surely be in the Pareto set. (The dictator will be made worse off if we move from the status quo.) In *SCIV*, Arrow addresses a deeper problem head on: the difficulty of *aggregating individual* welfares, judgments, or values into a meaningful indicator of *social welfare* by including procedural desiderata that go beyond the Paretian program.

However, if we rule out dictatorships—as many would, including Arrow—and tack on a few other criteria regarding the minimal reasonable properties of any procedure (such as simple notions of consistency), Arrow has shown, as indicated earlier, that we can all too quickly be driven beyond both Pareto and the possible. A quick and easy way to see how this impasse develops is to consider a simple example of the Condorcet paradox, in which the Pareto optimal outcomes are themselves dominated by another non-optimal outcome when pair-wise majority rule (PMR) is used.[26]

That a Condorcet paradox can threaten even Pareto is easily shown. Consider a situation (see table 1.1) in which three individuals (*i, j, k*) are voting to choose one of four outcomes (*a, b, c, d*). Item *d* is not in the Pareto set. (Note that all three voters prefer *c* to *d*.)

Yet if we use PMR, we can get the single nonmember of the Pareto set, *d*, to be the outcome of a sequence of votes. To illustrate, consider the results of the following pair-wise contests in table 1.2.

If the voting starts on the first line, it will end on the third, with *a* as the ultimate victor. If, on the other hand, it starts on the second line and works down the table, we would in fact end on the fourth line with *d*, the non-optimal outcome. Insisting on more from democracy—namely, that the outcome of a sequence of votes lead to a result in the Pareto set—might seem quite reasonable, but it cannot be guaranteed.

WHAT ONE GETS DEPENDS ON WHAT ONE'S GOT: ARE ORDINAL PREFERENCES THE PROBLEM?

What is to blame for these dismal conclusions? One obvious problem is that in all of the results discussed, preferences are restricted to ordinal information (perhaps) about the welfare of the individual.

Specifically, Arrow assumes that preferences—the "psychological engine of choice" (in microeconomics)—contain no more than ordinal information: that is, the individual's rankings of possible alternatives. As such, any aggregation has to be made of such stuff. As he asserts (1950, 2): "I quickly perceived that the ordinalist viewpoint, which I had fully adopted, implied that the only preference information that could be transmitted across individuals was an ordering."

Table 1.1   Pareto and Majority Rule

	Preferences of the Voters		
Rankings	i	j	k
1	a	c	b
2	b	d	c
3	c	a	d
4	d	b	a

Table 1.2   Outcomes and Pareto

| Contest | Victor | Voting for Winning | |
		Outcome	Vote Tally
d v. c	c	i, j, k	3,0
c v. b	b	i, k	2,1
b v. a	a	i, j	2,1
a v. d	d	j, k	2,1

Ordinal information is comparative, however, in only a minimalist sense. The fact that *j* prefers *x* to *y* does not tell us about the welfare *level* implied by either *x* or *y*. It is similar to my assertion that I was fatter at age twenty-two than at age fifty-six, and fatter at fifty-six than at age thirty-two. You do not have much information there. Certainly you do not know how fat I am, much less whether, at fifty-six, I am fatter than my lover was when she was fifty-four! And you are not even helped in that judgment to learn that she is fatter at fifty-four than when she was twelve, and so on. When using ordinal preferences, trying to get a measure of social welfare from an aggregation of preferences is analogous to trying to discover, from comparative age and weight statements of this sort, the width of the mattress we would need were my lover and I to sleep in the same bed.

In evaluating voting situations (for example, "I vote for Goodwin for mayor because I prefer him, on balance, to the candidates Black and Johnson"), one is often restricted to the same kind of minimal information that plagues the social choice literature.

Ordinal Voting

The results of a vote clearly reflect only ordinal preference information.[27] How does the process of voting as a choice device yield to analysis under the assumptions of preferences based on strictly ordinal information?

These slender assumptions do not prevent outcomes of certain votes from having ethically desirable properties. So, for example, if we restrict majority rule to a vote between only two alternatives, one can guarantee a Pareto improvement (May 1952). Or, if there are more than two alternatives and we restrict the preferences (and hence violate universal domain, one of the normative properties of democracy cited earlier), we can achieve some success. For example, if the majority feel passionately that some alternatives are undesirable, these alternatives will be rejected (Downs 1957). On the other hand, the unavoidable cycles may not be unequivocally undesirable. Nicholas R. Miller (1983) argues that although the conditions for democratic pluralism may be difficult to justify in social choice terms, the top cycle (Schwartz 1986) is Paretian and can be shown to be hit upon in at least every other decision.

Other voting regimes may satisfy other desiderata. For example, the voting literature has developed probabilistic voting models for elections. In these models, usually described spatially, the probability of *i* voting for option α over option β is assumed to go up as the distance between α and *i*'s preferred point decreases. From that perspective, there is an "analogy between market competition and political competition" (compare, Mueller 1989, 214). Many of the normative properties of market outcomes and equilibria carry over into the world of political campaigns. This constitutes substantial progress in the evaluation of voting. But probabilistic behavioral models pose problems of their own as leading to indicators of social welfare. Perhaps their value is best appreciated in the narrow sense of establishing that one might be able to reach social decisions.

As we pointed out earlier, however, Arrow's arguments address questions beyond voting. Across the wider agenda of social choice (see note 10), the bottom line is highly negative. Specifically, as far as the general issues of welfare judgments are concerned, the limitations of the information conveyed from *ordinal* and *interpersonally incomparable* preferences play a profound role in determining what one can conclude from patterns of preferences and choices.

WHAT HAVE WE GOT TO AGGREGATE?

In deciding what the best policies would be, we presumably would like to take into account the aggregate welfare implications of either the set of choices or the set of reports of individual welfare. It is clear that the information content of any aggregate outcome depends critically on the information content of what we aggregate. Can we assume that more information is available for welfare judgments than is contained in ordinal preferences that do not support interpersonal comparability?

In one respect, the utilitarians were right: were we able to make full interpersonal comparisons of welfare, we could aggregate the social consequences of all decisions in terms of welfare consequences. However, without interpersonal comparability, we are stuck with judgments no more powerful than Pareto (Soltan 1996). So what exactly is the interpersonally comparative status of the stuff we have to aggregate?

The Content of Preferences

In discussing the need to expand the content of preferences, Arrow has noted that it may be necessary to extend our conception of preference by considering *the domain of preferences.* As he put it in an early discussion (1950, 25):

> The failure of purely individualistic assumptions to lead to a well-defined social welfare function means, in effect, that there must be a divergence between social and private benefits if we are to be able to discuss a social optimum. Part of each individual's value system must be a scheme of socio-ethical norms, the realization of which cannot, by their nature, be achieved through atomistic market behavior. These norms, further, must be sufficiently similar among the members of the society to avoid the difficulties outlined here.

Hence, early on, Arrow saw that any solution to the social evaluation problem that relied on the aggregation of individual preferences required a (very) broad view of the notion of preferences and individual valuations of alternative social states. He was not the only one to feel this way. Earlier Vilfredo Pareto himself had argued that one needed to include a broad range of individual judgments in any aggregation procedure to get social evaluations (Arrow 1973b, 122). They each recognized that the welfare of one individual might be dependent on, or a function of, the welfare of others.

So the possibility of a sensible and justifiable (in Arrow's sense) social evaluation of a social choice must be built on the ethical aspects of individuals' preferences. The issue must be joined in two ways: What constitutes the basis of those ethical aspects? And how far can such a basis advance the problem of aggregation? Arrow points out that logic permits us to put no a priori restraints on those functions. It is merely that an individual's utility may be a nontrivial function of the welfare of others. As such, there is implicitly some subjective combining of the welfare of others *within* the individual: namely, $u_i = f(w_i, w_j)$. Viewed this way, individual preferences can be thought of as a sort of subjective social welfare function.

But of course, just because such a function is implicit in the preference structure of the individual does not endow the preferences with enough ethical content to allow it alone to be used as a justifiable basis for a social decision. Individuals would certainly be partial to situations that make *them* better off. It is therefore useful to remind ourselves that, virtually from the beginning, philosophers (certainly including the utilitarians; see Arrow 1973b, 123) urged that ethical content and judgments be based on some form of *impartial reasoning*. As far back as the first century B.C., Publius Syrus of Rome noted that when disputes arise, there is an inevitable problem of bias. His maxim to avoid this problem and get a fair settlement was, "No one should be judge in his own case." But nothing of this sort has been built into the argument. The ethical content, or the appropriate weighting for the welfare of other individuals, is left out of this argument (see Arrow 1973b, 124).[28]

Theories of social justice require not only a subjective preference structure but an interpersonal comparison of welfare. Arrow agrees that we must take that step if we want to make judgments regarding social justice. That is, there must be some comparative information that is meaningful *interpersonally*. (Sen [1973] argues this compellingly, especially in chapter 1, but also in Sen [1970a], chapter 9 and 9*.) Thus, for example, it must, at a minimum, be interpersonally meaningful to say that it is better to be Jack under circumstances α than Jill under circumstances β. Amartya Sen argues that this is precisely the interpersonal judgement that justice must be built on: the sort of empathy that allows us to put ourselves in each other's shoes and make comparative judgments regarding welfare. But precisely what form these judgments can and should take is less clear.

John Rawls's (1951, 1971, 1985) notions of justice, for example, require that a relatively limited interpersonal comparison be possible. So, for example, all that is required is an ability to select the "worst off." Such "positional" theories permit the development of consistent evaluation criteria for social choices, premised only on the notion that we can meaningfully transmit such positional information when we aggregate choices (see d'Aspremont and Gevers 1977; Arrow 1977b). This requires that we expand preferences to cover such comparisons as i prefers having the attributes of i under condition α to those of j under condition β. As Arrow puts it, this means substantially more than that the individual i is able to make the judgment that he is better off under α than he believes he would be as j under β (or $u_i(\alpha, i) > u_i((\beta, j))$). Rather, it means that it is factually the case that anyone would be better off as i in condition α than as j in condition β (or, now without subscripts, $u(\alpha, i) > u(\beta, j)$) (see Arrow 1977b, 152).

PREFERENCES OVER THE UNIVERSAL SET

In attempting to introduce such additional information about preferences in order to yield more determinate welfare judgments, Arrow (1977b) has made some useful, but not widely remarked upon, distinctions that can help us understand what it is "we've got": That is, the stuff we are aggregating. To begin with, he points out that preferences, as understood in economics, are assumed to be stable. He distinguishes between what he calls "tastes," which appear to be unstable, and preferences, which are stable. Preferences are an ordering of all the possible alternatives one might face (sometimes referred to as "over the universal set"), not just the alternatives available for choice at a given moment (usually referred to as "the feasible set").

To get a feel for the difference between these two sets, consider a wine aficionado going to buy a bottle of Merlot at a small corner store. She may have a clear ranking of all sorts of Merlots beyond both those she finds in the store and those available within her immediate budget.

As it turns out, this distinction, which may appear to be a quibble, is more than definitional. The insistence that preferences be defined over the universal set permits us to import considerable normative material into the discussion.[29] The universal set contains options we do not often consider. Arrow uses this to drive to some surprising conclusions:

> Among the characteristics which determine an individual's satisfaction are some which are not, at least at the moment, alterable. An individual who is ill can meaningfully be said to prefer being well. If in fact there were some medical means of cure, we would test this preference by asking if he would purchase the services. Clearly the preference would be there whether or not medicine was useful.[30] We may suppose that everything that determines an individual's satisfaction is included in the list of goods. Thus, not only the wine but the ability to enjoy and discriminate are included among goods. It is, in fact, true that only some of the goods so defined are transferable among individuals; others are not. But that consideration enters into the definition of the feasible set, not that of the ordering. If we use this complete list, then everyone should have the same utility function for what he gets out of the social state. This does not, of course, mean that individuals agree on the utility of a social state, since what they receive from a given state differs among individuals (Arrow 1977b, 159).

The notion that everyone has the same preference over the universal set, appropriately defined, would appear to come close to implying that only one representative individual would be required to evaluate the relative positions of all individuals. That is just a short step from saying that the means for an impartial judgment are within the grasp of any individual. Were any individual put behind a "veil of ignorance" in which she was unaware only of which role in the society she played, any choice of alternatives would, by assumption, overcome the difficulties Arrow identified in *SCIV*. Since all preference structures would be the same and any representative would be a dictator, the choice would be in the Pareto set. And all individuals, were they to vote from this impartial point of view, would presumably choose the same alternative.

Problems in Identifying the Universal Set

Of course, such a conclusion assumes that one's utility function is defined over the universal set that is common to all humanity, and hence that neither one's preferences nor the universal set is a function of one's particular experiences. Arrow acknowledges a possible difficulty with his construct (1977b, 160):

> If your satisfaction depends on some inner qualities that I do not possess, then I really have not had the experience which will enable me to judge the satisfaction one would derive from that quality in association with some distribution of goods. Hence, my judgment has a probability element in it and will not agree with your judgment.

In commenting on John Rawls, Arrow (1973a, 114) alludes to the difficulty of integrating potentially divergent perspectives on the universal set:

> To the extent that individuals are really individual, each an autonomous end in himself, to that extent they must be somewhat mysterious and inaccessible to one another. There cannot be any rule that is completely acceptable to all. There must be, or so it now seems to me, the possibility of unadjudicable conflict.

The difference Arrow draws between tastes over the feasible set and preferences over the universal set is an important and incisive one. We are not convinced, however, that it is reflective of individuals as they ordinarily make decisions. Perhaps Arrow's distinction does not go sufficiently deep (namely, close to bedrock; see Popper [1959], 111) to cope with recent observational difficulties about individual tastes and preferences. The assumption of a common utility function flies in the face of modern neurobiology (see, for example, Edelman 1992) and, on reflection, also runs counter to common sense.

The assumption of commonality is also problematic in another way. It assumes a strange ontology: the stable existence of the items in the universal set. If the items in the universal set are also a function of culture (was watching *The Simpsons* on channel 5 part of the universal set in 1970? in 1870?), then we must define those items in the universal set in terms of individuals' knowledge of the options they believe to be, or can imagine to be, available.

We conclude that both the domain of preferences and their functional form are more variable. Individual preferences must contain many unique aspects, and a uniform set of preferences over a universal set is most unlikely. Of course, that need not preclude the finding of some decisional consensus and hence the possibility of sensible aggregation of preferences over some domains. But the search for such consensus to gain leverage over the problems of social welfare needs to involve more than a simple polling of ambient preferences over some carefully defined but commonly understood feasible, or universal, set.

Indeed, we can now say that prior to an evaluation of the ethical, or even "welfare," content of a single preference structure, much less an aggregation of preferences, some groundwork must be done. If there can be no consensus regarding the content of the "universal set" of options, then one must specify the proper *domain* of alternatives over which the preferences operate.[31]

A common domain would identify the set of alternatives to be evaluated, including all relevant attributes of the alternatives. Arrow assumes that the alternatives, once fully specified, would be viewed from a single, unambiguous perspective and yield an unambiguous preference ranking. But more than agreement on a common domain is required. If more than one perspective is possible on the common domain, and if different perspectives yield different preferences, then the choice of an appropriate perspective from which to assess preferences must rest on a defensible normative element. For social welfare purposes, we argue later, an impartial frame of reference is often needed for a preference aggregation procedure to generate compelling results.

CONTEXT-DEPENDENT PREFERENCES

Putting it differently, both Arrow and the social choice theorists following him assume that preferences are fundamental. As such, institutional and other environmental aspects of the choice environment do not affect them. This permits social choice theorists to accept preferences as adequate representations of individual welfare. It then justifies the evaluation of social choice mechanisms on the basis of their *preference* aggregation properties. But we question the adequacy of a preference structure as unfiltered data. Hence, we reopen the problem of evaluation of the social choice mechanism by questioning the domain of the social choice function. Here we touch on some of the characteristics of preferences in light of recent findings in psychology. These findings indicate that preferences are both less "solid" and less fundamental than social choice theorists assume. Ironically, by considering the reasons for preference *instability*, we hope to arrive at an empirical mechanism with some improved hope for the sensible aggregating of preferences and with some desirable normative properties.

Among others, Amos Tversky, Daniel Kahneman, Kenneth May, George Quattrone, and Charles Plott have produced experimental results showing that individual choices, and hence revealed preferences, violate a number of the postulates of the choice model used by economists. Possibly the most famous example is that developed by Tversky and Kahneman (1981). In their study, the subject's response in a choice situation depended on the framing of the decision as about either a loss or a gain. Two verbally different, but logically equivalent, characterizations of a choice situation led subjects to display contradictory preferences over two alternatives.

Tversky and Kahneman (1981) attempt to explain this apparent contradiction by means of a new model of choice that they call "prospect theory." Their argument is that individuals make different choices in the "same" situation when the situation is "framed" as involving a "loss" as opposed to a "gain." Their theoretical representation of such behavior in "gain" versus "loss" situations uses a value function with a discontinuity in the first derivative at the status quo point.

Many articles have since been written arguing that the effects caught in these and other experiments are more general phenomena and play a profound role in choice behavior. We take a slightly more general approach than that put forward in prospect theory. From our perspective, the variability of individual choice is to be thought of as a result of the use of varying models of evaluation. In the case of the Tversky and Kahneman (1981) experiment, many people may have one model for dealing with losses, and another for dealing with gains. Interpreted this way, Tversky and Kahneman's diagram tries to encapsulate, in prospect theory, multiple views in a single model. As they argue, a situation can be framed as a potential loss situation or as a potential gain situation. We would characterize this as indicating that the models governing our preferences (hence, behavior) from these two perspectives are different, and it is for that reason that the framing affects our choices.

Although, on first blush, our characterization may appear to be a distinction without a difference, we think that a broader reading of the results on preference reversal may put this in a different light. Further, we hope to show that our interpretation may have direct implications for some of the questions Arrow raised in discussion of both the universal set and its implications for social aggregation of preferences.

Models, Framing, and Cues

Recent evidence from biology affords insight into how the brain makes sense of stimuli. Every concrete situation involves a potentially infinite number of aspects. Approaching any situation, we focus, because of our limited information-processing capabilities, on a small subset of the aspects of the situation that confronts us.[32] We "make sense" of the situation by means of a subset of our neural network that constitutes a cognitive model of the situation. The neural model is literally groups of neurons, each group roughly representing a concept, linked together in a network that is potentiated when appropriate stimuli are received from the environment (or from internal cognitive activity).

So, for example, walking past a school yard at recess time and seeing a group of students surround a girl, one might "understand" the situation either as "a game" or as an instance of dangerous "bullying." Which way one understands the situation determines what affect (value) one attaches to the situation, because in the brain the neuronal cognitive complex that represents "game" is linked to the limbic system differently than the one that represents "bullying." As such, they evoke differential emotional values when stimulated. What triggers the understanding can vary. For example, a sensory input at the time of the observation could help determine one's interpretation. Noticing tears, or a smile, could affect one's understanding of the situation. But that understanding might be a result of inputs received at a different time. Recent, or distant, exposure to media emphasis on problems of bullying in playgrounds (or one's own past playground experiences as a child) might induce one to favor one interpretation. By sharp contrast, media emphasis on the beneficial effects of recess on building peer solidarity might help determine quite a different "understanding" of one's visual inputs.

What is important to note is that in this situation, the individual has limited information, and the shifting "cues" and frames can be thought of as associated with learning. It may be that in many choice situations imperfect information, and hence learning, is associated with the instability of preferences over the choices available. But it is important to note that this potential for interpreting a situation in more than one way is not necessarily a function of not knowing what is "really" happening. Even in the playground example, there may be no unambiguous consensus, either among the children or within a given child, as to whether the situation is a game or an instance of bullying.

Judgments such as these can be fragile and at times may be a function of partial information. But fragile judgments, unstable preferences, and the like can stem from other causes. Kenneth May (1954), observing a high frequency of preference reversals, argued that unpracticed judgments can lead to unstable preferences in a situation even with good information.

Richard Larrick and Sally Blount's experimental studies (1997a, 1997b) of ultimatum games provide examples of framing effects that occur without any apparent learning component. In their studies, small changes in wording led to substantial shifts in the patterns of observed behavior.

Larrick and Blount developed an experiment in which structurally equivalent processes differ only in their verbal description of the choice options, not in the substantive structure of the choices. They utilized ultimatum games involving two persons. Characteristically in such games one subject is given some money (usually ten dollars) to divide between the two. The second then can accept the division (in which case the money is divided as prescribed by the offer) or reject the offer (in which case no money is given to either person). In their experiments, two treatments were applied. In one, the first person made an offer regarding the split in the ten dollars, and the second person could either accept or reject it. In the other treatment, the first person made a claim about the maximum amount she would offer, and simultaneously, not knowing how much the first person was offering, the second player made a claim about the lowest amount that she would accept. There was a common understanding that if the two claims added up to more than the total, no payment would be made. This difference in presentation affected both the average amounts offered and the average amounts accepted. Table 1.3 highlights the major results that illustrate the differences (see Larrick and Blount 1997b). Preferences about which divisions to offer and accept are clearly sensitive to the way in which the division problem is framed. Framing effects need not always be a function of learning or bad information.

These effects can be related to our discussion about how framing affects preferences. We would say that humans seem to understand (explain) the world by the use of cognitive models, and the models relate to specific aspects of situations. From the experimental results, it seems that framing the situation as one of coincident offers as opposed to sequential bids and acceptances or rejections evokes different models in subjects' minds. These small changes in emphasis, which leave the basic division problem intact, highlight different aspects of the situation or evoke different models, thus affecting behavior.

Arrow (1982, 268) has also written about some of this cognitive research. He summarizes:

> The drawing of inferences depends then on preconceptions, which may be true or false. The cognitive psychologists refer to the "framing" of questions, the effect of the way they are formulated on the answers. A fundamental element of rationality, so elementary that we hardly notice it, is, in logicians' language, its *extensionality*. The chosen element depends on the opportunity set from which the choice is to be made, independently of how that set is described. . . . The cognitive psychologists deny that choice is in fact extensional; the framing of the question affects the answer.

Table 1.3   Relative Frequency of Outcomes

	Reject/Accept (Percentage)	Claim/Counter claim (Percentage)
Person #1 offers 50–50 split to #2	48	57
Person #2 lets person #1 take all the money	8	37

Of course, as with the observation of the children on the playground, some observational learning may be going on. In those cases, preferences and behavior may be a function of cues that are used to "better understand" a situation and may reach an equilibrium value when enough information has been gathered. But in some cases, the instability appears to be more basic (as in the Tversky and Kahneman [1981] framing of gains and losses, or the Larrick and Blount [1997a, 1997b] examples). In those cases, the instability may be caused by the cues and framing and have nothing to do with learning. The instability may be inherent.

This cognitive interpretation is parallel to current arguments about cognition in the philosophy of science. Ronald Giere (1990) argues that scientific explanation conforms to this kind of cognitive processing. For him, explanation proceeds by a particular form of analogy. Explanation starts with the identification of aspects of a class of situations that may be germane to understanding the situation. The scientist then constructs an abstract (possibly mathematical) model. A theoretical explanation consists of identifying a class of phenomena, identifying certain aspects of that class of phenomena, and asserting that the class of phenomena resembles the model in that particular set of aspects and to a certain specified degree of accuracy.

A parallel between this notion of explanation and the notion of valuation can be drawn. Even when a domain of alternatives is developed for the purposes of a normative evaluation, the aspects of the phenomena that are abstracted and built into an explanatory model are not determined a priori or definitively by the specification of the alternative set. Rather, the evaluations are, at base, dependent on the neurophysiological maps of the individuals. Thus, competing explanations and framings of a given class of phenomena exist, each based on a subset of the neural maps that can be called up, and hence leading to models referring to different aspects of the phenomena in question. In a parallel way, individuals may place different valuations on the same alternatives as a function of differing cues. The cues lead to a focus on particular aspects of the alternatives and hence to the identification (or evoking) of a particular model to interpret and, indirectly, to evaluate those alternatives.

Hence, our understanding of a given situation is fluid, and the justification of our actions is predicated on our invoked interpretative models. Our chosen actions (or revealed choices) will then be a function of the different aspects of the situation that (quite literally) come to mind (or are emphasized). It follows that, as Tversky and Kahneman (1981, 458) note: "When framing influences the experience of consequences, the adoption of a decision frame is an ethically significant act."

HOW MIGHT FRAMING AFFECT A SOCIAL CHOICE PERSPECTIVE?

Let us spell out roughly how this perspective changes the fundamental notion of how values are related to preferences and choices. We will sketch some implications for preferences over welfare judgments. Suppose an individual, i, is to make a choice in a specified situation, A. The situation defines the feasible set available to i. The traditional economics model would have it that the individual examines the feasible set, identifies the possible outcomes associated with the feasible set of actions, and evaluates, through i's preferences, the alternatives on this basis (see figure 1.1).

Our modification of this simple scheme adds a layer to the decision process. It interposes a cognitive model that i uses to make sense of the situation. Conceivably, different models of the same alternatives are evoked by the perception of different aspects of the situation in question. And i is likely to attach different values to the alternatives in the different models of situations. These values may or may not be expressible in a simple coherent fashion as an ordering over the alternatives,[33] but the expression of them—here called preferences over the alternatives to be chosen— and indeed the outcomes themselves, are derivative not only of these values but by the way in which the situation is revealed (framed) and interpreted.

The cognitive schema in figure 1.2 can be juxtaposed with the simpler preference model of figure 1.1. In figure 1.2 it is assumed that the situation defines a feasible set and *a variety of evocable cues*. The difference is that each cue set (or frame) draws attention to a different set of aspects of the situation and evokes a different mental model in i. Each model leads to a different set of preferences and chosen behavior. The mapping of the feasible set to preferences, and indeed, to outcomes is now determined by the processing of cues by the individual actor. This processing may be thought of as occurring through the evocation of a set of models, conceptions, or images of the situation by the cues. To return to our earlier example, model M_1 could represent the interpretation of the children's behavior as play, and model M_2 could represent the same situation as bullying. The different models invoke different preferences and hence choices over the feasible set—say, whether to walk on, to intervene, and so on. These variable preferences are potentially rooted in a (not single-valued) set over the alternatives given the same situation.

This leads us to conclude that preferences are probably not founded on bedrock. There are likely to be no uniform preferences over a universal set. Preferences are a function of the specific cultural and individual experiences that determine our mental templates.[34] They are also likely to be filtered by the lenses we use to interpret situations. The structure of the decision environment itself (for example, a particular market or some other structure) may call forth a number of images[35] clustered around the item, each with its own set of attachments to the limbic system.[36]

Figure 1.1   The Traditional Economics Model Relating Choice to Preferences

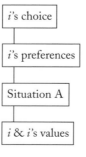

Figure 1.2   The Generation of Different Preferences in a Choice Context by Cues

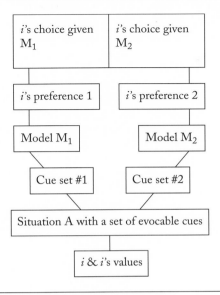

It follows that experience (and hence institutional arrangements, including those of preference expression and aggregation) is likely to affect the preferences expressed. This would be consistent with the evidence from psychologists regarding framing, and our interpretation of it. It could give us a theoretical basis for understanding choice (and hence voting) as a probabilistic ordinal expression.[37]

That may help to explain individual behavior, but what, then, is to be done with the indeterminacy of the mapping between the value structures of individuals and their preferences over concrete alternatives as they impinge on the questions of social choice? How is one to justify policies and institutions? Clearly, the complication we have introduced calls for some further normative qualification of which preferences and which domains are to be considered acceptable for this judgment.[38]

Thus, our approach leads to two difficulties. Which preferences of a given individual are to be taken into account in a social aggregation? And how can divergent preferences be aggregated in an acceptable way?

INTEGRATING DIVERSE PERSPECTIVES: THE EMPIRICAL CONNECTION

The potential multiplicity (and hence apparent instability) of preferences within any one individual can now be integrated into the evaluative task in Arrow's social choice program.

Arrow noted (1973a) that one of the big difficulties in the ethical program is that individual preferences, though containing "socio-ethical primitives," do not stem from an ethical "stance." We have noted that to choose from among divergent perspectives, which could yield different individual preferences, one needs a fixed point on which to stand. Put another way, if one wanted to tap an ethically valid preference structure of an individual, it would have to be invoked by cues that have the property that they are valid for such a purpose. But this is, after all, very much the same requirement that drove Rawls and his many forebears in ethics to call for the use of impartial reasoning. This is also the wisdom captured in the everyday instructions given to juries to be impartial—to exclude certain types of messages and appeals.

But inducing impartial reasoning to identify the "right" preferences may still not solve the problem of aggregation.[39] Arrow himself has considered the problem at various levels (see for example, Arrow 1952, 55; 1969, 87). He has wondered what level of consensus is likely to turn up through focused impartial cogitation on the social values of concern. In the end, in a discussion of Rawls (1973a, 106), he is pessimistic about overcoming all the difficulties of aggregation, although he feels that some progress is likely:

> Rawls assumes that individuals are egoistic, their social preferences being derived from the veil of ignorance. But why should there not be views of benevolence (or envy) even in the original position? All that is required is that there they not refer to named individuals. But if these are admitted, then there can be disagreement over the degree of benevolence or malevolence, and the happy assumption that there are no disagreements in the original position disappears.

If there were a single preference structure for all humanity, then impartial reasoning would lead to no disagreements. But given the caveats entered earlier, that is too much to expect. Let us examine the problem of the appropriate perspective for an individual to take so that she can access ethically acceptable preferences for a social decision on aggregate welfare.

Earlier we noted that a conclusion such as that reached by Rawls regarding the best way to distribute primary goods (leaving aside the issue of the specification of those goods) is that interpersonal ordinal comparisons of a particular sort are required. It means that for any two individuals i and j, not only does i prefer having the attributes of i under conditions α to those of j under condition β, but also conversely, and the judgment must be shared by all. It means $u(\alpha, i) > u(\beta, j)$. But of course, α and β are situations open to subjective evaluation in terms of individual models of the sort introduced earlier. What is the proper or appropriate perspective to take on α and β to evaluate i's and j's relative position under those conditions? First, an impartial point of view would appear to be appropriate. The evaluation should not be colored by particularistic concerns. But how can that be achieved? How can one take an impartial point of view?

Elsewhere (Frohlich and Oppenheimer 1992, 1997) we have argued that laboratory experiments in which conditions are manipulated to induce aspects of impartial reasoning among groups of subjects are a means of gaining information regarding preferences over principles of distributive justice and that a similar prescription might be effective in other ethically problematic situations.

There are two aspects of such an approach that recommend it as a way of generating insight into individual and group valuations of alternatives. First, as noted earlier, an impartial point of view—one that must take into account the outcome for all individuals in an evenhanded manner—is one that has normative weight. Second, individuals, discussing and deciding an issue in a group, possess an advantage over a set of the same individuals cogitating alone and reaching individual decisions. As the most rudimentary common sense tells us, each individual has private information, based on individual experiences, that is not accessible to the others unless that information is shared. If the common domain is to be well specified and understood, that understanding is likely to be fuller the broader the perspective taken on it. Group discussion is likely to broaden the perspective. Ideally it should reflect the perspective of all humanity, but at the least it should use the perspectives of all those affected by the decisions.

Group discussion in a structured environment is a way of bringing to bear wider information and a variety of perspectives so that individuals can expand their understanding of the domain of choice and refine their evaluations of the rankings of different alternatives in that set. If the ethical decision is sufficiently well specified, and if the sharing of information under impartiality yields a preferred perspective, then a unanimous decision based on a common understanding of the common domain (as it applies to that situation) may be obtainable.

A number of teams have conducted experiments to determine whether such a core of shared preferences about income distribution exist and can be evoked under conditions approximating impartial reasoning (Frohlich and Oppenheimer 1992; Jackson and Hill 1995; Lissowski, Tyszka, and Okrasa 1991; Oleson 1997; Saijo, Takahashi, and Turnbull 1996). In fact, significant consensus was obtained in Canada, three locations in the United States, Poland, Australia, and Japan. This speaks well for Arrow's original conjecture regarding the existence of a universal preference structure (at least over this limited domain). But it gives only qualified support to the notion of accessing any universal preference structure. It may be accessible under only the most precarious of conditions, and given the way in which our experiences structure how we perceive and evaluate the world, there may be wide divergence in individual preferences across other issues.[40] Yet the results may indicate the general existence of sets of *both acceptable* and *rejectable* options under properly specified conditions.

This perspective gives us language to use in a potentially meaningfully talk about interpersonal comparisons of welfare. It is possible to imagine, in principle, laboratory experiments designed to determine comparisons among different welfare states of hypothetical (or real) individuals. There is nothing simple, easy, or magical about conducting such experiments, and they are subject to a host of caveats and objections, but they do furnish a potential way of gaining insight into what exactly we are able to understand about one another and what we agree upon.[41] Whether there is a single, ethically justifiable preference over a set of alternatives in a particular domain is ultimately an empirical question. With the burgeoning of new experimental techniques in political science and economics (see for example, Kagel and Roth 1995), the time may be ripe for the application of empirical methods to some of the fundamental questions raised by Kenneth Arrow's works.

A FEW IMPLICATIONS FOR POLITICAL DISCOURSE

It now would be useful to identify some implications of these observations for the evaluation of social institutions.

As indicated earlier, we argue for the following as premises for the argument: (P1) The quality of governance is best measured by something like the aggregate welfare of the individuals subject to the governing institutions.[42] (P2) Democratic political institutions use a voting mechanism to aggregate individual choices (each of which can be thought of as a partial articulation of a voter's preference, and hence a welfare judgment) into a social choice. (P3) The preference any individual articulates varies as a function of the model used by the individual to understand the situation (or the choices to be made). Different frames may evoke preferences that assign different weights to the welfare of others. In particular, some frames may lead to an inappropriate discounting of others' welfare. (P4) Morality requires that the welfare of others play a nontrivial role in one's preferences.

These arguments lead us to conclude that: (C1) Some individual preference structures have greater moral standing than others.[43] In particular, those arrived at from a narrow and ill-informed perspective have less moral weight. (C2) In a given situation, with no change in political structures, a given set of individuals can generate different welfare aggregations depending on which preferences have been articulated. Hence, (C3) some welfare aggregations are morally "privileged."

We can be a bit more explicit about the social factors that may affect the way in which preferences are formed and articulated. (P5) The structural elements of the polity can profoundly affect the content of the political discourse in the society. Moreover, (P6) the content of the political discourse in a society affects the model used by an individual to determine her preferences. And further, as noted earlier, some structures and attributes of the political discourse in the society more readily generate preferences that have greater moral standing. It follows that: (C4) Such structures and attributes have greater moral standing.[44]

Put simply, in any democracy the outcome of the governmental process is sure to be a function of the cognitive models used by the individuals in their understanding and evaluation of the political alternatives. The models used by individuals are dependent on the framing of alternatives. The relative quality, if not the ethical standing, of the political outcomes is likely to be a function of the sorts of frames utilized by the individuals in their decisionmaking.[45] These frames are a function of the citizens' experience in the political arena as well as in other arenas. Thus, the welfare of the individuals in a democratic polity is a function of both the aggregation mechanisms of the polity and the structure and attributes of the political discourse in the society. Freer, broader, and more open discourse is preferable. Of course, in modern democracies governmental decisions are a function of many individual decisions, and no one frame occurs. But it would appear that a probabilistic weighting of these frames (an expectation) should be possible, as a function of the sorts of political perspectives that are emphasized and utilized in the designing and choosing of public policy.

To make these abstract observations more concrete we can consider some simplified examples. The prevailing American practice of interest group politics is usually justified normatively by the presumption that individual preferences, as they appear in the wild and as they are aggregated through a variety of democratic institutions, constitute an appropriate basis for achieving group welfare.[46] Given our arguments earlier, however, narrow interest group politics (which in its most extreme form might be characterized as identity politics) runs the risk of basing group demands on tastes or preferences formed on far too narrow a perspective. It is altogether reasonable to assume that broadly based public frames for the debate of issues might yield changes in outcomes.

To take another example, the change in the framing of racial issues in the United States during the 1960s changed the sorts of alternatives that were chosen. The same might be said of the provision of publicly funded medical care in Canada in the same era. It was framed as a fundamental right rather than as a commodity. In each case, alternatives emerged victorious in part as a result of the way various groups framed the situation and evaluated alternative courses of action.[47] And of course, the political structures of the two countries also played a role in bringing about the outcomes (as well as furnishing part of the explanation for why publicly funded medical care was more fully implemented in Canada).

Thus, the circle of inquiry begun in the 1950s comes around, in our discussion, to some of the same issues current then.[48] Now, as then, we are led to conclude that both structure and content matter. The quality of democratic regimes is not solely a function of the formal properties of the voting system and of the vote-counting procedures. The informal or civil properties of the discussion space can affect, to a considerable degree, the sorts of evaluations, and hence the choices, that citizens make.[49]

Arrow's insights into the problems of aggregation and the implications from cognitive psychology regarding the nature of the preferences that enter into the aggregation open new paths on the long trail that scholars have been exploring in their attempts to evaluate governments and political systems. In the early days of political analysis, Plato and Aristotle brought the knowledge of their time to bear on these nettlesome problems. The new insights we are gaining into the way people see, interpret, and make decisions about the world need to be integrated into that old quest. To do this, scholars will have to consider how the contributions of social choice, experimental techniques, and individual psychology cast light on the frames that individuals use in understanding and deciding their political fates.

This essay was written for presentation at the American Political Science Association annual meeting, Washington, D.C., September 1997, for a panel on Kenneth Arrow in the series on Nobelists in Economics. The panel was postponed, and the essay was presented at a Russell Sage Foundation panel, New York, November 13, 1997. We are deeply indebted to Michael Cain for his extensive and most helpful comments on an earlier draft. We are grateful to others, including Keith Dougherty, who also gave us helpful comments. We thank the Social Sciences and Humanities Research Council of Canada for its support of this project.

NOTES

1. The logic of his argument has been explored and elaborated upon by many, including, of course, Arrow himself (see, for example, Arrow 1977a; Plott 1976; Schwartz 1986; Sen 1970a, 1977a). In this essay, we focus primarily on some details of the fundamental behavioral assumptions necessary to develop empirical extensions of Arrow's findings.

2. See Farr and Seidelman (1993), especially the introductions to parts 1 and 2 by the editors and the essays by Ross, Merriam, Ricci, Gunnell, Dahl (1961/1993), and Easton (1985/1993).

3. Of course, von Neumann and Morgenstern extended this application to develop a weak (that is, non-interpersonally comparable) cardinal utility theory in their elaboration of the behavioral assumptions required to generate certain results. This cardinality held little difference for the logic of social choice theory (see Schwartz 1986). The commitment to the notion that preferences contain nothing more than ordinal information can be seen as one of the major breakthroughs in the analysis, and one of the great stumbling blocks for future work.

4. Of course, Arrow put forward one set of conditions but quite a few other sets have been proposed and shown to lead to a variety of similar difficulties. A particularly clear overview (if somewhat dated) can be had in Plott (1976).

5. Broader prohibitions, ruling out dictatorial decision power from subsets of the population, are shown to be the consequences of similar arguments, with relaxations of transitivity (see condition 5 later in the essay).

6. There has been some controversy over the "proper" specification of this criterion. Most outspoken has been Charles Plott (1976).

7. The implications of this assumption seem to conform to our notions of what is better and best. But see chapter 1 of Sen (1970a), an interesting discussion of how limited relaxations of this assumption can be consistent with other interpretations of evaluations of better and best. However, introducing other relaxations, as Dennis Mueller (1989, 389) puts it, brings "a degree of arbitrariness into the process." These relaxations spread "dictatorial power across a wider group" (Mueller 1989, 389), but none of them get us substantially out of the problem.

8. Again, a number of texts show versions of his proof: for an example, see chapter 20 of Mueller (1989).

9. This means that in using a democratic decision process, the defeat of some policy A by policy B, and B's defeat by policy C, might be followed by policy C's defeat by policy A, leaving no policy preferred to all others and calling into question the justification (on the basis of the normative qualities of its consequences), if not the utility, of the decision process.

10. Many examples of literature in this vein could be cited. The best would have to include such groundbreaking works as Schofield (1978), McKelvey (1979), and Miller (1983). A few others have endowed the problem with more importance. Gary Miller (1992), for example, questions whether there is a metric for strategies for efficiency in a firm when there are cycles. One might also look at Riker (1982) for a broader examination of the implications of the argument.

11. The Condorcet (or voters') paradox shows that, using majority rule, transitive individual preferences can aggregate into intransitive collective preferences. Hence, a majoritarian system cannot guarantee any consistency: The same profile of individual preferences can lead to various collective choices (see tables 1.2 and 1.3).

12. Amartya K. Sen (1977a) makes a helpful distinction between social choice theory, individual preference, and three different problems related to the social choice literature: voting and democratic institutions, social welfare judgments, and measures of social welfare. The first is concerned with the problem of choosing a best candidate or policy based on the preferences of a group. The second is concerned with what kinds of changes are best for the society given that some members gain and others lose. This kind of "preference" is a multidimensional comparative judgment about social states. The informational basis for this judgment is normally wider than for preferences in voting and democratic institutions, for which it has implications. The last is concerned with measures of poverty, national income, inequality, and so on, which have normative implications.

13. One similar approach is to look for general classes of cases that generate instabilities. One such class is vote trading (see Bernholz 1974; Kadane 1972; Oppenheimer 1975; and the generalization by Schwartz 1981).

14. Much of the work of Thomas Romer and Howard Rosenthal (1978), Kenneth Shepsle (1979), Barry Weingast (1979), Shepsle and Weingast (1981a, 1981b), and others has been oriented toward the discovery of how attributes of the institutional structure induce equilibria when otherwise one might predict cycles. For some disconfirming evidence on their hypotheses, however, see Eavey and Miller (1984) and Miller and Oppenheimer (1982).

15. Here the most successful work has been done by Coughlin (1984, 1988) and by Coughlin and Hinich (1984), but also see Feldman and Lee (1987) and Hinich (1977), and the useful discussion in Mueller (1989).

16. Arrow's methodology and assumptions lured scholars into explaining other political phenomena. Anthony Downs (1957) (a doctoral student of Arrow) extended Duncan Black's (1958) theory of spatial decisionmaking and Harold Hotelling's (1929) argument about economic competition in

a spatially differentiated market into a theory of political party competition—opening yet another field: political competition as spatial competition. (See Enelow and Hinich [1984] for a particularly lucid development of these arguments.)

17. We are not alone; there are many other social animals. For example, the relationship of the individual bee to its hive requires occasional relocation decisions that are made for the population of a hive (see Landa 1986; Wilson 1971; for a look at social choices among primates, see de Waal 1982). Such decisions would appear to be strongly related to the welfare and even survival of the communities that make them.

18. At a minimum, the family structure implies some collective action. Arrow identifies a number of aspects of our nature that generate the need for centralized or collective decisions, such as the need for public goods and the economies of scale in information (see Arrow 1974).

19. But even in that case, different assets carry different levels of risk, and the common measuring rod of current market value represents some aggregation of those risk preferences (not to mention any ambiguity or imperfections in information regarding the "true" value of some assets).

20. Part of the problem here can be seen to stem from the lack of comparability in health statements. Although one can crudely measure social aggregates of health by such things as average mortality rates, life expectancy, and the like, there is little available for sensible small-group or nuclear family comparisons (see U.S. Department of Health, Education, and Welfare 1969).

21. Such aggregation reflects only the ordinal information packed in the statements regarding the welfare of the individual (that is, that individual is better or worse off in one situation as compared to another). Again, we do not lack for indicators of social welfare for larger groups.

22. Indeed, the link between this aspect of "welfare economics" and the normative theories of the utilitarians is too obvious to belabor.

23. As Karol Soltan (1986) pointed out, Pareto optimality is what is left of utilitarianism when no interpersonal welfare (that is, utility) comparisons are allowed. There is an obvious relation between Pareto optimality and the voting rule unanimity: If you can improve some, without hurting anyone, and if people vote to improve themselves, then, theoretically at least, unanimity will lead to change until one is at a Pareto optimal point.

24. Actually, rationality and self-interest make even simple situations such as this one much harder to work out in reality than would appear to be the case if there were imperfect information. J, after all, has an incentive to exaggerate the harm the bridge would do him in order to demand higher compensation. Indeed, there is an entire area of scholarship devoted to this problem (for a discussion of demand revelation mechanisms, see chapter 8 of Mueller 1989; see also Miller and Hammond 1994).

25. The relationship between compensation schemes and social choice is quite direct. Arrow himself sketches that relationship in chapter 4 of *SCIV*. He considers whether there is a system of compensation that could be used as a social choice criteria. Along the way he discusses the Kaldor-Kicks criterion and other ideas for compensation that have been proposed.

26. Under PMR we include the property that any defeated item may not be reintroduced.

27. One can argue that, inasmuch as voting is costly, turnout rates may reflect intensity of preference. But that argument is tempered by the further observation that there are reasons for voting other than preference for one candidate over another (Downs 1957).

28. J. Marcus Fleming (1952) showed that if an individual is developing preferences as if he or she were an ethical judge, and if that individual is "capable of making social welfare judgements for part of the society independently of the remainder," his or her judgment will be consistent with a utilitarian ethical template (see Arrow 1973b, 124; see also Hamada 1973; Sen 1973).

29. The possibility that the preferences over the universal set could help determine some choices or evaluations in the feasible set caused Arrow to wonder about one of the conditions he imposed in his original argument: the independence of irrelevant alternatives. We take a similar perspective later in this essay, when we deal with the concept of latent, nonrevealed preferences. For when we consider framing as determining a preference over a pair, we are asserting that the preferences are not independent of an (irrelevant) framing factor. As Arrow said later of the univer-

sal set (1967, 76): "In many situations we do have information on preferences for nonfeasible alternatives. It can certainly be argued that when available this information should be used in social choice."

30. Indeed, recent findings in psychoneuroimmunology seem to hint that entertaining the notion of a cure and desiring it may, in some limited situations that are not yet well understood, affect the immune system and improve one's health.

31. As ought to be clear from the discussion later in the essay, we believe that the definition of the domain may be inseparable from the questions regarding cues and framing. But it is not clear to us yet how this aspect of the problem should be handled.

32. Indeed, a moment's reflection leads one to appreciate that even what constitutes "a situation" requires the selective abstraction of aspects of what confronts us.

33. Gerald Edelman (1992) explicitly identifies some of the neural structure that must underlie any manifest cognitive (or evaluative) judgment. The ambiguities of multiple maps and the likely probabilistic selection of those maps in any decision context are sufficient to generate the deeper structure to which we are alluding here.

34. This does not mean that there cannot be domains over which shared human experience in different cultures and settings may yield similar values and perspectives. We note later in the essay the possibility of agreement about some matters of distributive justice. But we would expect considerable divergence on many matters even within a given culture.

35. The word *images,* of course, is used metaphorically. The "mental images" may not be visual.

36. To push the matter even further, it may be a physiological fact that one cannot discover the meaning of an individual's preference between x and y without furnishing cues. And if one furnishes cues, one may be affecting i's preferences over the pairs, and indeed conceivably over other alternatives, s and t, in a subsequent decision. This would be a general limitation related to the irrelevance of other alternatives but also reflecting an uncertainty principle similar to the Heisenberg uncertainty principle.

37. In light of this, we can reconsider the example of the children in the school yard. There is no reason that the individual passerby needed to see tears to generate one frame or the other. The memories associated with such scenes will generate different affects depending on what is being tapped either by the scene or by other thoughts and happenings of the moment. Hence, the individual assessor would not be likely to have consistent evaluations of the scene were it to repeat itself (and yet catch her attention).

38. For an example regarding domains, see proposals by Richard M. Hare (1963), who ties the types of alternatives to the conditions of impartiality.

39. A substantial effort was undertaken by the authors to induce impartial reasoning in tests of Rawlsian conjectures (Frohlich and Oppenheimer 1992). They have been extended to other tasks and generalized (see Frohlich and Oppenheimer 1997). See also the conceptually related experimental literature (Frohlich and Oppenheimer 1984; Roth 1995) that has developed over the measure of self-interest's role in individual preference structures to begin to see how context generates substantive differences in preferences.

40. Of course, it is possible that although the decisions are consensual, some aspect of the frame of the situation *other than impartial reasoning* is driving the consensus. But we have tried in our experiments to test for the typical framing effects by running the experiments both as loss and as gain. None of these tests for framing seemed to matter (Frohlich and Oppenheimer 1992, 43 et seq., 84–87). It must be noted that the frame, or cues, supplied in the experiments helped determine the result. For example, when Oleson (1997) introduced the possibility of unemployment, the distribution of the principles chosen by the groups shifted. Other frames did not seem to affect the distributions.

41. Exactly what might constitute agreement, what sampling of humanity might be necessary to reach tenable conclusions, and what conditions would be appropriate are all contentious issues (Frohlich and Oppenheimer 1992, 1997).

42. This means that the government does not get credit for what it has not accomplished. Of course, by omission, we do not here intend to make light of the rights and liberties of individuals (which

must place constraints on centralized decisions) (Sen 1970b). Similarly, the distributive pattern of the welfares is an important aspect of the aggregate evaluation. We assume that many of these concerns are taken care of by arguing that only some sorts of preferences are morally privileged (see discussion later in the essay). Other procedural aspects of governance, such as fairness, openness, and equality of individuals, cannot be considered here but are closely parallel to the concerns of democratic procedures. So, for example, May (1952) has talked about anonymity—the property that the preferences of i and j will be handled in the same fashion by the institutions—as a desirable property of voting systems.

43. For example, preference structures induced by impartial reasoning may have a claim to being morally privileged.

44. In particular, political structures that induce more impartial perspectives can make some claim to being morally privileged.

45. Sen (1977b) went further. He argued that individuals have the ability to choose their preference structure. For him, they have a responsibility to get beyond an ordinalist metric of welfare and move on to an interpersonal comparative metric so as to make judgments regarding social welfare. In the argument, he also critiqued the notion that we should judge outcomes strictly as a function of the welfare of individuals. He conjectured that such a template is incomplete and that moral judgments need to be introduced in the aggregation process. It is in this spirit that we are proposing that the quality of the sociopolitical space be evaluated on the basis of the sorts of preference structures that the populace, in their roles as public citizens, are encouraged to adopt.

46. We leave aside, for the purposes of this discussion, the other deep questions of the difficulties of mobilizing large groups with diffuse interests against small groups with concentrated interests (Downs 1957; Olson 1965).

47. Indeed, one of the functions of political ideologies is to frame a whole set of situations within a grand interpretive schema so that alternatives disfavored by the proponents of the ideology are downgraded in the minds of those who buy into the ideology's worldview.

48. After all, it was only a few decades ago that those who sought to understand democracy began to consider the role of informal institutions.

49. Note how this points toward the perspective of Jurgen Habermas's "ideal speech situation," which may be viewed as an attempt to specify hypothetical conditions conducive to the discovery of important ethical insights (see Barry 1995; Habermas 1990; Honneth and Joas 1991). Careful attention to conditions such as these may furnish clues as to how one might structure environments of controlled observation to provide data useful in evaluating ethically "privileged" preferences and hence claims regarding social welfare. If there is validity in the identification of these theoretically identified conditions, then by attempting to replicate key components of their constructs we should be able to generate observations that illuminate the philosophical issues that underlie the evaluation of democratic systems.

REFERENCES

Arrow, Kenneth J. 1950. "A Difficulty in the Concept of Social Welfare." *Journal of Political Economy* 58: 328–46. Reprinted with a preface in *Collected Papers of Kenneth J. Arrow*, vol. 1, *Social Choice and Justice* (Cambridge, Mass.: Belknap Press of Harvard University Press, 1983), 1–29.
———. 1952. "Le Principe de rationalité dans les décisions collectives" [The Principle of Rationality in Collective Decisions]. *Économie Appliquée*, 5: 469–84. Translated and reprinted in *Collected Papers of Kenneth J. Arrow*, vol. 1, *Social Choice and Justice* (Cambridge, Mass.: Belknap Press of Harvard University Press, 1983), 45–58.
———. 1963a. *Social Choice and Individual Values*. 2nd ed. New Haven, Conn.: Yale University Press.
———. 1963b. "Uncertainty and the Welfare Economics of Medical Care." *American Economic Review* 8(5, December): 941–73.
———. 1967. "Values and Collective Decision Making." In *Philosophy, Politics, and Society*, edited by Peter Laslett and Walter G. Runiman (Oxford: Oxford University Press). Reprinted in *Collected Papers of Kenneth J. Arrow*, vol. 1, *Social Choice and Justice* (Cambridge, Mass.: Belknap Press of Harvard University Press, 1983), 59–77.

————. 1969. "Tullock and an Existence Theorem." *Public Choice* 6: 105–12. Reprinted in *Collected Papers of Kenneth J. Arrow*, vol. 1, *Social Choice and Justice* (Cambridge, Mass.: Belknap Press of Harvard University Press, 1983), 81–87.

————. 1973a. "Some Ordinalist-Utilitarian Notes on Rawls's Sense of Justice." *Journal of Philosophy* 70(May 10): 245–63. Reprinted in *Collected Papers of Kenneth J. Arrow*, vol. 1, *Social Choice and Justice* (Cambridge, Mass.: Belknap Press of Harvard University Press, 1983), 96–115.

————. 1973b. "Formal Theories of Social Welfare." In *Dictionary of the History of Ideas*, vol. 4, edited by Philip Wiener (New York: Scribner's), 276–84. Reprinted in *Collected Papers of Kenneth J. Arrow*, vol. 1, *Social Choice and Justice* (Cambridge, Mass.: Belknap Press of Harvard University Press, 1983), 115–32.

————. 1974. *The Limits of Organization.* New York: Norton.

————. 1977a. "Current Developments in the Theory of Social Choice," *Social Research* 44: 607–22.

————. 1977b. "Extended Sympathy and the Possibility of Social Choice." *American Economic Review*, 67(December): 219–25.

————. 1982. "Risk Perception in Psychology and Economics." *Economic Inquiry* 20: 1–9. Reprinted in *Collected Papers of Kenneth J. Arrow*, vol. 3, *Individual Choice Under Certainty and Uncertainty* (Cambridge, Mass.: Belknap Press of Harvard University Press, 1983), 261–70.

Barry, Brian. 1995. *Impartial Justice and Individual Discretion.* Oxford: Oxford University Press.

Bernholz, Peter. 1974. "Logrolling, Arrow Paradox, and Decision Rules: A Generalization." *KYKLOS* 27: 49–61.

Black, Duncan. 1958. *The Theory of Committees and Elections.* Cambridge: Cambridge University Press.

Coleman, James. 1966. "The Possibility of a Social Welfare Function." *American Economic Review* 56: 1105–22.

Coughlin, Peter. 1984. "Probabilistic Voting Models." In *Encyclopedia of the Statistical Sciences*, vol. 6, edited by Samuel Kotz, Norman Johnson, and Campbell Read (New York: Wiley).

————. 1988. "Expectations About Voter Choices." *Public Choice* 44(1): 49–59.

Coughlin, Peter, and Muelvin J. Hinich. 1984. "Necessary and Sufficient Conditions for Single-Peakedness in Public Economic Models." *Journal of Public Economics* 25: 323–41.

Dahl, Robert A. 1954. *A Preface to Democratic Theory.* Chicago: University of Chicago Press.

————. 1961. "The Behavioral Approach in Political Science: Epitaph for a Monument to a Successful Protest." *American Political Science Review* 55: 763–72. Reprinted in *Discipline and History*, edited by James Farr and Raymond Seidelman (Ann Arbor: University of Michigan Press, 1993), 249–67.

D'Aspremont, Claude, and Louis Gevers. 1977. "Equity and the Informational Basis of Collective Choice." *Review of Economic Studies* 44(June): 199–209.

De Waal, Frans. 1982. *Chimpanzee Politics: Power and Sex Among Apes.* New York: Harper & Row.

Downs, Anthony. 1957. *An Economic Theory of Democracy.* New York: Harper & Row.

Easton, David. 1985. "Political Science in the United States: Past and Present." *International Political Science Review* 6: 133–52. Reprinted in *Discipline and History*, edited by James Farr and Raymond Seidelman (Ann Arbor: University of Michigan Press, 1993), 291–310.

Eavey, Cheryl, and Gary Miller. 1984. "Bureaucratic Agenda Control: Imposition or Bargaining?" *American Political Science Review* 78(September): 719–33.

Edelman, Gerald M. 1992. *Bright Air, Brilliant Fire: On the Matter of the Mind.* New York: Basic Books.

Enelow, James, and Melvin Hinich. 1984. *The Spatial Theory of Voting.* Cambridge: Cambridge University Press.

Farr, James, and Raymond Seidelman (eds.). 1993. *Discipline and History.* Ann Arbor: University of Michigan Press.

Feldman, Allan M., and Kyung-Ho Lee. 1987. "Existence of Electoral Equilibria with Probabilistic Voting." Paper presented at the *Public Choice* meetings, Tucson, Arizona, March 27–30.

Fleming, J. Marcus. 1952. "A Cardinal Concept of Welfare." *Quarterly Journal of Economics* 64: 366–84.

Frohlich, Norman, and Joe A. Oppenheimer. 1992. *Choosing Justice: An Experimental Approach to Ethical Theory.* Berkeley: University of California Press.

————. 1997. "A Role for Structured Observation in Ethics." *Social Justice Research* 10(1, March): 1–21.

Frohlich, Norman, and Joe Oppenheimer, with Pat Bond and Irvin Boschman. 1984. "Beyond Economic Man." *Journal of Conflict Resolution* 28(1, March): 3–24.

Giere, Ronald N. 1990. *Explaining Science.* Chicago: University of Chicago Press.

Green, Donald P., and Ian Shapiro. 1994. *Pathologies of Rational Choice Theory: A Critique of Applications in Political Science.* New Haven, Conn.: Yale University Press.

Grether, David M., and Charles R. Plott. 1979. "Economic Theory of Choice and the Preference Reversal Phenomenon." *American Economic Review* 69(September): 623–38.

Gunnell, John G. 1993. "American Political Science, Liberalism, and the Invention of Political Theory." In *Discipline and History,* edited by James Farr and Raymond Seidelman (Ann Arbor: University of Michigan Press), 179–201.

Habermas, Jurgen. 1990. *Moral Consciousness and Communication Action.* Translated by Lenhjard and Nicholson. Cambridge, Mass:. MIT Press.

Hamada, Koichi. 1973. "A Simple-Majority Rule on the Distribution of Income." *Journal of Economic Theory:* 243–76.

Hardin, Garrett. 1968. "The Tragedy of the Commons." *Science* 162: 1243–48.

Hare, Richard M. 1963. *Freedom and Reason.* Oxford: Oxford University Press.

Hinich, Melvin J. 1977. "Equilibrium in Spatial Voting: The Median Voter Result Is an Artifact." *Journal of Economic Theory* 16(December): 208–19.

Honneth, Axel, and Hans Joas. 1991. *Communicative Action.* Cambridge, Mass.: MIT Press.

Hotelling, Harold. 1929. "Stability in Competition." *Economic Journal* 39 (1): 41–57.

Jackson, Michael, and Peter Hill. 1995. "A Fair Share." *Journal of Theoretical Politics* 7(2, April): 69–179.

Kadane, Joseph. 1972. "On Division of the Question." *Public Choice* 13(Fall): 47–54.

Kagel, John H., and Alvin E. Roth (eds.). 1995. *The Handbook of Experimental Economics.* Princeton, N.J.: Princeton University Press.

Landa, Janet. 1986. "The Political Economy of Swarming in Honeybees: Voting with the Wings, Decision-making Costs, and the Unanimity Rule." *Public Choice* 51(1): 25–38.

Larrick, Richard P., and Sally Blount. 1997a. "The Claiming Effect: Procedural Framing in Ultimatum Bargaining." Paper presented at the Economic Science Association, Tucson, Arizona, September.

———. 1997b. "The Claiming Effect: Why Players Are More Generous in Social Dilemmas Than in Ultimatum Games." *Journal of Personality and Social Psychology* 72: 810–25.

Lissowski, Grzegorz, Tadeusz Tyszka, and Wlodzimierz Okrasa. 1991. "Principles of Distributive Justice: Experiments in Poland and America." *Journal of Conflict Resolution* 35(1, March): 98–119.

May, Kenneth O. 1952. "A Set of Independent, Necessary, and Sufficient Conditions for Simple-Majority Decision." *Econometrica* 20(October): 680–84.

———. 1954. "Intransitivity, Utility, and the Aggregation of Preference Patterns." *Econometrica* 22 (1, January): 1–13.

McKelvey, Richard D. 1979. "General Conditions for Global Intransitivities in Formal Voting Models." *Econometrica* 47: 1085–111.

Merriam, Charles. 1993. "Recent Advances in Political Methods." In *Discipline and History,* edited by James Farr and Raymond Seidelman (Ann Arbor: University of Michigan Press), 129–46.

Miller, Gary. 1992. *Managerial Dilemmas: The Political Economy of Hierarchy.* Cambridge: Cambridge University Press.

Miller, Gary, and Thomas Hammond. 1994. "Why Politics Is More Fundamental Than Economics: Incentive-Compatible Mechanisms Are Not Credible." *Journal of Theoretical Politics* 6(1, January): 5–26.

Miller, Gary, and Joe A. Oppenheimer. 1982. "Universalism in Experimental Committees." *American Political Science Review* 76(2, June): 561–74.

Miller, Nicholas R. 1983. "Pluralism and Social Choice." *American Political Science Review* 77: 734–47.

Mueller, Dennis C. 1989. *Public Choice II.* Cambridge: Cambridge University Press.

Oleson, Paul E. 1997. "An Experimental Examination of Alternative Theories of Distributive Justice and Economic Fairness." Paper presented at the *Public Choice* meetings, San Francisco, March.

Olson, Mancur. 1965. *The Logic of Collective Action.* Cambridge, Mass.: Harvard University Press.

Oppenheimer, Joe. 1975. "Some Political Implications of 'Vote Trading and the Voting Paradox: A Proof of Logical Equivalence': A Comment." *American Political Science Review* 69 (3, September): 963–69.

Plott, Charles. 1976. "Axiomatic Social Choice Theory: An Overview and Interpretation." *American Journal of Political Science* 20(3, August): 511–94.

Popper, Karl. 1959. *The Logic of Scientific Discovery*. New York: Harper & Row. (Originally published in 1934)

Rawls, John. 1951. "Outline for a Decision Procedure for Ethics." *Philosophical Review* 60 (2, April): 177–97. Reprinted in *Ethics,* edited by J. Thomson and Gerald Dworkin (New York: Harper & Row, 1968).

———. 1971. *A Theory of Justice.* Cambridge, Mass.: Harvard University Press.

———. 1985. "Justice and Fairness: Political, Not Metaphysical." *Philosophy and Public Affairs* 14 (3, Summer): 223–51.

Ricci, David M. 1993. "Contradictions of a Political Discipline." In *Discipline and History,* edited by James Farr and Raymond Seidelman (Ann Arbor: University of Michigan Press), 165–74.

Riker, William H. 1982. *Liberalism Against Populism: A Confrontation Between the Theory of Democracy and the Theory of Social Choice.* Prospect Heights, Ill.: Waveland Press.

Romer, Thomas, and Howard Rosenthal. 1978. "Political Resource Allocation, Controlled Agendas, and the Status Quo." *Public Choice* 33(4): 27–43.

Ross, Dorothy. 1993. "The Development of the Social Sciences." In *Discipline and History,* edited by James Farr and Raymond Seidelman (Ann Arbor: University of Michigan Press), 81–104.

Roth, Alvin E. 1995. "Bargaining Experiments." In *The Handbook of Experimental Economics,* edited by John H. Kagel and Alvin E. Roth (Princeton, N.J.: Princeton University Press), 253–342.

Saijo, Tatsuyoshi, Shusuke Takahashi, and Stephen Turnbull. 1996. "Justice in Income Distribution: An Experimental Approach." Paper presented at the annual meeting of the International Studies Association, San Diego, April 18.

Schofield, Norman. 1978. "Instability of Simple Dynamic Games." *Review of Economic Studies* 45: 575–94.

Schwartz, Thomas. 1981. "The Universal Instability Theorem." *Public Choice* 37(3): 487–502.

———. 1986. *The Logic of Collective Choice.* New York: Columbia University Press.

Sen, Amartya K. 1970a. *Collective Choice and Social Welfare.* New York: North Holland.

———. 1970b. "The Impossibility of a Paretian Liberal." *Journal of Political Economy* 78(January–February): 152–57.

———. 1973. *On Economic Inequality.* New York: Norton.

———. 1977a. "Rational Fools: A Critique of the Behavioral Foundations of Economic Theory." *Philosophy and Public Affairs* 6(4, Summer): 317–44. Reprinted in *Beyond Self-Interest,* edited by Jane J. Mansbridge (Chicago: University of Chicago Press, 1990), 25–43.

———. 1977b. "Social Choice Theory: A Re-Examination." *Econometrica* 45 (January): 53–89.

Shepsle, Kenneth. 1979. "Institutional Arrangements and Equilibrium in Multidimensional Voting Models." *American Journal of Political Science* 23 (1, February): 27–59.

Shepsle, Kenneth A., and Barry R. Weingast. 1981a. "Political Preferences for the Pork Barrel: A Generalization." *American Journal of Political Science* 25(1, February): 96–111.

———. 1981b. "Structure Induced Equilibrium and Legislative Choice." *Public Choice* 37(3): 503–20.

Soltan, Karol. 1986. "Public Policy and Justice." In *Justice Views from the Social Sciences,* edited by Ronald L. Cohen (New York: Plenum), 235–68.

Tversky, Amos, and Daniel Kahneman. 1981. "The Framing of Decisions and the Psychology of Choice." *Science* 211(January 30): 453–58.

U.S. Department of Health, Education, and Welfare. 1969. "Toward a Social Report." Washington, D.C.: U.S. Government Printing Office.

Von Neumann, John, and Oskar Morgenstern. 1944. *Theory of Games and Economic Behavior.* New York: Wiley.

Weingast, Barry. 1979. "A Rational Choice Perspective on Congressional Norms." *American Journal of Political Science* 23(May): 245–62.

Wilson, Edward O. 1971. *The Insect Societies.* Cambridge, Mass.: Belknap Press of Harvard University Press.

CHAOS OR EQUILIBRIUM IN PREFERENCE AND BELIEF AGGREGATION

Norman Schofield

The great theorems of social mathematics discovered during the twentieth century can be separated into those that emphasize equilibrium and those that hint at "chaos," "inconsistency," or "irrationality."[1]

The equilibrium results all stem from Luitzen Brouwer's fixed point theorem (Brouwer 1910): A continuous function from the ball to itself has a fixed point. Since then the theorem has been extended to cover correspondences (Kakutani 1941) and infinite-dimensional spaces (Fan 1961) and has proved the fundamental tool in showing the existence of equilibria in games (Nash 1951; von Neumann 1928), in competitive economies (Arrow and Debreu 1954; Arrow and Hahn 1971; McKenzie 1959; von Neumann 1945), in coalition polities (Greenberg 1979; Nakamura 1979), and in evolutionary theory (Maynard Smith 1982).[2]

The first of the inconsistency results is the Gödel-Turing theorem on the decidability-halting problem in logic (Gödel 1931; Turing 1937): Any formal logic system (able to encompass arithmetic) will contain propositions whose validity (or truth value) cannot be determined within the system. Recently this theorem has been used by Roger Penrose (1989, 1994) to argue against Daniel Dennett (1991) that the behavior of the mind cannot be modeled by an algorithmic computing device. A version of the Turing theorem has been used even more recently to show that learning and optimization are incompatible features of games (Nachbar 1997).

The second fundamental inconsistency result is Arrow's impossibility theorem (Arrow 1950a, 1950b, 1951), which shows that apparently innocuous properties of a social welfare function are sufficient to ensure that it is dictatorial. My reading of these works by Arrow suggests to me that Arrow was concerned not simply with the possibility of "Condorcetian" voting cycles, nor with the intransitivity of domination in voting games (von Neumann and Morgenstern 1944). Rather, he was interested in the larger issue of the interaction between the political and economic realms, the topic that concerned political economists and philosophers such as Joseph Schumpeter, Friedrich von Hayek, and Karl Popper in the period around World War II. If I am correct in my inference, in order to understand Arrow's theorem it is necessary to set out the fundamental problem of political economy, namely, the nature and evolution of the social relationship between human beings. To do this I think it appropriate to briefly comment on my perception of the main themes of this debate since the time of Hobbes.

Since I understand this debate to focus on the possibility of equilibrium in contrast to disequilibrium (or disorder), I shall also mention what I judge to be the third significant anti-equilibrium discovery of this century: "chaos."

Stephen Smale (1966) is responsible for the key mathematical result: Structurally stable dynamical systems are not generic when the underlying space has three or more dimensions.[3] To illustrate, astronomers since the time of Pierre-Simon Laplace (1799) have believed that the solar system is structurally stable: Small perturbations in each planetary orbit (induced by other planets) cannot dramatically change the nature of the orbit. Although Isaac Newton was aware of the problem of perturbations (Newton 1687), even Henri Poincaré in his treatise of 1890 could not solve the differential equations.[4] However, Poincaré's work led to the beginning of differential topology and the work of Marston Morse, John Milnor, and Stephen Smale in this century. If the solar system were structurally unstable, or indeed chaotic, then it would be impossible to predict its evolution. In fact, it is not chaotic, although subsystems (such as asteroids) are.[5] As a result of popular books (Gleick 1987), we can conceive of natural phenomena (hurricanes) or even large-scale dynamic systems (such as climate) as potentially chaotic (Lorenz 1993). Although still a young science, human evolutionary theory suggests that chaotic transformations in weather may have had a profound effect on the human diaspora "out of Africa" (Boaz 1997; Calvin 1990; Stanley 1996). "Equilibrium"-focused evolutionary theory may also need revision (Eldridge and Gould 1972; Gould 1996).

Most scholars of human society believe (more or less as a requirement of their discipline) that society's evolutionary progress is intelligible, in the sense that predictions, of at least a qualitative form, can be made. This, I presume, is the understanding of economists when they base their reasoning on the fact of equilibrium. Even Douglass North (1990, 1994), in denying the utility of general (economic) equilibrium theory in explaining economic development, nonetheless appears to believe that an understanding of institutions allows us to infer something about the social "laws of motion." Contrary to North's suggestion that institutions are the "rules of the game," it appears to me that institutions are equilibria. If these equilibria are in constant motion (as seems obvious), then the dynamic that describes this motion (if indeed there is one) is just as likely to be chaotic as to be structurally stable.

It is, of course, possible that this belief, in the structural stability of society, is sustained by the apparent stability of the "world out there." Indeed, the bipolar world from the late 1940s until about 1990 did appear stable. Since then, the collapse of the Soviet Union, the disintegration of the Warsaw Pact, tumult in the Balkans, genocide and starvation in Africa, the troubles in Israel, and economic rumblings in Mexico and Southeast Asia all suggest something is amiss (see the discussion in Schofield 1999).

To tie the three instability theorems together in a kind of hierarchy, we may start with Penrose's argument that the Gödel-Turing theorem suggests that, at the fine level of analysis, individuals can display surprising, or apparently incomprehensible, behavior. Indeed, it is obvious that cognitive psychology can give only a very coarse-grained account of human motivation. One possible coarse-grained account is that each individual is "approximately" characterized by a preference correspondence (satisfying the usual properties assumed in microeconomics). However, game theory has made it obvious that the beliefs of agents are as important as (or even more important than) their preferences. Preferences are relatively easy to model, but beliefs are much more complicated. (In fact, they lie in function spaces.) Thus, while it is a standard formal procedure to use a Brouwer fixed point theorem (or better yet, the Fan theorem) to show the existence of optima in preferences, it is much more difficult to postulate conditions under which stable beliefs (a "belief equilibrium") can occur.

Arrow's theorem suggests that, even when individuals can be described by their preferences, only under particular circumstances can these preferences be aggregated to induce a "social vector field" that is "well behaved" in an appropriate sense. This is not to say that the social vector field can never exist; rather, there may be circumstances under which this field is badly behaved (or ill defined) in some sense. Obviously I am transposing Arrow's theorem from the discrete world where it was located to the continuous world of political economy. By a "social vector field" I mean a method of defining a direction of change compatible with the Pareto unanimity condition. If such a vector field could be defined, then in the usual political economy world (which is compact and convex), Brouwer fixed point arguments would give a singularity (a "social equilibrium"). The field could be badly behaved, for example, if it were not defined in some zone outside the Pareto set. Consequently, following the field would not lead into Pareto preferred outcomes. Arrow's theorem suggests that the only way to avoid such bad behavior is to pick one individual as dictator.[6]

Suppose now that Arrow's theorem is avoided by some device. For example, consider a world where everyone has strictly economic preferences and no public goods exist. In such a world, a competitive price equilibrium does exist. However, to attain it, we must imagine a price adjustment process (a vector field) based on excess demand. As an example by Herbert Scarf (1960) suggests, this vector field can be cyclic. Indeed, later results by Rolf Mantel (1974), Hugo Sonnenschein (1972), and Gerard Debreu (1974) show that it can be anything at all. As Donald Saari (1991) has emphasized, it could be chaotic.

This, of course, does not imply that the world is indeed chaotic. Some aspects of the political economic world may be chaotic without implying that the entire human universe is. To use the metaphor of the solar system, perhaps the overall process of human evolution is structurally stable but contains locally chaotic subsystems.

Whether equilibrium or non-equilibrium, chaos, appears to be a more satisfactory way of understanding the world depends, presumably, on the temperament of the scholar. It may be worth a detour to mention John von Neumann again, since his work touches on many aspects of social mathematics (as well as other fundamental areas of quantum mechanics, group theory, and so on).

Even before his game theory paper of 1928 and the work on general economic equilibrium (1945), von Neumann had published results on completing David Hilbert's program for proving the consistency of classical mathematics by finitary means. A recent biography of Kurt Gödel (Dawson 1997) notes that Gödel presented his inconsistency theorem at Konigsburg in 1930 to an audience that (aside from von Neumann) failed to grasp its significance. As far as I know, von Neumann ceased to work in formal logic after 1930.

Von Neumann met Alan Turing in Cambridge in 1935, and later during Turing's visit to Princeton in 1936 to 1937 (Hodges 1983), but appears to have paid little attention to Turing's results on the halting problem. However, von Neumann does appear to have made use of Turing's later work on computation during the Second World War, as well as Turing's essay on artificial intelligence (1950). Beginning in 1943, von Neumann was involved in approximate numeric solutions using some form of computing device. Turing's notion of a universal machine seems to have been indispensable to the design of British and American decoding devices during the war and to the construction of the computation machines (Edvac, Eniac, Maniac) necessary for the solution of nonlinear dynamical problems associated with the design of the hydrogen bomb (see Ulam and von Neumann 1947). Von Neumann took Turing's idea of a universal computing device and extended it to a model of the brain (von Neumann 1958) and of life (self-reproducing automata) in work later edited by Burks (von Neumann 1966).

What is interesting about this research is that Stanislaw Ulam, von Neumann's collaborator, had found chaos in a stochastic, or Monte Carlo, simulation of a relatively simple dynamical system (Fermi, Pasta, and Ulam 1955; see the discussion in Galison 1997). As far as I know, this is the first example of a computational model generating chaos. (It predates Edward Lorenz's meteorology simulation by seven years.) Monte Carlo simulation by von Neumann and his associates in numerical weather prediction and in their work on the bomb does not appear to have observed chaos (Galison 1997). If there had been chaos, there presumably would have been no hydrogen bomb.

In von Neumann's book with Morgenstern (1944) on cooperative game theory, the focus (as I understand it) is on trying to "equilibrate" the obvious cyclicity inherent in constant-sum voting games, using such devices as the von Neumann-Morgenstern solution. Later work in cooperative game theory also attempted to introduce equilibrium ideas (such as the bargaining set; see Aumann and Maschler 1964). These attempts seem unsatisfactory, and this may be why cooperative game theory is currently less influential than noncooperative game theory (and the powerful notion of Nash equilibrium).

Obviously, both the equilibrium perspective and the chaos implicit in the Gödel-Turing-Arrow theorems are relevant to understanding the world. In this essay, I consider some of the arguments that have been made in the past, which appear to have some bearing on both the equilibrium and chaotic views of the world.

HOBBESIAN AND LOCKEAN VIEWS OF SOCIETY

Thomas Hobbes returned to the England of the Protectorate in December 1651, ten years after his departure, three years after the execution of Charles I, and a few months after the publication of *Leviathan*. Hobbes's biographer (Rogow 1986, 109) quotes sources who suggest that during Hobbes's meeting with Galileo in Florence in 1635–36, "Galileo gave Hobbes . . . the first idea that the doctrines of ethics . . . can be brought to a mathematical certainty by applying the principles of geometry."

As Crawford B. MacPherson (1968, 26–27) says in his introduction to *Leviathan*:

> The resolutive part of Galileo's method was an exercise in imagination. What simple motions or forces could be imagined which, when logically compounded, would provide a causal explanation of the complex phenomenon which was to be explained? . . . The resolutive stage . . . consisted in resolving political society into the motion of its parts—individual human beings.

Although it is the appetites and aversions that move men, the effect is "a generall inclination of mankind, a perpetuall and restlesse desire of Power after power, that ceaseth only in Death" (161). Thus, "it is manifest, that during the time men live with-out a common Power to keep them all in awe, they are in that condition which is called Warre. . . . And the life of man [is] solitary, poore, nasty, brutish and short" (185–6).

Hobbes goes on to discuss the nature of contract or "Covenant":

> If a Covenant be made . . . in the condition of meer Nature . . . it is Voyd; But if there be a common Power set over them both, . . . it is not Voyd (196). . . . But when a Covenant is made, then to break it is *Unjust* (202). . . . A multi-tude of men, are made *One* person, when they are by one man, or one Person, Represented. . . . And if the Representative consist of many men, the voyce of the greatest number, must be considered as the voyce of them all (220–1).

On the form of the commonwealth, whether monarchy, democracy, or aristoc-racy, Hobbes suggests that the difference is not in power, but in "Convenience, or Aptitude to produce the Peace, and Security of the People" (241).

In chapter 18, Hobbes compares the benefits of life in the commonwealth with "the miseries, and horrible calamities, that accompany a Civill Warre." (238) In chapter 24, he discusses the economy of the commonwealth—the distribution of land, the nature of taxes, and, most important, the role of money, "the Sanguifica-tion of the Commonwealth."

In this chapter, Hobbes refers again to his somewhat shocking metaphor: "For by Art is created that great Leviathan called a Common-wealth, or State . . . which is but an Artificiall Man" (81).

Many political theorists of the recent past (Axelrod 1984; Schotter 1981; Sugden 1986; Taylor 1976, 1982) have interpreted Hobbes's argument for Leviathan in terms of the prisoners' dilemma. That is, the state of nature, of "Warre," is the Nash equilibrium (indeed, the joint dominant strategy in the game). All players prefer the state of cooperation, of peace, but it is unattainable without a covenant. The argu-ments have often proceeded to suggest that the "game form" is that of an *n*-person-iterated prisoners' dilemma. In such a game, cooperative equilibria may be possible if they are sustained by appropriate beliefs on the part of the agents. Much of the work of Michael Taylor (1982), Russell Hardin (1982), Robert Axelrod (1984), and Robert Sugden (1986) can be seen as an extension of Robert Nozick's famous book *Anarchy, State, and Utopia* (1974) to argue, contra Hobbes, that the state (Leviathan) is unnecessary for security. For example, Sugden argues that "conventions" (such as language, or driving on one side of the road) arise spontaneously as solutions to games of coordination and cooperation. But if we think of language as a convention, then it is obvious enough that it evolves quite rapidly. In Papua New Guinea, where human settlements are geographically separate, the evolving languages became extra-ordinarily diverse. (In fact, it has been estimated that there are about one thousand distinct languages, clustered in thirty phyla, among a population of about four mil-lion.) Although there may be some validity in Taylor's (1982) argument that "com-munity" can indeed sustain cooperation in the absence of a Hobbesian Leviathan, or state, the argument works only for small communities. Arrovian disorder between such communities would appear to be generic.[7] Moreover, the evolution of the "equi-libria" of these cooperative conventions would seem to be as indeterminate as the for-mal models of *n*-person-iterated prisoners' dilemmas (Kreps and others 1982). I return to this later when discussing "belief equilibria."

Locke's *Two Treatises of Government* was published anonymously in 1690 and is often taken as a response to both the Glorious Revolution of 1688 and Hobbes's *Leviathan*. However, Peter Laslett (1988), in his introduction to the *Treatises*, suggests that they were written approximately ten years earlier in response to Robert Filmer's essays "The Natural Power of Kings Defended against the Unnatural Liberty of the People" (1632) and "Observations concerning the origins of Government . . ." (1652). In *The Second Treatise*, Locke (1988, 97–98) develops further the notion of a contract but seems to remove the almost metaphysical Hobbesian conception of Leviathan.

> And Thus every Man, by consenting with others to make one Body Politik under one Government, puts himself under an Obligation to every one of that Society, to submit to the determination of the majority. . . . For if the *consent of the majority* shall not in reason, be received, as the act of the whole . . . nothing but the consent of every individual can make anything to be the act of the whole: But such a consent is next to impossible to be had.

Locke's version of the compact has obviously strongly influenced the twentieth-century contractarian visions of John Rawls (1972), David Gauthier (1986) and particularly Robert Nozick (1974). For Nozick, property (and especially labor) is a fundamental feature of Lockean Liberty. Nozick constructs what has been called a meta-utopian framework (Gray 1984), within which free individuals migrate to preferred communities, agree on public provision, and live in peace. The formal underpinning of this framework is that of the "core," the set of allocations that are coalitionally rational. But the conditions sufficient for the existence of a core (balancedness, "private" preferences, and so on) are likely to occur only in pure private goods economies. If power is a feature of the Nozickean political economy, then the appropriate formal model is not that of the exchange economy but the constant-sum game. In such a world, the core is generically empty and cycles or Arrovian intransitivities are pervasive (McKelvey and Schofield 1986). Nozick's anarchic utopia is thus void.

Gray (1984, 31) goes on to describe Hayek's (1944, 1948, 1973) meta-utopian framework in terms of the idea of a spontaneous order, of "self-organizing and self-replicating structures [that] arise without design or even the possibility of design." This framework is based on the inference that "unhampered markets display a tendency to equilibrium. . . . (In a world of constantly changing beliefs and preferences, of course, equilibrium is never achieved, but is to be viewed as a[n] . . . asymptote). . . . We find the spontaneous formation of self-regulating structures in the growth of language, [in] the development of law and in the emergence of moral norms."

Although Gray sees Hayek's ideas as Humean, contra Hobbes's "constructivist rationalism," it seems to me that the Hayekian vision of how social order comes into being is very similar to that of the Hobbesian Leviathan. Although the order is not based on a covenant and may not be intelligible to human analysis, it would seem to have an "artificiall life."

Somehow the beliefs of the members of society are "aggregated" in such a way as to generate the motion of this Leviathan. In an attempt to determine whether Hayek's view of order has theoretical justification, the next section extends the Arrovian notion of preference aggregation to that of belief aggregation.

CONDORCETIAN VIEWS OF TRUTH

As I intimated earlier, the Galilean logic of motion was developed by Newton to formally relate matter, motion, and space, first in his article on "Light and Colours" in 1672, then in *Principia* (1687) and finally in *Opticks* (1704). Voltaire's volume on *Newton's Philosophy* (1738) helped transmit Newton's underlying philosophy of science throughout Europe. Part of Newton's argument was against the "light of Reason" of Descartes' *Discource on Method* (1637) and for the "light of Nature"— that is, to follow the injunction to reason from the world, to find its underlying principles. I find it hardly surprising that Newton's awesome achievement in natural science sparked attempts by scholars, particularly in Britain and France, to construct a calculus of the moral or human sciences.[8]

Although Adam Smith was probably influenced by the French scholars Bernard Mandeville, Étienne Condillac, Richard Cantillon, and Anne-Robert-Jacques Turgot, it is Smith's work in moral philosophy and political economy that is particularly remembered. However, I wish to focus not on Smith but on Condorcet (1743 to 1794). As far as I know, Condorcet was viewed (and is generally still regarded) as a utopian theorist of little interest other than as providing provocation for Thomas Malthus's *Essay on the Principle of Population* (1798).

Condorcet, a protégé and friend of Turgot, was certainly influenced by him and by Smith, whom he met in Paris in 1766. The debt to Smith is most evident in Condorcet's *Esquisse d'un tableau historique des progrès de l'esprit humain* (edited by Condorcet's widow, Sophie, and published posthumously in 1795). But it is his work on the so-called jury theorem (Condorcet 1785, 1994), brought to light by Duncan Black (1958), that is of greater interest for the purpose of this essay. This theorem is part of Condorcet's attempt to construct a grand theory of human behavior, based on collective choice by a society in the presence of risk. Assuming that there is an external truth (a best choice out of the two alternatives), and supposing that each individual chooses the truth with probability at least one-half, then majority rule will be correct more often than the average juror. Moreover, as the jury increases in size, the probability that it will attain the truth approaches unity. The theorem assumes that voters are (pairwise) independent in their choices. As might be expected, however, if the average pairwise correlation between voter choices is low, then the theorem still holds (Ladha 1992, 1993; Ladha and Miller 1996). Moreover, it is not necessary to assume that each voter is described by a probability greater than one-half; it is sufficient if the average probability exceeds one-half (Boland 1989).

There have been attempts to develop models of "belief aggregation" in economics (Aumann 1976; Geanakoplos and Polemarchakis 1982; McKelvey and Page 1986), and Arrow (1986) has recently commented on these in the context of market behavior. I believe these are conceptually related to Condorcet's jury theorem. Before discussing these economic models, let us consider briefly the possible intellectual influence of Condorcet during the American and French Revolutions.

As Condorcet's biographers (Baker 1975; McLean and Hewitt 1994) have observed, Condorcet believed not in the notion of the "general will" (as had Rousseau) but in the possibility of the exercise of reason. In particular, he believed that political representatives would exercise their judgments (or beliefs) and be less swayed by the passions (or preferences) than would a mass of voters. In the years following the calling of the Estates-General (1789), up to his death in 1794, he was active as president of the French Legislative Assembly, as a member of the National Convention (1792), and as the architect of the "Girondin Constitution" of 1793. Prior to the trial of the king, Louis XVI, Condorcet had struggled to institute a constitutional monarchy, and during the trial (in January 1793) he spoke at length against capital punishment. With the expulsion of the Girondins in the Jacobin Terror in 1794, Condorcet's life was in danger. As Simon Schama (1989, 856) writes in his book on the French Revolution, "The great exponent of a state in which science and virtue would be mutually reinforcing, the Marquis de Condorcet, died in abject defeat. . . . He was locked up for the Revolutionary Tribunal but found dead in his cell."

As for the effect of Condorcet on the American Constitution, it is known that Condorcet and Thomas Jefferson were friends in Paris in 1786 (Randall 1993; Urken 1991), and Thomas Paine, of course, was in Paris and a member of the Legislative Assembly in 1792 to 1793. Jefferson and James Madison engaged in continual correspondence while Jefferson was in Paris (McLean and Urken 1992; Smith 1995).

I am no historian of ideas, but there appears to be quite a difference between the Lockean ideals of Jefferson circa 1776 and the views of Madison in 1787.[9] To some degree, Madison (writing as Publius in Federalist 10 in November 1787) develops Adam Smith's concern in *Wealth of Nations* for the power of "those rancorous and virulent factions which are inseparable from small democracies, and which have so frequently divided the affection of their people and disturbed the tranquillity of their governments" (1776/1976, book 5). As Madison writes:

> It may be concluded, that a pure Democracy, by which I mean, a Society, consisting of a small number of citizens, who assemble and administer the Government in person, can admit of no cure for the mischiefs of faction. . . . Hence it is, that such Democracies have ever been spectacles of turbulence and contention; have ever been found . . . short in their lives, as they have been violent in their deaths. (Federalist 10; see Bailyn 1993, 408)

Surely this is a very dramatic interpretation of Arrovian instability. On the other hand, Madison takes a very Condorcetian view of the nature of the republic, the political system of representation.

> A Republic, by which I mean a Government in which the scheme of representation takes place, opens a different prospect, and promises a cure for which we are seeking. . . . The two great points of difference between a Democracy and a Republic are, first, the delegation of the Government, in the latter, to a small number of citizens elected by the rest; secondly, the greater sphere of the country, over which the latter may be extended. . . . Under such a regulation, it may well happen that the public voice pronounced by the representatives of the people, will be more consonant to the public good. (Bailyn 1993, 409)

It seems to me that Madison is arguing that each representative must embody the preferences and beliefs of a large number of constituents and will therefore be unlikely to pursue any particular "electoral preference." Consequently, as Condorcet believed, the representatives can be considered to constitute a jury, acting so as to choose the "best" option in terms of the public good.

As the current form of the jury theorem suggests, low levels of (pairwise) behavioral correlation among the representatives are important for the ability of this political jury to find such wise options. By the term "greater sphere" I take Madison to refer to the heterogeneity of the beliefs that will be held by the representatives.

It is plausible, then, that Madison's argument rests on the postulate that belief heterogeneity is likely to result in choices that are for the public good. Of course, Condorcet's jury theorem is only valid for voting in binary decisions. He was unable to extend the theorem to three or more choices, and indeed, in attempting to so extend the theorem, he discovered the possibility of voting cycles. If we consider voting in terms of aggregation of preference, then not only will no equilibrium generally exist (Black 1958; Plott 1967), but the resulting cycles may fill the entire "policy space" (McKelvey 1976; Schofield 1978). This voting indeterminacy may reasonably be considered to be chaotic. Although these spatial voting theorems and Arrow's impossibility theorem are formally distinct, they do suggest that the greater the degree of preference heterogeneity, the more likely that the method of preference aggregation will be chaotic.[10] If political and economic decisionmaking should properly be viewed as belief aggregation, rather than as preference aggregation, and if the Madisonian postulate is justified, then we may infer instead that these processes will be reasonable.

The work by Robert Aumann (1976) and others, mentioned earlier, can be seen as an attempt to determine those conditions under which belief convergence occurs. The basic construction is one in which individuals, each with his or her own prior and private information, together generate a statistic (essentially a price vector). If the model that each individual employs is common knowledge, then every individual can compute a posterior belief on the basis of reasonable inferences about the nature of the other individuals' private information. After a few rounds, these posterior beliefs (probabilities) converge (McKelvey and Page 1986).

As Arrow (1986) has observed, however, this result does depend on seemingly very strong common knowledge assumptions. To illustrate, consider agents in a typical market trading assets of some kind. Unlike the standard picture of an exchange economy, the agents cannot really be said to have preferences for the assets. Whether an agent wishes to buy or sell an asset depends not so much on current prices as on expectations (beliefs) about the probable behavior of the prices. But these beliefs, of course, are determined by the agents' interpretation of the other agents' beliefs. In other words, unlike the Aumann problem, (which deals essentially with nature), this market is a game between rational actors. Formally analyzing such a game requires us to model the mental processes and strategic behavior of each agent. John Nachbar's theorem (1997) implies that each agent (in such a symmetric game) will adopt strategies that the agent believes cannot be adopted by the other players.

Of course, this interpretation of the game may be denied. That is, it could be argued that this market should be viewed as a decision-theoretic problem, in which each agent plays against nature and attempts to guess (statistically) how this nature behaves. Personally, I do not see how this argument can be valid. Indeed, Arrow (1986) suggests that the presumed advantage of markets (that they are effective decentralized methods of aggregating beliefs and preferences) rests on an unreasonable assumption: For the market to work, each agent must have (at least approximately) a model of every other agent's thought processes and a general economic equilibrium calculator to integrate everything. This is just impossible.

If we suppose instead that each individual responds, in a decision-theoretic fashion, to the overall behavior of the market, then it seems plausible that the aggregate behavior of the market could be indeterminate. Analyses of much simpler models of collective behavior (Hirschleifer, Bikhchandani, and Welsh 1992; Huberman and Glance 1995) have found complex bifurcations and cascades.

In his recent comments on the research carried out on complex systems at the Santa Fe Institute, Arrow (1988, 278) has gone on to observe that markets appear to have both homeostatic and chaotic features.

> Equilibrium Theory would tend to suggest that as technology spreads throughout the world, the per capita national incomes would tend to converge, but any such tendency is very weak indeed. . . . Instead of stochastic steady states, we observe that volatility tends to vary greatly over time, quiescent eras with little period-by-period fluctuations alternating with eras of rapid fluctuations. . . . These empirical results have given greater impetus to the closer study of dynamic models and the emphasis on application of new results on non-linear dynamic models. They have also given rise to criticism of the models themselves, and this goes far back; it suffices to mention the alternative theories of J. M. Keynes.

Some of the work being carried out under the auspices of the Santa Fe Institute (Holland 1988; Kauffman 1993, 1995) emphasizes the notion of complexity, of chaos generating order. These concepts are perhaps influenced by the work of Ilya Prigogine (1980) in the physical sciences; and before him by the ideas of John von Neumann (1966). As I suggested earlier, there appears to be a connection between the ideas of "order out of chaos" and the nonmathematical, neo-Hobbesian views of Hayek. These recent ideas are of very general applicability, and in the last section of the essay I discuss them in the context of some of the abstract models of the world that we have been considering.

A HIERARCHY OF MODELS

Figure 1.3 suggests how to relate the models of the world that we have been discussing. Newton's laws framed the first formal, mathematical model of "the world of the large"—the interaction of matter in space. The development of mathematics to deal with this world led to the new insights in differential geometry and topology of Poincaré, Smale, and others that we have discussed. This in turn led to the Brouwer fixed point theorem and the various applications in economic theory. For convenience, we can view this general class of game-theoretic models of "the social world" as belonging to the von Neumann research program. The focus of this program is to describe the interaction of individuals who are fundamentally described by "preferences," "utilities," and so on.

Game theory has been influenced by, and in turn has influenced, research in the Darwinian or evolutionary research program focused on "the biological world." The idea of "fitness" in the Darwinian research program is much like that of utility or preference, and the notion of the game-theoretic equilibrium has been modified to that of the "evolutionary stable strategy" (Maynard Smith 1982).

One might view Popper's work in the philosophy of science as being concerned with evolutionary models of knowledge or beliefs. As Popper (1972/1979, 261) has written: "[T]he growth of our knowledge is the result of a process closely resembling what Darwin called 'natural selection'; that is *the natural selection of hypotheses.*" In other words, Popper was concerned about how individuals form beliefs about the world, how they test these hypotheses, and how these beliefs "compete" with one another through their ability to describe the world. The more recent and related work of Aumann and others suggests that this process "converges to the truth."

Figure 1.3 distinguishes between the Popperian and Condorcetian research programs because I judge there to be an important difference between the two. Condorcet was interested in *collective* choice in an uncertain world; that is, once individuals have formed their judgments, how could these be aggregated in a sensible fashion?

It seems clear that Arrow, in his *Social Choice and Individual Values* (1951) and his two earlier papers (Arrow 1950a, 1950b), was also interested in the collective aggregation of values rather than simply tastes or preferences. However, the formal structure that he imposed on values was that of transitivity, a property natural to preferences. I thus distinguish between the Condorcetian and Arrovian research programs. As I have argued in the previous sections, the importance of Arrow's impossibility theorem is that it suggests that disorder of some kind is a real possibility. In this, it is very different from the orientation of the three other research programs in figure 1.3 (von Neumann, Popper, and Condorcet), which also attempt to structure the social world. It seems to me that Arrow gave the first formal demonstration of the possibility of social disorder of the kind hinted at earlier in the work of John Maynard Keynes (1936) and Joseph Schumpeter (1942).

Figure 1.3   A Hierarchy of Models

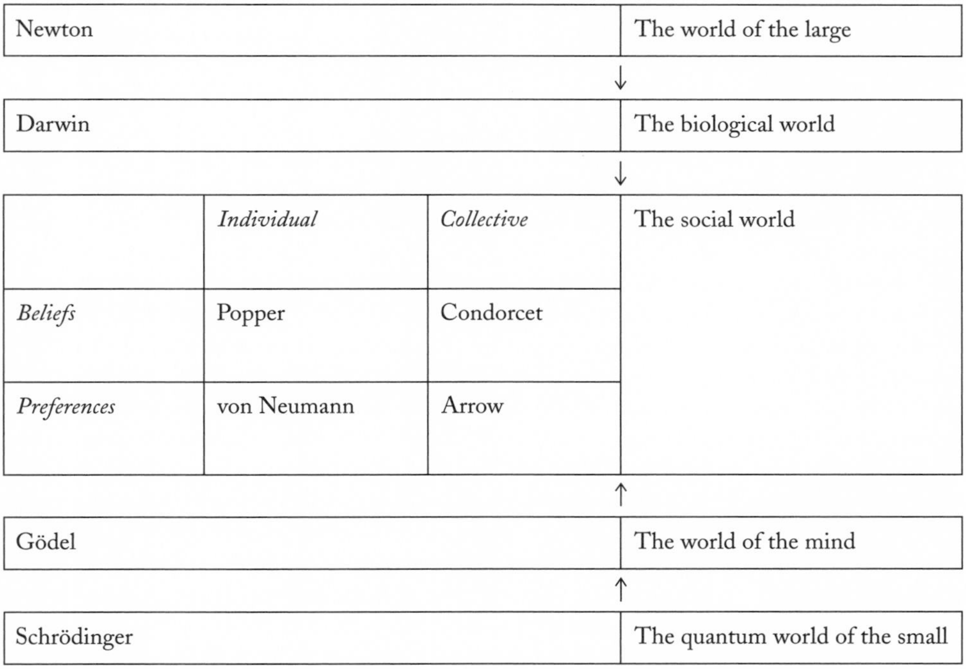

Newton			The world of the large
↓			
Darwin			The biological world
↓			
	Individual	*Collective*	The social world
Beliefs	Popper	Condorcet	
Preferences	von Neumann	Arrow	
↑			
Gödel			The world of the mind
↑			
Schrödinger			The quantum world of the small

To grapple with these themes of order and disorder, it may be worthwhile to consider the context within which Keynes, Schumpeter, Hayek, and Popper formulated their key ideas. Clearly the terrible political and economic events of the 1930s must have influenced their work. Keynes's argument (1936), I believe, was that under certain conditions a belief equilibrium can come into being that (contrary to the general equilibrium economic model) sustains high levels of unemployment and low levels of economic activity. Only the state, acting as Leviathan, can change the belief equilibrium to the advantage of all members of the society. Schumpeter (1942) wrote about the waves of technological innovations and the business cycles that can engulf the economy. With reason, we may interpret these cycles of economic activity as chaotic belief cascades.

In contrast, Popper (1945) saw democracy as an "optimal" institution that was compatible with open competition in ideas and beliefs. In the same way, he suggested that scientific development follows a process of natural selection that is "truth seeking." Hayek (1948), in a somewhat similar way, saw markets as "truth seeking" in their ability to generate and aggregate information efficiently. Out of competition in the market and polity come stable institutions.

Perhaps I do an injustice to Popper in ascribing to him the view that competition among scientific beliefs is "truth convergent." In his *Poverty of Historicism* (1957), he essentially argues that this process of truth seeking is "local" or piecemeal. In a later essay, "Of Clouds and Clocks," he argues against the "clockwork" characteristic of Newtonian mechanics and in favor of the metaphor of "clouds," of "physical systems which, like gases, are highly irregular, disorderly, and more or less unpredictable" (Popper 1979, 207). Of course, in contrasting determinism and disorder in this way, Popper was unable to make use of the notion of chaos, the idea that completely deterministic systems can be unlike clocks in being essentially unpredictable.

Let me examine more carefully this Popperian metaphor of "evolution," together with the more formal, current models of evolutionary game theory. I wish to show that Arrow's "anti-equilibrium" theorem in fact can be understood to be applicable to the von Neumann and Popper research programs. First consider evolutionary theory in biology. I find compelling Stephen Jay Gould's argument (Gould 1996, and elsewhere) that evolution is "nongradient": there appears to be no obvious tendency toward increasing complexity of form. Gould warns us to be suspicious of the nineteenth-century presumption that humankind is at the pinnacle of evolution. As we learn more about the likely evolution of homo sapiens in Africa, it seems increasingly plausible that this was the result of chaotic accidents of climatic and geological change.

But this is only one example. The general evolutionary models (Cziko 1995; Dennett 1995) conceive of each entity (whether a species or an idea or a language) to be undergoing natural selection in the context of a "fitness" landscape. Although it is easy to conceive of competition forcing the entity to the local maximum of the landscape, it can be forgotten that this landscape is generated by the behavior of other competing entities. In principle, these changes in the landscapes may be unrestricted. Thus, the Nash (1951) "equilibrium" of such an evolutionary game could move about in a chaotic fashion. The Nash equilibrium existence theorems nearly always "convexify" the landscape (by utilizing randomization) and thus have very little to say about such evolutionary processes.

But there is an even deeper problem with biological (and indeed social) evolutionary theory. We are now all familiar with the idea that the fundamental agents in biological evolution are genes (Dawkins 1976, 1986, 1996). However, it is not genes alone but *coalitions* of genes that effect evolutionary change. Arrow's theorem specifically demonstrates that nondictatorial, coalitional mechanisms of any kind can be disorderly.[11] The aspects of the social world that we would like to model using evolutionary game theory include convention, language, beliefs, ideas, technology, and science. But as I have attempted to indicate throughout this essay, all these phenomena are generated by the acts of groups of people (whether societies, cultures, economies, countries, institutions, professions, and so on). If the relevant family of groups is disjoint, then Arrow's theorem does not apply. However, as soon as there is overlapping membership, then the theorem is relevant. Thus, I infer that almost all activity in the social realm is governed, at least potentially, by Arrow's theorem.

Think, for a moment, about what this implies. Economists like to conceive of the market as ordered by the "invisible hand"—as obeying regular laws of motion. The metaphor of evolutionary game theory is used to account for this apparent social order. But if I am correct in my assertion that all activity, whether in the market or in the polity, is generated by groups, then one would not expect to observe rule-governed or "gradientlike" behavior. In particular, the attempts by John Hicks (1939), Nicholas Kaldor (1939), and others to found a science of welfare economics, in the period prior to Arrow's work, cannot succeed.

Finally, I wish to mention briefly what may be the deepest and most severe problem for game theory and therefore for any "equilibrium-based" social theory. Figure 1.3 locates the "world of the mind" beneath that of the "social world"and includes the name of Gödel to remind the reader of his inconsistency theorem. As I mentioned at the beginning of this essay, Penrose (1994) has put forward the case that the indeterminacy of the quantum world of the small (designated in the figure by Schrödinger's name) implies that the mind is non-algorithmic.[12] I find this connection between the quantum world and the world of the mind to be very tenuous. Nevertheless, I consider Penrose's argument that the mind is not like a computer to be very powerful. More important, the recent extension of Gödel's argument by Nachbar (1997) suggests that to play a "game" successfully each agent must already know an impossible amount about every other agent playing the game. In particular, "algorithmic" agents cannot learn enough about the other agents as the game progresses.

I am not denying here that computers can play games (after all, "Deep Blue" beat Kasparov at chess recently). I am denying that people play games like computers (see also John Searle, 1999, for a similar argument). More generally I would say that the kinds of games people play are like poker rather than chess. Predicting how people will play the game of life appears, to me at least, to be fruitless. Although each of us can gain some insight into the minds of other people, and may thus believe we understand something of the social world around us, we can never fully understand the acts of our fellows in the game of life. As Arrow (1973, 262) wrote (in a somewhat different context than we are considering here):

> To the extent that individuals really are individual, each an autonomous end in himself, to that extent they must be somewhat mysterious and inaccessible to one another, there cannot be any rule that is completely acceptable to all. There must be, or so it seems to me, the possibility of inadjudicable conflict.

The theoretical research on equilibrium and chaos, on which this essay draws, has been supported by the National Science Foundation (Grant SBR 97 30275) and owes much to conversations with Douglass North and Andrew Rutten. I am also indebted to Krishna Ladha and Iain McLean for discussions that we have had on the significance of Condorcet's work.

NOTES

1. The term "social mathematics" was first used by Marie-Jean-Antoine Nicolas, Marquis de Condorcet, in 1785 (see McLean and Hewitt 1994).

2. All of these equilibrium results depend on the intuition that a dynamical system (or "vector field") on certain types of spaces (like balls or tori or even-dimensional spheres) must have singularities ("equilibria"). This intuition allows one to develop the mathematics using the qualitative theory of global analysis (MasColell 1985; Schofield 1984; Smale 1973).

3. A structurally stable system is one that, when perturbed slightly, has identical qualitative properties. "Generic" means "almost all."

4. See the discussion on theories of the solar system in Peterson (1993).

5. Chaotic phenomena can, of course, have profound consequences. A chaotic event, an asteroid collision, may have led to the extinction of the dinosaurs.

6. To illustrate, voting mechanisms without vetoers (or collegia) can be badly behaved in the sense that voting trajectories ("following" the social vector field) may lead away from the Pareto set (McKelvey and Schofield 1986; Saari 1997).

7. Just to give an example, Avner Greif (1997) has analyzed the pattern of behavior in twelfth- and thirteenth-century Genoa. In the absence of an outside threat (the Holy Roman Emperor), Genoa collapsed into a thirty-year civil war. By "chance" the city adopted the idea of a podesta, a paid pivotal "Leviathan," with whom the Genoese families made a covenant. From 1190 to 1300, Genoa was able to engage extensively in trade with the countries of the western Mediterranean.

8. Richard Catillon published his *Essay on the Nature of Commerce in General* in 1730 in France, David Hume published *Essays Moral and Political* in 1742 in Scotland, Anne-Robert-Jacques Turgot published *Reflections on the Formation and Distribution of Wealth* in 1766 in France, and Adam Smith published *Theory of Moral Sentiments* in 1758 and *Wealth of Nations* in 1776. Bernard Mandeville's *Fable of the Bees; or Private Vices, Publick Benefits* (1714) is also of interest. See the discussion in Murray Rothbard (1995).

9. The terms used by Jefferson in, for example, *The Draft Constitution for Virginia* (June 1776) to describe George III and his "detestable and insupportable tyranny" (Jefferson 1984, 336) are similar to expressions used by Locke in his *Two Treatises* of 1690.

10. Conversely, if the preference profile satisfies certain "restriction properties" (which can be viewed as the degree of homogeneity), then preference aggregation by voting can be well behaved (Sen 1970). See also Harold Hotelling (1929) where this phenomenon was first discussed in the one-dimensional situation.

11. One way to demonstrate Arrow's theorem (Kirman and Sondermann 1992) is to show that "order" requires that the family of all effective coalitions of agents be an "ultrafilter" (namely, a family with a single dictator in common). Clearly the coalitions of effective genes cannot be an ultrafilter. One way out of the impossibility theorem is to assume that the collection of agents (or genes) is infinite. I do not believe this is a plausible escape from the theorem.

12. Actually, Popper (1972) also made a case that quantum indeterminacy provides the background for the operation of free will. Penrose is clearly influenced by Popper (particularly Popper and Eccles 1977), and his attempts to relate the worlds of the mind, of culture, and of nature (Penrose 1997) helped in the formulation of figure 1.3.

REFERENCES

Arrow, Kenneth. 1950a. "A Difficulty in the Concept of Social Welfare." *Journal of Political Economy* 58: 328–46.

————. 1950b. "An Extension of the Basic Theorems of Classical Welfare Economics." In *Proceedings of the Second Berkeley Symposium on Mathematics, Statistics, and Probability,* edited by Jerry Neyman (Berkeley: University of California Press), 507–32. Reprinted in *Readings in Mathematical Economics,* edited by Peter Newman. Baltimore: Johns Hopkins University Press, 1968, 365–90.

————. 1951. *Social Choice and Individual Values.* New York: Wiley.

————. 1973. "Some Ordinalist-Utilitarian Notes on Rawls's Sense of Justice." *Journal of Philosophy* 70: 245–63.

————. 1986. "Rationality of Self and Others in an Economic System." *Journal of Business* 59: S385–99.

————. 1988. "Workshop on the Economy as an Evolving Complex System: Summary." In *The Economy as an Evolving Complex System,* edited by Philip Anderson, Kenneth Arrow, and David Pines (Reading, Mass.: Addison-Wesley), 275–81.

Arrow, Kenneth, and Gerard Debreu. 1954. "Existence of an Equilibrium for a Competitive Economy." *Econometrica* 22: 265–90.

Arrow, Kenneth, and Frank Hahn. 1971. *General Competitive Analysis.* San Francisco: Holden Day.

Aumann, Robert. 1976. "Agreeing to Disagree." *Annals of Statistics* 4: 1236–39.

Aumann, Robert, and Michael Maschler. 1964. "The Bargaining Set for Cooperative Games." In *Advances in Game Theory,* edited by Melvin Drescher, Lloyd Shapley, and Albert Tucker. Princeton, N.J.: Princeton University Press, 443–76.

Axelrod, Robert. 1984. *The Evolution of Cooperation.* New York: Basic Books.

Bailyn, Bernard (ed.). 1993. *The Debate on the Constitution: Federalist and Anti-Federalist Speeches, Articles, and Letters.* New York: Viking.

Baker, Keith. 1975. *Condorcet: From Natural Philosophy to Social Mathematics.* Chicago: University of Chicago Press.

Black, Duncan. 1958. *The Theory of Committees and Elections.* Cambridge: Cambridge University Press.

Boaz, Noel. 1997. *Ecco Homo.* New York: Basic Books.

Boland, Philip. 1989. "Majority Systems and the Condorcet Jury Theorem." *The Statistician* 38: 187–89.

Brouwer, Luitzen. 1910. "Über Abbildung von Manningfaltigkeiten." *Mathematische Annalen* 71: 97–115.

Calvin, William. 1990. *The Ascent of Mind.* New York: Harmony Books.

Cantillon, Richard. 1964. *Essay on the Nature of Commerce in General.* Translated and edited by Henry Higgs. New York: Kelly. (Originally published in 1730)

Condorcet, Nicolas, Marquis de. 1785. *Essai sur l'application de l'analyse à la probabilité des décisions rendues à la pluralité des voix.* Paris: L'Imprimerie Royale.

————. 1955. *Sketch for an Historical Picture of the Human Mind.* Translated and edited by John Barraclough, and with an introduction by Stuart Hampshire. London: Weidenfeld and Nicholson. (Originally published in 1795)

————. 1994. "An Essay on the Application of Probability Theory to Plurality Decision-Making." Translated extracts in *Condorcet: Foundations of Social Choice and Political Theory,* Iain McLean and Fiona Hewitt. Aldershot, U.K.: Edward Elgar.

Cziko, Gary. 1995. *Without Miracles.* Cambridge, Mass.: MIT Press.

Dawkins, Richard. 1976. *The Selfish Gene.* Oxford: Oxford University Press.

————. 1986. *The Blind Watchmaker.* New York: Norton.

————. 1996. *Climbing Mount Improbable.* New York: Norton.

Dawson, John. 1997. *Logical Dilemmas.* Wellesley, Mass.: A. K. Peters.

Debreu, Gerard. 1974. "Excess Demand Functions." *Journal of Mathematical Economics* 1: 15–23.

Dennett, Daniel. 1991. *Consciousness Explained.* Boston: Little, Brown.

————. 1995. *Darwin's Dangerous Idea.* New York: Simon & Schuster.

Descartes, René. 1968. *Discourse on Method and Other Writings.* Edited by Frank Sutcliffe. Harmondsworth, U.K.: Penguin. (Originally published in 1637)

Eldridge, Niles, and Stephen Jay Gould. 1972. "Punctuated Equilibria: An Alternative to Phyletic Gradualism." In *Models in Paleobiology,* edited by Thomas Schopf (New York: Norton), 82–115.

Fan, Ky. 1961. "A Generalization of Tychonoff's Fixed Point Theorem." *Mathematische Annalen* 142: 305–10.

Fermi, Enrico, John Pasta, and Stanislaw Ulam. 1955. "Studies in Nonlinear Problems." Reprinted in *Analogies Between Analogies,* edited by Stanislaw Ulam (Berkeley: University of California Press). 139–54.

Filmer, Robert. 1949. *Patriarcha and Other Political Writings.* Edited by Peter Laslett. Oxford: Basil Blackwell. (Originally published between 1632 and 1652)

Galison, Peter. 1997. *Image and Logic.* Chicago: University of Chicago Press.

Gauthier, David. 1986. *Morals by Agreement.* Oxford: Clarendon Press.

Geanakoplos, John, and Herakles Polemarchakis. 1982. "We Can't Disagree Forever." *Journal of Economic Theory* 28: 192–200.

Gleick, James. 1987. *Chaos: Making a New Science.* New York: Viking.

Gödel, Kurt. 1931. "Uker formal unenstcheidbare Satze der *Principia Mathematica* und verwandter Systeme: 1." *Monatschefte für Mathematik und Physik* 38: 173–98.

Gould, Stephen Jay. 1996. *Full House.* New York: Harmony Books.

Gray, John. 1984. *Hayek on Liberty.* Oxford: Basil Blackwell.

Greenberg, Joseph. 1979. "Consistent Majority Rules over Compact Sets of Alternatives." *Econometrica* 41: 286–97.

Greif, Avner. 1997. "On the Interrelations and Economic Implications of Economic, Social, Political, and Normative Factors: Reflections from Two Late Medieval Societies." In *The Frontiers of the New Institutional Economics,* edited by John Drobak and John Nye (San Diego: Academic Press), 57–94.

Hardin, Russell. 1982. *Collective Action.* Baltimore: Johns Hopkins University Press.

Hayek, Friedrich von. 1944. *The Road to Serfdom.* London: Routledge & Kegan Paul.

———. 1948. *Individualism and Economic Order.* London: Routledge & Kegan Paul.

———. 1973. *Law, Legislation, and Liberty,* vol. 1, *Rules and Order.* London: Routledge & Kegan Paul.

Hicks, John. 1939. "The Foundations of Welfare Economics." *Economic Journal* 48: 696–712.

Hirschleifer, David, Sushil Bikhchandani, and Ivo Welsh. 1992. "A Theory of Fads, Fashions, Customs, and Cultural Change as Information Cascades." *Journal of Political Economy* 100: 992–1026.

Hobbes, Thomas. 1968. *Leviathan; or the Matter, Forme, and Power of a Common-Wealth, Ecclesiasticall and Civill.* Edited and with an introduction by Crawford MacPherson. Harmondsworth, U.K.: Penguin. (Originally published in 1651)

Hodges, Andrew. 1983. *Alan Turing: The Enigma.* New York: Simon & Schuster.

Holland, John. 1988. "The Global Economy as an Adaptive Process." In *The Economy as an Evolving System,* edited by Philip Anderson, Kenneth Arrow, and David Pines (Reading, Mass.: Addison-Wesley).

Hotelling, Harold J. 1929. "Stability in Competition." *Economic Journal* 39: 41–57.

Huberman, Bernardo, and Natalie Glance. 1995. "Beliefs and Cooperation." In *Chaos and Society,* edited by Alain Albert (Amsterdam: IOS Press), 309–28.

Hume, David. 1985. *Essays: Moral, Political and Literary.* Edited and with a foreword by Eugene Miller. Indianapolis, Ind.: Liberty Fund. (Originally published in 1742)

Jefferson, Thomas. 1984. "The Draft Constitution for Virginia." In *Writings,* edited and selected by Merrill Peterson, (New York: Literary Classics of the United States), 336–45. (Originally published in 1776)

Kakutani, Shizno. 1941. "A Generalization of Brouwer's Fixed Point Theorem." *Duke Mathematics Journal* 8: 457–59.

Kaldor, Nicholas. 1939. "The Foundations of Welfare Economics." *Economic Journal* 48: 696–712.

Kauffman, Stuart. 1993. *The Origins of Order.* Oxford: Oxford University Press.

———. 1995. *At Home in the Universe.* Oxford: Oxford University Press.

Keynes, John Maynard. 1936. *The General Theory of Employment, Interest, and Money.* New York: Harcourt, Brace.

Kirman, Alan, and Dieter Sondermann. 1972. "Arrow's Impossibility Theorem: Many Agents and Invisible Dictators." *Journal of Economic Theory* 5: 267–78.

Kreps, David, Paul Milgrom, John Roberts, and Robert Wilson. 1982. "Rational Cooperation in the Finitely Repeated Prisoner's Dilemma." *Journal of Economic Theory* 27: 245–52.

Ladha, Krishna. 1992. "Condorcet's Jury Theorem, Free Speech, and Correlated Votes." *American Journal of Political Science* 36: 617–74.

———. 1993. "Condorcet's Jury Theorem in the Light of de Finetti's Theorem: Majority Rule with Correlated Votes." *Social Choice and Welfare* 10: 69–86.

Ladha, Krishna, and Gary Miller. 1996. "Political Discourse, Factions and the General Will: Correlated Voting and Condorcet's Jury Theorem." In *Collective Decision-making: Social Choice and Political Economy,* edited by N. Schofield (Boston: Kluwer), 393–410.

Laplace, Pierre-Simon. 1799–1825. *Traité de Mécanique Céleste* (5 volumes). Paris: Gauthiers-Villars.

Laslett, Peter. 1988. Introduction to *Two Treatises of Government* by John Locke. Cambridge: Cambridge University Press.

Locke, John. 1988. *Two Treatises of Government.* Edited and with an introduction by Peter Laslett. Cambridge: Cambridge University Press. (Originally published in 1690)

Lorenz, Edward. 1993. *The Essence of Chaos.* Seattle: University of Washington Press.

MacPherson, Crawford. 1968. Introduction to *Leviathan* by Thomas Hobbes. Harmondsworth, U.K.: Penguin Books.

Malthus, Thomas. 1970. *An Essay on the Principle of Population and a Summary View of the Principle of Population.* Edited and with an introduction by Anthony Flew. Harmondsworth, U.K.: Penguin. (Originally published in 1798)

Mandeville, Bernard. 1924. *The Fable of the Bees or Private Vices, Publick Benefits.* Oxford: Oxford University Press. Reprinted, Indianapolis, Ind.: Liberty Fund, 1988. (Originally published in 1714)

Mantel, Rolf. 1974. "On the Characterization of Aggregate Excess Demand." *Journal of Economic Theory* 7: 197–201.

MasColell, Andreu. 1985. *The Theory of General Economic Equilibrium.* Cambridge: Cambridge University Press.

Maynard Smith, John. 1982. *Evolution and the Theory of Games.* Cambridge: Cambridge University Press.

McKelvey, Richard. 1976. "Intransitivities in Multidimensional Voting Models and Some Implications for Agenda Control." *Journal of Economic Theory* 12: 472–82.

McKelvey, Richard, and Talbot Page. 1986. "Common Knowledge, Consensus, and Aggregate Information." *Econometrica* 54: 109–27.

McKelvey, Richard, and Norman Schofield. 1986. "Structural Instability of the Core." *Journal of Mathematical Economics* 15: 179–98.

McKenzie, Lionel. 1959. "On the Existence of a General Equilibrium for a Competitive Economy." *Econometrica* 27: 54–71.

McLean, Iain, and Fiona Hewitt. 1994. *Condorcet: Foundations of Social Choice and Political Theory.* Aldershot, U.K.: Edward Elgar.

McLean, Iain, and Arnold Urken 1992. "Did Jefferson or Madison Understand Condorcet's Theory of Social Choice?" *Public Choice* 73: 445–57.

Nachbar, John. 1997. "Prediction, Optimization, and Learning in Repeated Games." *Econometrica* 65: 275–309.

Nakamura, Kenjiro. 1979. "The Vetoers in a Simple Game with Ordinal Preference." *International Journal of Game Theory* 8: 55–61.

Nash, John. 1951. "Non-Cooperative Games." *Annals of Mathematics* 54: 289–95.

Newton, Isaac. 1995. *Philosophiae Naturalis Principia Mathematica.* Translated, edited, and with an introduction by Andrew Motte. New York: Amherst. (Originally published in 1687)

———. 1704. *Opticks: Or, a Treatise of the Reflexions, Refractions, Inflexions and Colours of Light.* London: Smith and Walford.

North, Douglass. 1990. *Institutions, Institutional Change, and Economic Performance.* Cambridge: Cambridge University Press.

———. 1994. "Economic Performance Through Time." *American Economic Review* 84: 359–68.

Nozick, Robert. 1974. *Anarchy, State, and Utopia.* New York: Basic Books.

Penrose, Roger. 1989. *The Emperor's New Mind.* Oxford: Oxford University Press.

———. 1994. *Shadows of the Mind.* Oxford: Oxford University Press.

———. 1997. *The Large, the Small, and the Human Mind.* Cambridge: Cambridge University Press.

Peterson, Ivars. 1993. *Newton's Clock: Chaos in the Solar System.* New York: Freeman.

Plott, Charles. 1967. "A Notion of Equilibrium and Its Possibility Under Majority Rule." *American Economic Review* 57: 787–806.

Poincaré, Henri. 1993. *New Methods of Celestial Mechanics.* Edited and with an introduction by Daniel Goreff. New York: American Institute of Physics. (Originally published in three volumes, 1892–1899)

Popper, Karl. 1945. *The Open Society and Its Enemies.* London: Routledge & Kegan Paul.

———. 1957. *The Poverty of Historicism.* London: Routledge & Kegan Paul.

———. 1979. *Objective Knowledge: An Evolutionary Approach.* Rev. ed. Oxford: Clarendon Press. (Originally published in 1972)

Popper, Karl, and John Eccles. 1977. *The Self and the Brain.* Berlin: Springer-Verlag.

Prigogine, Ilya. 1980. *From Being to Becoming: Time and Complexity in the Physical Sciences.* San Francisco: Freeman.

Randall, W. 1993. *Thomas Jefferson: A Life.* New York: Holt.

Rawls, John. 1972. *A Theory of Justice.* Cambridge, Mass.: Harvard University Press.

Rogow, Arnold. 1986. *Thomas Hobbes: Radical in the Service of Reaction.* New York: Norton.

Rothbard, Murray. 1995. *Economic Thought before Adam Smith.* Cheltenham, U.K.: Edward Elgar.

Rousseau, Jean-Jacques. 1968. *The Social Contract.* Edited and with an introduction by Maurice Cranston. Harmondsworth, U.K.: Penguin. (Originally published in 1762)

Saari, Donald. 1991. "Erratic Behavior in Economic Models." *Journal of Economic Behavior and Organization* 16: 3–35.

———. 1997. "Generic Existence of a Core for q- rules." *Economic Theory* 9: 219–60.

Scarf, Herbert. 1960. "Some Examples of Global Instability of the Competitive Equilibrium." *International Economic Review* 1: 157–72.

Schama, Simon. 1989. *Citizens: A Chronicle of the French Revolution.* New York: Alfred Knopf.

Schofield, Norman. 1978. "Instability of Simple Dynamical Games." *Review of Economic Studies* 45: 475–94.

———. 1984. "Existence of Equilibrium on a Manifold." *Mathematics of Operations Research* 9: 545–57.

———. 1999. "The Heart of the Atlantic Constitution: International Economic Stability, 1919–1998." *Politics and Society* 27: 173–215.

Schotter, Andrew. 1981. *The Economic Theory of Social Institutions.* Cambridge: Cambridge University Press.

Schumpeter, Joseph. 1942. *Capitalism, Socialism, and Democracy.* New York: Harper.

Scitovsky, Tibor. 1941. "A Note on Welfare Properties in Economics." *Review of Economic Studies* 9: 77–88.

Searle, John. 1999. "I Married a Computer." *New York Review of Books* XLVI (6): 34–8.

Sen, Amartya. 1970. *Collective Choice and Social Welfare.* San Francisco: Holden Day.

Smale, Stephen. 1966. "Structurally Stable Systems Are Not Dense." *American Journal of Mathematics* 88: 491–96.

———. 1973. "Global Analysis and Economics I: Pareto Optimum and a Generalization of Morse Theory." In *Dynamical Systems,* edited by Mauricio Peixoto (New York: Academic Press), 531–44.

Smith, Adam. 1976. *An Inquiry into the Nature and Cause of Wealth of Nations.* Oxford: Oxford University Press. (Originally published in 1776)

———. 1976. *Theory of Moral Sentiments.* Oxford: Oxford University Press. (Originally published in 1758)

Smith, James (Ed.). 1995. *The Republic of Letters: The Correspondence between Thomas Jefferson and James Madison,* vol. 1. New York: Norton.

Sonnenschein, Hugo. 1972. "Market Excess Demand Functions." *Econometrica* 40: 549–63.

Stanley, Steven. 1996. *Children of the Ice Age.* New York: Harmony Books.

Sugden, Robert. 1986. *The Economics of Rights, Cooperation, and Welfare.* Oxford: Basil Blackwell.

Taylor, Michael. 1976. *Anarchy and Cooperation.* London: Wiley.

———. 1982. *Community, Anarchy, and Liberty.* Cambridge: Cambridge University Press.

Turgot, Anne-Robert-Jacques. 1973. "Reflections on the Formation and Distribution of Wealth." In *Turgot on Progress, Sociology and Economics.* Translated and edited by Ronald Meek. Cambridge: Cambridge University Press. (Originally published in 1766)

Turing, Alan. 1937. "On Computable Numbers, with an Application to the Entscheidungsproblem." *Proceedings of the London Mathematical Society* 42: 230–65.

———. 1950. "Computing Machinery and Intelligence." *Mind* 59: 422–60.

Ulam, Stanislaw, and John von Neumann. 1947. "On Combination of Stochastic and Deterministic Processes: Preliminary Report." *Bulletin of the American Mathematical Society* 53: 1120.

Urken, Arnold. 1991. "The Condorcet-Jefferson Connection and the Origins of Social Choice Theory." *Public Choice* 72: 213–36.

Voltaire, François. 1738. *The Elements of Sir Isaac Newton's Philosophy.* Translated from the French by John Hanna. London: Stephen Austen.

von Neumann, John. 1928. "Zur Theorie der Gesellschaftsspiele." *Mathematische Annalen* 100: 295–320.

———. 1945. "A Model of General Economic Equilibrium." *Review of Economic Studies* 13: 1–9. (Originally published in German in 1938)

———. 1958. *The Computer and the Brain.* New Haven, Conn.: Yale University Press.

———. 1966. *Theory of Self-reproducing Automata.* Edited by Arthur Burks. Urbana: University of Illinois Press.

von Neumann, John, and Oskar Morgenstern. 1944. *Theory of Games and Economic Behavior.* Princeton, N.J.: Princeton University Press.

COMMENTS ON THE COMMENTARIES

Kenneth J. Arrow

I am certainly grateful for the two commentaries on my work. Not only have they understood what I was trying to achieve, they have found meanings beyond those I was conscious of and have related my work to other currents. My late friend the writer Wallace Stegner used to say that an author is entitled to any meaning a critic can find in his work, and so I will not modestly say that I was unaware of these depths. Since the two essays have different orientations, I will comment on them separately.

I start by commenting on Norman Schofield's presentation. First, let me say a few words about the development of rational choice in politics and the study of the interaction between economic and political choice. "Arrow," says Schofield, "was concerned not simply with the possibility of . . . voting cycles . . . [but] rather, he was interested in the larger issue of the interaction between the political and economic realms, the topic that concerned political economists and philosophers such as Joseph Schumpeter, Friedrich von Hayek, and Karl Popper in the period around World War II." (33) Schofield is correct in referring to these authors, with special reference to Joseph Schumpeter, whose *Capitalism, Socialism, and Democracy* actually appeared in 1942. Indeed, Schumpeter gave a lecture to the Columbia Graduate Economic Society when I was a member that gave a fascinating account of the relation between the economic system and government; he argued that capitalists are intrinsically unfit to run a government because of their individualist bias and that successful governments depend on the existence of an aristocratic class. Schumpeter's book emphasizes the role of political competition and the entrepreneurial nature of political leadership. (It may be worth reminding ourselves that Schumpeter's book does not mention fascism, an extraordinary omission in view of the date. It is now fairly clear that Schumpeter was not without some sympathy for fascism.)

Socialism comes out surprisingly well in Schumpeter. It is true that he emphasizes its bureaucratic character, but he also holds that capitalism is moving into a bureaucratic phase. In his view, democratic socialism is possible, and with suitable planning based on decentralized flows of information, it can be reasonably efficient.

The difficulty I found with Schumpeter's book was that it contains no refutable propositions, which I was looking for as part of the generally positivistic orientation of the day, represented in economics especially by the writings of Paul Samuelson.

There was, to my mind, the beginnings of a genuine political theory in the literature, though I looked elsewhere than the authors cited by Schofield. I took for granted that the idea that an individual chooses in the polity with regard to his economic choices and status was already part of general knowledge. This concept probably goes back to Aristotle and surely anteceded Karl Marx. It was a staple of ordinary discourse among college students and many of their teachers, especially deriving from Charles Beard's *An Economic Interpretation of the Constitution* (1935), which my generation took as gospel, as well as from the work of Arthur Bentley (1935) on interest groups.

More relevant and fruitful were a few pages by my mentor, Harold Hotelling, in which he noted that a model of his for the analysis of spatial competition could also be applied to competition among political parties (1929). He stated, in somewhat loose form, the median voter theorem, a definite (and refutable) implication. Of course, John von Neumann and Oskar Morgenstern (1944) took for granted that all action, not just economic action, is governed by utility maximization in the context of games. In particular, what they called "simple games" were voting situations. Most explicit was the work of Duncan Black in a series of papers in the 1940s (incorporated into Black 1958). I read these works with great interest even before I took up the subject of social choice, but I regarded the idea that political action—and in particular voting—is governed by maximization under a preference ordering as obvious. Indeed, I think Black did too. The interest of Black's work lay in the specific theorems, above all the median voter theorem. In this, by the way, he was essentially anticipated by Howard Bowen (1943). Bowen took a very specific context, that of choosing a level of government expenditure, where the tax on each individual is proportional to the expenditure. The generality of his result was not obvious (I missed it when writing my book), but in fact the argument he gives has nothing to do with the specific institutional background.

The heart of Schofield's comments can be described as a broad perspective, a family of extended metaphors that will have to be made more specific to serve as a basis of analysis, normative or descriptive. But they appear to be fruitful. He compares two methodologies for analyzing dynamic systems, equilibrium and chaos. These are not, strictly speaking, antithetical; equilibrium describes the resting state or states of a dynamic system, and chaos is a possible kind of dynamic behavior. But equilibrium analysis will be useful primarily when the equilibria are stable. Studying a dynamic system by its equilibria is useful when the system is close to its equilibrium states for long periods, and this in turn requires that when a system is close to equilibrium, it remains there. This is precisely the definition of stability.

In a chaotic system, the equilibria have no special descriptive significance. On the contrary, small deviations can have large consequences. The modern revival of interest in chaotic behavior was begun when the meteorologist Edward Lorenz tried to make a weather forecast for several weeks ahead based strictly on physical theory (Lorenz 1993). To check, he repeated the calculation and found that the forecast was totally different. He found that this was due to a very small error in entering the initial conditions.

It should be added, however, that even for stable systems the descriptive power of equilibrium may be very poor if the system is far out of equilibrium. In the Robert Solow (1956) model of economic growth, national income and capital formation both converge to an exponential path, a kind of equilibrium. But in fact, the convergence to that path might be very slow; if the capital-labor ratio is far from its long-run equilibrium, it might take hundreds of years to get even reasonably close. Hence, both description and policy would be ill served by using the steady state solution.

Schofield contrasts different analyses of the economic system. The standard is still, despite all attacks, the competitive equilibrium, no doubt with some qualifications along the way. A frequent criticism, repeated by Schofield, is that we have evidence that if we embed competitive equilibrium in a dynamic system, there is no guarantee that the system is stable. As Schofield makes clear, the dynamic system he is considering is one in which excess demand raises the corresponding price and excess supply decreases it. But recent research (see Herings, van der Laan, and Venniker 1997; van der Laan and Talman 1987) has shown that a somewhat but not drastically modified dynamic system is in fact always convergent. It has long been known, of course, that there are dynamic systems that always converge to a competitive equilibrium (Scarf and Hansen 1973; Smale 1976), but these were not considered realistic. The newer systems are perhaps still somewhat artificial, but considerably less so. The point here is that in some sense we have, in economics, more intuition about the equilibria than about the dynamic system whose resting points they are.

As Schofield argues, political equilibria are much less likely to make sense. Indeed, their existence is at stake. What has been shown by Richard McKelvey (1976) and by Schofield (1978) is that the possible cycles that occur in Condorcet's work and in my own can be interpreted to give rise to chaotic behavior. This interpretation can be made when voting is applied to sequential procedures, such as the writing of legislation or a series of successive elections. The intransitivity or acyclicity can be interpreted in terms of temporal sequence. Chaotic behavior becomes possible, indeed almost universal, in the absence of a Condorcet candidate.

I find this account interesting and even compelling. But it does presuppose that we really know the dynamic system we are considering. There may be more than one plausible dynamic system that leads to the same equilibria, in political as in economic systems. For example, a political actor may well anticipate that if he or she makes a particular proposal, it will generate a counterproposal that will defeat it. In that case, the proposal may not be made.

Schofield states early on that chaotic behavior in the small may occur in a larger context that is basically stable. I am glad to see this view, because I have come to speculate on a similar possibility. The particular problem I was concerned with was more concrete and indeed had nothing to do with social choice. It was rather the nature of chaos in ecology and its implications for economics. These two subjects have very similar orientations, both involving complex systems whose movements are controlled by allocation of scarce resources. But ecologists have in recent years been emphasizing the possibility of chaotic dynamics. Earlier, they had more of an equilibrium orientation. For example, if a forest is destroyed, the species of trees that develop were held to have a fixed sequence leading to an equilibrium (called "climax") with a given set of tree species (depending, of course, on climate and soil). Then the doctrine changed; it was held that a destroyed forest would not necessarily come back to the same species composition. Now the pendulum seems to be resting somewhere in between. According to some ecologists and others, while the identical species do not recur, the species that do occur are metabolically equivalent to those that might otherwise have occurred. They are, in current ecological usage, of the same "guild."

Other examples come to mind. Australia, because of its isolation, has had its own evolution of mammals, with a great preponderance of marsupials, while placentals predominate elsewhere. Apparently the marsupials in Australia have specialized to have families similar in function to the placentals—for example, catlike marsupials, wolflike marsupials, and so forth.

In economic systems, the stock market certainly has violent fluctuations, most usually sudden drops. Yet there is a sense in which these falls, large as they seem at the time, are in the long run bounded in magnitude.

Is there some similar sense in which the accidents of legislative history may lead to results that differ but, broadly considered, are similar in nature and structure? This seems to me to be one of the possible implications of Schofield's essay.

Norman Frohlich and Joe Oppenheimer raise a different set of issues. Their main theme is the instability of the preferences themselves, rather than of the voting results derived from them. Much of what they have to say applies to individual preferences, to choice and belief by individuals. Indeed, the evidence cited is, for the most part, derived from experiments on individuals, as in the work of Daniel Kahneman, Paul Slovic, and Amos Tversky (1982) and in their own. The problem is descriptive. Of course, if expressed preferences are unstable—depending, for example, on the way choices are framed—then the descriptive problem becomes a normative one in the context of social choices. In one famous example (McNeill and others 1982), physicians were asked to choose between chemotherapy and surgery as a treatment for lung cancer. With surgery, there is about a 10 percent chance of dying during the operation, but the expected lifetime was greater (at the time of the study). The physicians were divided at random into two groups. One was given the outcome data in terms of probability of survival (90 percent chance of surviving the operation). The other was given the data in terms of the probability of dying (10 percent chance of dying). Trivially, the information was the same. But the choices were very different. A one-out-of-ten probability of dying on the table was very scary, and the physicians opted with high frequency for chemotherapy. A nine-out-of-ten probability of surviving the operation was very reassuring; thus presented, many more chose surgery.

Two related areas of social choice where this problem has become very practically acute are the development of environmental policy and the allocation of liability for environmental damages. What is the significance of what is known as "contingent valuation," that is, expressed statements of willingness to pay to avoid an environmental damage? Careful research by Kahneman (1986) and others has certainly shown some very odd and disturbing anomalies in the responses to contingent valuation questionnaires. In one study, they asked questions of two random samples from the population of Ontario. Each respondent in the first sample was asked how much he or she was willing to pay to clean a particular lake. Each respondent in the second sample was asked how much he or she was willing to pay to clean fifty lakes, including the one asked about in the first sample. The mean response was the same in the two samples.

Cognitive psychologists have come to question the notion of given preferences; rather, they say, preferences are "constructed" to fit into a particular context (Tversky 1996). This is especially true in relatively complex settings. The decisionmaker draws on past experience and on a consideration of a sequence of alternatives. But both processes take time; the more there is to draw upon, the less attention can be given to any given piece of past knowledge or of present alternatives. Thus, the sequence in which the information and range of alternatives is considered affects the decision finally made. In some circumstances, repetition of similar choices with knowledge of their consequences leads to learning. But many choice problems present new aspects; for example, durable goods such as automobiles are different each time they are purchased. Hence, choice involves guessing at the similarity to pre-

Comments on the Commentaries 55

vious experience, so the preference has to be constructed anew on each occasion. Political decisions similarly have always an element of novelty, so that the stability of preferences may have little significance.

Frohlich and Oppenheimer have expressed the tradition in which preferences to be used for social choice should be constructed in a social—that is to say, impartial—manner. But as they point out, once the instability of preferences and its dependence on neurological development is recognized, it is not easy to say that even the impartial perspective yields the consensus necessary to avoid social choice paradoxes.

They conclude by raising the proposition that preferences can be made more appropriate for social choice by dialogue. This fits into a viewpoint well represented in Europe and especially among German scholars. If differences arise simply because individuals have different information, then indeed, communication may bring them to a common viewpoint. This point was already made, as Schofield has noted, by Condorcet in his famous analysis of juries. But it can easily happen that better information may make clearer the irreconcilability of different viewpoints, especially if these are in part ego-driven. Apart from that, if differences in information arise from limits on the ability of any one individual to process information, communication may be equally difficult.

I want to conclude by expressing my appreciation for the careful and imaginative attention paid by the authors to the larger implications of my work.

REFERENCES

Beard, Charles. 1935. *An Economic Interpretation of the Constitution of the United States.* New York: Macmillan.

Bentley, Arthur. 1935. *The Process of Government.* Bloomington, Ind.: Principia Press.

Black, Duncan. 1958. *The Theory of Committees and Elections.* Cambridge: Cambridge University Press.

Bowen, Howard. 1943. "The Interpretation of Voting in the Allocation of Resources." *Quarterly Journal of Economics* 58: 27–48.

Herings, Jean-Jacques, Gerard van der Laan, and Richard Venniker. 1997. "The Transition from a Dréze Equilibrium to a Walrasian Equilibrium." Working Paper, Center, Tilburg University.

Hotelling, Harold. 1929. "Stability in Competition." *Economic Journal* 39(1): 41–57.

Kahneman, Daniel. 1986. "Comment." In *Valuing Environmental Goods: An Assessment of the Contingent Valuation Method,* edited by R. G. Cummings, David Brookshire, and William A. Schulze (Totawa, N.J.: Rowman and Allenfield), 185–93.

Kahneman, Daniel, Paul Slovic, and Amos Tversky (eds.). 1982. *Judgment Under Uncertainty: Heuristics and Biases.* Cambridge: Cambridge University Press.

Lorenz, Edward. 1993. *The Essence of Chaos.* Seattle: University of Washington Press.

McKelvey, Richard. 1976. "Intransitivities in Multidimensional Voting Models and Some Implications for Agenda Control." *Journal of Economic Theory* 12: 472–82.

McNeill, Barbara, A. S. Pauker, Harold Sox, and Amos Tversky. 1982. "Elicitation of Preferences of Alternative Therapies." *New England Journal of Medicine* 306: 1259–62.

Scarf, Herbert, with Terje Hansen. 1973. *The Computation of Economic Equilibria.* New Haven, Conn.: Yale University Press.

Schofield, Norman. 1978. "Instability of Simple Dynamical Games." *Review of Economic Studies* 45: 475–94.

Schumpeter, Joseph. 1942. *Capitalism, Socialism, and Democracy.* New York: Harper.

Smale, Stephen. 1976. "A Convergent Process of Price Adjustment and Global Newton Method." *Journal of Mathematical Economics* 3: 107–20.

Solow, Robert. 1956. "A Contribution to the Theory of Economic Growth." *Quarterly Journal of Economics* 70(1): 65–94.

Tversky, Amos. 1996. "Rational Theory and Constructive Choice." In *The Rational Foundations of Economic Behavior*, edited by Kenneth J. Arrow, Enrico Colombatto, Mark Perlman, and Christien Schmidt (Basingstoke: Macmillan; New York: St. Martin's Press/International Economic Association), 185–97.

van der Laan, Gerard, and A. J. J. Talman. 1987. "A Convergent Price Adjustment Process." *Economics Letters* 23: 119–23.

von Neumann, John, and Oskar Morgenstern. 1944. *Theory of Games and Economic Behavior*. Princeton, N.J.: Princeton University Press.

⚓ Chapter 2 ⚓

HERBERT A. SIMON
A Biographical Sketch

Herbert A. Simon was born on June 15, 1916, in a predominately German neighborhood of Milwaukee, Wisconsin. His father was an electrical engineer who emigrated to the United States, and his mother was a second-generation descendant of German immigrants to St. Louis. In addition to his strong precollege education, Simon was also an avid reader who spent hours in the local public library and museum exploring topics central to the social sciences as well as biology and physics. He entered the University of Chicago in 1933 (along with his lifelong friend Harold Guetzkow) very well prepared for a life of scholarship.

The University of Chicago was an excellent environment for a brilliant, inquiring, and independent mind. Since his excellent high school training went a long way toward preparing him for his second-year examinations, he soon began to audit upper-division and graduate-level courses. One of the more exciting courses, on price theory, was taught by Henry Simons, who provided Simon with a "glimpse of the applications of rigor and mathematics to economics." It almost led him to become an economics major: "I resolved to major in economics, until I learned that it required an accounting course. I switched to political science, which had no such requirement." A strange beginning, perhaps, for someone who was later to be a founding father of a business school and a Nobel laureate in economics. "As a result of that rather casual decision (a genuine fork in the maze), I did a great deal of work in both political science and economics" (Simon, 1991, 39). Simon continued to sample the rich array of faculty teaching at Chicago during this time—Nicolas Rashevsky, R. W. Shultz, and Rudolph Carnap, as well as the wonderful faculty that Charles Merriam had brought together in the Chicago Political Science Department, including Harold Gosnell, Harold Lasswell, and Merriam himself.

Another fork in the maze of Simon's life was constructed as a result of papers he wrote in courses on municipal government and his enrollment in Clarence Ridley's course "Measuring Municipal Government." At twenty-one, he had his first publication, with Ridley in the serialized version of "Measuring Municipal Activities" that was published in *Public Management* (Ridley and Simon 1938). (One of the co-editors of this book was so strongly influenced by this pioneering work as to spend fifteen years measuring the performance of urban governments.) This work led to an appointment by Samuel May at Berkeley to direct the program of studies of local government in California. He wrote his Ph.D. exams while in California and returned to Chicago for his orals.[1] His dissertation, *Administrative Behavior* (1947), would become one of the most influential books of this century. Simon would later explain that the dissertation "contains the foundation and much of the superstructure of the theory of bounded rationality that has been my lodestar for nearly fifty years" (Simon 1991, 86):

> The idea had its origins in the Milwaukee recreation study, was reinforced by what I had discovered about boundary conditions of rationality in the California tax incidence study, and was not contradicted by any of the management or other human experiences I had had in my six working years, or the years that preceded them.

Simon's first teaching appointment was at Illinois Institute of Technology in Chicago, where he stayed for seven years. His work there with Don Smithburg and Victor Thompson (Simon, Smithburg, and Thompson 1950) has influenced many generations of students in administrative theory. When the new Graduate School of Industrial Administration at the Carnegie Institute of Technology was in the planning stages, Simon served as a key adviser. He was then asked to become a full professor of administration in the new school, as well as chairman of the Department of Industrial Management. Given the vast resources that had just been given to the Carnegie Institute by the Mellon family, he made the difficult decision to move to what was to become his permanent academic home for the rest of his life. Not only did he help to build the Department of Industrial Management, but Simon turned his immense energies into building a new kind of business school, one based on rigorous social science research and empirical findings.

At Carnegie, Simon continued his extensive research on human decisionmaking. Like many of the other Nobelists included in this volume, he worked at the edges of many disciplines. In the early years of his research on human decisionmaking, he drew on the work of cognitive psychologists during an era when their work was scorned by behavioralists who reigned supreme. Throughout his career he drew on the work of mathematicians, logicians, economists, political scientists, philosophers, computer scientists, and psychologists, as well as the early contributors to what was to become the cybernetic revolution in the social sciences. His significant work with Allen Newell (Newell and Simon 1972) and Cliff Shaw (Newell, Shaw, and Simon 1962), on which the modern field of artificial intelligence is based, actually started at the RAND Corporation during the mid-1950s but has continued for more than four decades at Carnegie Tech.

Simon's major groundbreaking contributions to political science, economics, psychology, and computer science add up to a serious challenge to all social scientists: to build theoretical work on a realistic model of human decisionmaking that shows individuals learning heuristics that enable them to survive and flourish in the immensely complex situations in which they live.

Robert E. Goodin focuses on two of the major contributions Simon has made to political science (along with the multiple contributions he has made to economics, psychology, artificial intelligence, and cognitive science): his extensive work on bounded rationality, and his work on the "logic of appropriateness." Bryan Jones, on the other hand, focuses on the first contribution and digs into the empirical implications of bounded rationality. Jones argues that evidence from markets and political institutions is more consistent with bounded rationality than with maximization under the assumption of full rationality.

NOTE

1. At the time of his orals, the only graduate course for which Simon had credit was a "B" in boxing since he had relied primarily on the graduate work he did as an undergraduate, on his research assignments, and on self-education to prepare for his preliminary exams (Simon 1991, 84). This is something that few contemporary graduate students in political science could do.

REFERENCES

Newell, Allen, J. C. Shaw, and Herbert A. Simon. 1962. "The Processes of Creative Thinking." In *Contemporary Approaches to Creative Thinking,* edited by Howard E. Gruber, Glenn Terrell, and Michael Wertheimer (New York: Lieber-Atherton, Inc.), 63–119.

Newell, Allen, and Herbert A. Simon. 1972. *Human Problem Solving.* Englewood Cliffs, N.J.: Prentice-Hall.

Ridley, Clarence E., and Herbert A. Simon. 1938. *Measuring Municipal Activities.* Chicago: International City Managers' Association.

Simon, Herbert A. 1947. *Administrative Behavior.* New York: Macmillan.

———. 1991. *Models of My Life.* New York: Basic Books.

Simon, Herbert A., Don W. Smithburg, and Victor A. Thompson. 1950. *Public Administration.* New York: Alfred A. Knopf.

RATIONALITY REDUX:
REFLECTIONS ON HERBERT A. SIMON'S
VISION OF POLITICS

Robert E. Goodin

Even as Nobel laureates go, Herbert Simon's stretch is quite remarkable. His contributions range across administrative behavior and organization theory, management science and operations research, behavioral decision theory, cognitive psychology, and artificial intelligence. In each of these fields, furthermore, Simon is a major player. No academic interloper or mere intermediary, he speaks to each of these disciplines in its own terms. It is not so much that Simon's distinguished career has straddled four or five disciplines. Rather, he has led four or five distinguished careers in parallel.[1] The upshot is that each discipline knows a Simon all its own, in part a function of which side Simon has shown each of us, in part a function of how we collectively register and recall the lessons he has taught us.

Here I propose to examine Simon's contribution to political science. That contribution itself, I suggest, has two quite distinct strands, traced more fully later in this essay. Suffice it for now to say that the theme we political scientists most closely associate with Simon is "bounded rationality." This massively important contribution has helped us see how to relax overly taut mathematical models of behavior, bring greater realism into our decision theory, and fend off at least certain sorts of off hand dismissals of the whole project of mathematically modeling human behavior on rationalistic premises.

Important though notions of bounded rationality were—and still are—they seem by now to have been pretty well absorbed, at least in some minimalist way, into the received canon of political science. Good use will always be made of them by anyone deploying formal models to analyze the real world. Much more remains to be done to incorporate these notions formally into these models.[2] But as I show in the next section, the notion of bounded rationality now sits squarely—somewhat to Simon's own chagrin, and certainly not in quite the form he would most prefer—among the standard "tools of the trade" of political scientists, even those of the most archly rational-choice persuasion. Although Simon himself might prefer that analysis of psychological heuristics displace altogether hypotheses of rational expected utility maximization, political science has settled (rightly, I think, at least for now) on a more minimalist adaptation, taking cognitive heuristics onboard alongside and within rational maximization models.

There is a second strand to Simon's political science, less associated with his name but directly traceable to his influence, which seems to me to have lots more still to teach us. That is the notion of a "logic of appropriateness." That central tenet of

James March and Johan Olsen's (1995) "new institutionalism" is connected, through a remarkable string of coauthorships, all the way back to Simon's early work *Administrative Behavior* (1947). Furthermore, it is a topic on which someone like Simon, in his many different disciplinary guises, might have much to offer. Notions of what is or is not "appropriate," the informal logics governing those judgments, and the framing effects evoking them are obviously the province of cognitive psychology. There is much here that political scientists might usefully try to reappropriate. These are themes I explore, necessarily more tentatively, later in the essay.

BOUNDED RATIONALITY

Asked to name Simon's greatest contribution to political science, most of us— apparently including Simon himself (1985, 293)—would with little hesitation nominate the notion of "bounded rationality."[3] He originally phrased the central contrast as one between "optimizing" and "satisficing," between seeking the best outcome you could possibly get in the circumstances and settling for an outcome that you deem "good enough" (Simon 1955). Later he came to phrase it as a contrast between two models of rationality, with "substantive rationality" representing objective optimization and "procedural rationality" incorporating the cognitive limits reflected in his earlier notion of satisficing (Simon 1976, 1978, 1985). In his latest works, Simon (1979b, 1982) seems to have settled on the term "bounded rationality" as the most apt general characterization of that cluster of contrasts.[4]

The term "bounded rationality" captures particularly well what lies at the heart of Simon's distinctive account of decisionmaking. There are limits—bounds—to the cognitive capacity of the human brain. Real-world decisionmakers are restricted in the time and attention they can afford to devote to any one item. The mind is "scarce resource" (Simon 1978, 9); there are strict limits to its "computational capacities" (Simon 1976, 135).[5]

Still, Simon (1985, 297) insists that "bounded rationality is not irrationality." Bounded rationality remains a form of goal-seeking behavior on the part of intentional agents. Given the bounds within which their rationality operates, those goal-seekers inevitably err from time to time. Owing to their ignorance, oversights, or miscalculations, they sometimes choose the wrong course of action to achieve the goals they want. If rationality is defined in the substantive terms of making the "right choice," those wrong choices must necessarily be classed as "irrational." But it is "misleading," in Simon's (1985, 297) words, "to call them 'irrational.' They are better viewed as forms of bounded rationality." They are, to adapt a phrase from Russell Hardin (1988, ch. 1), merely manifestations of "rationality within the limits of [human] reason."

Simon Says "Psychologize"

Simon himself has always cast this contrast as a tug-of-war between economics (including its rational-choice offshoots in political science) and psychology. We must choose, he tells us (Simon 1985, 303), between "the nearly omniscient *Homo economicus* of rational choice theory or the boundedly rational *Homo psychologicus* of cognitive psychology." Our choice, he says, "makes a difference, a very big difference."

The economists' model of rational choice offers a spartan account of what goes on inside the human head. The economic model acknowledges constraints on human choice, to be sure, and the shape of the possibility frontier has an important impact on what we end up choosing. But the constraints recognized by economists are paradigmatically "outside the skin" of the choosing organism (Simon 1955, 100–101).

What Simon proposes to do is to open up the "black box" that is the choosing organism, exploring the decision mechanisms and processes that operate within it. He does so less with a Freudian view to discovering different decisional premises—hidden goals and drives of which the decisionmaker is unaware[6]—than with a view to discovering the factors that limit the cognitive capacity of the organism to optimize in the heroic ways hypothesized in statistical decision theory and its microeconomic analogues.[7] "To understand and predict human behavior," then, "we have to deal with the realities of human rationality, that is, with bounded rationality. There is nothing obvious about these boundaries; there is no way to predict, a priori, just where they lie" (Simon 1985, 297). Hence Simon's emphasis on the experimental, behavioral methods of psychology in preference to the a priori analytics of microeconomics.

Insofar as the aim is to explain particular actions and choices, detailed contextual knowledge of the decisionmakers, their information, and their interactions is obviously essential. Even insofar as the aim is to achieve some limited generalizations, certain sorts of characteristic cognitive constraints and interactions might map into certain characteristic responses to certain sorts of decision problems. Simon himself provides a variety of examples of this, in both economics and politics (Simon 1978, 1985). We may well want to incorporate some of those insights about how people actually make decisions—about the heuristics they use and the shortcuts they take—into our formal economistic models of rational choice.

It is unclear, however, whether importing those insights from behavioral psychology would necessarily make our theory a psychological *instead of* an economic model of decision. Surely it all depends on how much relative work is being done in the composite model by each component, the psychological complications versus the economic simplifications.[8]

In what follows, I suggest how we might start with the spartan economistic model of rational choice and complicate it only as much as necessary. Complications will prove both necessary and advantageous, in the various ways I shall show. The upshot will be a "rational choice theory with knobs on it," and some of those knobs will be of an indisputably psychological (and, in the section on the logic of appropriateness, sociological) sort. But at the end of the day it is still the theory rather than any of the knobs—the economics rather than the psychology or sociology—that is the driving force. It is the intentional, goal-seeking agent who does the choosing, however constrained. It is those choices, rather than any of the constraints, that provide the system's dynamics. By virtue of that fact, I am inclined to regard this mixed model as still very much a fundamentally economistic, rational-choice one.

In making these suggestions, furthermore, I am following what I take to be Simon's own procedure. He too starts with the spartan model of rational choice, handed down by statistical decision theory and microeconomics. He too complicates it as necessary. He too ends up with a model with knobs on it, but one that retains at its core an intentional, goal-seeking agent. Where we differ is merely in the description of the model we end up with—a difference, I suggest, that is mainly a matter of emphasis and audience. In the context of conversations with economists, Simon is right to say that his model is more "psychological" than theirs. But by any objective standard, and outside the narrow context of those conversations with economists, Simon's model must surely count as a distinctively rationalistic, economistic one—certainly, anyway, compared to other more deeply psychologized models of hidden drives and repressed desires, and maybe even as compared to more lightly psychologized models built on the foundations of tamer forms of cognitive psychology.

Alternatively, Rationalize

Economists themselves seem generally inclined to accept Simon's self-characterization as their archenemy.[9] Among political scientists, however, most rational-choice modelers have always (charitably, they always assumed)[10] regarded Simon's suggestions as friendly amendments from the point of view of their own models (Riker and Ordeshook 1973, 21–23).

There is warrant for this in Simon's own writing on the subject. He begins his classic 1955 paper "A Behavioral Theory of Rational Choice" by recalling that economic maximization is always subject to constraints. You are rational, economically, just so long as you get as much as you can of what you want within the constraints of your budget, within the constraints of existing technology, and so on. Absent those constraints, you would, of course, get more of what you want. But you cannot just wish them away. Economically rational decisionmakers simply have to take those "hard facts" about the world as "given" and chart a path for themselves within them.

Simon's 1955 paper goes on to point out that some of the constraints that must similarly be taken as given are "within one's skin." We are all limited by our physical capacities, for example.[11] So too, he says, should we be seen as limited in our decisions by constraints on our cognitive capacities. The scarcities of the mind—scarcities of information, attention, computing power—should on this account be seen as strictly on a par with the material scarcities. Both powerfully constrain the optimization exercises envisaged by economists.

Simon's 1955 paper then goes on to elaborate, both formally and discursively, some of those cognitive constraints. In his subsequent renditions of this account, as I have said, he has chosen to emphasize the "psychology-versus-economics" side of this story, and others have drawn the contrast more sharply still (March 1978). But his more charitable interpreters among political science's rational-choice fraternity have seized—in my view rightly—on the affinity between the constraints of the world and the constraints of the mind to "rationalize satisficing," so to speak.

The basic idea is straightforward. Economic rationality, everyone agrees, is a matter of maximizing subject to constraints. Let's just count the constraints of the mind as on a par with all others, and say that you are rational insofar as you are maximizing subject (inter alia) to the constraints of time, attention, information and computing power under which you are laboring. Then "satisficing" is not distinct from "optimizing" but merely a special case of it. Satisficing is just optimizing, taking account of the constraints of the mind (compare, Bell, Raiffa, and Tversky 1988, 19; Elster 1986, 25–26).[12]

Precisely this thought lies at the heart of Anthony Downs's (1957, chs. 11–13; Grofman 1993) theory of "rational ignorance."[13] Everyone starts out with a certain limited stock of information; acquiring more information is costly; it is rational to do that if and only if the utility you expect to derive from the new piece of information exceeds its expected costs (see, similarly, Radner 1975; Stigler 1961). Thus, it might be perfectly rational for everyone always to act partially in ignorance. It is perfectly comprehensible that asymmetrical information might give different people not only different perspectives but also differential power. These refinements have gone far toward enhancing the realistic feel and explanatory power of rational-choice models, both of politics (Ferejohn and Kuklinski 1990; Kinder and Palfrey 1993; Lupia 1994; Lupia and McCubbins 1998; Popkin 1991) and of social life more generally (Akerlof 1984; March 1972).

For only one recent example of that, consider Thomas Piketty's (1995) elegant analysis of different classes' voting behavior in terms of the different information available to them, within their different social milieux, about the probability of individual merit and effort being rewarded economically in the market. The prior expectation of working-class voters, from their own family histories, is that individual effort is rarely rewarded and that collective efforts at advancement are more likely to pay off. Given that expectation, they invest more heavily in collective efforts than in individual ones; investing less in individual efforts, they find that their individual efforts are less rewarded than their collective efforts, thus reinforcing their prior expectations. Middle-class voters experience the opposite self-reinforcing cycle: their prior expectation that individual effort will be rewarded leads to more individual efforts that are more rewarded. The differential information available to these two social groups, and the rational choices they make on the basis of it, thus lead working-class voters to support collectivist politics of redistribution and middle-class voters to support free-market solutions. This, I submit, is a classically Simonesque story.

Why Not?

If rational-choice political scientists are themselves so happy to accept Simon's satisficing as a friendly amendment to their standard models, why should Simon so staunchly spurn their friendly gesture?

Part of the explanation undoubtedly lies in the simple fact that differences with our close kin and near neighbors always loom the largest, if only because they make more practical difference in our day-to-day lives. Seen from the inside of his research program, what is interesting to Simon is what differentiates him from economic rationalists; seen from the outside and from a distance, however, what is more striking is what those two contrasting accounts share—an intentional, goal-seeking agent. That is the "family resemblance" by virtue of which satisficing and maximizing really ought to be grouped together in one broad family, one that is sharply distinct from other families of structural or phenomenological theories, for example.[14] Thus, I think Simon (1993) doth protest rather too much about being lumped together with economic theorists of politics.[15]

That said, it must also be said that there are important differences between Simon's model and ordinary microeconomic understandings. Here are three that have particularly exercised philosophical economists:

1. Simon says "satisfice": decide in advance what would be "good enough," and call off your search for further options once you have something that meets or exceeds that "aspiration level." Economists say that satisficing amounts to rational economizing on search costs. But, ask Simon's philosophical friends, how do you

know where to set your aspiration level in the first place? That part of the story, anyway, cannot be "rational," since ex hypothesi we know nothing of the merits of the unexplored options (Elster 1986, 25–26). Or for a variant on the same theme: Economists say "economize on information costs," but it is an analytic truism that it is impossible to know the value of an unknown piece of information.[16]

2. Simon and his philosophical friends would go on to say that there is no way of "knowing the future"—here, what the future would have held had you continued searching for better options rather than calling off your search once you had reached this particular aspiration level. It is another analytic truism, akin to the first, that you can never know what you will discover in the future. If you already knew it, you would already have discovered it (Popper 1964, vi–vii).

3. Finally, insofar as the information and foreknowledge concerned involves the actions and choices of other intentional agents, we can never know what others will do. Simon (1976, 140; 1978, 9–10) dubs this indeterminacy of game-theoretic solution concepts "the permanent and ineradicable scandal of economic theory," and many others would agree (Hollis 1987, ch. 7).

Economists have answers, of course. Where Simon sees "satisficing," they see ordinary "decisionmaking under uncertainty." They would have us simply maximize expected utility, resolving the uncertainties that plague Simon and his followers by assigning "subjective probability estimates" to the eventualities in view. Thus, we just offer up our best guess as to the probability of finding an option better than that picked out by each possible aspiration level we might set; then we set our aspiration level wherever the expected costs of continuing the search exceed the expected payoff in terms of better options the search would turn up. Or we guess the likelihood of discovering something dramatically different in the future, or of other people doing various things.[17]

Simon and his philosophical friends will remain unsatisfied. What goes on in the model after you have assigned those subjective probabilities may appear perfectly rational, they would say. But that is a charade, verging on a fraud, when the foundations upon which the whole apparatus rests—the subjective probability assessments—are themselves rationally groundless numbers plucked out of thin air.[18]

Fair enough. More does need to be said about the grounds for our subjective probability assessments. What can be said in their defense varies from case to case. But at least sometimes there seem to be good grounds for induction, for inferring from previous experiences in situations that we have good theoretical grounds for supposing to be relevantly similar. How do we know whether we have set our aspiration level correctly? Well, if we constantly find ourselves reaching it too easily, we can probably infer that we have set it too low;[19] if we find ourselves never reaching it, we can probably infer that we have set it too high. How do we know if we have correctly judged the chances of future surprises? If we find ourselves being constantly surprised, we can probably infer that we have set those chances too low, and conversely. Of course, we can never know exactly *what* will come up, but we can in these ways adjust our predictions that *something* significant will come up.

That does not work in all cases, and it may work particularly badly for the particular sorts of cases here in view. Induction is fine for settled situations, where the future is indeed much like the past. But the problems Simon and his friends point to are precisely the ones that arise where the future will be (or anyway may be) very unlike the past, not just in particulars (the specific things that happen) but also in general (the rates at which surprising things happen). Therein, of course, lies the "fallacy of induction" in general (Goodman 1955/1983). Just because in the past the future has always been broadly continuous with the past gives no ironclad guarantee that, in the future, it will always be. The fact that the sun has always risen in the east provides no ironclad guarantee that it will in the future.

Thus, we need to work up from induction to some higher-level theoretical understanding of the processes in view—here, some theories about human behavior and scientific discovery—and soon. Putting our complete faith in those theories will never be fully rational either, of course. They can never be completely "verified"; they always stand at risk of being falsified by some further fact. But if skepticism of *that* sort is all that Simon's philosophical friends can point to in alleging the irrationality of economistic optimizing of expected utility, then all I can say is that economistic optimizing is at least as rational as anything else any of us can ever conceive of doing in our lives—and that is good enough for me.

The "deep" problems Simon and his philosophical friends see in rationalizing his account of satisficing thus seem to me not to be problems. Or rather, they are no more problems for that project than they are for the whole enterprise of human understanding tout court. But Simon, fascinated though he rightly is by the magic and mystery of human cognition and artificial intelligence, is no party to mysticism as such. To attribute deep skepticism of that sort to him would be uncharitable in the extreme. Yet stopping anywhere short of that seems to me to leave us well equipped to give a perfectly rationalistic account of what is going on in satisficing.

If the deep philosophical problems prove relatively unworrying, the practical difficulties prove more so. Most of the practicalities here in view are almost wholly representational at root. The problem is one of finding elegant, simple symbolic representations of what in his Nobel lecture Simon (1979b, 504) called "the inelegancies of the real world." Mathematical economists, in particular, have been highly exercised by such worries. [20] Systematically accommodating imperfect, asymmetrical information into the general equilibrium theory that constitutes the crowning glory of modern economics proves devilishly difficult.[21]

Knowing the difficulty he has in selling the idea of bounded rationality to economists proper, Simon (1993, 49–50) is understandably wary of the rush of economists manqué in political science to embrace it. But, of course, the two disciplines analyze different things. Furthermore, for most of us most of the time, politics occupies a very small, confined corner of our lives, whereas the sorts of choices economists hope to capture are much more pervasive. Hence, it is not implausible to suppose that the sorts of complications to ordinary people's "objective functions" that might be needed to mimic their processes in reaching political decisions are just much less complicated, and hence a lot more formally tractable, than the ones involved in the fuller range of resource allocation decisions that economics hopes to map (much less the still fuller range that psychology hopes to map).

Why Bother?

Just how full an account we need of what goes on inside people's heads is indeed an "old debate" in the social sciences (Bell, Raiffa, and Tversky 1988, 19).[22] Having little hope of resolving it here, I will belabor it no further.

Let us next explore the more subversive possibility that perhaps the whole question—whether or how bounded rationality can be incorporated into the ordinary economic calculus, as applied to politics or anything else—is becoming increasingly moot. Recall the nature of Simon's bounds to rationality: "time, attention, information, and computational capacity," in the terms used to characterize them earlier. And then simply notice that with the advent of fast, powerful computer and communications technology, most of those constraints are (at least in certain respects) rapidly being relaxed.

That too is a familiar Simon theme. His early interest in the chess-playing computer as a model of human cognition grew into a larger interest in artificial intelligence and information technology more generally. In consequence, he was among the first to foresee the sorts of changes we are now seeing in our lives. Furthermore, as a student of organizational behavior as well as of the mind, Simon was among the first to give serious thought to what the growing power of computer technology might mean for the science of management (see, for example, Simon 1960/1977, 1969/1981, and 1982, chs. 6.1–6.7).

Enthusiasm for the computer revolution as a solution to all our managerial problems, so characteristic of the 1960s, has since waned, however, even within the Carnegie school. The increasing power of information technology might help decisionmakers evade problems of time, information, and computational capacity. But, as Simon now emphasizes, the problems associated with decisionmakers' limited "attention" will then loom larger than ever before. In Simon's (1985, 302) own words:

> The human eye and ear are highly parallel devices, capable of extracting many pieces of information simultaneously from the environment and decoding them into their significant features. Before this information can be used by the deliberative mind, however, it must proceed through the bottleneck of attention—a serial, not parallel, process whose information capacity is exceedingly small. Psychologists usually call this bottleneck short-term memory, and measurements show reliably that it can hold only about six chunks (that is to say, six familiar items of information). . . . The narrowness of the span of attention accounts for a great deal of human unreason that considers only one facet of a multi-faceted matter before a decision is reached.

This "limited attention" theme figures with increasing centrality in Simon's later presentations of his bounded rationality model (see, for example, Simon 1978, 13–14; 1983, 79–83; 1985, 302).

In the new "information-rich environment" (Simon 1960/1977, 106ff.) created for us by the information revolution, our principal task lies in selecting the signals that are significant, directing our attention to what really matters among all those data. That, Simon seems to think, is a different and much more difficult task with which information technology cannot really help.

But is that altogether true? Can we not just set "delimits" so that our machine calls our attention only to those things falling outside them? Think, for example, of the "tripwires" the Internal Revenue Service uses to choose which tax returns to audit. That would be just another example of bounded rationality, justified in the same constrained-maximizing economic terms as described earlier. We can conceive of those "delimits" as representing something like the "confidence interval" we associate with our best guesses as to what the right or real number is. We can adjust those delimits upward if we get too many up-side trips; if the converse, we can adjust them downward. We can justify not worrying about the slight differences within the range of untripped—broadly unsurprising—outcomes in terms of economizing on attention, which we can devote to tasks where it will (on our best present guess) do us the most good. We are in that way maximizing good outcomes, subject to constraint of limits on our attention.

Of course, the relative importance of constraints on our attention will grow as information technology increasingly eases the constraints on time, information, and computational capacity. Moreover, "delimits," like all decisional shortcuts, will never work perfectly. Even when they are working as they are designed to, they will always lead us into making marginal "errors" (wrong from the perspective of omniscience, reasonable from the perspective of constrained agents doing the best they can), and they will always break down occasionally, leading us into some really massive errors (think of all those "delimit" lights flashing in the nuclear power plant control room in *The China Syndrome*).

Rational choice as to where to direct your attention—as with so many other things—is not always so terribly rational from a God's-eye point of view. Alas, Her perspective is not one that we can (costlessly) share. Rational choice for humans consists in doing the best that is humanly possible, in the multiply constrained situation that constitutes the human condition.

Why Worry?

Within economics and psychology, in particular, there seems to be far more reluctance than we political scientists seem to think there should be to incorporate the decisional shortcuts, heuristics, and rules of thumb that real agents use in the real world into formal models of rational decision. There are, of course, genuine causes for concern: Mathematical messiness is one; a loss of parsimony is another. But what those considerations warrant, I submit, is a level of concern considerably more modest than is often in evidence among microeconomists or prescriptive decision theorists in psychology.

So why the exaggerated levels of concern? A large part of the explanation lies, of course, in the nature of the intradisciplinary battle lines within each of those disciplines. In economics, axiomatic theorists are the sworn enemies of experimentalists; in psychology, prescriptive decision theorists are the sworn enemies of descriptive ones. The "behavioralism" that lies at the heart of Simon-style heuristics and shortcuts makes those notions anathema to the formalists (axiomatic prescriptivists) of both disciplines.

These disciplinary divides, I think, go some way toward explaining the embarrassment those formalists feel at experimental findings that people are easily tripped up in artificial decision situations. People do not update their probability estimates nearly as much as Bayesian decision theory says they should; the "anchoring" heuristic has much more of a hold on them than ideally it ought to. People are unduly sensitive to the way questions are cast: They are far more reluctant to administer a vaccine when its effects are described in terms of how many people will die despite it than they are when its effects are described in terms of how many people it will save. People are unduly sensitive to losses as compared to gains. They are unreasonably sensitive to "earmarking," much more hesitant to carry on with a planned trip to the opera when they have lost a prepurchased ticket than when they have simply lost a bank note of equal value. Experimental psychology is full of such results (Abelson and Levi 1985; Kahneman, Slovic, and Tversky 1982; Tversky and Kahneman 1981), and formal decision theory is deeply embarrassed by them.

That embarrassment might well be explicable in terms of the gamesmanship that goes on inside each of those disciplines. But it is unwarranted in any larger sense, I would suggest. Social psychologists are cunningly clever at contriving experimental situations to trip people up in these ways. Showing that people can be tripped up, in just such "crucial tests," may well prove some deeper point under dispute within the discipline.

From the larger point of view of trying to explain what most people do most of the time, however, the thing to say about such experiments is just that they *are* fiendishly clever contrivances. (Just try designing one of those experiments yourself, if you doubt it.) As such, they are highly atypical of the sorts of situations that real decisionmakers characteristically meet in the real world. And, I suggest, the heuristics that so badly wrong-foot subjects in the situations that experimenters such as Daniel Kahneman and Amos Tversky have contrived actually serve the same people pretty well in the real world.

Thus, it is in general a good idea to react positively to helping keep people alive and negatively to letting them die.[23] In general, it is a pretty good idea to worry more about losses (which will necessarily entail alterations in your life) than about gains (which you can just bank if you do not want to be bothered). In general, it is a pretty good idea to make budgets and stick to them, however much fun experimentalists might poke at that "earmarking heuristic." Even insofar as Bayesian updating is concerned, there is much socially to be said for making up your mind and sticking to it rather than vacillating endlessly: making up your mind a little too early, and sticking to it a little too firmly, may well serve important social functions such as ensuring your reliability and trustworthiness.

In short, I submit that those heuristics are all perfectly good decisional shortcuts, rules of thumb that point us in the right direction in the vast majority of cases. What the experimentalists have done is simply to show that these shortcuts, like all shortcuts, can occasionally cause us to err. But we have always known that. The only question, from the point of view of the "rationalizing" project I proposed earlier, is whether those errors are (or rather, should reasonably be expected to be) sufficiently frequent and sufficiently grievous in their consequences that they eat up all the savings that come from employing the shortcuts in the first place. I can see no clear way of determining in advance and in general just how costly these errors might be. But I do think evidence for their relative rarity can be found in the very fact that it took such a cunningly contrived experimental design to isolate those pathologies in the first place.

From yet another disciplinary perspective—that of philosophy—these framing effects seem very untroubling indeed. It is a commonplace of contemporary action theory that all choice is "choice under some particular description." Any particular physical movement admits of a myriad of alternative descriptions. Characterizing it as "action" at all implies intentional agency; to further characterize it as a "choice" is to say that the agent intentionally selected it under some one or another of those alternative descriptions (Davidson 1980).[24]

In this connection, framing heuristics are highly useful devices, akin to the deci-sional shortcuts discussed earlier. They help us to identify the particular description(s) under which each choice situation should be regarded. They help us to see relevant points of similarity between this choice situation and others, past or in prospect (Tversky 1977). They help us, in that way, to achieve a measure of consistency across our choices—even if, in other ways beloved of experimental psychologists, they simultaneously introduce inconsistencies in other respects.

From a God's-eye point of view, of course, rational choosers would select their choices under *all* possible descriptions at the same time. They would look at *all* the attributes of each action, weighing the costs and benefits of each of those aspects of the act in the balance. The fact that each act has a potential infinity of alternative descriptions would be untroubling to a God with infinite capacities. The point, here as before, is simply that we are not She.

What Follows?

Rationalizing satisficing in this way constitutes a two-edged sword, so far as rational-choice modelers are concerned. If successful, that maneuver effectively neutralizes satisficing as a powerful external challenge to their theories. But it does so by domesticating satisficing, by incorporating it *within* the model of rational choice.

The upshot of that, in turn, is that rational-choice modelers can no longer simply ignore the sorts of heuristics and decisional shortcuts that satisficers characteristically employ. Those are no longer something "outside the model" that can properly be said to be the province of some other paradigm or some whole other discipline. Instead, they are now very much "within the model." As such, they are things that rational-choice modelers are obliged to study with all the care and attention they devote to any other component of their overall model.[25]

In "rationalizing satisficing," rational-choice modelers have *subsumed* satisficing, not subdued it. They have not vanquished a rival pretender to the title of "queen of the social sciences": rather, they have simply married into the competing dynastic line. The upshot of rationalizing satisficing is not that it can now be safely ignored, letting rational-choice theorists get on with their mathematics in peace. The upshot is, rather, that they must now seriously study it, employing all the impres-sive tools of modern cognitive psychology as well as all the fancy apparatus of mod-ern mathematical economics.[26]

In compiling composite models, it is an open question where the balance will even-tually be struck between the rationality postulates of economics and the decisional heuristics of cognitive psychology. Simon seems to suppose that in any such com-posite model virtually all the explanatory work will be done by the heuristics and virtually none of it by the rationality postulate. If so, then when we apply Occam's razor to cut extraneous premises out of our scientific models, the rationality postulate will have to go. In the fullness of time, of course, it is perfectly possible that Simon might be proven right in that speculation. Eventually we might learn enough about cognitive psychology for there to be no place left for the rationality that we so crudely postulate.

For now, however, all the best models employing decisional heuristics to analyze political phenomena really do seem to operate against a background assumption of goal-seeking, intentional agency. Those heuristics are shortcuts that lead, and mislead, those agents in quest of their goals. But in those accounts, agents are indeed modeled as intentional agents, as goal-seekers who are (however imperfectly) striving to find fitting means to their ends. And that fitting of means to ends is, of course, the hallmark of "rationality," as economically conceived.[27]

INTERLUDE: OUR TWO SIMONS

The "bounded rationality" story is the side of Simon's work more familiar to political scientists and indeed to economists. His notion of satisficing has served as an important counterweight to maximizing, enriching rational-choice models of politics at the same time as it has complicated them. His talk of bounded rationality has directed attention to the nature of the constraints under which politics (and much else) proceeds—constraints of time, information, attention, and sheer computational power, shamelessly glossed over in older "synoptic" models of decisionmaking borrowed from economics.

Tracing intellectual lineages, we might say that all this grew out of Simon's early observations about *Administrative Behavior* (1947, chs. 4–5). He proceeded to formalize those observations in his classic 1955 *Quarterly Journal of Economics* paper (and a companion piece, less well known among political scientists, published a year later in the *Psychological Review*). Simon himself went on to elaborate on those models in a great many places. But tracing his impact on political science as a profession, we can discern two important lines of influence emanating from that work. One is on Charles Lindblom's (1959, 1979; Braybrooke and Lindblom 1963; Dahl and Lindblom 1953) model of incremental adaptation and, through that, on various applied studies of political decisionmaking, perhaps the most distinguished of which remains Aaron Wildavsky's (1964/1984) study of public budgeting. The other path of influence is through Karl Deutsch's *Nerves of Government* (1963) and on to applications of cybernetic control theory in public administration (Steinbruner 1974). All are represented in the cluster of branches on the left-hand side of figure 2.1.

As foreshadowed in my introduction, however, there is a second side to Simon's influence. Like the first, it is rooted in his *Administrative Behavior* (1947). It proceeds through a remarkable series of collaborations—first between Simon and James March on *Organizations* (1958), then between March and Richard Cyert on their classic *Behavioral Theory of the Firm* (1963). It then flowed into the work of people like Oliver Williamson (1985), consolidating one important corner of the "new institutionalism" within economics, on the one side. On the other side, the March-Simon work on organization theory fed into March and Olsen's "garbage can theory" of organizational choice (March 1978; March and Olsen 1976), and thence into March and Olsen's (1989, 1995) classic works consolidating the "new institutionalism" within political science. All this is represented in the cluster of branches on the right of figure 2.1.

No intellectual history can ever be quite so neat as all that, of course. There have been lots of crosscurrents, lots of other influences, and so on. Besides, much of the influence was attenuated or at one remove. Still, Simon's work clearly set the academic agenda and constituted the intellectual background against which those further developments unfolded.

Figure 2.1   Simon's Intellectual Progeny

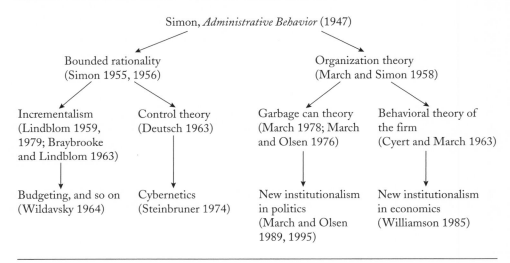

Although Simon's work constitutes the starting point for many of these later contributions, direct references to Simon and his work can in these discussions sometimes be surprisingly scarce. That is perhaps in part because Simon himself has been reluctant to tout his organization theory as a "second strand" independent from the first. Instead, he prefers to see the "logic of appropriateness" framing heuristics and so on as part and parcel of the first project—bounded rationality and its consequences. In a way, of course, it is. Rationality, its bounds, and our adaptations to its bounds can indeed be seen to swallow up virtually everything in the human sciences.

Whether this second strand is a genuinely distinct strand or whether it is merely a substrand of the first does not in the end matter greatly. What matters is merely that the second strand represents a genuinely important insight in itself, upon which many have profitably built; it offers considerable scope for further development of a richer understanding of political life after the fashion of Herbert Simon.

THE LOGIC OF APPROPRIATENESS

Let us now turn to consider that second strand of Simon's influence, the strand passing down from his work on organizational theory into the behavioral theory of the firm and garbage can models of organizational choice and thence into the new institutionalism in politics and economics.

New institutionalism itself is nowadays much discussed, and I propose simply to take much of it as read. What I want to do here is to highlight one crucial theme in those discussions, the notion of a "logic of appropriateness," which marks as crucial a departure from ordinary canons of rationality in these contexts, as did Simon's earlier notion of "bounded rationality" in others. I trace the ways in which the constellation of interests characterizing Simon's career (interests in rationality, in organizational dynamics, and in cognitive psychology) might help us extend those insights still further.

I should say from the outset, however, that I put these pieces together in ways that have no particular warrant in Simon's own disparate writings. I hope he might recognize just a little of himself in these reflections. Be that as it may, though, the ideas seem to me to have independent interest quite apart from their precise relation to Simon's view of his own works.

The Basic Idea

March and Olsen (1995, ch. 2) contrast what they call the "logic of appropriateness" with instrumental rationality's "logic of consequences." In an implicit echo of Max Weber's (1947, 115–18) distinction between zweckrational and wertrational, March and Olsen (1992, 38) say that their logic of appropriateness has embedded in it "ideas about the duties and obligations of citizenship and office, the commitment to fulfill an identity without regard to its consequences for personal or group preferences or interests."

"The core notion," as they describe it, "is that life is organized by sets of shared meanings and practices that come to be taken as given." They further explain (1992, 30–31):

> Political actors act and organize themselves in accordance with rules and practices that are socially constructed, publicly known, anticipated and accepted. Actions of individuals and collectivities occur within these shared meanings and practices, which can be called identities and institutions. . . . Institutions and identities constitute and legitimize political actors and provide them with consistent behavioral rules, conceptions of reality, standards of assessment, affective ties, and endowments, and thereby with a capacity for purposeful action. . . . [P]eople act, think, feel, and organize themselves on the basis of exemplary or authoritative (and sometimes competing or conflicting) rules derived from socially constructed identities and roles. . . . Rules and understandings frame thought, shape behavior, and constrain interpretation.

The bottom line is that "actions are expressions of what is appropriate, exemplary, natural, or acceptable behavior according to the (internalized) purposes, codes of rights and duties, practices, methods and techniques" specified by the group's institutions and the individuals' identities (March and Olsen 1992, 31).

This concept of "appropriateness" has both cognitive and normative aspects to it.[28] What is appropriate in the cognitive sense is that which has over time proven to work out well, to be adequate to certain sorts of situations. What is appropriate in the normative sense is that which is consonant with the morals of a specific community. Both give rise externally to expectations (a notion that similarly straddles the "statistically predicted" and the "normatively demanded"). Both give rise internally to a "critical reflective attitude," a propensity to assess one's prospective course of conduct according to standards of appropriateness (Hart 1961).

All this departs, once again, from rational maximizing across the board. It is, in a way, another instance of bounded rationality and constrained maximizing. But whereas before the bounds were set by "constraints of the mind"—time, attention, and cognitive capacity—here the bounds are set by social roles and what is deemed socially appropriate within them. Whereas satisficing might be said to amount to "rationality within the limits of human reason," behaving according to logics of appropriateness might be said to amount to "rationality within the limits of social roles."

Building Blocks

This notion of a "logic of appropriateness" has important resonances across a range of work in philosophy and the social sciences. Here I attempt to set out some of the "building blocks" that might usefully go into a more fully theorized account of the phenomenon. In so doing, I borrow shamelessly from philosophy, psychology, sociology, and organizational theory. Magpie-like, I will be gathering whatever glittering pieces happen to have caught my eye and seem, at least at first sight, to have roughly the right shape for doing the work we want them to do. Having assembled these pieces, however, I will (within the space of this paper, must perforce) leave to others the task of fashioning them fully to fit the task.

Situated Logics   In perhaps a subconscious echo of Karl Popper's (1964, 149) brief remarks on the "logic of the situation," March and Olsen (1992, 30) say that "appropriateness" in the logic they identify "refers to a match of behavior to a situation." The "logic" in view in both cases is a highly informal one. It has more to do with notions of "coherence" than deduction. It is more suggestive than directive, more flexible than determinate. Still, as another familiar philosophical model, the "coherence theory of the truth," teaches us, coherences of this sort might be as productive of right reasoning as any of the deductions found in the more standard deductive models.

The logic in view in both cases is, furthermore, a very partial one. The right thing to do, within this logic, does not derive from any large deductive apparatus tied back formally to a set of indubitable higher-order premises. It is simply, in the situation, the obviously right thing to do. There is a certain inexorability about that conclusion, derived from the situation rather than from any higher premises or formal structure.[29]

The further implication of this way of thinking is that different logics will operate in different situations, that different things will be appropriate in different circumstances. This "relativization" of logic, indexing its simplifications to the particular context, also marks an important departure from the classical logic of statistical decision theory and microeconomics. Again, however, there is a sophisticated body of philosophical work on "relevant logics" adapted to precisely this task.[30]

The "framing" heuristics discovered by experimental psychologists serve, I suggest, to define the "situation" for us in these respects. In addition to their other uses already discussed, these framing effects help us determine the proper "context" for any particular choice situation and thereby to determine which set of rules—which "decision logic"—to apply to it.

Some of this is already familiar. Organization theorists know of the importance of the "cognitive process of pairing problem-solving action correctly to a problem situation" from March and Simon's early work on *Organizations* (1958/1993, 10–13). Both that book and Cyert and March's sequel, *The Behavioral Theory of the Firm* (1963/1992), emphasize "the impact of rules of appropriateness and standard operating procedures in routine situations." March and Olsen (1992, 30–31) rightly recall both those early emphases. But it is, I think, fair to say that organization theorists have not mined these sources as fully as they might. The work of cognitive psychologists on pattern recognition and the intuitions grounded in it might well provide a platform for further advances in these connections (Simon 1969/1981, ch. 4; 1983, 25–29; Tversky 1977).

Realms of Rationality   Talk of situated logics appropriately operating differently in different contexts suggests something like different "realms of rationality" (March 1978). This in turn is evocative of Foucault's (1991) talk of "rationalities of governance," insistently in the plural. There is indeed much that these notions share. Both are founded on "rules and practices that are socially constructed" through discursive techniques (March and Olsen 1992, 30). Both are contextualized, situation-specific bodies of rules and practices, rather after the fashion of phenomenologists like Alfred Schutz (1943). Both evoke notions of "knowing how" rather more than of "knowing that," in one of Gilbert Ryle's (1949, ch. 2) more subversive distinctions.

Whatever our more general discomfort with postmodernists' larger claims, the phenomenon of different "realms of rationality" is itself comfortably familiar to us all. Both social critics and perceptive economists point to the various ways in which we intuitively operate with notions of separate *Spheres of Justice* (Walzer 1983). It is for an economist such as James Tobin (1970) a puzzling but undeniable fact that we practice "specific egalitarianism," distributing some goods and services (public housing, food stamps, jury duty) on an in-kind basis in a way that ensures that their distribution is more equal than is the distribution of money itself. Social anthropologists, of course, elaborate in great detail the ways in which we strive to keep certain sorts of people and certain sorts of things "in their place," in their "separate spheres," so that we will not be contaminated by rubbing up against inappropriate others (Douglas 1966, 1982; Douglas and Isherwood 1979), W. H. Auden's (1932, 5) "private faces in public places."

Role Rationality   Finally, note how within March and Olsen's (1992, 30) "institutional perspective, the axiomatics for political action begin not with subjective consequences and preferences but with rules, identities, and roles." It is a matter of matching action to "role expectations," sociologically understood.

There has, of course, been a plethora of sociologial work on role theory, much of it highly applicable here (Dahrendorf 1958/1968). But perhaps the most fruitful approach here would be less through sociology than through the psychology and philosophy of the social construction of the self (Benhabib 1992; Taylor 1989). There are certain things that you do, not because others expect you to, but simply because of the sort of person you think of yourself as being.

March and Olsen (1992, 31) evoke these considerations by talking about certain sorts of attitudes, behaviors, feelings, or preferences as "appropriate" to role occupants, in the sense that they are "essential" to being occupants of those roles at all. They are essential not just instrumentally, or "by arbitrary definitional convention," but rather in the sense that, without those attitudes, behaviors, feelings, and preferences, "one cannot claim to be a proper citizen, official, or farmer" at all. From a broader sociological perspective, that sense of the "essence" of being a proper occupant of all those roles is, of course, socially constructed. But from the inside, it is neither seen nor felt to be.[31]

Philosophers have from time to time toyed with the idea of developing models of "role rationality" (Benn 1976, 1979; Hollis 1977, 1987). Rational behavior, on this model, would consist of behavior appropriate to the role in question. There are various ways the story could be told. One would be to represent people's values as endogenously given by the roles they occupy, rewriting role occupants' objective functions so that the values they are trying to optimize are given to them by the roles they occupy. Alternatively, we might let people's values remain as exogenously given within our model and simply treat role expectations as constraints on what role occupants can do in pursuit of those goals. And, of course, we could do both at once, representing roles as both imparting new goals to people and imposing new constraints on what they can do in pursuit of their goals, both old and new.

The important fact to note about role rationality, in the present context, is that it is paradigmatically a situated logic. The rational thing to do in the context of one particular role is not necessarily rational outside that context. Roles thus create distinct "realms" of rationality, of just the sort discussed here. They are not the only way those distinct realms arise perhaps. But they are one clear way—and as I shall go on to show, one particularly important way in the context of the present discussion.

Bringing Social Relations Back In

Ronald Coase's (1937) early paper on "The Nature of the Firm" is rightly regarded as the starting point for one important strand of the "new institutionalism" within economics. Simon's (1951) paper "A Formal Theory of the Employment Relationship" ought to be resurrected and read alongside it. Coase asks why firms internalize the production process rather than buy components from subcontractors; he answers that question, in characteristically Coasian fashion, by referring to information and transaction costs—the relative costs of monitoring the quality of factor inputs from outside the firm as compared to within it.

The central concern in Simon's paper (foreshadowed in Simon 1947, chs. 7, 10, 11) is with the employment contract and the great difference between it and a contract for the sale of goods. Rather than specifying "a stated sum of money . . . in return [for] a specified quantity of a completely specified commodity," the employment contract is invariably incompletely specified. Furthermore, the employment contract establishes an ongoing relationship between employer and employee in a way that an ordinary contract between buyer and seller does not: "[T]he worker is interested in what the entrepreneur will want him to do" in a way that "the seller is not interested in the way his commodity is used once it is sold" (Simon 1951, 294). In these crucial ways, Simon's early paper went far toward anticipating the notions of incomplete and relational contracting that have come to dominate the new theory of the firm.[32]

These points about incomplete contracting are easily generalized into a theory of social relations. We have good reasons for forming ongoing relationships with others, setting up rules that govern our behavior within those relationships so as to give each other some reasonable expectation as to what we will do. We have all the better reasons for persisting in those patterns of ongoing social cooperation we have been born into, predating any active choices of our own.[33]

Writ small, we form—or persist in—trusting relationships of an intimate sort. Writ large, we establish—or persist in—general social standards of conduct, specifying some of the general sorts of expectations that we have of one another in each of the various roles in which we characteristically find ourselves. We trust others not to disappoint us in our expectations about how they will perform in their various roles. Those who behave in a trustworthy fashion acquire a good reputation for that behavior and become party to ever more trusting relations; those who betray our trust acquire a reputation for being untrustworthy and are deprived of the future benefits of trusting relations. All of this is by now tolerably well mapped by game theorists and others to varying degrees of formality and generality (Hardin 1993; Kreps 1990; Kreps and Wilson 1982).

In the present context, what I want to emphasize is how the "logic of appropriateness," working through notions of role rationality and the situated logics of role expectations, may be able to draw on models of imperfect, relational contracting. The result would be the further rationalizing of realms of life ordinarily thought resistant, if not impervious, to rationalization. And to some extent they will always defy complete rationalization. Whom exactly we trust, and what exactly we trust them to do, will always be somewhat indeterminate at the margins. But that we have institutions of trusting relations—roles and associated expectations, rewards and penalties for honoring or breaching them—is itself rationally perfectly explicable.[34]

Rationality Reformulated

All of this constitutes a genuine reformulation rather than just a marginal revision of ordinary models of rational choice as handed down to us by microeconomists, statistical decision theorists, and the like. Thinking as philosophers do of "choice" as always involving "choice under a description" (Davidson 1980; Sen 1980, 1983) emphasizes all the alternative descriptions under which any situation might be viewed, and hence under which any given action might be chosen. Psychological analyses of "framing effects" (Abelson and Levi 1985; Kahneman, Slovic, and Tversky 1982; Tversky 1977; Tversky and Kahneman 1981) and sociological accounts of norms of "appropriateness" help tell us "under what description" we see those situations and hence make our choices. But in all this, the relative importance accorded to "cueing" as opposed to "choosing," in any recognizably "rationally maximizing" way, has expanded considerably.

What then is left of "rationality" under this reformulation? Well, one thing that remains is "perspectival rationality." This is a matter of rational action from *within* a given perspective: rationality in the way you comprehend situations and in the way you act on them, from a particular point of view, from a particular perspective, from a particular standpoint.[35] This is perhaps more a hermeneutic, anthropological sense of rationality than an economic one (Hollis and Lukes 1982; Schutz 1943; Wilson 1970). But it is not necessarily any the worse for that—at least not from a philosophical or even social scientific point of view, if not from a more narrowly mathematical one.

What is also left might be a more frankly "prescriptive" sense of rationality, building on that perspectival one. Rational decisionmaking in this sense consists of recognizing and attempting as best you can to overcome the limits imposed by any one particular perspective on any given situation. Rationality is a recommendation to try to transcend narrowness, to try to "triangulate on the truth" by seeing the situation from as many alternative perspectives as possible. It is an old Enlightenment ideal, but again, it is none the worse for that. That ideal might not be an easy one to realize, and it might be one that is impossible ever to realize fully. Still, it is always worth trying to realize it to some extent, even in the most unfavorable circumstances.[36] And on average and across a wide range of times and circumstances, the closer we get to that normative ideal of rationality the better.[37]

CONCLUSION:
RATIONALITY REBOUND/RATIONALITY REBOUNDING

In Jon Elster's (1986, 26–27) summary judgment:

> Neoclassical economics will be dethroned if and when satisficing theory and psychology join forces to produce a simple and robust explanation of aspiration levels, or sociological theory comes up with a simple and robust theory of the relation between social norms and instrumental rationality. Until this happens, the continued dominance of neoclassical theory is ensured by the fact that one can't beat something with nothing.

The upshot of my discussion is that, while psychological and sociological contributions to our discussions can hardly be said to amount to "nothing," neither are they "everything" in these realms.

Simon and his progeny have emphasized the need to feed inputs both from cognitive psychology and from organizational sociology into political science's characterizations of people's decision functions if we are get reliable accounts of what people decide to do. Political scientists have gone some way toward the former, accommodating decision heuristics within their formal models of political behavior. There are many more such heuristics in the psychological lexicon than political scientists have yet managed to accommodate within their models (Abelson and Levi 1985), and much remains to be done truly to integrate decision heuristics into—rather than just tacking them onto—formally rationalistic models of behavior. But that first task is well under way and is already paying conspicuous dividends. The other Simon-inspired task—incorporating insights from organizational sociology and role theory—promises similar payoffs. The full political ramifications of alternative "logics of appropriateness" largely remain yet to be explored.

Where it will all end—whether cognitive psychology or organizational sociology (or some combination of the two) will eventually render the rationality postulate irrelevant—cannot be known in advance with confidence. But for now and the foreseeable future, it is still rationality that is in the driver's seat. Blend into our formal models such insights from cognitive psychology or organizational sociology as we will, what remains is still a model of rationality, however bounded—a logic, however qualified. Rationality of some recognizably means-ends sort is still providing the motive force within this enriched account of social decisionmaking. Thus, I conclude that, despite these impressive attempts to dethrone it, rationality is back on top—even if what it now sits atop is a rather more mixed bag of tricks.

This paper has its distant origins in conversations with Johan Olsen, Martin Hollis, and Brian Barry. I am grateful to them. For extensive comments on earlier drafts, I am thankful to James March, Elinor Ostrom, and, especially, Herbert Simon, from all of whom I doubtless learned less than I should.

NOTES

1. Moreover, starting in 1937, Simon has generated a publication list that is 873 items long and counting. For a complete bibliography up to the time of the Nobel Prize, see Ando (1979, 94–114).

2. If only so that they do not seem to be "ad hoc" let-out clauses for failures of prediction (Elster 1986, 26; Green and Shapiro 1994, 29–39).

3. Simon sees the notion of bounded rationality as his major contribution to economics as well, judging from his Ely lecture (1978) and his Nobel lecture (1979b).

4. The term itself is one that Simon has long been using, appearing as early as *Models of Man* (1957, 198). What is new is simply the centrality that Simon accords it in his present presentations.

5. His early interest in computational issues in particular led to fascinating forays into operations research, linear and integer programming, and artificial intelligence—all of which served to reimpress upon him the extraordinary computational demands involved in optimization in even apparently simple tasks (Simon 1978, 11–13). Chess is the classic example. There should, in principle, be a determinate answer to the question of what is the best move, but if in practice that involves scanning the 10^{120} possible moves in an average forty-round game, then no one will ever be able to perform the relevant calculations and everyone will always be left relying on the heuristics of what constitutes "good play" (Simon 1972, 166).

6. There was rather more of this in Simon's original presentation in *Administrative Behavior* (1947, ch. 5), but in subsequent presentations it seems to have dropped away (but cf. Simon 1985, 302).

7. Simon's (1957) two "models of man" are thus different from those of Martin Hollis (1977), whose Autonomous Man does indeed correspond to the microeconomic fiction but whose contrasting Plastic Man has much more social programming than Simon's initial satisficer necessarily manifested. Simon's more recent work on the evolutionary biological roots of altruism and social learning (1983, 1990, 1991, 35ff.) more generally constitutes an attempt, from within his model, to come to terms with Hollis's Plastic Man.

8. From recent correspondence, I take it that Simon's view is simply that all the work would be done by the psychological and inductive heuristics and none by the rationalistic and deductive simplifications. In support of that view, he points to his wonderful books *Scientific Discovery* (Langley, Simon, Bradshaw, and Zytkow 1987) and *Human Problem Solving* (Newell and Simon 1972). (Also see his passing remarks on new institutional economics [Simon 1991, 27] and his powerful demolition of the ostensible predictive success of Cobb-Douglas production functions [Simon 1979a].) Maybe. It is obviously an empirical question, the resolution of which will have to await an empirical answer. My own hunch, for what it is worth, is that the "assumption of rationality" serves as an essential adjunct to the "principle of charity" (Davidson 1980) for facilitating human interaction in real-world settings of any complexity, however dispensable cognitive psychologists or computer scientists might find them in the purer laboratory setting.

9. The reason may well be that they regard the intrusion of any "brute facts" as defiling the purity of their a priori deductive science. Political scientists, having earned their scientific spurs in the course of the behavioral revolution, are much more relaxed about brute facts and much happier to trade off a little parsimony for a lot more explanatory power.

10. There is something undeniably presumptuous about the "principle of charity"—interpreting their utterances as you would yourself have intended them, had they been yours—as applied to Nobel Prize winners who are honored precisely for having thoughts more profound than most of us could ordinarily muster. But we simply have no other way of proceeding if we want to engage in interpersonal communication at all (Davidson 1980).

11. We can, of course, invest time and resources in expanding those limits, just as we can invest time and resources in perfecting new technologies, but even those decisions to extend the limits have to be made within the constraints of existing limits.

12. There are, of course, forms of satisficing more extreme than this can capture: Buddhist self-denial is one example, Stoic moderation another. Some prescriptivists recommend such practices (Kolm 1979; Slote 1984), but not many actors in the real political world actually follow them.

13. Ironically, since Simon himself (1985, 294) presents Downs as the paradigm of the economistic opposition. The extent of the influence on Simon's 1955 article on Downs's (1957) work cannot easily be judged; although it appears in Downs's bibliography, it is nowhere cited in the text.

14. Or psychological ones either, insofar as non-intentional action is taken to be the defining feature of those models. Some psychological models (for example, Freudian ones) are like that; others (cognitive, for example) are not, or at least, not nearly so much so.

15. Though he was owed an apology, which Ted Lowi never quite managed to spit out in his *PS: Political Science and Politics* reply, for being dubbed "diabolical." What prompted Lowi's charge, I dare say, and what I suspect Simon might prefer to forget, was the profound influence of his 1957 exposé of the absurdity of the "maxims of public administration": Simon utterly undermined what many would still see as ancient and honorable traditions of public service and paved the way for their replacement by "scientific management" of a distinctly economic-rationalist bent.

16. Furthermore, in suggesting that we economize on information costs, these "theories do nothing to alleviate the computational complexities facing the decision maker . . . but simply magnify and multiply them. Now he needs to compute not merely the shapes of his supply and demand curves, but, in addition, the costs and benefits of computing those shapes to greater accuracy as well" (Simon 1979b, 504; see, similarly, Winter 1971; Elster 1984, 59, 135).

17. For small-group interactions, the problem of "outguessing" each other is indeed problematic; Simon (1979b, 505–6; see also 1978, 10) is right to complain that modern game theory provides "no definitive definition of the solution of a game," and hence no "unambiguous condition of rationality for this class of situation." Problematic though that may be for small-group interactions, and crucial though those are for certain classes of political problems, a great deal of political life involves each of us as essentially anonymous players "against the world," wherein others' choices really can be represented with little loss as stochastic events (compare, Hollis 1987, ch. 7).

18. As discussed in note 17, Simon enters similar complaints on different bases about the lack of any uniquely rational solution concepts in most of game theory, which is required for solving at least certain of the problems posed in the philosophical economists' third complaint.

19. Japanese economic planners take note, on Wildavsky's (1973) evidence.

20. So too, of course, have been psychologists. As David Bell, Howard Raiffa, and Amos Tversky (1988, 19) say, we can always rewrite decisionmakers' objective functions to take into account Simon-like complications, but that may well leave us working with objective functions that are so "horrendously complicated" that we would have been better off working with the same heuristics and decisional shortcuts used by the decisionmakers themselves. Indeed, that must always be true insofar as we are trying to explain the behavior of any particular decisionmaker: If parsimony is a prime goal of our explanatory models, then we should use the same shortcuts, for the same reasons, as does the decisionmaker herself. It is only in attempting to explain a large class of decisions, or the decisions of a large number of people, when the shortcut of postulating "rationality" with complications might yield more parsimonious explanations than just writing into our explanation the particular shortcuts used by particular decisionmakers. The variation in the shortcuts used among people and across decision realms may—or may not (compare, Kahneman, Slovic, and Tversky 1982)—be greater than the complications we need to introduce into rational economistic accounts of the decisionmaker.

21. Indeed, the 1996 Nobel Prize in Economics was awarded to James Mirrlees largely for his work in this area.

22. For the latest round, see Green and Shapiro (1994, 20–23) versus Satz and Ferejohn (1994).

23. The only irrationality there lies in not noticing that the experimenter's description of the situation has rendered the two equivalent descriptions of the same state of the world.

24. Amartya Sen (1980, 1983) provides a partial echo of these themes within economics.

25. As Simon (1991, 27) rightly says, a purpose of new institutional economics.

26. Simon himself (1984, 1986) enters powerful pleas to this effect as applied to models of economic dynamics (growth, business cycles, unemployment, and so on), although he would, of course, put it as more a matter of "psychologizing rationality" than of "rationalizing satisficing."

27. Thus, for example, when "contrasting rational and psychological analyses of political choice," George Quattrone and Amos Tversky's (1988) "psychological" model substitutes the value function specified by "prospect theory" for that specified by "expected utility theory," which prescriptive decision theory defines as "rational." But note that even within their modified "psychological" model, agents are presumed to be intentional, goal-seeking agents seeking (indeed, seeking to maximize) their value functions, thus respecified. Something similar seems broadly true of the various papers collected in, for example, Ferejohn and Kuklinski (1990) and Kinder and Palfrey (1993).

28. As Johan Olsen (letter to the author, May 15, 1997) has emphasized to me.

29. Work by Simon and others on pattern recognition, focusing on attention, intuition, and induction, obviously bears fairly directly on this process.

30. Within these logics, there is no necessary contradiction in asserting both P and not-P, so long as each assertion is contained within its own separate sphere of "relevance" and those spheres are always kept apart from one another. The most accessible version of this work for political scientists is "Anarchism" (1993) by Richard Sylvan, a leading figure in relevance logic who shows how such tools might be employed in the construction of decentralized anarchies.

31. There is a taken-for-grantedness here that has important action implications for the "engineering of choice" (March 1978). Indeed, once it ceases to be taken for granted, it usually ceases to work at all.

32. Williamson's *Economic Institutions of Capitalism*, dedicated to "his teachers" Coase and Simon among others, explicitly discusses Simon's treatment of the authority relation (1985, 218–21), as does Arrow (1974, 25, 63).

33. Which is simply to say path dependence matters here: There may be good reasons for contracting into such a scheme, de novo, but there are even better reasons for not contracting out of one once it is under way. I am grateful to Johan Olsen for reminding me of this point.

34. This is, admittedly, a Williamson-style way of putting the point that Simon has never embraced and from which, he says in recent correspondence (letter to the author, April 18, 1997), he would actually want to distance himself. His own preferred way of linking up bounded rationality and organizational loyalty is via evolutionary biology (Simon 1990; 1991, 30ff.; 1992; see also 1983).

35. Feminist epistemology, in particular, has made much of "standpoint theory" in just this way. See, for example, Smith (1987) and Harding and Hintinkka (1983).

36. For the worst-case scenario, suppose our responses are prompted by heuristics that are biologically hardwired into our genes. It nonetheless remains possible for us to get above our genes by looking at the problem from many different angles to see what different prompts evoke different responses from us. If we find that different prompts evoke different responses from us, we can then (to some extent or another) *decide*—in good Enlightenment "sovereign artificer" fashion—which of those prompts and associated response patterns to evoke from ourselves. The very fact that we can see the absurdity of our divergent responses to what is under one description the same underlying situation when psychological experimenters such as Kahneman and Tversky point it out to us suggests, I submit, that whatever genetic hardwiring is involved in these heuristics does not go so deep as to prevent us from *reflecting* at some other level on the desirability of acting on those prompts.

37. Which is to say, the "general theory of second best" (Lipsey and Lancaster 1956) is undoubtedly right to warn that that ideal is not *always* right. But it would be wrong to infer from that that it is always wrong.

REFERENCES

Abelson, Robert P., and Ariel Levi. 1985. "Decision Making and Decision Theory." In *Handbook of Social Psychology*, 3rd ed., vol. 1, edited by Gardner Lindzey and Elliot Aronson (New York: Random House), 231–309.

Akerlof, George A. 1984. *An Economic Theorist's Book of Tales*. Cambridge: Cambridge University Press.

Ando, Albert. 1979. "On the Contribution of Herbert A. Simon to Economics." *Scandinavian Journal of Economics* 81: 81–114.

Arrow, Kenneth J. 1974. *The Limits of Organization.* New York: Norton.

Auden, W. H. 1932. *The Orators.* London: Farber & Farber.

Bell, David E., Howard Raiffa, and Amos Tversky (eds.). 1988. *Decision Making: Descriptive, Normative, and Prescriptive Interactions.* Cambridge: Cambridge University Press.

Benhabib, Seyla. 1992. *Situating the Self.* Oxford: Polity.

Benn, Stanley I. 1976. "Rationality and Political Behaviour." In *Rationality and the Social Sciences,* edited by G. W. Mortimore and S. I. Benn (London: Routledge & Kegan Paul), 246–67.

———. 1979. "The Problematic Rationality of Political Participation." In *Philosophy, Politics, and Society,* edited by Peter Laslett and James S. Fishkin, 5th series (Oxford: Blackwell), 291–312.

Braybrooke, David, and Charles E. Lindblom. 1963. *A Strategy of Decision.* New York: Free Press.

Coase, Ronald H. 1937. "The Nature of the Firm." *Economica* 4: 386–405.

Cyert, Richard M., and James G. March. 1992. *A Behavioral Theory of the Firm.* 2nd ed. Cambridge, Mass.: Blackwell Business. (Originally published in 1963)

Dahl, Robert A., and Charles E. Lindblom. 1953. *Politics, Economics, and Welfare.* New York: Harper & Row.

Dahrendorf, Ralf. 1968. "Homosociologicus." In *Essays in Social Theory* (Stanford, Calif.: Stanford University Press), 19–87. (Originally published in 1958)

Davidson, Donald. 1980. *Essays on Actions and Events.* Oxford: Clarendon Press.

Deutsch, Karl W. 1963. *The Nerves of Government.* Glencoe, Ill: Free Press.

Douglas, Mary. 1966. *Purity and Danger.* London: Routledge & Kegan Paul.

———. 1982. *In the Active Voice.* London: Routledge & Kegan Paul.

Douglas, Mary, and Brian Isherwood. 1979. *The World of Goods.* London: Allen Lane.

Downs, Anthony. 1957. *An Economic Theory of Democracy.* New York: Harper.

Elster, Jon. 1984. *Ulysses and the Sirens: Studies in Rationality and Irrationality.* Cambridge: Cambridge University Press.

——— (ed.). 1986. *Rational Choice.* Oxford: Blackwell.

Ferejohn, John A., and James H. Kuklinski (eds.). 1990. *Information and Democratic Processes.* Urbana: University of Illinois Press.

Foucault, Michel. 1991. "Governmentality." In *The Foucault Effect: Studies in Governmentality,* edited by G. Burchell et al. (Hemel Hempstead: Harvester-Wheatsheaf), 87–104.

Goodman, Nelson. 1983. *Fact, Fiction, and Forecast.* 4th ed. Cambridge, Mass.: Harvard University Press. (Originally published in 1955)

Green, Donald P., and Ian Shapiro. 1994. *The Pathologies of Rational Choice.* New Haven, Conn.: Yale University Press.

Grofman, Bernard (ed.). 1993. *Information, Participation, and Choice: An Economic Theory of Democracy in Perspective.* Ann Arbor: University of Michigan Press.

Hardin, Russell. 1988. *Morality Within the Limits of Reason.* Chicago: University of Chicago Press.

———. 1993. "The Street-level Epistemology of Trust." *Politics and Society* 21: 505–29.

Harding, Sandra, and Merill B. Hintikka (eds.). 1983. *Discovering Reality: Feminist Perspectives on Epistemology, Metaphysics, Methodology, and Philosophy of Science.* Dordrecht: D. Reidel.

Hart, H. L. A. 1961. *The Concept of Law.* Oxford: Clarendon Press.

Hollis, Martin. 1977. *Models of Man.* Cambridge: Cambridge University Press.

———. 1987. *The Cunning of Reason.* Cambridge: Cambridge University Press.

Hollis, Martin, and Steven Lukes (eds.). 1982. *Rationality and Relativism.* Oxford: Blackwell.

Kahneman, Daniel, Paul Slovic, and Amos Tversky (eds.). 1982. *Judgment Under Uncertainty: Heuristics and Biases.* Cambridge: Cambridge University Press.

Kinder, Donald R., and Thomas R. Palfrey (eds.). 1993. *Experimental Foundations of Political Science.* Ann Arbor: University of Michigan Press.

Kolm, Serge-Christophe. 1979. La philosophie bouddhiste et les "hommes économiques." *Social Science Information* 18: 489–588.

Kreps, David M. 1990. "Corporate Culture and Economic Theory." In *Perspectives on Positive Political Economy,* edited by James Alt and Kenneth Shepsle (Cambridge: Cambridge University Press), 90–143.

Kreps, David M., and Robert Wilson. 1982. "Reputation and Imperfect Information." *Journal of Economic Theory* 27: 253–79.

Langley, Pat, Herbert A. Simon, Gary L. Bradshaw, and Jan M. Zytkow. 1987. *Scientific Discovery: Computational Explorations of the Creative Process.* Cambridge, Mass.: MIT Press.

Lindblom, Charles E. 1959. "The Science of Muddling Through." *Public Administration Review* 19: 79–88.

———. 1979. "Still Muddling: Not Yet Through." *Public Administration Review* 39: 517–26.

Lipsey, Richard G., and Kelvin J. Lancaster. 1956. "The General Theory of Second Best." *Review of Economic Studies* 24: 11–33.

Lupia, Arthur. 1994. "Shortcuts Versus Encyclopedias: Information and Voting Behavior in California Insurance Reform Elections." *American Political Science Review* 88: 63–76.

Lupia, Arthur, and Matthew McCubbins. 1998. *The Democratic Dilemma: Can Citizens Learn What They Need to Know?* Cambridge: Cambridge University Press.

March, James G. 1972. "Model Bias in Social Action." *Review of Educational Research* 42: 413–29.

———. 1978. "Bounded Rationality, Ambiguity, and the Engineering of Choice." *Bell Journal of Economics* 9: 587–608.

March, James G., and Johan P. Olsen. 1976. *Ambiguity and Choice in Organizations.* Bergen: Universitetsforlaget.

———. 1989. *Rediscovering Institutions: The Organizational Basis of Politics.* New York: Free Press.

———. 1995. *Democratic Governance.* New York: Free Press.

March, James G., and Herbert A. Simon, with Harold Guetzkow. 1993. *Organizations.* 2nd ed. Oxford: Blackwell. (Originally published in 1958)

Newell, Allen, and Herbert A. Simon. 1972. *Human Problem Solving.* Englewood Cliffs, N.J.: Prentice-Hall.

Piketty, Thomas. 1995. "Social Mobility and Redistributive Politics." *Quarterly Journal of Economics* 110: 551–84.

Popkin, Samuel L. 1991. *The Reasoning Voter.* Chicago: University of Chicago Press.

Popper, Karl. 1964. *The Poverty of Historicism.* 3rd ed. New York: Harper & Row. (Originally published in 1957)

Quattrone, George A., and Amos Tversky. 1988. "Contrasting Rational and Psychological Analyses of Political Choice." *American Political Science Review* 82: 719–36.

Radner, Roy. 1975. "Satisficing." *Journal of Mathematical Economics* 2: 253–62.

Riker, William H., and Peter C. Ordeshook. 1973. *An Introduction to Positive Political Theory.* Englewood Cliffs, N.J.: Prentice-Hall.

Ryle, Gilbert. 1949. *The Concept of Mind.* London: Hutchinson.

Satz, Debra, and John Ferejohn. 1994. "Rational Choice and Social Theory." *Journal of Philosophy* 91: 71–87.

Schutz, Alfred. 1943. "The Problem of Rationality in the Social World." *Economica* 10: 130–49.

Sen, Amartya. 1980. "Description as Choice." *Oxford Economic Papers* 32: 353–69.

———. 1983. "Accounts, Actions, and Values: Objectivity of Social Science." In *Social Theory and Political Practice,* edited by Christopher Lloyd (Oxford: Clarendon Press), 87–108.

Simon, Herbert A. 1947. *Administrative Behavior.* New York: Free Press.

———. 1951. "A Formal Theory of the Employment Relationship." *Econometrica* 19: 293–305. Reprinted in Simon, *Models of Man* (New York: Wiley, 1957), 183–95, and in Simon, *Models of Bounded Rationality* (Cambridge, Mass.: MIT Press, 1982), 2:11–23.

———. 1955. "A Behavioral Theory of Rational Choice." *Quarterly Journal of Economics* 69: 99–118. Reprinted in Simon, *Models of Man* (New York: Wiley, 1957), 241–60, and in Simon, *Models of Bounded Rationality* (Cambridge, Mass.: MIT Press, 1982), 2:239–58.

———. 1956. "Rational Choice and the Structure of the Environment." *Psychological Review* 63(2): 129–38. Reprinted in Simon, *Models of Man* (New York: Wiley, 1957), 261–73, and in Simon, *Models of Bounded Rationality* (Cambridge, Mass.: MIT Press, 1982), 2:259–68.

———. 1957. *Models of Man.* New York: Wiley.

———. 1972. "Theories of Bounded Rationality." In *Decision and Organization,* edited by C. B. Radner and R. Radner (Amsterdam: North-Holland), 161–76. Reprinted in Simon, *Models of Bounded Rationality* (Cambridge, Mass.: MIT Press, 1982), 2:408–23.

———. 1976. "From Substantive to Procedural Rationality." In *Method and Appraisal in Economics,* edited by S. J. Latsis (Cambridge: Cambridge University Press), 129–48. Reprinted in Simon, *Models of Bounded Rationality* (Cambridge, Mass.: MIT Press, 1982), 2:424–43.

———. 1977. *The New Science of Management Decision.* Rev. ed. Englewood Cliffs, N.J.: Prentice-Hall. (Originally published in 1960)

————. 1978. "Rationality as Process and as Product of Thought." Richard T. Ely Lecture. *American Economic Review* (Papers and Proceedings) 68(2, May): 1–16. Reprinted in Simon, *Models of Bounded Rationality* (Cambridge, Mass.: MIT Press, 1982), 2:444–59, and in David E. Bell, Howard Raiffa, and Amos Tversky (eds.), *Decision Making: Descriptive, Normative, and Prescriptive Interactions* (Cambridge: Cambridge University Press, 1988), 58–77.

————. 1979a. "On Parsimonious Explanations of Production Relations." *Scandinavian Journal of Economics* 81: 459–74. Reprinted in Simon, *Models of Bounded Rationality* (Cambridge, Mass.: MIT Press, 1982), 1:444–59.

————. 1979b. "Rational Decision Making in Business Organizations." Nobel Lecture. *American Economic Review* 69: 493–513. Reprinted in Simon, *Models of Bounded Rationality* (Cambridge, Mass.: MIT Press, 1982), 2:474–94.

————. 1981. *The Sciences of the Artificial.* 2nd ed. Cambridge, Mass.: MIT Press. (Originally published in 1969)

————. 1982. *Models of Bounded Rationality.* 2 vols. Cambridge, Mass.: MIT Press.

————. 1983. *Reason in Human Affairs.* Stanford, Calif.: Stanford University Press.

————. 1984. "On the Behavioral and Rational Foundations of Economic Dynamics." *Journal of Economic Behavior and Organization* 5: 35–55. Reprinted in *The Dynamics of Market Economies*, edited by R. H. Day and G. Eliasson (Amsterdam: North-Holland, 1986), 21–41.

————. 1985. "Human Nature in Politics: The Dialogue of Psychology and Political Science." James Madison Lecture. *American Political Science Review* 79: 293–304.

————. 1986. "Rationality in Psychology and Economics." *Journal of Business* 59(4, pt. 2): S209–24.

————. 1990. "A Mechanism for Social Selection and Successful Altruism." *Science* 250: 1665–68.

————. 1991. "Organizations and Markets." *Journal of Economic Perspectives* 5(2, Spring): 25–44.

————. 1992. "Altruism and Economics." *Eastern Economic Journal* 18(1): 73–83.

————. 1993. "The State of American Political Science: Professor Lowi's View of Our Discipline." *PS: Political Science and Politics* 26(1, March): 49–51.

Slote, Michael. 1984. "Satisficing Consequentialism." *Proceedings of the Aristotelian Society* (supplement) 58: 139–63.

Smith, Dorothy E. 1987. *The Everyday World as Problematic: A Feminist Sociology.* Boston: Northeastern University Press.

Steinbruner, John D. 1974. *The Cybernetic Theory of Decision.* Princeton, N.J.: Princeton University Press.

Stigler, George J. 1961. "The Economics of Information." *Journal of Political Economy* 69: 213–25.

Sylvan, Richard. 1993. "Anarchism." In *A Companion to Contemporary Political Philosophy*, edited by Robert Goodin and Philip Pettit (Oxford: Blackwell), 215–43.

Taylor, Charles. 1989. *Sources of the Self.* Cambridge: Cambridge University Press.

Tobin, James. 1970. "On Limiting the Domain of Inequality." *Journal of Law and Economics* 13: 363–78.

Tversky, Amos. 1977. "Features of Similarity." *Psychological Review* 84: 327–52.

Tversky, Amos, and Daniel Kahneman. 1981. "The Framing of Decisions and the Psychology of Choice." *Science* 211: 453–58. Reprinted in Jon Elster, *Rational Choice* (Oxford: Blackwell, 1986), 123–41.

Walzer, Michael. 1983. *Spheres of Justice.* Oxford: Martin Robertson.

Weber, Max. 1947. *The Theory of Social and Economic Organization.* Translated by A. M. Henderson and Talcott Parsons. New York: Oxford University Press.

Wildavsky, Aaron. 1973. "If Planning Is Everything, Maybe It's Nothing." *Policy Sciences* 4: 127–53.

————. 1984. *The Politics of the Budgetary Process.* 4th ed. Boston: Little, Brown. (Originally published in 1964)

Williamson, Oliver E. 1985. *The Economic Institutions of Capitalism: Firms, Markets, Relational Contracting.* New York: Free Press.

Wilson, Bryan (ed.). 1970. *Rationality.* Oxford: Blackwell.

Winter, Sidney. 1971. "Satisficing, Selection, and the Innovating Remnant." *Quarterly Journal of Economics* 85: 237–61.

BOUNDED RATIONALITY, POLITICAL INSTITUTIONS, AND THE ANALYSIS OF OUTCOMES

Bryan D. Jones

A key issue in the study of politics is the connection between the process of decisionmaking and the outputs from the operation of political institutions. Does one need to know only the barest outline of the rules and the nature of the inputs into the institution, or does one need to incorporate characteristics of the decisionmaker and aspects of the decisionmaking process to explain outputs?

One may crudely classify studies of politics into two camps: investigations based in bounded rationality, and those based in public choice.[1] In public choice based on rational axioms commonly applied in economics, decisionmakers are assumed to maximize given the incentives that political institutions provide. As a consequence of these assumptions, the characteristics of decisionmakers do not matter. All similarly situated decisionmakers behave similarly. If one assumes that decisionmakers maximize, one need not have a theory of decisionmaking processes. Herbert Simon (1985, 294) writes: "If the characteristics of the choosing organism are ignored, and we consider only those constraints that arise from the external situation, then we may speak of substantive or objective rationality, that is, behavior that can be adjudged objectively to be optimally adapted to the situation." In effect, the "constraints" from the external situation dictate outputs.

In bounded (or procedural) rationality, decisionmakers do not maximize, for two reasons. First, they are cognitively limited: They cannot. In the second place, they face a complex world that interacts with their limited cognitions: It is not so clear what they ought to maximize even if they could. A complex environment means that boundedly rational decisionmakers can actively choose—they would not necessarily be driven from the field if they do not maximize, because it is not so clear what ought to be maximized. One needs a theory of decisionmaking, because the characteristics of decisionmakers, and the processes by which they make choices, matter. Both internal constraints and the nature of the decisionmaker must be known to explain outputs.

In recent years public-choice theorists have made many of the major theoretical advances in the study of political institutions, demonstrating the power of the approach via the generation of captivating ideas. Yet the approach has generated controversy (Green and Shapiro 1994). There is disquiet among many political scientists, fueled by a discomfort with the strong rationality assumptions associated with public choice and a tendency to model "stylized facts" rather than subject models to rigorous empiricism—even given these important theoretical advances.

OVERVIEW OF THE ARGUMENT

In this essay, I reassert bounded rationality as a decisional foundation for the study of political (and indeed, human) institutions. I do so by focusing on the outputs of institutions. In particular, I show that many frequency distributions of outputs of decisionmaking in institutional settings are difficult to reconcile with rational analyses but are easier to reconcile with bounded rationality.

Economists have made strong predictions based on objective rationality in respect to the outputs of stock markets. The *efficient market thesis* implies that the distribution of returns from the market ought to be normally distributed. This is actually a powerful general theorem about human institutions. At least in the limit, the central limit theorem predicts that any input distribution based on numerous sources will be normally distributed. Efficient institutions—those in which actors take advantage of all information that is available—should reproduce this input distribution with an outcome distribution of their aggregate actions.

If individuals are boundedly rational, they will not reproduce the input distribution of information. What kind of output distribution will they produce? I show that findings from studies based in bounded rationality imply a particular kind of non-normality—a condition known as leptokurtosis—for *all* change data generated from outputs in human institutions. We are in a position, then, to compare output distributions, with strong implications for political theory. As a consequence, this essay is an attempt to deduce aggregate outcomes from the fundamental behavioral principles implied by bounded rationality. The use of the hypothetico-deductive method in this manner is associated with assumptions of rationality, but as I hope to demonstrate below, it need not be.

The essay proceeds as follows. First, I discuss the behavioral approach to the study of political organizations, an approach whose genesis may be traced to Simon's *Administrative Behavior* (1947), itself "one of the type specimens of Chicago political behavioralism" (Simon 1996a, 116). One of the primary aims of that approach is to link decisionmaking processes within organizations to their outputs. Then I detail key aspects of the efficient market thesis, showing how it embodies the notion of a proportionate decisionmaker (which follows from Simon's notion of objective rationality). That is, rational decisionmakers take action proportional to the information reaching them. Third, I show how findings from psychophysics, psychology, political science, and economics that illuminate characteristics of decisionmakers all imply nonproportionate or nonlinear decisionmaking.

The only question remaining is whether the assumption of proportionate decisionmaking embodied in the axioms of rational choice can explain the outputs of political and economic institutions. Data on the stock market, elections, and the federal budget all conform to the predictions from bounded rationality. I conclude that formal approaches ought to utilize such assumptions in the future.

INSTITUTIONS AND HUMAN BEHAVIOR

The study of institutions has come to play a fundamental role again in political science. Much of the current analysis of institutions is formal, and in general, scholars think of institutions interacting with the preferences of decisionmakers to produce policy outcomes according to Plott's fundamental equation:

$$\text{Preferences } (\times) \text{ Institutions} \rightarrow \text{Outcomes}$$

It may not be enough to know only actors' preferences and the structure of the institution to explain outcomes. Simon (1979, 8) has noted that the assumption of rational maximization allows economists (and now political scientists) to ignore the characteristics of decisionmakers: "The environment, combined with assumptions of rationality, fully determines the behavior." If decisionmakers are not fully rational but are boundedly rational, then the cognitive characteristics of decisionmakers beyond their preferences must be known.

Boundedly rational behavior is reasonable, nonmaximizing behavior based on the limited cognitive abilities (in comparison to those imputed in rational models of choice) of the decisionmaker (March 1978). In bounded rationality models of politics, the characteristics of the decisionmaker matter. Rather than assume that decisionmakers maximize, the characteristics are studied to see how they might affect the process of making decisions. Traditionally this approach was placed in a framework of *limited cognition;* that is, certain biological limits on the functioning of the human brain implied that decisionmakers could not be fully ("omnisciently") rational. Modern findings emerging in the cognitive sciences are providing a more optimistic view: Many of the so-called limitations are actually adaptive. In any case, the important premise is that the characteristics of decisionmakers cannot be assumed away, as they are in the public-choice approach, because they are fundamental to both the process and consequences of decisionmaking.

Unfortunately, in effect this adds additional unknowns to Plott's equation. A fully specified model of institutional decisionmaking would need to incorporate preferences, the institutional rules, and the characteristics of decisionmakers that, in effect, interfere with the smooth translation of preferences into outcomes.

The first issue, then, is how far rational and boundedly rational assumptions diverge in explaining decisions within institutions. The second issue is whether the incorporation of boundedly rational assumptions in models of political institutions improves the explanatory power of similar models with rationality assumptions.

BEHAVIORAL FOUNDATIONS OF PUBLIC ORGANIZATIONS

There has existed for half a century a vigorous literature in political science directed at understanding fundamental processes of government from the manner in which political actors make decisions. The approach, inaugurated by Simon (1947), insists that the study of political organizations be based on an understanding of how organizational life intersects with the limited cognitive capacities of decisionmakers (in comparison to the fully rational capacities assumed by neoclassical economics). The behavioral study of organizations was buttressed by the concept of bounded rationality, but because it treated rationality as contextual, it required that scholars examine the behavior of organizations empirically.

Over and over again students of the behavior of public organizations reported findings that did not comport with the demands of "objective rationality" (Simon 1985, 294). Search was incomplete, selective, and nonoptimal (Jones and Bachelor

1996; Simon 1985). Decisionmakers did not need simply to choose among alternatives, they had to generate the alternatives in the first place (Chisholm 1995; Simon 1983, 1996b). Problems were not givens; they had to be defined (Rochefort and Cobb 1994). Solutions did not automatically follow problems; sometimes actors had set solutions ready to apply to problems that could occur (Cohen, March, and Olsen 1972; Jones and Bachelor 1993; Kingdon 1996). Choice was based on incommensurate goals, which were badly integrated (Jones 1994; March 1978; Simon 1983, 1995). Organizations seemed to have limited attention spans and, at least in major policy changes, a serial processing capacity (Cobb and Elder 1972; Jones 1994; Kingdon 1996; Simon 1983).

The cognitive limits of human decisionmakers imposed limits on the ability of the organization to adjust to its environment. Rather than maximize, organizations tended to adopt *task performance rules,* which routinized even the most important decisions of the organization (March and Simon 1958). Firms routinized price and output decisions (Cyert and March 1963). Public-sector budgets were incremental because the fundamental uncertainties of large change caused decisionmakers to make small, reversible changes in policy (Lindblom 1959; Wildavsky 1964). Incrementalism was even criticized as too rational a characterization of budget processes, because of the adoption of roles by budget decisionmakers (Anton 1966: see also Fenno 1966; Meltsner 1971). Learning in organizations seemed to be a slow, evolutionary, conflictual process (Lounamaa and March 1985; Ostrom 1990; Sabatier and Jenkins-Smith 1993)—one that did not seem to "achieve intelligence through rational anticipatory, rational action" (Lounamaa and March 1985, 107).

Many of the behavioral studies were based on observations of *process.* But if organizational *outputs* were no different from those predicted by a comprehensively rational model, then the behavioral theory of organizations would be vulnerable to the criticism that it added complexity to the comprehensive rationality model. Maximizing models were to be preferred on Occam's criterion. One did not need to look inside the organization to understand the nature of its adaptation to the environment it faced.

Scholars from the behavioral school produced many studies over the years that demonstrated a connection between the decisionmaking processes within the organization and the outputs it produced. The most ambitious studies were in the area of public budgeting and the delivery of public services. Studies of budgeting at the national, state, and local levels linked performance routines and limited search procedures to changes in budget outcomes, which tended to be incremental (Anton 1966; Crecine 1969; Davis, Dempster, and Wildavsky 1966, 1974). The attention of policymakers was focused on a very constrained set of problems, and they used "extremely simple decision rules for 'solutions'" (Larkey 1979, 66).

In service provision, too, the performance rules of the organization dictated outputs. For the most part, disparities in service provision to city neighborhoods were caused not by explicit discrimination, not by the political power of the neighborhood, nor even by goal maximization. Rather, service distribution was dictated by organizational routines (Jones, Greenberg, and Drew 1980; Levy, Meltsner, and Wildavsky 1974; Mladenka 1978). Even when politics intruded into the delivery process, it tended to be routinized via *attention rules,* which specified what stimuli were to be attended to (Crecine 1969; Jones 1985). Parenthetically, these advances in linking service outputs to processes were accomplished because of the movement to improve measurement of the products of municipal service agencies—an approach pioneered by Clarence Ridley and Herbert Simon (1938) (for a look at the results of this movement, see Ostrom 1976).

In recent years bounded rationality has informed the study of electoral choice. Voters, once thought to be almost hardwired to a set of attitudes acquired very early in the socialization process (Campbell and others 1960) or assumed to be supremely rational (Downs 1957), are increasingly being studied as bounded rationalists (Popkin 1991; Sniderman, Brody, and Tetlock 1991).

The Incrementalism Controversy

In political science the zenith of the behavioral approach to governing organizations came in the study of budget incrementalism. Incrementalism was directly derived from bounded rationality put into institutional context. It linked process to output. And a proper theory of incrementalism had a role for externally generated "shocks" that could shift the size of the budgetary increment across the board (Davis, Dempster, and Wildavsky 1974). Yet the approach came under withering fire on both theoretical and empirical grounds (Gist 1982; Wanat 1974). James True (1997, 55), in his comprehensive review of budget decisionmaking, writes that incrementalism

> lacked a clear method for differentiating between incremental and non-incremental change. It finessed the tension between politics and administration [by failing to incorporate anything but budget rules]. . . . [I]ncrementalism did not fit the data very well. And it lacked any theoretical accounting of the large-scale changes which were observed in any comprehensive sample of budget activity.

There is some reason to speculate that the attack on the incrementalist model did considerable damage to the behavioral approach to understanding organizations. But, as I show later, incrementalism is not the proper implication embodied in bounded rationality—or rather, it is an incomplete implication.

BOUNDED RATIONALITY AND POLITICAL THEORY

Some weaknesses in the public-choice approach in practice (if not in theory) have led to vigorous criticism of the approach in political science. Much of that criticism has been directed at the poor quality of empiricism used to test formal theories (Green and Shapiro 1994). The charge has considerable merit, because of the reliance on the philosophy of instrumental positivism in economics and public choice. Instrumental positivism embodies the notion that good theories need not incorporate realistic assumptions; rather, theories should be judged by their predictions (Friedman 1996). That is, weaknesses in the assumptions of rationality are granted, but it is argued that the simplifications are more than compensated for by the heightened ability to use formal manipulations to derive predictions. But if the predictions are not tested in rigorous fashion, then the approach fails. Because one gives up one of only two logically possible links between theory and data (assumptions and derivations), the derivations become the only way to subject a theory to empirical scrutiny.

It has been noted, correctly, that the myriad of findings from psychological and bio-logical laboratory experiments cannot provide a satisfactory base from which to ground the study of complex institutions (see Goodin, this volume). On the other hand, Newell and Simon (1972, 789; see also Simon 1996b) have argued that adaptation implies that "only some rather general features of the structure of an adaptive [decisionmaker] can show through to task behavior." In theory building, then, a few simple postulates concerning bounded rationality should suffice to replace the unrealistic comprehensive rationality assumptions that characterize much of public choice. Unfortunately, this suggestion has gone un- (or under-) utilized. So public choice has many critics, but few have put forward a competing foundation for choice in politics. I am reminded of the comments attributed by S. S. Stevens (1961, 80) to G. T. Fechner regarding his psychophysical law (which related quan-titative objective magnitudes such as sound to subjective states). "The Tower of Babel was never finished because the workers could not reach an understanding on how they should build it; my psychological edifice will stand because the workers will never agree on how to tear it down." (Stevens, realizing that you cannot beat some-thing with nothing, was proposing a different form for the psychophysical law.)

In a limited number of studies, assumptions of bounded rationality have been incorporated into more formal approaches to the study of politics. Melvin Hinich and Michael Munger (1994, 2) see ideology as an informational short-cut, but one that is fundamental to human choice, not a matter of strategy. They argue that "rig-orous formal models of politics may someday account for emotion, history, and the idiosyncrasies of human cognition." The major lesson of the work of Hinich and Munger may be that we need not rely on the rational actor assumptions to do rig-orous formal analysis. In a similar vein, I have attempted to treat selective attention formally (Jones 1994), and William Riker (1996) incorporates non-expected utility approaches into his analysis of the campaign to ratify the American Constitution.

RATIONAL ASSUMPTIONS ON THE LINE: THE EFFICIENT MARKET THESIS

One problem in comparing the predictive efficacy of models based on rational, anticipatory action and those incorporating bounded rationality has been the lack of attention among rational-choice theorists to predictions about the outputs of organizational activity. Too many accounts of the activities of both politics and mar-kets take the form of "stylized facts" and even "just-so" stories.[2] The Nobel laureate Merton Miller, for example, has explained major market revaluations *in a single day* in terms of completely rational action (Malkiel 1996, 220).

Rational, anticipatory action was put into a testable form in the 1960s with the articulation of the *efficient market thesis*. According to this approach, stock mar-ket prices should follow a random walk in which all subsequent prices are serially independent of current prices. The reason is that rational investors will extract all incoming information instantaneously so that stock prices will be appropriately "discounted."

Fundamental to the efficient market thesis is the idea that rational decisionmakers make decisions proportionate to incoming information. Markets are driven by exter-nal events because rational and efficient players extract all information relevant to the movement of stocks. If new information relevant to returns becomes available, then some actor will take advantage of that information—at least up to the cost of the transaction. And efficient markets keep such transaction costs low. As in all theories of rational action, we need not rely on characteristics of decisionmakers; outputs (stock prices) are explained by inputs (information).

As a consequence, the distribution of market returns mimics completely the distribution of the relevant information that is input. We do not know what that distribution is. If, however, external events are randomly and independently distributed, they are basically error "shocks" to market prices. By the central limit theorem, they will be normally distributed. As a consequence, market prices are a random walk, and the distribution of daily changes in the market will follow a Gaussian, or normal, distribution. Eugene Fama (1964, 297), one of the developers of the efficient market thesis, puts it this way:

> If price changes from transaction to transaction are independent, identically distributed normal variables with finite variance, and if transactions are fairly uniformly spaced through time, the central limit theorem leads us to believe that price changes across differencing intervals such as a day, a week, or a month will be normally distributed since they are simple sums of the changes from transaction to transaction.

The efficient market thesis is actually a powerful theorem about the behavior of human institutions. Its power comes from its reliance on the central limit theorem (Mood and Graybill 1963, 149–53). If an input stream is composed of a large number of separate factors of finite variance, and act additively, then the input distribution observed by the actor will be normal. Under not-so-stringent assumptions, input distributions will be normal.

Considerable evidence has accumulated over the years that there is something awry with the efficient market thesis empirically (Mandelbrot 1960, 1963, 1964, 1983; Malkiel 1996; Peters 1991, 1994), but no satisfactory model has been developed to supplant it. Indeed, many financial time series display distinct leptokurtosis. In any case, the efficient market thesis stands as a standard for the operation of an efficient economic institution. Moreover, it is used to justify statistical studies of markets and notions about the composition of portfolios. One line of thought, for instance, associates volatility in markets with variance and suggests choosing stocks for their variability as well as their returns. For some non-Gaussian distributions, the variance is not defined, and hence the approach would not have a theoretical foundation (Mandelbrot 1964).

Would a rational politics theoretically result in Gaussian distributions? This is a harder question. Markets are established to promote exchange and are judged effective to the extent to which they do so. Political systems are not so designed and, in the United States, are designed in part to retard change and promote stability. In terms of policy outputs, there may well be too many constraints for actors, even fully rational actors, to respond proportionately to information. On the other hand, incoming information should change the balance of power within an institution, causing shifts in outputs. For example, changes in voter opinions have been linked to polity outputs (Page and Shapiro 1983; Stimson, MacKuen, and Erikson 1995). Moreover, certain aspects of politics might be far more responsive to incoming information than policy enactments. Elections, for example, ought to be distributed closer to Gaussian than policy outputs as rationally calculating, election-driven candidates offer policy packages to voters. The realignment thesis, however, implies non-normal distributions of election returns: distributions with "fat tails" for the realigning elections. But in any case, one expects election returns to be closer to Gaussian than policy actions.

DETECTING BEHAVIOR FROM OUTPUTS

In theory, rational actors and boundedly rational actors should differ in how they respond to incoming information. Rational actors should be proportionate information processors, while boundedly rational actors cannot be. By proportionate I mean a linear and uniform response to information flows: When relevant information comes into an institution, rational actors, being maximizers, will act on it. Boundedly rational actors will ignore much incoming information and then, as attention shifts occasionally to the new information, will rapidly respond to it. As a consequence, controlling for the distribution of incoming information, boundedly rational actors should fail to make moderate responses to incoming information but will rather tend to make either no policy change or a reasonably dramatic one.

The notion that it is important to distinguish boundedly rational behavior from fully rational behavior in models of institutional action must acknowledge the new rational-choice approaches based on incomplete information. These may, in the future, allow a merging of rational and boundedly rational approaches—a blending that, according to Robert Goodin (this volume), is well advanced in political science. For now, however, there remain critical differences, hinging on this distinction: In rational models of incomplete information, the decisionmaker faces a trade-off between acquiring more information or not. If he or she decides to acquire information, then he or she will further decide whether to institute "short-cuts" such as monitoring others' behaviors. A boundedly rational actor *cannot* attend to all aspects of a situation; his or her cognitive short-cuts are not strategies so much as unavoidable hardwiring. As a consequence, as I shall show later, the bounded decisionmaker is subject to both more conservatism *and* more radical change when faced with incoming information in comparison to a rational decisionmaker.

Observing and comparing outcome distributions without modeling the internal structure of the institution means that we cannot observe the processing of information directly. We will be in a position of making predictions about the shapes of distributions rather than making point predictions (Brady 1988, 138–43; King and others 1990). The study of outcome distributions has a rich history in the study of markets (Peters 1991, 1994) and in several branches of natural science (Bak and Chen 1991; Boss 1995; Mandelbrot 1983; Raup 1991; Rundle, Turcotte, and Klein 1996; Schroeder 1991; West and Deering 1995). But we surrender one of the important accomplishments of the behavioral study of organizations in political science: the careful empirical linkage between process and outcome. As a consequence, the prediction of different distributions for rational and boundedly rational decisionmaking, if empirically verified, should be a clarion call for a renewed vigor in the behavioral study of organizations (Simon 1998).

With a firm prediction about the distribution of market returns under rational action, we may compare predictions on distributions that would hypothetically result from bounded rationality. The distributional predictions I make later hinge on the notion of kurtosis. Kurtosis refers to the concentration of cases in a frequency distribution around the center. In particular, "[a] leptokurtic curve has a narrower central peak and higher tails than does the normal curve" (Croxton, Cowden, and Klein 1967, 190).

I argue that boundedly rational actions will lead to leptokurtic outcome distributions in comparison to rational actions *regardless of the nature of the institution in which they operate.* For rational actors, the nature of the input distribution will dictate the output distribution. If the input distribution is Gaussian, then the outputs of rational actors (in a perfectly efficient institution) will be Gaussian. Even if inputs are Gaussian, however, the outputs of boundedly rational actors *will not be Gaussian.* But only some kinds of non-Gaussian output distributions are consistent with bounded rationality—those with a sharp central peak and fat tails, known as leptokurtic distributions.

INSTITUTIONAL EFFICIENCY

If we rank institutions according to how efficiently they process information, kurtosis should be more in evidence as we move toward less informationally efficient institutions. This ranking is not as difficult as it may at first appear: All can agree, for example, that stock market returns should be more sensitive to incoming information than government budgets. Markets are designed to promote stable trade, but in the United States at least governing institutions are designed to slow the actions of popular majorities. In terms of response to incoming information, governments should be less efficient than markets. Elections and agenda-setting activities should fall in between markets and government policy outputs.

Differences in the purposes and operation of institutions can be used as leverage to help us understand the decisionmaking process. Efficiency may be defined in terms of responsiveness to the flow of information. For the time being, I offer the following definition of an institution's efficiency: the extent to which the responses of an institution are proportionate to incoming information relevant to the performance of the institution. Some institutions work better if they process information efficiently (markets), but others may need to balance other values (governments). This definition, however, at least allows us to begin to compare institutions whose functions are diverse.

It should be noted that this definition of efficiency is not the same as economic efficiency, which implies the matching of the actions of an institution with preferences. It is closer to efficiency in the engineering sense of the word.

THE NONTRIVIALITY OF NON-GAUSSIAN DISTRIBUTIONS

If stochastic factors operating on a specific causal process are independent of the causal factor and of each other, and act additively on the dependent variable and have finite variance, then (in the limit) the output distribution will be Gaussian, by the central limit theorem. If the distribution is non-Gaussian, then we know that the distribution cannot be the result of numerous additive and generally offsetting errors (West and Deering 1995, 87).

So the finding of a non-Gaussian distribution is not a trivial aggravation in the rush to apply standard Gaussian statistical models. Distributions are key to the adaptation process we are observing. In the general case, if we observe a non-Gaussian distribution of outcomes in any social process, one of the following has occurred:

- The flow of information is non-Gaussian.
- The characteristics of the decisionmaker are important—he or she is not maximizing.
- The institutional structure has inhibited (or facilitated) the response—the institution is inefficient.

Existing models of rational decisionmaking within markets—in particular, the efficient market thesis—imply that market returns are normally distributed. If returns are non-Gaussian, then we ought to conclude that either the behavior is not fully rational or the institution is not efficient.

What kind of distributions will emerge if actors are boundedly rational? Only John Padgett (1980, 1981) has studied this issue. Padgett's sequential attention model of budgetary behavior implies leptokurtic distributions for budget change data—exponential for homogeneous programs, Paretian for heterogeneous programs. Padgett thus implicitly suggests that boundedly rational behavior will lead to non-Gaussian distributions.[3]

NONPROPORTIONATE DECISIONMAKING

Differentiating between fully rational and boundedly rational actors in terms of their responses to information may be fairly simple, if Simon's "showing through" hypothesis is correct. My tentative hypothesis is that boundedly rational decisionmakers are nonproportionate decisionmakers, while fully rational decisionmakers would act proportionately to incoming information—at least in efficient institutions.

In detailing the general requirements of an organism operating under bounded (as contrasted with comprehensive) rationality, Simon (1983, 20–22) notes the following requisites:

- Some way of focusing attention
- A mechanism for generating alternatives
- A capacity for acquiring facts about the environment
- A modest capacity for drawing inferences from these facts

All of the following findings about the cognitive capacities of individual decision makers lead in the direction of nonproportionate response to information. Although several of the mechanisms listed here have implications for more than one category, we can nevertheless roughly categorize them according to Simon's requisites.

Acquiring Information and Focusing Attention

Experimental Psychophysics   Studies in psychophysics indicate that our responses to stimuli are not proportionate to the change in stimuli. That is, we do not perceive changes in sounds, or light intensity, or any number of continua, proportionately. The experimental psychophysicist S. S. Stevens (1975) established conclusively via experiment that the response and stimulus were linked via a power law:

$$\psi(x) = \alpha x^{\beta},$$

where x is the stimulus continuum and $\psi(x)$ is the response function. In Stevens's laboratory, experimental conditions, and in particular the distribution of the stimulus, could be controlled. Of course, the continua that Stevens was interested in were physical, but there is strong evidence that social stimuli are not perceived proportionately. For example, social status is not granted proportionately to critical stimuli such as income or education (Hamblin 1971; Shinn 1969). These relationships may not invariably be governed by a power function. Many, however, do seem to be, although Jones and Shorter (1972) report exponential relationships. In any case, responses are almost certainly not proportionate. It is easily seen that, outside the laboratory, a response function will not be Gaussian even if the distribution of stimulus intensity is Gaussian.

Selective Attention   Even in the case of the perception of simple stimuli, such as light or sound, both stimulus and sensation are multidimensional. Stevens (1975, 54) wrote that "attention must focus on one aspect or attribute, to the neglect of many other aspects that could be attended to." In the experimental psychophysics studies, selective attention is held constant because of instructions from experimenters. In a complex social situation it must come into play and is a critical facet of decisionmaking. One is never able to monitor all relevant aspects of a complex situation; rather, a decisionmaker focuses on a selected and limited number of relevant variables (Jones, 1994; Simon, 1983, 1985). Selective attention is thus disjoint and episodic, even if a relevant variable changes continuously. The operation of selective attention implies that, even if signals are normally distributed, responses cannot be.

Drawing Inferences

Conservatism in Human Information Processing   Laboratory studies indicate that human decisionmakers are conservative in the face of incoming information. Ward Edwards (1968, 18) writes: "It turns out that opinion change is very orderly, and usually proportional to numbers calculated from Bayes's theorem—but in insufficient amount." If decisionmakers underreact to information in the laboratory, they are likely to do so in the field—except that at some point they may have to overreact to "catch up."

Pattern Recognition   Howard Margolis (1987) has developed a theory of cognition based on pattern recognition. The problem for the decisionmaker is to decide whether a new pattern characterizes the information he or she is monitoring. If the same pattern is detected, then there is no reason to change current behavior. If a new pattern is detected, it might be desirable to change one's policies. Pattern recognition is thus fundamentally disjoint. There exists a fundamental conservatism in which a decisionmaker holds on to a response pattern that is directly related to "the intensity of unproblematical use" of the pattern (Margolis 1987, 140). (See Dodd [1994] for an analysis of how social "pattern recognition" exerts a conservative drag on political change but lurches forward when new patterns become accepted.)

Generating Alternatives

Heuristics or Cognitive Short-Cuts   The above mechanisms are fundamental to the operation of perceptual systems. Because they are hardwired, they are always present. Another category of mechanisms are available to the decisionmaker as aids to making decisions but may not always be present in any given decisionmaking situation. These are Simon's (1977, 1983) heuristics, or short-cuts. In this view, decisionmakers are cognitive misers, struggling with limited cognitive abilities in a complex world. Heuristics are rule-of-thumb short-cuts to decisions that allow the management of the overwhelming number of incoming stimuli with some degree of efficiency.

Some rational theorists have claimed that heuristics may be subsumed under rational analyses because information is costly and heuristics lower the costs of search. Although it is certainly true that hypothetically rational actors would not engage in complete search, noting that information is costly does not solve the heuristics problem. It makes a difference whether an actor uses heuristics to minimize information costs or to handle genetic limitations in cognitive abilities.

A major cognitive heuristic concerns *mimicking behavior* (Hirshleifer 1995). The information on which we act comes from only two sources: what we directly observe and what others tell us about what they observe. Acting based on others' observations (or acting on our own in combination with others where there are many others) causes behaviors to be intercorrelated. Mistakes (as well as correct actions) will cascade through a social system, becoming amplified (and violating the basic assumption of error independence critical in analyses based on the Gaussian distribution in the process).

Risk and Non-Expected Utility Theory   Rational decisionmakers are expected utility maximizers under conditions of risk. There is, however, considerable evidence that people are not maximizers of expected utility. Basically there are three problems: many people prefer certainty too much (compared to what expected utility would predict); people in effect dislike losses more than they like gains; and many people overestimate the effects of very small probabilities (for a review, see Riker 1996, 51–60).

Daniel Kahneman and Amos Tversky (1985) have offered *prospect theory* as an alternative to expected utility theory to explain behavior detected in laboratory behavior. In the general model, decisionmaking is composed of two stages. The first is an editing stage, which sets the neutral point, hence dividing the decision space into a domain of gains and a domain of losses. The second is a decision stage. Laboratory experiments have told us much about the decision stage, but much less about the editing stage. In any case, a decisionmaker operating under prospect theory will not offer proportionate responses to stimuli.

Behavioral Decision Theory   A great deal of recent work in behavioral decision theory has been produced that bears on the actions of decisionmakers within formal institutions (for some relatively recent reviews, see Baron 1994; and Payne, Bettman, and Johnson 1993). My initial survey of this literature (Jones 1996) suggests that a nonproportionate response function to information is generally supported. Behavioral decision theory also focuses on the nature of the adaptive process: how learning in complex situation occurs, for example (see Lounamaa and March 1985). The process of adaptation is critical, and unlikely to be instantaneous, but initially at least I ignore these processes.

BOUNDED RATIONALITY AND NONLINEAR DECISIONMAKING

The hypothetical boundedly rational decisionmaker has a response function that is affected by the ability to detect a signal (dictated by psychophysics, selective attention, and pattern recognition), the ability to conceive a plan of action (which can be related to heuristic short-cuts and behavior under risk), and the ability to take action (which can be related to the operation of institutions).

Boundedly rational decisionmakers are, in effect, nonlinear decisionmakers. They conservatively process information until the pattern carried by the new information undeniably affects their situation. Then they take rapid action.

To make these ideas a little more concrete, let us assume a rational decisionmaker and a bounded decisionmaker are responding to a similar stimulus (incoming information), but they do so according to a different response function. The rational decisionmaker responds proportionally according to the value of the information:

$$Y = 4X,$$

where 4 represents the value of the information.

The bounded decisionmaker is a nonlinear decisionmaker. Assume for the present that he or she responds according to Stevens's psychophysical function (the power function) with an exponent of 4:

$$Y = X^4$$

Figure 2.2 compares the response patterns of these two decisionmakers. The interpretation of the figure goes as follows. The rational decisionmaker makes proportionate decisions, adjusting his or her response to the incoming information continuously. The boundedly rational decisionmaker ignores the incoming information for relatively low levels of valuation, but then overresponds when a "threshold" is reached.[4]

Now here is where the operation of institutions comes in. A single rational decisionmaker, acting alone, in actuality would not respond linearly, because utility functions, even utility functions for information, are not generally taken to be linear. That is, he or she will not respond linearly *by choice*. Rather, there is a declining marginal utility for information. Collectively, however, the responses of rational decisionmakers *in efficient institutions* will be proportionate to incoming information, because if there is a part of the information that is unused by one actor, it will be utilized by another. This is a major implication of competition in markets. Boundedly rational actors will, by necessity, respond nonlinearly alone and in collectives.

PROCESSING INFORMATION: THE NATURE OF THE SIGNAL

Above I detailed the major reasons that decisionmakers do not react proportionately to information. In the laboratory, where the investigator can adjust stimulus magnitudes, this implies leptokurtic response (and response-change) distributions.[5] In the "field," output distributions are functions of decisionmaker response functions (as in the laboratory), as well as the nature of the input distribution. The fundamentally leptokurtic response functions of bounded decisionmakers imply that output

Figure 2.2   Comparing Fully Rational and Boundedly Rational Response Functions

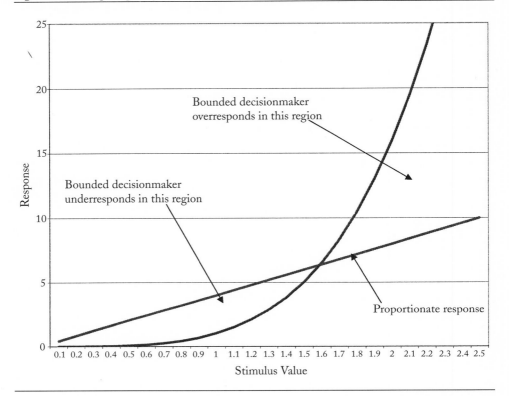

functions for institutions operated by bounded decisionmakers will not be Gaussian *even if* the decisionmakers face a Gaussian information flow.

There are some good reasons for assuming, at least to a first approximation, that information flows are Gaussian. The most persuasive reason is the central limit theorem. If lots of factors operate additively on a process, then the frequency distribution of that process will be Gaussian (so long as the numerous factors are independent, identically distributed random variables with finite variance). Assume a decisionmaker receives and observes *a signal + error*. In the long run, signals are numerous, independently distributed, with finite variance. Errors are drawn from a distribution of independently distributed random variables with finite variance. Hence, the observed distribution would be Gaussian.

On the other hand, information signals may be non-Gaussian. This may occur because *other decisionmakers* do not process information proportionately, and generally the action of other actors serves as informational input to a decisionmaker. This could violate one or more of the assumptions of the central limit theorem, particularly the independence assumption. For example, monitoring and mimicking behavior will violate the independence assumption and cause a decisionmaker to observe cascades and punctuations in the behavior of others. So every decisionmaker is enmeshed in a net of other nonproportionate decisionmakers, implying that the whole process is non-Gaussian.

In any case, it is difficult to conceive of a complex decisionmaking process with rational actors that does not involve a Gaussian distribution. On the other hand, one would not observe a Gaussian distribution if boundedly rational decisionmakers were involved.

TWO HYPOTHESES ABOUT RESPONSE DISTRIBUTIONS

Hypothesis 1—Decisionmaking Because of the bias toward conservatism in bounded models of choice, and because the factors necessary to generate a response interact multiplicatively rather than additively, distributions of responses will be leptokurtic. That is, they have strong central peaks and fat tails in comparison to the Gaussian. Conservatism is preferred until the perceptual and institutional resistance is overcome, and then punctuated change may occur. Mimicking cascades should also cause fat-tailed distributions.[6]

Hypothesis 2—Information Efficiency A second hypothesis comes from the problem of distinguishing cognitive constraints from institutional resistance in response distributions. The greater the institutional resistance to change, the more leptokurtic the distribution of outcomes should be. In particular, market outcomes should be less leptokurtic than political outcomes, but political outcomes should themselves be ordered. Changing the course of public policy is likely to generate more resistance than getting an item on the formal agenda of a decisionmaking body—scheduling a congressional hearing, for example.

Empirical Verification

In any study, one wants to ensure that the primary hypotheses have the potential of being rejected when confronted by data.

Evidence Against Hypothesis 1 Any distribution of outcomes that maps period-to-period changes in the decisions underlying the outcome distribution and is not leptokurtic in comparison to the Gaussian distribution will be evidence against the general decisionmaking model detailed here.

Evidence Against Hypothesis 2 The efficiency hypothesis is, at this point, less formalized than the general decisionmaking hypothesis, so that minor deviations may be less devastating to it. For example, elections are efficient in one political science literature, but far less so in a second. On the other hand, if markets and elections were more leptokurtic than budgets, clearly something is badly wrong with the general notion.

So the central hypotheses of this research are capable of rejection. As usual, evidence in favor does not establish the proposition, so an exploration of alternative hypotheses is necessary.

DETECTING DISTRIBUTIONS EMPIRICALLY

I set out above some theoretical expectations involving outcome distributions. The next issue involves how one detects these distributions empirically. The methodology is not common in political science, so I will illustrate the procedure I intend to follow with daily returns from the stock market as assessed by the Dow-Jones Industrial Average (DJIA).

Step 1   Is the distribution Gaussian? It is easy to detect non-Gaussian distributions simply by plotting the frequency distribution and comparing it to the theoretical Gaussian distribution. Statistical tests are available to allow the researcher to decide whether the differences between the empirical and theoretical Gaussian distributions could have occurred by chance (Chi-square and Kolmogorov-Smirnov). I have also found it useful sometimes to compare the empirical frequency with a simulated frequency based on the Gaussian.

In figure 2.3, I plot the daily DJIA percentage change along with a simulated random normal distribution with similar mean and variance.

We may compare the Dow data with the simulated normal data by subtracting the former from the latter. This yields figure 2.4, which clearly depicts the deviation of the actual stock market data from the expected based on the Gaussian. In particular, there is far more day-to-day stability than expected based on the Gaussian, and, simultaneously, far more major punctuations.

Step 2   What kind of distribution is it? Having shown that the distribution of stock market data is not Gaussian, we now turn to detecting the particular type of leptokurtic distribution. Figure 2.5 plots the stock market category frequencies against the midpoints of the categories, with the expected curvature clearly in evidence. The plot is presented for illustrative purposes; normal data would also exhibit curvature.

Figure 2.3   Daily DJIA Percentage Changes 1971 to 1996, Compared to Random Normal
            Numbers with Similar Mean and Variance

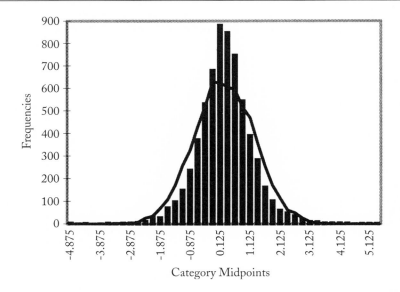

Figure 2.4   Differences in Frequencies Between the Normal Simulated Data and DJIA Daily
Percentage Differences, 1971 to 1996

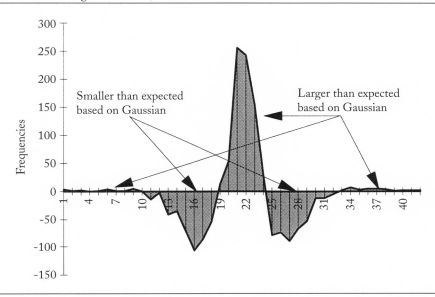

Exponential and Paretian distributions may be detected by plotting the frequencies against the category midpoints on semilogarithmic and logarithmic axes, because:

$$y = ae^{bx} \Rightarrow ln(y) = ln(a) + bX \tag{1}$$

$$y = aX^{b} \Rightarrow ln(y) = ln(a) + bln(X) \tag{2}$$

Figure 2.5   Stock Market Frequency Distribution Plotted in Linear Coordinates

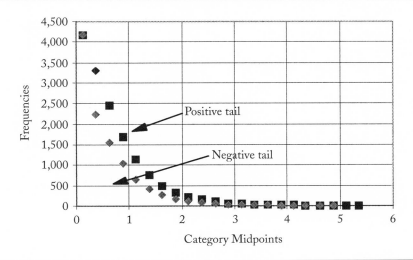

So (1) is linear in semilog coordinates, while (2) is linear in logarithmic coordinates. Graphing the frequencies of the category midpoints in semilog and log-log plots yields figures 2.6 and 2.7.[7]

It is clear that the semilog plot fits considerably better than the log-log plot, and regression/correlation analysis confirms this: $R^2 = .996$ for the semilog plot, but only .826 for the log-log plot (for the positive tails).[8]

I have studied U.S. stock market data for the following periods: 1896 to 1921, 1921 to 1946, 1946 to 1971, and 1971 to 1996. In each era, data are non-normal and are approximately exponentially distributed. The period 1921 to 1946 is more punctuated than the other three periods, indicating a distribution that is further from normal and hence less efficient.[9]

Some Preliminary Results

Thus far, I have examined the following data: daily returns for the Dow-Jones Industrial Average in four separate periods; election margins for county-level presidential election returns, 1828 to 1994; percentage changes in congressional hearings within topics, 1946 to 1994; and percentage changes in real congressional budget authority, by Office of Management and Budget (OMB) sub-function FY47–FY95. None of these distributions is Gaussian. All display pronounced leptokurtosis. The data for the stock market, elections, and congressional hearings all follow exponential distributions, but the budget data are markedly Paretian.

Election Margins

What output distribution would characterize election change? Here the political science literature has two contrary implications. The hypothesis that politicians are

Figure 2.6   Semilog Plot of Stock Market Data

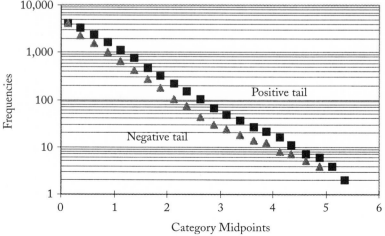

Figure 2.7   Log-Log Plot of Stock Market Data

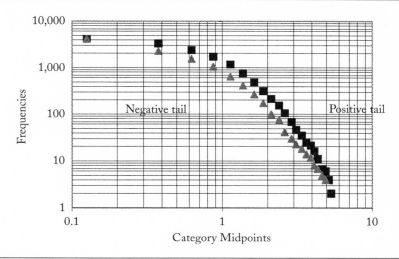

election-driven (and that parties are the creations of ambitious, election-driven politicians; see Aldrich 1995) suggests a relatively efficient response to information. Elections, under the hypothesis that elections are relatively informationally efficient, would have output distributions similar to those of the stock market. On the other hand, the realignment literature implies a highly leptokurtic distribution for election-to-election change. Either minor adjustments or new party alignments characterize a system of highly stable, but occasionally punctuated, change.

Peter Nardulli of the University of Illinois has constructed a county-level data set for election margin swings for presidential elections from 1828 through 1992. By pooling cross-sectional and time series data for his data, we can prepare histograms similar to that developed for the stock market. The resulting data are not normal and, indeed, are clearly exponential, as figure 2.8 indicates. A similar semilog graph of the positive election swings yields a similarly satisfactory fit.

U.S. National Budget Authority

If stock markets and elections are informationally efficient, policymaking should not be—at least not in pluralistic democracies such as the United States. Policymaking is the result of a series of stages (Jones 1977), each of which must be attained before policy is made. Once a policy is in place, it requires inordinate effort to change it. As a consequence, we expect that policy output distributions will be more leptokurtic than either market returns or democratic election swings. Policy changes cannot be expected to be normally distributed—or at least the central limit theorem, based as it is on independent additive processes, will not predict normality. Bruce West and Bill Deering (1995) argue that multiplicative processes, in many circumstances, yield Paretian distributions.

In collaboration with Frank Baumgartner and James True, I have examined the distribution of annual percentage changes of real congressional budget authority since

Figure 2.8   Semilog Plot of Cumulative Negative Changes in Election Margins

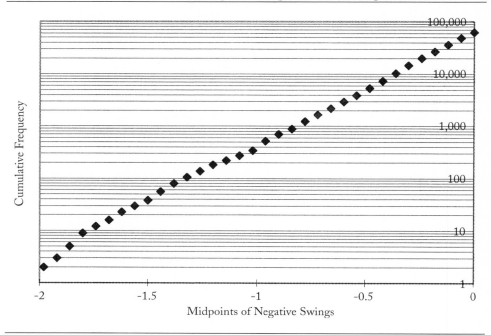

Source: Tabulated from Peter Nardulli, personal communication.

World War II (Jones, Baumgartner, and True 1996). The data were pooled across OMB subfunctions. The resulting histogram is clearly Paretian, as the diagrams in figure 2.9 show. Figure 2.9 diagrams the percentage changes of logged real U.S. budget authority. The severely leptokurtic shape of the distribution is clearly in evidence, even after logs were taken. For most budget subfunctions for most years, changes are minimal. But in some subfunctions in some years, major punctuations occur, and these punctuations involve both major increases and major decreases. What is far less in evidence than one might expect based on the Gaussian distribution are moderate changes. Adjustment in government budgets tends to be disjoint and episodic, against a very stable, incremental background pattern. A log-log plot for both the positive and negative changes indicates that the distribution is clearly Paretian.

Two tentative conclusions emerge from this early examination of the data. First, all the distributions are leptokurtic. Second, except for budgetary data, all the distributions I have examined are exponential. The budget data are clearly Paretian, and far more leptokurtic than elections or market data. It takes more to move government budgets than markets or elections, and the result is a distribution that is both more conservative and plagued by larger punctuations (represented in the "fat tails").

Potential Alternative Explanations

There are several alternative hypotheses that need to be explored. First, I note that we have juxtaposed a rational explanation of institutional outputs against a boundedly

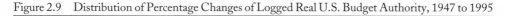

Figure 2.9   Distribution of Percentage Changes of Logged Real U.S. Budget Authority, 1947 to 1995

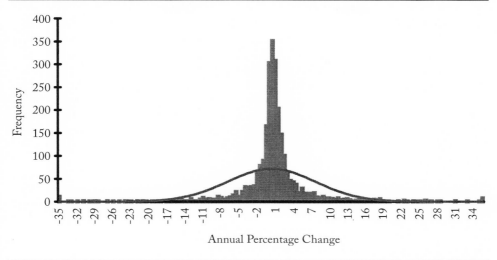

rational one. The evidence thus far supports the latter. Alternative hypotheses must show that rational decisionmakers will generate leptokurtic distributions as well. Any alternative hypotheses relevant to the thesis developed here will have to involve modifications of the efficient market thesis (moving in the direction of complexity, one of the complaints that rational theorists direct at boundedly rational studies). It also must be general, not covering all kinds of output distributions of the type discussed here—because the theory developed here is general.

At least the following are potential alternative hypotheses:

- Transaction costs
- Preference heterogeneity
- Attitudes toward risk
- An artifact of "shocks"

Transaction Costs   One possibility is that rational actors may take transaction costs into account in their decisions (even designing institutions to minimize them). Can transaction costs account for leptokurtic distributions in institutional outcomes by ensuring that decisionmakers do not act until these costs are deducted from the benefits that accrue from acting on information? First, let us note that transaction costs are real: Boundedly rational decisionmakers are just as subject to them as are fully rational actors. They are part and parcel of the institutional structure within which decisionmaking occurs. Second, it is possible that transaction costs would cause a delay in response to incoming information.

On the other hand, it is hard to see how fully rational actors would subject themselves to the wild punctuations that our distributions imply—at least in efficient institutions. In fully efficient markets, presumed competitive pressures should cause rational actors to respond in a highly efficient fashion. Arbitrage strategies should cause output distributions to approach input distributions.

Preference Heterogeneity   Actors in institutions may find that incoming information does not have uniform implications for their well-being. In politics, an exogenous change may benefit some actors more than others if they hold different preferences for policy actions. As a consequence, some actors may be motivated to block policy, others to initiate it. Even if all are rational, leptokurtosis may result.

In financial markets, however, actors have homogenous preferences. They all want to make money. If actors in markets respond with leptokurtic output distributions, then we are on firmer ground in inferring boundedly rational behavior. And if boundedly rational behavior occurs in the most efficient of institutions, then it must also occur in politics. (In any case, it is not immediately obvious that political systems should not adjust to relevant information inefficiently—especially in the case of elections.)

Attitudes Toward Risk   If market participants harbor differing attitudes toward risk, then it may be the case that the combination of a risk distribution and information distribution will produce a leptokurtic distribution.[10] Risk avoiders, however, are not utility maximizers—that is, they are not interested just in maximizing the returns from their investments. They are also interested in avoiding volatility. Riker (1996) has traced the implications for election campaigns of the tendency of many voters to be minimax-regreters (thus avoiding risk) rather than rational utility maximizers.

Risk avoidance is not something to be assumed; it needs to be explained because it does not comport with rational behavior. Indeed, the incrementalist theory of decisionmaking, the first embodiment of bounded rationality, was developed because of difficulties in dealing with risk. Incremental decisionmakers can be seen as minimax-regreters rather than utility maximizers. Even given this, risk maximization may not influence the distribution of market returns. If actor A undersupplies risk—he takes less risk than what would yield maximum returns—then actor B will oversupply it and pick up the returns that A has not been willing to "invest." Such a mechanism would push the market output distribution toward the input distribution.

An Artifact of Shocks   Finally, it may be objected that the distributions we observe are a statistical artifact of the aggregation process. Perhaps pooling is the source of the leptokurtosis, since this could transmit random exogenous shocks throughout the budget categories, for example, at a single point in time. This is an unlikely explanation. First, nonpooled data, in particular, daily stock market returns, are leptokurtic. Second, we have examined other public policy data series, for example, we examined outlay data for the U.S. government for the period 1800 to 1994, adjusted for inflation using the consumer price index (CPI), with the signature leptokurtosis clearly present (for result, see Jones, Baumgartner, and True 1996). Finally, data from market experiments in economics indicate that the "fat tail" problem exists in experimental data, in which the operation of exogenous variables and aggregation processes can be ruled out (Plott and Sunder 1982).

CONCLUSIONS

Knowing actors' preferences and the nature of an institution (and adding the assumption of maximizing behavior) does not seem to be enough to explain output distributions. One needs to add certain characteristics of decisionmakers to the mix to explain output distributions parsimoniously. Put boldly, *the distribution of outcomes in political and economic processes cannot be predicted from rational assumptions alone; boundedly rational processes are necessary to explain even this most basic facet of institutional activity.*

Rational decisionmakers are proportionate decisionmakers: they fully utilize the information coming to them in proportion to its relevance to the tasks they perform. Institutions are efficient to the extent that they allow such rational behavior. Hence, fully rational institutions produce outputs proportional to inputs. Boundedly rational individuals cannot be proportionate decisionmakers, for reasons that have to do with their genetic makeup, even in fully efficient institutions. Deviations from proportionate, or linear, efficiency can stem from either boundedly rational decisionmaking or institutional arrangements. But if outcome distributions from decisionmaking processes are consistently leptokurtic, no matter how efficient the institution, then we must conclude that the characteristics of decisionmakers are to blame.

In political science, formal approaches have almost always involved rational actor assumptions: formal analysis and public choice are virtually identical. It seems undeniable that the theoretical underpinnings of politics have been vastly improved by the infusion of economic approaches into the discipline. But there is no sound reason that rationality axioms have so dominated formal approaches to political theory. In this essay, I have shown how boundedly rational assumptions may be used to make systematic inferences about the distribution of institutional outcomes, and how these assumptions are superior to those employed by rational theorists in a direct comparative test.

These assumptions are not complex; they follow Simon's (1996b) dictum that in adaptive systems (such as markets and politics), only a few very general characteristics of decisionmakers will "show through" to the output distribution. These assumptions seem to be both more realistic and better predictors of output distributions. If boundedly rational decisional mechanisms are not responsible for the findings reported here, then what is the explanation? And if there is no other explanation, then why do we not return to the "Simon agenda" of empirical study of organizational and decisional processes in political institutions?

An earlier version of this essay was presented at the 1997 meetings of the American Political Science Association. A later version was presented at the University of Washington's Political Economy Drinks and Discussion Society. I appreciate comments from Jim Alt, Frank Baumgartner, Sandy Gordon, Margaret Levi, James March, Lin Ostrom, Herbert Simon, and the participants at PEDDS.

NOTES

1. Unfortunately, too many studies still fall into a third camp: they are empirical without any explicit foundation in the nature of the decisionmaking process.

2. "Just so stories" is Stephen J. Gould's term—from Rudyard Kipling—for the tendency of evolutionists to try to explain all form and function as a result of natural selection.

3. And that fully incremental budgeting will yield Gaussian outputs.

4. A power function with an exponent of less than 1 will yield a concave, rather than a convex, curve, implying an overreaction at low levels of the stimulus and an underreaction at higher levels. Exponents of less than and greater than unity have been reported in the psychophysics literature, depending on the stimulus continuum (Stevens 1975).

5. In the laboratory, decisionmakers operating according to a power function will produce lepto-kurtic response distributions and leptokurtic response-change distributions.

6. A stronger form of the hypothesis can be stated under somewhat more rigorous assumptions. If incoming information is Gaussian, and if decisionmakers detect and respond to information according to a power law, then we would expect response distributions to follow a Weibull distribution, which is closely related to the exponential—basically the exponential is a special case of the Weibull (Johnson, Kotz, and Balakrishnan 1994, 3). Details are available from the author.

7. I have plotted the cumulative frequencies rather than the raw frequencies in order to avoid taking logarithms of zero (which is not defined). Positive tails and negative tails of the distribution are graphed separately on each graph, with the break at the modal category, and the modal category is plotted for each side of the distribution. So the mode is to the left, and the tails to the right, on the graph; as a consequence, the slope is negative.

8. Actually, the tails of the distribution are close to Paretian—the problem for a Paretian fit is that there are actually too few cases close to the modal category.

9. If distributions tend to be exponential, then analyzing all distributions in terms of the same metric allows a direct comparison of coefficients. It turns out that the *lower* the coefficient from the exponential regression (of the log of frequencies versus the category midpoints), the more the distribution has "fat tails" and punctuations—and hence fewer moderate changes.

10. Sandy Gordon called my attention to this issue.

REFERENCES

Aldrich, John. 1995. *Why Parties?* Chicago: University of Chicago Press.

Anton, Thomas. 1966. *The Politics of State Expenditures in Illinois.* Urbana: University of Illinois Press.

Bak, Per, and Kan Chen. 1991. "Self-Organized Criticality." *Scientific American* 264(January): 46–53.

Baron, Jonathon. 1994. *Thinking and Deciding.* 2d ed. Cambridge: Cambridge University Press.

Boss, Alan. 1995. "Companions to Young Stars." *Scientific American* 273(October): 134–39.

Brady, David W. 1988. *Critical Elections and Congressional Policy Making.* Stanford, Calif.: Stanford University Press.

Campbell, Angus, Philip Converse, Warren Miller, and Donald Stokes. 1960. *The American Voter.* New York: Wiley.

Chisholm, Donald. 1995. "Problem-Solving and Institutional Design." *Journal of Public Administration Research and Theory* 5: 451–91.

Cobb, Roger, and Charles Elder. 1972. *Participation in American Politics.* Baltimore: Johns Hopkins Press.

Cohen, Michael, James G. March, and Johann Olsen. 1972. "A Garbage Can Model of Organizational Choice." *Administrative Science Quarterly* 17: 1–25.

Crecine, John P. 1969. *Government Problem-Solving: A Computer Simulation of Government Budgeting.* Chicago: Rand-McNally.

Croxton, Frederick E., Dudley J. Cowden, and Sidney Klein. 1967. *Applied General Statistics,* 3rd ed. Englewood Cliffs, N. J.: Prentice-Hall.

Cyert, Richard M., and James G. March. 1963. *A Behavioral Theory of the Firm.* Englewood Cliffs, N.J.: Prentice-Hall.

Davis, Otto A., M. A. H. Dempster, and Aaron Wildavsky. 1966. "A Theory of the Budget Process." *American Political Science Review* 60: 529–47.

———. 1974. "Towards a Predictive Theory of Government Expenditure: U.S. Domestic Appropriations." *British Journal of Political Science* 4: 419–52.

Dodd, Lawrence C. 1994. "Political Learning and Political Change: Understanding Development Across Time." In *The Dynamics of American Politics,* edited by Lawrence C. Dodd and Calvin Jilson (Boulder, Colo.: Westview).

Downs, Anthony. 1957. *An Economic Theory of Democracy.* New York: Harper & Row.

Edwards, Ward. 1968. "Conservatism in Human Information Processing." In *Formal Representation of Human Judgment,* edited by Benjamin Kleinmuntz (New York: Wiley), 17–52.

Fama, Eugene F. 1964. "Mandelbrot and the Stable Paretian Hypothesis." In *The Random Character of Stock Market Prices,* edited by Paul H. Cootner (Cambridge, Mass.: MIT Press), 297–306.

Fenno, Richard F., Jr. 1966. *The Power of the Purse: Appropriations Politics in Congress.* Boston: Little, Brown.

Friedman, Jeffrey. 1996. "Economic Approaches to Politics." In *The Rational Choice Controversy*, edited by Jeffrey Friedman (New Haven, Conn.: Yale University Press), 1–24.

Gist, John R. 1982. "'Stability' and 'Competition' in Budgetary Theory." *American Political Science Review* 76: 859–72.

Green, Donald, and Ian Shapiro. 1994. *Pathologies of Rational Choice Theory.* New Haven, Conn.: Yale University Press.

Hamblin, Robert. 1971. "Mathematical Experimentation and Sociological Theory: A Critical Analysis." *Sociometry* 34: 423–52.

Hinich, Melvin, and Michael Munger. 1994. *Ideology and the Theory of Political Choice.* Ann Arbor: University of Michigan Press.

Hirshleifer, David. 1995. "The Blind Leading the Blind: Social Influence, Fads, and Informational Cascades." In *The New Economics of Human Behavior*, edited by Mario Tommasi and Kathryn Ierulli (Cambridge: University of Cambridge Press), 188–215.

Johnson, Norman L., Samuel Kotz, and N. Balakrishnan. 1994. *Continuous Univariate Distributions.* 2nd ed. New York: Wiley.

———. 1995. "Genesis." In *The Exponential Distribution*, edited by N. Balakrishnan and Asit Basu (North Ryde, Australia: Gordon and Breach), 1–6.

Jones, Bryan D. 1985. *Governing Buildings and Building Government: A New Perspective on the Old Party.* Tuscaloosa: University of Alabama Press.

———. 1994. *Reconceiving Decision-Making in Democratic Politics.* Chicago: University of Chicago.

———. 1996. "Attributes, Alternatives, and the Flow of Ideas." Paper presented at the American Political Science Association, San Francisco (1996).

Jones, Bryan D., and Lynn Bachelor. 1994. *The Sustaining Hand.* 2nd ed. Lawrence: University Press of Kansas.

Jones, Bryan D., Frank R. Baumgartner, and James L. True. 1996. "The Shape of Change: Punctuations and Stability in U.S. Budgeting, 1947–1994." Paper prepared for the 54th annual meeting of the Midwest Political Science Association, Chicago (April 18–20).

Jones, Bryan D., Suadia Greenberg, and Joseph Drew. 1980. *Service Delivery in the City: Citizen Demand and Bureaucratic Rules.* New York: Longman.

Jones, Bryan D., and Richard Shorter. 1972. "The Ratio Measurement of Social Status: Some Cross-Cultural Comparisons." *Social Forces* 50:499–511.

Jones, Charles O. 1977. *An Introduction to the Study of Public Policy.* North Scituate, Mass.: Duxbury.

Kahneman, Daniel, and Amos Tversky. 1985. "Prospect Theory: An Analysis of Decision-Making Under Risk." *Econometrica* 47: 263–91.

King, Gary, James E. Alt, Nancy Burns, and Michael Laver. 1990. "A Unified Model of Cabinet Dissolution in Parliamentary Democracies." *American Journal of Political Science* 34: 846–71.

Kingdon, John. 1996. *Agendas, Alternatives, and Public Policies.* 2nd ed. Boston: Little, Brown.

Larkey, Partick D. 1979. *Evaluating Public Programs.* Princeton, N.J.: Princeton University Press.

Levy, Frank, Arnold Meltsner, and Aaron Wildavsky. 1974. *Urban Outcomes,* Berkeley: University of California Press.

Lindblom, Charles E. 1959. "The Science of Muddling Through." *Public Administration Review* 19: 79–88.

Lounamaa, Perth H., and James G. March. 1985. "Adaptive Coordination of a Learning Team." *Management Science* 33: 107–23.

Malkiel, Burton. 1996. *A Random Walk Down Wall Street.* New York: Norton.

Mandelbrot, Benoit. 1960. "The Pareto-Levy Law and the Distribution of Income." *Economic Review* 1: 79–106.

———. 1963. "New Methods in Statistical Economics." *Journal of Political Economy* 71: 421–40.

———. 1964. "The Variation of Certain Speculative Prices." In *The Random Character of Stock Market Prices*, edited by Paul H. Cootner (Cambridge, Mass.: MIT Press), 307–32.

———. 1983. *The Fractal Geometry of Nature.* New York: Freeman.

March, James. 1978. "Bounded Rationality, Ambiguity, and the Engineering of Choice." *Bell Journal of Economics* 9: 578–608.

March, James G., and Herbert A. Simon. 1958. *Organizations.* New York: Wiley.

Margolis, Howard. 1987. *Patterns, Thinking, and Cognition.* Chicago: University of Chicago Press.

Meltsner, Arnold. 1971. *The Politics of City Revenue.* Berkeley: University of California Press.

Mladenka, Kenneth. 1978. "Rules, Service Equity, and Distributional Decisions." *Social Science Quarterly* 59: 192–202.

Mood, Alexander, and Franklin Graybill. 1963. *Introduction to the Theory of Statistics.* 2nd ed. New York: McGraw-Hill.

Newell, Allen, and Herbert A. Simon. 1972. *Human Problem-Solving.* Englewood Cliffs, N.J.: Prentice-Hall.

Ostrom, Elinor. 1990. *Governing the Commons.* Cambridge: Cambridge University Press.

——— (ed.). 1976. *The Delivery of Urban Services.* Beverly Hills, Calif.: Sage.

Padgett, John F. 1980. "Bounded Rationality in Budgetary Research." *American Political Science Review* 74: 354–72.

———. 1981. "Hierarchy and Ecological Control in Federal Budgetary Decision Making." *American Journal of Sociology* 87: 75–128.

Page, Benjamin, and Robert Y. Shapiro. 1983. "Effects of Public Opinion on Policy." *American Political Science Review* 77: 23–43.

Payne, John W., James R. Bettman, and Erick J. Johnson. 1993. *The Adaptive Decision Maker.* Cambridge: Cambridge University Press.

Peters, Edgar F. 1991. *Chaos and Order in the Capital Markets.* New York: Wiley.

———. 1994. *Fractal Market Analysis.* New York: Wiley.

Plott, Charles, and Shyam Sunder. 1982. "Efficiency of Experimental Security Markets with Insider Trading." *Journal of Political Economy* 90: 692.

Popkin, Samuel. 1991. *The Reasoning Voter.* Chicago: University of Chicago Press.

Quattrone, George A., and Amos Tversky. 1988. "Contrasting Rational and Psychological Analyses of Political Choice." *American Political Science Review* 3: 719–36.

Raup, David M. 1991. *Extinction: Bad Genes or Bad Luck?* New York: Norton.

Ridley, Clarence A., and Herbert A. Simon. 1938. *Measuring Municipal Activities.* Chicago: International City Managers' Association.

Riker, William H. 1996. *The Strategy of Rhetoric: Campaigning for the American Constitution.* New Haven, Conn.: Yale University Press.

Rochefort, David, and Roger Cobb. 1994. *The Politics of Problem Definition.* Lawrence: University of Kansas Press.

Rundle, John B., Donald L. Turcotte, and William Klein (eds.). 1996. *Reduction and Predictability of Natural Disasters.* Reading, Mass.: Addison-Wesley.

Sabatier, Paul, and Hank Jenkins-Smith. 1993. *Policy Change and Learning.* Boulder, Colo.: Westview.

Schroeder, Manfred. 1991. *Fractals, Chaos, Power Laws.* New York: Freeman.

Shinn, Allen. 1969. "An Application of Psychophysical Scaling Techniques to the Measurement of National Power." *Journal of Politics* 31: 932–51.

Simon, Herbert A. 1947. *Administrative Behavior.* New York: Macmillan.

———. 1977. "The Logic of Heuristic Decisionmaking." In *Models of Discovery,* edited by R. S. Cohen and M. W. Wartofsky (Boston: D. Reidel).

———. 1979. "Rational Decisionmaking in Business Organizations." *American Economic Review* 69: 495–501.

———. 1983. *Reason in Human Affairs.* Stanford, Calif.: Stanford University Press.

———. 1985. "Human Nature in Politics: The Dialogue of Psychology with Political Science." *American Political Science Review* 79: 293–304.

———. 1995. "Rationality in Political Behavior." *Political Psychology* 16: 45–61.

———. 1996a. *Models of My Life.* Cambridge, Mass.: MIT Press.

———. 1996b. *The Sciences of the Artificial.* 3rd ed. Cambridge, Mass.: MIT Press.

———. 1998. "Theory Generation as a Task in Science." Paper presented at the conference "Taking Economics Seriously," Carnegie-Mellon University, Pittsburgh (April 11).

Sniderman, Paul, Richard Brody, and Philip Tetlock. 1991. *Reasoning and Choice.* Cambridge: Cambridge University Press.

Stevens, S. S. 1961. "To Honor Fechner and Repeal His Law." *Science* 133: 80–86.

———. 1975. *Psychophysics.* New York: Wiley.

Stimson, James A., Michael B. MacKuen, and Robert S. Erikson. 1995. "Dynamic Representation." *American Political Science Review* 89: 543–64.

True, James L. 1997. *Agenda Setting Politics, Policy Punctuations, and the Avalanche Budget Model.* Ph.D. diss., Texas A & M University, Department of Political Science.

Wanat, John. 1974. "Bases of Budgetary Incrementalism." *American Political Science Review* 68: 1221–28.

West, Bruce J., and Bill Deering. 1995. *The Lure of Modern Science.* Singapore: World Scientific.

Wildavsky, Aaron. 1964. *The Politics of the Budgetary Process.* Boston: Little, Brown.

THE POTLATCH BETWEEN ECONOMICS
AND POLITICAL SCIENCE

Herbert A. Simon

I am somewhat miscast in this conversation as one of the representatives of economics. Both of my academic degrees are in political science; a half-century ago I chaired a political science department; and I have never been a member of an economics department. Hence, my tribal allegiance is to political science.

In discussing the benefits that economics has conferred upon political science, I will echo Virgil: "Timeo Danaos et dona ferentis," which, if I may translate for those of you who were spared a classical education, means that I fear economists, even when they are bearing gifts. What is more, my own gift-bearing has gone in the opposite direction, and I have observed similar fears among the recipients at the economics end. Their belief that everyone is trying to maximize utility makes them skeptical about the intentions of altruists. As philanthropists soon discover, gift-giving is no easy occupation.

MUNICIPAL BUDGETING

To explain these remarks, I must go back to my first piece of research. In 1935, as an undergraduate at Chicago, and at the suggestion of Professor Jerry Kerwin, I spent some time in my native city of Milwaukee trying to understand the budgeting process in the city's recreation department, which was administered jointly by the school board and the department of public works. I came as a gift-bearing Greek, fresh from an intermediate price theory course taught by the grandfather of Chicago School neoclassical laissez-faire economics, Henry Simons.

My economics training showed me how to budget rationally. Simply compare the marginal utility of a proposed expenditure with its marginal cost, and approve it only if utility exceeds cost. However, what I saw in Milwaukee did not seem to be an application of this rule. I saw a lot of bargaining, of reference to the previous year's budget and incremental changes in it. If the word *marginal* was ever spoken, I missed it. Moreover, which participants would support which items was quite predictable. If the choice was between planting trees and hiring another recreation leader, the public works representatives opted for the former, the school representatives for the latter.

The whole affair was somewhat puzzling. Fortunately, I had had some other experiences that helped me to interpret what I saw. I was a great joiner in high school and loved the politics of organizations. I had learned that when people join an organization, their values and preferences begin to change. In particular, they become loyal to the organization and identify, to a greater or lesser degree, with its objectives.

Economists might say that their utilities change; actually, their representations of the world change. The change is not simply in values but also in what they know and believe. I could see a clear connection, in the recreation department, between peoples positions on budget matters and the values and beliefs that prevailed in their suborganizations.

I brought back from this experience to my friends and teachers in economics two gifts, which I ultimately called "organizational identification" and "bounded rationality." Of course, this did not all happen in one sudden "aha!" but developed gradually as I had opportunities to observe other organizations, to do research on the measurement of municipal activities, to study decisionmaking in public and business organizations at firsthand, and to brood about my experiences.

The gifts were not received with enthusiasm. Most economists did not see their relevance to anything they were doing, and they mostly ignored them and went on counting the angels on the heads of neoclassical pins.

THE GIFTS FROM ECONOMICS

The flow of gifts in recent years has been mainly in the opposite direction, labeled "public choice" and "game theory." Public choice endowed voters with the same utility functions that consumers were supposed to possess, and professional politicians with utility functions that valued power. Such proponents of public-choice theory as Anthony Downs and James Buchanan—and many others—relabeled many of the phenomena of politics that had been observed and recorded by Pendleton Herring, Charles Merriam and his associates and students, Paul Lazarsfeld and the Columbia group, and many others who had toiled in the vineyards of political science. The old wine was poured into new bottles. It has already been debated, at length, how far the relabeling advanced our understanding of political phenomena. Since I joined in that debate a decade ago, on receiving the James Madison Award (Simon 1985) and in a lecture at the London School of Economics (1987), I need not repeat it here, beyond reminding you of the key issue as I saw it.

That issue, already implicit in my Milwaukee experience, was that the public-choice theory could make no predictions until we had defined how the participants actually measure utility in each particular situation. All of the force of the theory depended on these auxiliary definitions and assumptions, and until they were nailed down, there was nothing to be tested, and nothing had been added to the earlier descriptions already available in the political science literature. Moreover, these were factual assumptions that acquired no validity from being made in an armchair but required empirical verification that they seldom received. Reinterpreting political behavior as following from utility maximization, in the absence of such empirical grounding, is an empty exercise.

The story of game theory is rather similar. The greatest contributions of John von Neumann and Oskar Morgenstern (1944) and of Kenneth Arrow in his classic work on social values (1951) were to show how elusive the concept of rationality is in the context of group decisionmaking. Many-person games have determinate solutions only under very specific assumptions about the "out-guessing" and coalition-forming that the participants engage in, and even then there is seldom uniqueness of solutions. This would seem to call for empirical study of the processes that human beings actually use to make decisions under highly ambiguous circumstances. Instead, until recently, the critical postulates, like those about utility, have simply been dreamed up with little or no empirical support.

A Dawning of Empiricism

But these clouds have silver linings. Increasing attention has been paid to the limits of human rationality, and these limits, implicitly or explicitly, have been introduced into the boundary conditions of the rational models and the operational definitions of the utility-maximizing processes. In economics, the term "bounded rationality" has recently become almost embarrassingly fashionable, but it is not often accompanied, unfortunately, by a recognition that nothing has been gained by adopting it unless the limits of rationality that affect a particular decision process are grounded in solid empirical evidence. The widespread adoption of the slogan of "bounded rationality" has as yet done only a little to curb armchair model building. For an egregious example of the latter (this time of new wine in old bottles), see Sargent (1993).

Similar comments may be made about game theory. If it is now widely recognized that securing definite solutions to games requires making assumptions about the "rational" processes used to play them, it is less well recognized that these assumptions are empirical and cannot legitimately be introduced without supporting evidence.

But another silver lining promises sunshine in the not-too-distant future. Increasingly, the empirical nature of the assumptions required for defining rational models, whether in public-choice theory, game theory, or economics generally, is being recognized. One form of this recognition is experimental economics, pioneered in the study of markets by Vernon Smith (1990), in public-choice theory by Charles Plott (1970), and in game theory by Reinhard Selten (Albers, Guth, and Hammerstein 1997, 4, 350, 360). Experimental economics uses human subjects to test the assumptions of human boundedness that go into models of rational decision.

I will mention just a couple of important findings, not irrelevant to political science, that experimental economics is producing. First, we are learning under what circumstances markets do and do not move to the theoretical equilibrium. Second, reaching equilibrium appears to have little to do with whether the participants are observing strict rules of rationality, for in simulated markets where participants are replaced by computer programs, quite "dumb" programs (for example, programs given only lower limits on selling prices and upper limits on buying prices) often bring markets rapidly to equilibrium (Gode and Sunder 1997). We must be cautious about assuming a high level of rationality when a very bounded rationality produces the same observed consequences.

The Gifts Not Brought

So far, the questions I have raised largely concern the value of the gifts that economics has brought to the potlatch. I am afraid that I must also complain about the neglect of other more valuable gifts that it has not brought because it does not manufacture them.

The decisionmaking theory that economics employs, and that its missionaries bring to the potlatch, is a theory of how choices are made among given sets of alternatives. Neoclassical economics has had almost nothing to say about how the alternatives are discovered or invented, and only a little to say about how they are diffused from their points of origin. Yet, if we inspect almost any decision process in public organizations, in legislatures, or, for that matter, in the design departments and marketing departments of business firms, we find that the bulk of the effort is given over to dreaming up new solutions to problems, new programs, new policies, new products, and new ways of marketing.

As I pointed out in my 1985 *American Political Science Review* paper, the Constitutional Convention was not preoccupied with choosing between constitutions that had been presented to it; it was involved in inventing a constitution. That same observation applies to almost every body or group, high or low, engaged in deciding, "What is to be done?"

Contrary to the views of the Preacher, there are indeed new things under the sun every day. Of course, the new does not spring forth whole from the brain of Zeus; it is generally fashioned by combinatorial processes from that which already exists. But creating it by searching through these possibilities is at the core of the decision process.

Political science, if it has produced no systematic theory of political or administrative innovation, has not neglected the phenomena, especially in the historical study of political institutions and in some of its literature on the decisionmaking process. Other social sciences have concerned themselves with innovation and discovery more intensively and systematically. In recent years, cognitive psychology and the history and sociology of science have given enormous attention to the processes that modify and adapt the old to create the new. If political science wants to sample such theories for their possible relevance to its own needs, potlatches with these other groups will be more profitable than exchanges with economics. As a starter, it could look at Langley and others, *Scientific Discovery* (1987), and the numerous references cited there. Innovation is closely related to another phenomenon that has been neglected by economics: selective attention. One of the important limits on human rationality is that we do not use all of the (incomplete) knowledge that we possess. When our attention is attracted to a particular issue or problem, we form a frame of reference for thinking about it and evoke from memory some of the things we know that are relevant as viewed from that frame of reference. Different foci of attention lead us to view the very same matter in quite different ways. A voter (even a voter who is mostly guided by selfish economic motives) will look at an election differently after the word *inflation* is mentioned than after mention of *unemployment*.

One of the important contributions of the voting studies that started in the 1940s was to call attention to focus of attention and shift of attention as central mechanisms (and as alternatives to persuasion) in political decision processes. Again, I have elaborated on these matters in my 1985 and 1987 papers and need not repeat that discussion here.

So one way we can balance the economic potlatch is with gifts to economics of theories of innovation and of the determination of the focus of attention.

ORGANIZATIONS

But the most serious blindness of economics to the facts of life, one that is particularly crippling for political science applications, is its inattention to organizations as decisionmaking systems that are as important to the operation of a society as are markets. The classical theory of the firm is a travesty of a theory of organizations—all skin and no bones, and surely no digestive tract or heart.

Again, the inadequacies derive from ignoring bounded rationality and, in particular, the forces of organizational identification. A "new institutional economics" strives to provide a more adequate organization theory by adding an employment market and introducing a plethora of other special forms of contract to take into account transaction costs and what is sometimes called "moral hazard."

All of these are still not able to explain the special properties of organizations. They continue to assume that employees and employers are motivated solely by economic interest; that, to a high degree, the marginal contributions of each to the organization's economic success can be measured; and that membership in an organization, whether as employer or employee, does not change either the values or beliefs of the members.

Whether these are really inadequacies, or whether they are dealt with by the new institutional economics, are empirical questions. They cannot be answered by building abstract models of organizations, but only by actually observing how people in organizations do behave, and in particular, what things they take into account in reaching their decisions, and by what means. We are back to the same point: Economics offers us models of organizations, but it does not offer us many facts showing that these are the right models.

Moreover, on the specific issue of the motivations that bind people to organizations and account for their decisions while they are in organizations, many facts that already exist point to the strength of organizational identification as often motivating quite different decisions than would be reached if the "selfish" motives assumed by economists were dominant (Simon 1997). Evolutionary arguments have been proposed in economics for accepting self-interest (usually in terms of economic goals) as the helmsman that steers behavior. Under assumptions of bounded rationality, even stronger reasons can be, and have been, given for introducing group identification as a basic source of motivation in organizations as well as in other social settings (nations, ethnic groups, and so on). (For a theory of identification deriving from assumptions of natural selection, see Simon 1990.)

The empirical study of organizations is not new. Sociologists, political scientists, and business school researchers have produced a large body of data about how decisions are actually reached within business firms. I need only to refer to the classic behavioral theory of the firm of my friends Dick Cyert and Jim March (1963), or to the more recent book by Phil Bromiley (1987) on corporate investment decisions. These are only two samples of a vast literature that, regrettably, still needs work on its methodologies, especially so that we can have greater confidence in the general conclusions we draw from very careful, but relatively isolated case studies.

The picture of organization that derives from such research shows a complexity that we must despair of capturing in a few algebraic or differential equations. It does not look at all like a cost curve and a demand curve. That simply means that we must go to newer and more powerful means of representation for our theories—in particular, to symbolic computer simulations, precisely the same kinds of models that are already being used in connection with experimental economics. And since these modeling tools have been progressively honed in cognitive psychology over the past forty years, there is a great body of methodological lore that we can now draw upon. Gift-giving between economics and the other social sciences can become a genuine exchange, going in both directions.

SCIENCE AND POLICY

We all agree, I think, that the special capability of science is to describe the world and how it works. Before we move from science to make proposals and prescriptions for changing the world, we must add values to our scientific knowledge, and there is no logical process that yields "oughts" in its conclusions without including some in its premises.

Nevertheless, when we take a closer view of the practice of applied science, whether it be public administration or public policy in economics, we find that particular scientific viewpoints seem to attract particular values. Specifically, history shows a high correlation between professional competence in neoclassical economics and the beliefs that markets are generally preferable to other institutional arrangements; that privately owned organizations are to be preferred to governmental organizations; and that governments should interfere minimally, if at all, with market institutions. You can all supply the necessary qualifications on these broad generalizations about economists' beliefs, but will perhaps accept them as a first approximation.

What I have said in the previous section about how people's views are shaped by organizational identifications might also lead us to conclude that political scientists too, by virtue of their profession, may tend to absorb certain values about public matters: for example, that government on the whole is a good thing, and that its health and vigor are essential to civil society. I would not deny our bias in this direction (again, with exceptions, like the Newt Gingrichs of our time), but at the moment I would like to examine the consequences of the value biases of neoclassical economics.

The value bias toward markets is a product of the Arrow-Debreu equilibrium theorems and the Pareto optima associated with them. The issues are well understood, in economics as well as in political science, and I need not rehash them here. The consequence of the bias is an antipathy to any redistribution of the social product that does not meet the conditions of Pareto optimization, a preference for efficient inequity, we might say, over inefficient equity.

The bias toward profit-making firms is a product of the theory of motivation that underlies neoclassical theories of organization, and whose inadequacy I have already discussed. Its consequence has been the spate of privatization efforts of recent years. If the theory of motivation is wrong, as seems to me almost certain, then these efforts are largely misguided.

The general mistrust of government as a positive instrument of a civil society is largely the product of the other two biases. I sometimes use the two words *Oklahoma City* to focus attention on some of the consequences of this generalized bias. Whether it is fair to use these two words, I have found that they certainly do have an attention-focusing effect.

REMARKS ON THE COMMENTS
OF PROFESSORS GOODIN AND JONES

Where does this leave us in relation to the thoughtful comments of Professors Goodin and Jones?

You will have observed that I am less sanguine than is Professor Goodin that the notions of bounded rationality "seem by now to have been pretty well absorbed into the received canon of political science." (Of course, many of these notions originated in political science.) But when Goodin says that "good use will always be made of them by anyone deploying formal models to analyze the real world," I must dissent, and have been dissenting throughout. The label of "bounded rationality" has been freely applied, but not the insistence on grounding formal models in solid empirical foundations. This is my answer to his "Why Not?" Why not join the public-choice movement? It is a movement that has frequently practiced a non-empirical methodology.

Now I must compound my ingratitude to Professor Goodin for the temperate tone of his paper, and the fascinating ideas it suggests. I do not recognize anything that distinguishes his "logic of appropriateness" from "bounded rationality," though the former phrase does focus attention on one facet of the latter. Goodin observes that, because of bounded rationality, we approach different situations with different frames of reference. That is quite true; it is also what bounded rationality and the processes of identification in particular are all about. Professor Goodin is correct in noting that psychological research, after focusing for many years on building a general picture of how the problem-solving search works, has been moving on to newer questions of how the search environment (the problem representation) is formed. A change in research focus should not be confused with a change in theory.

In summary, I think that Professor Goodin and I are out of synch to the extent that he, a philosopher, is looking at theories in terms of their appeal to reason, while I, an empirical scientist, am looking at them in terms of the empirical evidence we need to decide whether we should believe them and how we should go about obtaining such evidence. I suppose that such a division of labor between philosophers and scientists is not surprising.

Professor Jones takes what I have just called the "scientific" rather than the "philosophical" tack, and I have no problems with what he says. He builds several theoretical models of a market or a political process, some proceeding from assumptions of classical rationality, others from assumptions of bounded rationality. He then deduces some phenomena that should be observed if one or another of the models describes reality, and compares how well the phenomena agree with the predictions.

In the cases he describes, the outcomes he observes are statistical distributions that may be Gaussian, or non-Gaussian, in several ways. On the basis of his data, he concludes that the observed distributions are consistent with certain models of bounded rationality, but not with models of global rationality. This is standard hypothetico-deductive (H-D) procedure that I can and do applaud. I would only add (and I have no reason to suppose that Professor Jones would disagree) that this is one way in which empirical science proceeds: from hypotheses to predictions, and then to empirical tests of their correctness. Another way (sometimes called abduction) is from observed phenomena (which may have been observed accidentally, and without a theory in mind) to hypotheses that could account for them. We can find numerous examples of both of these kinds of sequences, and others, in the histories of any of the sciences.

To sum up my remarks in a sentence: What we need in political science is much more empirical research, whether to test the predictions of theories that have been proposed or to so immerse ourselves in the real-world phenomena that striking observations will stimulate the generation of promising theories that can then be tested further. That is a long sentence, but it is mostly captured in the first clause.

REFERENCES

Albers, Wulf, Werner Guth, and Peter Hammerstein (eds.). 1997. *Understanding Strategic Interaction: Essays in Honor of Reinhard Selten.* Heidelberg: Springer-Verlag.

Arrow, Kenneth J. 1951. *Social Choice and Individual Values.* New York: Wiley.

Bromiley, Philip. 1987. *Corporate Capital Investments: A Behavioral Approach.* Cambridge: Cambridge University Press.

Cyert, Richard M., and James G. March. 1963. *A Behavioral Theory of the Firm.* Englewood Cliffs, N.J.: Prentice-Hall.

Gode, Dhananjay K., and Shyam Sunder. 1997. "What Makes Markets Allocationally Efficient?" *Quarterly Journal of Economics* (May): 604–30.

Langley, Pat, Herbert A. Simon, Gary L. Bradshaw, and Jan M. Zytkow. 1987. *Scientific Discovery: Computational Explorations of the Creative Processes.* Cambridge, Mass.: MIT Press.

Plott, Charles R. 1970. *Recent Results in the Theory of Voting.* Lafayette, Ind.: Purdue University Press.

Sargent, Thomas J. 1993. *Bounded Rationality in Macroeconomics.* Oxford: Oxford University Press.

Simon, Herbert A. 1985. "Human Nature in Politics: The Dialogue of Psychology with Political Science." *American Political Science Review* 79: 293–304.

———. 1987. "Politics as Information Processing." *London School of Economics Quarterly* 1: 345–70.

———. 1990. "A Mechanism for Social Selection and Successful Altruism." *Science* 250: 1665–68.

———. 1997. *Administrative Behavior.* 4th ed. New York: Free Press.

Smith, Vernon. 1990. *Game Theory and Experimental Economics: The Early Years.* Durham, N.C.: Duke University Press.

von Neumann, John, and Oskar Morgenstern. 1944. *Theory of Games and Economic Behavior.* Princeton, N.J.: Princeton University Press.

Chapter 3

JAMES M. BUCHANAN
A Biographical Sketch

James Buchanan, Harris University Professor at George Mason University, has provided an entertaining autobiographical account called *Better Than Plowing* (1992). He was born in rural Tennessee, educated locally at Middle Tennessee State Teachers College (where he supported himself by milking cows), and then had a year of graduate study in economics at the University of Tennessee. Naval service during World War II delayed his education but led to a GI subsidy on which he went to the University of Chicago to earn a Ph.D. in economics. Since then he has taught at the University of Virginia, UCLA, and Virginia Tech, before joining George Mason. He has a dozen honorary doctorates from universities in at least seven countries and has won various awards, including the Seidman Award and the Nobel Prize in Economic Science, awarded in 1986. Of his many books, probably *The Calculus of Consent* (with Gordon Tullock; 1962), *The Limits of Liberty* (1975), *Freedom in Constitutional Contract* (1978), *The Power to Tax* (with Geoffrey Brennan; 1980), and *The Reason of Rules* (with Brennan; 1985) are most familiar to political scientists. Buchanan has also written extensively in other areas, including ethics and public finance.

On arriving in Chicago, Buchanan believed himself a "libertarian socialist," but exposure to price theory with Frank Knight quickly converted him to classical liberalism. Though retaining his libertarian values, he came to believe through Knight that the market rather than government is the organizational form most consistent with those values. Nevertheless, while only individuals choose, Buchanan came to believe that economics could not be studied properly outside of politics (Boettke, forthcoming). Efficiency in the public sector would be guaranteed only under a rule of unanimity for collective choices.

Buchanan's early contribution to political analysis was a new view of the consequences of "externalities" and decision costs. Already believing that politics as well as economics should be viewed as exchange (not maximizing), he brought the concept of gains derived from mutual exchange between individuals out of the exclusive realm of economic markets and into the realm of political decisionmaking. Collective decisions about, say, taxes impose externalities on those outside the decisive coalition. As Thomas Schwartz points out in his chapter, by doing this Buchanan expanded public economics into public choice by making it encompass the political process. We end up with the same individuals wearing two hats, that is, the consumers and producers of economics are also citizens in politics. Some of them are politically active, and so the same actors can affect narrowly economic outcomes in two ways, both now accommodated in one analytic approach.

Buchanan has had a lifelong interest in public finance, much of which has been picked up and developed by others in the public choice literature. In *Public*

Finance in a Democratic Process (1967), Buchanan revived interest in the concept of fiscal illusion, the belief among voters that they are taxed more or less than they really are (the "illusion" of being under- or overtaxed). Buchanan drew attention to practices—including general fund financing and the separation of voting on taxes and the expenditures they finance—that he believed increased the incompleteness of voter information, possibly leading to unwarranted expansion of government. Others followed Buchanan's lead in studying the connection between the visibility of a tax and voter support for it.

Partly because economics is about a game played within rules, the choices among different rules of the game cannot be ignored. In his later work, Buchanan turned to constitutional analysis of the state, mainly from a contractarian point of view. In his constitutional work, he came to distinguish between three states: the "protective" state, which enforces agreed-to rights that emerged out of the pre-constitutional moment; the "productive" state, which coordinates the plans of actors through collective action unavailable through individual action; and the "redistributive" state, transformed from productivity by rent-seeking motives and political actions, which transfers value from one party to another through the tool of collective action. While preconstitutional analysis opens up the discourse over the rules of the game, postconstitutional analysis reflects an examination of the strategies players adopt within the defined rules; political economy, properly understood, is the tacking back and forth between these two levels of analysis. This is, in the end, the message of the public choice revolution.

Seen this way, constitutional analysis applies at many levels of human association. However, it always involves an interaction between constitutional rules and cultural ("civic religion") elements, which are not only involved in the choice of rules (as Buchanan elaborates in *The Reason of Rules*, with Brennan) but learned as a consequence of living under rules. Vincent Ostrom's chapter elaborates on this connection. He shows how Buchanan took constitutional analysis out of the study of law by combining methodological individualism and considerations of costs to create logical foundations for the rational choice of collective decision rules in a wide range of associational contexts. Ostrom argues that while Buchanan (originally) neglected both the moral dimension of constitutional analysis and the importance of norms, he produced a valuable, general way to discuss the logical foundations of constitutions.

Another enduring legacy of Buchanan's work is the question of whether the rent-seeking and externalities that arise under supermajority procedures are better for us than the ones that arise under majoritarian procedures. Schwartz builds on Buchanan's critique of majoritarianism and shows that—somewhat *contra* Buchanan—there is something special about simple-majority rule but—very much in line with Buchanan—what is special is not necessarily a good thing. Schwartz argues that extremely large externalities can arise from unanimous decisions when simple majorities could have been decisive.

REFERENCES

Boettke, Peter M. Forthcoming. "James M. Buchanan and the Rebirth of Political Economy." In *Against the Grain: Dissent in Economics*, ed. Steve Pressman and Ric Holt (Aldershot: Edward Elgar Publishing).

Brennan, Geoffrey, and James Buchanan. 1985. *The Reason of Rules.* New York: Cambridge University Press.

Buchanan, James M. 1967. *Public Finance in a Democratic Process.* Chapel Hill: University of North Carolina Press.

———. 1975. *The Limits of Liberty.* Chicago: University of Chicago Press.

———. 1978. *Freedom in Constitutional Contract.* College Station: Texas A&M University Press.

———. 1992. *Better Than Plowing and Other Essays.* Chicago: University of Chicago Press.

Buchanan, James M., and Geoffrey Brennan. 1980. *The Power to Tax.* New York: Cambridge University Press.

Buchanan, James M., and Gordon Tullock. 1962. *The Calculus of Consent.* Ann Arbor: University of Michigan Press.

TAKING CONSTITUTIONS SERIOUSLY: BUCHANAN'S CHALLENGE TO TWENTIETH-CENTURY POLITICAL SCIENCE

Vincent Ostrom

James M. Buchanan is a maverick among economists. He is preoccupied with constitutional economics and public finance, not market economics and price theory. He is a challenge to twentieth-century political scientists because he takes constitutions and the constitutional level of analysis seriously. Failing to take constitutions seriously is largely a twentieth-century way of thinking among political scientists. Leading men of affairs were preoccupied with the constitutional level of analysis in the founding era and in the early decades of the United States of America. At the end of the nineteenth century, a paradigmatic shift occurred and constitutions came to be viewed as literary theories and paper pictures. Logical positivism based on a natural science approach to the social sciences came to prevail. James Buchanan and Gordon Tullock's *The Calculus of Consent* (1962), by focusing on the constitutional level of analysis in the longer tradition of political inquiry going back at least to Hobbes and Montesquieu, if not Aristotle, has contributed to the revival of a concern for theory at the core of efforts to conceptualize and design systems of political order and to study the conduct of political experiments in field settings. We are taking part in the creation of a "new science of politics" for a "new world," as Alexis de Tocqueville anticipated in his introduction to *Democracy in America* (1835/1990, 1:7).

A PRELUDE TO CONSTITUTIONAL ANALYSIS

Before political science became a specialized academic discipline, eminent American intellectuals, including John Adams, Alexander Hamilton, James Kent, Thomas Jefferson, and James Madison, were knowledgeable about the great works in political philosophy and jurisprudence, and they seriously devoted themselves to the formulation of constitutions grounded in what Hamilton ([1788], 524) referred to in Federalist 81 as "the general theory of a limited constitution." *The Federalist*, authored by Alexander Hamilton, John Jay, and James Madison, effectively distinguished between constitutions and ordinary laws, addressed the rationale for constitutions as fundamental law in constitutional republics, and offered a careful analysis of the document prepared by the Philadelphia Convention of 1787 to inform the deliberations over the ratification of the Constitution of the United States. Establishing "good government" by reflection and choice implied deliberation through processes of constitutional choice both in formulating and revising constitutions as governable charters.

In the opening paragraph of Federalist 1, Alexander Hamilton ([1788], 3) directed attention to the problem of "whether societies of men are really capable or not of establishing good government from reflection and choice, or whether they are forever destined to depend for their political constitutions on accident and force." Revolutions, coups d'état, and military conquests yield constitutions decided by force. The course of politics decided by minimal winning coalitions through instrumentalities of government might be viewed as the accidents of history—decided by the changing fortunes of electoral contestation through time. The possibility of reflection and choice was abandoned to accident and force when attention shifted to winning elections rather than constitutional reform.

THE AMBIGUOUS ROLE OF CONSTITUTIONS IN TWENTIETH-CENTURY POLITICAL SCIENCE

On the eve of the twentieth century, such an eminent scholar and political personality as Woodrow Wilson had in *Congressional Government* (1885/1956) rejected the explanations offered in *The Federalist* as "literary theories" (37) and "paper pictures" (31). Wilson saw an irreconcilable conflict between "the Constitution of the books" and "the Constitution in operation" (30). In his quest to study the living reality—the living Constitution—Wilson offered the following methodological advice to the reader:

> It is, therefore, the difficult task of one who would now write at once practically and critically of our national government to escape from theories and attach himself to facts, not allowing himself to be confused by a knowledge of what that government was intended to be, or led away into conjectures as to what it may one day become, but striving to catch its present phases and to photograph the delicate organism in all its characteristic parts exactly as it is today; an undertaking all the more arduous and doubtful of issue because it has to be entered upon without guidance from writers of acknowledged authority. (30)

Instead, Wilson presumed that, in all systems of government, "there is always a [singular] centre of power." The burden of the analyst is to determine "where in this system is that centre? in whose hands is *self-sufficient authority* lodged and through what agencies does that authority speak and act?" (1885/1956, 30, my emphasis). Wilson's response in 1885 was that "the predominant and controlling force, the centre and source of all motive and of all regulative power, is Congress" (31). In the 1900 preface to the fifteenth printing of *Congressional Government*, Wilson questioned his earlier conclusion and pointed to the "new leadership of the Executive" as offering the prospect of substituting "statesmanship for government by mass meeting." *Congressional* government was being replaced by *presidential* government. Wilson observed that these developments might "put this whole volume hopelessly out of date" (23). The course of partisan electoral politics and the place of America in world affairs was rendering "the Constitution of the books" and *Congressional Government* obsolete. The implication was that accident and force rather than reflection and choice prevail in the constitution of power relationships.

The mainstreams of American political science through the eras of Wilson, Roosevelt, and Nixon have followed in the intellectual tradition established by

Wilson and the inspiration that he drew from Walter Bagehot's search for a *single* center of power in British government, which Bagehot identified with Cabinet government in *The English Constitution* (1865/1964). The behavioral revolution sought to identify the realities of power in the American political system by focusing variously on presidential government, congressional government, and judicial supremacy.

The search for the realities of power in the *living* constitution placed an emphasis on logical positivism that, in some sense, put Alexander Hamilton's question of "whether societies of men are really capable or not of establishing good government from reflection and choice" beyond the scope of a political science. Harold Lasswell, whom I regard as the premier American political scientist in the twentieth century, conceptualized political science as "the shaping and sharing of power" (Lasswell and Kaplan 1950, xiv). Lasswell defined *power* as "the making of decisions: G has power over H with respect to the values K if G participates in the making of decisions affecting the K-policies of H" (75). "A *decision*," then, "is a policy involving severe sanctions (deprivations)" (74, Lasswell and Kaplan's emphasis).

Recourse to "severe sanctions" places political relationships beyond the realm of economic relationships involving a *voluntary* exchange of goods. Recourse to coercion in the sense of mobilizing severe sanctions and imposing deprivations means that political relationships are somewhat more analogous to a Faustian bargain than an exchange of goods in a market economy. However, market exchange relationships are themselves rule-ordered relationships, and the concept of property rights, the enforcement of contractual relationships, and the exchange of goods depend on the use of severe sanctions to foreclose theft, fraud, and other perverse strategies that are in the realm of possibilities. There is a living political reality in the shadow of market transactions.

Hamilton's question of whether societies of men are capable of establishing *good government* from reflection and choice is itself concerned with some set of possibilities that would be conducive both to an exchange of goods and the possibility of yielding conditions compatible with liberty and justice in the constitution of governmental authority. The concept of *good government* would be compatible with the realization of *public goods*. In exploring such *possibilities,* human beings would need to have recourse to conceptions in which hypothetical conditions might be specified among the necessary conditions to yield anticipated consequences. Normative considerations thus have a place in relation to positive explanations. The realization of possibilities is contingent, then, on human motivation to use conceptions to create specifiable design conditions to achieve desired consequences, as in any experimental venture.

James Madison had explicitly referred to the experimental character of what had been formulated at the Philadelphia Convention in Federalist 10, 14, and 51. Alexis de Tocqueville wrote many years later, in a transitional paragraph at the end of the first chapter in *Democracy in America* (1835/1990, 1:25):

> In that land the great experiment of the attempt to construct society upon a new basis was to be made by civilized man; and it was there, for the first time, that theories hitherto unknown, or deemed impracticable, were to exhibit a spectacle for which the world had not been prepared by the history of the past.

By contrast, Milovan Djilas, in his critique of what might be called the Soviet experiment, was concerned with the relationship of "ideas" to "deeds" when acting on the basis of theoretical conjectures intended to evoke desired consequences. The experiment conducted "in the name of doing away with classes," according to Djilas, had resulted in achieving "the most complete authority" by the Communist Party as a new ruling class. "Everything else is sham and an illusion" (1957, 36). Some theoretical conjectures may provide a warrantable basis for creating a system of constitutional government; other theoretical conjectures may create illusions of classless societies while serving as the intellectual facade for a new despotism and for the entrapment of those who place their faith in illusions.

Alongside these considerations bearing on "literary theories," "paper pictures," "a great experiment to construct society upon a new basis," "shams," and "illusions," we need to recognize that political analysts are plagued by wishful thinking and by the opportunistic behavior of political actors who find ways to use severe sanctions to gain dominance and exercise control over others. A preoccupation with politics as a study of *who gets what, when,* and *how* (Lasswell 1936) can be the source of endless narratives of curious interest to people in democratic societies.

Against this background of ambiguity and indecision about the meaning of constitutions in political realities, American political scientists face the anomaly that James Buchanan, a maverick economist, won the Nobel Prize in Economic Science for his contribution to the constitutional level of analysis. I shall proceed by considering the mode of analysis undertaken in *The Calculus of Consent: Logical Foundations of Constitutional Democracy* (1962), which Buchanan coauthored with Gordon Tullock. I shall then proceed to further reflections on the ideas that Buchanan advances in some of his subsequent work on the constitutional level of analysis. Serious intellectual issues need to be confronted as we take constitutions seriously in relating *ideas* to *deeds* and as Homo sapiens—the thinking one—considers what it means to be human.

THE CALCULUS OF CONSENT

The key to Buchanan's basic challenge is to be found in *The Calculus of Consent.* The subtitle, *Logical Foundations of Constitutional Democracy,* reveals the foundational and normative orientation of scholarship concerned with liberty and justice in democratic societies. Tullock, who was trained as a lawyer at the University of Chicago law school, began his career as a foreign service officer. In my judgment, Tullock was somewhat more committed to the application of neoclassical economic theory to nonmarket decisionmaking. Buchanan has been more focused on constitutional political economy, with a strong concern for the moral and philosophical foundations of constitutional democracy.

Tullock's *The Politics of Bureaucracy* (1965) was an important complement to *The Calculus of Consent* in my own paradigmatic concerns about democratic administration as an alternative to bureaucratic administration in highly fragmented, pluralistic democratic societies. Buchanan and Tullock's *The Calculus of Consent* and Tullock's *The Politics of Bureaucracy* were important antecedents to "The Organization of Government in Metropolitan Areas" (1961), an article I coauthored with Charles Tiebout and Robert Warren, and to my analysis in *The Intellectual Crisis in American Public Administration* (1973/1989). These foundations have provided the theoretical formulations for an extended series of studies concerned with public economies in metropolitan areas over the last three decades.[1]

If we are to understand Buchanan's challenge, it is necessary to examine the basic elements expounded in *The Calculus of Consent*, reinforced by some of the basic theses advanced in the more traditional treatments of the problems of constitutional choice. In reflecting on their own work, Buchanan and Tullock (1962, 301) suggest that they had "come to appreciate more fully the genius of the Founding Fathers in the construction of the American system." They add:

> The rather bewildering complex of institutions that makes up the American decision-making system does not seem openly to contradict the fundamental hypotheses of our model [approach]. This is the extent to which our construction serves as a rationalization for what is, or perhaps more aptly stated, what is supposed to be.

The correlative proposition might also be expected to hold: *Those familiar with traditional political theory,* including those theoretical formulations used in the conception and design of "The American decision-making system," *might be expected to find the formulations in* The Calculus of Consent *to have close parallels to works with which they are familiar.* The language of economists addressing the constitutional level of analysis will have a familiar ring to earlier formulations advanced by American Federalists and the Scottish philosophers, among others. It is with this possibility in mind that I shall attempt to review the basic elements and presuppositions of Buchanan's challenge.

The Importance of the Individual Level of Analysis

The strong emphasis in Buchanan's work is his commitment to *methodological individualism,* meaning that it is individuals who think, make choices, act, and do whatever it is that human beings do. In a market economy, it is individuals who function as autonomous decisionmakers engaging in voluntary exchanges with one another. In applying economic reasoning to constitutional choice, it is individuals who are presumed to be engaged in constitutional decisionmaking. The analysis takes the perspective of *hypothetical individuals* to think through the calculations that would apply to the choice of *rules* to be included in a constitution.

This is equivalent to presuming that hypothetical citizens are engaged in the deliberations that establish the rules to be applied to systems of governance. In other words, citizens are presumed to be sovereign in much the same way that economists presume that producer and consumer sovereignty prevails in market economies. The equivalent decision rule to achieve a binding agreement between buyers and sellers is *unanimity.* The term *conceptual unanimity* recognizes that potential holdouts, if absolute unanimity were required, could prevent consensus about the fundamental rules that would prevail among reasonable individuals engaged in constitutional choice. Absolute unanimity gives way to conceptual unanimity because some individuals might pursue a holdout strategy to gain extraordinary bargaining power.

A point of dispute between economists and political scientists is apt to arise when political scientists presume that those in leadership positions need to take the perspective of the society as a whole in addressing particular problems of that society. Such a perspective is sometimes identified with that of an *omniscient observer*—one who can see the whole picture. Woodrow Wilson and many others have presumed that such a perspective is necessary for those who govern. Jeremy Bentham, for example, presumed that a representative assembly or parliament would be composed of men of goodwill who knew what promoted the greatest good for the greatest number and who could thus exercise the prerogatives of government.

The problem of human fallibility casts doubt about using the perspective of the omniscient observer as the basis for proceeding with an analysis bearing on the constitution of order in human societies. The rationale for checks and balances in a constitution arises because human beings cannot be omniscient. The neoclassical theory of markets has its own difficulties when market participants are presumed to have either perfect or complete information. Neither omniscient observers in political affairs nor perfect or complete information in economic affairs is possible. These presumptions do not withstand critical scrutiny.

The key question is how particular types of institutional arrangements evoke information. Competitive pricing expressed in monetary units and contestability among contenders in political processes are ways of evoking information to enlighten the choices that human beings make. Taking constitutions seriously relates, then, to the possibility that conflict and contestation can be engaged in through due processes of inquiry to enhance levels of information, extend human knowledge about public affairs, and stimulate innovation as a way of achieving conflict resolution.

Constitutional choice can be distinguished from collective choice. Buchanan emphasizes the choice of rules that apply to the prerogatives of government rather than the choice of who will fill particular positions of governmental authority and what funds will be spent for the purposes characteristic of collective choice. We can anticipate that choices about personnel and budgets will involve winners and losers. If rule-ordered relationships are conceived as games, many of the "games" of life involve winners and losers. Nevertheless, it is still necessary that players agree to sets of rules, play in accordance with the rules, and adhere to the rules in making judgments about the fairness of the game. Complex games may require the presence of officials to enforce rules as the game is played and observers to judge the play of the game according to how both players and officials adhere to the accepted rules of the game. Conceptual unanimity applies in devising rules to games that involve winning and losing in efforts to meet standards of fairness.

Cost Calculus

In *The Calculus of Consent,* Buchanan and Tullock develop a *cost calculus* applicable to the constitutional level of analysis: They demonstrate that those participating in formulating the rules for taking collective decisions would be justified in unanimously agreeing to decision rules of less than unanimity for taking collective-choice decisions. Their cost calculus includes *decision costs*—the time and effort expended on decisionmaking—and *external costs*—the costs imposed on others. Time and effort costs would be reduced to a minimum if some *one* individual could render a binding decision. External (deprivation) costs would be expected to decline as an increasing portion of those affected would have a voice in taking the decision. In extreme emergencies, it would be rational to authorize anyone to command the service of a fire department, for example, or to designate an official to invoke emergency measures in case of a disaster. Various forms of plurality and majority voting would be justified in taking other forms of collective decisions by some unit of government.

Types of Goods and the Nature of Public Goods

Both decision costs and external (deprivation) costs would need to be taken into account in light of the *type of good or service* to be provided. If there are no significant external costs, and if transaction costs are to be minimized, market arrangements afford an optimal resolution for those goods and services that are conceptualized as *private*. Mancur Olson's *The Logic of Collective Action* (1965) is widely recognized by political scientists as addressing the nature of public goods. In *The Demand and Supply of Public Goods* (1968), Buchanan further develops a theory of public goods and delineates the constitutional issues created by the nature of public goods. He indicates that the important issues bear on jointness of *use* or *consumption*. Patterns of interdependence among the community of users need to be taken into account. The degree of indivisibility needs to be related to the size of the interacting group in addressing the collective organization of the public sector. Buchanan quite explicitly states, "Nothing in the discussion implies anything about the actual *organization of production*" (186, Buchanan's emphasis). The key problems pertain to patterns of consumption or use. In the conclusions he offers to the question "Which Goods Should Be Public?" (187), Buchanan comments:

> Any positive approach to this question must proceed on a case-by-case basis and provisional conclusions [be] reached only after comparison of institutional alternatives in the broadest sense. The descriptive character of a good or service, the technology of common-sharing, and the range of such sharing, are important determinants of organizational efficiency. Care should be taken, however, not to presume that these characteristics, taken alone, allow *a priori* judgments to be made. . . . The predicted working properties of the institutional structures, imposed as constraints on individual behavior, must be evaluated.

These formulations are fully consistent with the concept of *the public* treated in "The Organization of Government in Metropolitan Areas" (V. Ostrom, Tiebout, and Warren 1961). Buchanan also gave considerable attention to club goods, which might also be viewed as toll goods. The good is enjoyed in common, such as in a country club, theater, or toll road, but a price is placed as a condition of entry. Open access to public roads may generate a tragedy of the commons, such as the rural coal-haul roads of East Kentucky (Oakerson 1978). Some resources used in common may be subject to subtractibility in use or consumption. At some threshold, any one person's added use will diminish the supply of the resource available to other users. Common-pool resources such as water, fisheries, forests, and wildlife are examples (Blomquist 1992; Hess 1996a, 1996b; Keohane and E. Ostrom 1995; Lam 1998; E. Ostrom 1990; Schlager and E. Ostrom 1992; Tang 1992). Joint use of toll goods, common-pool resources, and public goods may require collective choice to secure effective results, but Buchanan's advice about taking a case-by-case approach still holds.

SIMILAR FORMULATIONS IN EARLIER TRADITIONS

In *The Federalist*, Alexander Hamilton emphasized that the exercise of the prerogatives of government must apply to the person of the individual if justice is to be done. His treatment is fully consistent with Buchanan's emphasis on method-ological individualism. The authors of *The Federalist* assumed that individuals are fallible but capable of learning through contestation and deliberation (V. Ostrom 1971/1987). Hamilton further held that acts contrary to the constitution cannot be accepted as a valid exercise of governmental authority. Penalties imposed on collectivities imply that deprivations are being imposed on innocent bystanders. Justice cannot be done when governments presume to govern other governments and seek to impose penalties on collectivities, as in a confederation. The essays in *The Federalist* are surprisingly consistent with the analytical methods developed in *The Calculus of Consent*, as I have demonstrated in *The Political Theory of a Compound Republic* (V. Ostrom 1971/1987).

In *Leviathan* (1651/1960), Thomas Hobbes not only conceptualized individuals as the basic unit of analysis in addressing the problem of order in human societies but devoted the introductory section of some sixteen chapters to the treatment "Of Man" prior to his treatment "Of Commonwealth." He gave priority to the characteristics of individuals because man is both the *matter* that is constitutive of commonwealths and the *artificer* that creates commonwealths.

His advice to readers was that when proceeding in an inquiry about the nature of commonwealths, one must be prepared to *"read thyself"* (1651/1960, 6, Hobbes's emphasis)—a version of methodological individualism. He went on to explain that there is a basic "similitude" of thoughts and passions characteristic of all mankind. The objects of one's thoughts and passions will vary in light of one's particular expe-rience and education, but the matter of how human beings think and feel is common to all mankind. All voluntary actions are grounded first in thought derived from a knowledge of cause-and-effect relationships and in sentiments and passions that can be characterized as appetites and aversions. Alternatives are conceptualized and then weighed in a process of deliberation entailing choice.

Hobbes anticipated that multiple equilibria will exist within human societies that vary according to the learning and levels of knowledge prevailing among their mem-bers. In a state of nature devoid of the arts derived from language, Hobbes anticipated that human beings will end up fighting with one another when the bounty of nature is inadequate to meet their demands. However, that condition is contrary to the motivation of individuals to seek their own good because fighting with one another yields misery instead. For human beings to find their way to peace as an alternative to war, Hobbes indicated that the Golden Rule provides a method of normative inquiry when expressed as *"Do not that to another, which thou wouldest not have done to thyself"* (1651/1960, 103, Hobbes's emphasis). In other words, Hobbes was sug-gesting that an individual can use his or her resources as a human being to come to an understanding of other human beings given the similitude of thoughts and passions characteristic of all mankind.

By using the method inherent in the Golden Rule, Hobbes argued that the meaning of his laws of nature as articles of peace will become "intelligible" even to a man of "the meanest capacity" if

> when weighing the actions of other men with his own, they seem too heavy, to put them into the other part of the balance, and his own into their place, that his own passions, and self-love, may add nothing to the weight; and then there is none of these laws of nature that will not appear unto him very reasonable (1651/1960, 103).

By such a method of inquiry, human beings establish the moral precepts that constitute the foundations of human community.

Although such precepts are binding in conscience, they do not necessarily bind in actions. Opportunities may arise that override conscience. It is necessary to have recourse to those who exercise the authority of a sovereign representative to enforce rules and make them binding in human societies.

Hobbes conceptualized a democracy as a society ruled by an assembly of all citizens who would come together. He neglected to consider the problem of how the rules of an assembly are to be formulated and made binding. The failure of an assembly to place limits on its assignment of authority to agents acting on its behalf is the source of the condition marking the "death of the people" (Hobbes 1642/1949, 97) in a democracy. Under those conditions, a democracy fails and is replaced by the type of agency to which the assembly has extended unlimited authority.

The specification of limits on the representatives acting on behalf of people in constitutional democracies implies that a division of labor is necessary to the allocation of authority among those performing governmental functions. Limited authority thus implies a separation and sharing of powers among those performing diverse functions in the governance of the society. Adherence to the limits established in any set of rule-ordered relationships is a construction that is normative in character, implying "what is supposed to be" rather than "what is." Incentives always exist for some to act in ways that are at variance with the rules if by so acting they can gain an advantage over others.

PUZZLES ABOUT THE THEORY OF CONSTITUTIONAL CHOICE

A profound tension exists in all political systems. There are exceptionally strong incentives for those engaged in political pursuits to play the game to win, even if winning comes at the cost of maintaining a system of rules that meet essential requirements of liberty and justice for all who participate in systems of rule-ordered relationships. Those who set and enforce rules dominate the allocation of values in any society. If citizens in a democratic society do not have a conscious awareness of the essential importance of the logical conditions of constitutional democracy and do not develop a civic culture for relating responsibly to one another and to those who act as agents on their behalf, democratic societies are placed at risk (V. Ostrom 1997).

These circumstances create a rather serious dilemma for the development of political theory. Simple models that are assumed to have universal application lead to abstractions that lose their meaning and to theory that is confined to doctrine and lacks contact with reality. Those who would take economics seriously need to read Walter Eucken's *The Foundations of Economics* (1940/1951) to avoid the pitfalls of using simple theoretical models when the relevant experience is one of artifactual construction embedded in multiple levels reflecting the three worlds of constitutional considerations, collective choice, and operational choice (Kiser and E. Ostrom 1982). Unless readers are prepared to interpret Buchanan's work in the broader context of European schools of economics, which are more sensitive to the type of critique offered by Eucken, they are in serious danger of misconstruing what Buchanan has to say. I often find myself troubled about how to interpret what I read.

Buchanan, for example, is frequently emphatic about the fundamental importance of relying on a rigorous model of Homo economicus in the analysis of rules and their place in rule-ordered relationships. Yet he is distinguished for having advanced the thesis that human beings have reflective capabilities that enter into the development of their personal character structure. In other words, character structure is an artifactual creation (see Buchanan 1979, ch. 5, "Natural and Artifactual Man"). This possibility is also expressed in relation to the human potential for developing *meta-preferences* and *meta-rules* and acting on the basis of moral precepts. Instead of being driven only by appetites and aversions in their expression of preferences, humans can reflect on their appetites and aversions in light of the consequences evoked and develop a higher order of response to stimuli. Such a meta-level of ordering preferences is commonplace in moral and religious teachings and becomes an integral part of the customs and traditions of people. Tocqueville referred to such considerations as habits of the heart and mind and identified religion as having the first order of importance in shaping American democracy, even though religion took no direct part in the government of society.

Buchanan's emphasis on Homo economicus also has its place because resorting to opportunistic self-serving strategies that impose deprivations on others is also a recurrent phenomenon in all political systems. The opportunism associated with Homo economicus may contradict standards of moral judgment. I construe Buchanan's emphasis on both Homo economicus and meta-preferences to be similar to Tocqueville's distinction between "egoism," "individualism," and "self-interest rightly understood" (1840/1990, 2:98–127). These contingencies prevail in human experience and thus need to be taken into account in ways that Elinor Ostrom (1998) suggested in her 1997 presidential address to the American Political Science Association.

The concept of rational choice need not be narrowly construed. Instead, principles of meta-rationality might be applied to processes of mediating conflict and searching for conflict resolution that enable human beings to emphasize the creative potentials of conflict rather than allow conflict to escalate to violent confrontations (Boulding 1963; Follett 1924/1951). The concept of due process in the exercise of problem-solving capabilities has recourse to principles (rules) of methodology that imply the development of meta-rationality among human beings. A theory of rational choice would presumably be a form of rationality taking account of meta-preferences and meta-rules.

The explicitly normative character of Buchanan's work—not unlike the normative foundations in Hobbes—is elaborated in *The Reason of Rules* (1985), coauthored with Geoffrey Brennan. There they express

> the hope that **a new "civic religion"** is on the way to being born, a civic religion that will return, in part, to the skepticism of the eighteenth century concerning politics and government and that, quite naturally, will concentrate our attention on the *rules that constrain governments* rather than on innovations that justify ever expanding political intrusions into the lives of citizens. **Our normative role, as social philosophers, is to shape this civic religion, surely a challenge sufficient to us all.** (150, Brennan and Buchanan's emphasis in italics, my emphasis in boldface)

Walter Lippmann (1955) would have characterized such a "civic religion" as a "public philosophy." The place of such a system of thought in providing the logical foundations of constitutional democracy not only draws on methods of normative inquiry compatible with a search for conceptual unanimity in human communities but also provides the basis for building the shared communities of understanding that are constitutive of the cultural and social sciences and the humanities that address themselves to the social dilemmas that plague human affairs.

The possibility of a theory of constitutional choice is inevitably plagued by numerous puzzles, many of which have been addressed by Buchanan. Taking constitutions seriously is of a fundamental magnitude in the development of a political science that can address itself to the logical foundations of constitutional democracy. Rather than assuming that there can be a general theory of politics, I presume that we face the problem of specifying the elements of a framework that would need to be taken into account in any analytical effort. Individuals acting in situations composed of relevant material conditions, rule-ordered relationships, and shared communities of understanding (culture) would be among those essential elements of such a framework. Those elements are covered by Buchanan's emphasis on methodological individualism; the nature of goods; the cost calculus applicable to rule-ordered relationships, and to the shared communities of understanding applicable to meta-preferences; and the importance of a civic religion.

Representative individuals acting in specifiable situations are the active agents who are making choices among alternative possibilities. The conjectures advanced about the action tendencies of representative individuals in those action situations are formulations about the relationship of hypothetical conditions to outcomes. This is equivalent to hypotheses about action tendencies of an artifactual nature, which are the analogue of cause-and-effect relationships. The world of rule-ordered relationships is composed of the soft constraints of human creation rather than the hard constraints of natural phenomena.

The logical conditions of constitutional democracies can be addressed only by taking constitutions seriously. Buchanan and his colleagues have rendered an essential service to the political science of the twenty-first century by providing us with the rationale for grounding our work in the constitutional level of analysis. Prior centuries provided sufficiently rich traditions of work with regard to the constitutional level of analysis that Buchanan's essential contribution may be neglected in references and bibliographies. His essential service was to persist in emphasizing the importance of taking constitutions seriously.

Every scholar in the cultural and social sciences and humanities needs to face the normative implications of their own endeavors. Is enlightenment value-free? Or does enlightenment have tendencies that affect the shaping and sharing of all values in the emergence of human civilizations? Was Tocqueville correct when he asserted: "It is evident to all alike that a *great* democratic revolution is going on among us" (1835/1990, 1:3, my emphasis)? Is this "the most uniform, the most ancient, and the most permanent tendency that is to be found in history" (1:3)? Is it the first of our duties "to educate democracy" (1:7)? What is the "new science of politics" that "is needed for a new world" (1:7)? What is the place of the logical foundations for constitutional democracy—a calculus of consent—in a new science of politics for a new world?

Critical reflection requires careful attention to the comparative analysis of other patterns of order in human societies, particularly conceptions and conditions that are constitutive of various types of regimes. John Clark and Aaron Wildavsky's *The Moral Collapse of Communism* (1990), Antoni Z. Kaminski's *An Institutional Theory of Communist Regimes* (1992), Brian Loveman's *The Constitution of Tyranny* (1993), Alexander Obolonsky's "The Drama of Russian Political History" (1996), Philip G. Roeder's *Red Sunset* (1993), Amos Sawyer's *The Emergence of Autocracy in Liberia* (1992), Mark Sproule-Jones's *Governments at Work* (1993), James Wunsch and Dele Olowu's *The Failure of the Centralized State* (1990/1995), and Tai-Shuenn Yang's "Property Rights and Constitutional Order in Imperial China" (1987) are among the contemporary works that take constitutions seriously in examining the aggregate structures of political regimes.

All such studies owe a substantial debt to Buchanan and his colleagues for taking constitutions seriously, whether or not that debt is acknowledged. Buchanan and his colleagues made the challenge, and many political scientists are rediscovering their roots in the long-standing traditions of political philosophy and jurisprudence. There is a place for reflection and choice in the constitution of order in human societies.

NOTE

1. Robert Warren's *Government in Metropolitan Regions* (1966) examines the political history that was constitutive of the system of local government authorities in Los Angeles County. Robert Bish's *The Public Economy of Metropolitan Areas* (1971) extends the mode of analysis developed in V. Ostrom, Tiebout, and Warren (1961). Elinor Ostrom, in the late 1960s, initiated studies of policing in the Indianapolis, Chicago, and St. Louis metropolitan areas (E. Ostrom and others 1973; E. Ostrom and Whitaker 1974; E. Ostrom, Parks, and Whitaker 1978). The National Science Foundation initiated a larger series of metropolitan studies with Lois MacGillivray, Elinor Ostrom, and E. S. Savas serving as principal investigators concerned with fire, police, and solid waste disposal, respectively. The Advisory Commission on Intergovernmental Relations (ACIR) later initiated a series of reports on *The Organization of Local Public Economies* (1987), on *Metropolitan Organization: The St. Louis Case* (1988), and on *Metropolitan Organization: The Allegheny County Case* (1992). Extended bibliographies are to be found in each of these publications and in a two-volume bibliography prepared by Fenton Martin (1989, 1992).

REFERENCES

Advisory Commission on Intergovernmental Relations [Ronald J. Oakerson]. 1987. *The Organization of Local Public Economies.* Washington, D.C.: ACIR.
——— [Ronald J. Oakerson, Roger B. Parks, and Henry A. Bell]. 1988. *Metropolitan Organization: The St. Louis Case.* Washington, D.C.: ACIR.
——— [Roger B. Parks and Ronald J. Oakerson]. 1992. *Metropolitan Organization: The Allegheny County Case.* Washington, D.C.: ACIR.
Bagehot, Walter. 1964. *The English Constitution,* ed. R. H. S. Crossman. London: C. A. Watts. (Originally published in 1865)
Bish, Robert L. 1971. *The Public Economy of Metropolitan Areas.* Chicago: Markham.
Blomquist, William. 1992. *Dividing the Waters: Governing Groundwater in Southern California.* San Francisco: Institute for Contemporary Studies Press.
Boulding, Kenneth E. 1963. "Towards a Pure Theory of Threat Systems." *American Economic Review* 53(May): 424–34.
Brennan, Geoffrey, and James M. Buchanan. 1985. *The Reason of Rules.* Cambridge: Cambridge University Press.

Buchanan, James M. 1968. *The Demand and Supply of Public Goods.* Chicago: Rand McNally.

———. 1979. *What Should Economists Do?* Indianapolis: Liberty.

Buchanan, James M., and Gordon Tullock. 1962. *The Calculus of Consent: Logical Foundations of Constitutional Democracy.* Ann Arbor: University of Michigan Press.

Clark, John, and Aaron Wildavsky. 1990. *The Moral Collapse of Communism: Poland as a Cautionary Tale.* San Francisco: Institute for Contemporary Studies Press.

Djilas, Milovan. 1957. *The New Class: An Analysis of the Communist System.* New York: Praeger.

Eucken, Walter. 1951. *The Foundations of Economics.* Chicago: University of Chicago Press. (Originally published in 1940)

Follett, Mary Parker. 1951. *Creative Experience.* New York: Peter Smith. (Originally published in 1924)

Hamilton, Alexander, John Jay, and James Madison. [1788]. *The Federalist,* edited by Edward M. Earle. New York: Modern Library.

Hess, Charlotte. 1996a. *Common Pool Resources and Collective Action: A Bibliography.* Vol. 3. Bloomington: Workshop in Political Theory and Policy Analysis, Indiana University.

———. 1996b. *Forestry Resources and Institutions: A Bibliography.* Bloomington: Workshop in Political Theory and Policy Analysis, Indiana University.

Hobbes, Thomas. 1949. *De Cive or the Citizen.* Ed. Sterling P. Lamprecht. New York: Appleton-Century-Crofts. (Originally published in 1642)

———. 1960. *Leviathan or the Matter, Forme, and Power of a Commonwealth Ecclesiasticall and Civil,* edited by Michael Oakeshott. Oxford: Basil Blackwell. (Originally published in 1651)

Kaminski, Antoni Z. 1992. *An Institutional Theory of Communist Regimes: Design, Function, and Breakdown.* San Francisco: Institute for Contemporary Studies Press.

Keohane, Robert O., and Elinor Ostrom (eds.). 1995. *Local Commons and Global Interdependence: Heterogeneity and Cooperation in Two Domains.* London: Sage.

Kiser, Larry L., and Elinor Ostrom. 1982. "The Three Worlds of Action: A Metatheoretical Synthesis of Institutional Approaches." In *Strategies of Political Inquiry,* edited by Elinor Ostrom (Beverly Hills, Calif.: Sage), 179–222.

Lam, Wai Fung. 1998. *Governing Irrigation Systems in Nepal: Institutions, Infrastructure, and Collective Action.* Oakland, Calif.: Institute for Contemporary Studies Press.

Lasswell, Harold D. 1936. *Politics: Who Gets What, When, How.* New York: McGraw-Hill.

Lasswell, Harold D., and Abraham Kaplan. 1950. *Power and Society: A Framework for Political Inquiry.* New Haven, Conn.: Yale University Press.

Lippmann, Walter. 1955. *The Public Philosophy.* New York: New American Library/Mentor Books.

Loveman, Brian. 1993. *The Constitution of Tyranny: Regimes of Exception in Spanish America.* Pittsburgh: University of Pittsburgh Press.

Martin, Fenton. 1989. *Common-Pool Resources and Collective Action: A Bibliography.* Vol. 1. Bloomington: Workshop in Political Theory and Policy Analysis, Indiana University.

———. 1992. *Common-Pool Resources and Collective Action: A Bibliography.* Vol. 2. Bloomington: Workshop in Political Theory and Policy Analysis, Indiana University.

Oakerson, Ronald J. 1978. "The Erosion of Public Highways: A Policy Analysis of the Eastern Kentucky Coal-Haul Road Problem." Ph.D. diss., Department of Political Science, Indiana University.

Obolonsky, Alexander. 1996. "The Drama of Russian Political History: System Against Individuality." Workshop in Political Theory and Policy Analysis, Indiana University. Unpublished paper.

Olson, Mancur. 1965. *The Logic of Collective Action: Public Goods and the Theory of Groups.* Cambridge, Mass.: Harvard University Press.

Ostrom, Elinor. 1990. *Governing the Commons: The Evolution of Institutions for Collective Action.* New York: Cambridge University Press.

———. 1998. "A Behavioral Approach to the Rational-Choice Theory of Collective Action." *American Political Science Review* 92(1, March): 1–22.

Ostrom, Elinor, William Baugh, Richard Guarasci, Roger Parks, and Gordon P. Whitaker. 1973. *Community Organization and the Provision of Police Services.* Beverly Hills, Calif.: Sage.

Ostrom, Elinor, Roger B. Parks, and Gordon P. Whitaker. 1978. *Patterns of Metropolitan Policing.* Cambridge, Mass.: Ballinger.

Ostrom, Elinor, and Gordon P. Whitaker. 1974. "Community Control and Governmental Responsiveness: The Case of Police in Black Communities." In *Improving the Quality of Urban Management,* edited by David Rogers and Willis Hawley. *Urban Affairs Annual Reviews,* vol. 8 (Beverly Hills, Calif.: Sage), 303–34.

Ostrom, Vincent. 1987. *The Political Theory of a Compound Republic: Designing the American Experiment.* 2d ed., rev. and enlarged. San Francisco: Institute for Contemporary Studies Press. (Originally published in 1971)

————. 1989. *The Intellectual Crisis in American Public Administration.* 2d ed. Tuscaloosa: University of Alabama Press. (Originally published in 1973)

————. 1997. *The Meaning of Democracy and the Vulnerability of Democracies: A Response to Tocqueville's Challenge.* Ann Arbor: University of Michigan Press.

Ostrom, Vincent, Charles M. Tiebout, and Robert Warren. 1961. "The Organization of Government in Metropolitan Areas: A Theoretical Inquiry." *American Political Science Review* 55(December): 831–42.

Roeder, Philip G. 1993. *Red Sunset: The Failure of Soviet Politics.* Princeton, N.J.: Princeton University Press.

Sawyer, Amos. 1992. *The Emergence of Autocracy in Liberia: Tragedy and Challenge.* San Francisco: Institute for Contemporary Studies Press.

Schlager, Edella, and Elinor Ostrom. 1992. "Property-Rights Regimes and Natural Resources: A Conceptual Analysis." *Land Economics* 68(3, August): 249–62.

Sproule-Jones, Mark. 1993. *Governments at Work: Canadian Parliamentary Federalism and Its Public Policy Effects.* Toronto: University of Toronto Press.

Tang, Shui Yan. 1992. *Institutions and Collective Action: Self-Governance in Irrigation.* San Francisco: Institute for Contemporary Studies Press.

Tocqueville, Alexis de. 1990. *Democracy in America.* 2 vols. Edited by Phillips Bradley. New York: Alfred A. Knopf. (Originally published in 1835 [vol. 1] and 1840 [vol. 2])

Tullock, Gordon. 1965. *The Politics of Bureaucracy.* Washington, D.C.: Public Affairs Press.

Warren, Robert O. 1966. *Government in Metropolitan Regions: A Reappraisal of Fractionated Political Organization.* Davis: Institute of Governmental Affairs, University of California.

Wilson, Woodrow. 1956. *Congressional Government: A Study in American Politics.* New York: Meridian. (Originally published in 1885)

Wunsch, James S., and Dele Olowu (eds.). 1995 [1990]. *The Failure of the Centralized State: Institutions and Self-Governance in Africa.* 2d ed. San Francisco: Institute for Contemporary Studies Press. (Originally published in 1990)

Yang, Tai-Shuenn. 1987. "Property Rights and Constitutional Order in Imperial China." Ph.D. diss., Department of Political Science, Indiana University.

JAMES M. BUCHANAN'S CONTRIBUTION TO PUBLIC ECONOMICS, POLITICAL PHILOSOPHY, AND POLITICAL SCIENCE

Thomas Schwartz

For a half-century or so, James Buchanan has invested prodigiously in a scheme to thwart the purpose of this book: the quantity and variety of own writings and those of his followers make a fair accounting of his contribution to political science impossible in a single essay. Instead, I shall highlight three Buchanan themes, all found in his landmark *The Calculus of Consent* with Gordon Tullock (1962), though not there alone: the reformation of public economics, the refinement and extension of contractarianism, and—for the sake of illustration as well as intrinsic interest—the critique of majoritarianism.

THE REFORMATION OF PUBLIC ECONOMICS

It is no wonder political science has imported the work of Buchanan and the public-choice school he founded. Political science has long been marked by an imbalance of trade, acquiring most of its theories and methods from elsewhere—from sociology and social psychology, from history and philosophy, from law and rhetoric and other subjects, not least economics. But Buchanan himself was less an exporter seeking foreign markets for preexisting economic products than a producer within economics of a new product, a generalization of economics itself. Because it patently helps explain the operation and effects of democratic institutions, this generalization found a ready market in import-hungry political science.

Economics is at least about markets, whose outcomes affect and are affected by government. There are market failures, positive and negative externalities and consequent inefficiencies, and the government might or might not intervene to remove or reduce them. Also, market outcomes reflect the distribution of initial endowments and the definition of property, and willy-nilly the government acts to preserve or change these things too. In public economics broadly conceived—in welfare theory, macroeconomics, and public finance—the interaction between markets and politics was central. But the polity was portrayed pretty much as a deus ex machina, a single exogenous actor. From a positive point of view, this actor was assigned no particular goal. From a normative point of view, it was the benevolent recipient of economic advice.

Buchanan generalized public economics to encompass the political process, the public choices that interact with private ones to produce economic outcomes, and to model and evaluate the two in much the same way, basing even the public ones on economic-like microfoundations. In this public choice approach, the ineluctable deus ex machina gives way to a cast of real characters. Like consumers and producers, these citizens and politicians and bureaucrats act in singly explicable ways, rationally pursuing their respective goals. Constitutional and other public procedures turn their several decisions into one public choice—public rather than private, yet still the creature of naught but individual decisions. Four things made this approach fruitful as well as possible:

Interaction Because, as public economics had always emphasized, economic outcomes cannot be explained in isolation from political ones, public choice was much more than an analogy, much more than an economic style of reasoning applied to political behavior. It was an attempt—a successful one, allowing for the fact that no single style of analysis can explain everything all at once—to capture the political economy in one theoretical swoop.

Two Hats Consumers and producers are also citizens, some of them politically active: the same actors directly affect even narrowly economic outcomes in two ways, both now accommodated by one analytical approach. An analytical separation of these political and economic hats is often convenient and sometimes unavoidable but never fully general. It is akin to analytically separating markets, to ignoring the effects of a petroleum shortage on the prices of ponies and pogo sticks. Like money, democracy gives economic actors more strategies for pursuing their economic goals.

Similar Behavior Economics treats of the exchange of endowments, if anything, but much of politics likewise involves the exchange of endowments. Sometimes legislators explicitly trade votes on separate bills or parts of bills. More often they achieve the same effect implicitly: they vote on single package bills drafted by "market"-making political "brokers." Similarly do electoral candidates offer larger packages to voters, brokering enormous multilateral trades. *The Calculus of Consent* is probably best remembered among political scientists for its celebration of the importance of political exchange, thus broadly conceived.

Similar Problems Perhaps Buchanan's greatest insight was that the externalities and inefficiencies that had occasioned welfare economics are mirrored, maybe magnified, in the public sector. Government might be able to eliminate or lessen some of the externalities of private exchange, but to allow the government to do so, at least by familiar means, is to let political actors create similar externalities: the public doctor who treats private disease might catch and spread it. Indeed, if market externalities are somewhat exceptional, political ones are rather the rule. For example, except when unanimous, winning majorities perforce impose external costs on losing minorities. The benefits of government intervention may be worth such costs, in particular cases, or in general, or on balance, but then again they may not be. Either way we cannot know until we have generalized economics *au Buchanan* by modeling the behavior of citizens in their dual capacity.

  None of this is meant to suggest that Buchanan has plumped for a "rational-actor paradigm" to replace all other analytical styles in political science. Other styles are legitimate, sometimes better, even in narrowly political-economic contexts. For example, Buchanan's (1960, 59–64) own well-known idea of "fiscal illusion" is more cognitive than rationalistic: democratic polities tend to overspend on projects that concentrate benefits and diffuse costs because voters find the former more salient than the latter. Again, Brennan and Buchanan (1985) argue that the durability of democracies depends on a sociological factor, a shared "civic religion." Buchanan's contribution to political science was to expand what had been economics, not to shrink what had been political science: his manifesto called for more politics in economics rather than more economics in politics. His general approach and specific findings did spread to political science, but that is because he lured some bright young political scientists, such as Vincent Ostrom and the late William Riker, to the commodious umbrella of public choice that they might help him replace despotism with democracy in public economics, because political science is always on the lookout for new imports, because the behavioral revolution in political science had matured enough to tolerate some institutionalist balance, which *The Calculus of Consent* promised and the public-choice school quickly started to provide, and because, as I have argued elsewhere (Schwartz 1989b), Buchanan's school continued the theoretical tradition of the Federalist Papers, long honored but lately neglected by political scientists.

Public economics had always been normative, and so is public choice. Buchanan is a contractarian: for him, the acceptable political constitutions are those that could be the creatures of unanimous consent, of a social contract. That is why his advice about the choice of constitutional arrangements is offered to the typical citizen—and why his advice is mostly about the choice of constitutional arrangements.

Of course, public choice is positive too, concerned with explanation and prediction as well as evaluation and prescription. Though a work of normative theory in its stated purpose and its very name, *The Calculus of Consent* repeatedly accentuates the positive. The reasons are two. First, among the countless observations of behavior in an institutional context that one might conceivably try to explain or predict, one must select but a few, and Buchanan's normative criterion offers a principle of selection: look for behavior of concern to the typical citizen, whose preferences bear on the contractarian test. Second, the evaluation of institutions requires explanation and prediction of the behavior they allow and encourage: to evaluate institutions, one must first discover how they work, not only what they allow and forbid but what incentives they create, hence what individual strategies and public choices are likely to follow their adoption. This positive prerequisite of normative inquiry is hidden from view when public economics ignores the *process* of public choice by fancying a benevolent despot who can touch his scepter to any point in the production-possibility set and instantaneously effect a final distribution of all public and private products and their costs.

REFINEMENT OF CONTRACTARIANISM

Political science has long been anchored, if loosely so, in a literary canon, the timeless classics of political philosophy. Because it neatly solves a problem that had always bedeviled attempts to formulate the social-contract theory, *The Calculus of Consent* must be regarded as an addition to that canon.

Absent government, the denizens of any society would suffer from a massive problem of cooperation, or collective action. They would find themselves in an n-person prisoners' dilemma composed in a way of many smaller ones: all would benefit from certain patterns of mutual cooperation—keeping contracts, respecting property, paying taxes for the common defense—but the benefit to each would come from the cooperation of others, not himself, his own cooperation benefiting them and not him. So each would have some incentive to defect from those patterns (break contracts, steal, refuse to pay taxes) for want of a common enforcer. Thus, a well-drawn social contract to establish government would be mutually advantageous and command unanimous consent in a suitably constructed bargaining situation. The contractarian test of a just (or otherwise commendable) constitution is that it *could* be the creature of such a contract; obviously it is too much to demand an actual historical contract.

But this formulation leaves an apparent gap: which constitutions would thus command unanimous agreement appears to depend on the *base point*, the initial situation in which the fancied agreement is to be struck. Consider the Crusoe-Friday "society" portrayed in figure 3.1. For base point A, a mutually advantageous contract must create a constitution expected to put Crusoe's and Friday's utility incomes somewhere inside ABC but not on AB or AC. To represent a reasonable bargain, not just something they would accept in lieu of A, such a constitution must move their expectations to somewhere around the middle of BC. Because base point A is unfairly biased in Crusoe's favor, would be a contract that moved their expectations from A to any other point in ABC.

Here I have made an interpersonal comparison of utility, but that was inessential. We can make the point in terms of generalized (not necessarily two-dimensional) Edgeworth boxes based on physical goods—including the negative goods of investment—that are available to Crusoe and Friday and determine their welfare: if the basepoint distribution of initial endowments is skewed in Crusoe's favor, so will be the contract locus.

The devil of contractarianism has always been the difficulty of defining a fair base point. For Thomas Hobbes (1651) it was the state of nature, or complete anarchy. There one finds a state of "war of all against all," in which the life of man is "solitary, poor, nasty, brutish, and short." There one also finds a sort of unstable equality, or better, an equality borne of instability. Though some men are naturally more powerful than others, the individually weak can seek power in numbers, friends to fight foes. But alliances shift, leaving no subgroup in permanent control. A problem with this idea and some later ones is that it is hard for real people to imagine themselves in the state of nature: in assuming away government we must assume away much more, else

Figure 3.1 Base-Point Bias in a Two-Person Social Contract

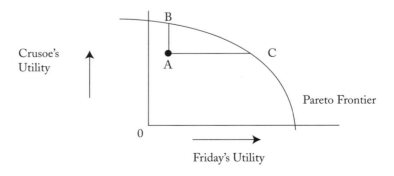

there is no advantage in government, but it is hard to tell just how different we and our circumstances would be. Another problem is that if all of society can make an effective contract then so can subgroups, and if subgroups can then one of them might conquer and dominate the rest, destroying Hobbes's shaky equality. Indeed, Hobbes argued that one person or small group would receive the surrender of all others, creating as skewed a contract as one can imagine. To defend it one must show what plainly is not so: that no fairer constitution is feasible.

John Locke's (1689) base point was a more benign state of nature, a condition of abundance in which each person acquired property by mixing his labor with nature—by tilling a field, for example—but always leaving "as much and as good" for others. Offhand, that condition seems fair enough to ensure a fair contract, but its meaning is obscure. A water polluter does not leave water for others that is "as good," but what if he leaves manufactured goods more prized by others than pristine water? And how different is he from a farmer who paints his barn red to the acute irritation of his red-averse neighbor? If hunting takes time and effort, then a hunter who bags a stag has probably depleted the *local* stag pool enough that his neighbors must travel a bit farther to find some. Has he left as much and as good for them? More generally, men in Locke's state of nature enjoy "natural rights" to "property"—to "life, liberty, and estate"—which the contract must protect while adding the advantages of mutual cooperation, but it is far from clear where a man's rights leave off, and to mark them off with any precision is to make their definition and not the contract bear most of the normative burden when the good constitutions are winnowed from the bad.

For Jean-Jacques Rousseau (1762) the base point was a condition of equal property—whatever that means—in a very small society with a simple agricultural economy. To real societies, obviously, such a base point can have no application.

For all three theorists, and for the contemporary Lockeans Robert Nozick (1974) and David Gauthier (1986), the base point is a *point of reversion*, the outcome in default of any government, hence any contract. For John Rawls (1971) there is no point of reversion: like dutiful jurors, Rawls's fancied contractors *must* agree to *something*—if nothing else then a continuation of anarchy. Rawls does have a base point of sorts. It is still the fancied circumstance in which a contract is struck, but it is no longer the point of reversion, there being none. Specifically, it is a circumstance of utter ignorance about one's own peculiar condition: no one knows his social status, nor his distinctive talents and disabilities, and no one knows anything about his own utility function except that it is positive in "basic goods," these defined by an ad hoc list. Then there is no self-interested bias that might skew the contract. Then, however, the individual's calculus of consent is driven by little more than his attitude to uncertainty. Yet he cannot even know what that attitude is unless it is part of his general knowledge of mankind. Because people do differ in attitudes to uncertainty, I fail to see how anything much can be deduced, and I am not surprised that Rawls himself substitutes assertion for deduction. Some have partly filled the gap by assuming uniform attitudes to uncertainty, but as is well known, what can be deduced about the content of the social contract depends on what specific attitude is assumed (Harsanyi 1975).

Buchanan too allows contractors a fair measure of uncertainty. But he does not do so to achieve fairness, or a lack of bias. Instead, he does so because he is concerned with the contractual choice of constitutions rather than concrete policies. Under complete certainty the chosen constitution would be extremely specific, tantamount to a policy package except where certain questions are left to chance as a way of securing either arbitrary coordination or a convex combination of conflicting policies.

Hobbes, Locke, Rousseau, and Rawls all start with purportedly fair base points (equal power, equal rights, equal property, equal ignorance) to ensure fair contracts. Consequently, their normative test is not consent—or not only consent—but independent criteria of fairness, applied to their base points and reflected in any contracts struck therein. By contrast, *Buchanan has no normative test but consent.* His base point is real, not fancied, and it is not a point of reversion. There people know everything real people do know about themselves and their circumstances, but no one, however powerful and prosperous, can use such knowledge to demand a contract biased in his favor because the base point does not automatically prevail in default of any contract.

Buchanan sidesteps the base-point problem by making the chosen constitution all-encompassing. It says how public choices are made, but also which choices are to remain private. No rights or liberties or spheres of privacy are marked off in advance as part of a reversion point: *there is no point of reversion.* No personal distinctions are hidden in advance, behind a Rawlsian "veil of ignorance": *there is no artificial ignorance* about invidious differences. Whether we are free to wiggle our noses without government regulation is part of the contract. Because everything is up for grabs, no one has any protected endowments to use for bargaining advantage. Contractors would quickly agree to nose-wiggle freedom and much else. But agree they must or wiggle they won't. You may know that your nose-wiggling ability is superior to mine, but you cannot use that fact to secure a better contract by threatening to outwiggle me if no agreement is reached: nasal freedom is not marked off in advance, as part of a reversion point. True, a wealthy and powerful person might see some advantage in not contracting, in entering into a relation of anarchy with those who do. But once in the contracting game, he must bargain (or we are to fancy that he must) from a base point where all liberties and possessions are left to the contract: To preserve his superior wealth and power, he must secure the consent of fellow contractors. The outcome in default of any agreement is not the status quo, and it is not the status quo minus government, minus the depletion of resources, or minus all self-knowledge. *There is no default outcome,* or if there is then it is a society of us—like mannequins, figures just like us but immobile, three-dimensional cross-sections of four-dimensional us, unable to exploit any actual endowments for want of a contract to specify their rights and liberties.

Objection Absent a point of reversion, it is hard to predict a reasonable solution to the bargaining game among social contractors, to say what a fair bargain—the content of the contract—would be.

Reply So it is. But even with a point of reversion there is a problem: what we count as a fair bargain, or a reasonable solution to the bargaining game, is quite sensitive to what we assume, and in this field there is a variety of reasonable-looking assumptions that have conflicting and sometimes paradoxical consequences (see, for example, Roth 1985). On the other hand, the want of any reversion point does not block solvability. Except that they know less about future distributions of benefits and costs, contractors are like divorcing marriage partners who must somehow divide their children and pets, their cars and artworks and whatnot, or find a rule or procedure for doing so. There is no reversion division that prevails in default of any agreement; even a judge or arbitrator would try to figure out what the divorcing couple themselves, or their cooler-headed counterparts, would be willing to accept. Steven Brams and Alan Taylor (1996) have couched this reversion-free bargaining problem in very broad terms and shown that a straightforward generalization of the old "you divide, I choose" procedure yields a solution in every case.

Buchanan assumes people are rational in the sense of maximizing utility functions. Whether all real or reasonable choice functions are rationalizable by real-valued functions, weak orderings, or binary relations of any sort is open to question (Schwartz 1972), but he uses his assumption most in admittedly simplified models, and the basic approach would probably survive a relaxation of the classical conditions of "rational" choice. More important, Buchanan assumes that people are rational in the sense of attending to consequences and seeking to fulfill their own goals, but I do not see why anyone would object to that. Often Buchanan speaks of self-interested individuals. But he never insists on any sharp or narrow definition, and for him as for James Madison, self-interest is an "even if" hypothesis (Schwartz 1989b). Devils and lunatics, who might selflessly seek evil goals, are ignored, but a good social contract should not require that men be angels. It should be acceptable and durable *even if* men are self-interested.

Buchanan's contractarian test for constitutions is still pretty abstract, but its applicability is enhanced by three means. First, some normative judgments are drawn from a weaker test, Pareto efficiency—weaker because every unanimously agreeable contract must at least be Pareto-efficient, but pretty clearly only certain Pareto-efficient ones are unanimously agreeable. Second, much of Buchanan's reasoning is about the benefits and costs of alternative institutions to a typical individual whose distinguishing characteristics are not material to the given argument. This use of a "veil of ignorance" is merely heuristical: unlike Rawls, Buchanan does not postulate any normative test independent of unanimous consent. Last and most important, much can be learned about better and worse institutional arrangements short of finding an ideal constitution, the exact content of the fancied contract. As discussed later, for example, *The Calculus of Consent* argues that a typical citizen might well find simple-majority rule in a unicameral legislature more costly than supermajority rules or bicameralism.

EXTENSION OF CONTRACTARIANISM

Hobbes thought his contractarian test would select an absolute sovereign, maybe an assembly but more likely a dictator. Many regimes are imaginable, but the denizens of Hobbes's kakatopia must agree to one. To solve their cooperation problem they must solve a *coordination* problem: how to achieve a common goal when more than one pattern of behavior (general obedience to any of several candidates for sovereignty) would do the job but all must follow the same pattern (obey the same sovereign). If we agree to meet in Moscow at a certain time but fail to say where, each of us would likely head for Red Square. It is the focal solution, the most salient of the possible solutions. Hobbes's Red Square was the de facto sovereign, or the closest approximation to one—the strongest baron, war lord, or gang leader around. Locke thought this remedy for the external costs suffered in the state of nature was probably worse than the disease, and he proposed instead a system of limited, representative government. There was still a coordination problem: citizens agree that elected representatives should govern, but what if there are two candidates? The focal solution is numerical: let majorities choose. Rousseau too thought majority rule a reasonable way to coordinate, but on policy in an assembly of the whole: his city-states were direct democracies. None of these three theorists supply much more detail. Nor does Rawls, whose contractarian test picks certain principles of justice that in turn pick liberal democracies with a social safety net, or so he contends: the steps from test to principles to constitution require more faith than I have.

By contrast, Buchanan offers more than a name or short sketch of a regime type, though of course less than a full-blown constitution for any particular state. He has initiated a potentially prodigious body of theory about constitutional details, the incentives they create, and their consequent costs and benefits for the typical individual evaluating them as a party to the social contract. What is important here is Buchanan's insight that the relevant questions about the effects of alternative institutional arrangements require theory in the best sense: a growing, testable, revisable, deductively articulated body of findings.

What has been found so far, and how much can be attributed to Buchanan? A great merit of Buchanan's contractarianism is its breadth: virtually any finding, deductive or empirical, about the consequences of adopting an institution contributes to the general enterprise. Of course, there are specific ideas bearing Buchanan's signature; I discuss the most famous in the next section. Also, there are strands of reasoning that he initiated or plainly influenced by offering the first sustained treatment of certain ideas (vote trading, political externalities, the citizen's calculus of consent, majority versus unanimity rule, and fiscal illusion, to mention a few); Dennis Mueller (1989, 1997) has collected many of these strands, which continue to be visible in *Public Choice, Constitutional Political Economy,* and other periodicals. Buchanan has also worked to find diverse scholars whose research bears on the contractarian enterprise and to gather them round the standard of public choice that they might see each other as collaborators. It is largely through him that the Anglo-American world knows of the voluntarist and other Continental schools of public finance (among other things, he translated Wicksell and Lindahl from German), and through him that we see the works of Duncan Black and Kenneth Arrow, Anthony Downs and Mancur Olson, James Coleman and William Riker and other founding fathers as contributions to the same intellectual enterprise. Alone and with Gordon Tullock, he himself authored some of the founding ideas, but he also did more than the others to organize them, in part by starting the Public Choice Society and in part by framing the unifying themes of a political economy that encompasses the political process and of a modernized, simplified contractarian test that invites a bounty of research findings.

CRITIQUE OF MAJORITARIANISM

Buchanan's most famous constitutional recommendation, and the one most fully elaborated in *The Calculus of Consent,* is that simple-majority rule is often inferior, from the typical social contractor's point of view, to unanimity and other special-majority rules. Thus, Buchanan had to challenge the conventional wisdom that there is something special and especially democratic about simple-majority rule. I shall challenge the challenge: it is partly true, no more. Still, the reasons for its partial truth are sweeping in their implications (some drawn out later in this essay), and half a truth is invaluable when it shows orthodoxy to be half false.

The Challenge

The basic point (from Buchanan 1954) I have already remarked: unless unanimous, winning majorities always impose external costs on the losing minorities. Unanimity rule would bar such externalities. Ordinarily, however, a unanimous winning majority would be costly to negotiate: in effect, it would require brokering a vote trade that gave something to everyone, something each valued enough to pay his share for it plus other "somethings" for everyone else. For any given category of centralized collective decisions, we might require a quota $q > n/2$ to take a decision. As q gets larger, external costs decrease, totaling 0 when $q = n$, when there is no losing minority to suffer the external cost. But decision costs increase, hitting a maximum when $q = n$. Therefore, total net costs, assumed to be of naught but these two sorts, are minimized at some point q_m with $n/2 < q_m < n$. In some cases, q_m may be a bare majority, but in others it is n, in still others in between.

Like market externalities, the external costs created by simple-majority rule—or, more generally, by quota rules with $q_m < n$—can lead to Pareto-inefficient outcomes. To cite the simplest version of the *Calculus of Consent* road-repair example (originally from Tullock 1959), assume simple-majority rule and suppose Messrs. 1, 2, and 3 must vote on three bills, *a, b,* and *c,* that distribute net benefits as in figure 3.2. Each bill would benefit a majority, which has an incentive to pass it and impose an external cost on the loser. For example, *a* would benefit Messrs. 1 and 2 at the expense of 3. Each bill is inefficient: net cost exceeds net benefit. That is to be expected if the bill is written by or on behalf of the majority. In writing *a,* for example, Messrs. 1 and 2 are likely to set expenditures above a cost-effective level because they pay only part of the cost: simple-majority rule lets them foist part of it on Mr. 3. But if all three bills pass, each voter nets −1—compared with 0 if none pass. Majority-ruled government might eliminate some of the prisoners' dilemmas, or collective-action problems, that would arise in an unregulated private sector, but it can also create new ones. Here we have a three-player prisoners' dilemma, the players being all the two-person coalitions.

Figure 3.2 External Costs of Majority Decisions

	Mr. 1	Mr. 2	Mr. 3
a	4	4	-9
b	4	-9	4
c	-9	4	4

Messrs. 1, 2, and 3 can avoid the problem by making a deal—a vote trade of sorts—that requires them to vote against all three bills, or to vote for variants of those bills that lower spending to cost-effective levels. Then, of course, they incur greater decision costs, but that is part of Buchanan's point.

True, the collective-choice rules found in practice are not all quota rules, a rather simple category used for easy illustration of the social contractor's decision calculus and of the too-easy equation of democracy with simple-majority rule. *The Calculus of Consent* shows, for example, that in a bicameral legislature with simple-majority rule in either house, how much the houses differ in their bases of representation—how much their constituencies cross-cut rather than coincide—works like the magnitude of q_m: it diminishes external costs.

The Problem of Private-Sector Externalities

Suppose each bill would limit or eliminate a private-sector external cost caused by the unregulated actions of the loser. So, for example, Mr. 3 might be an air polluter and *a* might ban or reduce his polluting behavior. Then, it may seem, the cost of *a* must include not only the decision cost, minimized by simple-majority rule, and the external cost of voting, minimized by unanimity rule, but also the external cost of Mr. 3's private behavior, again minimized by simple-majority rule. *The Calculus of Consent* treats of the costs *ignored* by traditional welfare economics but apparently ignores the costs *addressed* by welfare economics.

Even under unanimity rule, however, Messrs. 1 and 2 can cut 3's pollution by buying his consent with an additional benefit for him. Sometimes that sort of thing seems reasonable, sometimes not. But if it is not, then it must be too costly. Then the added cost is a decision cost, a cost of negotiating a more inclusive vote trade. The individual's decision calculus needs no separate parameter for private-sector externalities because they are already reckoned in decision costs. In saying so, of course, we must take care to appreciate that decision costs include more than the time cost of transactions. They also include the tax cost of financing some benefit for every consenter, hence something for everyone when unanimous consent is required. *The Calculus of Consent* might have been clearer about this point. It does not refute Buchanan's thesis about which decision rules minimize which sorts of cost. It does show the case for unanimity and against simple-majority rule to be weaker than it had seemed, the decision costs of unanimity being greater.

The Locke-May Objection

Consider a voting rule, *R*, for choosing between alternatives two at a time. When *R* is used, there are two feasible alternatives, say *x* and *y*, everyone votes for one of them or abstains, and the outcome is *x* or *y* or a tie. Suppose R meets three ostensibly democratic conditions. One is *anonymity*, or independence of the labeling of voters: if *x* is chosen over *y*, and if two voters switch votes, each voting (or abstaining) as the other had, then *x* is still chosen. Another condition is *neutrality*, or independence of the labeling of alternatives: if *x* is chosen over *y*, and if *x* and *y* are now replaced by *x'* and *y'* on everyone's ballot (abstainers still abstaining), then *x'* is now chosen over *y'*. The third condition is *positive responsiveness*, or fragility of ties: if *x* ties *y* with some voters abstaining, and if some of the abstainers now vote for *x*, all else staying the same, then that is enough to break the tie in x's favor. Obviously simple-majority rule has all three properties. Kenneth May's (1952) famous theorem says that *only* simple-majority rule does.

This argument does not conclusively show that simple-majority rule must be adopted in all cases. How could it, given the Pareto inefficiency shown before? It does show that *there is something special* about simple-majority rule (further, see Rae 1969). Take any quota rule with quota $q > n/2 + 1$; maybe $q = n$. The condition it flouts is neutrality. In a choice between collective action x and collective inaction y (status quo or other default outcome), the assumed quota rule is biased in y's favor. Suppose half the voters vote for x, the rest for y. Because x has fewer than q supporters, y wins. Now replace x by $x' = y$ and y by $y' = x$ on every ballot. Because x still has fewer than q supporters, y still wins, contrary *neutrality*.

Obviously Buchanan has assumed that the typical individual's decision calculus depends on more than external and decision costs: it reflects a bias in favor of collective inaction, the status quo. That is often reasonable, I think: to plan their lives, citizens must be able to count on some questions as more or less settled, on some prevailing policies as hard or impossible to change without their consent. Still, the bias is sometimes unjustified. It is always unjustified in Locke's fancied case, where it has been agreed to elect a government with certain powers and voters must coordinate round one of two contenders. There, at least, neither alternative is privileged, so neither can be singled out in advance as "inaction," as the default outcome when no real "choice" is made. In such cases, neutrality is reasonable, and so for that matter are anonymity and positive responsiveness, making simple-majority rule uniquely acceptable.

Still, if *The Calculus of Consent* overstates the case against simple-majority rule, it states an underappreciated case: the too-easy equation of democracy with majoritarianism cannot be extended much beyond Locke's problem of mere coordination without ignoring those externalities that may be somewhat exceptional in unregulated markets but abound in politics.

PARTIES

Buchanan's insight about the importance for constitutional choice of majority-rule externalities carries profound lessons, positive and normative, some not yet fully drawn or widely grasped. One concerns the emergence of political parties.

To appreciate the virtues and shortcomings of simple-majority rule, let us ask how a majority-ruled legislature (or town meeting) might sidestep the Pareto inefficiency of our little example. Compared with electors, legislators are few enough that they might agree to abide by a norm of unanimity though constitutionally allowed to flout it. That changes the distribution of net benefits in the example from $(-1, -1, -1)$ to $(0, 0, 0)$.

But if three legislators can reach and abide by an agreement to vote en bloc, so can any two. Messrs. 1 and 2, for example, can agree to stick together on all votes, or all votes of a certain category. Presumably they would then vote for a and against b and c. That further changes the distribution to $(4, 4, -9)$, worse for Mr. 3 but better for Messrs. 1 and 2. Even if we contrive to let only efficient bills reach the floor—changing 4 to 3 and -9 to -5, for example—Messrs. 1 and 2 still gain from sticking together.

To the extent that a legislative majority acts thus as a permanent bloc, not a fugacious vote-trading coalition, it resembles a *political party*. Yes, as any good student of Buchanan would quickly remark, party platforms are *implicit* vote trades. But as the best among them would quickly add, so are practically all legislative acts. Still, a coalition of legislators who trade votes on some issues need not stick together on all or most issues, and those who do are very like political parties (though also like disciplined *coalitions* of parties). So far the One-Two Party is only legislative, not electoral. However, it has an incentive to protect its brand name at election time, and those left out have an incentive to mount a challenge. The election rule might encourage fragmentation of the legislative majority party, but some do not.

Of course, even the most disciplined legislative parties find it hard to discipline their electorates: electoral competition induces periodic realignments. That may temper the ruthlessness of winners in imposing external costs on losers. But it also means that our *a–b–c* scenario, now blocked in the short run, can recur over a longer period at the electoral level, the three successive and winning bills replaced by three successive and winning party manifestos. Since parties encourage responsibility for broad policy, that may not be so bad: I simply do not know whether the typical citizen should favor the unanimity or partisan solution to *The Calculus of Consent*'s Paretian problem.

What you and I do know is that the partisan solution is a widely observed one when simple-majority rule is constitutionally allowed. So I have argued elsewhere (Schwartz 1989a). John Aldrich (1995) has used this argument, drawn from *The Calculus of Consent*, as the basis for a novel analysis of the history and behavior of political parties in America. Here is a good example of the nonobvious potency of Buchanan's idea about the importance of majority-rule externalities.

However explicable, the structural incentive to form a majority party may seem unfair. Some contend that a fairer system would have no majority party but several smaller ones, represented in proportion to their electoral votes. I have shown elsewhere, however, that there simply is no such thing as fair representation (Schwartz 1995). A summary of my argument would take us too far afield. I mention the matter in part because that argument is yet another lesson drawn directly from Buchanan's insight that simple-majority voting can be unacceptably costly to losing minorities.

PORK

Pork-barrel legislation in Congress presents a paradox for Buchanan. *Distributive legislation*—legislation providing separate local benefits, or pork, for the several constituencies of the winning majority—is notable for its inefficiency, but also for its unanimous support (Schwartz 1994, 15–16, note 1). As David Stockman (1975) showed, pork is not peculiar to public works: once passed, the initially controversial social and educational policies of the Great Society quickly turned into pork barrels, inefficient but unopposed. How can unanimity spawn inefficiency? *The Calculus of Consent* suggests that the explanation must be the decision cost of building a winning coalition or else the external cost of majority voting. But if the former is the culprit, then why do coalition builders not stop building long before unanimity is secured? And if the latter, then where is the losing minority that must bear the external cost?

Start with the "electoral connection" assumption that each of n legislators is a good agent of his constituents: his maximand is not their welfare as such but his *marginal product* for them, how big a difference he has made in their behalf. Assume simple-majority rule, but suppose the legislature constructs a pork-barrel omnibus by letting each legislator pick an amount x to be spent on projects for his constituents. Let $B(x)$ be the benefit his constituents get from expenditure x, and $C(x)$ the cost to them (not to others) of x. To keep things manageably simple, let all n constituencies have the same benefit and cost functions, B and C. Because costs are spread through the tax systems, the *total* cost of x is not $C(x)$—that is only one constituency's share—but $nC(x)$. And because all n legislators join the pork-barrel coalition, the cost of the legislation for one constituency is not $C(x)$ but again $nC(x)$. Assume as usual that B increases at a decreasing rate ($B'(x) > 0 > B''(x)$), while C increases at a constant or increasing rate ($C'(x) > 0 \leq C''(x)$). Then, if a legislator were a dictator, he would pick x^* in figure 3.3.

That would maximize $B(x) - C(x)$, a dictator's marginal product and the net benefit for his constituents. Of course, a U.S. congressman is no dictator. But his marginal product for his constituents is still a dictator's whopping $B(x^*) - C(x^*)$. That is what his constituents would lose if he dropped out of the pork-barrel coalition: presumably the other $n - 1$ legislators would stay in and not raise or lower x^* for their own constituencies since doing so would only reduce their own marginal products, likewise $B(x^*) - C(x^*)$. Why should a small majority let every legislator join the coalition? Because, if we start with a moderate-size winning majority, each legislator has a maximum marginal product of $B(x^*) - C(x^*)$, and that does not decrease when the coalition expands. The obvious efficiency problem is that each *legislator* fares best at x^*, but each *constituency* would fare better at x^{**}; such is the most notable peculiarity of the two-level voting required by representative democracy—an institutional complication ignored by *The Calculus of Consent* and much later literature.

Besides assuming a particular procedure for the construction of pork-barrel omnibuses, I have assumed that all constituencies have the same B and C. But none of that is essential to the demonstration that perfect agency makes the winning coalition unanimous and the consequent legislation inefficient (Schwartz 1994).

Figure 3.3 The Porcine Incentive of Local Agents

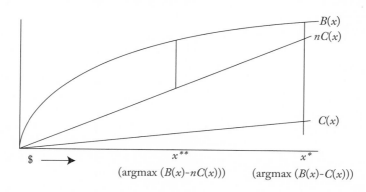

Although a plausible legislative-agency model explained the observed combination of unanimity and inefficient pork, it assumed simple-majority rule—or anyway a decision rule short of unanimity. Oddly, perhaps, a constitutional *rule* of unanimity would have blocked this pork-barrel paradox. The reason $B(x^*) - C(x^*)$ is any given legislator's marginal product for his constituency is precisely that unanimity is not required, that his vote is not needed for the rest of the pork barrel: if he alone defected, all others would still pick x^*, and the net benefit for his constituency would drop from $B(x^*) - nC(x^*)$ to $-(n-1)\,C(x^*) = C(x^*) - nC(x^*)$, making his marginal product from x^* equal to the one minus the other, or $B(x^*) - nC(x^*) - (C(x^*) - nC(x^*)) = B(x^*) - C(x^*)$. Now assume unanimity rule. Then if one legislator defected from the coalition behind x^* and insisted instead on x^{**}, his constituency's net benefit would rise from $B(x^*) - nC(x^*)$ to $B(x^{**}) - nC(x^{**})$, making his marginal product from x^* no longer the large positive $B(x^*) - C(x^*)$ but the negative $B(x^*) - nC(x^*) - (B(x^{**}) - nC(x^{**}))$. It is precisely because unanimity is not required that Congress unanimously adopts inefficient distributive legislation: the unanimous support for inefficient projects actually vindicates Buchanan (contrary to Schwartz 1994, 4, where I fallaciously contended that the inefficient universalism observed in Congress refutes Buchanan and Tullock—along with Wicksell and Lindahl).

CONCLUSION

There is no need to marshal evidence of the value for political science of the work of a Nobel laureate in economics who has spent much of his life theorizing about political institutions. Instead, I have dusted off some long-familiar but long-neglected themes from *The Calculus of Consent*. Jim Buchanan took up politics, not to conquer political science but to reform public economics. He revived the old social-contract idea as a selection principle for constitutions, but he also *revised* that idea, showing how consent can serve as a normative test independent of others—something the classical contractarians and Rawls failed to do. Instead of wielding that test, as others had done, to defend one very general form of government, he used it to start an open, unending inquiry into innumerable questions of institutional architecture, himself addressing a few of them—an important few, but still and inevitably a few. Instead of taking majority rule for granted as the defining ideal of democracy and fussing about how to approximate it when the ideal is somehow ill defined or not practicable, he questioned whether it is a good idea at all, taking a critical tack whose lessons, positive and normative, still unfold.

Thanks to the UCLA Senate for financial support, to James Alt for an apt critique of an earlier draft, to Brian Yano for able assistance, and to Pradhip Mehta, Charles Plott, and the late, great Mancur Olson for early advice.

REFERENCES

Aldrich, John H. 1995. *Why Parties?: The Origin and Transformation of Party Politics in America*. Chicago: University of Chicago Press.

Brams, Steven J., and Alan D. Taylor. 1996. *Fair Division*. Cambridge: Cambridge University Press.

Brennan, Geoffrey, and James M. Buchanan. 1985. *The Reason of Rules.* Cambridge: Cambridge University Press.

Buchanan, James M. 1954. "Individual Choice in Voting and the Market." *Journal of Political Economy* 62: 334–43.

———. 1960. *Fiscal Theory and Political Economy.* Chapel Hill: University of North Carolina Press.

———. 1975. *The Limits of Liberty.* Chicago: University of Chicago Press.

Buchanan, James M., and Gordon Tullock. 1962. *The Calculus of Consent.* Ann Arbor: University of Michigan Press.

Gauthier, David. 1986. *Morals by Agreement.* Oxford: Clarendon Press.

Harsanyi, John C. 1975. "Can the Maximin Principle Serve as a Basis for Morality?: A Critique of John Rawls's Theory." *American Political Science Review* 69: 594–606.

Hobbes, Thomas. 1946. *Leviathan,* edited by Michael Oakshott. Oxford: Basil Blackwell. (Originally published in 1651)

Locke, John. 1960. "An Essay Concerning the True Original, Extent, and End of Civil Government." In *Two Treaties of Government,* edited by Harold Laslett. Cambridge: Cambridge University Press. (Originally published in 1689)

May, Kenneth O. 1952. "A Set of Independent, Necessary, and Sufficient Conditions for Simple-Majority Decision." *Econometrica* 20: 680–84.

Mueller, Dennis C. 1989. *Public Choice.* Cambridge: Cambridge University Press.

———(ed.). 1997. *Perspectives in Public Choice.* Cambridge: Cambridge University Press.

Nozick, Robert. 1974. *Anarchy, State and Utopia.* New York: Basic Books.

Rae, Douglas W. 1969. "Decision Rules and Individual Values in Constitutional Choice." *American Political Science Review* 63: 40–56.

Rawls, John. 1971. *A Theory of Justice.* Cambridge, Mass.: Harvard University Press.

Roth, Alvin (ed.). 1985. *Game Theoretic Models of Bargaining.* Cambridge: Cambridge University Press.

Rousseau, Jean-Jacques. 1923. *Le contrat social.* In *The Social Contract and Discourses,* translated by G. D. H. Cole. London: Dent/Everyman's Library. (Originally published in 1762)

Schwartz, Thomas. 1972. "Rationality and the Myth of the Maximum." *Noûs* 6: 97–117.

———. 1989a. "Why Parties?" University of California at Los Angeles. Unpublished paper.

———. 1989b. "Publius and Public Choice." In *The Federalist Papers and the New Institutionalism,* edited by Bernard Grofman and Donald Wittman. (New York: Atherton), 31–38.

———. 1994. "Representation as Agency and the Pork-Barrel Paradox." *Public Choice* 78: 3–21.

———. 1995. "The Paradox of Representation." *Journal of Politics* 57: 309–23.

Stockman, David. 1975. "The Social Pork Barrel." *The Public Interest* 39: 3–30.

Tullock, Gordon. 1959. "Problems of Majority Voting." *Journal of Political Economy* 67: 571–79.

RESPONSE TO OSTROM AND SCHWARTZ

James M. Buchanan

I am both embarrassed and flattered that the American Political Science Association would organize a whole session devoted to my work, and, particularly, that two scholars of the standing of Vincent Ostrom and Thomas Schwartz would be willing to take the time and effort required to prepare papers. In my view, both essays are quite laudatory; hence, it is unnecessary for me to mount a defensive counter to any of their arguments.

I shall, accordingly, say only a few things directly related to their essays. Little did I know that, in the 1960s, the state of American political science was indeed as woeful in its neglect of basic constitutional inquiry as it is described by Vincent Ostrom (1997). As Thomas Schwartz (1997) notes, I have from the outset of my own research program been highly critical of the simplistic majoritarianism that seemed to characterize much normative analysis of democratic politics. But I surely did not sense that constitutional foundations were basically beyond the limits for mid-twentieth-century academic concerns. As Thomas Schwartz indicates, the specific sources of my early work are in public economics, or, more narrowly, in theoretical welfare economics in its extended application to the public or political sector. In this work, the primary influence was Knut Wicksell, who tried to extend the efficiency norm beyond the realm of market relationships. The constitutional implications simply emerged more or less "naturally" as this line of inquiry was followed up. And while Ostrom is correct in distinguishing my own philosophical bent from that of Gordon Tullock, this feature of my effort was more emergent than initially motivational.

Rather than wax autobiographical, however, I want to devote most of this response to a brief discussion of two elements that I did not fully appreciate when we wrote *The Calculus of Consent*—elements that did not really inform the analysis of that book or my other early efforts, at least in any direct or explicit sense (Buchanan and Tullock 1962).

Only within the last half-decade have I come to recognize the critical relevance and importance of the *endogeneity* of the choice alternatives that are presented to the collectivity and, more specifically, of the essential dependence of these alternatives on the rules for reaching collective decisions. In looking over some of my earlier thinking, it seems as if I bought into the mindset of social choice theorists, who constructed their analyses on the presupposition that the alternatives for collective choice are simply "out there," as a menu from which selections are to be made, for the most part through a sequence of pairwise comparisons.[1] Once stated so baldly, the intellectual vulnerability of this presupposition becomes evident. Choice alternatives (just like economic goods) must come from somewhere; they must be created, or, better said, invented. And the alternatives created will depend on the rules that are used to make the selection. Clearly, we must predict that majority rule will, in itself, tend to generate choice alternatives that embody distributional discrimination between members of majority and minority coalitions. (For elaboration of the analysis here, see Buchanan 1995a.)

If, somehow, there could be some sort of guarantee that the set of choice alternatives is genuinely *exogenous* to the process, then the familiar defenses of majority rule, discussed by Schwartz in connection with the May theorem, would become analytically legitimate. Absent any such guarantee, however, how are "public interest" alternatives to be distinguished from those that are deliberately invented by political entrepreneurs who seek to further the limited interests of members of potential majority coalitions?

The second element that was missing from my early work was any explicit recognition of the importance of *rent-seeking,* as first elaborated by Gordon Tullock (1967) in his seminal paper. As with all seminal ideas, this one seems simple, once stated. If potential value exists, persons will make efforts to capture it. And if value is artificially created through political action, for example, by market restrictions, efforts to secure the rents represent social wastage of resources that could otherwise be used to produce goods and services. We need only think of the thousands of highly skilled lawyers who almost exclusively devote their efforts to devising ways and means through which clients may secure differential gains or avoid differential losses from the maze of politically orchestrated regulations, not the least of which is the tax code, recently made even more complex.

The rent-seeking element relates to the endogeneity point in the following way. Unless constitutionally constrained, majorities will tend to generate differentially advantageous economic value for their own members. The potential value to be gained from majority coalition membership surely serves as an attractor for investments aimed at securing such membership (Buchanan 1995b). Majoritarian rent-seeking, even as very roughly measured by the increasingly apparent efforts to influence electoral results, clearly emerges as a basis for arguments in support of either more inclusive decision rules, which was our focus in *The Calculus of Consent,* or of explicit constitutional constraints against discriminatory political treatment. My most recent book, *Politics by Principle, Not Interest,* written with Roger Congleton, analyzes this second approach in some detail (Buchanan and Congleton 1998). One application of the argument will suffice. When all is said and done, the argument for the flat tax may not rest on either simplicity or fairness, but on *political efficiency.*

NOTE

1. Thomas Schwartz (1986) is himself an exception to this generalization. In his book *The Logic of Collective Choice,* Schwartz devotes a whole chapter to "Choosing the Set from Which to Choose."

REFERENCES

Buchanan, James M. 1995a. "Foundational Concerns: A Criticism of Public Choice Theory." In *Current Issues in Public Choice,* edited by José Casas Pardo and Friedrich Schneider (Cheltenham, Eng.: Edward Elgar), 3–20.

———. 1995b. "Majoritarian Rent-Seeking." Center for the Study of Public Choice, George Mason University. Unpublished paper.

Buchanan, James M., and Roger D. Congleton. 1998. *Politics by Principle, Not Interest: Toward Nondiscriminatory Democracy.* Cambridge: Cambridge University Press.

Buchanan, James M., and Gordon Tullock. 1962. *The Calculus of Consent: Logical Foundations of Constitutional Democracy.* Ann Arbor: University of Michigan Press.

Ostrom, Vincent. 1997. "Buchanan's Opening to Constitutional Choice and Meta Levels of Analysis." Workshop in Political Theory and Policy Analysis, Indiana University. Unpublished paper.

Schwartz, Thomas. 1986. *The Logic of Collective Action.* New York: Columbia University Press.

———. 1997. "What James Buchanan Has Contributed to Public Economics, Political Philosophy, and Political Science." Department of Political Science, University of California at Los Angeles. Unpublished paper.

Tullock, Gordon. 1967. "The Welfare Costs of Tariffs, Monopolies, and Theft." *Western Economic Journal* 5(June): 224–32.

~ Chapter 4 ~

GARY S. BECKER
A Biographical Sketch

G ary S. Becker won the Nobel Prize in 1992. He has also been the recipient of the prestigious Seidman Prize and has served as president of the American Economic Association. He is currently Professor of Economics and Sociology at the University of Chicago, a research associate at the Economics Research Center at the National Opinion Research Center, and a senior fellow at the Hoover Institution. He also writes a monthly column for *Business Week*.

Becker's career has been devoted to demonstrating how the assumption of rational, maximizing agents explains behavior in a wide variety of domains and accounts even for behavior generally considered irrational or habitual. Perhaps best known for his work on human capital, Becker has also contributed to research on fertility, discrimination, crime and punishment, addiction, the family, pressure groups, regulation, tastes and preferences, and, most recently, social capital. He is famous—in some circles infamous—for treating children as durable consumer goods and for arguing for the rationality of addiction. Economists, as well as other social scientists, initially treated his approach with skepticism; they believed he was asking economics to do what it could not do. But Becker believed otherwise, and ultimately the members of his chosen profession and the Nobel Academy came to agree with him.

Born in 1930 in Pottsville, Pennsylvania, Becker grew up in Brooklyn, where his family moved when he was a small child. Neither of his parents went to school beyond eighth grade. As an undergraduate at Princeton, Gary Becker combined an aptitude in mathematics with a keen "desire to do something useful for society" (1997). In an introductory course in economics, he was intrigued by Paul A. Samuelson's textbook, particularly the sections on microeconomics, which he found "concise and mathematically formulated, and yet they dealt with interesting problems" (Swedberg 1990, 28). By his senior year, however, he worried that economics was insufficiently relevant to social problems. He briefly flirted with sociology, but his reading of Talcott Parsons discouraged him. In 1951, having completed his degree in three years, Becker graduated from Princeton and entered the Ph.D. program at the University of Chicago. There his interest in economics was immediately reinvigorated by Milton Friedman, who emphasized the use of economics as a powerful tool for analysis of significant social and political questions. By 1952 Becker was beginning to explore new territory for economics; stimulated by Schumpeter's *Capitalism, Socialism, and Democracy,* he wrote a paper applying microeconomic theory to politics. The profession was not yet ready, and the *Journal of Political Economy* rejected his piece. (It would publish a shorter version in 1958.)

After his third year at Chicago, Becker accepted an assistant professorship at Columbia with a joint appointment at the National Bureau of Economic Research. He returned to Chicago in 1970, a decision motivated in part by his feeling that the Columbia administration did not take sufficiently strong action against what he believed was student intimidation during the 1968 strike.

The University of Chicago proved an excellent environment for Becker. Discussions with George Stigler produced several important pieces of research and revived his earlier interest in applying economic theory to politics. Becker also developed a strong bond with the sociologist James Coleman. In 1983 he accepted a joint appointment in the Department of Sociology. One result was the establishment of the extremely influential Becker-Coleman Seminar on rational choice in the social sciences. Interdisciplinary and wide-ranging, the seminar allowed Becker and Coleman to raise the standards and push the boundaries of economic reasoning in political science, sociology, and related disciplines.

Becker rigorously adheres to the assumption of individuals as purposeful and maximizing, and he stringently applies microeconomic theory to a range of human behaviors usually outside the scope of economic theory. His formalization and elaboration of the microfoundations of the human capital model made possible a general framework for investigating returns on training and education. Human capital refers to the level of skills and knowledge an individual possesses. As with physical capital, human capital can grow, given appropriate investments and markets, and different individuals and different countries can vary in the supply of human capital they possess. Using the same model of human behavior, Becker has also explored discrimination as a rational behavior in which the discriminator is willing to bear a cost for his beliefs, and criminality as rational behavior under uncertainty about the probability of punishment. His work on family decisions as rational allocations of time and labor under shifting wage constraints continues to produce insightful and controversial explanations of the division of household labor, the number of children a family has and what education they receive, and the rate of divorce.

Becker has clearly made a mark in sociology, but he is also an eminent political economist. A longtime editor of the *Journal of Political Economy* and the author of some of the earliest papers to apply microeconomic theory to political problems, he plans to continue to explore political processes and institutions in future work. Given Becker's significance as a theorist, his wide range of policy-related interests, and his specific research on regulatory and pressure-group behavior, it is noteworthy that political scientists have generally failed to integrate his findings into their own work. Most citations in political science journals use Becker as an example of the imperialism of neoclassical economics; few actually use his theories and models or take on his findings in a systematic fashion. The relative lack of influence Becker has had is the puzzle that Ronald Rogowski's chapter raises and analyzes. His conclusions are something of an indictment of the profession. Rogowski believes that Becker is insignificantly appreciated by political scientists because of the parochialism of Americanists, the technical deficiencies of comparativists combined with Becker's technical proficiency, political correctness, and a general disdain for "normal science."

In recent discussions and writings, Becker is turning once again to questions of central interest to political scientists. He may do more work on pressure-group politics, and he has begun to develop a concept of social capital as a means to explain the link between individual values and decisions and collective outcomes. Russell

Hardin, in his chapter, contrasts Becker's approach to social capital with those of Robert Putnam, Francis Fukuyama, Wendy Rahn and John Brehm, and James Coleman, all of whom have had a significant impact on political science. Hardin argues that Becker's formulation of social capital may be more powerful than the formulations of others who use the term and is certainly more precise. Although he criticizes some of Becker's approach, Hardin recognizes and sympathizes with Becker's effort to provide a corrective, based in rigorous analysis, to simplistic theories of self-interest. However, in retaining the rigorous microeconomic foundations that so many political scientists resist, it will be interesting to see whether Becker's model of social capital and his renewed efforts at political analysis succeed in capturing the attention of political scientists any better than his other efforts.

REFERENCES

Becker, Gary S. 1997. "Autobiography." Nobel Prize Internet Archive, available at: http://www.nobel.se/laureates/economy-1992-autobio.html.
Swedberg, Richard. 1990. *Economics and Sociology*. Ch. 1. Princeton, N.J.: Princeton University Press.

GARY S. BECKER: AN APPRECIATION, SOME MODEST PROPOSALS, AND A DISCIPLINARY SELF-CRITIQUE

Ronald Rogowski

Few economists can have written so much of relevance to political science, across so broad a spectrum of interests, as Gary Becker. Discrimination, interest groups, the family, human capital, the allocation of time (for example, between politics and other pursuits), crime and punishment—all are central to students of politics, or at least to some subfield of political science.

More important still for those of us who pioneered the "rational-choice" approach in political science, Becker showed brilliantly how classical methods of optimization could illuminate the most nonmonetary and seemingly irrational parts of human behavior, and he gave no quarter in denouncing as unscientific and intellectually lazy the culturalist and normative "explanations" of those behaviors on which most of us had been weaned. His description of the social sciences (including much of economics) in the introduction to his collection of essays *The Economic Approach to Human Behavior* (1976, 11–13) thrilled us then and has lost none of its force or accuracy today:

> [A]llegations of irrational behavior, unnecessary ignorance, folly, and ad hoc shifts in values . . . simply acknowledg[e] defeat in the guise of considered judgment.

> War is said to be caused by madmen, and political behavior, more generally, dominated by folly and ignorance. . . . [C]hanges in preferences [are] conveniently introduced ad hoc to explain puzzling behavior.

> With an ingenuity worthy of admiration if put to better use, almost any conceivable behavior is alleged to be dominated by ignorance and irrationality, values and their frequent unexplained shifts, custom and tradition, the compliance somehow induced by social norms, or the ego and the id.

This was, and remains, nothing less than the manifesto of the rational-choice method in political science,[1] and that method has gone on to dominate virtually all major university departments and the central journals of the discipline.

It therefore seems astonishing that Becker's work, as opposed to his philippics, has inspired such meager sustained interest among political scientists. He is cited at only a respectable rate—in fifty-two articles in the top dozen journals[2] over the last dozen years,[3] or about once every third year in the average journal[4]—but the citations are mostly cursory, not infrequently distorted or trivial,[5] and often enough dismissive (usually not just of Becker, but of the "Chicago School"). The published papers in this period that attempt seriously to apply, extend, or rebut Becker's work can literally be counted on the fingers of one hand.

I propose in this essay to say, by way of appreciation and exhortation, how much political scientists *should* have learned from Becker and to indicate directions in which they can, and should, extend his pathbreaking work; to examine more closely the actual pattern of citation to, and learning from, Becker since 1986; and as an exercise in disciplinary forensic pathology, to suggest why even the most sympathetic political scientists have resisted the seemingly obvious allure of Becker's work.

WHAT POLITICAL SCIENTISTS *SHOULD* HAVE LEARNED FROM BECKER

Three areas of Becker's work have particularly significant, and mostly unexploited, implications for political science: discrimination, pressure groups, and human capital.[6]

Discrimination

The comparative study of intergroup conflict (usually ethnic, often religious, occasionally regional) is of urgent and growing concern but, as many students have lamented, remains pathetically underdeveloped theoretically.[7] The common thread in such conflicts is discrimination, perceived or genuine, against some characteristic (skin color, language, religion) that people can change only with great difficulty, if at all; it is little short of amazing that Becker's insights on precisely that issue have resonated so feebly in political science.

Becker's fundamental breakthrough, it will be recalled, was to apply to inter*ethnic* economic relations the basic Heckscher-Ohlin framework for the analysis of inter*national* exchange. A dominant group almost always possesses more human and physical capital per person than a dominated one;[8] hence, absent the barrier of discrimination, the dominant group exports capital (or capital-intensive products) and imports labor (or labor-intensive goods and services), and the dominated group does exactly the opposite.

Discrimination, as a barrier to trade, diminishes social welfare and normally harms the dominated group more than the dominant one; however, it actually benefits dominant-group workers and dominated-group holders of human and physical capital. If (again, the canonical case) the dominant group discriminates more than the dominated one—for example, in the traditional U.S. case many whites would not employ blacks, but most blacks would accept employment with whites—then increased discrimination by the dominated group (nationalism, or separatism) harms dominated-group workers still more but benefits dominated-group elites.

From this standpoint, it is easy to see why dominant-group elites are often more "liberal" (less discriminatory) and, equally, why dominated-group elites often embrace ethnic nationalism and separation (compare, Breton 1964). One needs only the Rybczynski theorem to begin to explain why, when the advantage of the dominant group in skill or physical capital grows, dominated-group elites so often become frantic and violent in their demands for separation—or, indeed, for the physical annihilation of dominant-group possessors of capital and skill (compare, Horowitz 1985; the tragic scenario was played out again most recently in Rwanda).

From the nineteenth century down to the present day, analysts have observed with befuddlement that liberalized international trade is actually associated with more virulent nationalism among previously oppressed minorities (see, for example, Hobsbawm 1979, ch. 5; Hobsbawm 1992). But the Samuelson factor-price equalization theorem tells us that, in most cases, trade in goods achieves the same equalization of returns as migration of factors; hence, under increased foreign trade, oppressed minorities gain most of what they would have achieved by a repeal of discrimination and can contemplate a "divorce" from their oppressors that earlier would have seemed unacceptably expensive.

Finally, Becker's perspective casts an unsparing light on quotas or "proportionality": efforts to remedy discrimination against the dominated group by reserving population-proportional numbers of elite positions for them regardless of training or ability.[9] In Beckerian terms, quotas guarantee that dominated-group elites will receive a wage in excess of their marginal product (MP), and dominant-group ones a wage less than their MP, while dominant-group workers will usually receive more, and dominated-group workers less, than their MP. Paradoxically, this conduces ineluctably to greater, and more rational, discrimination: buyers devoid of any "taste" for discrimination will come to infer that a dominant-group professional is the better bargain (and, equally, that one gets better value for the money from a dominated-group worker than from a dominant-group one). A policy intended to erode segregation has the perverse effect of intensifying it.[10]

All of this flows, I think straightforwardly, from the original Becker insight. It resolves many of the puzzles that still surround our comparative study of ethnic conflict. And I am bound to believe that what I have indicated here barely scratches the surface of what can be done with Becker's model.

Pressure Groups

Interest groups have been a central concern of political science since the pioneering work of Arthur Bentley (1908) and were much studied cross-nationally in the 1950s (Ehrmann 1958; compare, Almond 1997, 12). More recently, students of international political economy have inquired into the kinds of groups that attempt to influence trade policy (Alt and others 1996; Frieden and Rogowski 1996). Political scientists generally have been drawn to the economic debates over rent-seeking, deadweight loss, and political instability (see, inter alia, Buchanan, Tollison, and Tullock 1980; Gray and Lowery 1988; Krueger 1974; Olson 1982).

Becker's seminal paper "Competition Among Pressure Groups" (1983) powerfully illuminates these issues and carries implications for other major political questions. Viewing pressure-group competition as a simple negative-sum game—winners' benefits amount to losers' taxes, minus the deadweight costs of redistribution—resolved by the relative influence that groups bring to bear, Becker arrives at three powerful conclusions: political leaders *and pressure groups* have strong incentives to minimize deadweight costs; shifts in the total amount and distribution of subsidies mostly reflect changes in efficiency, either of redistribution (an increase or decrease in its deadweight costs) or of pressure-group mobilization (with the same effort by leaders and members, greater pressure can be mobilized); and exogenous economic gains normally increase a group's political influence, while economic losses normally decrease them.

The first point is utterly convincing once stated. Consider two states of the world: in both, group A gets subsidy S at the expense of group B, but in the first, deadweight costs are markedly greater. By moving to the situation of lower deadweight costs, the tax on B can be reduced, the rents to politicians increased, or both; by assumption, group A incurs no loss. If the second option is available, why not take it?[11]

Becker, of course, is no Pangloss; he recognizes that seemingly inefficient transfers (quotas instead of tariffs, restrictions on acreage or entry instead of subsidies) often occur (Becker 1983, 386). But his rather Coaseian point about deadweight-cost minimization forces us, instead of merely shaking our heads about the irrationality of politics, to think seriously about why seemingly more efficient methods might not guarantee similar levels,[12] or beneficiaries,[13] of transfer.

Becker's analysis also suggests research avenues on the sustained growth of government, and in particular of transfer payments, in all industrial societies since the 1960s (compare, Lindert 1996) and on the recent "deregulatory revolution" in many countries. The rapid growth of government spending, and in particular of transfer payments, can hardly have resulted from anything other than equally sudden reductions in the deadweight costs of taxation and spending.[14] Among the likely candidates are both improved data handling (from computerization) and less distortionary taxes (in particular, the value-added tax). An interesting secondary question is whether Becker's approach leads us toward an explanation of "Wagner's Law," that is, the tendency for government's share of gross domestic product (GDP) to rise (cross-sectionally and dynamically within countries) with GDP per capita.

The shift away from regulation, similarly, must arise from either a radical increase in regulation's deadweight costs (surely a defensible view in such sectors as telecommunications) or a drastic change in efficiency of mobilization, either in favor of its previous victims or against its previous beneficiaries. The relevance of Becker's analysis to deregulation has at least been noticed by students of politics (Mitchell and Munger 1991, 534), but as we shall see later, the many other research paths opened by his perspective have so far remained largely exploited.

Finally, Becker's view that economic gainers increase, and economic losers decrease, pressure and influence would be questioned by many political scientists. We believe almost reflexively that *losers* from exogenous economic change (for example, autoworkers threatened by Japanese imports) mobilize more readily, and win more frequently, than winners (for example, software firms that dominate world markets), yet Becker's model implies the contrary unless (as seems hardly probable) political pressure is an inferior good, that is, one on which one spends less as income rises.[15] What I think the seeming paradox actually suggests is a need to inquire into the microfoundations of political activity by uniting with his work on pressure groups an earlier strand of Becker's work, namely, that on allocation of time. Among other things, I would conjecture that *younger* "losers" would be likelier to mobilize politically (amortizing resultant costs over a longer lifetime and, if successful, garnering a much higher present-value lifetime income stream) than older ones.

Human Capital

While few political scientists work specifically on issues of education or training, many have been drawn to *corporatism* (Berger 1981; Katzenstein 1984) and its frequent concomitant, "active labor-market policies" that continually retool workers for new demands (Scharpf 1991, 93–94). From Becker's perspective, we can see at once why such policies arise only, and almost always, where national-level bargaining imposes a "solidaristic wage" on broad categories of workers.[16]

Consider a situation of perfect competition in which there are only two types of workers, skilled and unskilled, and in which each firm hires only one type or the other. The wages of each type of worker will equilibrate, and any exogenous shock—for example, increased world demand for the products of the skilled sector—will be accommodated by a shift in relative wages (in this case, in favor of skilled workers). Over the longer run, such a change will induce more otherwise unskilled workers to become skilled: according to standard Beckerian analysis, younger workers are more likely to acquire skills (since for them skills have higher present value), and where skills are firm-specific, firms are likely to pay workers in training less than, and workers post-training more than, their marginal product (Becker 1993, ch. 3).

But now suppose that a "solidaristic wage" compels firms in the unskilled sector to pay more, and workers in the skilled sector to accept less, than marginal product. Firms in the unskilled sector will massively substitute capital for labor, and firms in the skilled sector will seek to substitute labor for capital, but wage changes (being forbidden)[17] can no longer equilibrate these shifts. The certain result is unemployment in the unskilled sector, overemployment in the skilled sector, and, given the likelihood of continuing wage compression, little incentive for unskilled workers—and none whatever for mature workers, whose seniority would shield them from unemployment—to acquire skills. Absent wage changes, only subsidization of training could reallocate labor.

All of this seems pretty obvious once stated (and perhaps equally obvious is the inevitable failure of the scheme over the longer term), but the amazing point is how few of the corporatist systems' starry-eyed admirers in the world of political science have perceived the link.

WHAT POLITICAL SCIENTISTS *HAVE* LEARNED FROM BECKER

Between 1986 and the present, the article by Becker most frequently cited (some fifteen times) in leading political science journals has been the one on *pressure groups* (1983). Sometimes he is cited as the authority for by now relatively familiar points (that smaller groups fare better, that groups exert pressure in dictatorships as well as in democracies: see, respectively, Runge and von Witzke 1990, 254; Wintrobe 1990, 854); more often (and more important) he is cited for his argument about minimization of deadweight cost (Grove 1991, 59; Przeworski and Wallerstein 1988, 13) or for his translation of economic into political power (Rogowski 1987b). Students of U.S. politics, rather missing the point,[18] sometimes chide Becker for inattention to the geographic aspects of representation (Bendor and Moe 1986, n.4; Levitt and Snyder 1995, fn.962; Roberts 1990, 36n.), or they incorrectly attribute to him the view that institutions scarcely matter (McCubbins and Schwartz 1988, 389).

So far as I can determine, precisely two articles have devoted concentrated attention to Becker's work on interest groups. William Mitchell and Michael Munger (1991), in a useful review article intended to acquaint political scientists with economists' work on interest groups, devote several pages to a textbooklike exposition. More intriguingly, Wendy Hansen (1990) attempts seriously to operational-ize and test one of Becker's chief hypotheses.[19] If politicians and interest groups endeavor to minimize deadweight loss, Hansen (1990, 35) argues, then protection against imports should be granted most often to those commodities with the most inelastic demand.[20] The record of anti-dumping cases before the U.S. International Trade Commission, however, fails to support that hypothesis; if anything, a more inelastic demand makes protection *less* likely.

Cited second most frequently (in some dozen articles) is Becker's work on *crime and punishment*—addressed, not as one might suspect, by specialists on public pol-icy or criminal justice, but either by scholars of international relations interested in mutual deterrence or enforcement of international agreements (for example, Chayes and Chayes 1993; Legro 1996; Lipson 1991; Wittman 1989) or students of compar-ative politics who analyze corruption or repression (Kiser and Tong 1992; Lichbach 1987, 1990; Nas, Price, and Weber 1986). Again, most invoke Becker fleetingly to make a minor point (typically, that infractions are reduced chiefly by raising the probability of detection); only two papers (Chayes and Chayes 1993, 202; Tsebelis 1989, 79) take issue with Becker's underlying assumptions or with the testability of his theory. None, unless it has eluded my attention, seriously extends or applies Becker's work on this topic.

A distant third in political science citations is Becker's work on *human capital and the allocation of time*. Four articles make use of it from very different perspectives: to explain women's underrepresentation in certain occupational categories (Saltzstein 1986, 144–45); to explain the greater support for European unification among pro-fessionals and white-collar workers (Gabel and Palmer 1995, 7); to question, from a normative standpoint, Becker's distinction between "political" and "full" income (Grafstein 1990, 24); and to hypothesize how various resource constraints might affect individual propensity toward political participation (Brady, Verba, and Schlozman 1995). No article in this category can be counted as a major challenge to, or extension of, Becker's work.

The remaining citations are either scattered across other lines of Becker's work or are even more cursory than those already indicated. Little attention has been given to Becker's work on *discrimination* (two citations), and again, no serious effort has been made to test or extend it.

WHY POLITICAL SCIENTISTS HAVE (SEEMINGLY) EXPLOITED BECKER SO LITTLE

As I indicated at the outset, Becker has probably influenced political science indirectly—by unconscious borrowing, or by example and attitude—more than he has directly. Nonetheless, the question persists: why, in a discipline normally so lacking in compunction about the appropriation of neighbors' tools, have the shiny and powerful utensils of Becker's workshop gone mostly untouched, if often admired from afar?

For one set of political scientists, the answer is obvious: they utterly reject Becker's vision of social science and find comfort (which they are pleased to call "explanation") in precisely the "unexplained shifts in values" that Becker has so eloquently denounced. But political scientists of this stripe are a species moving rapidly toward extinction. As I noted earlier, the dominant tendency in recent political science would have led one to expect a far more eager reception of Becker's work.

Opposition to science is not the problem. Rather, I suggest six main reasons.

The Parochialism of Americanists Specialists in American politics have made the most important theoretical breakthroughs of the last two decades in political science and have been among the most receptive to economic modes of thought and analysis. They are the natural audience for Becker's work on pressure groups. Yet too few Americanists have even a vague awareness of institutions or political processes outside the United States. Becker's models, intended to apply generally, strike many Americanists as alien to (or excessively abstracted from) the reality they know, or, notably in Becker's analysis of discrimination, they run too great a risk of political incorrectness (see later discussion).

Technical Deficiencies of Comparativists Mathematical and microeconomic skills have so far tended to be localized among Americanists; comparativists, particularly those of the area-studies persuasion, have been among the weakest in their grasp of these tools. Becker's work—I say entirely in admiration—is hardly among the most inaccessible or technically dense in economics, yet a lot of it remains beyond the grasp of all but a few comparativists. They therefore grasp it, if at all, only in diluted translation. This means that the natural audience for a lot of Becker's work on human capital and discrimination cannot receive the transmissions.

Becker's Predilection for Reduced-Form Modeling[21] Even empirically astute Americanists and formally adept comparativists, however, often find Becker's models too spare to apply readily to the political problems that most concern them. The inclinations of regimes toward free trade or protection, to take a classic example, cannot readily be analyzed without considering the relative power of pressure groups (Grossman and Helpman 1994) or such institutional detail as constituency size (Lohmann and O'Halloran 1994) or electoral mechanism (Rogowski 1987a). The same can be said of governmental commitment, particularly in the area of monetary policy (see, for example, Grilli, Masciandaro, and Tabellini 1991; Roubini and Sachs 1989). More broadly, formal modelers in both economics and politics have discovered that they can gain enormous purchase by adding to a spare Beckerian model of pressure-group influence so simple a detail as a left-right ideological dimension (Dixit and Londregan 1996). Becker's pronounced taste for parsimony and his ruthless wielding of Occam's razor have not meshed easily with more recent theorists' efforts to unpack the "black box" of political processes.

The Remaining Gap Between Comparative Politics and International Relations Political scientists like to believe that the line between comparative politics (analysis of countries' domestic institutions) and international relations (the study of states' interactions) has all but disappeared. It has not, as anybody who has tried recently to place a student in either field will know. Students of international relations, or at least of international political economy, will usually know the Heckscher-Ohlin model of international trade that underpins Becker's analysis of discrimination but most of them will also have little interest in the topic (or in comparative ethnic conflict). Comparativists will often be passionately interested in comparative ethnic conflict but will seldom know, or care about, the economics of international trade.

Political Correctness For all its pretension to value-neutral social science, political science remains in important respects a bastion of totalitarian thought control. Hard or radical thinking about such topics as discrimination, affirmative action, or the family (even in the context of human capital) is all but foreclosed; the political incorrectness of such arguments is taken as conclusive proof of their falsity (cf. Booth 1994, 656–57), and scholars—particularly younger scholars—who address such questions do so at peril to their careers.

Disdain for "Normal Science" Brian Barry (1974, 79–80) observed almost a quarter-century ago that political science respected and rewarded the authors of "in" books—that is, ones that advanced some bold new thesis that could be summarized in a sentence (so that nobody actually had to read the book). The larger point was cynical and (slightly) exaggerated; the smaller one—that political scientists avoid and slight the arduous detail work of elaboration, operationalization, and testing—was, and mostly remains, accurate. Scholars still make their careers by advancing large (even if ultimately wrong) new theories, not by proposing modest (even if clearly right, and damned clever) extensions or emendations of others' work. That Becker has advanced brilliant theories of important political phenomena is, for many, reason enough to work on other topics, where one's own second-magnitude star will not be obscured by Becker's sun.

The good news, I think, is that most of the disciplinary obstacles are falling. The best Americanists are now eager to extend their gaze abroad;[22] comparativists—at least at places like Harvard, Rochester, and UCLA—are leapfrogging into a high level of technical skill; young comparativists do not readily find jobs if they are ignorant of international political economy; and journals like *American Journal of Political Science, International Organization,* and lately even *American Political Science Review* have begun to welcome "normal" science. Only political correctness remains a significant institutional impediment: it will probably be some time yet before vulnerable (that is, pre-tenure) younger scholars dare to publish really heterodox work on such subjects as discrimination and the family.

More problematic is the growing "disconnect" between the institutionally informed work of most of today's formal theorists and Becker's much more reduced-form models. To the newer group, Becker's work will probably continue to serve more as inspiration than as direct source. My own hunch is that Becker's draconian parsimony will prove the better road, but it is, just now, the one less taken.

CONCLUSION

Gary Becker's work is in danger of attaining scriptural authority in rational-choice political science: that is to say, like the Gospels in Christianity or *Das Kapital* in Marxism, it is revered more than read, and almost never taken as a serious guide to action. If the recent literature is a guide, Becker is invoked offhandedly, far more often as a warrant for assertions than as a starting point for serious analysis.

At the same time, his example and approach have had a wide and important influence. By telling (and more important, by showing) us how good social science should be done, and what its criteria are, he has taught two generations of political scientists what to emulate and what to avoid.

Still, our widespread disciplinary failure to extend and apply the specific aspects of Becker's work that most directly address political concerns—a very few of which I have indicated here—demands reconsideration of our own training, organization, and incentives. Why have we welcomed the messenger and ignored so much of the message?

NOTES

1. What is more remarkable, of course, is that Becker was denouncing first and foremost *economists'* explanations of such phenomena.

2. A personal but not idiosyncratic selection: in alphabetical order, *American Journal of Political Science, American Political Science Review, British Journal of Political Science, Canadian Journal of Political Science, Comparative Political Studies, Comparative Politics, European Journal of Political Research, International Organization, Journal of Conflict Resolution, Journal of Politics, Polity,* and *World Politics.* Margaret Levi (private communication) has suggested that journals in public administration, law, and public policy (particularly touching on crime and health) might show a higher rate of citation. I grant the point (without having at all examined the evidence) but note that none of those journals would be counted among the leading ones in political science. Obviously, the survey undertaken here excludes citations in books, but there is little reason to think those would be more numerous.

3. Actually, January 1986 through June 1987.

4. In nineteen articles over the dozen years in *American Political Science Review,* in nine in *American Journal of Political Science,* in none in either *Comparative Political Studies* or *Polity;* in between two and four articles in each of the other journals.

5. One, apparently innocent of the concept of a Giffen good, cites Becker as authority for the proposition that a higher price always entails reduced demand.

6. A fourth area, crime and punishment, holds implications for students of public policy and—as several have recognized—for students of international strategy. About this I shall have much less to say, largely because of my own disciplinary limitations.

7. My own earlier jeremiad is contained in Rogowski (1993). Among the best, but still highly unsatisfactory, efforts have been the psychological approach of Donald Horowitz (1985), Michael Hechter's work on internal colonialism (1975), David Laitin (1988, 1992) on "language games," and James Fearon (1994) on the uses of interethnic terror.

8. Among the rare exceptions was probably Russian dominance over the highly educated and entrepreneurial Balts and Armenians within the former Soviet Union.

9. Americans will probably be chagrined to learn that the policy was invented, and carried through much more rigorously, in the Netherlands around 1918 as a way of combating religious discrimination (see Lijphart 1968).

10. In the Netherlands, which had no open-accommodation or equal opportunity laws, the policy of proportionality led to almost total segregation in housing and employment.

11. One answer is that, when voters' information about both policy effects and politicians' positions is imperfect, deadweight loss need not be minimized (Coate and Morris 1995).

12. A simple example: in the U.S. system, tariffs can be entrenched in law subject only to later repeal; subsidies must be reappropriated annually. The default value on a tariff is therefore a continued tariff; the default on a subsidy is no subsidy. The institutional remedy for this seeming inefficiency is multi-year appropriations.

13. One could, for example, benefit *farmers* more efficiently by lump-sum buyouts, but subsidizing only crops and land guarantees that farm *suppliers* (particularly merchants in small rural towns) survive. It is the latter who are the natural constituency of the (mostly Republican) representatives of rural constituencies.

14. Peter Lindert's (1996, 3) objection—that such a change cannot explain cross-sectional *variation* in the level of social spending among countries—seems to me beside the point. In Becker's analysis, the level of spending can result from country-specific variation in interest-group strength and efficiency, but universal *change* in levels would have to have a common cause.

15. In Becker's comparative statics, pressure is nondecreasing in the amount spent per member (Becker 1983, 377), and unless pressure is an inferior good, this amount will rise with members' income.

16. In the (extreme) Swedish case, all workers with similar qualifications were in theory paid the same wage wherever employed, and the wage gap between skilled and unskilled workers was steadily narrowed (Scharpf 1991, 91).

17. Wage changes are forbidden in theory; in practice, considerable "wage drift" occurs at the firm level (Scharpf 1991, 90–91).

18. The joke, of course, is that, outside the United States, few countries (France, the United Kingdom and its former colonies, until recently Japan, in very recent years Italy) elect representatives from small geographic districts. In my experience, this news comes as a shock to most Americanists.

19. Wendy Hansen, according to my APSA biographical directory, holds her Ph.D. from Cal Tech.

20. The argument has weak links but is not insupportable: basically, one must assume that both import shocks and prior efficiency of organization are stochastically distributed across sectors.

21. Remarks by Thomas Romer and Charles Cameron, in discussing an earlier draft of this paper at the Russell Sage Foundation, persuaded me on this point.

22. Mat McCubbins, for example, has collaborated in research on Japan and is now leading a project on comparative budgetary procedures.

REFERENCES

Alt, James E., et al. 1996. "The Political Economy of International Trade: Enduring Puzzles and an Agenda for Inquiry." *Comparative Political Studies* 29: 689–717.

Almond, Gabriel A. 1997. "The Future of Comparative and Area Studies in the United States." Address to Plenary Session of World Congress of International Political Science Association, Seoul, Korea, (August 1997).

Barry, Brian. 1974. "Review of article 'Exit, Voice, and Loyalty.'" *British Journal of Political Science* 4: 79–107.

Becker, Gary S. 1976. *The Economic Approach to Human Behavior.* Chicago: University of Chicago Press.

———. 1983. "A Theory of Competition among Pressure Groups for Political Influence." *Quarterly Journal of Economics* 98: 371–400.

———. 1993. *Human Capital: A Theoretical and Empirical Analysis, with Special Reference to Education.* 3rd ed. Chicago: University of Chicago Press.

Bendor, Jonathan B., and Terry M. Moe. 1986. "Agenda Control, Committee Capture, and the Dynamics of Institutional Politics." *American Journal of Political Science* 80: 1187–1207.

Bentley, Arthur Fisher. 1908. *The Process of Government: a Study of Social Pressures.* Chicago: University of Chicago Press.

Berger, Suzanne D. (ed.). 1981. *Organizing Interests in Western Europe: Pluralism, Corporatism, and the Transformation of Politics.* Cambridge: Cambridge University Press.

Booth, William J. 1994. "On the Idea of the Moral Economy." *American Political Science Review* 88: 653–67.

Brady, Henry E., Sidney Verba, and Kay L. Schlozman. 1995. "Beyond SES: A Resource Model of Political Participation." *American Political Science Review* 89: 271–94.

Breton, Albert. 1964. "Economics of Nationalism." *Journal of Political Economy* 72: 376–86.

Buchanan, James, Robert Tollison, and Gordon Tullock (eds.). 1980. *Toward a Theory of the Rent-Seeking Society.* College Station: Texas A&M Press.

Chayes, Abram, and Antonia Handler Chayes. 1993. "On Compliance." *International Organization* 47: 175–205.

Coate, Stephen, and Stephen Morris. 1995. "On the Form of Transfers to Special Interests." *Journal of Political Economy* 103: 1210–35.

Dixit, Avenash, and John Londregan. 1996. "The Determinants of Success of Special Interests in Redistributive Politics." *Journal of Politics* 58: 1132–55.

Ehrmann, Henry W. (ed.). 1958. *Interest Groups on Four Continents.* Pittsburgh: University of Pittsburgh Press/International Political Science Association.

Fearon, James D. 1994. "Ethnic War as a Commitment Problem." Paper presented at Annual Meeting of American Political Science Association, New York (September 2, 1994).

Frieden, Jeffry A., and Ronald Rogowski. 1996. "The Impact of the International Economy on National Policies: An Analytical Overview." In *Internationalization and Domestic Politics,* edited by Robert O. Keohane and Helen Milner (Cambridge: Cambridge University Press), ch. 2.

Gabel, Matthew, and Harvey D. Palmer. 1995. "Understanding Variation in Public Support for European Integration." *European Journal of Political Research* 27: 3–19.

Grafstein, Robert. 1990. "Missing the Archimedean Point: Liberalism's Institutional Presuppositions." *American Political Science Review* 84: 177–93.

Gray, Virginia, and David Lowery. 1988. "Interest Group Politics and Economic Growth in the American States: Testing the Olson Contract." *American Political Science Review* 82: 109–32.

Grilli, Vittorio, Donato Masciandaro, and Guido Tabellini. 1991. "Political and Monetary Institutions and Public Financial Policies in the Industrial Countries." *Economic Policy* 13: 342–91.

Grossman, Gene M., and Elhanan Helpman. 1994. "Protection for Sale." *American Economic Review* 84: 833–50.

Grove, D. John. 1991. "Education and the Ethnic Division of Labor in Reform-Minded Societies." *Comparative Political Studies* 24: 56–75.

Hansen, Wendy L. 1990. "The International Trade Commission and the Politics of Protectionism." *American Political Science Review* 84: 21–46.

Hechter, Michael. 1975. *Internal Colonialism: The Celtic Fringe in British National Development, 1536–1966.* Berkeley: University of California Press.

Hobsbawm, Eric J. 1979. *The Age of Capital, 1848–1875.* New York: New American Library.

———. 1992. *Nations and Nationalism Since 1780,* 2nd ed. Cambridge: Cambridge University Press.

Horowitz, Donald L. 1985. *Ethnic Groups in Conflict.* Berkeley: University of California Press.

Katzenstein, Peter J. 1984. *Corporatism and Change: Austria, Switzerland, and the Politics of Industry.* Ithaca, N.Y.: Cornell University Press.

Kiser, Edward, and Xiaoxi Tong. 1992. "Determinants of the Amount and Type of Corruption in State Fiscal Bureaucracies: An Analysis of Late Imperial China." *Comparative Political Studies* 25: 300–331.

Krueger, Anne O. 1974. "The Political Economy of the Rent-Seeking Society." *American Economic Review* 64: 291–303.

Laitin, David D. 1988. "Language Games." *Comparative Politics* 20: 289–302.

———. 1992. *Language Repertoires and State Construction in Africa.* New York: Cambridge University Press.

Legro, Jeffrey W. 1996. "Culture and Preferences in the International Cooperation Two-Step." *American Political Science Review* 90: 118–37.

Levitt, Steven D., and James M. Snyder. 1995. "Political Parties and the Distribution of Federal Outlays." *American Journal of Political Science* 39: 958–980.

Lichbach, Mark I. 1987. "Deterrence or Escalation: The Puzzle of Aggregate Studies of Repression and Dissent." *Journal of Conflict Resolution* 31: 266–97.

———. 1990. "Will Rational People Rebel Against Inequality?: Samson's Choice." *American Journal of Political Science* 34: 1049–76.

Lijphart, Arend. 1968. *The Politics of Accommodation: Pluralism and Democracy in the Netherlands.* Berkeley: University of California Press.

Lindert, Peter H. 1996. "What Limits Social Spending?" *Explorations in Economic History* 33: 1–34.

Lipson, Charles. 1991. "Why Are Some International Agreements Informal?" *International Organization* 45: 495–538.

Lohmann, Susanne, and Sharyn O'Halloran. 1994. "Divided Government and U.S. Trade Policy: Theory and Evidence." *International Organization* 48: 595–632.

McCubbins, Matthew D., and Thomas Schwartz. 1988."Congress, the Courts, and Public Policy: Consequences of the One Man, One Vote Rule." *American Journal of Political Science* 32: 388–415.

Mitchell, William C., and Michael C. Munger. 1991. "Economic Models of Interest Groups: An Introductory Survey." *American Journal of Political Science* 35: 512–46.

Nas, Tevfik F., Albert C. Price, and Charles T. Weber. 1986. "A Policy-Oriented Theory of Corruption." *American Political Science Review* 80: 107–19.

Olson, Mancur, Jr. 1982. *The Rise and Decline of Nations.* New Haven, Conn.: Yale University Press.

Przeworski, Adam, and Michael Wallerstein. 1988. The Structural Dependence of the State on Capital. *American Political Science Review* 82: 11–29.

Roberts, Brian E. 1990. "A Dead Senator Tells No Lies: Seniority and the Distribution of Federal Benefits." *American Journal of Political Science* 34: 31–58.

Rogowski, Ronald. 1987a. "Trade and the Variety of Democratic Institutions." *International Organization* 41: 203–23.

———. 1987b. "Political Cleavages and Changing Exposure to Trade." *American Political Science Review* 81: 1121–37.

———. 1993. "Comparative Politics." In *Political Science: The State of the Discipline II,* edited by Ada W. Finifter, (Washington: American Political Science Association).

Roubini, Nouriel, and Jeffrey Sachs. 1989. "Political and Economic Determinants of Budget Deficits in the Industrial Democracies." *European Economic Review* 33: 903–33.

Runge, C. Ford, and Harald von Witzke. 1990. "European Community Enlargement and Institutional Choice in the Common Agricultural Policy." *American Journal of Political Science* 34: 254–268.

Saltzstein, Grace Hall. 1986. "Female Mayors and Women in Municipal Jobs." *American Journal of Political Science* 30: 140–64.

Scharpf, Fritz W. 1991. *Crisis and Choice in European Social Democracy.* Translated by Ruth Crowley and Fred Thompson. Ithaca, N.Y.: Cornell University Press.

Tsebelis, George. 1989. "The Abuse of Probability in Political Analysis: The Robinson Crusoe Fallacy." *American Political Science Review* 83: 77–91.

Wintrobe, Ronald. 1990. "The Tinpot and the Totalitarian: An Economic Theory of Dictatorship." *American Political Science Review* 84: 849–872.

Wittman, Donald A. 1989. "Arms Control, Verification, and Other Games Involving Imperfect Detection." *American Political Science Review* 83: 923–45.

SOCIAL CAPITAL

Russell Hardin

Although the term "social capital" itself is a recent coinage, concern with the things that have been discussed under that label has been long-standing in sociological theory.[1] James Coleman has been the most influential proponent of viewing these as systematically related. In his first treatment of social capital (Coleman 1988, S98; see also Coleman 1990, 302–4), he discussed it as follows:

> Social capital is defined by its function. It is not a single entity but a variety of different entities, with two elements in common: they all consist of some aspect of social structures, and they facilitate certain actions of actors—whether persons or corporate actors—within the structure. Like other forms of capital, including human capital, social capital is not completely fungible but may be specific to certain activities. A given form of social capital that is valuable in facilitating certain actions may be useless or even harmful for others.

In his applications of the idea of social capital, Coleman considers the lower-level structures of ongoing relationships, family, work groups, and so forth (Coleman 1990, 300–21, 361–63, 590–93, 595–96). These structures enable us, as individuals or corporate actors, to do many things, including cooperate successfully with each other in manifold ways.

Perhaps the most surprising exponent of a notion of social capital is Gary Becker, who says that social capital "incorporates the influence of past actions by peers and others in an individual's social network and control system" into "preferences or tastes." He pairs it with *personal capital,* which includes "the relevant past consumption and other personal experiences that affect current and future utilities" (1996, 4). Like Coleman, Becker is concerned with using social capital to help explain the relation of individual values and actions to collective or structural outcomes, but it has this effect through the utility function.

Other recent users of the term typically do not define it specifically but rather refer to instances of it or give very general characterizations of it. By social capital, Robert Putnam (1995, 665–66) means "social connections and the attendant norms and trust" that are "features of social life . . . that enable participants to act together more effectively to pursue shared objectives." John Brehm and Wendy Rahn (1997, 999) define social capital as "the web of cooperative relationships between citizens that facilitates resolution of collective action problems." Francis Fukuyama shares this general view with Brehm, Rahn, and Putnam. Of these scholars, he gives the most general statement of what social capital is: "the ability of people to work together for common purposes in groups and organizations" (Fukuyama 1995, 10).

For yet a third vision of the workings of social capital, one way to read the burgeoning literature on the relational theory of contract (and other) law is as an account of the ways social capital can enable us to cooperate without the use of the sanctions of the law as much more than a backdrop to protect us against the worst abuses we might experience (Macauley 1963; Macneil 1980; see also Williamson 1985). Hence, social capital (norms and relationships) can be used to displace what might be considered another form of capital (legal institutions) that is putatively less effective or efficient. Similarly, in much of the neo-institutional account of the success of firms, the focus is on the informal devices of social capital that displace or augment the formal devices of hierarchical control (Williamson 1975, 1981).

For the political scientists Brehm, Fukuyama, Putnam, Rahn, and others, the interest in social capital

> is motivated primarily by the linkage between levels of social capital and collective outcomes; high levels of social capital appear to be crucial for such measures of collective well-being as economic development, effective political institutions, low crime rates, and lower incidences of other social problems such as teen pregnancy and delinquency. (Brehm and Rahn 1997, 1000)

They focus on trust, norms, and networks, all of which seem to be at the individual level. But for them, the central concern is with how individual-level factors *facilitate the working of institutions,* including the whole of government. Hence, at least initially, the view of Putnam and these others is strikingly different from that expressed by Coleman in the passage quoted earlier. They tend to reverse Coleman's characterization, in which various instances of social capital *"facilitate certain actions of actors."* Although he also mentions corporate actors as beneficiaries of social capital, in Coleman's actual applications of the notion, the function of social capital is to enable individuals (and groups of individuals) to achieve things they could not otherwise achieve so well, as in the examples he gives of student political groups, doctor-patient relations, neighborhood child care, and a Cairo bazaar (Coleman 1990, 302–4).

For the political scientists, it is social capital at the individual level that allows groups and societies to manage at the highest collective level. In particular, individual-level social capital contributes to the working of the institutions of government and the performance of the economy. The causal relation is a bit loose, and indeed, it is chiefly merely asserted from various correlations. The main correlation for Putnam and others who are worried about the possible decline of government effectiveness over time is a putative and simultaneous decline in so-called generalized trust and in trusting government over the past few decades in the United States. The main, somewhat loose correlation for Fukuyama is between cross-societal differences in general trusting and in economic performance.

Causally, the main difference between these political scientists and Coleman is the direction of their causal arrows. Coleman's arrow generally goes from the level of social relations (which ground social capital) to the individual level. For the political scientists, the causal arrow goes from the individual level to the institutional level. The difference can be exemplified by the nature of the concern with trust in the two visions. For Coleman, various relationships enable individuals to trust each other; for the others, individual-level trust enables institutions to work well.

Hence, under the rubric of social capital, we seemingly cover several quite varied and often amorphous *causal relations:* the effects of lower-level social interactions that facilitate individual achievements for Coleman; between individual-level trust and social institutions and other collective-level outcomes in the recent work of political scientists; and the displacement of some institutional-level devices by individual-level relationships in the relational theory of law. Still others see social capital at work in facilitating the relations between organizations (see, for example, Leeuw 1997, 484). Notably missing from the list are the *effects of institutions on lower-level interactions.*

Despite the variations, this recent wave of work on social capital may be one of the most interesting and potentially most important moves in recent social theory. And its multifaceted and possibly even incoherent character might reflect nothing more than the usual effort to grapple with a new idea before getting it nailed down and making it useful in our explanations. I think, however, that much of the variation in the discussions can be clarified easily and that, if it is, the concepts at issue become much more useful to our understanding of relevant causal effects.

The conceptual difference between Becker and the others is substantial. For Becker, social capital works at the level of the individual, so much so that it can be incorporated into the individual's utility function, and *its causal impact is on the individual.* Social capital is the influences that others have on shaping my tastes. My tastes then determine the degree of pleasure or other welfare benefit I receive from consuming various things. Some might prefer not to call Becker's social capital an instance of capital because, traditionally, the chief role of capital is to help produce goods. But there is no point in merely producing goods—the point is to produce goods that contribute to welfare. Becker's social and personal capital contribute to welfare by affecting the level of benefit one gets from consuming particular goods.

The titles of works by Brehm and Rahn (1997), Fukuyama (1995), and Putnam (1993) suggest that, in their view, levels of social capital have a strong causal role in the general levels of governmental and economic performance. But the variant visions of social capital may be sufficiently diverse as to permit some aspects of such capital to go *into the utility function* as though they directly yield welfare rather than merely causally contribute to the production of other things that yield welfare. For example, my relationship with you might be a direct good to me, although it might also facilitate my achievement of many things I value. What makes it a good to me largely also makes it facilitative, so that it has a role both in my utility function and in the category of those things that produce utility for me. But the fact that some bit of my social capital fits in this way in my utility function is not a concern of Coleman or the political scientists, and its role there is not that which Becker envisions.

In this essay, I distinguish Becker's social capital from the various things Coleman and the political scientists call social capital. I use the term "interpersonal capital" for the latter. That is a more informative label for what Coleman, Putnam, and others mean: the relationships with others that enable us to do various things. Whether particular factors other than merely rich relationships, such as norms or trust, belong in interpersonal capital turns on explanatory or causal understandings of such factors. Including them merely by definition makes using the concept relatively messy when, in Coleman's case, that concept is used to explain trust and, in the case of Putnam and others, it is supposed to include trust.

One might prefer other labels for interpersonal capital, such as "relational" or "network" capital, which also capture its sense better than the relatively amorphous term "social capital." That amorphous term is more fitting for the social norms, expectations, and so forth that Becker's analysis focuses on, because these things have the same causal function in Becker's account. But the labels per se do not matter, and no doubt many of these authors will continue to lay claim to the term "social capital" and will continue to mean quite different things by it. What matters is how the various conceptions fit into explaining behavior and social outcomes.

To make sense of Becker's social capital, I will first fit it into utility theory as the theory has developed over the past couple of centuries. Putting Becker's social and personal capital into the utility function is a complex move whose significance and even meaning might not be readily apparent. It should come as no surprise that Becker's is analytically the most acute contribution to this literature. A main thesis of what follows, however, is that inclusion of social and personal capital in human capital (Becker 1996, 4) is wrong in an important sense. Or at least there is good analytical reason to separate the human capital on which Becker has done much of the foundational work (Becker 1964/1975) from his social and personal capital. The reason is related to the claim that what Putnam and others call social capital is not Becker's social capital.

THE UTILITY FUNCTION

Utility theory has developed remarkably from its early years in economics, when, as in the quotidian usage of the word, utility was taken to be a property of objects. This quotidian view was expressed well by Jeremy Bentham, for whom utility was the central moral concept. His opening definition in his most influential work is: "By utility is meant *that property in any object,* whereby it tends to produce benefit, advantage, pleasure, good, or happiness [or] to prevent the happening of mischief, pain, evil, or unhappiness to the party whose interest is considered" (Bentham 1789/1970, 12; my emphasis).

Part of the problem with the very term "utility" is that it derives indirectly from the Latin utilitas, meaning useful. Bentham was rather like a dictionary run wild, a lunatic for definition, who defined terms within definitions of terms and with his own inventions of the linguistic derivations of words. As a definitionalist, he would have found it difficult to escape the sense of utility as useful even though, in adopting utility as the foundation of his moral theory, he distorted his own program. Under his influence, a modern dictionary defines utility first as "usefulness" and then makes the seemingly illicit or incoherent move of adding the meanings "the power to satisfy human wants" and "happiness," which is essentially satisfied wants. From meaning "the power to satisfy wants" the term moves to meaning the satisfaction itself. Such creeping evolutions in meaning are often creepy, as in this case.

From at least Adam Smith forward, the traditional view that utility inheres in objects rather than in the use people make of them is contrary to good sense. It is only a short conceptual step from Smith's demand and supply view of price to the view that utility is in the person's valuing rather than in what is valued. Bentham's opening definition of utility is even contrary to the utilitarian program that he helped to initiate with the book that defines utility so badly. That program, after all, is based on the "benefit, advantage, pleasure, good, or happiness" of the individual, not on the value of the objects the individual consumes or uses. Bentham, unfortunately, has burdened us with his terminology: to untutored ears, his moral theory, "utilitarianism," is often heard as pragmatic or crude self-interest.[2] His actual theory should better be labeled "welfarism" or some other relevant term, because his actual interest was in the panoply of welfarist notions in his "benefit, advantage, pleasure, good, or happiness."

Hence, Bentham by himself represented the bifurcation of economic theory into two contrary lines. One of these was the line that focused on the value inherent in objects, which ended with the dismal labor theory of value of Karl Marx, a theory that wrecked much of the work of one of the otherwise greatest minds of his century. The other is the line that focused on the value people get out of using or consuming objects and out of other activities, which is still in development today in modern utility theory, although many modern writers seem uncomfortable with the term "utility" and often eliminate it and speak only of "preferences."

The utility function today often has an abstract aura. Various items are included in it, and its functional form is commonly left unspecified. Recall that Becker includes personal and social capital in the individual's utility function. It is striking that he did not do this with his earlier, extremely influential account of human capital, such as in skills and training (Becker 1964/1975), although he says of social and personal capital that they are merely part of human capital (1996, 4). Although human capital clearly contributes to utility—in the causal sense discussed earlier— Becker did not make it simply a part of the utility function.

I think Becker's earlier decision not to put human capital in the utility function was conceptually correct, and on some accounts of social capital, it would therefore seem similarly correct to exclude social capital from the utility function, even though it obviously *contributes causally* to those things that are in the utility function. Becker (1996, 5) says that conceiving the utility function without social capital in it and without specific goods, but only with their effects on welfare, would be a "more fundamental approach," in which

> utility does not depend directly on goods and consumer capital stocks, but only on household-produced "commodities," such as health, social standing and reputation, and pleasures of the senses. The production of these commodities in turn depends on goods, consumer capital, abilities, and other variables. The utility at any time is then only a function of commodities produced at the same time, and not of any commodities produced in the past.[3] Nevertheless, the past, present, and future are still linked through the capital stocks that determine the productivity of commodity production. Present accumulation of personal and social capital changes household productivity in the future.

This is the "more fundamental approach" of Becker's earlier efforts to work out a "new theory of consumer behavior" with Robert Michael (Becker 1976, 131–49) and George Stigler (Becker 1996, 24–49). Becker uses this conception of the utility function to great effect in his work on the family (Becker 1981, 7–12). The point of the

earlier efforts was to reduce the vast catalog of goods and services that might be arguments in an individual's utility function to a smaller set of beneficial effects on the
household from its consumption of market goods and services *in its own production of
this smaller set of beneficial effects.* These effects are the "health, social standing and reputation, and pleasures of the senses" mentioned earlier. This smaller set of effects
would be far more stable over time than the set of particular consumptions that go into
their production. Hence, focusing on this smaller set of beneficial effects fits Becker's
desire to define stable utility functions that are useful in making predictions over time.

In his discussion of social capital, Becker appears to take an intermediate position
between the standard form of the utility function, with its multifarious consumptions of ordinary goods and services, and this greatly simplified (more fundamental) utility function. He does so by *entering social capital into the utility function* along
with consumption goods—this yields his "extended utility function"—to account for
the conversion of goods by the individual or the household into their beneficial
effects. This would make sense of his otherwise odd omission of traditional material
capital, such as machinery, which is used in producing the ordinary goods that go
into the utility function, thence to be further affected by social and personal capital to
produce benefits.

This extended form of the utility function has the conspicuous benefit, at least
abstractly, of representing the fact that my personal capital might produce very different benefits for me than your capital would produce for you *from the same set of goods
and services.* (If we are in the same milieu, however, our social capital must be quite
similar.) If we cannot represent that personal difference, then each person's (or household's) utility function must be entirely independently defined, with quite different
functional relationships between all the inputs of goods and services. Furthermore,
each individual's function has to change over time to accommodate changing personal
and social capital. It is, of course, each individual's differences in personal and social
capital that make the conversion of specific goods and services into beneficial effects
idiosyncratic. One person's personal capital makes caviar a sensory treat worth its high
price; another's makes caviar a source of revulsion.[4] With Becker's more refined
extended utility function, therefore, we can highlight such facts and more readily make
sense of them, especially when we wish to predict behavior over time.

The more fundamental form and the extended form of the utility function that
Becker uses in his analysis of social and personal capital are alternative ways to sta-
bilize the utility function. The more fundamental approach that includes only the
small set of beneficial effects of the consumption of a vast range of goods gives all
individuals a similar utility function but quite different utility levels. In the more
recent vocabulary of social and personal capital, the differences in utility levels
depend on our variant holdings of personal and social capital.

In what follows I wish both to highlight several conceptual issues that tend to get
in the way of coherent argument and to focus attention on causal issues. I organize
discussion around the conceptual issues first; causal issues come up throughout these
discussions, and I turn to them most specifically in the section on trust and interpersonal capital and in concluding remarks on the larger programs of all these scholars. It should become clear that what Becker wishes to explain is quite different from
what the others here attempt to explain with their variant notions of social capital.

INTERESTS, CONSUMPTIONS, WELFARE

We speak, sometimes almost interchangeably, of interests, consumptions, and welfare, but these are conceptually quite different. Our interests are what put us in a position to consume, and consumption typically brings welfare. I have an interest in amassing resources, but resources are of no value per se—I want them only in order to be able to consume. Obviously, interests and consumptions trade off with each other. If I consume some things, I must expend some of my resources. Some social theorists argue that we should ground our normative theories in resources rather than in welfare, that certain conceptual problems in welfare make it finally an unworkable normative principle (Sen 1982, 353–69). Without resolving that issue, we may all readily grant that resources are means without intrinsic value and that what gives them instrumental value is the welfare they can bring us. In some contexts, however, resources can stand proxy for consumptions—as is commonly true, for example, when we speak of the interests of various groups that want higher income or profit.

Having resources is in our interest because they can be used to enable consumptions, which produce or have utility. Interests are therefore merely proxy for the utility of eventual consumptions. Interests are a useful proxy for alternative consumptions just because they constitute a far less varied category than do consumptions and because they are fungible across many possible consumptions (Hardin 1988, 200). This suggests that a utility function in interests alone would be even simpler than Becker's fundamental form of the utility function. But the costs of consumptions need not be linearly related to their utility or the enjoyment of them, because of the ways Becker's social and personal capital work on them, but also because price and benefit are not at all equivalent for any particular consumption and because there may be complementarities and substitutabilities among consumptions.

Using interests as a proxy for consumptions is therefore potentially misleading, although it might often be relatively sensible. The cardinal value theory of John von Neumann (von Neumann and Morgenstern 1944/1953, appendix) and Thomas Bayes (1764/1958) might apply to simply conceived interests but not so readily to a panoply of consumptions with their complementarities and substitutabilities. To put this the other way around, focusing on interests allows us, perhaps wrongly, to think cardinally; focusing on consumptions virtually forces us to think ordinally. Becker's fundamental form of the utility function takes these ordinal issues into account so that it is a better form than the even simpler form that includes only interests.

If we include all consumptions now and into the future in our choice function, as in Kenneth Arrow's (1951/1963) fully determined states of affairs, interest drops out (see Hardin 1987). Note that interests and consumptions trade off against each other. It is against my interest to consume an opera tonight, but if I could not do such things, I would have little reason for living. It is the very point of my interest in various resources that they enable me to consume various things, and the point of consuming them is that consumption brings benefits or welfare. The Japanese novelist Yasunari Kawabata (1974, 49) elegantly frames the relation between interests and consumptions: "When one spends money, one remembers spending it even after it's gone. But when one loses the money one has saved, the very thought of saving is a bitter memory."

CAPITAL

We may distinguish several forms of capital, including financial, physical, human, interpersonal, and Becker's social and personal capital. All of these contribute to our welfare because they enable us to purchase or produce goods for consumption or to turn those goods into welfare for ourselves and others. In traditional accounts, there were only financial and physical capital. Theodore Schultz (1963) and Becker (1964/1975) are the main early developers of the analysis of human capital, which is principally education and training that enable us to produce, just as physical capital in machines enables us to produce. Financial capital enables us to purchase other kinds of capital, to invest in other ways, or to purchase consumption goods directly. Physical and human capital have the quality that they do not convert into goods for consumption but do enable us to produce goods for consumption, in a sense, far more cheaply. Hence, for example, with a relevant machine and training I can produce far more of some good in any given period of time than I could without the machine or the training. An instructive way to put this claim is that such capital is often superadditive with other inputs, such as effort.

Hence, money is often different from other forms of capital such as physical and human capital, and unless it is used to purchase those forms of capital, it typically does not have the multiplier or productive effects of those other forms. It is also different in that it is typically more fungible than, say, material capital in machinery or human, social, or personal capital. Physical, human, social, and personal capital all have potential multiplier effects. The productive quality of such capital seems to fit uneasily with the goods that we consume as part of a single utility function.

Human capital differs from social and personal capital in a significant way. Human capital, such as education and training, is itself useful directly in the production of goods. Social and personal capital come in later at the point of converting the consumption of goods into welfare. Financial capital is embodied in money and other financial instruments, physical capital typically in machinery, and human capital in educated abilities and knowledge. In Coleman's phrasing, social capital is "embodied in the *relations* among persons" (1990, 304). Indeed, he suggests it is dependent on iterated interactions, even perhaps iterated prisoners' dilemma or exchange interactions (743). Becker's vision is superficially similar. But because of the way social capital works in transforming the value of consumptions rather than in directly producing the goods that are consumed, he puts his social capital in the utility function. Hence, "the utility function at any moment depends not only on the different goods consumed but also on the stock of personal and social capital at that moment" (Becker 1996, 5). (He also includes personal capital in the utility function because it similarly works by affecting the level of benefit one gets from particular consumptions [4].)

These differences can be summarized by instantiating them. The (alas, paltry) bit of money in my pocket is an instance of financial capital. The computer on which I write this is obviously an instance of physical capital. The years I spent in education and the evenings I spent in the Becker-Coleman seminar at the University of Chicago contributed to my human capital (although they also provided many moments of immediate pleasure). My ongoing relations with colleagues and many others ground instances of interpersonal capital—or social capital in the sense of

Coleman, Putnam, and others. And the social influences of my peers, community, or reference group on my tastes are instances of my social capital in Becker's sense. What I have directly experienced that has affected my tastes for some consumption goods is an instance of personal capital. Taken together, most of these benefit me through the consumptions they enable me to enjoy, while Becker's personal and social capital affect me through their influence on how much I benefit from various consumptions.

All of these effects on consumption and its enjoyment not only interact with each other causally but also sometimes interact through my welfare and at cost to my interests. For example, I may indirectly gain great benefit from writing something (I must publish or perish) while also gaining great pleasure from it directly. Hence, keeping the separate categories of capital or the categories of capital, welfare, consumptions, and interests completely separated analytically is often difficult or impossible.

If capital is viewed simply as a resource, as clearly financial capital is, then it does not belong in the utility function. It brings beneficial effects or welfare only after it is converted into, produces, or enhances goods that are consumed. Purely resource terms essentially represent future consumptions. Becker's social and personal capital cannot be resource terms in this sense because they do not convert into goods. Rather, *they act on me* to make my consumption of goods more (or less) rewarding. Putting financial capital into the utility function would constitute double counting, as though having the capital now and using it for consumptions to enhance my welfare later both added to my welfare. Putting social capital into the utility function does not have this flaw if its role there is the functional one of affecting the conversion of consumed goods into richer benefits. But the interpersonal capital of Coleman, Putnam, and others is essentially a resource. Hence, it cannot be put into Becker's extended utility function.

On an expansive reading of Coleman's general statement characterizing social capital (quoted at the outset of this essay), a well-functioning family structure, a system of norms to regulate cooperation and social interactions to the benefit of typical individuals, a working legal system for enforcing contracts, and a working language might all seem to be instances of social capital. In Coleman's actual discussions of instances of social capital, however, only the first two examples come up. Similarly in the work of Putnam and others, the focus is on interpersonal considerations grounded in informal networks of interaction. Hence, these scholars evidently do not count the more substantial institutional structures of government and large organizations as instances of their version of social capital, although these structures may contribute to its creation in other contexts. And the mastery of a native language may or may not be an instance of social capital for them, although having English rather than, say, Navajo as a native language is enormously more enabling for many purposes.

Yet institutions and language enable us in many ways. For example, the legal institutions that stand behind contracting enable us to enter into exchanges that would be prohibitively risky without legal enforcement of relevant obligations. We may call this *institutional capital*. It is very different from financial, physical, and human capital in that it does not directly produce goods or benefits. But it is like these insofar as it indirectly enables us to produce by protecting us against intrusions into our efforts and providing infrastructures that make production more efficient. Institutional capital is sometimes more nearly like social and personal capital in that it enables us to make the most of whatever goods we do produce and consume.

But it also differs from human, social, and personal capital in that it is largely outside us. The theorists of relational law and the new institutional economists might claim that the institutional capital in the legal system is far less than we might have thought because very much of what makes, say, contracts work is interpersonal capital.

The institutional capital in the government of the United States is enormously enabling to me. As far as I am concerned, however, it is essentially a matter of external luck that that government exists and governs over my territory. I may contribute slightly to the continued existence and power of that government and to its specific workings in particular contexts, much as I might contribute to the improvement of a machine I use in production. And of course, it would be hard finally to abstract that government from the inputs and supports of 260 million Americans. But the contribution of any one of us is too slight to make the government seem modally to be anything other than external to us.

Should Becker include such institutional capital in his extended utility function or exclude it? Its role is not so much to enhance the value of various consumptions once we have them, as social capital does, but actually to enable us to have them at all. Hence, its role would seem to be external to the utility function as Becker sees it, along with financial, physical, and human capital. Its role in producing benefits is externally causal rather than functional in the sense that personal and social capital are functional within Becker's utility function. Along with financial, physical, human, and interpersonal capital, institutional capital therefore does *not* belong in the utility function. All of these work by affecting what consumptions are available. Hence, their effects are largely external to the actor. The effects of Becker's social and personal capital are more or less entirely within the actor. For example, your personal capital may enable you to enjoy an extravagantly expensive wine far more than mine allows me to do. And your social capital may enable you to get a great kick out of conforming especially well to your group's dress code while I get little or no special kick from the way I dress, even though I might spend far more on dress than you do. In both cases, the same external expenditure buys more internal benefit for you than for me. [5]

In sum, various forms of capital, ranging from financial to social and personal capital, cross the distinctions between interests, consumptions, and welfare. Financial capital constitutes mere resources or interests. Physical and human capital produce or enhance the production of resources and consumptions. Interpersonal and institutional capital enable us more readily to produce consumptions. Becker's social and personal capital work on consumptions to produce welfare. The logics of these forms of capital are therefore quite varied.

PROBLEMS IN THE NOTION OF PREFERENCE

Discussions of preferences, utility, and welfare often range over several distinctions that undercut coherent arguments. I wish to consider two pairs of views on the nature of preferences. The two views in each pair are mutually exclusive, or at least potentially in conflict. To ask which of the views in either of the pairs is correct may or may not make sense, depending on what is meant by correct. But making claims that are grounded sometimes in one of these pairs and sometimes in the other, without carefully distinguishing these, often clearly does not make sense. The significance of these pairs for present purposes is in how they relate to Becker's utility functions that include social and personal capital as arguments and in how they help us to make sense of these.

Momentary Versus Lifetime Utility

Becker's reason for including social and personal capital as arguments in the individual's (extended) utility function is that doing so makes the utility *function* stable into the future even though levels of capital might change. Not including these capital terms makes utility functions unstable over time because what I prefer tomorrow might depend on what I consume or do today if that affects my capacities for enjoying various things tomorrow. Of course, although Becker's utility functions do not change over time, *levels* of utility do change (Becker 1996, 5–6), as should follow from the fact that we may be able to produce and consume far more at one time than at another. Becker wants stable utility functions because they enable us to make reasonable predictions about behavior at future times from current utility functions.

If we put the individual's social or personal capital in her utility function, we need not rewrite that function every time these change. Against this concern, note three classes of problems: exogenous reasons for changing utility functions, time-dependent variations in welfare from experiences and consumptions, and limited personal identification over time. The latter two classes of problems suggest the traditional concern with the discounting of future consumptions. Discounting futures in order to take uncertainties into consideration is not problematic. But Jon Elster characterizes a strong present orientation as "consistently irrational" (Elster 1979, 70), and Becker seems plausibly to agree (Becker 1996, 10–12, 48–49).

What I discuss here, however, is neither discounting to take account of uncertainty nor the pure discounting that troubles Elster and Becker. Rather, under "time dependence" I am concerned with the present enjoyment I derive from a past or future consumption. And under "limited identification with the self" I am concerned with the degree to which I even care about my future self.

Exogenous Changes   First, unfortunately, utility functions may actually be unstable over time for reasons other than changes in capital. Some of these reasons are as orderly and predictable as any of Becker's concerns with explanation from utility functions. For example, there are chemical changes that make an individual's preferences change over time, and these changes may be reasonably predicted from the relevant biological theory. One change that has been mooted recently is in the chemicals that supposedly influence romantic love and its emotions. There is reputedly a cycle of these chemicals that commonly runs for about four years before their effect diminishes substantially or ceases altogether (Fisher 1992). Hence, the remarkable fact that many marriages seem to end after about four years might not reflect changing judgments of the other person or judgments of particularly irksome experiences of them, but merely biological changes that terminate the intensity of feelings for the other. If this is what is happening, then trying to explain this change as merely a straightforward endogenous preference change grounded in a stable utility function seems less satisfactory than explaining it chemically.

Still, one might agree with Becker that economic explanations of changing preferences in many contexts are more satisfactory and less ad hoc than such biological explanations or than various psychological and other explanations. In large part, they are more satisfactory because they are more systematic and because, as in Becker's (1981) treatise on the family, they work remarkably well. But biological and other explanations of changing preferences may trump economic accounts of some phenomena, as they surely do in many developmental or ethological accounts of behavior.

Time Dependence in Welfare   Becker remarks that one's utility at any time is "only a function of commodities produced at the same time, and not of any commodities produced in the past" (Becker 1996, 5). Contrary to this view, there may be some residue of the wonderfully enjoyable meal I accidentally ate at the Quilted Giraffe on Madison Avenue in June 1992. But if I had a choice today between having eaten that meal and finding the money it cost in the pocket of an old jacket, I would have a hard time supposing that the present residue of the enjoyment of that meal is worth the one hundred dollars that the meal cost. Was the then-present enjoyment of that meal worth that much at the time? Arguably, yes. If consumptions of the past enhance my welfare today, they do so because of this typically very slight—and increasingly slight as time passes—present residue of pleasure and because of other causal effects they may have had on my current consumptions and my enjoyment of these. In the latter case, for example, as a result of what I learned from experiencing that meal, I may receive greater pleasure from other meals today. That is, in Becker's terms, some past consumptions contribute to my personal capital and thereby have a multiplier effect on my current efforts to achieve pleasure through fine food.

Of course, that 1992 experience might perversely also have reduced my welfare today by setting a standard that I cannot often afford and that reduces the pleasure I might otherwise have had in meals of a less extraordinary quality. For example, adults who have discovered Italian gelato or French dark chocolate may never again find much pleasure in ordinary American variants.[6] In that case, I might wish I had different, cheaper preferences. But I do not act on that wish because my actual capital stocks constrain my choices and the utility I get from them no matter how much I may regret "the amount and kind of capital" I inherited form my past (Becker 1996, 21–22).

Similarly, of course, anticipation of future consumptions may greatly enhance my welfare today. For example, anticipation of the pleasures of being with someone or of taking a trip to Paris next week or next month—perhaps especially the pleasure of taking that trip with that someone—may be enormously enjoyable today. Contrariwise, anticipation of a future misery might reduce my pleasure in today's consumptions.

We should include all of these effects in my present utility function because they all affect my present enjoyment. Including them with their present remembered or anticipated pleasures is not double counting them because the relevant consumptions are actually enjoyed now in addition to the moment in which the relevant goods are actually or directly consumed. If people differ with respect to their capacities for enjoying either remembered or anticipated pleasures, they should choose to experience more of their consumptions either sooner or later, respectively.

Limited Identification with the Self   One might argue that Becker's move to the extended form of the utility function that includes social capital as well as goods is a move to presentiate future benefits that depend on such capital. This is analogous to the claim in contract theory that future actions are presentiated—that is, brought into the present—by a contract that requires future actions. If that is what the extended form of the utility function does, however, it runs against the problem of weak identification.

There is a huge literature on personal identity and its consistency over time. A more compelling issue is *personal identification* over time (Hardin 1988, 191–201). I may have relatively limited identification with the person who succeeds me in, say, 2008, or with the one who preceded me in 1958 or 1988. Suppose I do not identify at all with RH-1958. I may still be glad that RH-1958 had certain experiences that contributed to the character and capacities of RH-1998. Indeed, if my identification with past and future selves is weak, I must wonder whether I would even identify with RH-1998 if my experiences had been significantly other than what they were, because different experiences would have produced a different person in many respects. Still, in some vague sense I might wish RH-1958 had been better disciplined about learning to play the piano or that RH-1968 had studied economics. But as Becker says, RH-1998 is stuck with what those other RHs did: "We are all to some extent prisoners of experiences we wish we never had" (Becker 1996, 128). Our sunk costs are us (Hardin 1995, 69).

There may be a problem with the idea of a consistent utility function over a lifetime that is more nearly philosophical. Thomas Nagel (1970) argued that those who care about the enjoyments of their own future selves should as well worry about the present enjoyments of other people, to whom they are about as strongly attached and whose enjoyments they could at least as readily share. One could as forcefully argue the contrary, namely, that one should be no more concerned about one's distant future enjoyments than about the present enjoyments of others. That is what weak personal identification would imply.

If I identify little or not at all with my moderately distant future self, then I make little or no investment in personal capital for that future self. Or at least, I do not deliberately make any, although I might have experiences that, for reasons of their present benefit, do contribute to my personal capital as an unintended consequence or by-product. If I have such weak identification, then my utility function should include only present and near-present consumptions, so that we would speak only of my immediate welfare. If I have strong identification with RH over time, then I must also be concerned with interests, resources, and capital that are proxies for welfare that is yet to come (Hardin 1988, 201). Whether I would then have an integrated utility function over time, a function that includes my personal and social capital, such as Becker wants, might still be an open question for other reasons. But if I have very limited identification, it would be odd to put my personal capital into my current utility function. One might think to qualify this claim with some such phrase as "except insofar as that capital gives me richer experiences now." But insofar as it does this, my utility function already captures everything it should without adding in and, therefore, double counting my capital.

It is not meaningless to speak of interests, or resources, on the weak identification view of a self, but there is little need to speak of them. We need not speak of them because all we want from them is present consumptions. We cannot, however, do without concern with interests on the strong identification view. We do not know enough about all our plausible consumptions to bring them into a full evaluation. We therefore virtually require some such proxy notion as interests in order to bring future consumptions and their welfare into our utility function. Then we can trade off future consumptions against present consumptions through their similar effect on our interests (Hardin 1988, 200).

In sum, we surely do wish, as Becker does, to explain the changes that might be taken as evidence of changes in utility functions, but we might think they should often be explained by things that are not in the utility function or that are not matters of changes in social, personal, or other capital.

Instant Versus Reasoned Preferences

Often we have instant or gut-level preferences that are out of keeping with some seemingly more reasoned preference we may have. For example, F. Y. Edgeworth—with plausibly most others who have ever drunk it with pleasure—supposed that our preference for wine is a function of how much we have already had. My instant preference for wine at tonight's party, with its tendency to substantial consumption, might, however, be one that I would prefer both ex ante not to act on and ex post not to have acted on. In some sense, then, I seem to have a reasoned preference that conflicts with my instant or gut-level preference. It is not necessary to get that sense right for present purposes so long as we grant that there is some issue at stake here. (Anyone who attempts to get it right is likely to founder on the thousands of pages written on the issue.)

There are many treatments of so-called meta-preferences, rational preferences, and so forth, both by philosophers and by quasi- and not so quasi-psychologists. All of these discussions that I know are too simplistic to be finally compelling. For example, in the philosophical tradition, such preferences are often invoked in discussions of weakness of will. If my will were strong, presumably I would not drink too much, break my moral rules, fail to exercise, and on and on. Unfortunately, one might wonder just where or what the rational will is that it somehow gets the values right while the momentary person gets them wrong. In particular, one might suppose that the mind is a royal (or plebeian) mess that simply gets things differently in some parts than in others, and one might suppose further that there is no authoritative part of the mind that can rule on such matters (Hardin 1988, 193–97). Analytically, we may have no better claim to make than that my ex ante and ex post preferences can be out of line with my present preferences.

In part, the issues here are related to those of time dependence discussed earlier. At the gut level, I might prefer many consumptions now to having had them in the past or to having them in the future. I might have such a preference even though I might grant that I am better off at this moment from having had a pattern of experiences over many years, even decades. Indeed, it is those experiences that give me much of my present personal capital and that enable me to enjoy present experiences as much as I do. I might suppose this to be true even if I do not strongly identify with my past selves.

TRUST AND INTERPERSONAL CAPITAL

Institutional capital suggests the concern of the ancient Greek "Anonymous Iamblichi" (Gagarin and Woodruff 1995, 294), according to which: "The first result of lawfulness is trust, which greatly benefits all people and is among the greatest goods. The result of trust is that property has common benefits, so that even just a little property suffices, since it is circulated, whereas without this even a great amount does not suffice." The context of the remark is a list of the benefits of lawfulness. Law (or government) enables people to trust each other enough to risk exchanges with each other, to their great benefit. The anonymous Greek author shared the central vision of Thomas Hobbes (1651), for whom stable government enabled us to profit from our own efforts by protecting us from the depredations of others.

For Putnam and others, it is interpersonal relationships of trust that enable us to trust government, which enables government to work. Or perhaps we can say only that for them the problematic concern is with the seeming correlation between levels of interpersonal trust and levels of trust in government—and possibly with levels of performance of government. This correlation is problematic because it may suggest declining performance in the United States and some other Western nations and obstacles to performance in many developing nations (but see Hardin, 1999). What is wanted still is an explanatory account of why these correlations appear to be what survey research suggests they are (for graphic representation of the correlations in the United States, see Putnam 1995).

A central issue for understanding levels of trust in various societies is to grasp whether trust follows from interpersonal capital of other kinds or whether it is itself a major category of interpersonal capital. Fukuyama, Putnam, and many others seem to see it as a major category of interpersonal capital. There may very well be some conceptual confusion in their claims, because the actual interpersonal capital, if there is any with respect to trust, is *those things that enable people rationally to trust, not the trust itself.* That we perhaps successfully teach our children to be trustworthy, that we design institutions to give added incentive to be trustworthy, and that we have ongoing networks of relationships with others give us grounds to trust people in many contexts. The ongoing networks are part of our interpersonal capital.

We might also suppose that the learned capacity to judge trustworthiness, both in judging specific other individuals and in judging the context in which we are dealing with them, constitutes a form of interpersonal capital. That capacity can vary substantially across individuals and may depend heavily on early upbringing (see the learning model of Hardin 1992). Hence, families and societies that give infants and children a sense of the trustworthiness of others may thereby create substantial interpersonal capital that enables their children later to enter into cooperative arrangements relatively optimistically.

In an ongoing (roughly iterated) exchange relationship I may be able to trust you with respect to some matter in the sense that I can expect it to be your interest to take into account my interest in your fulfilling the trust. There are many visions of what trust is, but this one—trust as encapsulated in the interest the trusted has to fulfill the trust (Hardin 1991)—gives rich explanations of many phenomena of apparent trusting and trustworthiness. In particular, it compellingly fits the pattern of those whom we trust—who are those with whom we are in especially rich ongoing interactions of essentially iterated exchange. If, as in this model, trust is grounded in a rich ongoing relationship, the trusted has substantial incentive to be trustworthy in order to maintain the relationship.[7] But then it is not trust but rather the ongoing relationship (which enables trust by encouraging trustworthiness) that constitutes our interpersonal capital. It is that relationship that allows us to trust and to be trusted. It is important, of course, for me to be able to be trusted, because then I can enter into cooperative arrangements with others.

A commonplace claim is that trust does not fit the encapsulated interest model because it is inherently normative. Perhaps seeing it as normative would fit it into interpersonal capital. To address this possibility, note that, more generally, Coleman, Putnam, and others include norms in what they call social capital and what I have here labeled interpersonal capital. Becker includes them in his social capital. Do norms work in such different ways as to fit them in some of their workings into Becker's notion and in some into the notion of interpersonal capital? For Becker, norms belong in social capital only to the extent that they affect one's valuations of one's consumptions. For Putnam and others, they belong in interpersonal capital only to the extent that they facilitate cooperative activities at the interpersonal level. Note, oddly, that norms work *on the individual* in Becker's social capital but work on the interpersonal relationships—that is to say, *on others*—in interpersonal capital. For Coleman, Putnam, and others, one benefits from the norms that guide the behavior of others.

It seems likely that norms commonly do have both these functions, so that, in different ways, they belong in both Becker's social capital and in interpersonal capital. Norms, loosely defined, might make me shrink from doing many things, such as eating pork, and hence might radically affect my welfare from various consumptions, so that they fit as functional terms in Becker's extended utility function.[8] They might also cause me to be a calculating Kantian, who cooperates only if enough others do in various endeavors, so that they contribute to the interpersonal capital of those in my milieu by facilitating our cooperation.

But what of trust as a norm? There clearly cannot be a sensible norm merely to trust, because far too many people would be utterly untrustworthy in various contexts in which trusting them would cause harm to the truster or others. There might be a norm to be trustworthy. If so, then cooperative endeavors would prosper more readily because trustworthiness would beget trust. This follows because *your being trustworthy gives me incentive to trust you* in some context in which doing so would lead to cooperation that would be beneficial to me. Hence, trustworthiness might be part of interpersonal capital. It is part of that capital *not so much to the trustworthy person as to others who are enabled by it*. Trust that is relatively blind, rather than grounded in the incentives of an ongoing relationship or in the normative trustworthiness of another, would enable others also. But it would enable them to take one-sided advantage of the gullibly trusting. Hence, trust is either a conceptual proxy for trustworthiness in the claims of Putnam and others, or it does not belong in interpersonal capital (see further, Hardin 1996).

This conclusion goes some way toward drawing the supposedly normative sting of their analyses because it could hardly come as news that trustworthiness is a good thing. (They should therefore be concerned with assessing declining trustworthiness rather than its resultant declining trust.) Moreover, on the encapsulated interest vision of trust, their interpersonal capital is predominantly to be seen as grounded in the rationality of maintaining a cooperative stance in ongoing relationships. This, of course, recommends the use of institutional capital as well as, probably to a limited extent, norms to secure cooperation at the interpersonal level.

CONCLUDING REMARKS

All of the forms of capital discussed here can interact with each other, whether causally or functionally or both. The institutional capital represented by the American government is enormous in its impact on American and other lives and their welfare. (Indeed, a large part of the difference between, say, Russian and American economic and social life turns on the differences in the quality of the two nations' institutional capital.) The interpersonal capital that contributes to successful collective endeavors at lower levels might, through these lower-level activities and also perhaps directly, also be enormous in its impact on the workings of that government. The program of political scientists such as Putnam and others is to work out this particular causal role. To date they have given us some limited arguments for how interpersonal capital can causally affect institutional performance and capital. Certain forms of interpersonal capital enable individuals to perform their tasks within institutions better than they could do otherwise and, hence, to contribute to those institutions and the institutional capital that they represent.

Becker's social capital affects my welfare through its impact on the beneficial effects on me of my consumptions, that is, on my valuations of my consumptions. He is surely right to suppose that this is an important phenomenon and a corrective to simplistic self-interest theorizing. Coleman is right that interpersonal capital is important for facilitating lower-level interactions. Oliver Williamson is right that institutional harnessing of interpersonal capital to work around hierarchical and legal constraints can be efficient. The relational lawyers are likely right that interpersonal capital often does much of the work of facilitating contracts. Because it can make particular firms more efficient and can help to overcome the inefficiencies of legal devices, then Fukuyama is likely right that interpersonal capital positively affects overall economic success. It would also be right, therefore, to suppose that interpersonal capital is important in making specific government agencies work more efficiently and effectively because of the way such capital is harnessed *within* the agencies.

But is it right that interpersonal capital is important for making democracy work? That it is important in this way is in essence the claim of Putnam and others. While the Colemanesque argument seems to work for the other cases of facilitating cooperation, firm success, governmental agency success, and economic performance, there is as yet no argument that unpacks, in this microlevel way, the relationships between interpersonal capital and the general performance and responsiveness of democratic government. Perhaps getting the arguments and the causal relations clearer will lead to insights into what the microlevel relationships are.

Suppose interpersonal capital does affect institutional success in the general way that Putnam and others suppose. Then there may be substantial feedback between it and institutional capital, which enhances the prospects of interpersonal cooperation. If so, then we might expect both political and economic development to have self-reinforcing qualities that, once started, allow them to take off suddenly. This would follow already from the arguments of Williamson, the relational lawyers, and Fukuyama. And it would be reinforced still further if the arguments manqué of Putnam and others could be put into compelling form.

This seems roughly to be the story of the beginnings of the new regime of the United States under its Constitution of 1788. James Madison's design of institutions under the Constitution and Alexander Hamilton's monetary policies as secretary of the Treasury through the early years of the new government were the crucial moves in building institutions that could underwrite individual confidence in dealings with others across a very broad range of actors. Any given individual must have had many trustworthy partners for various undertakings, but the institutional devices of Madison and Hamilton greatly expanded the range of people with whom the typical individual engaged in the economy could deal. That those institutions were so beneficial may then have encouraged support for them.

Finally, note that all of these forms of capital are commonly invoked as enabling. Often, however, as Becker emphasizes, they are constraining: past "experiences, and the attitudes and behavior of others, frequently place more far-reaching constraints on choices than do mistakes and distortions in cognitive perceptions" (1996, 22).[9] They do so by contributing social capital that can detract from the benefits of various consumptions. Interpersonal and institutional capital can similarly get in our way. Widespread customs and even very local practices of personal networks can impose destructive norms on people, norms that have all of the structural qualities of interpersonal capital. Institutional capital can also wreak its destructive hold, as in the Eastern nations that are now trying to build new economies and political systems while partially still in the grip of old institutions.

Original version prepared for the Russell Sage Foundation–American Political Science Association panel on the contributions of Gary Becker to political science.

NOTES

1. James Coleman attributes the term to Glenn Loury (1977, 1987), but it was used even earlier in roughly the relevant sense by Jane Jacobs (1961, 138) and Lyda Hanifan (1916). I thank Robert Putnam for the latter reference.

2. A remarkably well educated colleague of mine at the University of Chicago once asked me how I could think of myself as a utilitarian, since that meant I was merely crudely self-interested. The even better educated Philippa Foot dismisses utilitarianism as virtually the opposite: as beneficence run wild.

3. But see the discussion later in the essay of residues of past enjoyments and anticipations of future enjoyments.

4. This example is complex. Perhaps I have come to eat caviar despite my distaste for it because of the social pressure but now I actually like it very much. My present taste for it is therefore based both on social pressure and on experience; it is a case of both social and personal capital.

5. Becker's versions of social and personal capital give an analytical way to deal with so-called utility monsters and other cute stories in debates over fairness.

6. When I once derided the minimal pleasures of instant coffee in comparison to what I called the real thing, Jon Elster remarked that it was merely a different consumption. I have often since then wished that I could as successfully compartmentalize my enjoyments into more narrowly defined categories to rescue some of them from the low state they have for me.

7. The incentive might be trumped by other considerations, so that even the best of trusting relationships can fail when the stakes get high.

8. The Rabbi Joshua J. Hammerman (1998) notes that the Oreo cookie has now become kosher and that, in contemplating that middle-Americanization of his diet, he begins "to understand that a faith community cannot live by food taboos alone." But he still has pork as a barrier to total assimilation.

9. This comment is made in a brief discussion of the large body of recent work on irrational aspects of choice behavior. Much of this work focuses on anomalies and gives sly and sometimes cute explanations of them.

REFERENCES

Arrow, Kenneth J. 1963. *Social Choice and Individual Values.* 2nd ed. New Haven, Conn.: Yale University Press. (Originally published in 1951)

Bayes, Thomas. 1958. "An Essay Toward Solving a Problem in the Doctrine of Choices." *Biometrika* 45: 293–315. (Originally published in 1764)

Becker, Gary S. 1975. *Human Capital: A Theoretical and Empirical Analysis, with Special Reference to Education.* 2nd ed. New York: Columbia University Press. (Originally published in 1964)

———. 1976. *The Economic Approach to Human Behavior.* Chicago: University of Chicago Press.

———. 1981. *A Treatise on the Family.* Cambridge, Mass.: Harvard University Press.

———. 1996. *Accounting for Tastes.* Cambridge, Mass.: Harvard University Press.

Bentham, Jeremy. 1970. *An Introduction to the Principles of Morals and Legislation.* Edited by J. H. Burns and H. L. A. Hart. London: Methuen. (Originally published in 1789)

Brehm, John, and Wendy Rahn. 1997. "Individual-Level Evidence for the Causes and Consequences of Social Capital." *American Journal of Political Science* 41: 999–1023.

Coleman, James S. 1988. "Social Capital in the Creation of Human Capital." *American Journal of Sociology* (supplement) 94: S95–S120.

———. 1990. *Foundations of Social Theory.* Cambridge, Mass.: Harvard University Press.

Elster, Jon. 1979. *Ulysses and the Sirens: Studies in Rationality and Irrationality.* Cambridge: Cambridge University Press.

Fisher, Helen. 1992. *Anatomy of Love.* New York: Norton.

Fukuyama, Francis. 1995. *Trust: The Social Virtues and the Creation of Prosperity.* New York: Free Press.

Gagarin, Michael, and Paul Woodruff (eds.). 1995. *Early Greek Political Thought from Homer to the Sophists.* Cambridge: Cambridge University Press.

Hammerman, Joshua J. 1998. "The Forbidden Oreo." *New York Times Magazine,* January 11, 66.

Hanifan, Lyda J. 1916. "The Rural School Community Center." *Annals of the American Academy of Political and Social Science* 67: 130–38.

Hardin, Russell. 1987. "Rational Choice Theories." In *Idioms of Inquiry: Critique and Renewal in Political Science,* edited by Terence Ball (Albany: State University of New York Press), 67–91.

———. 1988. *Morality Within the Limits of Reason.* Chicago: University of Chicago Press.

———. 1991. "Trusting Persons, Trusting Institutions." In *The Strategy of Choice,* edited by Richard J. Zeckhauser (Cambridge, Mass.: MIT Press), 185–209.

———. 1992. "The Street-Level Epistemology of Trust." *Analyse und Kritik* 14 (December): 152–76; reprinted in *Politics and Society* 21 (December 1993): 505–29.

———. 1995. *One for All: The Logic of Group Conflict.* Princeton, N.J.: Princeton University Press.

———. 1996. "Trustworthiness." *Ethics* 107 (October): 26–42.

———. 1999. "Do We Want Trust in Government?" In *Democracy and Trust,* edited by Mark Warren (Cambridge: Cambridge University Press), 22–41.

Hobbes, Thomas. 1651. *Leviathan.* London: Andrew Cooke.

Jacobs, Jane. 1961. *The Death and Life of Great American Cities.* New York: Random House.

Kawabata, Yasunari. 1974. *The Lake.* Translated by Reiko Tsukimura. Tokyo: Kodansha.

Leeuw, Frans L. 1997. "Solidarity Between Public-Sector Organizations: The Problem of Social Cohesion in the Asymmetric Society." *Rationality and Society* 9 (November): 469–88.

Loury, Glenn C. 1977. "A Dynamic Theory of Racial Income Differences." In *Women, Minorities, and Employment Discrimination,* edited by P. A. Wallace and A. Le Mund (Lexington, Mass.: Lexington Books), ch. 8.

———. 1987. "Why Should We Care About Group Inequality?" *Social Philosophy and Policy* 5: 249–71.

Macauley, Stewart. 1963. "Non-Contractual Relations in Business: A Preliminary Study." *American Sociological Review* 28: 55–67.

Macneil, Ian R. 1980. *The New Social Contract: An Inquiry into Modern Contractual Relations.* New Haven, Conn.: Yale University Press.

Nagel, Thomas. 1970. *The Possibility of Altruism.* Oxford: Oxford University Press.

Putnam, Robert. 1993. *Making Democracy Work: Civic Traditions in Modern Italy.* Princeton, N.J.: Princeton University Press.

———. 1995. "Tuning in, Tuning out: The Strange Disappearance of Social Capital in America." *PS: Political Science and Politics* (December): 664–83.

Schultz, Theodore W. 1963. *The Economic Value of Education.* New York: Columbia University Press.

Sen, Amartya. 1982. "Equality of What?" In Sen, *Choice, Welfare and Measurement* (Cambridge, Mass.: MIT Press), 353–69.

von Neumann, John, and Oskar Morgenstern. 1953. *Theory of Games and Economic Behavior.* 3rd ed. Princeton, N.J.: Princeton University Press. (Originally published in 1944)

Williamson, Oliver E. 1975. *Markets and Hierarchies: Analysis and Antitrust Implications.* New York: Free Press.

————. 1981. "The Economics of Organization: The Transaction Cost Approach." *American Journal of Sociology* 87: 548–77.

————. 1985. *The Economic Institutions of Capitalism: Firms, Markets, Relational Contracting.* New York: Free Press.

COMMENTS

Gary S. Becker

I want to begin with a story about myself. I almost wrote a thesis in political science. In the summer after my first year at Chicago, I wrote a paper on a political competition approach to democracy. I showed it to Milton Friedman and Aaron Director, and they were both quite enthusiastic about it. I submitted it to the *Journal of Political Economy*, whose editors at first gave me a very positive response and indicated they would publish it. However, it was unusual to publish a student's paper in a journal as prestigious as the *Journal of Political Economy*, and they decided not to do it after a negative review by Frank Knight. I have preserved his comments.

Knight's criticism is partly relevant to a number of things Russell Hardin says about the difference between normative and positive theory. Knight always looked at political democracy from a normative point of view, in which one discusses and reaches some kind of consensus. I took a more cynical approach, stimulated by Schumpeter's *Capitalism, Socialism, and Democracy*, which attempted to offer a positive theory of democracy, regardless of the system's merits.

The journal finally rejected the paper based on Knight's very flimsy discussion of it, and I got a little bit discouraged. Fortunately for me, I was also working out some ideas on discrimination at the time. I had to make the choice: Should I write a dissertation on democracy or discrimination? And I made the choice for good or bad to work on discrimination. Five years later I published a very short note on this sort of competitive approach to democracy.

I tell this story to illustrate my long interest in political science, not necessarily as a venue for applying economic reasoning—although in fact I have tried to do that—but as an area of enormous importance. It was even more important in those days, the early 1950s. Government is a major factor in the economy and in social life, and economists in particular have been very lax in giving government its due credit. By due credit I am not making a normative statement but referring, from a positive point of view, to government's enormous influence on what happens in an economy. That issue has continued to attract me. So I was very happy on this occasion to have a discussion with two eminent political scientists, Russell Hardin, who is, of course, a friend and long-term colleague at Chicago, and Ron Rogowski, whose commentary gives me good reason to become more familiar with his work.

The essays are very different. Hardin's is a general discussion and analysis of the role of self-interested and rational-choice behavior in general, of values, and of social capital. Rogowski's essay is an analysis and evaluation of my contributions and why it may be they did not have as much of an influence as he, I am gratified to see, thinks they should have had in political science.

Let me start out first with Hardin's essay. He offers a fine clarification and defense of values and of normative versus positive approaches. I have always thought it logically possible to have a normative science without having a positive one. From a practical point of view, however, to evaluate whether an action is good or bad, you have to have some discussion of its consequences. To take a controversial issue in economics in recent years as an example, the state raises the minimum wage. Most people would support the minimum wage if it had little effect on unemployment. To discuss the normative issues, you have to have a positive model, whether it is rational choice or something else. It is only at the very abstract and rather empty level that one can have a normative theory without having a positive theory.

Let me make one other point. Hardin raises the issue of whether, as societies get richer, economizing or being rational is no longer as important. Actually, Keynes wrote an article in the 1930s in which he predicted that thirty or forty years later, in the 1970s, the West would be so rich that the economic problem would be trivial. We would only have to worry about what operas we should see and similar decisions, and economists would be out of business.

But fortunately for most of us, we are not out of business. Why? There is a basic fallacy in those type of arguments, which is the fallacy that while one can get richer in goods, behavior is still constrained by limited time. As one gets richer in goods, the value of time goes up; the value of goods *relative* to time may go down, but the value of time relative to goods goes up. These are mirror images of each other. So, richer people are much more economical with their time than poorer people. In poor societies, people may be lolling around much of the time because they really do not have much to do; there are not enough goods. For richer people, the biggest problem is how to make effective use of time. Rich societies have a lot of goods, but the problem lies in spending the amount of goods per hour efficiently, limited by the number of hours. Rich countries may be more careless with goods; this is just another way of saying the rich are more careful with their time than their goods because time is so much more important for them. The economic problem, in this broader sense, is far from resolved.

One final comment on the various points Hardin raises. I believe individual choice has a lot to contribute to understanding community. It is what Glenn Loury and the late Jim Coleman called "social capital," a very popular term now. We are lacking a good theory of how social capital or norms—the concept goes under a lot of different names—gets formed and then dissolves. In a manuscript called *Social Markets,* my coauthors and I build an analysis of the formation and ultimately the dissolution of both personal capital and social capital. Progress will be faster when we consider the role of peer pressure and similar variables within a rational-choice context.

I am reminded of the comment made by Harvard economist James Dusenberry when I wrote my first paper on fertility: that economics is all about choice, and sociology is about why people do not have a choice. I did not quite know what it meant, but I thought it was a neat statement. I now think I understand what it means, and it is wrong, although the statement has insight. It is wrong because sociology is about a different set of choices than the ones that economists (and political scientists) address. Sociology is about how people choose their friends, their peers, their neighborhoods, their way of life. Mary Douglass, a very fine anthropologist, once made the statement that the major decision we make in life is about our way of life.

It is not saying that we do not make choices; it is saying that the important choices are who we marry, what profession we go into, what neighborhood we live in, what friends we have, what religion we adopt. Those are all choices, and in *Social Markets* we use a rational-choice framework to discuss these so-called sociological choices. These choices are made by individuals, but they lead to very important group influences over behavior.

Let me now turn to Rogowski's essay. I thank him for his complimentary remarks. He discusses three contributions—regarding discrimination, human capital, and interest groups. I am not going to say much about human capital, although I do believe it is one of the most important things I have done, but it is less relevant to some of the issues discussed here. I am going to say a few things about discrimination, but I am going to concentrate on interest groups, partly because I am currently working on this issue again and want to get some reaction to my current research.

Rogowski has good insights on the political implications of discrimination, only some of which I was aware. I have often argued that in South Africa white capitalists were opposed to much of apartheid because it really hurt them. The beneficiaries were white workers, and apartheid was generally promoted by trade unions and workers' groups, for obvious reasons—they tried to keep out competition from black workers in mines and elsewhere in South Africa. Some of the same benefits to workers may have accrued to white workers in the American South, but South Africa is a better example because discrimination there was even more extreme. Political aspects become important because different groups are affected differently by discrimination; that is the point Rogowski stresses. He is absolutely right that it is an implication of applying the fundamental model of discrimination, or applying simple international trade theory to discrimination.

An additional point Rogowski makes is that as international trade has grown in the world, ethnic and other groups have split up rather than stayed together. This is a point I have been making, in several *Business Week* columns. There has been enormous growth in trade since 1950, relative even to world income, and very rapid growth since the 1960s. A model of discrimination combined with trade would suggest greater ethnic separations. There has been an enormous expansion in a number of countries since the 1950s. A small nation no longer needs to be part of a large internal market. A comparison of whether large nations or small ones have grown faster in per capita income since 1960 reveals that small nations have a slightly faster rate of growth. This calculation is not adjusted for any variables other than initial per capita income, and perhaps a sophisticated analysis would yield different results. Still, this is an extremely important question to which economists have not paid much attention. Perhaps political scientists have done more on what determines the number of nations or the structure of nations. With international trade possible, a group need not put up with intense discrimination for it can trade with others. That is a point Rogowski emphasizes and should be followed up with further applications of the discrimination analysis.

Let me turn to interest groups. Perhaps my model of discrimination will be a useful contribution to political science ultimately, but I have always thought my most important direct contribution to political science is the discussion of interest-group competition developed in two articles: in 1983 in the *Quarterly Journal of Economics,* and in 1985 in the *Journal of Public Economics.* These articles have had more of an impact on some economists' work on political economy than apparently they have had on political science. I am going to come back also to the discussion of this analysis and the question of why it has received so little attention in political science.

I am currently engaged in additional work on this problem, jointly with a young colleague, Casey Mulligan. He and others are doing independent work trying to extend this interest-group type of model to a number of issues in political economy. To be honest, I do think it is a useful model for understanding some political processes, for the reasons Rogowski mentions, including that it emphasizes deadweight costs, which are very important in understanding political power.

People sometimes believe I am arguing that these groups are directly worried about the social consequences or deadweight costs of their behavior. On the assumption that these are self-interested—in Hardin's terms, selfish—groups, deadweight costs only indirectly influence the incentives to spend time and money trying to gain political influence. Interest groups have may or may not be concerned about social consequences. Nevertheless, indirectly they are influenced by deadweight costs because these costs make it more expensive for them to obtain subsidies and make it more costly to taxpayers when they have to be paying taxes. It is because of these private effects that deadweight costs become crucial determinants in these models of political competition among interest groups.

Rogowski mentions several implications, all of which I fully agree with. I want to emphasize the deregulation movement of the 1970s and 1980s, which covered banking—or finance more generally, including securities—telecommunications, transportation, airlines, and trucking. Why did this movement happen? Why did deregulation occur not only in the United States but in other countries as well? I very much agree with Rogowski on the necessity of getting beyond simply looking at the United States to evaluate political models.

Sam Peltzman, an economist at Chicago, evaluated interest-group models in terms of how well they explain the U.S. deregulation movement in the 1970s and 1980s. With one exception, he concluded that they do very well. In banking, stock exchanges, airlines, and telecommunications, deadweight costs grew over time. The influence of the subsidized groups consequently decreased, and it was unsurprising that they lost power. The model does not work well for trucking. Peltzman did not find any comparable increase in deadweight costs over time from the extensive trucking regulation in the United States, and yet there was sharp deregulation of interstate trucking. Still, I would say that five out of six is pretty good in research.

Some people believe that there has been an overall deregulation movement, but there has not. Regulation in various industries decreased, but regulation increased in labor markets and environment, to take two of the biggest areas. Why has deregulation happened in some areas at the same time that regulation has increased in others? I do not believe anybody has adequately discussed these very important questions. The jury is still out on whether an interest-group model is successful overall in understanding regulation and deregulation, but it has been pretty successful in understanding the deregulation movement that started in the United States and spread elsewhere. Now there is a worldwide deregulation of banking. The deadweight costs for any one country trying to maintain regulatory banking and finance when capital markets are becoming more global would have been enormous, so it is not surprising that one by one countries have been forced to open up their capital markets. The analysis goes well beyond the United States political system.

I disagree with Rogowski on one thing. I do not know the study by Wendy Hansen that he mentions, in which she tests the implications of the interest-group model with tariffs. Apparently, however, her data rejected the supposed implication of the analysis that industries with more elastic demands should be more likely to obtain tariffs. That is not the implication. Consider the extreme case of completely inelastic demand, there is no deadweight cost. The deadweight cost of a given percentage increase in price is smaller for less elastic demand; that is a general result well known in economics. Therefore, I was very happy to see her result since it supports the theory.

Elasticities also help explain why declining industries are often more successful politically than growing industries. This issue is discussed in my 1985 paper, that asks: Why are declining industries often more successful at getting political support? If there is a lot of industry-specific investment in most industries, then initially as they decline, supply curves would be inelastic. It would take a really big decline for any firm to want to get out of these industries. The amount invested in steel-making skills is not useful if a worker produces computers instead. Declining industries would, therefore, be expected to have considerable power because deadweight costs are smaller there.

There are a couple of other points. There is a fair bit of support by economists for a flat tax. Why? They show that a change from a progressive tax to a flat tax or other more efficient tax would reduce the deadweight costs of raising the same amount of revenue. Every economist more or less agrees that, holding government spending constant, a move to a flat tax, like a social security tax or flat consumption or flat income tax, reduces deadweight costs and perhaps some administrative costs. There is nothing wrong with that conclusion, but I am not sure how relevant it is, for with a flat tax there will be more government spending and tax revenue. An immediate implication of interest group analysis is that a flat tax would increase government spending. Rogowski mentions this in his essay as one reason why government spending grew over time.

This is a prediction of the theory, but is it right? Well, Casey Mulligan and I have done a little work looking at some flat taxes. The two most important are the VAT (value-added tax)—important not in the United States but in South America and Europe—and the social security tax, which is typically pretty flat, with often a cut-off at the top. Casey and I linked these taxes to the size of government spending, holding some things constant. Ours is not the last word on the empirical side, but we do find some connections between the flatness of the tax structure and the increase in government spending over time and the size of government. We may not be right, but it is not legitimate to assume that government spending is going to be independent of the tax structure.

There are many proposals for privatization of social security, and some suggest that the transition be financed in the United States by introducing a new federal sales tax. In my view, the authors of these proposals have not thought through the implications for what government will do, whether this tax will increase over time, and what will be the effect on the size of government. The interest-group model is an engine for analyzing these questions. People who use this this model can reach whatever normative conclusions they want, but they should get the positive side of the analysis straight.

Another implication of the interest-group analysis deal with the effect of an exogenous increase in government receipts on other taxes. The theory implies that other taxes would go down, yet government spending would go up. Casey Mulligan and I find some confirmation of this implication.

Suppose there is an exogenous increase in government spending—say a war breaks out—and military spending goes up. What happens to total taxes and to other government spending? We predict total taxes increase, but other government spending falls. This is not such an obvious implication, but we find some support at the federal level of spending during World War II.

I will discuss one more question, one that may be of more interest to economists than to political scientists, to whom the answer is probably obvious. Economists, macroeconomists in particular, argue there is often an incentive to repudiate public debt because it is very hard to commit future governments to repay debt. Thomas Sargent has an interesting paper comparing the French and the British in the eighteenth century, when the French repudiated their debt and the English generally did not. Economists predict repudiation sometimes through inflation. However, usually government debt is not repudiated, and not only for reputational reasons.

An interest-group model can explain why debt is not reputational when held by powerful interest groups. They not only prevent repudiation of the debt of their own nations, but sometimes use powerful governments like the United States to force the Brazilians and Mexicans to pay off their debt to these groups. These governments also encourage the International Monetary Fund and others to bail out debtor governments, so they can repay their debt. The role of interest groups in debt repudiation should receive more attention from macroeconomists.

I will focus my final comments on the question Rogowski raises—and it is a question I have puzzled over on a number of occasions—of why political scientists and economists interested in formal political theory have not been more influenced by an interest-group analysis, whether by me or anybody else. Rogowski makes several good arguments. I want to emphasize one of them, and then add another. The one I want to emphasize is the claim that the interest-group analysis ignores the details of a political system, which it looks at as a black box. My justification for this has been that interest group analysis is a reduced form, and that many political systems are similar in a reduced form even though they have very different structures. The reduced form has benefits and costs to people maximizing, and I have always believed that is something that transcends many details of the political system.

I agree that ultimately an interest-group model should be combined with an analysis of political institutions. Still there is much commonality among policies across different systems: which industries have tariffs, the deregulation of banking and national airlines, private or public ownership of railroads, the regulation of securities, the growing environmental movement, regulations of labor markets (more in Europe than the United States but growing here in the United States).

Why so much common behavior? If mainly the political structure mattered, surely there would be much greater differences. So something more fundamental than structure must be operating here, although structure also matters.

The second difficulty that many formal theorists have with interest-group analysis is that it does not deal explicitly with voting. Yet virtually all the formal analysis in political science is based on median voter models. I do not deny that the analysis would be more powerful with a voting model, but I do not believe the voting models currently used are appropriate since they are very poorly grounded in rational choice.

People vote, but where do they get the preferences that determine how they vote and who they vote for? The so-called voting paradox has long recognized that people do not have an incentive to vote, but I believe that has been overblown as an issue. The more fundamental issue is that how they vote makes very little difference to outcomes.

Preferences are endogenous in the sense discussed in my *Accounting for Tastes* (1996); and political preferences are influenced by interest groups. The economist, statistician, and political scientist, Simon Newcomb wrote *Principles of Political Economy* (1985) at the end of the nineteenth century. He asks why small interest groups have so much influence. He concludes that day after day, the typical person hears the arguments advanced by these groups, and many eventually are persuaded of their merits, and vote as the groups have persuaded him. We need a theory of how people vote, and for that we need an endogenous theory of preferences.

Most voting models ask whether a person is going to be made better off or worse off if the Democrats get into power. If she is made better off, she votes for the Democrats, if worse off, she votes for the Republicans. Some people might vote that way, but a relevant theory should take account of the influence on voters of interest-group activities and expenditures, how friends and peers are voting, and social capital. The challenge is to develop a theory of how they vote when individual votes do not affect outcomes. That is a whole different calculus.

Let me conclude by repeating how gratified I am that this volume was arranged by three eminent political scientists, and for the discussion of my work by two other eminent political scientists. It is valuable to see the work of six economists being discussed and evaluated for what it adds to political science.

I am not concerned that I have received so few citations in the political science literature, especially given the excessive number of citations I have received in economics and elsewhere. However, I do agree with Ron Rogowski's statement that my interest-group analysis and, perhaps more so, my analysis of discrimination does have important political aspects. Perhaps it would be useful if political scientists paid somewhat more attention to them.

These comments were transcribed by Sara Colburn and edited by Margaret Levi and Gary Becker from Gary Becker's remarks at the Russell Sage Foundation in November 1997.

REFERENCES

Becker, Gary S. 1983. "A Theory of Competition among Pressure Groups for Political Influence." *Quarterly Journal of Economics* 98(3): 371–400.

———. 1985. "Public Policies, Pressure Groups, and Dead Weight Costs." *Journal of Public Economics* 28(3): 329–47.

———. 1996. *Accounting for Tastes*. Cambridge, Mass.: Harvard University Press.

Coleman, James S. 1990. *Foundations of Social Theory*. Cambridge, Mass.: Belknap Press.

Mulligan, Casey B., and Xavier X. Sala-i-Martin. 1999. "Social Security in Theory and Practice." *National Bureau of Economic Research Working Papers 7118, 7119,* May 1999. Cambridge, Mass.: National Bureau of Economic Research.

Newcomb, Simon. 1885. *Principles of Political Economy*. New York: Harper.

Peltzman, Sam. 1989. "The Economic Theory of Regulation after a Decade of Deregulation." *Brookings Papers of Economic Activity*. Special Issue, 1–41. Washington, D.C.: Brookings Institution.

Sargent, Thomas J., and Francois R. Velde. 1995. "Macroeconomic Features of the French Revolution." *Journal of Political Economy* 103(3): 474–519.

Schumpeter, Joseph Alois. 1947. *Capitalism, Socialism, and Democracy*. New York, London: Harper & Brothers.

Chapter 5

DOUGLASS C. NORTH
A Biographical Sketch

Douglass C. North was the corecipient of the 1993 Nobel Prize in Economic Science, an honor he shared with Robert Fogel for their pioneering but quite different work in economic history. He was also the first economic historian to receive the John R. Commons Award, one of the highest honors in the economics profession. He has served as president of the Economic History Association and as the second president of the International Society for the New Institutional Economics. North is the inaugural Spencer T. Olin Professor in Arts and Sciences at Washington University and a senior research fellow at the Hoover Institution.

North's early work applied neoclassical economic theory to the analysis of long-term secular and technological change, but he soon realized that neoclassical theory required modification if it was to be applicable to the issues of economic development and performance that most concerned him. Influenced by the Nobel laureate Ronald Coase, North began to explore the role of property rights and transaction costs and, in the process, helped pioneer the new economic institutionalism. His most recent work takes up the challenge of cognitive science as a means to improve the rationality assumption and thus develop better theories of ideology, culture, and, more generally, path dependence and preference formation. Robert Fogel (1997, 18) argues that, in his criticism of the contemporary confusion between mathematical models and economic theory and in his emphasis on the importance of history as a source of theory, "few theorists have made more effective use of history than Douglass C. North."

Douglass North was born in 1920 in Cambridge, Massachusetts. His family moved numerous times during his childhood, living in Canada and Europe as well as the United States. A triple major in political science, philosophy, and economics, North received his undergraduate degree from the University of California at Berkeley in 1942. He discovered Marxism at Berkeley and became a liberal activist and opponent of World War II. He spent the war in the merchant marine.

North's early professional passion was photography. He remains quite proud of numerous prizes won in an international competition for high school and college students. In 1941 he worked with Dorothea Lange, then head of the photographic division of the Farm Security Administration. When the war was over, Lange tried to persuade North to become a photographer, but her husband, the economist Paul Taylor, succeeded in convincing him to begin graduate study in economics instead. North received his Ph.D. from Berkeley in 1952.

North was a member of the faculty of the University of Washington from 1950 until 1983, when he joined the faculty at Washington University. In Seattle he developed his capacities in economic history and economic theory as part of a group of scholars working on transaction cost theory and property rights. He also rediscovered Marxism and political economy as sources of ideas about long-term technological and institutional change. In St. Louis he expanded his skills in modern political economy and began to explore cognitive science. His work on path dependence, on the one hand, and mental models, on the other, are among the many results.

North has exerted considerable institutional as well as intellectual influence. He directed and helped put on the map the Center in Political Economy at Washington University. With James Alt, he founded and co-edited "The Political Economy of Institutions and Decisions," an important series for Cambridge University Press. Most recently, he helped initiate the International Society for the New Institutional Economics and is the current president (1997–99). In addition, he has served as an adviser to the World Bank and to numerous heads of states, although his policy prescriptions are not always what his audience wants to hear. For North, informal as well as formal institutions need to change if economic performance is to improve, and there is no easy way to transform norms and culture.

North continues to emphasize the importance of institutions and the dimension of time in understanding and transforming economies, and he continues to seek explanations of how markets are shaped and constrained. Increasingly, however, he also challenges economists and political economists to rethink their models of rationality and choice.

The process of applying Northian analysis to important problems in political science tends to modify the initial model. Barbara Geddes, for example, relies on the work North did primarily in the 1970s and 1980s, particularly his "neoclassical theory of the state," to account for contemporary conflicts over privatization and corruption. In her analysis, however, she finds it necessary to replace North's assumption of the wealth-maximizing ruler with the assumption that political leaders maximize access to office. With this modification of her North-inspired model, she is able to identify the conditions under which contemporary political leaders will maintain inefficient property rights in the form of state ownership and corruption.

Robert Keohane considers the same sources Geddes uses as well as more recent work by North on transaction cost models of institutions and the role that ideology and cognition play in creating, maintaining, and transforming institutions. Keohane then applies these Northian tools to critical problems in international political economy, a domain in which North's significance is recognized but in which there has been little empirical exploration within the Northian program. Keohane too concludes that North offers a powerful mode of analysis, but one that needs some fine-tuning to make it applicable to the problems that political scientists investigate.

As evidenced both by his response and by his recent research, North himself agrees with the importance of putting his models to the test and of developing a still better model yet. He continues to push the boundaries of political economy. His interests in path dependence and cognitive theory combine with his development of the new institutionalism to augur a refined and improved behavioral model of political, economic, and social behavior.

REFERENCES

Fogel, Robert W. 1997. "Douglass C. North and Economic Theory." In *The Frontiers of the New Institutional Economics,* edited by John N. Drobak and John V. C. Nye (San Diego: Academic Press), 13–28.

North, Douglass C. 1997. "Autobiography." Nobel Prize Internet Archive, available at: http://www.nobel.se/laureates/economy-1993-2-autobio.html.

DOUGLASS C. NORTH AND INSTITUTIONAL CHANGE IN CONTEMPORARY DEVELOPING COUNTRIES

Barbara Geddes

The work of Douglass North has transformed the way political scientists think about economic development, institutional change, and that particular institution most central to our endeavor but most difficult to understand, the state. North locates the cause of increases in productivity through the ages in changes in property rights; develops a theory about why property rights conducive to development are adopted at some times and places but not others; and generalizes the explanation of property rights institutions into a theory of institutional choice and change that links the perpetuation of inefficient institutions to transaction costs.

This strand of North's work was initially motivated by the question: Why are some societies so much poorer than others? After identifying property rights as the root cause of changes in economic performance (North and Thomas 1973; see also Alchian and Demsetz 1973), North shifted his attention to explaining why inefficient property rights could persist over long periods of time when one would expect competitive pressures to cause their demise. To answer this question, he developed a theory of the state in which decisionmaking power is vested in a ruler who seeks to maximize revenue but whose choices are constrained by the power of those from whom the revenue must be extracted and available technology, which in turn determines the transaction costs associated with different revenue-raising techniques. Particular property rights institutions are thus a by-product of the interaction between the ruler's quest for revenue and the constraints he faces (North and Weingast 1989). Inefficient property rights may be chosen, even though they lower overall productivity and hence potential revenue, if they reduce the transaction costs of collecting revenue and hence increase net gain to the ruler (North 1981, 1989a). North then generalized the argument developed first to explain property rights institutions, emphasizing the importance of the bargaining power of different actors, limited information and possibly erroneous mental constructs, and the effect of transaction costs on the gains that can be realized from various institutional innovations in different settings (North 1985, 1989b, 1990).

North's ideas have obvious relevance for contemporary developing countries struggling to initiate reforms that will set them on the path to more rapid growth. During the 1980s an international price shock of the kind North and Thomas (1973) identify as the source of institutional changes occurred, and it has created strong incentives for institutional change in most of the developing and ex-Communist world. In this essay, I use North's seminal ideas to make sense of the political battles currently raging over what these new institutions should be.

BACKGROUND

North's research has focused mostly on the United States and early modern Europe, but his ideas, as shown here, also clarify contemporary events in developing countries. For several decades prior to the beginning of the debt crisis in 1982, most developing countries followed an economic policy strategy emphasizing import-substitution industrialization (ISI). Typically, the ISI strategy included high levels of protection for domestic industry, overvalued exchange rates that subsidized inputs into manufacturing at the expense of exports produced by other sectors, substantial state investment, high rates of state ownership and regulation, and low taxes. This set of policies routinely resulted in trade and budget deficits, which were in turn routinely covered by inflows of foreign money, mostly in the form of loans. Through the 1970s, low real interest rates kept the cost of the ISI strategy relatively low, and consequently this strategy survived in most countries even though its inefficiencies were well understood by at least some citizens and policymakers. The ISI strategy, combining policies, organizations to implement them, and institutions to govern their implementation, is thus a highly visible example of a set of long-lasting inefficient institutions of the kind North sought to explain.

The debt crisis suddenly and dramatically raised the international cost of money. In consequence, the cost of pursuing the ISI strategy leaped, and economies that had been muddling along suddenly faced hyperinflation and other symptoms of economic disaster. In response to the price shock, the struggle over institutional change began. Among the reforms recently initiated or currently under discussion in many countries are liberalizing the exchange rate, lowering tariffs, reforming tax systems,[1] reducing regulation, and privatizing state-owned enterprises.[2] The ideas of North and some of those whose work he has influenced can illuminate the institutional choices now being made.

In this essay, I use North's ideas to explain the persistence of two phenomena usually considered inefficient, corruption and state ownership.[3] Most prior treatments of corruption have either focused on description or proposed analyses founded on an assumption of individual greed (Rose-Ackerman 1978; Shackleton 1978; Soskice, Bates, and Epstein 1992). Most prior treatments of state ownership and its current decline have similarly either focused on description or proposed models grounded in the interests of private-sector actors.[4] In both areas of research, economic models tend either to ignore or to distort the strategic behavior and motivations of the political leaders who actually make many of the relevant decisions.[5] Descriptive treatments more often discuss the actions and motivations of political leaders but usually fail to incorporate them into systematic explanations.

I build on North's extensive work on institutional choice and change to propose a systematic explanation for the persistence of corruption and state ownership over long periods of time, despite ill effects on overall productivity. I begin with a very brief sketch of North's argument about the relationship between the interests of rulers and the creation of new institutions. I then extend the argument in a direction consistent with the thrust of North's work. I conclude with some preliminary evidence that the argument fits events in the real world.

THE NORTHIAN FRAMEWORK

The Northian image of government draws on an extended implicit analogy between entrepreneurs and rulers. Rulers are assumed to maximize revenue, as entrepreneurs are assumed to maximize profit. The strategic choices of both are constrained by the cost and availability of technology and the transaction costs associated with different modes of organizing production and different forms of extracting revenue. The availability of close substitutes for the ruler drives the price of her services down, that is, forces her to lower the tax rate or provide better-quality defense and law, in the same way that competition among the producers of widgets drives their price down or quality up (North 1981, 23–24).

This analogy has proved useful as a means of bringing order to, and suggesting new interpretations of, large quantities of historical detail. Perhaps its most fruitful use, however, has been to direct concentrated attention toward places where the analogy breaks down. What many scholars would consider North's most important contribution to understanding economic history, the argument about property rights, explains the consequences of one way in which a ruler is *not* like an entrepreneur.

Entrepreneurs, in the standard stylized portrait, are driven to innovate by the profit motive and competition. The connection between invention and competition is unproblematic because entrepreneurs are assumed to live in a legal and political environment of stable property rights conducive to innovation and investment. In his work on economic development, North has drawn out the implications of relaxing the assumption of stable and "appropriate" property rights, an assumption that would be highly implausible for most of human history. He argues that in the absence of appropriate property rights, investments in productivity-increasing innovations will not be made, and hence that economic development depends on prior innovations in institutions affecting property rights.

This insight leads immediately to the question: If a change in property rights institutions could lead to large increases in productivity, such as those associated with the spread of settled agriculture or the industrial revolution, why are they not adopted as soon as people understand their potential effects? In particular, if a ruler is like a profit-maximizing entrepreneur, why does he not adopt such productivity-enhancing innovations? North's answer to this question is that, although one can usually assume that productivity increases benefit entrepreneurs, revenue collection by rulers is not always maximized by the same institutions that would maximize productivity. Consequently, suboptimal property rights often remain in place for a long time (North 1981, 24–25; 1989a).

These basic Northian ideas can be extended to illuminate another area in which the analogy between entrepreneurs and rulers fits imperfectly: the bifurcation between ownership and management that develops over time as economies and polities modernize. Over time three trends have changed the nature of rulership: The locus of competition among potential rulers has become concentrated within the territorial state; the resource most essential to winning this competition has shifted from arms to votes; and political managers chosen by stockholder-citizens have replaced owner-operator monarchs as primary decisionmakers.

To continue the analogy, a monarch in early modern Europe was like a firm owner who manages his own business, or at least keeps a close eye on it. Throughout most of human history, retaining a throne—and in fact, ensuring the continued existence of political entities in which a throne might be retained—has depended directly on military might, which in turn depends on revenue. It thus makes sense to think of early rulers as maximizing revenue in the same way that entrepreneurs maximize profit. Monarchs may have genuinely cared most about wealth, which could be passed down to heirs, and being king may have seemed the best way to amass it. Alternatively, monarchs may have cared most about holding on to kingdoms, and in the conditions of the time, revenue maximization may have been a necessary means to that end (North and Thomas 1973, 94, 100). One reason to believe that the second alternative better describes the motivations of most monarchs is that few principalities have been bought from their rulers, though buyouts are common in the business world. Most states resulted from conquest or consolidation through marriage, a means of ensuring the survival in office of one's descendants. Whichever goal motivated them, however, most monarchs would have needed to maximize revenue.

Important changes have occurred in the political context since the historical period on which North focuses most of his attention. The contextual change most relevant to this essay was the shift in the primary weapons of the struggle for rulership from arms to votes and in the locus of political competition from partly external to almost entirely internal. When survival in kingly office was frequently challenged by rulers of other states at the head of armies, and when internal challengers were also usually armed, staying in office did literally require squeezing sufficient revenues out of one's domain to support an adequate army. In the case of internal competitors, the monarch's need to squeeze would be checked to some extent by the concurrent need to offer subjects benefits in order to retain their support (North 1981, 27–28, 139).

In the case of external competitors, however, this constraint would be minimal. To the average peasant, the origin of the ruler might make little difference. But the nobility could expect to gain power, wealth, and land if a conqueror were resisted or expelled; for them, a foreign competitor was rarely a close substitute. In European history, it is during drives to expel conquerors that we see dramatic increases in crown revenues, innovations in the forms of revenue extraction, and the loss of rights by the nobility to consent to, and thus limit, taxation (North and Thomas 1973, 120–31).[6] In other words, far from increasing the bargaining power of subjects, competition in the form of threats of hostile takeover may lead powerful subjects to acquiesce in the reduction of their own income and rights.

When the main challengers come from within, however, and arms have ceased to play a large role in internal political conflict, competition among potential rulers drives down the profits of rule and leads to increases in the income and rights of subjects. Competitors for office must offer some combination of lower taxes, transfers of money (subsidies, pork), opportunities for rent (such as monopolies and regulation), better services, or public goods, including property rights, in order to attract support (Riker and Sened 1991, 954). Revenue maximization might in some particular circumstance be the best strategy for providing better services, such as better defense in time of war, but it would not in general be the optimal strategy for achieving or surviving in office.

The development of more modern forms of rule also leads to a split between management and ownership analogous to that in the economic sphere; modern political leaders are analogous to managers and the dominant coalition, that is, "the group or class of which the ruler is the agent" (North 1981, 25) to stockholders. This split creates even more serious agency problems in politics than in the firm. In the rest of this essay, I first draw out the theoretical implications of the split between political ownership and management and then discuss corruption and privatization in light of these ideas.

Political managers face different incentives than do managers of firms. Managers of firms keep their jobs and maximize their own incomes by maximizing the income of stockholders, so for them all good things go together: profit, personal income, and job security. In democratic systems, however, political managers cannot usually maximize revenue, survival in office, and personal income at the same time.[7] In the economist's stylization of democracy, stockholders—the coalition that elects political leaders—delegate to the political managers the task of maximizing income for the coalition and try to make survival in office contingent on accomplishing this task (compare, Levi 1988, 46). Because revenue collected in a democratic polity, unlike profit, cannot be simply transferred to the ruling coalition, revenue maximization would not in general serve the coalition's interests and thus would not increase the likelihood of survival in office.

Since revenue maximization does not seem closely linked to political survival in modern polities, it seems more useful to assume that the interests of politicians center on access to office, whether because they care more about power than money, because they want to influence policy and can do it best from a position of power, or because political power is the surest road (for them) to wealth. And because political managers are highly imperfect agents of their supporters, their interest in survival must be taken seriously in any effort to explain what governments do.

In short, the argument up to this point is that the standard assumption of political scientists about the motives of political leaders—that they maximize access to office—should be substituted for the assumption that they maximize revenue when analyzing contemporary events.[8] The political science assumption has greater descriptive accuracy and fits quite well into the Northian model of institutional change.[9] The change in assumptions is needed, as will be shown later, in order to explain the resistance of corruption and state ownership to efforts to change them.

IMPLICATIONS FOR CONTEMPORARY ECONOMIC DEVELOPMENT

This change in motivational assumptions leads to a change in expectations about the circumstances in which political leaders promulgate appropriate property rights and other public goods. Political leaders are most likely to provide public goods (and other policies) conducive to economic development when they expect doing so to contribute to their own political survival. It might seem that, given competition, the best way for the political leader to maximize support would be to provide a set of optimal property rights and other public goods in order to maximize production, which would maximize the welfare and hence support of citizens. The state could then tax its highly productive subjects at some optimal level, use the money to pay for more productivity-enhancing public goods, and so on.

This "careful husbandman"[10] image, however, shatters in the face of short time horizons and agency problems. The "husbandman"—that is, the politician—knows that he will lose the farm at some point, though he may not know when. Unlike a monarch, he cannot usually pass his office on to his children, and he cannot sell it and retire on the proceeds.[11] Consequently, his time horizons are relatively short.[12] While he controls the farm, he would prefer it to be a successful, profit-making concern, but he has little incentive to make long-term investments or to initiate innovations that will benefit his successors. And if his control is challenged by competitors, as it often is, he does not hesitate to slaughter some of the milch cows to raise money to defend his control. In short, the political manager has no secure property right in either the wealth or the revenue of the state, a situation that, as North has shown, tends to result in suboptimal investment.

Political leaders can get away with slaughtering some milch cows because, in the real world of scarce and expensive information (especially emphasized in North 1990), citizens have limited ability to monitor the performance of their representatives. Citizens, in other words, face an agency problem. The citizenry, through its vote for parties and candidates, chooses a set of policies expected to result in particular distributional outcomes. To implement citizens' choices, politicians must enact necessary laws and allocate adequate resources.

The agency problem is caused by an interaction between information asymmetries and conflicts of interest between principal and agent (Moe 1984). In developing countries the information asymmetry between citizens and politicians looms very large. Where levels of education are low and few read newspapers, most citizens have little ability to monitor the policy-relevant activities of politicians.

> In formulating policies [politicians] do not feel tightly bound by citizen preferences (except on occasional highly salient issues). Rather, they feel constrained to have those policies appear successful by the time of the next election. Politicians need not discern the precise policy preferences of their constituents. They need only *anticipate* the *reactions* of their constituents to the conditions brought about by the policy instruments they adopt. (Fiorina 1981, 11, Fiorina's emphasis)

For most people, in consequence, judgments of politicians depend on cheap and easily obtained information (North 1990; compare, Fiorina 1981; Downs 1957). Most citizens know whether they have received individual help from local representatives of the ruling party or government, and they can assess the overall performance of the economy. These are the bases on which they decide what incumbents have done for them lately. These bases are poor indicators of the fulfillment of policy promises, however. Politicians can often provide particular benefits without carrying out the distributional policies preferred by voters. And although major disasters cannot be hidden from citizens, politicians have a number of instruments at their disposal for fooling "all of the people some of the time and some of the people all of the time" about how the economy is doing during the months preceding elections.[13]

In short, citizens often lack the information necessary to judge whether politicians are fulfilling their policy promises and therefore cannot make credible threats to use votes, demonstrations, or other means to punish those who fail to do so. This information asymmetry has the expected effect of reducing the citizenry's ability to select the candidates most likely to provide the public policies they prefer. Citizens' limited ability to monitor permits politicians considerable autonomy when it comes to deciding which policies to support (Kalt and Zupan 1984, 1990; North 1990, 138).

Because citizens cannot adequately monitor politicians' policy performance and thus vote decisions depend heavily on the availability of particular benefits, electoral machines become essential to the successful mobilization of the vote. Electoral machines play a role in contemporary struggles for office analogous to that of armed retainers in medieval times. Instead of trying to defeat the armed followers of competitors, they try to outbid them in the provision of individual benefits.[14] These benefits include such things as coupons entitling pregnant women to free milk or schoolchildren to free lunches, places in better schools, help initiating pension payments, titles to land, and many other government services to which citizens have legal claims but no real access without partisan intervention.

To reach large numbers of voters with individual benefits, politicians need extensive political machines staffed by party activists and workers. Party workers and campaign contributors have to be paid for their help with jobs, contracts, licenses, and other favors. Politicians' ability to deliver individual benefits thus depends on the extent to which members of their parties occupy positions in the bureaucracy, the importance of partisan loyalty to bureaucratic recruitment and promotion, and the extent of state penetration of the economy. Where the state has traditionally intervened in the economy in a multitude of ways, politicians rely on the distribution of state largesse to cement party loyalties. Just as early modern rulers required revenues to pay for the armies needed to defend themselves, so contemporary political managers need other kinds of resources to win the competitions they face.

With this version of the political world in mind, let us now consider how corruption and state ownership fit into the picture. Corruption, state ownership, and other forms of state intervention in the economy are highly important sources of the money and other benefits that political leaders need in order to reward their supporters. They substitute to some extent for policies that might be paid for by taxes, allowing political leaders to include low taxes or tax evasion in the package of benefits they offer to potential party supporters.

Some of the income earned through corruption goes into personal consumption by officials, but in most countries, most is spent by officials to maintain their informal political support networks and party machines. The distribution of corruption income between these personal and political uses varies by country and individual, but officials in many developing countries use income from corruption for the routine building and maintenance of political support.

State intervention in the economy plays an even larger role in greasing the wheels of political machines. Contracts for public works, import licenses, and access to foreign exchange go to campaign contributors (whether contributions are legal or in the form of kickbacks or bribes). Prices are manipulated to benefit politically crucial groups. Jobs in state enterprises can be given to supporters.

The state enterprise emerged as the institution of choice for rewarding large numbers of midlevel party activists in nearly all developing countries because, though often economically inefficient, it reduces the cost of enforcing the implicit contract between party leaders and party workers (see North 1990, 54–60). It would be hypothetically more efficient to reward party workers with equivalent opportunities in the private sector, but any kind of reward one can imagine (such as simple payments in money or jobs in private firms owned by supporters) would entail high transaction costs, both to measure political effort by the activist and to enforce the terms of the implicit contract. The delivery of individual benefits is both information- and labor-intensive, and party workers are strongly tempted to shirk the time-consuming tasks associated with maintaining high levels of political support in high-participation political systems. It is easy to imagine that party workers rewarded with help finding jobs in the private sector might, over a period of time, forget their gratitude and find better uses for their time.

Employment of party workers in the state sector reduces the cost of monitoring and contract enforcement. Immediate superiors and coworkers are likely to be copartisans with an interest in preventing others from shirking, and serious violations of the implicit contract can lead to demotion or even unemployment.

We would expect, then, that just as early modern rulers might have perpetuated inefficient property rights that helped them raise the revenues needed to stay in office, contemporary political leaders might fail to privatize or curb corruption because state ownership and graft provide some of the political resources they need to survive in office. In the following sections, I build on the logic elaborated so far in order to make some systematic arguments about circumstances likely to give political leaders incentives to privatize or reduce corruption. The theoretical sections are followed by an empirical investigation of privatization. Analogous empirical work on corruption is impossible because of the absence of adequate data.

CORRUPTION

Because corruption provides some of the resources used by politicians in the fight for office, economic models of corruption as an agency problem fail to capture an essential feature of the problem. Although freelance corruption (which could be modeled as an agency problem) undoubtedly occurs, it is much more common for hierarchical superiors to benefit from and collude in the corruption of those lower in the hierarchy.[15] Sometimes this benefit involves a personal cut of the money, but it need not and often does not. A bureaucrat who buys her posting from the ruling party is, on the one hand, buying a license to collect bribes in return for services, and on the other, providing the party with some of the income it needs to run political campaigns and buy votes (Wade 1982, 1984, 1985). A legislator who collects the funds needed for a winning campaign through kickbacks from contractors is an energetic and successful member of his party's team, not someone party leaders would stop if they could figure out a way to monitor him better. If corruption is not an agency problem, then policies aimed at increasing superiors' ability to monitor subordinates will not reduce it.

A second implication of the usefulness of corruption in political competition is that much corruption is motivated by political ambition, not greed. In some models, it may not matter whether greed or ambition is assumed to motivate corruption (since they often go together). Models that assume a trade-off between greed and political ambition, however—that is, models assuming that greed is constrained by the fear of detection and consequent loss of office—simply fail to capture an essential feature of political reality in many developing countries. In countries where either individuals or parties routinely finance their campaigns and hold their political machines together with resources drawn from some form of corruption, it is very difficult for a scrupulous candidate to achieve political office in the first place.

In such systems, few politicians' hands are entirely clean. Reporters, publishers, and judges also often have partisan affiliations that constrain their willingness to expose and punish corruption. Even the few politicians and judges with unsmirched records are prevented from exposing their opponents by the fear of reciprocal exposure of their copartisans. Once such collusive norms are violated, whole party systems can unravel, as has happened recently in Italy, ending the political careers of much of the political class. One cannot expect that exposure would be undertaken lightly in such systems.

Needless to say, political competition does not automatically reduce corruption, contrary to what is often assumed. Let us consider more carefully why not. Two standard arguments support the idea that competition reduces corruption: That competition increases the likelihood that corruption will be detected, since the press is freer in competitive systems and politicians can improve their own electoral fortunes by exposing the misdeeds of their opponents during campaigns; and that competition drives down the price of bribes. The first of these arguments describes reality in some countries but not others, for the reasons noted earlier.

The second argument has little applicability in real-world politics. Imperfections in political competition undermine its potential effects on the price of bribes. It would seem that parties in competition with each other would offer lower bribe prices as part of their effort to attract supporters, and that this competition would drive the price down. Political competition, however, is both limited and sporadic. In most established political systems, barriers to the entry of new parties or independent candidates are quite high. Collusion develops easily among established parties. Further, competition occurs only at intervals, every few years, with monopoly or collusive oligopoly the rule in between. Parties and individuals do in fact make offers to reduce bribes during campaigns, in the form of promises to clean up corruption. They sometimes even carry out these promises, especially when the accused belong to opposing parties or factions. Between campaigns, however, competition wanes. The offices through which bribes can be extracted may all be held by a single party; they may be shared out among coalition partners; or, where offices are protected by civil service, collusive agreements may have developed among permanent bureaucrats from different parties. Whatever competition occurs at the points where members of the public actually interact with officials is among citizens competing for services, access, exceptions, contracts, licenses, and so on, not among officials competing to serve them.

The fruits of corruption may indeed become more important to politicians as political systems become more inclusive and competition intensifies. Increases in political participation increase the number of votes that need to be "bought" by successful politicians. These votes can be bought with policies that appeal to groups of voters, such as promises to end corruption. Or they can be bought more literally with particularistic goods distributed to individual voters. It is said that a vote in the Philippines during the Marcos presidency cost two cigarettes. Gary Cox (1986) has argued persuasively that as the number of participants rises, politicians prefer to switch from particularistic goods to policy goods that can be supplied to large numbers more efficiently. Yet voters may still want particularistic goods for the reasons noted earlier. In fact, such goods continue to play a very large role in the political strategies of politicians in developing countries. Particularistic benefits, unlike most policies, are easily excludable and thus give citizens selective incentives to vote. Furthermore, two cigarettes have higher expected value than a vote for one's favorite candidate (given the very low probability that a single vote will affect the outcome).[16]

Candidates, of course, try to arrange for the state to pay for these goods and their distribution, but they must often foot some of the bill themselves. For this reason, politicians facing a strong demand from voters for particularistic goods have great difficulty fulfilling their promises to end graft. Knowledgeable observers estimate that winning congressional candidates in Brazil now spend an average of more than $1 million each on their campaigns (Ames 1995). It is difficult to imagine how that kind of money could be raised legally in a relatively poor country with stringent limitations on legal campaign contributions. About fifteen parties are currently represented in the Brazilian Chamber of Deputies; in Brazil's open-list system, candidates run not only against opposing parties but also against other members of their own parties. All this means that a very large number of would-be deputies exist at any particular time. Many of them precede their campaigns with a stint as a local elected official or bureaucrat in a state agency, where they try to put together a campaign chest of $1 million-plus any way they can.

Intense political competition can also lead to the multiplication of sites of corruption. In fragmented party systems, presidents from small parties are elected fairly often. To put together an effective majority in the legislature, such a president has to distribute cabinet seats and the control over hiring, contracting, and distribution they entail to representatives of several parties. The parties use their control over the ministries and their subordinate agencies to hire their own loyalists, who tend to see the needs of their own partisans as most compelling. This leads to the transformation of entitlements—such as the initiation of pension payments, the distribution of building materials to slum dwellers, or the granting of titles during land reform—into rewards for partisan loyalty. Corruption in the strict sense may also increase, as party activists who have achieved a bureaucratic niche attempt to build the resource base needed to move either into electoral politics, higher in the bureaucracy, or to a more lucrative posting. The control of different agencies by different parties, or by different personal cliques in countries where parties are either unimportant or unable to impose discipline on their members, can multiply the number of bribes or kickbacks needed to accomplish a project (Shleifer and Vishny 1993).

The one consequence of competition that often leads to reduced corruption is the entry of new competitors into the field. When the leader of a new party assumes office and finds herself at the head of a government filled with opposition party cadres, the logic of corruption shifts sharply, giving the new party incentives to pursue reform with a partisan vengeance. Privatization, as shown later, is likely to occur under the same circumstances.

Given the usefulness of the fruits of corruption in political combat, we should not be surprised that it persists, mutates, and even at times seems to multiply during democratization. As North has noted (1990, 16): "Institutions are not necessarily or even usually created to be socially efficient; rather they . . . are created to serve the interests of those with the bargaining power to devise new rules."

This discussion also implies some predictions about the factors that are likely to reduce corruption. Reforms that increase the independence of the judiciary from parties and rulers tend to decrease the expected benefits of corruption because they increase the likelihood of detection and punishment. The transition from partisanship to professionalism in the press also increases the likelihood of detection; as the industry professionalizes, career rewards go increasingly to journalists who uncover hidden information, including corruption. Most important, corruption tends to decline as citizens become more informed and affluent. With greater information and wealth, voters value the individual benefits distributed by politicians less since they can get them from other sources, and citizens have a greater ability to assess politicians' policy performance. For both these reasons, the value of corruption to politicians declines, and reforms aimed at reducing it become easier to initiate. None of these predictions are novel or surprising, but it seems worth mentioning them since they derive in a straightforward way from the earlier argument. No additional claims about culture or values are needed to explain either the general persistence of corruption in developing countries or the rise in public intolerance for it in a number of countries during the last ten years.

PRIVATIZATION

State ownership, like corruption, generates resources that politicians can exchange for support. In consequence, many of the same considerations that prevent politicians from ending corruption also affect decisions about privatization. The privatization of state-owned firms, like most other market-extending reforms, reduces officials' discretion over the distribution of individual benefits and thus reduces their access to politically valuable resources (compare, Waterbury 1992, 1993). When considering privatization, politicians have to assess not only its expected effect on groups in society but also its direct effect on their ability to deliver benefits to especially useful supporters. Privatization almost always results in layoffs of both blue-collar and managerial personnel, but even when no layoffs occur, employees cease to owe their posts to politicians. They can no longer be required to work during the campaign, contribute a percentage of their salaries to their parties, or expedite the business of copartisans.

Jobs in the bureaucracy have traditionally been the most important currency for paying party workers in many countries. In Uruguay, for example, state-owned enterprises,

> in general, are refuges for failed politicians, that is, candidates for deputy who have lost elections; this is a consolation prize; it assures them a salary and [future] electoral possibilities through the illicit use of power. They have a duty to satisfy the demands of the party with regard to appointing employees, granting credits, pensions, giving prompt service. (Real 1965, 67)

The ability to provide the individual constituency services that are the meat and potatoes of successful party maintenance depends on having party loyalists in relevant bureaucratic agencies. The more the state intervenes in the economy, the more benefits are potentially available to distribute. More state enterprises make possible the distribution of more jobs and contracts. In short, privatization and reductions in state employment potentially threaten politicians' "internal constituencies"—those who canvass neighborhoods on the candidate's behalf, organize transportation to the polls, bring constituents' needs and grievances to the candidate's attention, and make large campaign contributions.[17]

The fruits of state ownership differ from the fruits of corruption, however, in this respect: They go mainly to the parties that secured niches in the state enterprise sector while it was growing; the fruits of corruption, in contrast, can be gathered by whatever party currently staffs relevant offices. As a result of this difference, privatizing depends more on specific political circumstances and less on long-term secular trends than does curbing corruption.

In most countries, the state enterprise sector has contributed heavily to the maintenance of the party or parties in power during the time when the public sector grew rapidly. Many partisans of these parties got their appointments during the early days of massive hiring, and over time they rose to supervisory positions from which they could hire others. In most countries with democratic histories, the partisan hires of one administration were not dismissed by the next.[18] Though the new administration may have wished to be rid of them, they were deterred by civil service laws, the fear of violence, or the expectation of retaliation the next time they found themselves in opposition. Military governments have sometimes been more willing to fire the appointees of previous administrations. The military in Argentina, for example, sacked not only large numbers of Peronist bureaucrats but even Peronist university faculty.

One can often infer the costs and benefits of privatization or large-scale dismissals of state employees if one knows the party affiliation of the executive and which party's loyalists predominate in staffing state agencies.[19] In other words, it is not sheer numbers laid off that matter so much but *whose* partisans face layoffs. Layoffs caused by politician X can hurt politician Y by leading to the disorganization and demoralization of Y's political machine. X need not worry about the wrath of those hurt by the decision because Y's supporters would not have voted for him anyway.

Whether these policies are carried out should then depend on who has decision-making power and whether their supporters are concentrated in state agencies and firms. This is a very simple idea. It does not take into account many factors that observers recognize as important, such as the extent of the economic crisis the country faces, societal economic interests that will be affected by privatization, and public attitudes toward capitalism. But this simple idea, as shown later, goes a surprisingly long way toward explaining the differences in the experiences of a large number of developing countries.

During the last fifteen or so years, executives have faced intensifying pressures from the external economic environment to privatize and reduce public employment. These reforms are relatively quick and, in some circumstances, attractive ways to cut budget deficits, reduce outstanding debt, secure revenue inflows, and make international agencies happy. The benefits of such reforms are thus quite substantial and, at least since about 1990, have been well understood by political leaders in developing countries. Executives, however, must also consider the costs to their own future political viability and that of their parties.[20]

Whether executives advocate extensive privatization depends on whether their own party or faction occupies a disproportionate number of positions in the bureaucracy or state enterprise sector. Executives opposed by factions or parties heavily reliant on control of state positions are especially likely to favor privatization as a means of reducing the political resources available to opponents. Although some privatizations are accomplished through executive decree, extensive programs of divestiture require legislative and judicial acquiescence except in the most autocratic regimes.

Consequently, the extent of privatization depends not only on the executive's interests but also on those of the parties that dominate the legislature and judiciary.

EVIDENCE

With this North-inspired picture of the political uses of state ownership in mind, let us now take a look at the privatization experiences of developing countries. Table 5.1 summarizes the experiences of fifteen countries in Latin America, the European periphery, and Africa.

Column 1 lists each administration in the fifteen countries, beginning with the executive in office when international pressure for economic reforms began and ending with those who assumed office early in 1996. Anyone elected after that date would have had very little time to carry out privatizations.

Columns 2 and 3 show ordinal assessments of the amount of privatization proposed and carried out during each administration. These assessments are based on the *Economist* Intelligence Unit's *Country Reports* for each country, ending in mid-1997. In making these judgments, I have taken into account the size of the public sector prior to the beginning of privatization and the size of the economy. For example, $100 million in revenues from privatization in Tanzania is considered evidence of greater privatization than would the same amount of revenue in Mexico because the Mexican economy is so much larger. The "coding" rules for assigning amounts of privatization to categories are as follows: "None" means that no privatization is reported in the relevant *Country Reports;* "minimal" means that the government sold some small firms of little political or economic significance, such as hotels or small tea factories, and/or small amounts of stock in large public utilities; "modest" means that a number of firms were sold, bringing in revenues of between $100 million and $500 million in an average-size country; "substantial" means that much of the public sector was sold off, with revenues often reaching the billions; "radical" means that not only was most of the public sector (with the possible exception of the main extractive industry) sold very rapidly, but even such public services as sewerage treatment, water supply, and highways were leased to private operators.

Column 4 lists the party affiliation of the executive in column 1. Column 5 identifies the party or parties likely to lose the most in terms of administrative jobs and access to state resources as a result of privatization. In most cases, these are the parties that ruled during the years when the state enterprise sector was expanding. In recently democratized countries, however, retired officers and supporters of military rule occupied many posts in the public sector at the time of the transition, and the partisan appointments of earlier democratic governments had been purged. I have followed the literature on Mexico in identifying presidents de la Madrid, Salinas, and Zedillo as members of the technocratic wing of the Partido Revolucionario Institucional (PRI), and the main beneficiaries of state-sector employment as loyalists of the more traditional wing (see, for example, Graham 1990; Middlebrook 1994).

Columns 6 and 7 describe the executive's level of support in the legislature. Column 6 refers to the proportion of seats in the legislature held by the executive's party. "Majority" means that the executive's party held at least one seat more than 50 percent of all seats. "Working" means that the executive's party by itself controlled between 40 and 50 percent of the seats and could routinely call on the

Table 5.1   Relationship Between Executive's Interests and Privatization

	Privatization		Party Affiliation		Legislature	
	Proposed	Achieved	Executive	Patronage	Majority	Disc.
Argentina						
Alfonsín	Minimal	Minimal	UCR	Military, UCR	Mixed	High
Menem '89	Radical	Radical	PJ	Military, UCR	Working	Medium
Menem '95	Radical	Radical	PJ	Military, UCR	Majority	Medium
Brazil						
Sarney	Minimal	Minimal	PFL	PDS, PFL, PMDB	Minority	Low
Collor	Substantial	Modest	PRN	PDS, PFL, PMDB	Minority	Low
Franco	Modest	Modest	None	PDS, PFL, PMDB	Minority	Low
Cardoso	Substantial	Modest	PSB	PDS, PFL, PMDB	Coalition	Low
Chile						
Pinochet	Radical	Radical	Military	Traditional parties	No legislature	
Ghana						
Rawlings '81	Substantial	Substantial	PNDC	Traditional parties, military	(No legislature)	
Rawlings '92	Modest	Modest	NDC	Traditional parties, military	Majority	High
Greece						
Papandreou '81	None	None	PASOK	PASOK	Majority	High
Papandreou '85	None	None	PASOK	PASOK	Majority	High
Mitsotakis	Modest	Minimal	ND	PASOK	Working	Medium
Papandreou	Reverse	None	PASOK	PASOK	Majority	High
Simitis	Minimal	Minimal	PASOK	PASOK	Majority	High
Kenya						
Moi '78	None	None	KANU	KANU	Majority	High
Moi '92	Modest	Modest	KANU	KANU	Majority	High
Mexico						
De la Madrid	Modest	Modest	Technocratic PRI	Traditional PRI	Majority	High
Salinas	Substantial	Substantial	Technocratic PRI	Traditional PRI	Majority	High
Zedillo	Substantial	Substantial	Technocratic PRI	Traditional PRI	Majority	High
Peru						
García	None	None	APRA	APRA	Majority	High
Fujimori '90	Substantial	Minimal	C90	APRA	Minority	Low
Fujimori '93	Substantial	Substantial	C90	APRA	Majority	Medium
Fujimori '95	Substantial	Substantial	C90-NM	APRA	Majority	Medium
Senegal						
Diouf '83	None	None	PS	PS	Majority	High
Diouf '88	Minimal	Minimal	PS	PS	Majority	High
Diouf '93	Modest	Minimal	PS	PS	Majority	High

(*Table 5.1 continues on page 214.*)

Table 5.1   *Continued*

	Privatization		Party Affiliation		Legislature	
	Proposed	Achieved	Executive	Patronage	Majority	Disc.
Spain						
Suárez	None	None	UCD	Franquist	Working	Medium
González '82	Substantial	Substantial	PSOE	Franquist	Majority	High
González '86	Substantial	Substantial	PSOE	Franquist	Majority	High
González '89	Substantial	Substantial	PSOE	Franquist	Coalition	High
González '93	Substantial	Substantial	PSOE	Franquist	Coalition	High
Aznar	Substantial	Substantial	PP	Franquist	Coalition	High
Tanzania						
Mwinyi '85	None	None	CCM	CCM	Majority	High
Mwinyi '90	Minimal	Minimal	CCM	CCM	Majority	High
Mkapa	Modest	Modest	CCM	CCM	Majority	High
Turkey						
Özal '83	Minimal	Minimal	Motherland	Motherland	Majority	High
Özal '87	Minimal	Minimal	Motherland	Motherland	Majority	High
Demiral	Modest	Minimal	True Path	Motherland	Coalition	Medium
Ciller	Substantial	Modest	True Path	Motherland	Coalition	Medium
Erbakan	Substantial	Modest	Welfare	Motherland	Coalition	Medium
Uruguay						
Sanguinetti	Minimal	None	Colorado	Colorado, Blanco	Coalition	Low
LaCalle	Modest	Minimal	Blanco	Colorado, Blanco	Minority	Low
Sanguinetti	None	None	Colorado	Colorado, Blanco	Coalition	Low
Venezuela						
Lusinchi	None	None	AD	AD, COPEI	Majority	High
Pérez	Modest	Minimal	AD	AD, COPEI	Working	High
Caldera	Substantial	Minimal	CN	AD, COPEI	Minority	Low
Zambia						
Kaunda	None	None	UNIP	UNIP	Majority	High
Chiluba	Substantial	Substantial	MMD	UNIP	Majority	High

Source: Economist Intelligence Unit, Country Reports (multiple years).

support of one or more small parties in order to pass legislation. "Coalition" means that the executive's party formed a stable alliance with one or more other parties sufficiently large or important to demand positions in the cabinet or important policies in return for their support. "Mixed" means that the executive controlled one house but not the other in a bicameral system in which the support of both was needed in order to pass legislation. "No" means that the executive's party held a minority of seats in the legislature and coalitions did not last; new coalitions had to be put together to pass different pieces of legislation. Column 7, which provides a judgment of the level of party discipline within the executive's party or coalition, is included because in some cases the executive's interests diverged from those of the rest of the party, which sometimes, in the absence of discipline, caused legislators from the president's party to refuse support.

Table 5.1 shows that, on average, the experience of privatization in these countries has been consistent with expectations generated by the Northian argument. In Latin America the most radical privatizations were carried out by Carlos Menem of Argentina and Augusto Pinochet of Chile. Carlos Salinas of Mexico, Alberto Fujimori of Peru, and Fernando Collor and Fernando Henrique Cardoso of Brazil also pressed for extensive privatization, though not all were able to achieve their goals. The most extensive privatization in democratizing southern Europe occurred in Spain during the government of Felipe González. In Africa, Frederick Chiluba of Zambia and Jerry Rawlings of Ghana have undertaken more privatization than other leaders. All but Salinas of Mexico came from parties different from those that stood to lose most from privatization.

The least privatization was proposed and achieved by Adolfo Suárez of the Unión del Centro Democrático (UCD) in Spain, Kenneth Kaunda, founder and leader of the United National Independence Party (UNIP) in Zambia, Jaime Lusinchi of Acción Democrática (AD) in Venezuela, and Andreas Papandreou, founder and leader of the Panhellenic Socialist Movement (PASOK) in Greece. The Spanish UCD was a recently formed center-right catchall party that included many former Franco supporters. The state enterprise sector in Spain developed during Franco's long rule, and many Franquista supporters were employed in it (Bermeo 1990). In the other administrations during which no privatization was proposed, the party that had benefited most from state intervention in the economy controlled both the executive and legislative branches.

Additional insights and clarification of some interpretations can be gained from examining some of the cases shown in table 5.1 in a bit more detail. Let us begin by taking a closer look at two cases in which standard interest-based theories would not have predicted extensive privatization: the Menem administration in Argentina and the González administration in Spain. In both, labor party governments carried out wide-ranging privatizations that led to layoffs for large numbers of their own union-ized supporters, as well as other economic reforms leading to increased unemploy-ment. Although severe economic crisis and hyperinflation in Argentina had reduced the options open to Menem, Spain faced only moderate economic problems. In short, standard arguments cannot explain privatization in these two countries.

The radical economic liberalization implemented by President Menem of Argentina initially astonished observers, not only because of his affiliation with the Partido Justicialista (PJ or Peronist party), but because of his previous career as governor of the backward state of La Rioja. As governor, Menem became famous for increasing public-sector employment in the state by 50 percent, an increase rumored to include hundreds of his own relatives and in-laws. Most unionized public employees, the backbone of the Peronist party, strongly opposed privatiza-tion. Nevertheless, Menem's government carried out one of the most rapid and extensive privatizations in the world. Between 1990 and the end of 1992, the Argentine government earned $17.6 billion from privatizations that included not only state-owned enterprises but leases on federal highways and concessions for the operation of water and sewerage systems.[21]

Most of the blue-collar workers laid off in the course of privatization were Peronists, that is, members of the Peronist external constituency. Since democ-ratization, however, higher-status jobs in the federal administration have not played the role in Peronist party maintenance they once did because Peronist bureaucrats were purged by military rulers, first during the 1950s and again in the 1970s. When Menem came to power, the Peronists had not had an opportunity to control federal appointments for nearly fifteen years, and the Peronist politi-cal machine did not depend on distributing such jobs. Consequently, although the cost of privatization to the Peronists' *external* constituency was high, its cost to the *internal* constituency was not. The military itself controlled and staffed some of the largest public enterprises, such as the oil and petrochemical industries. Among the least controversial privatizations in Argentina were the assets controlled by the military. Laying off retired military officers was not politically costly for the Peronists.

The Partido Socialista de Obrero Español (PSOE) in Spain, like the Peronist party in Argentina, had been allied with unions since its founding. And again as in Argentina, unionized workers have borne major costs during Spain's economic reform: Official unemployment hovered in the vicinity of 20 percent for five years straight during the 1980s (ILO 1990) and returned to those levels again during the mid-1990s. Although generous unemployment benefits and increased spending on social welfare reduced the burden (Maravall 1993), the González government's policies eventually caused the alliance between the Socialists and the unions to break down (Gillespie 1990), indicating that, despite side payments, reforms had high costs for the external constituency. From the point of view of PSOE's internal constituency, however, the privatizations were costless. Because of the state sector's links to the Franco regime, PSOE had no stake in its perpetuation. In contrast, the center-right UCD, which included in its ranks many Franco supporters, carried out no privatizations, though it liberalized moderately in other ways. In fact, employment in state enterprises increased by 11 percent between 1975 and 1980, and budgetary transfers to public enterprises increased by 500 percent between 1977 and 1982 during UCD rule (Bermeo 1990, 140).

Privatization by the conservative, anti-labor Pinochet government in Chile, in contrast to the Argentine and Spanish experiences, has never been considered surprising. It may thus come as a surprise to non–Latin Americanists to learn that the Pinochet government was the only one of the conservative Latin American military governments to carry out substantial privatization, despite considerable liberalization in other areas and strident free market rhetoric. In Chile, as in the other countries that succumbed to bureaucratic-authoritarian regimes during the 1960s and 1970s, the state sector had grown rapidly in the decades preceding military intervention. During that time all major parties had opportunities to find niches for themselves in the state enterprise sector (Valenzuela 1977). The Pinochet government had no interest in perpetuating the parties' access to state resources, and it implemented the earliest radical privatization. Military governments in other countries, however, were not equally disinterested in the state sector. Argentine and Brazilian officers had run some of the largest state enterprises for decades before they seized power, and they had no more desire to give up these valuable political resources than did civilian political leaders (Biglaiser 1996). Military rulers in various African countries have also used state enterprises in the same fashion, as the source of benefits to be distributed to supporters. In short, a conservative antilabor ideology and support coalition predict privatization no better than do a prolabor social democratic ideology and support coalition.

At first glance, Mexico's experience seems inconsistent with the argument advanced here. A president from the long-dominant PRI oversaw a massive privatization campaign that without doubt hurt the PRI's internal constituency. To understand the politics behind Mexico's privatization, one must take account of the bitter factional fight inside the PRI during the 1980s. Two characteristics distinguish Mexico from many other single-party regimes: federalism and a regular,

institutionalized succession process. Federalism has allowed divergent developments in the operating procedures and interests of state-level party organizations
within the PRI. In consequence, the PRI has become polarized between a more
modern wing, with support concentrated in the more developed states, and a traditional wing, dominant in more backward areas, that continues to rely on exchange-
based politics (Graham 1990).

The process of choosing successors has resulted in a series of presidents allied
with the more modern faction. Most rulers of single-party regimes have built
the party around themselves and rely on its members for support. They are thus
beholden to party activists and ignore at their peril these activists' interest in continued state ownership. But the secret procedure for nominating future presidents
in Mexico, in which only a small number of officials are consulted, has had the
unforeseen consequence of weakening the link between the president and the traditional PRI electoral machine. Recent presidents have all risen from within party
and government bureaucracies, not through electoral politics. No Mexican president since 1970 had previously held elective office. Meanwhile, party and government administration in Mexico have become increasingly professionalized since
the 1960s, thus increasing the likelihood that a person who rose to prominence
within this milieu would combine a technocratic outlook with the more usual
political gifts (Graham 1990). Professionalization of government administration
per se is not unusual. In fact, it is occurring in segments of the bureaucracy in virtually all developing countries. But the selection of presidents from among this
group is uncommon.

By 1987, when Salinas was nominated for the presidency, Mexico had been
undergoing the rigors of austerity for five years. Real wages are estimated to have
fallen about 50 percent between 1982 and 1988. This period of austerity and
decline seriously undermined the old party machine that had delivered the votes
so regularly for nearly fifty years. Unable to deliver the carrots to voters, it could
no longer deliver the vote for PRI candidates. Furthermore, the traditional wing
of the PRI had fought against Salinas's nomination, opposed the economic reforms,
and hindered at every turn efforts to transform the party and the Mexican economy. Many from the traditional wing of the PRI deserted it to vote for Cuauhtémoc
Cárdenas in the 1988 presidential election. After winning the first closely con-
tested election in Mexico's history,[22] Salinas aggressively attacked the political
resource base of the traditional wing of the PRI, not only through extensive privatization but also through well-publicized assaults on some of the most powerful
unions in Mexico. The vast number of layoffs in the state-owned oil industry,
mining, and railroads were made more palatable to the rank-and-file by generous
severance pay, but the old union elite, the cogs and wheels of the old PRI
machine, were forced out in several unions (Middlebrook 1994). In short, the costs
of Mexico's privatization were concentrated among members of the faction
that opposed President Salinas. Their loss of offices and resources strengthened
Salinas's faction.

PATTERNS IN THE EVIDENCE

Since it is difficult to perceive patterns in a complicated table—especially interactive ones such as those hypothesized here—and even more difficult to discern
them in the clutter of case sketches, I turn now to regression to show the basic

patterns in the evidence. The data used in the regressions reflect the information in table 5.1.[23]

Table 5.2 reports a test of the simplest and most basic argument, that executives' support for privatization depends on whether their own supporters occupy large numbers of administrative positions in the state enterprise sector. To control for the effects of international economic pressures, which have intensified over time, a measure of the years since international pressures for reform began is included in the regression.[24] This proxy reflects the increasing pressure from donors to privatize, as well as the effects of continuing financial crisis in countries that have been slow to do so. As can be seen in table 5.1, there is a trend toward more privatization over time. Including this variable holds that trend constant.

The left-hand panel in table 5.2 shows the effect on proposals to privatize of the executive's belonging to the party that has historically controlled white-collar hiring in state firms. As can be seen, the coefficient for this variable is −2.02, indicating that the average level of privatization proposed by executives who belong to the same party as most state employees is about two categories lower than it would be if they belonged to different parties. A two-category difference is that between minimal and substantial privatization or between modest and radical. In other words, it is a very big difference. This result is highly statistically significant. Date, the proxy for international pressures, has the expected effect of increasing proposed privatizations over time, and it is also statistically significant at conventional levels in a one-tailed test. These two variables explain 71 percent of the variance in the amount of privatization proposed by executives.

The right-hand side of table 5.2 shows the effect of a difference in party affiliation between the executive and those who will bear the heaviest costs of privatization on the actual achievement of privatization. This effect is −1.95, about the same as its effect on proposed privatization, and it is also highly significant. But the effect of international pressure, as proxied by date, is decreased by about half and is no longer statistically significant. The overall variance explained also drops a bit, to .59. I interpret these differences in the two results as tentative evidence, first, that international pressures have a stronger effect on proposals than achievements and, second, that achievements are more affected than proposals by other political factors not included in these initial regressions.

These first results demonstrate the powerful effects of party interest on the proposal and achievement of privatization, but they leave out a great deal. The next regression attempts to capture a somewhat broader and more realistic picture of the

Table 5.2   Relationship Between Privatization and Shared Party Affiliation

	Proposed Privatization		Privatization Achieved	
	B	Significance	B	Significance
Executive's party controls hiring in state firms (range 0–1)	−2.02	.00	−1.87	.00
Date (range 0–17)	0.04	.03	0.02	.20
Intercept	2.36	—	2.22	—
N of cases		49		49
Adjusted R-squared		.71		.59

Note: Both dependent variables have a range from 0 (no privatization) to 4 (radical privatization).

political world facing executives under pressure to privatize. The most important factor left out of the first regressions is the strength of the executive's party in the legislature. The regression results in table 5.3 and figure 5.1 incorporate this factor into the analysis. We would expect that an executive affiliated with a party not very dependent on the public sector for political resources and supported by a disciplined majority in the legislature would have the best chance of carrying out extensive privatizations. In contrast, an executive with similar legislative support but leading a party heavily dependent on the public sector would be unlikely to propose extensive privatization and likely to face intense legislative opposition if he did. I use an interaction between the two variables, "same party" and "legislative support," to capture this idea. Because the coefficients from interactive regressions are difficult to interpret in numerical form, I focus on the graphical display of the regression coefficients shown in figure 5.1.[25]

The left side of figure 5.1 shows the combined effects of legislative support and shared party affiliation on proposed privatization. As the gap between the upper and lower lines shows, executives whose parties do not control large numbers of positions in the public sector are likely to propose markedly more extensive privatization than those who do. Legislative support affects the two types of executives differently: Legislative strength leads executives who belong to the same party as white-collar state employees to propose less privatization and executives who do not belong this party to propose more. Legislative strength thus has a multiplier effect on party interest: The greater an executive's strength in the legislature, the more vigorously he promotes party interests.

The right sides of table 5.3 and figure 5.1 show the results of the same regression as shown on the left, but with achieved privatization as the dependent variable rather than proposed privatization. The differences are rather interesting. Proposals are much more affected by the party affiliation of the executive than achievements are. Again, the effects of the interaction can best be seen graphically. The two graphs are fairly similar except for this important difference: Legislative support has notably more effect on the achievement of privatization than on its mere proposal.

In the graph on the right side of figure 5.1, the top line shows that when the executive is not affiliated with the party that has dominated hiring in the public sector, privatization increases sharply as legislative support increases. Over the range of legislative support in this set of cases, the amount of privatization achieved

Table 5.3   Relationship Between Privatization and Shared Party Affiliation

	Proposed Privatization		Privatization Achieved	
	B	Significance	B	Significance
Executive's party controls hiring in state firms (range 0–1)	−1.11	.02	−0.50	.15
Legislative support (range 0–7)	0.08	.11	0.30	.00
Leg. Support X Exec. Party	−0.19	.03	−0.31	.00
Date (range 0–17)	0.05	.02	0.05	.02
Intercept	1.90		0.65	
N of cases		49		49
Adjusted R-squared		.72		.71

Notes: Both dependent variables have a range from 0 (no privatization) to 4 (radical privatization). "Legislative support" was formed by summing "party discipline" and "majority party" in table 5.1.

Figure 5.1   The Effect of Presidential Interest and Legislative Support on the Proposal and Achievement of Privatization

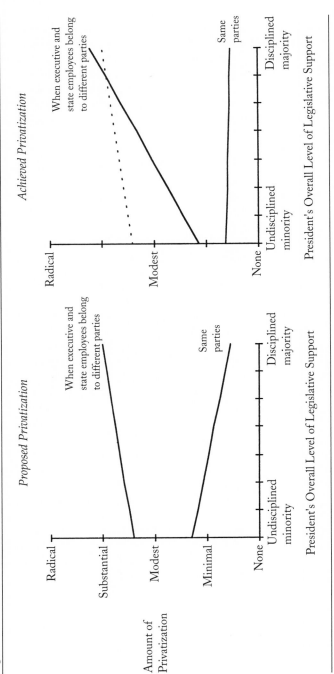

Note: Figures are based on cases in table 5.1 and OLS regression coefficients in table 5.3.

rises, on average, from just above minimal to just above substantial. When, however, the executive's party dominates state firms, privatization is minimal at best, and legislative support has little effect. To facilitate comparison between the left and right sides of the figure, the top line on the left side is transposed onto the graph on the right side as a dotted line. The difference between the dotted line and the top solid line shows that, although executives having no vested interest in state ownership often propose extensive privatization, they do not achieve very much unless they command the support of a disciplined party in the legislature.

Taken altogether, these regressions offer strong support for the North-inspired argument that the interests of political leaders drive the politics of privatization, as they do the politics of other institutional changes. They show, first of all, that executives under pressure to privatize are much more likely to *propose* doing so when it serves their narrow political interest, that is, when the state workers who would be sacked or transferred to private employment are cadres of the opposition party. To go further and explain how much privatization is actually *achieved*, the partisanship of the whole management team, including the legislature, must be taken into account. When the executive has an interest in privatization but the opposition party dominates the legislature, little privatization occurs. Only when executive interest coincides with disciplined party strength in the legislature does extensive privatization occur.

REDUCING CORRUPTION, INCREASING PRIVATIZATION

Let us step back now from the detailed analysis of the interconnections between corruption, state intervention, and politics to consider a couple of the big questions posed by current events. Why, after decades of increasing intervention in their economies, have most developing countries now begun to privatize? And why, after centuries of unremarked and routine corruption, have citizens in a surprising number of countries suddenly become fed up, thrown out governments, and abandoned parties that had counted, sometimes for more than a generation, on their unquestioning loyalty?

The short answer is that the worldwide economic crisis, usually dated from 1982, and the collapse of communism between them have resulted in the ouster of more incumbent political leaders and parties during the last fifteen years than in any other decade and a half in world history. At the same time, the media are playing an ever larger role in influencing vote choice, reducing the power of parties even in long-established democracies. In short, we are living in an era that, because of regime change, the party fluidity that sometimes results from regime change, increasing availability of information, and internal party democratization, provides unusual opportunities for political outsiders.

The interests of outsiders often differ from those of incumbents, and consequently these changes in personnel at the top have resulted in a remarkable spate of reforms. Because the political benefits of both corruption and state ownership tend to accrue to incumbents, political outsiders can, in some circumstances, improve their own competitiveness by reducing corruption and privatizing. In economically normal times, there is little incentive, even for outsiders, to initiate these kinds of changes. Ordinarily, new leaders might simply want to make arrangements to get their cut and create new agencies to employ their own supporters. The international price shock of the 1980s, however, reduced the feasibility of this politically sensible risk-averse strategy. Political leaders for at least the last ten years have faced intense pressures to reduce budget deficits; they cannot hire a lot of new people. Through privatization, they can, however, disorganize opponents' support networks and, at the same time, generate new revenues to use to help balance the budget, reduce the debt, and create new distributive networks tied to themselves. Since "institutions . . . are created to serve the interests of those with the bargaining power to devise new rules" (North 1990, 16), and the interests of incumbents differ from those of newcomers, the general reduction in the number of both authoritarian and democratic incumbents during the 1980s and 1990s has led to widespread privatization and a large number of anticorruption initiatives.

CONCLUSION

This study began with the observation that Douglass North has transformed the way political scientists understand economic development and institutional change. I have attempted to demonstrate the effect of these ideas by using them to illuminate the current struggles in developing countries over institutional changes expected to reduce economic inefficiencies. To summarize the argument, during the 1980s an international price shock created strong pressures for institutional change in most of the developing world (North and Thomas 1973). Given the change in relative prices, North's argument would lead to the expectation that political leaders would have tried to initiate institutional changes when they could themselves benefit from doing so (North 1990, 16), and the analysis of privatization proposals in this study shows that leaders of contemporary developing countries have behaved as expected. North's argument would also lead to the expectation that leaders' ability to make the institutional changes they prefer would have been constrained by the interests and bargaining power of other powerful political actors, and the analysis of achieved privatization shows that they have been.

North has repeatedly emphasized the importance of transaction costs in explaining why political leaders would in some circumstances prefer inefficient institutions even though they reduce overall productivity, and I have suggested that transaction costs explain why state enterprises have historically played such a large role in rewarding party activists. Employment in state enterprises reduces the cost to party leaders of enforcing the implicit contract with party activists and preventing shirking. As this mode of organizing party machines has become prohibitively expensive, we see long-established parties historically based on patronage and clientelism struggling for survival in many parts of the developing world. This form of party organization may simply not be able to survive in the era of mass politics without a large state sector. If no new way of keeping down the transaction costs of running political machines can be found, parties in developing countries may be forced to appeal to voters with policy promises rather than particularistic goods.

At one time observers thought that democratic governments would be deterred by popular opposition from imposing liberal economic reforms such as privatization and that only authoritarian governments would be able to do so. These observers have turned out to be wrong, but conventional theories cannot explain why they are wrong. North's approach provides the theoretical tools for explaining why so many contemporary developing democracies have begun substantial privatization. It focuses attention on political leaders and their interests as a critical element in explanations of institutional change. Taking that approach, this investigation of privatization shows that new rulers, regimes, and governments often have interests different from old ones, and thus the costs of institutional change to them may be lower, indeed negative. Today most new regimes and governments are more democratic than those they succeeded. Because they are new, privatization and other institutional changes associated with economic liberalization are less costly to them than to the parties and leaders they replaced.

NOTES

1. Prior to the crisis, a large share of revenues in most developing countries came from tariffs, taxes on exports, and the sale of minerals by state-owned producers. Income taxes were relatively low, and compliance rates in many areas very low. Margaret Levi (1988, 114) suggests explanations for these practices. Taxes on trade, as she notes, are among the easiest to measure and monitor and may therefore be preferred by rulers who cannot depend on a competent and honest bureaucracy to collect other forms of tax, even though such taxes reduce the volume of trade and consequently the gains from exchange. Levi's argument (1988, 177) that "the income tax is possible only where there are representative institutions" may explain traditionally low compliance rates in countries such as Argentina in which representative government has been repeatedly interrupted.

2. For a North-influenced treatment of privatization and regulation in the telecommunications industry, see Levy and Spiller (1996).

3. It has been argued, most prominently by Nathaniel Leff (1964), that when states intervene in the economy, corruption can be efficient in the sense of creating an informal way to circumvent even more inefficient state regulations. Without denying this possibility, I think that most observers of developing countries would now agree that corruption usually reduces investment, productivity, and growth (Alam 1989, 1990; Kaufman 1997; Mauro 1995; Shleifer and Vishny 1993; Wade 1985).

4. During the 1970s much more was written on state ownership than could possibly be listed here. In most of this literature, "the state" was an important actor, but it reflected either the interests of dominant economic groups or a vaguely defined "public" interest. Among the most influential were Evans (1979), Moran (1974), and Baer, Newfarmer, and Trebat (1976). Since the mid-1980s hundreds of studies of privatization have been produced. Recent analytic or comparative studies include Chua (1995), Cowan (1990), Dinavo (1995), Milor (1994), Ramanadham (1994), Sader (1993), Waterbury (1993), and World Bank (1995). A useful bibliography covering countries large and small from all regions of the world can be found in Berend (1994).

5. A conspicuous exception is Shleifer and Vishny (1994).

6. North (1981, 148–50) interprets the increase in crown rights and revenues during drives for national consolidation of territory in France and Spain somewhat differently—namely, as the price paid by subjects for peace and order in situations of extreme disorder and violence. My point is that the advantages to indigenous nobles of the reconquest of territory go beyond peace and order to include tracts of land, high office, and the spoils of war.

7. Political managers in oligarchic and autocratic governments often face incentives similar to those of firm managers: Policy decisions that maximize income for their narrow coalition of supporters, and thus maintain their support, often also maximize their personal income.

8. Assumptions are intellectual constructs used in theory building and thus can be useful even when not plausible. Levi's book on tax practices, for example, makes effective use of the revenue maximization assumption in both ancient and modern societies by treating the survival imperative as a constraint (1988, 13).

9. In fact, North himself often relies on a survival maximization assumption in more historically detailed passages (see, for example, North and Thomas 1973, 94, 100). Other analysts sometimes finesse the issue by assuming that "rulers maximize toward some goals, which include the possession of resources, tax income, the authority and emoluments of office, and even sometimes benevolent public service" (Riker and Sened 1991, 954). My point is that one can get some additional theoretical leverage on the subject under study here from making a narrower and more concrete and descriptively accurate motivational assumption.

10. Mancur Olson's metaphor. For an extended discussion of this idea (in different language), see Olson 1993.

11. In democracies the children of executives have advantages in future competitions, but no certainty of achieving office. Dictators often hope to pass office on to their children but rarely succeed. In only 4 of the 163 dictatorships in existence at any time between 1946 and 1996 did the son or son-in-law of an autocrat succeed to his father's powers (figures from a data set collected by the author that includes all post-World War II dictatorships lasting three or more years in countries with one million or more inhabitants).

12. With an image of authoritarianism drawn from such long-lasting rulers as Francisco Franco, Mobutu Sese Seko, and Hafez al-Asad, one might suppose that autocratic political leaders have long time horizons, but in reality the average dictator can expect a relatively short term in office. The modal term for dictatorships within the data set cited in note 11, which excludes those of less than three years, is five years.

13. Although the original model of a "political business cycle" in industrialized democracies has been challenged (Hibbs 1987), observations of government efforts to manipulate economic outcomes during the run-up to elections are commonplace in studies of developing countries. Barry Ames (1987) has shown that government spending increases in Latin American countries during the year preceding elections. Mexico's recent economic disaster is routinely attributed to the government's determination to keep the currency overvalued in order to encourage a consumer spending binge during the months before the 1994 election.

14. The literature on clientelism and machine politics in developing countries is enormous. Among the more useful and interesting studies are Abueva (1966), Diniz (1982), Leal (1949), Leal Buitrago and Dávila (1990), Powell (1970), Schmidt and others (1977), Scott (1969, 1972a, 1972b), Strickon and Greenfield (1972), Valenzuela (1977), and Waterbury (1973, 1976).

15. This point will come as no surprise to observers of politics in the United States or any developing country, but seems not to have made its way into most economic models of corruption. For studies of corruption that are both theoretically imaginative and empirically careful, see Manion (1996), who shows the effects of changing the incentives facing Chinese bureaucrats in different hierarchical contexts.

16. Thus, turnout is less paradoxical in many developing countries than in the more advanced.

17. Harold Demsetz (1990) uses the phrase "internal constituency" to distinguish party activists and contributors from the "external constituency" of voters.

18. Colombia before 1958 is a well-known exception. In Venezuela opposition supporters claimed that eighty thousand of their number lost their jobs when Carlos Andrés Pérez came to power in 1974, but these dismissals violated norms (Karl 1982, 267). The more common situation is captured by a Chilean simile: Public administration is like an onion, with the partisan composition of each layer reflecting the administration during which it was hired and individual partisanship predictable from the date of hiring.

19. In regimes dominated by a single party, making inferences about the interests of different leaders and figuring out which factions control more patronage is more difficult because reform and antireform factions are both part of the same party.

20. It might seem that presidents in many democratic systems would not share the concerns of legislators and prime ministers in maintaining party and personal political machines since nearly all countries have term limits, most of only one term. Nevertheless, the interest of presidents in political survival does not differ greatly from that of legislators. They want to maintain their party base while in office in order to govern effectively. Many face midterm legislative, gubernatorial,

or municipal elections that can be interpreted as plebiscites on presidential performance. And finally, even though they may not be able to run for office again immediately, most wish to continue their political careers as party leaders, and many hope to win the presidency again after a term or two has elapsed. The hope of achieving the pinnacle of power again is very widespread and not as unrealistic as one might at first suspect. Carlos Andrés Pérez and Rafael Caldera of Venezuela, Fernando Belaúnde of Peru, Juan Perón of Argentina, Carlos Ibáñez of Chile, and Getúlio Vargas of Brazil were all elected to another term as president after being out of office for at least one. And many others have schemed and campaigned for second terms without achieving them.

21. *Chronicle of Latin American Affairs,* January 7, 1993, 2, and June 17, 1993, 2–6.

22. Some observers believe that an honest vote count would have resulted in a PRI loss, and that Salinas won only by fraud. It is impossible to know for sure.

23. In order to carry out the statistical analysis, the qualitative descriptions in table 5.1 must be converted into quantitative descriptions. In the table, I describe five levels of privatization—none, minimal, modest, substantial, and radical. For purposes of statistical analysis, I have converted these descriptions into integer values running from 0 to 4. Columns 4 and 5 identify the party affiliation of the executive and of most occupants of administrative jobs in state firms. When the same party is named in both columns, I give the same-party variable a value of 1, and 0 otherwise. Measuring an executive's level of support in the legislature is slightly more complicated. The table includes two indicators of legislative support: the strength of the executive's party in the legislature, which takes the values of "minority," "mixed" (meaning control of one house), "coalition," "working majority," "majority," and "no legislature"; and level of discipline within the executive's party, which runs from low to middle to high. Converting these ordered descriptions into values from 0 to 5 and from 0 to 2 and adding them together produces a variable, "legislative support," that runs from 0 (undisciplined minority) to 6 (disciplined majority). Heads of military governments, who can do whatever they want because they have no legislatures to hold them in check, are scored 7, the highest value. Given the roughness of the original descriptions, there is no loss of information in this conversion.

24. The measure is the midpoint of the executive's term minus 1979 (the earliest midpoint in the data set). For executives elected after 1994, I used 1996 as the midpoint. This variable ranges from 0 to 17.

25. To make this graph, the date was set at 1989, about midway between the onset of the crisis and 1997.

REFERENCES

Abueva, José. 1966. "The Contribution of Nepotism, Spoils, and Graft to Political Development." *East-West Center Review* 3: 45–54.

Alam, M. S. 1989. "Anatomy of Corruption: An Approach to the Political Economy of Underdevelopment." *American Journal of Economics and Sociology* 48(4): 441–55.

———. 1990. "Some Economic Costs of Corruption in LDCs." *Journal of Development Studies* 27(1): 89–97.

Alchian, A., and Harold Demsetz. 1973. "The Property Rights Paradigm." *Journal of Economic History* 33: 16–27.

Ames, Barry. 1987. *Political Survival: Politicians and Public Policy in Latin America.* Berkeley: University of California Press.

———. 1995. "Electoral Rules, Constituency Pressures, and Pork Barrel: Bases of Voting in the Brazilian Congress." *Journal of Politics* 57(2): 324–43.

Baer, Werner, Richard Newfarmer, and Thomas Trebat. 1976. "On State Capitalism in Brazil: Some New Issues and Questions." *Inter-American Economic Affairs* 30(3): 69–91.

Berend, Ivan (ed.). 1994. *Transition to a Market Economy at the End of the Twentieth Century.* Südosteuropa-Studie 54. Munich: Südosteuropa-Gesellschaft.

Bermeo, Nancy. 1990. "The Politics of Public Enterprise in Portugal, Spain, and Greece." In *The Political Economy of Public Sector Reform and Privatization,* edited by Ezra Suleiman and John Waterbury (Boulder, Colo.: Westview), 137–62.

Biglaiser, Glen. 1996. "Policy Choices Under Military Rule: The Effect of Institutions and Ideas on Policy Outcomes." Ph.D. diss., University of California at Los Angeles.

Chua, Amy. 1995. "The Privatization-Nationalization Cycle: The Link Between Markets and Ethnicity in Developing Countries." *Columbia Law Review* 95: 223–303.

Cowan, Gray. 1990. *Privatization in the Developing World.* Contributions in Economics and Economic History 112. New York: Greenwood Press.

Cox, Gary. 1986. "The Development of a Party-Oriented Electorate in England, 1832–1918." *British Journal of Political Science* 16: 187–216.

Demsetz, Harold. 1990. "Amenity Potential, Indivisibilities, and Political Competition." In *Perspectives on Positive Political Economy,* edited by James Alt and Kenneth Shepsle (Cambridge: Cambridge University Press), 144–60.

Diniz, Eli. 1982. *Voto e máquina política: Patronagem e clientelismo no Rio de Janeiro.* Rio de Janeiro: Paz e Terra.

Dinavo, Jacques. 1995. *Privatizing in Developing Countries: Its Impact on Economic Development and Democracy.* Westport, Conn.: Praeger.

Downs, Anthony. 1957. *An Economic Theory of Democracy.* New York: Harper & Row.

Evans, Peter. 1979. *Dependent Development: The Alliance of Multinational, State, and Local Capital in Brazil.* Princeton, N.J.: Princeton University Press.

Fiorina, Morris. 1981. *Retrospective Voting in American National Elections.* New Haven, Conn.: Yale University Press.

Gillespie, Richard. 1990. "The Break-up of the 'Socialist Family': Party-Union Relations in Spain, 1982–1989." *West European Politics* 13: 47–62.

Graham, Lawrence. 1990. *The State and Policy Outcomes in Latin America.* New York: Praeger/Hoover Institution Press.

Hibbs, Douglas. 1987. *The Political Economy of Industrial Democracies.* Cambridge, Mass.: Harvard University Press.

International Labour Organization. 1990. *1989–90 Year Book of Labour Statistics 1990.* Geneva: International Labour Office.

Kalt, Joseph, and Mark Zupan. 1984. "Capture and Ideology in the Economic Theory of Politics." *American Economic Review* 74: 279–300.

———. 1990. "Apparent Ideological Behavior of Legislators: Testing for Principal-Agent Slack in Political Institutions." *Journal of Law and Economics* 33: 103–31.

Karl, Terry. 1982. "The Political Economy of Petrodollars: Oil and Democracy in Venezuela." Ph.D. diss., Stanford University.

Kaufman, Daniel. 1997. "Corruption: The Facts." *Foreign Policy* (Summer): 114–31.

Leal, Victor Nunes. 1949. *Coronelismo, enxado, e voto.* Rio de Janeiro: Forense.

Leal Buitrago, Francisco, and Andrés Dávila. 1990. *Clientelismo: El sistema político y su expresión regional.* Bogotá: Tercer Mundo Editores.

Leff, Nathaniel. 1964. "Economic Development Through Bureaucratic Corruption." *American Behavioral Scientist* 8 (November): 8–14.

Levi, Margaret. 1988. *Of Rule and Revenue.* Berkeley: University of California Press.

Levy, Brian, and Pablo Spiller (eds.). 1996. *Regulations, Institutions, and Commitment: Comparative Studies of Telecommunications.* Cambridge: Cambridge University Press.

Manion, Melanie. 1996. "Corruption by Design: Bribery in Chinese Enterprise Licensing." *Journal of Law, Economics, and Organization* 12: 167–95.

Maravall, José María. 1993. "Politics and Policy: Economic Reforms in Southern Europe." In *Economic Reforms in New Democracies,* edited by Luis Carlos Bresser Pereira, José María Maravall, and Adam Przeworski (Cambridge: Cambridge University Press), 77–131.

Mauro, Paolo. 1995. "Corruption and Growth." *Quarterly Journal of Economics* 110(3): 681–712.

Middlebrook, Kevin. 1994. *Organized Labor and the State in Mexico.* Baltimore: Johns Hopkins University Press.

Milor, Vedat (ed.). 1994. *Changing Political Economies: Privatization in Post-Communist and Reforming States.* Boulder, Colo.: Lynne Rienner.

Moe, Terry. 1984. "The New Economics of Organization." *American Journal of Political Science* 28: 739–77.

Moran, Theodore. 1974. *Multinational Corporations and the Politics of Dependence: Copper in Chile.* Princeton, N.J.: Princeton University Press.

North, Douglass. 1981. *Structure and Change in Economic History.* New York: Norton.

———. 1985. "Transaction Costs in History." *Journal of European Economic History* 14: 557–76.

————. 1989a. "Institutions and Economic Growth: An Historical Introduction." *World Development* 17: 1319–32.

————. 1989b. "A Transaction Cost Approach to the Historical Development of Polities and Economies." *Journal of Institutional and Theoretical Economics* 145: 661–68.

————. 1990. *Institutions, Institutional Change, and Economic Performance.* Political Economy of Institutions and Decisions Series. Cambridge: Cambridge University Press.

North, Douglass, and Robert Thomas. 1973. *The Rise of the Western World.* New York: Cambridge University Press.

North, Douglass, and Barry Weingast. 1989. "Constitutions and Commitment: The Evolution of Institutions Governing Public Choice in Seventeenth-Century England." *Journal of Economic History* 49 (December): 803–32.

Olson, Mancur. 1993. "Dictatorship, Democracy, and Development." *American Political Science Review* 87: 567–76.

Powell, John D. 1970. "Peasant Society and Clientelistic Politics." *American Political Science Review* 64: 411–25.

Ramanadham, V. V. (ed.). 1994. *Privatizing and After: Monitoring and Regulation.* London: Routledge.

Real, Alberto Ramón 1965. *Las estructuras políticas y administrativas uruguayas en relación con el desarrollo.* Montevideo: n.p.

Riker, William, and Itai Sened. 1991. "A Political Theory of the Origin of Property Rights." *American Journal of Political Science* 35(4): 951–69.

Rose-Ackerman, Susan. 1978. *Corruption: A Study in Political Economy.* New York: Academic Press.

Sader, Frank. 1993. *Privatization and Foreign Investment in the Developing World, 1988–1992.* Working Paper 1202. Washington, D.C.: World Bank, International Economics Department.

Schmidt, Steffen, et al. (eds.). 1977. *Friends, Followers, and Factions: A Reader in Political Clientelism.* Berkeley: University of California Press.

Scott, James C. 1969. "Corruption, Machine Politics, and Political Change." *American Political Science Review* 63: 1142–58.

————. 1972a. *Comparative Political Corruption.* Englewood Cliffs, N.J.: Prentice-Hall.

————. 1972b. "Patron-Client Politics and Political Change in Southeast Asia." *American Political Science Review* 66: 91–113.

Shackelton, J.R. 1978. "Corruption: An Essay in Economic Analysis." *The Political Quarterly* 49: 25–37.

Shleifer, Andrei, and Robert Vishny. 1993. "Corruption." *Quarterly Journal of Economics* 108 (3, August): 599–617.

————. 1994. "Politicians and Firms." *Quarterly Journal of Economics* 109: 995–1025.

Soskice, David, Robert Bates, and David Epstein. 1992. "Ambition and Constraint: The Stabilizing Role of Institutions." *Journal of Law, Economics, and Organization* (October): 547–60.

Strickon, Arnold, and Sidney Greenfield (eds.). 1972. *Structure and Process in Latin America: Patronage, Clientage, and Power Systems.* Albuquerque: University of New Mexico Press.

Valenzuela, Arturo. 1977. *Political Brokers in Chile: Local Government in a Centralized Polity.* Durham, N.C.: Duke University Press.

Wade, Robert. 1982. "The System of Administrative and Political Corruption: Canal Irrigation in South India." *Journal of Development Studies* 18(3): 297–38.

————. 1984. "Irrigation Reform in Conditions of Populist Anarchy: An Indian Case." *Journal of Development Economics* 14: 285–303.

————. 1985. "The Market for Public Office: Why the Indian State Is Not Better at Development." *World Development* 13(4): 467–97.

Waterbury, John. 1973. "Endemic and Planned Corruption in a Monarchical Regime." *World Politics* 25: 533–55.

————. 1976. "Corruption, Political Stability, and Development: Comparative Evidence from Egypt and Morocco." *Government and Opposition* 11: 426–45.

————. 1992. "The Heart of the Matter? Public Enterprise and the Adjustment Process." In *The Politics of Economic Adjustment,* edited by Stephan Haggard and Robert Kaufman (Princeton, N.J.: Princeton University Press), 182–220.

————. 1993. *Exposed to Innumerable Delusions: Public Enterprise and State Power in Egypt, India, Mexico, and Turkey.* Cambridge: Cambridge University Press.

World Bank. 1995. *Bureaucrats in Business.* Policy Research Report. New York: Oxford University Press.

IDEOLOGY AND PROFESSIONALISM IN INTERNATIONAL INSTITUTIONS: INSIGHTS FROM THE WORK OF DOUGLASS C. NORTH

Robert O. Keohane

Douglass North has searched throughout his career for the "Holy Grail of the ultimate sources of economic performance"—understanding what makes economies rich or poor (North 1997, 3). Seeking to explain variations across countries and time in economic performance led him to an interest in institutions, which he has defined as "the humanly devised constraints that structure human interaction," composed of formal constraints, informal constraints, conventions, and their "enforcement characteristics" (North 1994, 360). Neoclassical growth theory takes for granted an institutional structure in which individuals have incentives to undertake socially desirable activities (North and Thomas 1973, 2). The neoclassical formulation, he writes (North 1981, 5), "begs all of the interesting questions" by assuming a frictionless world "in which institutions do not exist and all change occurs through perfectly operating markets. In short, the costs of acquiring information, uncertainty, and transactions do not exist."

In the real world that North studies as a historian, however, transaction costs—the costs of acquiring information and enforcing agreements—are high. Coercion and opportunism are real problems, ignored at the historian's peril. Institutions are not always efficient: Indeed, they vary greatly in their ability to protect property rights, reduce uncertainty and opportunism, and ensure that credible commitments can be made. Hence, to understand economic growth, one must understand institutions.

Studying institutions has taken North into the domain of political science; indeed, his reputation in political science rests chiefly on his transaction cost theory of institutions. Ronald Coase (1937/1990) introduced the concept of transaction costs to explain the existence of firms and later showed (1960/1990) that transaction costs are the key to the significance of institutions in economics. Another economist who has made a big impact on political science, Oliver Williamson (1985), built on Coase's insights by elaborating the concepts of credible commitments, opportunism, and especially asset-specificity, which he used to generate comparative static propositions that are subject to operational specification and empirical testing. North, by contrast, went beyond the firm to analyze "the transaction costs that determined overall economic performance" (North 1997, 7; see Myhrman and Weingast 1994).

Although North is normally classified as an economist or economic historian, his work is closer than that of many political scientists to the classics of the discipline, since he is interested in the big questions that have dominated political science since Aristotle. How do the institutions ("constitutions") of polities differ? What are their behavioral effects? How do they change over time? North's concern is the core issue of comparative politics: the problem of the state. By insisting that a cogent analysis of the state requires an analysis of property rights, and by emphasizing the tensions between efficiency and rulers' interests, North has reformulated, in modern economic terms, fundamental questions of constitution-making, so well addressed by James Madison and his colleagues in 1787. How can institutional arrangements enable the state as an organization to provide public goods without becoming predatory (Levi 1988)? In other words, how can the state be limited without being crippled? In joint work with Barry Weingast, North has used institutional theory to show how the new institutions of Parliamentary supremacy after the English Glorious Revolution of 1688 "provided a clear and dramatic credible commitment that the government would honor its promises and maintain the existing pattern of rights" (North and Weingast 1989/1996, 156). The result, they show, was a sudden and sharp rise in government borrowing and spending—a "necessary condition," they argue, for its success in war with France (163). North's institutional theory may be as essential to understanding issues of war and peace as questions of economic development.

Political scientists in international relations as well as comparative politics have been quick to recognize the significance of North's work for their subject. A survey of citations to his work in political science turned up 185 references, heavily concentrated in journals specializing in international relations or comparative politics. Authors citing North three times or more during this period included such scholars as Robert Bates, Judith Goldstein, Stephan Haggard, Margaret Levi, Ronald Rogowski, and John Ruggie.[1] However, despite the relevance of North's work to international relations, his own empirical efforts, and those of most of his followers, have remained focused on the state, in relationship to a society and a domestic economy taken as given. Two recent edited volumes on the new institutional economics contain articles on topics as varied as medieval and early modern economic development, economic reform in the Soviet system, property rights in Africa and the Amazon, and American public debt—but nothing on relations between states, much less on broader relationships between organizations and institutions in world politics (Alston, Eggertsson, and North 1996; Drobak and Nye 1997).

In this essay, I will show how North's insights could illuminate some important problems in the study of the world political economy. North's work is motivated by a recognition that economic growth requires investment, innovation, and exchange, none of which will be forthcoming in significant quantity without secure property rights. These property rights, he argues, must be secured by the state—hence his attempt to develop a theory of the state as a necessary condition for a meaningful theory of economic development. However, in a global economy growth requires that extensive transactions take place across international boundaries, taking advantage of great variations across countries in factor prices. The issue of property rights, so important to North's account of the origins and differential successes of modern states, reappears in the contemporary international setting: "international transactions often make parties vulnerable to one another's opportunistic actions" (Yarbrough and Yarbrough 1994, 244). Economic growth in a globalized economy requires institutions that reduce such vulnerability. How are such institutions possible in the absence of world government? The first section of this essay discusses this question.

Although North is best known in political science for his transaction cost theory of institutions, he has long pointed out that transaction cost economics provides an inadequate basis, by itself, for understanding institutions. He observes that the transaction cost literature is "full of references to simple self-interest versus self-interest with guile (in opportunistic behavior); sometimes individuals will take advantage of each other and sometimes they won't; sometimes individuals are hardworking and sometimes not" (North 1981, 44). As he points out, the transaction cost framework does not account for such differences in behavior. Indeed, the emphasis of transaction cost economics on the costs of monitoring and enforcing rules, and the prevalence of opportunism, implies that the costs of monitoring and enforcing rules on individuals should be prohibitive. How, then, can a transaction cost framework explain the existence of institutions?

Economic history, and by extension, political science, therefore need what North calls a theory of ideology. For North, ideology is "the subjective perceptions (models, theories) all people possess to explain the world around them" (North 1990, 23).[2] Ideology persuades people to act in ways that are consistent with social welfare even when they are not subject to monitoring and punishment. It is apparent that North's broad conception of ideology includes a variety of causal mechanisms: Normative constraints on self-interested behavior, causal beliefs, and broad worldviews are all included within this umbrella concept. One problem with such a broad definition is that after the fact almost any anomaly can be accounted for as the result of an ideology known only post hoc; without a clear prior theory of ideology, the concept provides little basis for rigorous explanation. Recognizing this problem, North has turned in his recent work to cognitive psychology to seek stronger analytical foundations for his emphasis on the role of subjectivity and beliefs (Denzau and North 1994). In this essay, however, I neither seek to criticize the analytical gaps in North's use of ideology nor to develop a cognitive argument; instead, my purpose is to see how his very insightful and suggestive (if not rigorous) arguments about ideology can throw light on *other processes*, involving scientific knowledge, professional networks, and reputation, that may reduce the transaction costs entailed in forming and maintaining international institutions.

North's skepticism about monitoring and enforcement, and his emphasis on high transaction costs, raise serious questions about the institutions underpinning globalization of the world economy. In a world of self-interested states, with considerable strategic capabilities and capacity for opportunism, could international rules ("international regimes") ever be monitored and enforced at an acceptable cost? The implication of the transaction cost argument is that they could not, yet we observe such regimes. How is this potential anomaly to be resolved? Does North's concept of ideology, or other causal processes that substitute for ideology, help us understand how international regimes can continue to exist, and even to grow? This is the subject of the second section of the essay.

If monitoring and punishment are prohibitively costly or even unavailable, North's analysis suggests that effective rules require widespread voluntary compliance. For such compliance to occur, the actors must accept the rules as legitimate—that is, as conforming to standards of fairness. On this argument, effective international regimes require development of a regime-supporting ideology. Yet it has usually been assumed that states act in a "self-interested" fashion, in the sense

that their leaders either seek to serve their own interests directly (without significant regard for general principles of justice or the interests of others) or act as agents
for the self-interested demands of their constituents. In this sense, self-interest
has been the classically accepted principle of state behavior, and the advent of democracy in the nineteenth century is often interpreted as having provided an additional justification for egoistic behavior by states. Leaders of states are accountable
to their people and required, legally as well as morally, to serve their interests rather
than to identify with the interests of outsiders. The third section begins by inquiring about prospects for an ideology that would promote compliance with the rules.
I do not envisage the emergence of a comprehensive cosmopolitan ideology elevat-
ing international institutions above the nation-state; widespread acceptance of such
a worldview appears highly unlikely in the foreseeable future. Hence, I turn from
ideology to the consideration of *substitutes* for ideology that could help solve the
problem of high transaction costs that North identifies. I suggest that transnational
networks composed of individuals operating according to professional norms can
substitute to some extent for such an ideology. These networks can create and
legitimate new causal ideas or help to interpret the relevance of normative ideas to
practices of international regulation.

THE STATE AND INTERNATIONAL REGIMES

North defines a state as "an organization with a comparative advantage in violence,
extending over a geographic area whose boundaries are determined by its power
to tax constituents" (North 1981, 21). In *The Rise of the Western World,* he flirts
with a functional theory of the state, in which the state is the result of a contract:
Government is seen "simply as an organization that provides protection and justice in return for revenue" (North and Thomas 1973, 6). When he wrote *Structure
and Change* (1981), however, North acknowledged that this argument was vulnerable to serious objections. States could not have arisen from market demand, since
they predate markets (North 1981, 41). Most fundamentally, North and Thomas
had "put the relationship into the framework of a contract" and "did not lay sufficient stress on the one-sided nature of the arrangement" (North 1981, 130). The
contract theory presupposes "an equal distribution of violence potential among
the principals," whereas a "predatory theory" assumes an unequal distribution
(Levi 1988, ch. 2). The predatory theory of the state seems both historically and
theoretically more valid than the contractual one: as Charles Tilly (1990, 67) has
famously expressed the point, "war made states." Recognizing the force of these
points, North retreated from an attempt to provide a functional explanation of
the origins of the state, although he insists on the crucial functions that the state
performs for the economy.

North also discusses international arrangements to secure property rights,
although they are not the principal focus of his analysis. Informal rules and practices have governed trade for many centuries: Athens controlled the international
grain trade of the fifth century B.C. (North 1981, 106); the "law merchant" was a
significant figure in medieval trade (Milgrom, North, and Weingast 1990); and the
colonial powers of the early modern period imposed rules for trade within their
colonies and between the colonies and the mother countries (North 1981, 144–45).
The establishment of property rights, internationally as well as nationally, "provided

incentives to use factors of production more efficiently and directed resources into inventive and innovative activity" (North 1981, 148).

Formal, negotiated international regimes on a significant scale date only from the late nineteenth century and are principally a product of the post-1945 world (Murphy 1994). Perhaps owing to their recency, and to the small role they therefore play in the grand sweep of Western history, they receive little attention in North's work. However, they are institutions in North's sense, since they constitute the underlying rules of international relations, distinct from the organizations—states, international governmental organizations (IGOs), nongovernmental organizations (NGOs), and business corporations—that operate within the rules or seek to reshape them (North 1990, 3–5). These international regimes are constructed by states and therefore do not challenge constitutional sovereignty; however, they do restrict the "operational sovereignty" of modern states by limiting their legal freedom of action. States accept these restraints because the benefits they can make by restricting others' freedom of action, in situations of high interdependence, outweigh the costs they incur by limiting their own legal freedom of action (Keohane 1995, 174–77). In North's terms, one could say that the transaction costs of making and enforcing these agreements are lower than the transaction costs incurred by governments and firms in the absence of such agreements.

With respect to their origins, these modern international regimes differ from states in two crucial respects. First, unlike states and the informal international regimes of the past, they postdate the development of a market economy, so their existence could in principle be explained on functional grounds. States, whose leaders seek to gain from more efficient regulation of world markets, or from redistribution of benefits in their favor, create these international institutions. Since international regimes are created purposively by rational individuals occupying roles in organizations, a functional explanation could be illuminating. Second, modern international regimes are the result of negotiations between formally equal states, and states can refuse to join without being subject to physical coercion. Hence, contractual theory is prima facie more applicable to the creation of international regimes than to either the violence-laden origins of states or the rules imposed by states concomitant with the development of international markets. Contractual theory does not require equality of participants: Clearly, the opportunity costs of refusing to join a regime may be higher for small and weak states than for large and strong ones, and the weak are likely also to have had less influence on the nature of the rules.

The functional theory of international regimes views regimes as devices designed by states (often with predominant input from a hegemonic power) to reduce uncertainty by providing information and to reduce transaction costs by providing regular rules for decisionmaking, establishing arrangements (often including organizations) to monitor members' actions, and enforcing rules through decentralized action, largely as a result of reciprocity and reputation (Keohane 1984, chs. 5, 6). What the theory establishes is a "demand for international regimes" (Keohane 1982)—theoretically grounded reasons that such regimes are created despite their at least nominal derogation from sovereign state autonomy. The theory of international institutions that has emerged over the last decade and a half is indebted to, and broadly consistent with, work in the new institutional economics. The essential problem to be solved is to ensure the credibility of commitments so that asset-specific investments may rationally be made (Lake 1996). In a sense, this literature follows the mainstream of the new institutional economics more closely than does North's own work, since it is more willing to accept the contractual assumption at the heart of the new institutional economics.[3]

A prime example of an international regime is the World Trade Organization (WTO), which comprises rules, practices, and organizations to govern international trade. Other examples include the rules and organizations governing production and trade in chlorofluorocarbons (CFCs), which deplete the protective stratospheric ozone layer; the rules and organizations regulating airline safety; agreed-on technical standards in many industrial sectors; arrangements to limit intentional oil pollution by tankers at sea; and the now-defunct Bretton Woods monetary regime.

Some of these regimes, such as those that govern airline safety or establish technical standards, may be self-enforcing: Once in place, no one has an incentive unilaterally to violate them. In such situations of "coordination," bargaining problems prior to agreement may be serious, but once agreements are reached, monitoring and enforcement are not significant issues. However, for regimes of "collaboration," which entail issues of potential cheating (as in the prisoners' dilemma), the problem that North raises for the state seems even more serious: How can they monitor and enforce their rules at reasonable cost?[4]

The solutions to this problem are various. The General Agreement on Tariffs and Trade (GATT) and now the WTO have relied on a "fire-alarm" system (McCubbins and Schwartz 1984) in which states have interests in monitoring others' activities. WTO enforcement takes the form of authorized retaliation. The Montreal Protocol on the Ozone Layer of 1987 includes provisions for trade sanctions against nonmembers or violators (Benedick 1991, 91–92). The "Marpol" regime on oceanic pollution requires certain equipment for entry into key ports (Mitchell 1994). But monitoring is imperfect. There is a black market in CFCs, and for decades previous rules prohibiting discharge of oily wastes at sea were ignored. Enforcement is also weak: The Bretton Woods monetary regime never had effective enforcement tools, and the WTO has to be cautious when major interests of the European Union or the United States are at stake. North's insight—that monitoring and enforcement are of critical importance and that the transaction costs involved are often high—is valid in this domain.

THE TRANSACTION COSTS OF INTERNATIONAL REGIMES

Monitoring activities across jurisdictions is inherently more difficult than doing so within them, since common reporting standards and coordination practices have to be worked out among independent authorities with their own standards and practices. A natural step is to establish international organizations, which universally seem to have information gathering as one of their functions. Yet these organizations do not have the legal or political authority of national governments to compel the provision of information; they have to work through governments to be effective. As a result, their monitoring costs are relatively high.

The disabilities of international regimes in efforts to enforce rules are, if anything, even greater. Large-scale coercion is still monopolized by states, which jealously guard this privilege. Whatever international organizations do, they are not quasi-states that enforce rules through hierarchical bureaucracies. Whatever enforcement takes place is decentralized, implemented by states, perhaps under authorization from international regimes. Very little such enforcement is evident. The United States has engaged in a number of military interventions in the Caribbean since 1965, in violation of article 2 of the United Nations Charter (Wood 1985); the Soviet Union intervened in Afghanistan and elsewhere. Trade barriers in violation of the GATT or WTO have been common, with the United States—a chief proponent of the WTO—prominent among the violators (Hudec 1990; Lowenfeld 1996). Compliance has been a serious problem with respect to enforcement of the Convention on International Trade in Endangered Species, known as CITES (Jacobson and Weiss 1995). For many years rules limiting oil discharges by tankers were systematically violated (Mitchell 1994). The Soviet Union and some East European socialist countries, in the 1980s, dumped radioactive materials in the oceans and falsified their compliance records under the European acid rain regime. Cheating on international regimes may not be the rule, but it is endemic (Downs, Rocke, and Barsoom 1996). The evidence is over-whelming that international enforcement is difficult and that the transaction costs of such enforcement are quite high (Yarbrough and Yarbrough 1994). North's generalization about high transaction costs within societies certainly applies to international relations.

The two principal means of ensuring compliance on which international regimes have relied are reciprocity and reputation. Reciprocity and reputation, although often conflated, are quite different. Reciprocity in the sense used here refers to a pattern of interaction in which the actions of each party are contingent on the prior actions of the others in such a way that good is returned for good, and bad for bad. Fear of reprisal, or at least of the loss of a flow of benefits from the commitment, is the key mechanism by which reciprocity leads states to maintain commitments that would otherwise be more burdensome to keep than to reject. The operation of reci-procity does not depend on uncertainty; indeed, greater certainty may be expected to increase its deterrent effect.

The causal mechanism involving reputation does depend on uncertainty. It refers to how members of an audience—observing others' behavior without necessarily being involved—update their beliefs about the reliability of an actor, and therefore the credibility of its commitments, as a result of such observation. Despite the absence of a threat of retaliation, leaders of a government could fear that the credi-bility of commitments they have made would be jeopardized, for some audience, by reneging on a set of commitments that have become inconvenient. To summarize the distinction, incentives based on reciprocity derive from the anticipation of con-tingent actions that one's current partner may take in response to one's reneging on an agreement with it, whereas the reputational mechanism operates through anticipation of how one's actions are likely to affect others' estimates of one's own reliability at some future date.

For reciprocity to constitute an effective mechanism for fulfillment of commit-ments, another state must have both the capability to retaliate in a significant way and incentives to make a credible commitment to do so. The key questions are whether threats of retaliation, in response to finessing or nonfulfillment, are credi-ble, and whether such retaliation is likely to be sufficiently costly to make it worth taking into account. On grounds of reciprocity, we should expect governments to keep commitments toward highly motivated powerful counterparts, but not toward weak or irresolute states. The asymmetrical ability of strong states to be predatory is therefore the most prominent flaw in the reciprocity-based commitment pathway. The weak cannot enforce the rules against the strong. Anticipating this incapacity, they may be less disposed to agree to international rules ex ante.

The key argument for the reputational pathway is that reputation is like a political capital asset, increasing the ability of its possessor to engage in political exchange:

> Under conditions of uncertainty and decentralization, governments will decide whom to make agreements with, and on what terms, largely on the basis of their expectations about their partners' willingness and ability to keep their commitments. A good reputation makes it easier for a government to enter into advantageous international agreements; tarnishing that reputation imposes costs by making agreements more difficult to reach. (Keohane 1984, 105–6; see also Snidal 1985, 938; Milgrom, North, and Weingast, 1990)

The key problem with reputation as a guarantee against opportunism is that opportunistic actors, especially if they are powerful, may be able to differentiate situations in which they renege on commitments from the hypothetical situations about which they wish to reassure their partners. Often, commitments can be obfuscated, owing to vague rules or poor monitoring. Since no two situations are exactly alike, circumstances can be distinguished from one another. In the past the victim of reneging could be characterized as "uncivilized" (as the United States characterized the American Indian nations with which it had made agreements); now the victim may be an international organization like the United Nations, which no powerful state has an incentive (owing to collective action problems) to defend. If the reneging actor is very powerful—consider unilateral U.S. intervention in the Caribbean during the Cold War—others may be unwilling to challenge it. They may also be unable to find other partners for important international agreements. Enacting unilateral trade sanctions in the Helms-Burton Act of 1996 may damage the reputation of the United States, but its major trading partners cannot avoid negotiating with it on trade issues. Like reciprocity, the reputational mechanism for ensuring compliance is biased by asymmetries of power.

As the new institutional economics would suggest, international regimes can increase the gains from political exchange by reducing uncertainty and lowering transaction costs. They make it more difficult for potentially predatory states to be opportunistic.[5] But as North would lead us to expect, the transaction costs of monitoring and enforcing the regimes typically remain very high. It is therefore a fair inference that many potentially beneficial agreements are not made because of ex ante fears of opportunism (Downs, Rocke, and Barsoom 1996). Following North a step further, it appears that global economic growth is hampered by a disjunction between the social and private benefits of innovation and investment: Fearing opportunism, potential innovators and investors refrain from making certain cross-border investments that would have positive social utility.

Since it is difficult even for well-structured states to monitor and enforce rules outside their jurisdictions, it follows that in a world of states that had established sensible internal property rights, a lack of effective international regimes would nevertheless be a hindrance to economic growth. The more open the national economy, the more severe will be the consequences of a lack of effective international regimes—worse, for instance, for Hong Kong before July 1, 1997, than for China. There is little reason to expect that, in the absence of such regimes, states will punish their own nationals for opportunistic behavior. As students of international relations such as Jean-Jacques Rousseau have long observed, states are typically biased in favor of their own citizens, acting unjustly abroad even if they behave justly at home (Hoffmann 1965; Waltz 1959).

I conclude that in a world of egoistic states, international regimes can exist and may help promote cooperation. But the transaction costs associated with them will be high, and they will provide a suboptimal level of security: In North's terms, they will fall far short of creating an institutional structure that equates social and private benefits.

North's solution to this problem at the domestic level is "ideology." Does his theory of ideology hold promise for solving this problem at the international level?

TRANSNATIONAL NETWORKS OF PROFESSIONALS AS CARRIERS OF IDEAS

North (1990, 23) defines ideology broadly as "the subjective perceptions (models, theories) all people possess to explain the world around them." He observes that these theories and models are colored by normative views. Elsewhere he remarks that ideology provides individuals with a "worldview" to help them understand their environments and simplify decisionmaking (North 1981, 49). For North, "ideology" is equivalent to the beliefs held by individuals—what others have referred to simply as "ideas." Three types of beliefs can be distinguished: worldviews, comprehensive intellectual constructs as in religions, as well as in ideologies such as communism; principled beliefs, involving criteria for distinguishing right from wrong and just from unjust; and causal beliefs, which specify cause-effect relationships (Goldstein and Keohane 1993, 8–10).

North does not claim to have a theory of ideology; rather, he proposes an original way of looking at the problem of the role of beliefs in politics, along with some tentative hypotheses. When he focuses on ideology, his interest is fundamentally in the sociology of knowledge. In this section, I try to extend some of North's insights about ideology and knowledge in order to help us understand how international regimes seem to function despite the high transaction costs identified earlier.

North approaches the issue of ideology in a novel way, through the free-rider problem. In a rational-choice framework, Mancur Olson (1965) has shown why collective goods are undersupplied. But, North observes, Olson's theory seems to predict the absence of groups that fail to provide selective benefits to individuals, as well as a lack of mass protest movements. Olson "points up the instability of farm protest movements that did not have side benefits, but he neglects the point that they should not have existed at all under his model." Nor can Olson account for mass movements. What is missing from Olson's account, for North, is "evolving ideological perspectives that have led individuals and groups to have contrasting views of the fairness of their situation and to act upon these views" (North 1981, 58).

For North, ideology is the key to explaining why people sometimes do not act as free-riders: The more legitimate they view the system as being, the more willing they are to obey its rules even when those rules are not likely to be enforced against them. Well-functioning institutions, which guarantee personal security, guard against economic retaliation and protect freedom of speech, reduce the price people have to pay for acting on their convictions, therefore enhancing the role of individual beliefs in institutional change (North 1990, 85–86). As evidence of the importance of beliefs in the legitimacy of a system, North points to the huge investment in education in which almost all societies engage. Much of this investment "is obviously directed at inculcating a set of values rather than investing in human capital." Neoclassical economists have ignored "an essential ingredient of every society" (North 1981, 54). For North, this investment is explicable in transaction cost terms: It produces legitimacy, which dramatically reduces the transaction costs involved in monitoring and enforcing rules.

I am going to assume that North has a valid point about domestic society. Do his insights about ideology help us understand how international regimes can overcome problems of free-riding and opportunism?

Taken literally, and restricted to the conception of ideology as a set of normative constraints on self-interested behavior, the idea does not seem very promising. Sovereign states come fairly close to monopolizing large-scale coercive force—their only rivals are nonstate revolutionary groups, not supranational organizations. States command broad police powers over their economies, although globalization constrains their exercise of many of these powers toward mobile organizations such as multinational corporations. States are organized as hierarchies whose leaders are formally responsible at most to the people of their own societies (and often only to a small elite subset of those people). No global educational system exists to inculcate an ideology of cosmopolitan ethics or responsibility to a hypothetical "world community." On the contrary, the dominant view almost everywhere is that governments are responsible for promoting the welfare of their own people, not for some vague world welfare function. Hence, the ideological causal mechanism that North proposes—societies educate their young to accept the legitimacy of rules, thus reducing the costs of monitoring and enforcing compliance—surely does not operate on a world scale.

Since North's broad conception of ideology equates it with beliefs—that is, ideas—another approach would simply be to point out that both causal and normative ideas can promote international cooperation by reducing ambiguity and uncertainty (Goldstein and Keohane 1993). North's emphasis on both rational action subject to calculations of shifting marginal costs and the role of ideology helps us to reconcile these two important strands of thought. However, we can make such arguments more specific, tracing the causal mechanisms more convincingly, if we reconceptualize the nature of world politics in the contemporary world, emphasizing the role of transnational networks as well as states. The ideas that North emphasizes are developed, institutionalized, and legitimized in these transnational networks by individuals behaving in conformity with norms of professionalism.

Transnational Networks and World Politics

The simple models that we carry around in our heads may frame international relations simply as the interactions of units called states: This is what Arnold Wolfers (1962, 19) called the "billiard-ball model" of world politics. It has the virtue of simplicity, which facilitates modeling of games between these "actors."

The functional theory of international regimes, discussed in the first section of this essay, deliberately accepts this unitary-actor assumption as a basis for explaining why regimes exist.

However, as Wolfers pointed out, the billiard-ball model radically oversimplifies reality. Thousands of multinational corporations operate across national boundaries, many of them with resources greater than those of scores of states. Transnational networks have dramatically expanded in recent years, most notably in finance but also in almost every other domain of human activity: Nongovernmental organizations promote causes from preservation of tropical forests to human rights; scientific networks exchange information on diseases from AIDS to cancer; multinational corporations build cars in many different countries; criminals transport drugs and use their resources to subvert governments.[6] Modern governments themselves are not unified hierarchies: Transgovernmental relations link bureaucracies of different countries in areas of high interdependence, and national judiciaries pay some attention to decisions elsewhere. The countries of the European Union engage in the pooling of sovereignty in novel ways that contradict the billiard-ball model of international relations in almost every way.

These networks between societies, and between bureaucracies at different levels, have transformed the conduct of international relations. It is *not* the case that world politics is being controlled more and more by supranational organizations with bureaucracies staffed by international civil servants. Between 1981 and 1992 the number of IGOs increased only from 1,063 to 1,147—less than 8 percent in eleven years (Shanks, Jacobson, and Kaplan 1996, 593). During roughly the same period, international capital flows quintupled (Turner 1991). The United Nations has been in persistent financial crisis owing largely to the withholding of payments by the United States, and the United States almost single-handedly engineered the replacement of Secretary-General Boutros Boutros-Ghali in 1996—illustrating effectively where real power lies. Even the much-maligned bureaucracy of the European Union is small compared to the bureaucracies of its member states. The future does not seem to belong to international bureaucracy.

Yet we do observe a marked increase in international rule-making. This rule-making trend is very clear in international trade. GATT had a simple set of articles of agreement that could be read and understood in an afternoon; the WTO has volumes of rules that require an army of lawyers to interpret.[7] The North American Free Trade Agreement (NAFTA) contains another complex set of rules, with novel joint administrative arrangements for interpretation and dispute settlement (Goldstein 1996). The European Union also has a highly complex structure of rules, which are interpreted by the European Court of Justice and are binding on member states through their national judicial systems (Burley and Mattli 1993). International environmental regulations have become much more extensive in recent years, led by the ozone regulations resulting from the Montreal Protocol of 1987 (Caldwell 1996).

What is most interesting about these agreements for our purposes is that the process by which they are created involves transnational and transgovernmental *networks of professionals* as well as national diplomats. Governmental officials still have to negotiate the final specifications of binding agreements; the top leaders of governments have to agree to sign them; and in some countries they can be ratified only after legislative consent has been obtained. But both before and after the formal negotiations, networks of professionals play a major role.

I will illustrate this argument briefly by discussing the role of scientific professionalism in environmental issues and the role of bureaucratic and legal professionalism in interpreting agreements. My emphasis on transnational and transgovernmental networks is distantly related to some writing by Joseph S. Nye and myself long ago (Keohane and Nye 1974, 1977). However, my current thinking on these issues is especially indebted to the work of Anne-Marie Slaughter (Slaughter 1995, 1997), who has developed the concept of transgovernmental networks in a remarkably persuasive and encompassing way.

Negotiating Agreements: The Role of Scientific Professionalism

Consider international environmental issues, in particular the current question of global climate change. In 1988 two United Nations agencies, the World Meteorological Association (WMO) and the UN Environment Program (UNEP), created the Intergovernmental Panel on Climate Change (IPCC) to assess whether human actions are having significant effects on the global climate, and what those impacts might be. Although the IPCC is an intergovernmental body, most of its work is carried out through three scientific working groups, run by scientists using extensive peer review, with twenty to sixty reviewers per chapter. In other words, the IPCC institutionalizes scientific assessment in such a way as to produce comprehensive, systematic statements of what is scientifically known about climate, and it does so repeatedly. In its first seven years, the IPCC went through two assessment cycles, in each of which its three working groups issued lengthy comprehensive reports (IPCC 1996). When Working Group I concluded in 1995 that the evidence, on balance, suggests that human activities are altering the global climate, this finding became the basis for a similar declaration by the president of the United States at a UN conference in June 1997.

In a purely political intergovernmental negotiating process, the issue of whether human beings are altering the global environment would have become an issue for political negotiation. We could have expected both opportunism and free-riding. Governments that expected to pay heavily for remedial measures could have sought to resist regulation by denying any connection between human activity and climate change—as governments that expected to bear the cost of measures against the international spread of disease did during the nineteenth century. Governments that expected regulation to occur but did not want to pay their share could have sought to free-ride by arguing either that the connection did not exist or that they would not be harmed (or even helped) by climate change, and should not therefore be required to contribute to its alleviation. In North's terms, the transaction costs of negotiation could have been very high indeed. As Richard Cooper (1989, 194) has pointed out, over forty years elapsed between an international sanitary conference on cholera and plague in 1851 and the institution of an international sanitary convention on cholera.

The point of institutionalizing scientific assessment on climate change is to reduce these transaction costs. But why does scientific assessment reduce these costs? Why aren't problems of opportunism and free-riding merely reintroduced into the process under the guise of science? The answer to this question takes us back to North's concept of ideology. Science depends on adherence to established methodologies for the gathering and assessment of evidence, and the reputations of individual scientists depend on adherence to these accepted practices. A scientist who contests a finding reached by other scientists, without strong scientific justification, risks jeopardizing her reputation with her peers. A diplomat could offer poor scientific arguments in the service of political ends while maintaining his reputation as a competent diplomat; a scientist would pay a high price for engaging in the same behavior.

The issue, then, is one of legitimacy, not the normative legitimacy about which North writes, but scientific legitimacy. A process is normatively legitimate if it is regarded as fair, and North asserts that people will have a greater tendency to obey processes they regard as fair than those they see as unfair or unjust. A process is scientifically legitimate if it has followed established scientific practices, such as assigning the work to the scientists in the field who have the best reputations and subjecting their papers to rigorous peer review. Establishing institutionalized processes that are scientifically legitimate reduces the transaction costs of negotiation by excluding certain causal issues from the political process. Professional scientific norms and reputational networks among scientists insulate this process from direct political interference. Admittedly, the scientific practices at issue have been socially constructed—that is, created by selected groups of human beings and reflecting their values, and therefore the values of the societies from which they are drawn. Modern science is Western science, which causes political problems. But once the decision on whether human action is leading to climate change is delegated to an institutionalized scientific process, what counts as a relevant argument changes. To count, arguments must be credible to independent scientists.[8]

Interpreting Agreements: The Role of Bureaucratic and Legal Professionalism

After agreements are made by governments, they have to be interpreted. International regimes are forms of incomplete contracts, since they cannot specify the eventualities that may arise under their rules. Under a strictly interstate system characterized by self-help, each state is the judge of its own compliance. The scope for opportunism under these conditions is obviously enormous, and the transaction costs of monitoring and enforcing agreements are high.

Transnational communities may help restrain opportunism under these conditions. Reputations will be important for individual professionals, since interactions are repetitive. Indeed, individuals may take reputation more seriously than governments. Individuals, who possess biological continuity through time, cannot reduce costs to their personal reputations by blaming their predecessors, nor can they externalize the costs of a bad reputation onto their successors. They are rarely powerful enough to be able to avoid the adverse consequences of reputational degradation. National as well as international bureaucrats will value their reputations for probity and good faith, as will members of transnational networks not employed by governments. As long as there is a common understanding of what constitutes good faith, and of how facts are to be ascertained, repeated play may therefore promote cooperation by inhibiting opportunism.[9]

The significance of individual reputations, in the context of professional networks, can be illustrated with examples from the European Union, the Canada-U.S. Free Trade Agreement, and the GATT. Within the European Union the elaborate system of intergovernmental committees for policymaking fosters repeated inter-action, in which "the group pressure to internalize basic interaction norms is quite considerable" (Wessels 1991, 146). The Canada-U.S. Free Trade Agreement estab-lished a system of binational panels whose members were chosen from a panel of individuals, most of whom were lawyers. These panels could issue binding judg-ments overturning decisions by the U.S. trade bureaucracy (Goldstein 1996). One way of interpreting this institutional innovation was that it transferred authority from national bureaucrats (prone to bias against foreign producers and therefore to opportunism) to binational panels, whose decisions would be governed by evolving standards of a network of professionals. Each of these professionals had an interest in maintaining his or her reputation for fairness, not only in order to serve on future panels but to be hired by a variety of clients as a lawyer. During the first three years of operation of these panels, anti-dumping orders by the United States against Canada dropped dramatically, apparently as a result of the reputation that these panels developed for being skeptical of the bureaucracy's decisions (Goldstein 1996, 550–51). Finally, GATT panels developed a substantial body of trade law during the 1980s, even though their decisions were not binding (Hudec 1993); this body of law is being further developed in the World Trade Organization, whose legal processes, involving panels and an appellate process, are binding on members.

These examples, not surprisingly, come from organizations whose members share fundamental values. At the other extreme, where there is no such commonality—as in the Iran-U.S. claims tribunal set up under the Algiers Accords of 1981—opportunism may be severe. Self-interested action in the Iran-U.S. claims tribunal has even included a physical assault by two young Iranian arbitrators on one of their elderly neutral colleagues (Feldman 1986, 1004). When almost no values are shared, as in the Iran-U.S. claims tribunal, the role for professionalism is likely to be minimal.

Judiciaries also play an important interpretive role. As Slaughter (1995) has shown, democratic courts show more deference to the views of courts in other democracies than to courts of states not governed by the rule of law. Professional standards of interpretation may converge when the basic normative framework is similar; deference to other courts' decisions certainly reduces the transaction costs of interpretation and dispute settlement.

Ideology and Knowledge

North (1990, 76) couples ideology with knowledge: "The way in which knowledge develops influences the perceptions people have about the world around them and hence the way in which they rationalize, explain, and justify that world, which in turn influences the cost of contracting." The implication of this conception—that processes of knowledge creation affect people's ideologies—is particularly interesting to a student of world politics, since we seem to observe an increasing number of institutionalized arrangements for the creation and systematization of knowledge on important topics, as in the IPCC assessment process, the creation of a body of trade law, and the specification of technical standards for a large num-ber of products that are traded internationally. These activities are based on an underlying ideology, or worldview: that of Western scientific rationalism. Peer review, the codification of law, and the specification of technical standards all take issues out of the strictly political arena—where power and interests, rather than reason, are trump, and where opportunism is to be expected as standard modus operandi—and into an arena governed by professional standards. These standards are guarded by a self-identified community; maintaining a reputation for adherence to them is central to the identities and livelihoods of that community's members.

These institutionalized practices depend on ideology in the sense of a worldview, although as pointed out earlier, they may limit the role of ideology in the sense of normative constraints on behavior. However, they also change ideology in the sense of causal beliefs. Such changes are very clear on environmental issues. Does human energy consumption change the climate, and if so, how? What will the economic impact of such climate change be? If a given set of policy changes were initiated, what effects could we expect to experience? Institutionalized, knowledge-creating practices also change ideology in the sense of normative beliefs at an applied level. Is it wrong for the European Union to give preference to bananas produced in its former colonies, or for the United States to apply a strict version of anti-dumping law to Canadian producers? "Wrong" in this sense means inconsistent with a set of rules that are themselves justified in terms of higher principles, such as fair trade.

These processes of professional knowledge creation coexist, of course, with contradictory trends in world politics. Even if the notion of a "clash of civilizations" (Huntington 1996) is vastly overstated, there are fundamental differences of values among societies. One only has to think of the vast disparity in values among the United States, Japan, Iran, and China to recognize this point. The argument I am making is not therefore one that presages the "end of ideology," much less of history. Not all trends go in the same direction; rationalism has been overwhelmed by barbarism more than once in the past. My point is to use North's transaction cost-based insights into ideology to illuminate one set of trends in world politics, not to generalize this trend into a theory of history.

CONCLUSION

Douglass North's work displays a subtle understanding of both the value of transaction cost economics and its limitations for understanding institutions. Transaction cost theory plays a crucial role in understanding how states and societies operate, but we must also appreciate the role played by ideas, which North refers to as ideology. However, ideology is more significant in world politics when conceived of in terms of broad worldviews and conceptions of causality than as specific normative constraints on opportunism. Indeed, mechanisms involving reciprocity, reputation, and transnational and transgovernmental networks do more to substitute for internalized normative constraints than to provide them. Yet with proper adaptation, North's insights into the role of ideas are highly relevant for understanding how international cooperation takes place, among independent states, through institutions known as international regimes.

Transaction cost theory has been used for fifteen years to explain the origins and operation of these institutions, but students of international relations have been slower to appreciate the role played, within a transaction cost framework, by ideas. In general, causal and normative ideas lower transaction costs by reducing ambiguity. But this process of reducing uncertainty is not simply one by which leaders of unitary states come to consensus on causal or normative beliefs, thus promoting cooperation. Crucial to the causal mechanism are transnational professional networks, which gather information, set standards, and interpret rules. Crucial aspects of the negotiation and implementation of agreements are separated from direct political bargaining. The scope for opportunism and free-riding is thereby narrowed, and the transaction costs of cooperation reduced. In world politics—as North pointed out with respect to the state—transaction cost theory is incomplete without an appreciation of the role played by ideas in the operation of institutions. Transnational networks develop, institutionalize, and legitimate the ideas that grease the squeaky wheels of international regimes.

The author is grateful for the research assistance and comments of Imke Risopp-Nickelson, and for comments on earlier drafts by Peter Haas, Lisa Martin, Justin Pearlman, and the editors of this volume.

NOTES

1. The period surveyed was 1956 to 1995, with the preponderance of citations coming in the most recent years. Fifty-seven citations were from international relations journals, 46 from comparative politics journals, and six in *World Politics,* which is almost equally divided between the two fields. Sixty-one of the citations were in general political science journals. Most cited were North (1981) (68 citations) and North (1990) (33 citations). Margaret Levi led the list of citers of North with eight citations. In addition to those authors listed in the text, others with three or more citations included W. J. Booth, M. Pastore, Douglass C. North, and myself. I am grateful to Imke Risopp-Nickelson for carrying out this work. Robert Fogel (1997, 25–26) reports that in a comprehensive survey of citations to North's work over the period between 1972 and the early 1990s, about one-quarter of the citations were by social scientists outside of economics, particularly political scientists and sociologists.

2. For a more recent elaboration, see Denzau and North (1994).

3. The institutionalist reliance on contractualism has been severely criticized, on the grounds that it fails to explain well the origins of institutions, as opposed to their effects, and that in examining effects it underemphasizes distributional issues. Both of these criticisms have some force, but they do not negate the powerful insights that contractual theory provides into both the demand for institutions and their effects. For these criticisms, see Bates (1988) (on explaining institutional origins) and Krasner (1991) (on distributional politics).

4. For a lucid discussion of the distinction between coordination and collaboration games, see Martin (1992).

5. One might ask: What keeps regimes themselves from being predatory? The answer is that most regimes are not coherent actors: They consist of generalizable rules that nominally apply equally to all of their members and therefore tend to counterbalance inequalities of power. However, certain regimes, especially those led by a single hegemonic power or run by a small set of countries, could be considered predatory toward outsiders. Such might have been the Soviet perception of the COCOM (Coordinating Committee on Multilateral Export Controls) regime, by which Western countries controlled exports of strategically sensitive products and materials to the Soviet bloc during the Cold War. I am indebted to Margaret Levi for asking this question.

6. According to *The Economist* (June 28, 1997, 44), the cross-border traffic in illegal drugs, estimated at $400 billion per year, is greater than the cross-border traffic in cars.

7. I am indebted for this observation to Professor Abram Chayes of Harvard Law School.

8. On the role of scientific "epistemic communities" in international negotiations in general, see Haas (1992) and Sebenius (1992). On their role in the ozone negotiations, see Litfin (1994).

9. Justin Pearlman (private communication, July 1997) has pointed out to me that the causal mechanisms by which reputation operates are in some ways the opposite of those for ideology. Repeated, reputation-based interaction by professionals makes bureaucratic action more publicly visible, whereas ideology (in the sense of normative constraints on self-interest) "encourages compliance with norms when decisions are private or undetectable to other actors." This point, of course, is consistent with the theme of this essay—to sketch processes that may substitute for ideology rather than to rely on ideology itself as the basis for international institutions.

REFERENCES

Alston, Lee J., Thrainn Eggertsson, and Douglass C. North (eds.). 1996. *Empirical Studies in Institutional Change.* Cambridge: Cambridge University Press.

Bates, Robert H. 1988. "Contra Contractarianism: Some Reflections on the New Institutionalism." *Politics and Society* 16: 387–401.

Benedick, Richard Elliot. 1991. *Ozone Diplomacy: New Directions in Safeguarding the Planet.* Cambridge, Mass.: Harvard University Press.

Burley, Anne-Marie, and Walter Mattli. 1993. "Europe Before the Court: A Political Theory of Legal Integration." *International Organization* 47(1): 41–76.

Caldwell, Lynton Keith. 1996. *International Environmental Policy.* 3rd ed. Durham, N.C.: Duke University Press.

Coase, Ronald L. 1937. "The Nature of the Firm." *Economica* 4(November). Reprinted in Coase, *The Firm, the Market, and the Law* (Chicago: University of Chicago Press, 1990), 33–55.

———. 1960. "The Problem of Social Cost." *Journal of Law and Economics* 3(October): 1–44. Reprinted in Coase, *The Firm, the Market, and the Law* (Chicago: University of Chicago Press, 1990), 95–156.

Cooper, Richard N. 1989. "International Cooperation in Public Health as a Prologue to Macroeconomic Cooperation." In *Can Nations Agree?,* edited by Richard N. Cooper et al. (Washington, D.C.: Brookings Institution), 178–254.

Denzau, Arthur T., and Douglass C. North. 1994. "Shared Mental Models: Ideologies and Institutions." *Kyklos* 47(1): 3–31.

Downs, George, David M. Rocke, and Peter N. Barsoom. 1996. "Is the Good News About Compliance Good News About Cooperation?" *International Organization* 50(3): 379–406.

Drobak, John N., and John V. C. Nye. 1997. *The Frontiers of the New Institutional Economics.* San Diego: Academic Press.

Feldman, Mark B. 1986. "Ted L. Stein on the Iran-U.S. Claims Tribunal—Scholarship Par Excellence." *Washington Law Review* 61(3).

Fogel, Robert William. 1997. "Douglas C. North and Economic Theory." In *The Frontiers of the New Institutional Economics,* edited by John N. Drobak and John V. C. Nye (San Diego: Academic Press), 13–28.

Goldstein, Judith. 1996. "International Law and Domestic Institutions: Reconciling North American 'Unfair' Trade Laws." *International Organization* 50(4): 541–64.

Goldstein, Judith, and Robert O. Keohane. 1993. "Ideas and Foreign Policy: An Analytical Framework." In *Ideas and Foreign Policy,* edited by Judith Goldstein and Robert O. Keohane (Ithaca, N.Y.: Cornell University Press), 3–30.

Haas, Peter M. 1992. "Epistemic Communities and International Policy Coordination." *International Organization* 46(1): 1–36.

Hoffmann, Stanley. 1965. "Rousseau on War and Peace." In Hoffmann, *The State of War: Essays on the Theory and Practice of International Politics* (New York: Praeger).

Hudec, Robert E. 1990. "Thinking About the New Section 301: Beyond Good and Evil." In *Aggressive Unilateralism: America's 301 Trade Policy and the World Trading System,* edited by Jagdish Bhagwati and Hugh T. Patrick (Ann Arbor: University of Michigan Press), 113–59.

———. 1993. *Enforcing International Trade Law: The Evolution of the Modern GATT Legal System.* Salem, N. H.: Butterworth Legal Publishers.

Huntington, Samuel P. 1996. *The Clash of Civilizations and the Remaking of World Order.* New York: Simon & Schuster.

Intergovernmental Panel on Climate Change (IPCC). 1996. *Climate Change 1995.* 3 vols. Reports of Working Groups I, II, and III. Cambridge: Cambridge University Press.

Jacobson, Harold K., and Edith Brown Weiss. 1995. "Strengthening Compliance with International Environmental Accords: Preliminary Observations from a Collaborative Project." *Global Governance* 1 (2, May–August): 119–48.

Keohane, Robert O. 1982. "The Demand for International Regimes." *International Organization* 36 (1, Spring): 325–55.

———. 1984. *After Hegemony: Cooperation and Discord in the World Political Economy.* Princeton, N.J.: Princeton University Press.

———. 1995. "Hobbes's Dilemma and Institutional Change in World Politics: Sovereignty in International Society." In *Whose World Order?: Uneven Globalization and the End of the Cold War,* edited by Hans-Henrik Holm and Georg Sorensen (Boulder, Colo.: Westview), 165–86.

Keohane, Robert O., and Joseph S. Nye. 1974. "Transgovernmental Relations and World International Organizations." *World Politics* 27 (1): 39–62.

———. 1977. *Power and Interdependence: World Politics in Transition.* Boston: Little, Brown.

Krasner, Stephen D. 1991. "Global Communications and National Power: Life on the Pareto Frontier." *World Politics* 43 (3): 336–66.

Lake, David A. 1996. "Anarchy, Hierarchy, and the Variety of International Relations." *International Organization* 50 (1): 1–34.

Levi, Margaret. 1988. *Of Rule and Revenue.* Berkeley: University of California Press.

Litfin, Karen T. 1994. *Ozone Discourses: Science and Politics in Global Environmental Cooperation.* New York: Columbia University Press.

Lowenfeld, Andreas F. 1996. "Congress and Cuba: The Helms-Burton Act." *American Journal of International Law* 90 (3): 419–33.

Martin, Lisa L. 1992. "Interests, Power, and Multilateralism." *International Organization* 46 (4): 765–92.

McCubbins, Matthew D., and Thomas Schwartz. 1984. "Police Patrols Versus Fire Alarms." *American Journal of Political Science* 28: 165–79.

Milgrom, Paul R., Douglass C. North, and Barry R. Weingast. 1990. "The Role of Institutions in the Revival of Trade: The Law Merchant, Private Judges, and the Champagne Fairs." *Economics and Politics* 2 (1): 1–24.

Mitchell, Ronald B. 1994. *Intentional Oil Pollution at Sea: Environment Policy and Treaty Compliance.* Cambridge, Mass.: MIT Press.

Murphy, Craig N. 1994. *International Organization and Industrial Change: Global Governance Since 1850.* Cambridge: Polity Press.

Myhrman, Johan, and Barry R. Weingast. 1994. "Douglass C. North's Contributions to Economics and Economic History." *Scandinavian Journal of Economics* 96 (2): 185–93.

North, Douglass C. 1981. *Structure and Change in Economic History.* New York: Norton.

———. 1990. *Institutions, Institutional Change, and Economic Performance.* Cambridge: Cambridge University Press.

———. 1994. "Economic Performance Through Time." *American Economic Review* 84 (3): 359–68. Reprinted in *Empirical Studies in Institutional Change,* edited by Lee J. Alston, Thrainn Eggertsson, and Douglass C. North (Cambridge: Cambridge University Press, 1996), 342–55.

———. 1997. "Prologue." In *The Frontiers of the New Institutional Economics,* edited by John N. Drobak and John V. C. Nye (San Diego: Academic Press, 1997), 3–12.

North, Douglass C., and Robert Paul Thomas. 1973. *The Rise of the Western World: A New Economic History.* Cambridge: Cambridge University Press.

North, Douglass C., and Barry Weingast. 1989. "Constitutions and Commitments: The Evolution of Institutions Governing Public Choice in Seventeenth-Century England." *Journal of Economic History* 49 (4, December). Reprinted in *Empirical Studies in Institutional Change,* edited by Lee J. Alston, Thrainn Eggertsson, and Douglass C. North (Cambridge: Cambridge University Press, 1996), 134–65. (page references from that volume).

Olson, Mancur. 1965. *The Logic of Collective Action.* Cambridge, Mass.: Harvard University Press.

Sebenius, James K. 1992. "Challenging Conventional Explanations of International Cooperation: Negotiation Analysis and the Case of Epistemic Communities." *International Organization* 46 (1): 323–66.

Shanks, Cheryl, Harold K. Jacobson, and Jeffry H. Kaplan. 1996. "Inertia and Change in the Constellation of International Governmental Organizations." *International Organization* 50(4): 593–627.

Slaughter, Anne-Marie. 1995. "International Law in a World of Liberal States." *European Journal of International Law* 6: 503–38.

———. 1997. "The Real New World Order." *Foreign Affairs* 76(5): 183–97.

Snidal, Duncan. 1985. "Coordination Versus Prisoners' Dilemma: Implications for International Cooperation and Regimes." *American Political Science Review* 79(4): 923–42.

Tilly, Charles. 1990. *Coercion, Capital, and European States, AD 990–1990.* Cambridge: Basil Blackwell.

Turner, Philip. 1991. *Capital Flows in the 1980s.* BIS Economic Paper 30. Basle: Bank for International Settlements (April).

Waltz, Kenneth N. 1959. *Man, the State, and War.* New York: Columbia University Press.

Wessels, Wolfgang. 1991. "The EC Council: The Community's Decisionmaking Center." In *The New European Community: Decisionmaking and Institutional Change,* edited by Robert O. Keohane and Stanley Hoffmann (Boulder, Colo.: Westview), 133–54.

Williamson, Oliver. 1985. *The Economic Institutions of Capitalism.* New York: Free Press.

Wolfers, Arnold. 1962. *Discord and Collaboration: Essays on International Politics.* Baltimore: Johns Hopkins University Press.

Wood, Bryce. 1985. *The Dismantling of the Good Neighbor Policy.* Austin: University of Texas Press.

Yarbrough, Beth V., and Robert M. Yarbrough. 1994. "International Contracting and Territorial Control: The Boundary Question." *Journal of Institutional and Theoretical Economics* 150(1): 239–64.

RESPONSE TO GEDDES AND KEOHANE

Douglass C. North

In evaluating these two comments on my work, I want to begin by spending a little time on a paper of mine that neither of my discussants uses but that I think is useful in looking at the very interesting analyses that they employ. The paper, "A Transaction Cost Theory of Politics," appeared in the *Journal of Theoretical Politics* in 1990. I like it, and I hope that I can encourage some of you to expand on it, because you all have a lot of the knowledge and expertise that could turn what is a very imperfect and partial work into something more complete.

The transaction cost approach concerns the costs of measuring and enforcing agreements. That sounds very, very pedestrian and uninteresting, but it is not if we look at the resources that occupy a major part of the total costs of societal operations. In a study that I did with one of my former students, we looked at the size of the transaction sector in the American economy between 1870 and 1970. We found that in 1870 the transaction sector occupied 25 percent of GNP; by 1970 it was 40 percent of GNP; and today it is well over half. What these figures tell us is very straightforward: Most people do not produce anything. What they do is devote their resources to organizing and running economic, political, and social systems. The costs of organizing and running a society are overwhelmingly more important than production costs. A lot of the societal costs, of course, are costs associated with the way in which the polity and the bureaucracy run political and economic systems.

We talk about the costs of measurement and enforcement. Included are the costs of defining and specifying ownership rights and how they are used and the costs of measuring how to specify the characteristics of what is being exchanged. A standard contract in an economic exchange today typically is an enormously complex document that runs to dozens, sometimes hundreds, of pages because you must specify the multiple dimensions of an exchange. When you exchange a good or a service, you are not exchanging a unit-dimensional good. We economists used to talk about buying and selling widgets. A widget is a unit-dimensional product, and one widget is just like another widget. But when you buy and sell automobiles, when you buy and sell any other goods, or—very important—when you are talking about principal-agent relationships in both the polity and the economy, you are talking about many dimensions.

Let me illustrate. For many years I was chairman of the economics department at the university where Margaret Levi and I worked. My job, of course, was to monitor and meter the performance of the economics faculty and then, in turn, to decide whether they should get raises, tenure, and other rewards. You say, that is easy to do: All you have to do is see how productive they are, how much they produce, and how effective they are as teachers. But that is not all you are concerned with; you are concerned about whether faculty are using the telephone to call their sweethearts in Hong Kong at department expense, whether they go skiing on Thursdays when they are supposed to be meeting their classes, whether they are drunk when they meet their classes—I could go on for a long time. And even when you think about the simple things, when you talk about such straightforward things as measuring output in terms of teaching and research, there are difficulties. We do not have a good measure of teaching. The modern way is to have teaching polls, which measure how popular you are with your students according to whether you give them good grades and tell good jokes in class. As for research, you can count the number of pages, but you and I know that about 90 percent of the research that is published is not worth anything. So you are concerned not only with quantity but with quality.

Therefore, evaluating the principal-agent performance in something as simple as the academic world is enormously difficult and very costly in terms of time and in terms of monitoring effects. A whole society is immensely complex, and the costs of measurement are big, big costs in the society. And indeed, the costs of enforcement build on the costs of measurement. If you have low-cost measurement of the performance characteristics of the players and principal-agent relationships, or you have low-cost measurement of the characteristics of the goods and services being exchanged, then it is easy to enforce contracts. (I tell the law professor with whom I coteach a course in law and economics that ambiguity is built into the description of contracts so that lawyers will have lots of cases coming up in court.) The ambiguity may make it impossible to define whether the contract is being fulfilled. I want to emphasize this because when you get into the measurement and enforcement characteristics, you get into a jungle. But exploring measurement and enforcement characteristics holds enormous promise for increasing our understanding of economics performance as well as political performance. The exploration depends on the promise of the new institutional economics.

The new institutional economics, as applied to firms and as pioneered by people like Ronald Coase and Oliver Williamson, is doing a good job of increasing our understanding of the economy. I think similar applications can be made to the polity. Let me show you how. In economic exchange, it is relatively easy to measure what is being exchanged, either in terms of the physical dimensions of the goods being exchanged or in terms of legal criteria, even despite all the things I just said. In well-functioning markets you have competition, which makes enforcement unnecessary for a great many of the things required to make the market work well. Additionally, there is a judicial system that, when it works, provides a way to undertake enforcement of contracts. In the political system measurement is very difficult—what is being exchanged? Perhaps it is an exchange between voters and legislators of votes for promises, or it may be exchange also within legislatures of promises for votes. The incentive of the voter to be informed is something that we have talked about at great length, so I will not go into it anymore except to say that there is not very much incentive to be informed, and voters generally are not informed. Enforcement is very difficult; indeed, you cannot enforce most agreements directly. Competition plays a much more effective role in the economic marketplace than it does in the political marketplace. Thus, political markets are inherently much more imperfect than economic markets because of the inability to clearly measure what is being exchanged and because of a lack of enforcement abilities.

In the economic markets we devise institutional structures that are designed to overcome transaction costs. An efficient economic market is a market in which the costs of measurement are carefully made so that they are very low and the costs of enforcement are very low; indeed, what Ronald Coase was awarded the Nobel Prize for was pointing out that where you have zero costs of transacting—a world we do not have—markets work perfectly and you have efficiency. But you get something close to efficient economic markets where transaction costs are very low. It is very hard to get that economic market. I now spend quite a bit of my time in Third World and transition economies, trying to devise institutions that will structure the economic markets so that they will have low costs of transacting. That is a lot harder to do in political markets, because the tools you have at hand, the institutional ways to devise a structure, are not available so that you can make such markets as efficient. There is an interesting and growing political science literature looking at this. Barry Weingast and Bill Marshall, in an interesting paper in the *Journal of Political Economy* (1988), looked at the relative efficiency of the U.S. Congress as a legislative structure; they looked at the informal as well as formal institutional structure, and at why the structure tended to produce forms of relative efficiency in exchange.

All of this is another way of saying that the transaction cost approach to economics or politics builds on two ingredients missing in standard rational-choice models. One, which actually we have not talked about right now, is the subjective model of the actors, that is, the way the actors perceive the world. The way the actors perceive the world is a function of their belief systems, their ideology—to use a word that Bob Keohane uses that I now step away from for all the trouble it has gotten me into. The second ingredient is the efficiency of economic and political institutions that either do or do not encourage efficient political or economic exchange.

Now let me use that background to talk about both of these interesting essays. Let me start with Bob Keohane. Keohane deals with three issues. One is, with respect to international institutions in the absence of third-party enforcement, how do you get enforcement? Two, could international rules ever be monitored and enforced at an acceptable cost? And three, professionalism is a source of legitimacy. I have to say right away that I think these are really interesting issues, but I have never said much about them, as Keohane, I think, hints at very delicately in his remarks. What he has to say not only is fascinating but points to, I hope, a research agenda that I think would profit from a transaction cost approach.

Keohane points out rightly that where you have international agreements and where they are self-enforcing, no one has an interest in violating them. But of course, the agreements we are interested in, as in agreements in exchange in the economic and internal political markets, are the agreements whose players stand to gain by violating them and whose measurement costs are significant. I would suggest trying to structure agreements in international markets so that the measurement costs of what constitutes adherence to or violation of the agreement would be clear and low. I am impressed that in a number of cases in which I have been involved simply trying to rewrite contract structures so as to make clear and unambiguous exactly what constitutes contract agreement versus contract violation has been a big step in being able to publicize the violations that all parties agree exist (in contrast to a situation in which there is ambiguity about whether in fact a violation has occurred). I am sure I am not telling Keohane anything that he does not already know.

Keohane also talks about reciprocity and reputation. Both have limits, and indeed, he points out that the limits are very real. But again, there are ways by which reciprocity and reputation are built. Keohane refers to a paper that Barry Weingast and I and a game theory economist (1990) wrote in which we looked at the way agreements were developed among merchants from diverse entities and political bodies to fulfill a contract across what at least today we would consider to be national boundaries. We described in some detail a voluntaristic structure that was erected in the Champagne fairs in the twelfth and thirteenth centuries; this agreement was designed to make it costly for a merchant to violate it because the violation would be recorded with the law merchant and the law merchant would publicize the violation in a larger area. This was an effective device: It enabled medieval trade to grow over a vastly larger horizon than ever could have occurred in its absence. It has limits that I am sure Keohane would remind me of because eventually the market got so big that a merchant could go ahead and violate a contract in the Champagne market and then go to Leipzig, where nobody knew him and he could get away with being a bum there too. So ultimately there are limits to the reputation mechanism, but surely it is a mechanism that is useful for a lot of the ways in which we try to enforce exchange when we cannot have third-party enforcement.

This raises the final point that Keohane makes. It is a very interesting one, and I will not do it justice either. Keohane talks about ideology. It is true that I have sneaked up on the problem of ideology with a simple point, and that is that one could not otherwise explain the degree to which human beings live up to agreements when they could violate them frequently or, conversely, act the other way in positions where they do not perceive the legitimacy of the situation. And I said that therefore ideology helps us to understand something about the degree to which polities have been able to have contract enforcement over their subjects and indeed to have order in a larger world than the one that we have with personal exchange. Ideology, as I conceived it, was an opening wedge to explain a lot of things that I thought were important. The reason I cavil at the term "ideology" is that it carries too much of a burden. In the work I now do in cognitive science I use the term "belief systems"; it is more normal, and it does not get me into as much trouble. "Ideology" connotes the Marxist notion of false or correct beliefs. I do not mean either; I mean that everybody has belief systems. Belief systems enable us to interpret that part of reality that we are trying to understand and build into models for ourselves so that we have both a positive and always a normative perspective on that world. So in that much broader sense, ideology—now "belief system"—is something that we all have, and indeed, it plays a bigger part in shaping performance, I suggest, than anything else that we have been talking about. Keohane deals with ideology rather narrowly when he looks at professionalism among professional groups, but I think he has a very interesting point. Scientific legitimacy is a way to have force in agreements. That is a start. I think we can go further. I think belief systems deeply underlie the way in which societies evolve through time. And to the degree that we evolve belief systems that heavily emphasize trust and cooperation, we indeed reduce the cost of enforcement. We are trying to understand what makes for increased trust, what makes people live up to agreements when they do not have to. We are a long way from completely understanding what is going on here.

Let me go on to Barbara Geddes. In her essay, Geddes takes the institutional framework that I have developed and applies it to a fascinating range of issues in politics. She begins by critically evaluating some of the assumptions that I make. She argues that the fundamental behavioral assumption of economics, the wealth-maximizing assumption, is not necessarily the correct one when applied to rulers. However good the wealth-maximizing behavioral assumption is for economics, the political model requires a more complicated one about the utility functions of the actors. In particular, her point concerning the changing structure of the competitive constraints on political entrepreneurs is an important one. She talks about the shift from external threats to survival of the ruler to internal competition—a shift really from ruler-owners to something approximating managers. All of this, I think, is a nice addition and adds a much more realistic behavioral assumption to our analysis.

The next point Geddes makes is equally important. She emphasizes something that I am struck by in my role as an adviser to a number of governments, and that is the difference in the time horizon of the economic adviser from the time horizon of the politician. The time horizon of politicians is traditionally the next election. Typically the kinds of economic reforms that the economist adviser would like to suggest may take anywhere from three to twenty years to be realized; in many cases, therefore, they are impractical pieces of advice in the face of the competitive constraints of the ruler.

With this background then, we can explore the major issues that Geddes's essay confronts, which are those of corruption and state ownership of assets. Both are major problems in development. Overall I think Geddes's analysis is excellent, and it integrates very well with a lot of my experiences. My main suggestion is one that I think comes from my comments preceding Keohane's and Geddes's essays, and that is that the analysis could be highlighted, and greater insights could be gathered, by using a transaction cost framework. The transaction costs of corruption certainly relate to the cost of information and the cost of enforcement, the two underlying sources of transaction costs. If we had costless measurement of what is being exchanged in the political process and costless enforcement, then obviously the corruption process would be eliminated. But with a positive cost of information and positive enforcement characteristics, a lot of the features that Geddes highlights so effectively come into play. I think it is worth putting it this way because when we focus on policy reforms we wish to focus on the reduction of information costs or on enforcement characteristics. Policies that increase, for example, the transparency of exchanges are obviously high on the list. Geddes's emphasis on the crucial role of improving the performance of the judiciary is particularly important. With an independent and professionally trained judiciary, the costs of corruption rise dramatically.

Geddes provides an important contribution in her exploration of the characteristics of state ownership and the sources of privatization. I would add only two points to her discussions, although they are implicit and indeed partially explicit in the statistical exercises she has done. The first is that in order to have the assets shifted from public hands to private hands, one must first have a framework of property rights and enforcement characteristics that makes it worthwhile for people to acquire the assets. I am particularly sensitive to this because of my experience as an adviser to President Rafael Caldera of Venezuela. When he was attempting to shift assets from public to private hands, we could find no takers. It was easy to see the reason. The market structure in Venezuela makes it very difficult to have an enforceable contract; at the same time, one incurred a variety of costs, such as the cost of severance pay obligations. The second point related to the maximizing characteristics of rulers, which I discussed earlier. I do not want to give up completely the idea that wealth-maximizing behavior plays a major role. In the case of Argentina and Venezuela, the income derived from the sale of assets was a major incentive for rulers to privatize.

Let me conclude with a point that has run through our discussion. That is, ideas matter, and it is not possible to observe the shift into the selling off of state-owned assets without recognizing the important role of ideology and particularly of the successes of privatization in the process. With the demise of the Soviet Union and the improved performance of a lot of economies that have shifted assets from public to private hands, it has become fashionable, perhaps too fashionable, to view uncritically the sale of assets from public to private hands as a panacea for a country's problems. It is not a panacea. The sale of assets must be accompanied by secure property rights and by markets structured to make them efficient, none of which happens automatically. Nevertheless, I want to end by emphasizing that ideas matter. It is beliefs, ideas, dogmas, and ideologies that ultimately shape polities and economies.

REFERENCES

North, Douglass C. 1990. "A Transaction Cost Theory of Politics." *Journal of Theoretical Politics* (October): 355–67.

North, Douglass C., and John S. Wallis. 1986. "Measuring the Transaction Sector in the American Economy, 1870–1970." In *Long-term Factors in American Economic Growth,* edited by S. L. Ergomand and R. E. Gallman (Chicago: University of Chicago Press).

Weingast, Barry R., and William Marshall. 1988. "The Industrial Organization of Congress." *Journal of Political Economy* 96: 132–63.

Weingast, Barry R., Douglass C. North, and Paul Milgrom. 1990. "The Role of Institutions in the Renewal of Trade: The Law Merchant, Private Judges, and Champagne Fairs." *Economics and Politics* 2: 123.

Chapter 6

REINHARD SELTEN
A Biographical Sketch

Reinhard Selten was born on October 5, 1930, in Breslau, Germany. He attended high school in Melsungen, where he served in his junior and senior years as the librarian in the America-house at Melsungen. His voracious appetite for reading across the social sciences and the world of literature (including science fiction) was whetted at this time. He entered the University of Frankfort/Main and received his Ph.D. in mathematics in 1961 under the direction of Ewald Burger. His first postdoctoral academic appointment was on the team of Heinz Sauermann in the Economics Department of the University of Frankfort/Main. Selten has taught on the faculty of economics at the Free University of Berlin, at the University of Bielefeld, and at Bonn University. He was awarded the Nobel Prize in Economic Science with John C. Harsanyi and John F. Nash in 1994. He has been awarded honorary doctoral degrees from the University of Graz in Austria and the University of Breslau in Poland. He served as president of the European Economic Association in 1997.

Selten and Sauermann initiated the German School of Experimental Economics, and Selten has continued doing experimental work and encouraging others to do experimental research ever since. Selten and Sauermann undertook a series of experiments on the behavior of subjects presented with the payoff structure of an oligopoly game (Sauermann and Selten 1959). These early experiments had an extremely important impact on Selten's intellectual development.

Selten's most influential paper, in which he presented his theory of subgame perfection (Selten 1965), was written in an effort to provide a theoretical explanation for the behavior he had observed in these oligopoly experiments. At that time scholars presumed that oligopolists engage in tacit coordination by sending signals to one another so as to arrive at a collusive and Pareto-optimal outcome. This did not happen in the lab. Instead, Selten observed behavior much closer to that of Cournot's theory of oligopoly. In the dynamic game they were studying with demand inertia, the counterpart to the Cournot solution was not clear. As Selten (Albers and others 1997, 5) reflects on his discovery of subgame perfection:

> It took me a long time to answer this question. Finally I found an equilibrium solution by backward induction. However, while I already was in the process of writing the paper, I became aware of the fact that the game has many other equilibrium points. In order to make precise what is the distinguishing feature of the natural solution I had derived, I introduced subgame perfectness as a general game theoretic concept. This was only a small part of the paper but, as it turned out later, its most important one.

Selten has been a methodological dualist ever since these initial experiments. "The 'naive rationalist' thinks that people must act rationally and it is only necessary to find out what is the right rational solution concept" (Albers and others 1997, 4). At the time there were many debates about what constituted the right rational solution concept. The experimental findings of Kalisch and others (1954) had also convinced Selten that a "purely rational theory is not a good theory" for explaining what had happened in their experiments. Soon after, Selten read some of Herbert Simon's work, and this helped to consolidate his views on the importance of an empirically based descriptive theory different from the normative theory of rational choice. Again in his own words (Albers and others 1997, 4):

> Shortly after I had begun to run oligopoly experiments I read Herbert Simon and I was immediately convinced of the necessity to build a theory of bounded rationality. At first I still thought it might be possible to do this in an axiomatic way, just by pure thinking, as you build up a theory of full rationality. But over the years I more and more came to the conclusion that the axiomatic approach is premature. Behavior cannot be invented in the armchair, it must be observed in experiments. You first have to know what really happens before forming an axiomatic theory.

Thus, throughout his career, in addition to his major contributions to increasing the rigor and precision of noncooperative game theory, Selten has continued to examine how individuals actually make decisions in experimental and field settings.

Because of his methodological dualism, colleagues have at times referred to "the three Seltens." The first Selten has made extensive, theoretical contributions to normative theories of rational behavior. Selten and John Harsanyi have worked for many years on developing a general theory of equilibrium selection in games (Harsanyi and Selten 1988). The existence of multiple equilibria in many kinds of noncooperative games has been a major problem for theorists who view game theory as a normative theory of advice. The goal was to establish which equilibrium from a candidate set should be chosen by a rational actor. The book that Harsanyi and Selten wrote on the subject circulated among game theorists and was used in many graduate-level seminars for at least a decade before it was published. It is essential reading for all game theorists in all disciplines. It presents a coherent approach to the selection of a single equilibrium in all games. Although not all aspects of their theory sustain the challenge of other theoretical approaches, Harsanyi and Selten's general normative theory is the starting place for all work in the area.

The second Selten has done extensive empirical work in the experimental laboratory in order to gain a better descriptive theory of human behavior. This Selten has written extensively about bounded rationality and extended Simon's work in this domain (see Selten 1990). In a further development of the concept of bounded rationality, Selten in his paper with Mitzkewitz and Uhlich (1997) develops a heuristic called "measure-for-measure" to characterize the actions actually taken by experienced players in duopoly experiments.

The third Selten has made pathbreaking contributions to the study of human behavior within the context of evolutionary game theory. Selten's extensive contributions to evolutionary game theory are also closely related to his interests in a positive theory of human choice. After all, human beings are a product of evolution, and understanding how animals acquire heuristics or strategies as a result of evolution-ary pressures is an important foundation for understanding how decisions are made.

All three Seltens have made important contributions to political science. Norma-tive game theory forms the foundation for analyzing how rational political actors with complete information and knowledge of game structure should act if they want to be rational. If political scientists are more interested in how actors do behave than in how game theory advises them to behave, Selten's work on boundedly rational behavior is, along with the work of Herbert Simon, a major foundation. When we are interested in behavior that has evolved over long periods of time, Selten's work on evolutionary game theory is directly relevant. The chapter by Kenneth Shepsle in this volume focuses primarily on the implications of normative game theory for political science, and David Laitin's chapter examines the importance of evolutionary approaches.

REFERENCES

Albers, Wulf, et al. (eds.) 1997. *Understanding Strategic Interaction: Essays in Honor of Reinhard Selten.* Berlin: Springer-Verlag.

Kalisch, Gerhard K., John W. Milnor, John Nash, and Evar D. Nering. 1954. "Some Experimental N-Person Games." In *Decision Processes,* edited by Robert M. Thrall, Clyde H. Coombs, and R. L. Davis (New York: Wiley), 301–27.

Harsanyi, John C., and Reinhard Selten. 1988. *A General Theory of Equilibrium Selection in Games.* Cambridge, Mass.: MIT Press.

Sauermann, Heinz, and Reinhard Selten. 1959. "Ein Oligopolexperiment." *Zeitschrift für die gesante Staatswissenschaft* 115: 427–71.

Selten, Reinhard. 1965. "Spieltheoretische Behandlung eines Oligopolmodells mit Nachfrageträgheit." *Zeitschrift für die gesamte Staatswissenschaft* 121: 301–24, 667–89.

———. 1990. "Bounded Rationality." *Journal of Institutional and Theoretical Economics* 146(4): 649–58.

Selten, Reinhard, Michael Mitzkewitz, and Gerald R. Uhlich. 1997. "Duopoly Strategies Programmed by Experienced Players." *Econometrica* 65(3): 517–55.

GAME THEORY, STRUCTURE, AND SEQUENCE: THE CONTRIBUTIONS OF REINHARD SELTEN TO POLITICAL ANALYSIS

Kenneth A. Shepsle

The earliest analyses of strategic interactions among politicians and other agents of the political economy were typically static—indeed, they were often one-shot stylizations of some critical feature of political or economic life. The two features given the most attention were provocative analytical dilemmas—the first is the idea of an *inefficient equilibrium,* as in the "equilibrium trap" constituted by the dominant strategies of a prisoners' dilemma. Duncan Luce and Howard Raiffa (1957) popularized this feature for political science, underscoring its disturbing quality by declaring (tongue in cheek) that "there ought to be a law against this type of game." The second feature given attention was the notion that more than one configuration of behaviors could constitute an equilibrium, as in the *multiple equilibria* of the "battle of the sexes" game. The puzzle here was one of coordination—that is, how could the players seize the dividend available to them if they could arrange collectively to correlate their strategy choices.

These paradoxes, while counterintuitive, provocative, and engaging, were ultimately unsatisfactory as theoretical characterizations of real phenomena—fundamental building blocks perhaps, but clearly insufficient. It was not that they entailed abstraction, for this is what any science does. Rather, it was that they removed the strategic interaction from the broader context of structure and process with which more conventional political analysis was concerned. Political activity takes place within institutional, cultural, and behavioral contexts, on the one hand, and unfolds over time, on the other. The static, institution-free formulations of the early students of strategic interaction did not engage or exploit these structural and temporal dimensions. Indeed, in some quarters theorists thought it to be a step backward to incorporate these features because it would entail specializing rather than generalizing an argument.

The noncooperative game theory revolution, especially its emphasis on the extensive form of a strategic interaction, permitted two crucial enrichments. First, it became possible to think of the extensive form itself as an abstract characterization of "institutional ways of doing things." A game form, in this view, *is* an institution. It specifies the players, how they interact, their strategic options at every opportunity they have to do something, what they know at each specified decision opportunity, and the consequences that follow from their choices at these decision opportunities. (Add preferences of actors to the mix and this game form is transformed into a game.) A theorist may render an extensive form as intricate and elaborate as he or she wishes, balancing the gains from verisimilitude against the losses in accessibility to interrogation. Rather than suppressing these details, as one inevitably does in the reduced-form rendition of the normal form of a game, the extensive form allows one to make institutional features and parameters explicit, thus enabling "comparative statics" exercises on precisely the *political* features of a strategic interaction that primarily interest political scientists. It enables "what if" questions, the answers to which elucidate the impact of particular institutional features on strategic outcomes. They allow one to see, for example, how institutional features sustain, change, or destroy equilibrium.

Complementing this institutional enrichment, the noncooperative game theory revolution admitted the possibility of temporal enrichment. History is more than "one damn fact after another," as a wag once put it. Looking backward, it is a foundation on which contemporaneous opinions and beliefs may be updated. Looking forward, it is something to be anticipated and hence factored into contemporaneous calculations. It allows a strategic agent to bring experience to bear on his or her current situation, as well as to engage the imagination in conjectures and forecasts about future possibilities for the agent and his or her allies and adversaries. That is, the extensive form recognizes that strategic interaction has a temporal flow. By putting time and sequence back in, so to speak, the extensive-form representation allows us to think of political actors as engaged in intertemporal calculation and planning.

The noncooperative game theory revolution has had far-reaching effects in economics and evolutionary biology. I shall have little to say about the latter field. Regarding economics, nearly every field of this discipline now possesses game-theoretic foundations. In recognition of this fact, the Nobel Prize for Economic Science in 1994 was awarded to three distinguished scholars, John Harsanyi, John Nash, and Reinhard Selten. Harsanyi pioneered the study of strategic interaction in informationally incomplete and imperfect settings. Nash, nearly a half-century ago, provided the key concept of *equilibrium point* that now bears his name. Selten facilitated and gave altogether new meaning to the influence of structure, sequence, and time on social equilibrium through the development of the notion of a *subgame perfect equilibrium point*. This last contribution, giving theoretical leverage to game-theoretic analysis of institutionally structured, intertemporal, strategic settings, is the principal focus of my essay. Selten's contributions, in short, provide the underpinnings for the "new institutionalism" that enjoys so much cachet in contemporary political science and political economy.

In asking for an assessment of Selten's contributions to political science, the editors of this project have set a difficult task for me. Selten is a mathematician by training, having completed both a master's thesis and a Ph.D. thesis in this subject. His habilitation thesis was in economics, and he has been a professor of economics since 1969 in various German and American universities, including Bielefeld, Bonn, and Berkeley. His professional contributions are primarily in pure game theory, decision theory, experimental methods, economics, and evolutionary biology. He is widely read in all the social sciences and many of the biological sciences, and he has written papers across a broad spectrum of subjects. However, he would not, I suspect, self-identify with political science. Nor would he be widely recognized by political scientists, even those who might have a passing familiarity with the contributions of other Nobel laureates. Even the Swedish Academy, in detailing Selten's contributions, failed to mention anything that could be interpreted as of direct *political* significance.

To give some quantitative precision to this claim, I did a citation count of all the articles appearing in the *American Political Science Review* since 1980 to determine how frequently Selten's work was explicitly referenced. The very first citations appeared in Axelrod (1986) and Morrow (1986). Over the entire seventeen-year period there were sixteen citations, all but one to Selten (1975). Oddly, his famous paper "The Chain Store Paradox" (Selten 1978) has never (through mid-1997) been cited in the *American Political Science Review*. I have no baseline against which to compare this frequency, but my subjective hunch is that the number is low in comparison to references to the work of game-theoretically inclined political scientists, or even to the citations of many of the Nobel laureates whose contributions are elaborated elsewhere in this project.

Influence, however, works in mysterious and indirect ways. Commenting on the frequency of citation reported here, one of my wiser colleagues observed that Selten's seminal ideas, once grasped, seem so natural as to be taken for granted and not to require explicit citation. ("Do we cite Aristotle every time we use a syllogism?" he asked!) And the idea of subgame perfection is indeed a natural one, deriving initially in response to a purely game-theoretical dissatisfaction with the plethora of Nash equilibria in many strategic settings. Because of this naturalness, it served as a methodological approach to refining the Nash concept. In the press release announcing the prize, the Swedish Academy put it thus:

> The problem of numerous non-cooperative equilibria has generated a research program aimed at eliminating "uninteresting" Nash equilibria. The principal idea has been to use stronger conditions not only to reduce the number of possible equilibria, but also to avoid equilibria which are unreasonable in economic terms. By introducing the concept of subgame perfection, Selten provided the foundation for a systematic endeavor.

Selten, that is, provided a method to identify and eliminate outcomes that otherwise satisfied the technical requirements of a Nash equilibrium point but were unreasonable in the sense that they required behavior that could not be rationalized. In ordinary language, they required actors to use or to be influenced by threats and promises that a rational individual would not subsequently implement or fulfill.

This seems like a technical contribution, one of interest only to those absorbed in the deep logic of game theory and not to those whose interest extends primarily to deploying game-theoretic principles in the service of substantively relevant theoretical arguments in political science, sociology, and economics. However, this seemingly technical contribution, I will claim, stands at the heart of an appreciation of how structure, sequence, and time conspire in providing regularity to social, economic, and political life. It also may account for the relative invisibility of Selten to mainstream political scientists. Just as many of the latter make frequent recourse to statistical methods like regression analysis without being able to identify Johann Gauss or Andrey Markov, they are increasingly employing the logic and concepts of sequential strategic analysis while being only vaguely familiar with the seminal thinkers upon whose contributions such analysis depends.

Before commencing to my claims, let me note a second sense in which the editors of this collection have posed a challenging task for me. I am not certain that Professor Selten will concur with or take comfort in the contributions to political science I attribute to his work. It is indisputable that some of his most significant work is devoted to refining and embellishing the ways in which "strong-form rationality" has an impact on social outcomes. An appreciation of how this rather demanding form of rationality can be utilized to reduce the number of equilibria in a social setting, and thereby to sharpen one's predictions of how such circumstances will work out, is no more in evidence than in Selten (1965, 1975). It is also clear, from some of his earliest papers right up to his most recent, that he is not convinced of the usefulness of rationality in its strong form as an explanatory factor for social phenomena. This perspective is made evident in a second classic paper (Selten 1978), in the large body of work he has contributed on themes in evolutionary biology in which he abandons entirely the rationality hypothesis, and more recently in his presidential address to the European Economic Association (Selten 1997). In the body of work associated with subgame perfection, he is engaged in refining equilibrium based on a strong-form rationality hypothesis. In the corpus of work critical of rationality in its very strong form, he is engaged in a form of Schumpeterian "creative destruction" of a game theory, decision theory, and economics altogether too enamored of a demanding view of individual calculation and decision. Indeed, his words in a recent paper (Selten 1990, 650) on bounded rationality have a decidedly Schumpeterian ring to them: "The refutation of widely held views about decision making [that is, strong-form rationality] cannot be more than the demolition of a decrepit structure with the purpose to make room for a new construction." In short, there is a tension between these two facets of Selten's research—the Selten of backward induction and subgame perfection, and the Selten of a more layered and nuanced rationality that manages to avoid the strictures of what he calls the "induction problem."[1]

His Schumpeterian instincts are on target in economics; other eminent economists have joined him in trying to accommodate bounded rationality, imperfect and incomplete information, and cognitive limitations, as well as the costs of transacting and deciding. Economic models incorporating agents with more limited cognitive capacities have become something of a light industry recently, in no small measure because of Selten's discomfiture with induction arguments that make enormous demands on actors and fail to square with experimental and experiential evidence. Yet it is the models based on strong-form rationality—based on Selten (1975), that is— that have allowed political scientists more effectively to come to grips with institutional and intertemporal phenomena than ever before. So I find myself admiring Selten's creative destruction of economic formalisms while, at the same time, recognizing the creative *construction* in political science that has been enabled by some of his seminal contributions. Political science, being in an earlier state of formal theoretical development than economics, has drawn especially on the Selten of strong-form rationality (though an emerging scholarly thrust encouraged by the cognitive sciences will undoubtedly draw on the Selten who emphasizes bounded rationality).

The bulk of this essay is on sequence, time, and institutions. I give a brief introduction to the extensive form, but I want to make clear at the outset that this is not a technical rendition of game theory. Neither this author nor, I suspect, most readers are prepared to deal with a deeply technical presentation.

THE EXTENSIVE FORM

The "natural" way to think about an instance of strategic interaction is given by a structure known as the *extensive form*. It is, loosely speaking, a description of behavioral possibilities in a strategic context and is given by a botanical metaphor—

a tree with nodes and branches.[2] Assigned to each node is a player who has the opportunity to determine down which branch emanating from that node the process of interaction will proceed. Once the player chooses (deterministically or stochastically), the process moves to the very next node on the chosen branch, where another player is confronted with a choice. There is an initial node (into which no branch enters) and a set of terminal nodes (from each of which no branch exits). Attached to each of the latter is a vector of payoffs for the players, since the strategic interaction ends at one of these locations. (There is no player name attached to any terminal node, since there are no subsequent choices to be made there.) All other nodes have a branch flowing in and more than one flowing out (and thus have player names attached).

A *strategy* is a plan of action for each player. In effect, it is a declaration of the choice a player will make at each node to which his or her name is attached if that node should be reached. Chastened by the analytical messiness entailed in all but the simplest of game trees, John von Neumann and Oskar Morgenstern (1947) thought it theoretically more promising to desert the extensive form for an analysis entirely in terms of player strategies. Called the *normal form* (or *strategic form*), this characterization requires each player to choose one of his or her strategies from the set of that player's contingency plans. Each combination of strategy choices—one for each of the players involved—maps into a terminal node in the extensive form and thus into a vector of payoffs.

Equilibrium points of a normal form are combinations of player strategy choices that have the property that each is a "best reply" to all the others. No player has an incentive to switch to some other contingency plan if his or her strategy is a best reply to all the others, since switching in this circumstance will not yield the player a higher payoff. John Nash labeled best-reply combinations of this sort *equilibrium points,* and they are now known as *Nash equilibria.*

The problem with the normal form and its associated Nash equilibria is that it often offers "too much." To see this, let us return to the notion of strategy. The idea of a strategy is simply to summarize exactly how a rational player would play at *every* node at which he or she *might* be called on to make a choice. It is important that the contingency plan be *complete*—that a choice is indicated at every node with the player's name attached—or the strategy will not be implementable if the play of the game should reach a node for which no provision has been made. *But this includes even those nodes that will never be reached in rational plays of the game.* Some equilibrium points, as a consequence, will be predicated on irrational moves occurring somewhere in the game, even though they satisfy the technical definition of an equilibrium point. It is these equilibrium points that are "uninteresting" in a purely rational analysis.

Consider one variation of the Ultimatum Game in figure 6.1, where players A and B announce, in sequence, any number between 0 and 100. If the announcements sum to no more than 100, each player receives the number he or she announced. If the sum exceeds 100, then each gets 0. In the figure, two such announcements (from among the 101 possible) are given for A, and two responses for each of those are given for B. Both (99,1) and (1,99) are equilibrium points in the technical sense that each announcement is a best response to the other. But the latter equilibrium requires A to behave irrationally, since he could induce a superior outcome for himself by a different choice. The set of Nash equilibrium points contains many such equilibria that depend on irrational behavior. Surely we would want a more refined notion of equilibrium, one based only on rational behavior at every

Figure 6.1   The Ultimatum Game

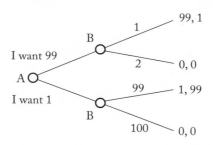

stage of the game. The normal form, however, requires B to make contingency plans for *every* possible selection A could make, even the irrational ones. Thus, there are 101 possible choices for A of the form "I want—, " and for each of these there are 101 possible choices for B of the form "If A demands—, then I want—." Among these, there is a choice by B that is a best response to A's demand and also renders A's demand the best A could do given B's choice. Consequently, for *every* choice A makes—rational and irrational alike—there is a choice by B that makes the two choices an equilibrium point according to the Nash standard.

To make the point more strongly, suppose there were two moves before those portrayed in figure 6.1. In an "announcement phase" of the game, each player announces the choice he or she *intends* to make in the Ultimatum Game proper. This provides an occasion for A or B to make a threat or promise. In particular, suppose B announces that she will ask for 99, "no matter what," hoping to induce A to play "I want 1." By her threat, that is, B seeks to produce an equilibrium more to her liking. The threat, however, is not credible. There is no reason for A to take her seriously—he should conclude that she is just posturing—since once he actually selects the "I want 99" branch, she is left to choose between a payoff for herself of 0 and 1. Nothing else is on the table at that point. Consequently, the sequence of choices in this amended Ultimatum Game—A announces nothing, B announces, "I will demand 99 no matter what," A then plays "I want 1," and B plays "I want 99"—induces, loosely speaking, a Nash equilibrium in the Ultimatum Game proper. But it is one based on A's irrational response to B's noncredible threat. In short, though it is one of the many Nash equilibria of this game, it is probably one we would not want to take seriously as a plausible prediction of play.[3]

It took several decades for the message illustrated by this example to be taken on board. Influenced by von Neumann and Morgenstern's (1947) initial aversion to the extensive form, game theorists took the normal form as basic, only occasionally appreciating the baggage of imperfect Nash equilibria this approach carries. This is not to say there were not scholars raising the problems just described, but many, like Thomas Schelling (1960), were "waltzing before a blind audience." Selten's very early paper (Selten 1965) was one of the opening salvos of the noncooperative game theory revolution that sought to formalize the problem and thereby breathe life into what became an elaborate program of refinement of the Nash equilibrium point concept.

There is surely a detailed and fascinating story to tell about this intellectual revolution. But just as surely this would take us into technical areas that are neither the present author's comparative strength nor the present readers' relative interest. Instead, let us simply stipulate that a scientific revolution of Kuhnian proportions unfolded over a ten- or fifteen-year period, so that by about 1980 economists had begun to elaborate models of strategic interaction in market settings that exhibited the fruits of the Nash refinement program. By the 1990s this methodological approach had captured industrial organization in its entirety and made substantial inroads into nearly all the fields of economics.

For political scientists of an analytical bent, all this activity in a cognate field did not go unnoticed. Actually, the influence of game theory had been felt in political science for quite some time. Following the development of cooperative, normal-form game theory by von Neumann and Morgenstern, a handful of political applications were developed. The most prominent of these concerned the formation of coalitions in voting bodies (Riker 1962; Shapley and Shubik 1954).[4] These, in turn, produced a flood of studies of coalitional phenomena (for example, Groennings, Kelley, and Leiserson 1970), and the general approach remains to this very day an integral feature of the study of coalition government and parliamentary democracy (see, for example, Laver and Schofield 1990).

Normal-form, game-theoretic studies of coalitional phenomena remain a light industry in European political science, but they no longer figure prominently among analytical political scientists in America (though they have been kept alive on this side of the Atlantic almost single-handedly by Norman Schofield). Instead, attention in American political science shifted two decades ago to the kinds of institutional analysis that the revolution in noncooperative game theory permits.[5] The "new institutionalism"—at least in its explicitly analytical form—has adopted a thoroughgoing strategic perspective and, like parallel developments in the economics of industrial organization, has sought to explain the regularities of institutional life in terms of the equilibria of extensive-form representations. I want to turn to these developments shortly, but first let me briefly describe the breakthrough that allowed this progress to be made.

SUBGAME PERFECTION

The linchpin idea for analyzing games in extensive form (and perfect information) derives from dynamic programming. From this perspective, the first operative principle in deciding how to choose at each decision point is: "Today is the first day of the rest of my life." The second operative principle is: "The first operative principle will be used at every occasion of choice." Together these principles focus the chooser's attention on the future, not the past.

From the first principle, each choice is the beginning of a new game, a *subgame* of the overall game. Strategic decisions from this point on will be taken only with respect to this subgame, not with respect to the history by which the process arrived at this subgame, and not with respect to any other subgames to which the process might have been taken. The second principle, in requiring generalization of the first principle to all such choice opportunities, permits the methodology of *backward induction* to be employed. According to this methodology, we can deduce how individuals, if they follow the two principles, will play throughout the game. In particular, we can apply the first principle to the "last" subgames (those that conclude only in terminal nodes and therefore are the initial node for *no* further subgames).[6] This yields a straightforward decision about what is best to do among a finite set of options, each with a known payoff. Once this has been determined, we can effectively "eliminate" these terminal subgames from the analysis; if ever one of these nodes is reached, all will know how play will transpire from that point on. Now the analysis can move up one level, conditioned on the fact that we now know the consequences of play "one level down" (namely, that it will lead into one of the terminal subgames that we have already solved). Thus, we can now solve how play will transpire from nodes "one level up." Repeating this process, we can solve the entire game—that is, we can determine the path of rational play.

In effect, the two principles and the backward-induction methodology they entail generate a set of equilibria that satisfy the Nash requirement—individual strategies are best replies to one another—but exclude those Nash equilibria that do not involve "sensible" play in every subgame. That is, they forbid threats and promises about subsequent subgame behavior that, if the relevant subgame is ever reached, the promiser or threatener will have no incentive to honor. Selten called the subset of Nash equilibrium strategies that are characterized by sensible behavior in this sense *subgame perfect*.

The insight of the dynamic programming algorithm that Selten exploited is nicely summarized by Eric van Damme (1983, 7):

> Since [non–self-enforcing] commitments are not possible, behavior in a subgame can depend only on the subgame itself and, therefore, for an equilibrium to be sensible, it is necessary that this equilibrium induce equilibria in every subgame. . . . For games with a finite time horizon and a recursive structure, the subgame perfectness criterion is very powerful in reducing the set of equilibria which are qualified to be chosen as the solution.

It is illustrated in the modified Ultimatum Game described earlier, in which player B's declaration in the "announcement phase" that she intends to ask for 99 no matter what is not credible since, after A announces, "I want 99," in the actual play of the game, B has no incentive to carry out the threat. In this game, therefore, the full set of Nash equilibria is {(99,1), (98,2), (97,3) . . . (3,97), (2,98), (1,99)} (and some others as well), but the only one of these that is subgame perfect is (99,1).[7] As van Damme (1983, 8) puts it, "[T]he subgame perfectness concept severely reduces the set of eligible equilibria."[8]

INSTITUTIONS

The revolution in equilibrium analysis spawned by the work of Selten and others revitalized interest in writing down extensive form games to characterize instances of strategic interaction instead of repairing to a reduced-form version that focuses only on strategies. At about the same time (whether causally connected or not is difficult to discern), political scientists were growing weary of arid formalizations of politics that were both institution-free and removed from broader contexts. Partly this weariness came from a condition exactly the opposite of that which stimulated the Nash refinement program—rather than a plethora of equilibria, there was, in the case of majority voting and coalition formation activities, an absence of equilibrium. Kenneth

Arrow's famous possibility theorem, given geometric application to majority rule in the famous spatial instability theorems of Richard McKelvey (1976, 1979), Norman Schofield (1983), and McKelvey and Schofield (1987), characterized instances of group politics stripped of all but individual preferences and a mechanism for aggregating them into group choices. That these latter were essential building blocks in a theory of group choice was plausible to many of us. That more was required was becoming increasingly manifest.

Some of us interested in these abstract renditions of group choice were also attracted to an impressive empirical literature on the decisionmaking of what must be the most studied of all decisionmaking groups, the U.S. Congress. In stark contrast to the spartan environment in which abstract group choice took place, however, the Congress was layered with institutional detail and laden with a long history of institutional development. Abstract models that began, "Assume a set N of agents, each endowed with preferences and a vote, a set A of alternatives, and a majority-rule preference-aggregation mechanism . . . ," seemed to obscure the fact, increasingly apparent in empirical settings in real-world legislatures, that subsets of N, as well as N itself, often are politically relevant; that A is not given exogenously and it too has an internal structure that conditions decisionmaking; and that the preference-aggregation mechanism is often a much elaborated version of pure majority rule.

As a consequence, Luddites of various stripes in substantive fields of political science thought the abstract models absolutely irrelevant to the study of real decision-making groups and concluded that the budding rational-choice approach in political science was no more than a fad that would quickly lose steam. Others, more sanguine about the relevance of pure majority-rule models to real majoritarian politics, began casting about for a methodology that would permit appropriate enrichments. The new institutionalism was born of an enthusiasm for institutional detail and a genuine appreciation for an older descriptive tradition that relished it, but also of a parallel enthusiasm for scientific progress (see, for example, Riker 1980; Shepsle 1979). Thick description was not the principal objective for these scholars, and this is what made the new institutionalism new. Though steeped in historical and institutional details, the work of these scholars was focused on "why" and "what if" questions—on causal and counterfactual inquiries. The former required regularities that could be explained as the equilibrium tendencies of some process (something in rich supply in the empirical scholarship on the U.S. Congress). The latter required parameter-rich institutional specifications of equilibrium so that, through comparative statics exercises, one could derive expectations of equilibrium change in response to perturbations in parameter values. In this latter sense, one could *compare* different institutions (that is, institutions that differed on some institutional parameter) in terms of the equilibrium tendencies each displayed. One could also *explain* reformist sentiments and activities in terms of the (more desirable) equilibrium that some change in institutional parameters would yield.

STRUCTURE, PROCEDURE, AND SEQUENCE

The new institutionalism in political science sought not to qualify or neutralize the scope of rationality in political life but rather to embed it in a context. The complaints about pure majority rule were not complaints about goal-seeking, maximizing, or calculating on the part of politicians in legislatures like the U.S. Congress.

To the contrary, much of the lore about the U.S. Congress had always been rich in stories about strategic maneuvering. Indeed, legislative language conveys a strategic tone with terms like "agenda-setting," "gatekeeping," "veto points," "credit-claiming," "blame-ducking," "position-taking," "killer amendments," "protecting committee turf," and "rolling the committee." And as suggested in note 2, parliamentarians and legislative leaders are well aware that they are constructing a game form when they choreograph a piece of legislative deliberation. It was therefore not an objection to the inherently strategic nature of institutional decisionmaking to which students of the new institutionalism responded. It was the spartan institutional environment of the pure majority-rule setup and the discrepancy between it and the nonchaotic regularities we observed in empirical settings.

The new institutionalist chorus sang its philosophy of science in positivist octaves, so it was clear that we did not object in principle to abstracting away "attendant circumstances" (Friedman 1953), since science does this all the time. To claim, therefore, that the earlier pure majority-rule approach threw out too much of the baby with the bathwater, it was necessary to demonstrate that bringing institutions back in enriched our theories, generated possibly different equilibrium tendencies, and managed to accommodate empirical and experimental evidence more satisfactorily than the more spartan specifications. It turned out to be easy to do the first: An institutionally enriched model provided a hitherto unavailable menu of parameters that captured institutional features and allowed, through comparative statics, an assessment of the impact of institutional arrangements on political outcomes. The second too proved a possibility with an enriched model. The absence of equilibrium in pure majority-rule specifications of group voting yielded to the existence of structure-induced equilibrium when structural and procedural features of institutions were taken into account. The sequencing of activities, also a feature of an institutional specification, proved just as rich as scholars adapted Rubinstein-like bargaining models to the features of legislative politics (Baron 1995; Baron and Ferejohn 1989a; Rubinstein 1982).[9] The third requirement—that institutionally enriched specifications accommodate empirical and experimental evidence—is the subject of ongoing assessment. At the very least, the fact that these richer models yield equilibria is nominally more in tune than sparser models with legislative phenomena that appear to be regular and patterned (that is, the empirical stuff of equilibrium).

A simple, tremendously important paper by Thomas Romer and Howard Rosenthal (1978) made clear to many of us that the incorporation of institutional features would enrich our understanding of political life. Their paper, though about popular voting on tax-rate referendums rather than about legislative bodies, nevertheless provided a way forward. They demonstrated that, in a world of single-peaked preferences over a unidimensional set of alternatives (property tax rates), the centripetal tendencies associated with the median voter theorem were attenuated in the presence of an agenda-setter—in their case, a proposer in a referendum election—with first-mover advantages protected by restrictive procedures. Specifically, a *structural* feature (an agenda-setter with monopoly power to propose changes in the status-quo tax rate), a *procedural* feature (the agenda-setter's proposal came to the voters in "take it or leave it" form with no amendments permitted), and a *sequential* feature (the agenda-setter had first-mover advantage and thus could "keep the gates closed," thereby unilaterally retaining the status quo) implied not only that there was an equilibrium but also that it was different from the median voter's optimum *because of the institutional context in which the group choice was taken.* Put differently, the comparative statics implication of Romer-Rosenthal contrasts with that of the median voter theorem. The latter implies that the majority-rule equilibrium continuously tracks the ideal point of the median voter. The comparative statics implications of the enriched Romer-Rosenthal model, on the other hand, suggests that equilibrium can vary, and not necessarily continuously, with the identity of the proposer, the degree of monopoly power of the proposer, the degree of protection from modifications afforded proposals, the sequence in which alternative proposers can move, and so on.

At about the same time I sought to incorporate analogous features into models of legislative politics (Shepsle 1979). A division- and specialization-of-labor committee system (later extended to ministerial arrangements in parliamentary government by Laver and Shepsle [1996]) was the legislative analogue to the Romer-Rosenthal agenda-setter (the *structural* feature). In effect, a committee has disproportionate influence over proposals to change the status quo in its own jurisdiction. Restrictive legislative rules, a *procedural* feature, constitute the analogue to the Romer-Rosenthal agenda-setter's "take it or leave it" motion-making authority. In the legislative context, a closed rule, in which no amendments to a bill are permitted, plays precisely this role. Extending the idea, a legislative proposal may be governed by less restrictive amendment-control rules. A germaneness rule, for example, would permit amendments, but only those that are germane to the bill in question in the sense that they deal with matters in the same jurisdiction from which the bill is drawn. *Sequence* is present in the sense that the rules of procedure that govern legislative practice demarcate a sequential process in which the agenda-setting committee moves first, other motion-makers move next with amendments (if permitted), the floor of the chamber then gets an opportunity to choose among the alternatives on offer in accord with a rule-governed amendment decision tree, and, in bicameral settings, legislative differences between the chambers are typically resolved in a procedure dominated by the relevant committees of jurisdiction (Baron and Ferejohn 1989a; Shepsle and Weingast 1987).

At the time Romer and Rosenthal's paper appeared (and mine the next year), Selten's paper on subgame perfection had been available for only a couple of years. It was just being taken on board by economic theorists and had not yet penetrated the collective consciousness of analytical political science. Neither Romer and Rosenthal nor I even formulated our arguments in explicitly game-theoretic form; we were much more influenced at the time by social choice theory and spatial representations. But the game-theoretic revolution in economics was moving into high gear, the Nash refinement program was continuing apace, and the methodology of building stylized models (a quintessential instance of which was Rubinstein's divide-the-dollar game) was becoming increasingly common, even in political science. These developments, including Ariel Rubinstein's famous paper (1982), were directly dependent on the logic of backward induction and the insights associated with equilibrium refinements like perfectness.[10]

TIME

To our rich comprehension of the politics of left, right, and center, we can usefully add an equally rich comprehension of the politics of early, later, and late. (Fenno 1986, 9)

I noted at the beginning of this essay that the early program of rational-choice and game theory approaches to politics looked at simple, static settings and were especially fascinated by the puzzles and anomalies of these stage games. Time did not figure at all in these one-shot formulations. Just as the stage game was extracted from a broader institutional context, so too was it removed from any temporal flow. In the latter case, this gave rational choice an especially bad name among substantive political scholars because it necessitated generalizing *to an entire temporal domain* a conclusion about cold-blooded, hard-hearted, narrowly conceived self-interest, commonly associated with end-game behavior in a temporally richer setting. It forced the analyst to defend one-shot behavior even in contexts that could easily be conceptualized as something more than one shot. Once one allows for the possibility of more than one shot, however, one also allows for a considerably broader set of behavior patterns.

In political science the breakthrough came from Robert Axelrod's (1984) compelling studies of repeat-play prisoners' dilemmas. Time enters into an agent's thinking in two key ways. First, the agent can express *impatience,* as measured by the rate of increase in compensation he or she requires to defer a particular compensation for a period of play. A perfectly patient agent is one who is indifferent about accepting the same compensation tomorrow as he would accept today. An impatient agent, on the other hand, requires more tomorrow to make her indifferent to deferring compensation today. Second, an agent can incorporate the prospects of her mortality. That is, instead of being absolutely certain of one play of the game after which everyone packs up and goes home—that is, dies—there is a probability that the game will be repeated in the next period (or equivalently, there is a probability that the agent will live to play again). *Uncertainty* thus joins impatience as a second aspect of time that opens up a vast array of new strategic possibilities.

Space precludes going into detail here about the impact through repeat play of time on strategic considerations. It should be emphasized, however, that the Nash refinement program played an essential role in permitting the casual chat about supergames, as in the discussions in Luce and Raiffa (1957), to be transformed into a rich body of theoretical ideas about equilibrium tendencies over time. Foresight, anticipation, and planning, anomalous in a static setting, make sense in an extended temporal setting.

Let me mention one last family of phenomena that may be accommodated in a modeling context that explicitly incorporates time. The earlier discussion suggests that an individual can be thought of in terms of temporal markers—young, middle-aged, or old in life generally; a rookie, regular, or veteran on a team; a novice, journeyman, or master in a profession; a youth, warrior, or elder in a tribal setting—as well as in terms of various seniority-based grades and ranks within organizations like the military, civil service, legislature, and university. His or her attitude toward various prizes at different stages of a temporally extended game—attitudes toward risk and impatience, for instance—is nicely captured by temporal parameters. Organizations themselves may be characterized in terms of time, allowing, for example, a short-lived politician who discounts the future heavily and is impatient for immediate gratification (like winning the very next election) to be contrasted with a long-lived political party or interest group for which the future takes on an altogether different meaning (like balancing off future elections against the present one, or future political relationships against a present windfall, respectively).

Thus, an organization may be thought of as distinct from any of the individuals temporarily occupying a niche in it. Organizations may also be thought of as holding companies for generations of individuals. That is, the temporal aspect allows us to consider time-relevant *compositions* of individuals in organizations and the strategic tensions implicit in individuals of varying time horizons and attitudes toward the future interacting with one another in an organizational setting. Jacques Cremer (1987) developed the logic of strategic interaction among overlapping generations of agents in an organizational setting, an idea first broached by Paul Samuelson (1958). The overlapping-generations logic, which incorporates Nash refinements in repeat-play contexts, has been adapted to the study of seniority in legislatures (McKelvey and Riezman 1992), legislating in temporally diverse legislatures (Diermeier 1995), more general seniority structures (Shepsle and Nalebuff 1990), and age-grading in primitive societies (Bates and Shepsle 1996), among other applications.

If structure, procedure, and sequence as features of ongoing political activity in institutional settings were the first enrichments of the more spartan social-choice and spatial models enabled by the Nash refinement program and the new institutionalist agenda it fostered, then the next step, currently under way, has emphasized temporal markers and rhythms. Though not fully dynamic, this program of research nevertheless does bring time into play and characterizes individuals not only by preferences and resource endowments but also by temporal properties. This development promises to be rich in possibilities.

CONCLUSIONS

Let me conclude with, and elaborate briefly on, several caveats. First, this has surely not been a comprehensive intellectual biography of the contributions of Reinhard Selten.[11] Even if the reader accepts the simplification of a "Selten A" associated with backward induction and subgame perfection and a "Selten B" who focuses increasingly on weaker, bounded forms of rationality, I have all but ignored the latter. This is an injustice, for Selten is both a theorist and an empiricist. Although it may be a pragmatic decision to separate these two facets of his scholarship, both sides of the man inhere in the same body and are inextricably interwoven.

Selten (1978, 133) makes this crystal clear in his almost self-critical examination of the chain store paradox:

> My experience suggests that mathematically trained persons recognize the logical validity of the induction argument, but they refuse to accept it as a guide to practical behavior. . . . The fact that the logical inescapability of the induction theory fails to destroy the plausibility of [more practical ways of playing an extensive form game] is a serious phenomenon which merits the name of a paradox.

Selten concedes that a compelling theory—one of his own invention and one that has proven a valuable and durable foundation for a new generation of game theory, economics, and analytical political science—simply does not entirely square either with the way otherwise reasonable individuals behave or with how he and other "mathematically trained persons" would behave. This intellectual tension, and the direct honesty with which Selten acknowledges it, has been a stimulus not only for his own experimental and revisionist theoretical activities but also for a substantial record of scientific progress by others on problems of imperfect or "weaker-form" rationality. This creative destruction has affected game theory and the decision sciences and is beginning to be felt in economics. It is also making an appearance in political science as analytically oriented rational-choice scholars engage the cognitive sciences (see Lupia and McCubbins 1998).

Second, I have suggested that Selten's primary influence in political science has been to provide a theoretical orientation and analytical methodology for the new institutionalism. This surely was not what he set out to do, so the sins and successes of the new institutionalism should not be placed at his door. But there is no gain-saying that the noncooperative game theory revolution, in which he was a principal coconspirator, and the model-building methodology of extensive-form game theory and equilibrium selection have been the lifeblood of analytical political science for the past two decades. In qualification, I would only add (as Selten himself would) that he is not alone in this respect.

Finally, let me be intentionally provocative in suggesting that the scientific revo-lution wrought by noncooperative game theory, though elaborated most exten-sively in economics and evolutionary biology, is fundamentally about politics. *This is because the game itself is the structure of politics.* Within this structure, when players are endowed with preferences, the possibility for conflict or cooperation, for isolated action or collective action, for individual enterprise or coalition formation, all become part of the strategic agenda. How these things actually get worked out, both in theory and in practice, depends essentially on the game—on the structure of politics.

In this important sense, Selten's contributions to political science are profound. Although his important papers on strong-form rationality may be accessible chiefly to more technically inclined, game-theoretic political scientists, and explicit citations to these papers appear only occasionally in *APSR* bibliographies, his ideas have contributed to a veritable revolution in political science.

NOTES

1. This tension allows the following interpretation—namely, that Selten writes some of the time as a mathematician engaged in providing normative advice on how to play strategically, and at other times as an empirical scientist eager to provide plausible and persuasive characterizations and explanations of strategic play in real empirical settings. I thank Elinor Ostrom for conversations on this point.

2. In a conversation once with one of the parliamentarians of the U.S. House of Representatives about game-theoretic approaches to legislative politics, I was chastised for "getting it all wrong." The game-tree description, he thought, was perfectly all right to describe the process of motion-making and amendment activity on the floor of the House. But in his office they drew amendment trees *across* the page, not up and down the way it often appears in game theory texts. We political scientists should be so "all wrong" in other aspects of our work!

3. "Yes and no," I can hear Professor Selten saying. In a model embodying strong-form rationality, where players are stipulated to be sophisticated and invulnerable to the limitations on pure rationality, we would indeed want to refine the set of Nash equilibria as stipulated here. On the other hand, in a particular real-world instance of this game—A is an adult, and B is a small child—B's nominally noncredible threat may well be taken quite seriously by A. In such cases, so-called imperfect Nash equilibria nevertheless constitute reasonable predictions of how this game will unfold.

4. A harbinger of things to come, another prominent early entry in the applied game theory literature that related to politics was Schelling (1960). Although not highly formal, the collection of papers in Schelling's volume highlighted the problem of multiple equilibria and the need for refinement. His contribution was to emphasize credibility, on the one hand, and focal points, on the other. The former shares with Selten a belief that equilibria based on noncredible threats and promises should be excluded, and the latter emphasizes the importance of the context in which a game is played and the manner in which seemingly strategy-irrelevant features can focus attention.

5. Coalition theory, as it is presently practiced, also reflects this shift. See the work of David Austen-Smith and Jeffrey Banks (1988, 1990), David Baron (1991), Daniel Diermeier (1995), John Huber (1996a, 1996b), and Michael Laver and Kenneth Shepsle (1990, 1996). All of these rely on noncooperative game models.

6. I am being very loose and inexact here and will continue in this mode, since I promised (credibly!) to avoid technical elaboration.

7. I suppose that (100,0) and (0,100) could be included as Nash equilibria as well, since each involves choices that are weakly "best replies" to one another. If, however, one elaborates the model to allow an individual to randomize—for example, over all best replies to which he or she is indifferent— we can safely exclude these two points.

8. Selten's original 1965 paper, and its elaboration in Selten (1975), provided the major impetus for the program of refining Nash equilibria. The game-theoretic literature of the last three decades has extended Selten's thrust to increasingly subtle "sensibleness" requirements, on the one hand, and to richer contexts (for example, imperfect and incomplete information, infinite horizon), on the other.

9. The equilibria of Rubinstein's bargaining model—called "divide the dollar"—are derived from Selten's subgame-perfection refinement.

10. By this time there were additional refinements, perhaps the best known of which is sequential equilibrium (Kreps and Wilson 1982). These are reviewed in van Damme (1983) and elaborated in game theory texts (for example, Fudenberg and Tirole 1991).

11. An outstanding one is Guth (1994).

REFERENCES

Austen-Smith, David, and Jeffrey Banks. 1988. "Elections, Coalitions, and Legislative Outcomes." *American Political Science Review* 82: 405–22.

———. 1990. "Stable Portfolio Allocations." *American Political Science Review* 84: 891–906.

Axelrod, Robert. 1984. *The Evolution of Cooperation.* New York: Basic Books.

———. 1986. "An Evolutionary Approach to Norms." *American Political Science Review* 80: 1095–1113.

Baron, David P. 1991. "A Spatial Bargaining Theory of Government Formation in Parliamentary Systems." *American Political Science Review* 85: 137–65.

———. 1995. "A Sequential Choice Theory Perspective on Legislative Organization." In *Positive Theories of Congressional Institutions,* edited by Kenneth A. Shepsle and Barry R. Weingast (Ann Arbor: University of Michigan Press), 77–101.

Baron, David P., and John A. Ferejohn. 1989a. "Bargaining in Legislatures." *American Political Science Review* 83: 1181–1206.

———. 1989b. "The Power to Propose." In *Models of Strategic Choice in Politics,* edited by Peter C. Ordeshook (Ann Arbor: University of Michigan Press), 343–67.

Bates, Robert H., and Kenneth A Shepsle. 1996. "Intertemporal Institutions." In *The Frontiers of the New Institutional Economics,* edited by John N. Drobak and John V. C. Nye (New York: Academic Press), 197–213.

Cremer, Jacques. 1987. "Cooperation in Ongoing Organizations." *Quarterly Journal of Economics* 101: 33–49.

Diermeier, Daniel. 1995. "Commitment, Deference, and Legislative Institutions." *American Political Science Review* 89: 344–56.

Fenno, Richard F. 1986. "Observation, Context, and Sequence in the Study of Politics." *American Political Science Review* 80: 3–17.

Friedman, Milton. 1953. "The Methodology of Positive Economics." In *Essays in Positive Economics,* edited by Milton Friedman (Chicago: University of Chicago Press), 3–43.

Fudenberg, Drew, and Jean Tirole. 1991. *Game Theory.* Cambridge, Mass.: MIT Press.

Groennings, Sven, E. W. Kelley, and Michael Leiserson (eds.). 1970. *The Study of Coalition Behavior.* New York: Holt, Rinehart, and Winston.

Guth, Werner. 1994. "On the Scientific Work of John C. Harsanyi, John F. Nash, and Reinhard Selten." Discussion Paper, Economic Series. Berlin: Humboldt-Universitat Wirtschaftswissenschaftliche Fakultat.

Huber, John D. 1996a. "The Vote of Confidence in Parliamentary Democracies." *American Political Science Review* 90: 269–82.

———. 1996b. *Rationalizing Parliament.* New York: Cambridge University Press.

Kreps, David M., and Robert Wilson. 1982. "Sequential Equilibria." *Econometrica* 50: 863–94.

Laver, Michael, and Norman Schofield. 1990. *Multiparty Government.* Oxford: Oxford University Press.

Laver, Michael, and Kenneth A. Shepsle. 1990. "Coalitions and Cabinet Government." *American Political Science Review* 84: 873–90.

———. 1996. *Making and Breaking Governments.* New York: Cambridge University Press.

Luce, R. Duncan, and Howard Raiffa. 1957. *Games and Decisions.* New York: Wiley.

Lupia, Arthur, and Matthew D. McCubbins. 1998. *The Democratic Dilemma: Can Citizens Learn What They Need to Know?* New York: Cambridge University Press.

McKelvey, Richard D. 1976. "Intransitivities in Multidimensional Voting Models and Some Implications for Agenda Control." *Journal of Economic Theory* 12: 472–82.

———. 1979. "General Conditions for Global Intransitivities in Formal Voting Models." *Econometrica* 47: 1085–1112.

McKelvey, Richard D., and Raymond Riezman. 1992. "Seniority in Legislatures." *American Political Science Review* 86: 951–65.

McKelvey, Richard D., and Norman Schofield. 1987. "Generalized Symmetry Conditions at a Core Point." *Econometrica* 55: 923–33.

Morrow, James D. 1986. "A Spatial Model of International Conflict." *American Political Science Review* 80: 1131–51.

Riker, William R. 1962. *The Theory of Political Coalitions.* New Haven, Conn.: Yale University Press.

———. 1980. "Implications from the Disequilibrium of Majority Rule for the Study of Institutions." *American Political Science Review* 74: 432–46.

Romer, Thomas, and Howard Rosenthal. 1978. "Political Resource Allocation, Controlled Agendas, and the Status Quo." *Public Choice* 33: 27–43.

Rubinstein, Ariel. 1982. "Perfect Equilibrium in a Bargaining Model." *Econometrica* 50: 97–109.

Samuelson, Paul A. 1958. "An Exact Consumption-Loan Model of Interest With or Without the Contrivance of Money." *Journal of Political Economy* 66: 467–82.

Schelling, Thomas. 1960. *The Strategy of Conflict.* Cambridge, Mass.: Harvard University Press.

Schofield, Norman. 1983. "Generic Instability of Majority Rule." *Review of Economic Studies* 50: 695–705.

Selten, Reinhard. 1965. "Spieltheoretische Behandlung eines Oligopolmodells mit Nachfragetrageheit." *Zeitschrift fur die gesamte Staatswissenschaft* 12: 301–24.

———. 1975. "Reexamination of the Perfectness Concept for Equilibrium Points in Extensive Games." *International Journal of Game Theory* 4: 25–55.

———. 1978. "The Chain Store Paradox." *Theory and Decision* 9: 127–59.

———. 1990. "Bounded Rationality." *Journal of Institutional and Theoretical Economics* 146: 649–58.

———. 1997. "Features of Experimentally Observed Bounded Rationality." Presidential address, European Economic Association. Toulouse.

Shapley, L. S., and Martin Shubik. 1954. "A Method of Evaluating the Distribution of Power in a Committee System." *American Political Science Review* 48: 787–92.

Shepsle, Kenneth A. 1979. "Institutional Arrangements and Equilibrium in Multidimensional Voting Models." *American Journal of Political Science* 23: 27–60.

Shepsle, Kenneth A., and Barry Nalebuff. 1990. "The Commitment to Seniority in Self-Governing Groups." *Journal of Law, Economics, and Organization* 6: 42–72.

Shepsle, Kenneth A., and Barry R. Weingast. 1987. "The Institutional Foundations of Committee Power." *American Political Science Review* 81: 85–104.

van Damme, Eric. 1983. *Refinements of the Nash Equilibrium Concept*. Berlin: Springer-Verlag.

von Neumann, John, and Oskar Morgenstern. 1947. *The Theory of Games and Economic Behavior*. Princeton, N.J.: Princeton University Press.

IDENTITY CHOICE UNDER CONDITIONS
OF UNCERTAINTY: REFLECTIONS ON SELTEN'S
DUALIST METHODOLOGY

David D. Laitin

> Behavior cannot be invented in the armchair. It has to be observed.
> Therefore, the development of theories of bounded rationality needs an
> empirical basis. Laboratory experimentation is an important source of
> empirical evidence. Of course, also field data are important, but they are
> more difficult to obtain and harder to interpret. (Selten 1998, 414)

Reinhard Selten is a methodological dualist. On the formal side, his mathematical solutions to equilibrium selection problems in game theory, as Kenneth
Shepsle rightly emphasizes in this volume, have had an immense impact on contemporary political science and especially on its study of institutions (Shepsle, this
volume). On the experimental side, his contributions to economics, in which he
has shown how oligopolists—and not a computational god—make strategic choices,
have become foundational in the descriptive theory of bounded rationality. As
Elinor Ostrom underlined in her presidential address to the American Political
Science Association, this sort of experimental work is likely to have an increasing
role as the political science discipline develops (Ostrom 1998).

Selten combines his formal and experimental work (in collaboration with Peter
Hammerstein) in his work on evolutionary models, and in a way that should become
increasingly useful to political scientists. Formal theorists are likely to note that in
this work Selten has mathematically derived criteria for an evolutionarily stable
strategy (ESS)—defined as a strategy that "has reproductive success against any
mutant that might arise within its population" (Hammerstein and Selten 1994,
932)—that parallels his work on subgame perfection. Experimentalists are likely to
highlight Selten's concern for empirical data that are sometimes "impossible" to get
in the field (Hammerstein and Selten 1994, 975). The solution to evolutionary
equilibria is especially susceptible to Selten's dualist approach.

Relying on a dualist methodology, as he has done especially in his work on evolution, Selten retains the rigor and intuitions of game theory without being forever
tied to its analytically strong (but descriptively weak) assumptions concerning rationality. In analyzing strategic situations, we need not assume that the actors are
rational calculators, but rather that in their heuristic behaviors under real-world conditions they are engaged in strategies that are evolutionarily stable. As Hammerstein
and Selten (1994, 931) put it: "Originally game theory was developed as a theory of
human strategic behavior based on an idealized picture of rational decision making.
Evolutionary game theory does not rely on rationality assumptions but on the idea

that the Darwinian process of natural selection drives organisms towards the optimization of reproductive success." Evolutionary theory may therefore—as Selten pointed out in the Russell Sage seminar in preparation for this volume—serve as a bridge between normative (the formal Selten) and descriptive (the experimentalist Selten) theory.

Selten's dualism has profound implications for future research in political science in general, and particularly in my subfield, comparative politics. In this essay, I promote a dualist methodology by moving back and forth between the formal and the empirical. I also promote the view that formal evolutionary models have great promise for political scientists, in large part because we can postulate intergenerational optimizations that require far less calculating genius than do models of a single actor over time. But because my own field of research is that of cultural transmission, I propose here the dualism that Selten (in the epigraph) feels is riskier, and harder to interpret: that between formal theory and field data collected through ethnography.

I promote the ethnographic (in place of the experimental) method as the complement to formal theory for culturalists in particular and for comparativists in general for three reasons. First, as opposed to experimental data, the field data collected through the ethnographic method provide information about choices in "natural task environments" (Goldstein and Hogarth 1997, 8), an issue I deal with in the conclusion. What look like antinormative biases in the laboratory might turn out to be in accord with normative theory in the real world of natural task environments. Therefore, field data provide a check on the claims of experimentalists. Second, as opposed to pure theory, field work exposes researchers to strategies that are rational in the normative sense but were never conceived of in theory. We should see as a goal of field research to identify political strategies that have not been identified theoretically but look immensely successful in the real world. Close observations in the field can yield hypotheses about strategic behavior that at first glance look incredible to game theorists but that turn out to be evolutionarily stable. A good example of this in biology is the so-called handicap principle: Signalers evolve handicaps (such as antlers) in order to make their "fight" signals costly, and therefore credible. "This shows nicely," Hammerstein and Selten (1994, 980) note, "how biologists may sometimes learn more quickly about game rationality from studying real animals than by dealing with mathematical models." In this sense, field data should push theorists to expand (or revise) the choice set in their models. While Selten (Selten and Ockenfels 1998) has discovered new strategies that cannot easily be interpreted by standard models of utility maximization mostly from experimental data, here I want to show that field data can also provide, through apparently anomalous behaviors by subjects, a compelling justification for respecifying standard economic models. Third, even when field work cannot provide the necessary quantitative data to demonstrate the rationality of a path of play, observations from the field can inform simulations that are constructed to compare the yield of different strategies played over many generations. Hammerstein and other collaborators have done innovative work in simulations based on field observations; for example, from a long-term field study of spiders, they estimated "game payoffs as changes in the expected lifetime number of eggs laid." Simulations were developed from the data in calculating lifetime egg mass comparing, for example, a healthy owner of a web to a healthy wanderer (that is, a spider who gave up his web without a fight) (Hammerstein and Selten 1994, 975–78). In sum, comparativists, in observing real people in real political settings, should be attentive to strategies that were unknown to formalists and not considered by experimentalists, yet have high expected returns.

In the first section of this essay, I introduce my own research program—looking at how diasporic groups adapt culturally in their new political environments, and suggesting why, counter to most scholarship in the field of culture, I adopted a rationality-based approach to the subject. In the second section, I give a formal representation to this problem, which I define as identity choice under conditions of uncertainty. Here I rely on Thomas Schelling's tipping game for my formal model.

The question then arises as to whether people in the situation I describe can act in ways that the formal model predicts. In the third section, I pose a potentially powerful experimental critique of the use of game-theoretic models (and the normative model of expected utility) that is inspired by the studies of Amos Tversky and Daniel Kahneman, and I focus on judgments under conditions of uncertainty that are subject to heuristics and biases (hereafter "heuristic theory"). But in the fourth section, going back to my field data and relying on game-theoretic analysis, I suggest that my informants were not biased in their judgments in the way heuristic theory suggests they would have been. These suggestions form my basis for preferring ethnographic to experimental data in analyzing the relevance of rational models to social choice.

In the fifth section, I introduce an evolutionary approach to strategic choice under conditions of uncertainty, especially as it has been appropriated by economists working in the Selten tradition. Then, relying on foundational work by Robert Boyd and Peter J. Richerson (1985) in the application of evolutionary theory to issues of culture, I show how my informants may well have been biased by evolutionary heuristics that have different qualities from those developed in Tversky and Kahneman's heuristic theory. In other words, my field work uncovered biases in judgment, but ones that have been highlighted in the field work-oriented evolutionary tradition (Boyd and Richerson) rather than the ones highlighted in the experimental tradition (Tversky and Kahneman). I develop this point further in the sixth section. Relying on observations from the field, I identify a strategy for playing the tipping game under conditions of uncertainty that has not been identified in the theoretical literature but appears to have a "best response" quality to it, much in line with some recent evolutionary theorizing about tipping.

In the conclusion, I return to the points I have already outlined concerning Selten's dualist methodology and elaborate on directions for future work in political science that are in part inspired by Selten's work on evolution.

THE PROBLEM OF IDENTITY CHOICE

In *Identity in Formation: The Russian-Speaking Populations in the Near Abroad* (Laitin 1998), I describe the trauma suffered by Russian speakers who found themselves in diaspora, living in the now-independent republics of the former Soviet Union. They had suffered from a double cataclysm. The first cataclysm occurred in 1989, when all the non-Russian republics of the union passed new language laws that effectively threatened the presumed rights of Russian speakers in the union republics to remain monolingual in Russian and yet still maintain full job mobility prospects in those republics. The second cataclysm struck in 1991, when the Soviet center collapsed and the union republics became sovereign states. With their red passports in de jure desuetude, Russian speakers were no longer sure about which country was theirs. The twenty-five million Russian speakers who did not consider themselves native to the republics in which they lived had to make decisions about their language repertoires and their national membership—questions that are at the heart of cultural identity—under conditions of enormous uncertainty.

The uncertainty was palpable. In the course of my field work, I lived with a Russian-speaking family in the town of Narva, a stone's throw from Russia, where some 95 percent of the population is Russian-speaking. One morning, over coffee with Liuba, the mother of three children, we heard on the radio about the newest in a series of regulations concerning the crossing of the border to Russia. Liuba shook her head and complained that now she feels like a small child. Every day, she moaned, she needs to learn new ways to cope, since all the old strategies for getting through the day became obsolete in 1991. She complained that she does not know who she is, what a market is, or what country she is from. For someone who prides herself on knowing where each item in the market was grown and what a fair price for it should be—and thereby protecting her family (and me!) from fruits she believed were still tainted by the Chernobyl nuclear disaster—she was suffering from immense uncertainty. Although part of this uncertainty was shared by all who made the transition from a state socialist economy, the Russians in the "near abroad," especially those who had citizenship only in a defunct country (the Soviet Union) faced heightened uncertainty.[1]

Here are conditions that the sociologist Ann Swidler (1986, 278–80) would classify as "unsettled . . . cultural periods when people are learning new ways of organizing individual and collective action." In unsettled times, Swidler reasons, "people formulate, flesh out, and put into practice new habits of action. In such situations, culture may indeed be said to directly shape action." By this she means that there will be purveyors of doctrine and heavy policing of cultural practices, and that therefore "people developing new strategies of action depend on cultural models to learn styles of self, relationship, cooperation, authority." She concludes this discussion by arguing that "culture has independent causal influence in unsettled cultural periods because it makes possible new strategies of action—constructing entities that can act (selves, families, corporations), shaping the styles and skills with which they act, and modeling forms of authority and cooperation."

A market model of identities in general, or of language in particular, would seem at first blush to be inappropriate for a situation in such unsettled times, when the modeled actors are outraged, indignant, and uncertain. It seems intuitive that Russians, living in the detritus of the Soviet Union, suddenly finding themselves without a homeland, and fearing violence, deportation, and split families, would lash back at titulars, or state authorities, like "bent twigs" (Berlin 1972, 11). Perhaps more realistic, Russians under these circumstances could not make choices at all, and their identities would be altered purely by stochastic processes, depending on new trade and migration patterns that they could not control (Deutsch 1954; Friedman 1977). Or at least, given Swidler's (1986, 278) analysis, people would be subject to the attractions of "explicitly articulated cultural models, such as ideologies, [which would] play a powerful role in organizing social life . . . in such periods, [because such] ideologies—explicit, articulated, highly organized meaning systems . . . —establish new styles or strategies of action."

Despite what we might have expected from such analyses, ethnographic research carried out among the Russian-speaking populations in four of the republics of the near abroad—Estonia, Latvia, Ukraine, and Kazakhstan—reveals highly conscious calculations about the costs and payoffs to linguistic assimilation and national re-identification.[2] In fact, as should be apparent, here we have individuals competing for scarce jobs, status, marriage opportunities, and access to the state. One of the key decisions that affects their or their children's opportunities to obtain these scarce resources is their investment in language and other cultural repertoires. With the survival of one's culture and the success of one's children at stake, we can suppose that formal models (the first element of the dualism) emphasizing calculation would be appropriate.

THE LINGUISTIC TIPPING GAME

To capture the essence of the strategic problem faced by Russian speakers in the near abroad, I adapted the tipping game first modeled by Thomas Schelling (1978, ch. 7). Tips and cascades are common features of social life and seem to be associated with situations of considerable uncertainty. In U.S. urban areas, for example, stable "white" neighborhoods have experienced the arrival of one or two "African American" home-owners. All of a sudden, the remaining white families, fearing that they will be the last whites in the neighborhood, with concomitant lower property values, all seek to sell out at the same time. But now only African Americans are willing to buy. Consequently, the neighborhood becomes a stable African American zone. We can say that the neighborhood "tipped" from stable white to stable African American.

In the late 1980s cascades of protest in Eastern Europe had similar characteristics. From a situation of stability in which street protesting was nonexistent, these societies experienced sporadic demonstrations that were not quickly put down. Protesting suddenly reached revolutionary proportions. Thoroughly hopeless and demobilized societies made a rapid shift to become highly mobilized and active societies. Political protest in 1988 seemed impossible; in 1989 it was normal (Kuran 1991; Lohmann 1994).

These cascades occur because people condition their actions on what they think others are going to do. If I think that none of my neighbors will sell his house if a few African American families move close by, I will have no incentive to sell mine. But if I think many others will—or better, if I think many others will think that many others will—then I will have an interest in selling my house before these others do, that is to say, before property values plummet. By the same token, if I think that no one will be out picketing in the streets, I know I will be an easy target for the police if I do so. But if I think that others will be out—or if I believe that many others will be sure that many others will be out—prudence no longer dictates that I remain quiescent at home.

Both of these situations (at least in the standard models) have two stable equilibrium outcomes: an all-white or all-African American neighborhood, and streets with no protesters or streets filled with protesters.

Language shift, like neighborhood shift, has cascade possibilities.[3] Language repertoires, despite being what are often considered essential aspects of people's identities, are subject to rapid intergenerational shift. We hear stories of language retention despite all efforts by a state to erase a language,[4] as well as stories of mother tongues being lost within a couple of generations—for example, the Lutheran children in nineteenth-century Ohio who mocked their ministers who insisted on speaking German. Both story lines are accurate. When my grandparents came to New York in the late nineteenth century, their parents knew that other children of Yiddish speakers would be learning English and that it would be irrational for them to seek to maintain the intergenerational transmission of Yiddish. Meanwhile, when Russians moved into the "virgin" lands of Kazakhstan at that same time, they fully expected other Russians to maintain the linguistic repertoires they had had in the Russia heartland. Here we have examples of opposite, and extreme, equilibria. In New York, after a generation, there were hardly any monolingual Yiddish speakers. In Kazakhstan, after a generation, there were very few descendants of Russian migrants who could speak any Kazakh at all.

Taking mother tongue as a proxy for national identity, the tipping model helps resolve a debate raging in the literature on nationalism as to whether identities are natural or constructed. Schelling's model applied to national identity can account for both the constructed nature (to those who study it) and the naturalness (to those who live it) of social identities. At any equilibrium it appears to actors that the world is completely stable. In this situation, identities are not in question. There is (by the definition of equilibrium) no incentive for anyone to explore new identities. It is obvious to people who in fact they are. A point of coordination, in which there is a tacit understanding among all people in a community that this is an aspect of their identity (for example, that Russians will address all others living in Kazakhstan in Russian), is an example of what Schelling has called a "focal point" (Schelling 1960). Exogenous events (such as the independence of Kazakhstan), however, can bring some instability, with certain people exploring new identities (such as a Russian-Kazakhstani). At such times cultural entrepreneurs of the once stable identity come out of the woodwork, trying to stem any tide away from the old equilibrium, and seek to naturalize, or essentialize, the status quo ante. Those claims will appear compelling, for the very fact that there was coordination at a particular equilibrium over generations does indeed look like a law of nature. Other cultural entrepreneurs, more forward-looking, will seek to induce a cascade toward a new equilibrium, and if they are successful, the change will be thought of as natural, or inevitable. The tipping game therefore shows why identities are powerful "focal points" of coordination yet are also subject to change.

For the Russian speakers in the near abroad, the tipping calculus suggests that there might be—if all Russian speakers feared that other Russian-speaking families were investing in linguistic assimilation—rapid assimilation into the national language even if all parents agreed that it would be better if all Russian-speaking families held together and nurtured their home culture in each of the post-Soviet republics. Indeed, as suggested by figure 6.2, the rate of change might be slow at first until the number of people who switch their children to a medium of instruction school in the national language begins to increase. As more Russians equip their children for fluency in the titular language, their neighbors will perceive the trend and will calculate that the payoffs for not speaking the titular language will, before too long, be lower than for learning it. As this occurs, and the feeling spreads that the direction of change is toward the language of the national state, the rate of change will rapidly increase.

Figure 6.2   The Linguistic Tipping Game: Russian Speakers Sending Their Children to
              Titular-Medium Schools

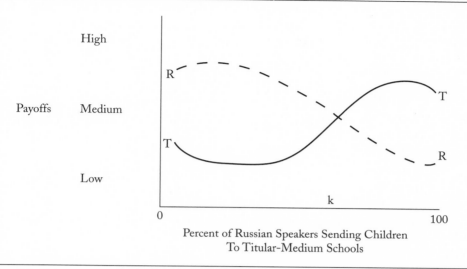

Percent of Russian Speakers Sending Children
To Titular-Medium Schools

Notes: RR=Utility function for family sending child to Russian-medium school; TT=Utility function for family
sending child to titular-medium school; k=Tipping point

Ethnographic data support this notion that Russian speakers in the near abroad were caught in a tipping game. Consider the point made by Alexander Nicklass in the *Baltiiskaia gazeta*. Nicklass, a loyal Soviet citizen, insisted that he had no nationality but lamented that in the Latvia of his day (1994), since citizenship was tied to nationality, being a non-national was not so easy. "One thing worries me," he wrote. "While one part of the population [Latvians] is off finding its national distinctiveness and other interesting things, what is the other part supposed to do . . . those people who aren't concerned by all of this? And what should be done with the nationality listed in the passports of these people who 'aren't doing the right thing'?" The logic of the post-Soviet world had forced Nicklass, and countless others, to think strategically about matters that had held little meaning for them months earlier. His language repertoire—or that of his children—now had to be reassessed. One factor in the assessment was, of course, the likely decisions of other Russian speakers in Latvia. "Nature," game theorists might say, put Nicklass into a choice node in a linguistic tipping game.

In developing the tipping model for *Identities in Formation,* and relying on the theoretical groundwork of Roger Petersen (1989), I hypothesized that the utility function for expanding one's language repertoire had three elements exogenous to the game dynamic. The first was the expected economic returns less learning costs for adding the national language to one's repertoire. The second was the loss of ingroup status that a potential assimilant might have to pay should he or she learn the national language yet be considered a "sellout" by members of his or her network of friends and relatives. The third was the potential gain in outgroup status—whether members of the titular nationality would fully accept linguistic assimilants into their society and as potential spouses for their children—that would come if he or she learned the national language.

The actual research for the book found considerable evidence that these calculations were important to Russian speakers in trying to make sense of their unexpected new situation as minorities in sovereign states led by non-Russians. Yet other calculations were also shown to be important. Russian speakers were attuned to whether the titular populations were serious about the promotion of the national language—to the extent that they were serious, the expected returns for learning it went up. Russian speakers also considered the costs and benefits of what might be called playing different games. For example, the costs of emigration to Russia (where linguistic assimilation would be unnecessary) were calculated. Also, Russian speakers considered the possibilities of political protest, in the hopes of getting government support for autonomous Russian-speaking zones in the republics. Here the cost of "voice" was weighed against the cost of assimilation. Despite the limits of a single tipping game to encompass the whose range of activities that Russian speakers engaged in during a period of crisis, I concluded that Russian speakers were strategically calculating expected returns conditioned on the choices that their fellow Russian speakers were likely to make, and therefore that a game-theoretic approach to culture in unsettled times had considerable yield. However, as described in the next section, I did not build tests into my research program to see whether the calculations concerning assimilation were reasonable approximations of the objective situation or subject to systematic biases. It was to address this issue that I turned to the work of Tversky and Kahneman.

HEURISTIC THEORY AND THE NORMATIVE MODEL

In this section I first describe how the expected utility model was modified to handle situations of choice under uncertainty. I then outline the critique of it that is based on its assumptions about human computational capabilities.

Expected Utility: The Normative Model

In the game theory of the "formal" Selten, developed for situations in which all payoffs and probabilities are common knowledge, it was assumed that decisionmakers need to lay out a set of mutually exclusive and exhaustive possibilities so that the sum of the probabilities of all possibilities equals one. Applying this approach to situations of uncertainty required some modifications in the standard models (von Neumann and Morgenstern 1944; Savage 1954). In game theory language, uncertainty refers to a choice situation in which at least some of the objective probabilities (that is, long-run frequencies) associated with all possible outcomes are either unknown to the decisionmaker or not well defined. In such situations, there are two crucial modifications necessary for game-theoretic techniques to be applicable.[5]

First, if the range of outcomes under conditions of uncertainty is unknown, a fiction needs to be created so that the sum of probabilities will add up to one. John Harsanyi (1977) dealt with this problem of unforeseen events by stipulating that there are only two possible outcomes, e (the event that the researcher is seeking to predict—in my case, linguistic assimilation) and $\bar{e}$ (that set of outcomes that does not involve linguistic assimilation). $\bar{E}$ is called a complementary event, and Harsanyi implies that it is possible for $\bar{e}$ to be a whole range of nonspecified alternatives, so that e and $\bar{e}$ are together exhaustive.

The second problem is in stipulating the probabilities of outcomes. With uncertainty, Harsanyi (1977, 41, 47) stipulates, expected utility must be computed through each decisionmaker's own "subjective probabilities, which [the decision maker] assigns to events whose objective probabilities are unknown to him." Some have criticized this extension of the Bayesian approach as requiring nothing more of the decisionmaker, in the formation of his subjective probabilities, than consistency with the basic laws of probability. "But in any practical application of the Bayesian approach," Harsanyi retorts,

> there is always an implicit recognition of the principle that the decision maker must choose his subjective probabilities in a rational manner, i.e., in the light of the best information available to him. We will call this the principle of best information. Our own principle of mutually expected rationality is essentially a specialization of this principle of best information. It represents an application of the latter principle to game situations in which each player has good reasons to believe, on the basis of the best information available to him, that the other players are also intelligent individuals, likely to display rational behavior in the game.

In the case at hand, Russian speakers need to update their probabilities of other Russian speakers taking the route toward linguistic assimilation, assuming those others to be engaged in a mirror calculus to theirs. If this is a correct assumption, then expected utility for assimilation is the sum of the payoffs for learning the titular language at each value of the percentage of Russian speakers who learn it (that is, at each point on the x axis), multiplied by the subjective probability of that percentage of Russian speakers learning it. This would be the rational calculation of whether to assimilate in the language tipping game.

The Critique of the Normative Model   Selten is one of the few formalists who recognizes that only a god can make such calculations, but the seminal critiques of the normative model go back to Herbert Simon and James March, both of whom insisted that real people, even in the best of conditions, do not have the calculating capacity to act in ways that the normative model demands. Maximization, Simon warned, is impossible; the best that real people can do is "satisfice" through small behavioral adjustments, correcting for past error. Nearly three decades after his classic *Models of Man* (1957), with the normative model still in ascendance in economics, Simon was exasperated. Lecturing at the Graduate School of Business at the University of Chicago, he urged that

> we stop debating whether a theory of substantive rationality and the assumptions of utility maximization provide a sufficient base for explaining and predicting economic behavior. The evidence is overwhelming that they do not. We already have in psychology a substantial body of empirically tested theory about the processes people actually use to make boundedly rational, or "reasonable," decisions. (Simon 1986, S223)[6]

Tversky and Kahneman, building on the Simon-March critique, systematically used experimental data to illustrate the biases that limit the usefulness of game theory as a predictive tool. In their critique of the normative approach, Tversky and Kahneman (1982, 19, 504) wrote, "Modern decision theory regards subjective probability as the quantified opinion of an idealized person." But they find numerous problems with this "normative" model and suggest in its stead a more psychologically plausible model that I have been calling "heuristic theory." They point out, in regard to situations that I have been analyzing, that "naturally, the biasing factors . . . are likely to have most impact in situations of high uncertainty." Shelley Taylor (1982, 191), writing in the Tversky and Kahneman paradigm, says these heuristics are especially useful for social judgments, which share the uncertainty of nonsocial judgments but "include new sources of uncertainty. Information about people is more ambiguous, less reliable, and more unstable than is information about objects or non-social events, since people do not wear their personal attributes on their faces the way objects wear their color, shape, or size."

The important contribution of the work of Tversky and Kahneman and complementary literature is that there has developed an inductive theory of systematic distortions from the normative model of rationality. From this work, we can make predictions about choice (especially under uncertainty) that deviate from expected utility analysis. These authors have identified, specified, and illustrated many heuristics that people systematically use and that are in technical violation of the normative model. Indeed, the ethnographic data from the Russian-speaking population that I collected reveal applications of some of the standard heuristics.

Yet the data and analysis from my field work suggest limits to heuristic theory. In my critique of it, I hope to give some insight into why game theorists abjured formal development of the psychological approach to heuristics and biases and instead moved to address the problems identified in heuristic theory through the adoption and development of evolutionary models. Rather than give a full account of the non-normative heuristics, here I limit myself to those three from Tversky and Kahneman that appear in the reasoning of my Russian-speaking informants.

Availability Heuristic The assessment of probability of an outcome based on the ease with which instances of that outcome can be brought to mind. In assessing the danger of a particular expedition, Tversky and Kahneman (1982, 13) point out that risk "is evaluated by imagining contingencies with which the expedition is not equipped to cope. If many such difficulties are vividly portrayed, the expedition can be made to appear exceedingly dangerous, although the ease with which disasters are imagined need not reflect their actual likelihood."

Anchoring Heuristic The assessment of change that is "anchored" by the point of the status quo, not by an objective estimate of the expected outcome. Subjects, for example, who are asked to give estimates of the product of $8 \times 7 \times 6 \times 5 \times 4 \times 3 \times 2 \times 1$ in a very short time frame come up with much higher guesses, on average, than those asked to multiply $1 \times 2 \times 3 \times 4 \times 5 \times 6 \times 7 \times 8$; this is because the anchoring point for the first set is 56 (8×7) while the anchoring point for the second set is 2 (1×2). Projections from the point where calculations stopped—

when time ran out—were systematically lower for the second group owing to the anchoring bias. A related anchoring phenomenon has to do with the probability assessment of conjunctive events, such as drawing a red marble seven times in succession, after replacement, from a bag containing 90 percent red marbles and 10 percent white marbles, as opposed to disjunctive events, such as drawing a white marble at least once in seven successive tries, after replacement, from the same bag. Subjects overestimate the probability of conjunctive events and underestimate the probability of disjunctive events. This bias, Tversky and Kahneman (1982, 14–16) warn, has implications for planning. Experts may well overestimate the safety of systems that have long chains of high-probability successful operations and underestimate (the perhaps higher-probability situation) of one of a large set of components breaking down.

Asymmetry Heuristic This suggests that people under conditions of uncertainty rely heavily on causal schemas (which tend to be highly determinative), and therefore overpredict on the extremes of a possible distribution, when the normative ideal would be to predict closer to the mean.

FIELD OBSERVATIONS CONCERNING HEURISTIC THEORY

In this section, I give evidence as to why I favor ethnographic over experimental data. Here I return to my field notes in order to evaluate the challenge to the normative model posed by the three biases associated with Tversky and Kahneman's heuristic theory described in the previous section. I show that while the use of these heuristics is common under the conditions of my research, they are not so clearly violations of the normative model as leading experts such as Tversky and Kahneman suggest. In fact, the heuristics, as they are actually applied, may serve as reasonable approximations of expected utilities, especially when the decisionmaker has no precise way to calibrate expected returns.

Availability

Under conditions of uncertainty, a stunning event or example serves as a proxy for a general trend. I give four examples.

Kazakhstan The newly independent government renamed Kazakh State University, which had been named after Kirov in Soviet times, to Al Farabi. Shortly thereafter the monument to Kirov became a target of vandalism. His ears and nose were smashed. No one removed it or repaired it over a three-year period. It stood, for many Russian speakers, as the signal of the future when the *nekul'tur'e* (the uncultured ones) were expected to take over the state.

Ukraine Marina Diatlova, an official of Tovaristvo Rus', which is monitoring the rapid Ukrainization of Kiev schools, noted that in world literature classes in secondary schools students are reading translations of Pushkin into Ukrainian. Reflecting on this utterly absurd practice (since all the students read Russian, and Pushkin is a master of Russian prose), Diatlova foresaw a general "threat to Russian culture" in Ukraine.

Estonia The government has required the teaching of Estonian in Russophone schools and agreed to pay higher salaries to teachers of Estonian in Russian schools. Nina Sepp, the rector of the Narva Teachers' Training Center, told me that this has induced many Russian students to study Estonian seriously, as it is mostly Russians who are taking advantage of these salary opportunities. The availability of a few jobs under conditions of high unemployment led many students to invest heavily in language, without any assessment of the likelihood of getting such a job given that many other students were studying Estonian, or the costs of learning Estonian in order to qualify for these jobs. The publicized availability of these opportunities weighed heavily indeed.

Transdneister A final example of the use of the availability heuristic has to do with the well-publicized information about ethnic violence in Transdneister (and reported incidents involving Russians in Tajikistan, Abkhazia, and Baku). The behavior of my informants often seemed conditioned on the chaotic and threatening situation for Russians as exemplified by these events, which were regularly reported on television, rather than on the statistical fact that Russian civilians were almost nowhere else the direct targets of ethnic violence in the former Soviet Union.

Despite these examples of the power of availability—as opposed to statistical probability—there is good reason to oppose a rigid dichotomy between the normative model and the availability heuristic when it comes to real-life situations under conditions of uncertainty. I would like to make five points showing the rationality of reliance on available data.

Availability Is a Proxy for a Low-Probability but Disastrous Outcome

Consider the following report on the fourteenth session of the Odessa city council in the spring of 1993. A vote was taken twice on whether to discuss the issue of bilingualism. Although it was finally passed, V. Tsymbaliuk, the local leader of Rukh, the Ukrainian nationalist party, said during the debate (Laitin 1998, 107–8): "In the five years of its existence in Odessa, Rukh never raised the language problem. We are against a referendum or any discussion on this question. It would not lead to a solution, but to an acute polarization of opinions in the council and in the streets. The experience of our neighbor Transdneister attests to that."

Suppose the probability of working out a Pareto-superior language policy for Crimea were much greater than the probability that a failure would yield ethnic war in the streets. Even if the statistical probability of a Transdneister were low, the reason the events in Moldova were so available is that Russians throughout the former Soviet Union put an enormous negative value on that outcome. The "asymmetry of the stakes," as Robert Bates, Rui de Figueiredo, and Barry Weingast (1998) show in regard to the former Yugoslavia, because they threaten low-probability but potentially disastrous outcomes, gives the "available" information its high value in expected utility terms.

Availability Is Endogenous   In the experimental literature, availability is carefully delimited and set by the investigator. In the real world, people search for good cues, or stunning examples, in order to make the best updates of their subjective probabilities of various outcomes. In the hypothesized language tipping game, Rus-

sian speakers searched for clues as to the success of the national language program among titulars themselves.[7] If the titulars were privately subverting the language program—by maintaining Russian as an essential element of their repertoires—it would not be necessary for Russians to go beyond symbolic learning of a few titular phrases. My data showed considerable search for such clues. Consider this incident. In the Tallinn Central Market in January 1994, two Estonian women in their thirties were walking around the outdoor stalls, and one said to the other in Estonian: "Imagine that! I've nearly forgotten all of my Russian! Now that's a problem!" This suggests that she was still willing to switch languages in order to communicate with Russian-speaking sellers, who once predominated in the market. But the need for this had been declining rapidly, and she announced her recognition of a "problem" with a kind of pleasant surprise—she never thought she would not really need the language. In many places in Estonia, the development of what might be called "Russian-free zones" also has a stunning effect on residents' sense of the future value of Russian monolingualism. At the University of Tartu, the premier institution of higher learning in Estonia, where many of the children of my informants from Narva aspired to enroll, there was hardly a public sign in Russian. I even had a hard time finding a single Russian-language newspaper. It is no wonder that Russian-speaking students aspiring to a college education, despite the university's public pronouncements of no linguistic discrimination, were convinced that they would not earn a place at the university (in most departments) unless they could demonstrate Estonian competence in their interviews. Such examples suggest that no Russian living in Estonia could possibly miss the point that Estonians are systematically altering their language repertoires in a way that will make Russian a rare weapon in any Estonian's linguistic arsenal. This implies that for Russians to be able to communicate with state authorities in the future, they will need to speak Estonian.

In Kazakhstan, despite energetic struggles by committed nationalists, Kazakhs cannot demonstrate seriousness of purpose in their quest to reduce significantly the presence of Russian, even among Kazakhs. Thus, Kazakh nationalists are unable to make a credible threat to the Russian speakers that their future in Kazakhstan will require fluency in Kazakh, and in fact they "privately subvert" their own language laws by inter alia sending their children to Russian-language schools.[8] In Kazakhstan, one tactic in the private subversion strategy is to accept the notion that a few words in Kazakh are enough to demonstrate fulfillment of the program. My research assistant Bhavna Dave met a couple, Farida and Yerik, both highly educated in technical fields, and Kazakh-speaking Kazakhs by their self-descriptions. Yet once Dave and Yerik each proved that they could maintain a conversation in Kazakh, conversation switched to Russian.

"Private subversion" has an element of deviousness to it, as we can see from Dave's interview with A. Dokuchaeva, the leader of Lad, the Slavic movement. A teacher at the Mathematics Institute of the Kazakh State University, Dokuchaeva (1993) wrote in *Mysl'*:

> It is necessary to mention that a large number of teachers, philologists, and scholars are now engaged in the work on revival of the Kazakh language. Sincerely concerned by its fate, these activists come to schools and to lecture halls to tell their cocitizens about the beauty and the high culture of Kazakh speech. But we also know that in the course of the last three years since the

Law [making Kazakh the state language] was passed, the state—implying its bureaucrats and the governmental institutions—are not all that excited about improving the state language or studying it. There is a lot of "slyness" beneath the taunts directed toward those "unwilling" to learn it."

The slyness refers to the public display of Kazakhization alongside the private use of Russian. These examples of private subversion are picked up on by Russian informants, who come to the conclusion that the nationalization of language is not serious and therefore they need not make an investment in it.

There are, to be sure, attempts to demonstrate a commitment to the Kazakh language and culture. By moving the capital from Almaty, which is a thoroughly Russianized city, the government wants to Kazakhize the political center of the country. Outside of urban areas such as Almaty (except for the heavily Russianized industrial areas in the northeast), Russian is less widely spoken. A powerful movement to Russify urban Kazakhs has been unremitting for well over a century; the Russian language has spread into every nook and cranny of urbanized and high-status Kazakh life. Ultai Zhunispeisova mentioned to Dave how Kazakh adaptation to Russification has sometimes reached absurd proportions. Kazakhs, she bemoaned, gave up their beautiful historical names for meaningless terms from the Soviet era. One comes across names like Kolkhozbek, Traktorbek, Kosyurga (an abbreviation for the cosmonaut Yurii Gagarin, a name that abounded in the Baikanour cosmodrome region) even in the Kazakh rural villages. To add injury to insult, the Kazakh mankurty (the insulting term for the cosmopolitans who have "forgotten" their culture) are neither disappearing from public sight nor preparing themselves for a reentry as Kazakh-dominant intellectuals. They defend their interests publicly. Nurbulat Masanov and Nurlan Amrekulov, in a subtle essay in *Karavan*, a Russian-language newspaper in Kazakhstan, supported the country's privatization campaign. Though the authors do not mention it explicitly in this article, their contention was that the promotion of Kazakh as the state language was a step in the direction of ethnocracy in a multiethnic society; they considered it a protectionist measure on the part of the nomenklatura, who were basically afraid of real market-like competition based on merit and efficiency. To say that the Russian speakers' unwillingness to learn Kazakh shows that they are non-normatively swayed by available data is not quite right: They searched the landscape for cues that would help them maximize their linguistic returns.

The Availability Heuristic Implies a Reluctance to Update   Informants in my study were updating constantly, trying to apply new models to make sense of their situation. Consider the Grigor'evs, the family with whom I lived. Husband and wife talked to each other repeatedly about future opportunities for the next generation. Pavel, Liuba's husband, determined that while engineering was the skill of the Soviet period, language was the skill of the new market. Their youngest child, in fifth grade, was therefore transferred into a school, requiring a one-hour bus ride daily, that specialized in language instruction, both in English and Estonian. They are not the only ones to have done this: The school that developed this specialization suddenly had far longer waiting lists for students than the school with the highest ranking in traditional academic subjects.

Compare this again with the situation in Kazakhstan. Slava Kozlov, a young Russian engineer who himself planned to learn Kazakh, told Dave and me: "The only way to get a good job is breaking through family networks. No one," he said, "will lose his job due to not knowing Kazakh. But on the other hand," he insisted, "no one will get a good job just for learning Kazakh." Despite his good intentions, Slava saw no returns for an investment in knowing Kazakh, and this, I believe, was why he postponed learning it.

On the question of whether to invest in exit—that is, a return to Russia, the putative homeland—there was endless calculation and updating. In all four republics, Russians were quite ambivalent about Russia. On the one hand, many (even non-Russian Russian speakers) did see Russia as their ancestral home. On the other hand, Russian informants resident in all four republics, but especially in Estonia and Ukraine, gratuitously told me and my research team on many occasions that Russia was "chaotic" and that Russians from Russia were "foreign" to them. They learned this not by watching the fantasy world of advertisements on Russian television, but by reading between the lines. They were especially affected by the few clips they were able to see of the October 1993 storming of the Russian Parliament by President Boris Yeltsin's troops. Nina Sepp felt that she knew why there was so little migration to Russia from Estonia. "Fear of chaos, or disorder," she told me in September 1993, "is far greater than the fear of loss of identity or dignity that they face in Estonia." It is surely true that the clips Russian speakers get of Russia on television are not representative of the general situation there. Nonetheless, experienced Kremlinologists that they are, they could see that the expected returns of exit were dangerously low.

Moreover, informants developed, through poking around, a catalog of values concerning the transaction costs of migration. First there was the problem of the illiquid housing market. One resettler told Vello Pettai of being robbed of $1,100 by an unscrupulous firm. Fear of high and unregulated transition costs holds back explorations of new possibilities in Russia. Similarly, Russians underemployed at an electronics factory in Narva told me that the market for flats situated near comparable factories is equally dry in Russia, so they cannot take the risk of moving.

Second, there was the problem of insufficient resources. One group of Russians from Narva had organized themselves to homestead in Russia. They heard of the resettlement funds available from Estonian organizations and sought to tap into those resources. L. Shliminov, a correspondent from the *Narvskaia gazeta*, interviewed them and found they were utterly disgusted that the actual funds available to them were paltry. They gave up their effort.

Third, there was the problem that there was no real "homeland" to return to. Few Russians in Estonia could provide me with a locality that was their home. For example, in the Estonian-language class that I participated in for the unemployed, an early dialogue required us to say (in Estonian) where we were from. More than half of the students who did not say "Estonia" reported places outside of the core Russian zone, such as Uzbekistan, Kazakhstan, Moldova, and Siberia. I surmised that many of their parents grew up in prison camps, and very few Russians were courageous enough to explain to their children where the family's roots were. For most Russians in Estonia whom I have talked to, there is no village, no neighborhood, no housing bloc in Russia, that represents their "real" home.

Fourth, the collapse of the Soviet Union led to declining links to Russia. Russia has since 1991 slowly begun to fall beyond a horizon for Russians in Estonia. Trade data tell the big story: 95 percent of Estonian trade was with Soviet states in 1991, but that figure had fallen to 26 percent by 1993. The story is retold in real people's lives. Lena in Tallinn saw free access to Russian television (Ostankino, but in 1995 it became ORT) as her link to the homeland. "If they cut Ostankino," she told Pettai, "it will cut the last thread we have left to Russian culture. We all grew up on Ostankino and learned about culture through it. All our favorite actors and artists are there. We know them all. Now we will lose them." Liuba Grigor'ev was affected in another way, living halfway between Saint Petersburg and Tallinn. It used to be, she said, that if you needed to get your cat spayed, you would take it to Saint Petersburg, since there was no such facility in Narva. But now the border is too slow, and it is better to do that kind of business in Tallinn. Russia is slowly disappearing from Russian-Estonian consciousness as their "exemplary center" (Geertz 1980).

Finally, there was the problem of a lack of job opportunities in Russia—knowledge of which was based on the reports of returned migrants as well as general knowledge of the economic situation in Russia. It is therefore clear that Russian speakers were carefully monitoring trends in life opportunities for themselves and their families in both Russia and their republic of residence.

Implausible but Available Signals Are Discounted   Tversky and Kahneman (1982, 5), discussing the representativeness heuristic, show the power of "worthless information" in biasing people's assessments of probability. The data from my research show that under conditions of uncertainty—with real things at stake—people are rational skeptics and throw away a lot of bad information. There is also a question of the scale of information. In the Tversky and Kahneman experiments, only tidbits are given to subjects, thus orienting them toward using whatever cues are available (even something as meager as a number written on the blackboard of the room in which the experiment took place). In the real world, people get too much information, and it is rational for them to engage in a form of informational triage rather than take useless but available cues. The rational discounting of available information weakens, in the real world, the biases of the availability heuristic.

Consider the analysis in *Karavan,* the Russian-language newspaper in Kazakhstan. An article on the declining situation of Russians says: "Russians would have packed their bags even earlier, if only the Russian-speaking reader were able to read some of the [inflammatory] publications in Kazakh-language press." Yet Russian informants were looking at the actual situation with an eye to their own jobs and futures, not with a sensitivity to the extremist rhetoric. Our informants told Dave and me repeatedly that the Kazakhs cannot do without them for many years, and therefore it is reasonable for them to remain, but prudent to prepare their children for the job market in Russia.

Signals sent by titulars about the value of assimilationist probes by outsiders face rational scrutiny by Russians wondering whether to assimilate linguistically. Titulars in all four republics, to different degrees, consciously sent signals that emphasized the extremely limited payoffs that would accrue to linguistic assimilants. Estonians, for example, made assimilation seem like the situation faced by Alice on the Queen's chessboard—the criteria for success kept changing. New barriers were erected as well. On the legal front, with the passage of the Aliens Law in 1993, a whole new vocabulary to delegitimate Russians was put into service. The terms "migrant," "colonizer," and "occupier" were part of social delegitimization on the popular level. But the legal terms "non-Estonian" (muulane), "noncitizen" (mitte-kodanik), and "alien" (välismaalane) were added. An exasperated Klara Hallik from the Estonian Academy of Science, an Estonian with Russian roots of generations ago who was a leader in the Popular Front period, commented to Pettai: "Who would have thought that the noncitizens' registration could now be interpreted [by Estonian authorities] as merely giving them the right to apply for a temporary residency permit in the Republic of Estonia?" New legal barriers to entry, no matter what Russians were trying to do, sent clear signals that should have lowered the expected payoffs for linguistic assimilation.

Russians in Estonia picked up these signals. Members of the Narva city council, after voting in February 1993 to commit themselves to a constructive process of international peace, decried stories of the "Estonian decolonization fund." Although the Estonians talked of the "velvet" application of international human rights norms with their "decolonization fund," one member said sardonically that their goal of having the republic become 80 percent Estonian would mean a "velvet expulsion." Or in the words of one Russian woman from Tallinn, born and bred in Estonia, and interviewed by Estonian television: "It's as if they [the Estonians] are saying, 'I want you to leave, I want your kids to leave, there is no higher education for them. . . .' They look down upon us from on high. . . . I didn't feel any problems or obstacles at first. I wasn't a Russian person. But later I began to feel it."

Nonetheless, Russians queued up to study Estonian and made extraordinary efforts to get their children educated in it. There is a small element of Huck Finn in this kind of reasoning—if you want to get long queues for a night at the theater, it is best to announce that women and children will be prohibited from attending, thus raising the value of a ticket. High citizenship barriers raise the value of achieving citizenship. I think the overriding mechanism operating here is that Russians in Estonia have discounted the "available" anti-Russian rhetoric as a bad predictor of the future; they watch the progress of the economy and the actual human rights record of the regime to update their expected values of achieving citizenship.

The "Focal Point" Reality of Available Signals   As Schelling pointed out in his classic *The Strategy of Conflict* (1960, 54–58), people who want to coordinate rationally make extensive searches for patently available signals, and these become the basis for coordination. At the time of the field work, Russian speakers in central Ukraine felt that the linguistic situation in the streets, in the shops, and in people's homes was predominantly Russian. Yet they also felt that a tip to Ukrainian was possible, given the fluid political situation. In 1994 Leonid Kuchma, a Ukrainian by nationality but a Russian-speaking monolingual, was elected president, with great support from the Russian-speaking east. Immediately after winning the election, he began assiduously to study Ukrainian, and in all his public appearances as president he has relied exclusively on Ukrainian. Those who take the president's language studies as a signal that the tip is going in the direction of Ukrainian might be accused of falling for the bias of availability. Yet if Russian speakers assume that others will fall for that bias, and they want to coordinate with others, they will fall for that bias not because of any lack of statistical acumen but because they assume that others assume that they will take such a public event (Kuchma speaking Ukrainian) as a signal that there will be a tip toward Ukrainian. Thus, in coordination games, conditioning behavior on availability has a "focal point" rationality.

Anchoring

The "Soviet" world was one in which Russian speakers could be monolingual everywhere but non-Russians had to be bilingual to achieve success. Ironically, Russian monolingualism by the 1970s was being hailed by authorities as a manifestation of internationalism; meanwhile, bilingualism in this same period was developing a negative connotation and, if publicly displayed, was considered an example of national chauvinism. The Soviet norm—high status for remaining monolingual in Russian—was internalized by Russians living in the union republics outside of the Russian federation. And as a norm, it served as an "anchor" from which all trends were assessed. In this sense, it provided a conservative bias to probability assessments.

Consider this example. A common response of Russian speakers to the question of whether they would send their children to Estonian-medium schools, especially in areas where Estonian is not at all known by parents, is incredulity at the very thought of intergenerational linguistic shift. Nataliia Berezhkova lives in a Russian-dominated neighborhood in Tallinn. She has studied Estonian and is working hard to pass the citizenship exam. She works as an activities coordinator at a Russian-language secondary school. When asked what would happen to the Russian-medium schools if most parents chose to enroll their children in Estonian-medium institutions, Nataliia had a look of disbelief: "It is not possible," she answered.

In their discussion of anchoring, Tversky and Kahneman mention the overvaluing of conjunctive probabilities and the devaluing of disjunctive ones. A good example comes from my experience living with the Grigor'evs. Pavel has a beautiful dacha, about five kilometers from his home. The dacha is in a swamp that in the early 1960s was made available by the government to kokholzniky and various other people whom it allowed to "buy" a plot of land. One beautiful day in October, overlooking his harvest, Pavel said to me, "This is why Russians don't want to leave Estonia!" For those who do, the risks to their property are high. His next-door neighbor, an agronomist at a Saint Petersburg agricultural institute, was the one who provided the saplings for the luscious apple trees we were then picking. The neighbor had not been to his house since 1991, because of problems with crossing the border, or so Pavel said. The agronomist has papers showing that he is the owner, but under current law he owns the house but has only a ninety-nine-year lease on the land. Pavel, however, since he is a citizen, owns both his house and the land it sits on, and he has the right to sell all of it to another citizen. He would not do that given that his dacha is where he has a guaranteed food supply and where he has spent virtually all his free time for thirty years, constructing his private castle. With property of this sort, if Pavel were not given citizenship for his "service to the state," he would have studied Estonian, as his wife was about to do, in order to receive it.

Pavel's reasoning went something like this. The government will surely continue to grant property rights only to citizens. The government is likely to force out of their property rights noncitizens who acquired those rights in the Soviet period, since these rights are no longer recognized. To protect those property rights, it is best to legalize yourself. The biggest burden for legalization is the language. Therefore, you should study the language quickly in order to secure your property. Even if all these probabilities individually are high, Tversky and Kahneman suggest that decisionmakers who put a high probability on all of them being fulfilled are violating the normative model. This is because the disjunctive possibility—for example, that a rabid nationalist would come to power in Estonia and evict all Russians—although quite low, is only a single event and no chain is necessary for it to be fulfilled. Yet if that happened, it would break the entire conjunction that is leading Russians (with dachas) to learn Estonian.

Asymmetry

In Kazakhstan, whatever the job possibilities involved, many Russians cannot take the study of Kazakh seriously. One Russian pontificated to Dave that the Kazakhs do not really have a language, they merely have dialects. A somewhat more academic version of this negative view came from A. Zhovtis, who told Dave and me that "it is absurd to transform a spiritual folkloric language into a technical one." Zhovtis, who was strongly supportive of Kazakh independence, further told us that it is "not possible" for the Russian-speaking population to learn Kazakh, even if they wanted to. It was an absurd thought, even to raise it theoretically.

Zhovtis has a strong theory about language: there are real languages of science, and there are folk languages of affection, and it is impossible to transform the second into the first. He has therefore assessed the probability of Kazakh becoming a language of education, science, and administration at the zero point. A weaker schema, one more open to data about language revivals elsewhere in the world (for example, Israel), might have led Zhovtis to put the probability somewhat above zero, although he probably would still have given it a low number. This is an example of what Tversky and Kahneman call asymmetry, and it certainly has a powerful effect on strategic choice in regard to adding to Russian speakers' linguistic repertoires.

A Final Note on Heuristic Theory   In reviewing my field data, in which people were making cultural decisions under conditions of uncertainty, I found many examples of reliance on the judgments posited in heuristic theory, with the implication that these heuristics violated the normative model of expected utility. My preliminary judgment on these examples is that in the real world these violations do not seem as stark as they do in the laboratory. Real people seek out multiple clues from the messy environment (and thus availability is partially endogenous). To be sure, people are anchored to norms of the status quo ante, and to old schemas, but they are impressed by new information, for which they are hungry. My guess is that the use of Tversky and Kahneman's heuristics do not lead to great deviations from what would be predicted from analysis based solely on the normative model (Gizerenzer 1991).

EVOLUTIONARY THEORY

Selten's methodological dualism leads him to juxtapose the expectations of his formal models with experimental research in the Tversky and Kahneman tradition (see, for example, Selten 1998, 415). But the heuristics uncovered by that tradition have not been informative in evolutionary models. Of course, the Tversky and Kahneman tradition ignores strategic choices by individuals over time, and it has not addressed intergenerational adaptation. Perhaps this is why the Tversky and Kahneman heuristics did not appear all that biasing in the cases I examined. Especially in the realm of culture, in which the effects of choice span generations, perhaps choice is biased through quite different mechanisms. In this section, I follow Selten's path into evolutionary theory to see whether it provides some clues as to how to interpret cultural choice.

The attraction of evolution for game theorists like Selten is easily explained. First, in a classic treatise by John Maynard Smith (1982), rudimentary game models are used to describe animal behavior in a powerful and cogent manner. Second, these models do not have to rely on unrealistic rationality assumptions. Third, evolutionary models posit strategic situations that are frequently encountered and sufficiently simple to allow for mathematical representation. Finally, through a combination of learning (by actors) and selection (through intergenerational reproduction), equilibria are attained, and these equilibria can be predicted from the mathematical representations of the strategic situation.[9]

Evolutionary Biases

Evolutionary theory, like the psychological theory of Tversky and Kahneman, postulates that actors will rely on heuristics. More so than the psychologists, however, evolutionary biologists assume that these heuristics are reasonably good tools, or else, through processes of selection, they would have disappeared. Although Selten is prudent to caution me (at the Russell Sage seminar) about the quite distinct evolutionary mechanisms in the biological and social worlds, Hammerstein and Selten's papers (which establish mathematical correspondences between subgame perfection in human strategy and ESS in animal behavior) implicitly invite the application of evolutionary theory to the social sciences.

One can begin by acknowledging, as do Boyd and Richerson, that humans acquire much of their behavior culturally rather than genetically, and therefore human evolutionary processes are indeed distinct from those of other animals. Yet, by seeing "the transmission of culture in humans [as a] system of inheritance," Boyd and Richerson model cultural evolution with many of the same mathematical models that are used in genetics and population biology (Boyd and Richerson 1985, 1–2, 20).

The bulk of Boyd and Richerson's analysis centers on combining two learning mechanisms—the adoption of behavior that is culturally transmitted and the development of behavior that is individually learned—into a general learning model that they call "guided variation." The authors analyze a mathematical model of guided variation showing that under conditions of rapid environmental change, cheap learning, and relative accuracy of individual to social learning, natural selection should favor individual learning; the opposite conditions should favor selection based on culture (or social learning) (Boyd and Richerson 1985, 98, 106, 116, 126). Not only do humans have a capacity for cultural transmission, they argue, but under certain parameter values they have an incentive to favor it over individual learning. Cultural transmission is therefore cost-effective and rational.

But unlike most sociobiologists, Boyd and Richerson consider the possibility of evolutionary learning that is individually irrational; that is, they examine evolutionary biases that are parallel to Tversky and Kahneman's heuristic theory. Two of their biases merit attention here, because they compel me to reconsider my field data.

Runaway Bias or "Herding"   Boyd and Richerson identify "indirect bias" as a force generating change in the variation of characteristics in a population when high-status individuals become models for naive individuals and traits not directly connected with their status (for example, their dress) are adopted. There are "indicator" traits that correspond with success and are easier to observe than the underlying trait that gives the model his or her wealth, power, or prestige. Transmission is indirectly biased if naive individuals prefer some model over others based on examination of indicator traits. Since it is costly to find out precisely what to copy in a successful model, naive individuals can economize by copying all traits, whether relevant to success or not.

Boyd and Richerson provide real-world examples of indirect bias that can easily cascade into what they call "runaway bias," which helps to explain maladaptive characters. A well-known example in the animal world is the exaggerated tail on peacocks. To illustrate this process in our cultural world, Boyd and Richerson give an example from sociolinguistics to show how dialects spread down and up status hierarchies. Dialect, they assume, is not really a choice, but an adaptation of behavior toward the indicators of people whose lifestyle is worthy of emulation. Relying on William Labov's (1972) work on Martha's Vineyard, they suggest that "salty talk" is an indicator trait showing the independence of fisherman, and that it has prestige given the encroachment of the modern world that threatens the Vineyard's culture. If teenagers from the Vineyard imitate those who use more than the mean salty talk, Boyd and Richerson's model suggests, the mean for the next generation will rise. Over generations, if this mechanism repeats itself, a slight difference between the salty dialect of fishermen and the more stolid dialect of the mainland population could cascade into a rigid linguistic difference (Boyd and Richerson 1985, 8–9, ch. 8).

Indirect bias has parallels with the phenomenon of "herding" analyzed by several economists, for example, in papers by Abhijit Banerjee (1992) and by Sushil Bikhchandani, David Hirshleifer, and Ivo Welch (1992). Banerjee (1992, 797–9) notes that people often "decide on what stores and restaurants to patronize or what schools to attend on the basis of how popular they seem to be." The key to Banerjee's model is that "paying heed to what everyone else is doing is rational because their decisions may reflect information they have and we do not. . . . But this suggests that the very act of trying to use the information contained in the decisions made by others makes each person's decision less responsive to her own information and hence less informative to others." In any sequential decision process, "the second person's decision to ignore her own information and join the herd therefore inflicts a negative externality on the rest of the population." This he calls the "herd externality." Extending the range of this model, Bikhchandani, Hirshleifer, and Welch theorize about "information cascades" that help explain not only volatile asset markets but fads, fashions, and voting landslides. Although the herding phenomenon (unlike the Tversky and Kahneman heuristics) is not a violation of the normative model, it does suggest that the suboptimal social outcomes are due to the considerable underweighting of one's own information relative to assumptions about the quality of other players' information. Or in Boyd and Richerson's formulation, where it is an evolutionary bias, the indicator (the number of people patronizing a restaurant) is used as a proxy for an underlying but hard-to-evaluate trait (a high-quality restaurant).

But herding, in the sense of losing information owing to sequencing, does not seem to be happening under the conditions I studied in the former Soviet Union. Consider this report (Giller and Shatskikh 1993) from Kazakhstan.

> The prices of apartments are rapidly falling in Almaty as well as in other cities of Kazakhstan, supply of apartments exceeds demand, every day there are hundreds of 3–5-ton containers labeled "to Russia" leaving the capital of Kazakhstan. In all "Russian-speaking" kitchens, without any exaggerations, conversations center on who has already left, who's settled where, who's selling apartments, how much he settled for, and so on.

This accords with what all of us in the field experienced in virtually every kitchen of Russian speakers in the non-Russian republics of the former Soviet Union.

The assumption in the herding models is that decisionmakers are aware only of the decisions of people who moved before them. With tight networks of people probing each others' intentions— those who have moved and those who have not— information is not being lost in the potential exit cascade from Kazakhstan. In fact, networks are so dense among the Russian-speaking populations in the republics that even the tipping game —which assumes that no actor knows anyone else's threshold—is suspect. Adding to the socially unstructured tipping game a small degree of social structure—people sharing information with people in their network—allows for coordination (without lost information) at far greater levels than the simple tipping game allows.[10] We have clear evidence of such gossiping networks— where thresholds are revealed—and at minimum this renders irrelevant the herd externalities that we see in volatile asset markets in analysis of culture shift.

Frequency-Dependent Bias   Adding social structure (and gossiping networks) to the picture leads us to a different evolutionary bias, one that Boyd and Richerson call "frequency-dependent bias." In this bias, naive individuals adopt the behaviors of the majority, even when such behaviors are known by personal experience to be ineffective. To the extent that people rely on it, they are disproportionately likely to acquire the more common variant in the population. (We can see that it deviates some from the normative model under certain conditions, for example, when most members of the society are playing "nice" strategies in an iterated prisoners' dilemma game. A rational maximizer would choose always to defect under such conditions, but a naive individual trying to copy the most frequent strategy as a proxy for evolutionary fitness would choose the nice strategy.) Conformist frequency-dependent bias has two effects:

> [F]irst, in a spatially varying environment, it can provide a simple general rule that improves the chance of acquiring the locally favored cultural variant, and second, it increases the amount of cultural variation among groups relative to

the amount of cultural variation within groups. This in turn can cause selection between groups to favor cultural variants which enhance the success of the group at the expense of the individual. (Boyd and Richerson 1985, 205–6)

The ex ante premise of my rendition of the tipping model is that people under conditions of threat and uncertainty are driven by a frequency-dependent bias. Or in other words, the tipping game is an appropriate model to analyze cultural shift under conditions of uncertainty because individuals condition their behavior on the frequency of each choice made by members of their social network. One can speculate that the explanatory power of the tipping game is a result of the fact that frequency-dependent choice evolved under conditions of uncertainty. In a sense, then, calculation within the tipping model is normative in the expected utility sense, but the tipping game is the appropriate metric for the study of culture shift under conditions of uncertainty owing to an evolutionary bias. An attractive aspect of reliance on evolutionary bias (as opposed to those in heuristic theory) is that if the strategy is an ESS—something Boyd and Richerson do not claim—we can account for why it has not disappeared with the arrival of a breed of hypercalculating mutants. Future work on frequency-dependent bias and its resistance to mutants therefore merits attention.

OPTIMAL HEDGING: A STRATEGY OBSERVED FROM THE FIELD

The real beauty of Selten's methodological dualism is in the discovery of rational strategies that would never have been seen if a tree were invented on an armchair and research involved calculations based on backward induction. Observing behavior sensitizes the researcher to branches that were ignored for purposes of simplification or never even considered. Those branches, observed in the wild, compel the dualist to respecify the game. In this section, I illustrate an example of theory-relevant clues popping up in the course of field work.

To be more specific: Field workers, if they are attentive to formal models, will undoubtedly discover paths of play that formal theorists, given their "small world" assumption, have never included in their game structures. Yet these paths may well be followed given some parameter values. For example, amid field work performed in 1987 in India, I first became aware of cultural hedging. A middle-class respondent in Bombay whose mother tongue was Marathi told me that he had one son who specialized in Hindi, another in German, and yet another in French; all, of course, spoke English as well. He made sure that all his daughters spoke Gujerati, since that language might help them in the local marriage market. I laughed at this differentiated story and then learned that it is repeated all over the country, because people cannot be sure of the returns for different linguistic investments (Laitin 1993a).

I found similar hedging strategies in my field notes concerning Russians in the near abroad. In Almaty, Volodiia is a Russian-speaking physicist who was quick to assume Kazakhstani citizenship. He protested against Dave's question about which citizenship he would choose, and responded, "Where's the question of choosing?" as if it were obvious that he and his wife were natives of Kazakhstan. Yet a year later he acknowledged to Dave and me that his willingness to stake his future with Kazakhstani citizenship was based partly on his assurance that should all hell break loose, Russia would accept all the ethnic Russians in the near abroad no matter what deadlines are currently set for committing to Russian citizenship. Furthermore, Volodiia has used his connections in the physics world to get his son a fellowship in Tomsk, where he will be pursuing an advanced degree in science and setting roots in Russia, where he never lived. His daughter became well educated in English and is a secretary for a foreign firm; earning far more than her father, she is now capable of emigrating to the West. Finally, Volodiia's mother was a descendent of an ethnic German, giving him a presumptive right to citizenship in the Federal Republic. He is careful to keep all those papers in order—and to at least maintain his weak knowledge of the German language—just in case life requires that he evacuate from the entire former Soviet world. In one sense, Volodiia "chose" to remain in Kazakhstan and to learn the language sufficiently for his professional standing; in another sense, with great uncertainty about the future, Volodiia has diversified his (family's) cultural portfolio.

To be sure, the strategy of hedging is not unknown in the economics field. The finance literature suggests that investors, in seeking to find the best portfolio for their needs, were once irrationally limited in their portfolios. That is to say, their portfolios were insufficiently hedged.[11] Under conditions of high risk and high variance in the projected yield of each asset, the literature now shows how it is rational to diversify one's portfolio far more than does the typical investor. Perhaps this can be extended to questions of cultural choice. In "unsettled times," do people insufficiently hedge their cultural bets? Unfortunately, there seems to be no psychological research on financial decisionmaking of this sort.[12] To apply diversification models to problems of everyday choice, the normative model would require covariance matrices reflecting expected values (and variances) of each asset, or else it would not be possible to assess whether subjects are rational diversifiers. Nonetheless, it is useful to know that diversification strategies do manifest themselves under conditions of uncertainty, on issues having to do with cultural investments.

Can I claim that my informants were rational cultural hedgers? Some empirical work in political economy claims that when it comes to diversifying fields, peasants are rational hedgers (Popkin 1979; Townsend 1993). Yet given the costs of traveling from one field to another, it is difficult indeed to specify an optimal hedging strategy. Similarly here: I can claim only that under conditions of uncertainty and high variance of subjective probabilities some hedging is rational, and that our informants did engage in cultural hedging. However, with no theory of optimal hedging or even a well-specified psychological heuristic that shows a bias against such hedging, neither the normative model nor heuristic theory points to a clear conclusion as to the rationality of this hedging.

Evolutionary theory suggests an alternative way to analyze hedging. Evolutionary biologists distinguish between two forms of polymorphic equilibria. A population state is monomorphic if every member uses the same strategy, and polymorphic if more than one strategy is present. Polymorphic states may be polymorphic for strategy in two ways. First, different members of the population may play different pure strategies; the proportion of players adhering to a given strategy is determined by the optimum percentage of each strategy, given the payoffs and the model for mixing among members, that determines the context in which a strategy is played. For example, with random mixing, each strategy encounters the others in proportion to the representation in the population. With positive assorting, each strategy plays more frequently against itself than expected with random mixing, and with negative assorting, a strategy plays against a different one more often than expected with random mixing. Second, all members of the population may play the same mixed or conditional strategies. In this case, despite the uniformity of the members, variations (that is, polymorphism) in strategy occur because of the context dependence and prior history of the players. Within evolutionary biology, a further distinction is made between genetic polymorphism and behavioral polymorphism. The second situation is behaviorally polymorphic but genetically monomorphic. It is also believed that all conditional or mixed strategies began as genetic polymorphisms for single strategies and evolved from that starting point by modifiers to conditional strategies. That is, a conditional strategy represents a more highly evolved state.

In the Schelling tipping game presented earlier, each of the two equilibria (when reached) is monomorphic, with all players playing the same strategy. But before an equilibrium is reached, all players are assumed to be playing pure strategies. Suppose, however, as in many evolutionary games, we assume a polymorphic state, in the sense of all players mixing optimally. Consider a state in which two-thirds of the Russians sent their children to Russian schools and one-third sent them to titular-medium schools. This state would have the same population distribution in the school system as a state in which Russians sent two-thirds of their children to Russian schools and one-third to titular-medium schools. The two populations would have the same mean fitness, but the individual variance in the pure strategy state would be higher. Genetic models solve for changes in population fitness—in this case, with the same mean fitness in two populations but with different variances. With such models, we should be able to determine whether hedging is a rational strategy in cultural evolution.

Evolutionary thinking allows for another modification of the tipping model Schelling-style. By distinguishing learning from selection, evolutionary theory suggests a way to model the Russian situation in the near abroad more realistically than I did earlier. These Russians are learning in their rather chaotic new environments the relative merits of investing in different languages, emigrating to Russia, and organizing for political rights as Russians within their republics—all of this without knowing which selection processes will be operating in the future. That is, they are uncertain as to what the principal axis of coordination will be once some degree of stability returns to the environment. Thus, short-term learning and longer-term selection ought to be separated yet modeled interactively. Evolutionary models that build in polymorphic strategies and distinguish learning from selection hold high promise for the study of cultural shift.

CONCLUSION

In *Identity in Formation* (1998), I relied on a range of data sets to code for expected economic returns, and ingroup and outgroup status, in order to account for variations on a dimension I called "propensity for assimilation." The additive function that I patched together—with a little curve fitting—helped account for the values on the dependent variable for the four countries I studied. In this sense, an expected utility framework was quite useful in assessing cultural shifts in the tumultuous world of post-Soviet politics. The strategic calculus of cultural assimilation that I identified strongly suggests that a special model of ideologically driven behavior for "unsettled times," as postulated by Ann Swidler (1986), is unnecessary.

This essay takes the next logical step. Post-Soviet diasporas may well have calculated strategically, but they might still have deviated from the normative expected utility model. From the reexamination of my field notes induced by these doubts concerning the degree to which the calculations of my informants were in accord with the normative model, and reflecting on Selten's evolutionary models, two of the general points I made at the outset of this chapter can be elaborated.

First, game-theoretic models need no longer rest on unrealistic assumptions about human capacities to calculate. In reviewing my field data, in which people who were making cultural decisions under conditions of uncertainty, I found many examples of reliance on heuristics, with the implication that these heuristics violated the normative model of expected utility. But under real-world conditions, these deviations from the normative model as identified in heuristic theory did not loom all that large. Therefore, from observations in the field, the everyday decisionmaker of the experimental Selten may not make decisions that deviate very greatly from those of the godlike calculator of the formal Selten.[13] To the extent that a bias is detected, it may more usefully be accounted for as due not to psychological deviations from expected utility thinking, but as due to an evolutionary bias that may meet the criterion of an ESS. An evolutionary bias, unlike those in heuristic theory, does not lead to the question any game theorist would ask: Why and how does it persist over time? Thus, evolutionary theory, as Selten has suggested, allows formal theorists to drop unrealistic assumptions about rationality without giving up analyses that predict behavior based on "best responses" to strategic situations.

Second, this essay alters one element of Selten's dualism, at least for the set of problems involving cultural shift. It argues that field work should remain a vital complement to formal theory. To rely only on experimental work entails the cost, long recognized by psychologists working in the Brunswikian tradition, of ignoring information from "natural task environments" (Goldstein and Hogarth 1997, 8).[14] Making availability endogenous, as I suggested was necessary, is an insight based on field work that weakens the power of the availability deviations identified in the laboratory.

Perhaps a more significant contribution of field work is in its ability to identify strategies with Nash qualities that were missed in purely formal renditions of games. The hedging of cultural identities appears to be strategically rational, but it was not part of the choice set in the tipping model. Rather than throw away data that do not fit formal models, it is best to reconfigure models based on field observations, since this will enrich our understanding of the social world. The reconfigured models will, of course, have an initial appearance of "curve fitting," as in the description of the results of cultural hedging as an evolutionarily advanced polymorphic strategy. But the next methodological step is to test the observable implications of the enriched model on data that did not inform the reconfiguration.

A final role for field work, as Hammerstein and Selten (1994) suggest, is to give guidance to simulation, which can be a vital tool for the testing and elaboration of models. The great weakness of the substantive discussion in this essay is the impressionistic evaluation of the data, without any quantitative support. In *Identity in Formation*, through surveys and experiments, I was able to amass quantitative data on elements of the utility function concerning assimilation. But on the calculations discussed here, it may be far more difficult to accrue reliable data from surveys. A clear alternative is to develop models of cultural shift similar to the cellular automata games developed by Axelrod (1997). In Axelrod's simulations, the rules for cultural shift were quite primitive, though exceedingly interesting. A future task would be to encode into the algorithms some of the calculations that field workers have observed in real cases of culture shift. Although Axelrod's cells are responsive to frequency-dependent factors, it would be exciting, for example, to see the long-run implications of cells that hedge their cultural bets.

A principal purpose of this essay is to suggest that Selten's methodological dualism, not yet fully accepted in political science, provides an invitation for comparativists to inaugurate a new sort of research program connecting formal theory with empirical data. Selten's work in evolution (including his specification of an ESS) suggests that the cognitive requirements in standard economic theory can be greatly relaxed once we think in terms of intergenerational adaptation. Although Selten, for his purposes, has relied more heavily on experimental data for the second element of his dualism, I have suggested that for many of the problems associated with research in comparative politics, the collection of ethnographic data—even if they are harder to interpret—is more appropriate. By introducing game-theoretic thinking into a new realm (that of culture), linking game theory to field observations, and appealing to the notion of evolutionarily stable strategies (thereby relaxing the need for a computational hyperrationality among one's subjects), I hope to have shown the potential of Selten's methodological dualism for future research in comparative politics.

This essay was presented at faculty seminars at the Departments of Political Science at the University of Michigan (November 21, 1996), Columbia University (December 2, 1996), Yale University (December 3, 1996), McGill University (January 10, 1997), New York University (January 21, 1997), and Princeton University (April 7, 1997), and at the Nobelist panel held at the Russell Sage Foundation (November 13, 1997). I am grateful to my hosts and to the seminar participants who gave me many ideas for improvement. I owe special thanks to James Fearon, Margaret Levi, Jonathan Bendor, Michael Wade, James Alt, and Elinor Ostrom for their suggestions.

NOTES

1. The term "near abroad" is a euphemism in Russian official discourse. It refers to the former union republics of the Soviet Union and implies that Russian policy toward those now-independent states is not "domestic" but also not quite "foreign."

2. Supported by NSF Grant POLS/SES 92125768, I put together an ethnographic research team with a coordinated data collection routine. I did the field research in northeast Estonia; Vello Pettai conducted the research in western Estonia and in Latvia; Dominique Arel did the field work in eastern Ukraine; and Bhavna Dave worked in southern Kazakhstan. As principal investigator, I had full access to the field notes of my collaborators. A full description of our research methods is available in a special issue of *Post-Soviet Affairs* 12, no. 1 (January–March 1996).

3. Indeed, Selten, an activist in the Esperanto Society, has with Jonathan Pool modeled the probability of a cascade toward an auxiliary language (such as Esperanto) as a language of intergroup communication. Science, however, trumped ideology: Despite the model's assumption of low relative learning costs of the auxiliary language, backward induction worked in favor of learning a natural language (Selten and Pool 1991).

4. This is a principal theme in Toivo Raun (1987, 224). He cites the nineteenth-century poem of Kristjan Jaak Peterson ("May not the language of this land/On winds of song and/Rising to the heavens/Seek eternity?") to show how commitment to a Finno-Ugric identity could overcome historically powerful Germanic and Russian efforts to stamp out an autonomous Estonian identity.

5. Here I am relying on the post-Savage synthesis of Harsanyi (1977, 22–25, 41, 47).

6. Simon's (1986) critique is less cogent today, ten years later, given that so much work is now being done at the center of game theory in which models do not stipulate all possible future states of the world ex ante.

7. Violating the normative principle of representativeness, however, Russian speakers among our informants never took the statistical frequency of success for a set of nationalizing countries throughout the world as a benchmark for the likely success of the national language program in the republic in which they were living.

8. I develop the notion of the "private subversion of a public good" in Laitin (1993b, 233).

9. These points summarize chapter 1 of Samuelson (1997), which represents the fullest incorporation of evolutionary models into standard economic theory.

10. For a development of this point, see Chwe (1998).

11. For a recent discussion of hedging theory in macroeconomics, see Culp and Miller (1995).

12. This is a preliminary assessment by Richard Thaler (personal communication, November 8, 1996), a leading researcher on psychological tests of the normative model.

13. Boyd and Richerson (1985, 93) report on the work of McNamara and Houston (1980) on "optimal foraging theory," which demonstrates that animals learning to forage in unpredictable environments rely on the representativeness heuristic, leading to bad choices in the laboratory but good ones in the field.

14. Goldstein and Hogarth (1997) are reviewing Brunswik (1956). For another source questioning the value of the laboratory in the examination of rationality, see Nisbett and Ross (1980).

REFERENCES

Axelrod, Robert. 1997. "The Dissemination of Culture: A Model with Local Convergence and Global Polarization." *Journal of Conflict Resolution* 41 (2): 203–26.

Banerjee, Abhijit V. 1992. "A Simple Model of Herd Behavior." *Quarterly Journal of Economics* 107 (3): 797–817.

Bates, Robert, Rui J. P. de Figueiredo Jr., and Barry Weingast. 1998. "The Politics of Interpretation: Rationality, Culture, and Transition." *Politics and Society* 26 (4): 603–42.

Berlin, Isaiah. 1972. "Bent Twig: A Note on Nationalism." *Foreign Affairs* 51 (October): 11–30.

Bikhchandani, Sushil, David Hirshleifer, and Ivo Welch. 1992. "A Theory of Fads, Fashion, Custom, and Cultural Change as Informational Cascades." *Journal of Political Economy* 100 (5): 992–1026.

Boyd, Robert, and Peter J. Richerson. 1985. *Culture and the Evolutionary Process.* Chicago: University of Chicago Press.

Brunswik, E. 1956. *Perception and the Representative Design of Psychological Experiments.* 2nd ed. Berkeley: University of California Press.

Chwe, Michael Suk-Young. 1998. "Structure and Strategy in Collective Action: Communication and Coordination in Social Networks." *Rationality and Society* 10 (1): 47–75.

Culp, Christopher, and Merton Miller. 1995. "Hedging in the Theory of Corporate Finance: A Reply to Our Critics." *Continental Bank Journal of Applied Corporate Finance* 8 (1): 121–27.

Deutsch, Karl. 1954. *Nationalism and Social Communication.* Cambridge, Mass.: MIT Press.

Dokuchaeva, A. 1993. "O iazyke: Ot emotsii-k zdravomu smyslu." *Mysl'* 5: 38–43.

Friedman, David. 1977. "A Theory of the Size and Shape of Nations." *Journal of Political Economy* 85: 59–77.

Geertz, Clifford. 1980. *Negara.* Princeton, N.J.: Princeton University Press.

Giller, Boris, and Viktor Shatskikh. 1993. "Opredelenie berega: Russkoiazychnyie v Kazakhstane." *Karavan*, December 12, 1–3.

Gizerenzer, Gerd. 1991. "How to Make Cognitive Illusions Disappear: Beyond 'Heuristics and Biases.'" *European Review of Social Psychology* 2: 83–115.

Goldstein, William M., and Robin Hogarth. 1997. "Judgment and Decision Research: Some Historical Context." In *Research on Judgment and Decision Making*, edited by William M. Goldstein and Robin M. Hogarth (Cambridge: Cambridge University Press), 3–65.

Hammerstein, Peter, and Reinhard Selten. 1994. "Game Theory and Evolutionary Biology." In *Handbook of Game Theory*, vol. 2, edited by Robert J. Aumann and Sergiu Hart (Amsterdam: Elsevier), 929–93.

Harsanyi, John. 1977. *Rational Behavior and Bargaining Equilibrium in Games and Social Situations.* Cambridge: Cambridge University Press.

Kahneman, Daniel, and Amos Tversky. 1979. "Prospect Theory: An Analysis of Decision Under Risk." *Econometrica* 47: 263–91.

———. 1982. "On the Study of Statistical Intuitions." In *Judgment Under Uncertainty: Heuristics and Biases*, edited by Daniel Kahneman, Paul Slovic, and Amos Tversky (Cambridge: Cambridge University Press), 493–508.

Kuran, Timur. 1991. "Now out of Never: The Role of Surprise in the East European Revolution of 1989." *World Politics* 44 (1): 7–48.

Labov, William, 1972. *Sociolinguistic Patterns.* Philadelphia: University of Pennsylvania Press.

Laitin, David. 1993a. "Migration and Language Shift in Urban India." *International Journal of the Sociology of Language* 103: 57–72.

———. 1993b. "The Game Theory of Language Regimes." *International Political Science Review* 14 (3): 227–39.

———. 1998. *Identity in Formation: The Russian-Speaking Populations in the Near Abroad.* Ithaca, N.Y.: Cornell University Press.

Lohmann, Susan. 1994. "Dynamics of Informational Cascades." *World Politics* 47 (1): 42–101.

McNamara J., and A. Houston. 1980. "The Application of Statistical Decision Theory to Animal Behavior." *Journal of Theoretical Biology* 85: 673–90.

Maynard Smith, John. 1982. *Evolution and the Theory of Games.* Cambridge: Cambridge University Press.

Nisbett, Richard, and Lee Ross. 1980. *Human Inference: Strategies and Shortcomings of Social Judgment.* Englewood Cliffs, N.J.: Prentice-Hall.

Ostrom, Elinor. 1998. "A Behavioral Approach to the Rational-Choice Theory of Collective Action." *American Political Science Review* 92 (1): 1–22.

Petersen, Roger. 1989. "Rationality, Ethnicity, and Military Enlistment." *Social Science Information* 28 (3): 563–98.

Popkin, Samuel. 1979. *The Rational Peasant.* Berkeley: University of California Press.

Raun, Toivo. 1987. *Estonia and the Estonians.* Stanford, Calif.: Hoover Institution Press.

Samuelson, Larry. 1997. *Evolutionary Games and Equilibrium Selection.* Cambridge, Mass.: MIT Press.

Savage, Leonard J. 1954. *Foundations of Statistics.* New York: Wiley.

Schelling, Thomas. 1960. *The Strategy of Conflict.* Cambridge, Mass.: Harvard University Press.

———. 1978. *Micromotives and Macrobehavior.* New York: Norton.

Selten, Reinhard. 1998. "Features of Experimentally Observed Bounded Rationality." *European Economic Review* 42 (3–5): 413–36.

Selten, Reinhard, and Axel Ockenfels. 1998. "An Experimental Solidarity Game." *Journal of Economic Behavior and Organization* 34 (4): 517–39.

Selten, Reinhard, and Jonathan Pool. 1991. "The Distribution of Foreign Language Skills as a Game Equilibrium." In *Game Equilibrium Models IV*, edited by Reinhard Selten (Berlin: Springer-Verlag), 64–87.

Simon, Herbert A. 1957. *Models of Man.* New York: Wiley.

———. 1986. "Rationality in Psychology and Economics." *Journal of Business* 59 (4, pt. 2): S209–S224.

Swidler, Ann. 1986. "Culture in Action: Symbols and Strategies." *American Sociological Review* 51 (April): 273–86.

Taylor, Shelley E. 1982. "The Availability Bias in Social Perception and Interaction." In *Judgment Under Uncertainty: Heuristics and Biases,* edited by Daniel Kahneman, Paul Slovic, and Amos Tversky (Cambridge: Cambridge University Press), 190–208.

Townsend, Robert. 1993. *The Medieval Village Economy.* Princeton, N.J.: Princeton University Press.

Tversky, Amos, and Daniel Kahneman. 1982. "Judgment Under Uncertainty: Heuristics and Biases." In *Judgment Under Uncertainty: Heuristics and Biases,* edited by Daniel Kahneman, Paul Slovic, and Amos Tversky (Cambridge: Cambridge University Press), 3–20.

von Neumann, John, and Oskar Morgenstern. 1944. *Theory of Games and Economic Behavior.* Princeton, N.J.: Princeton University Press.

RESPONSE TO SHEPSLE AND LAITIN

Reinhard Selten

It is a great pleasure for me to see my work appreciated by an outstanding political scientist. There is much room for fruitful applications of game theory in political science. Kenneth Shepsle writes about my contribution to the noncooperative revolution in game theory. He also comments on my experimental research and my work on bounded rationality and then finds a contrast between the "early" Selten associated with hyperrational game-theoretic concepts like trembling hand perfection and the "later" Selten who seems to be out to destroy what he helped to build up. These are not exactly Ken's words. He knows that my relationship to the problem of rationality is more complex than that.

Maybe not for his benefit, but for that of others who have read his paper and are less familiar with my work, let me explain my epistemological position on methodological dualism. In my view, there is a fundamental difference between normative and descriptive decision and game theory. Normative decision and game theory has the aim of exploring full rationality and its consequences. Full rationality is an ideal about the adequacy and coherence of decisionmaking. It is not meant to be descriptive of how human beings actually behave, but rather of what they think about the structure of the behavior of an idealized decisionmaker without any cognitive limitations. This idealized decisionmaker is a mythical hero, whom we may call "fully rational man." Real people have limited powers of logical deduction and computation, but fully rational man has instant access to everything that needs to be logically deduced or computed for adequate and coherent decisionmaking.

Bounded rationality understood in the tradition of Herbert A. Simon as the rationality exhibited by real people is very different from full rationality. It is not just optimization under constraints on memory size or some other cheaper version of full rationality. It is not something that can be thought up in the armchair. It must be explored empirically. Bounded rationality is a descriptive concept.

Why should we be interested in full rationality at all? One may think that it is completely useless to indulge in the sophistries of normative game theory. This is not what I want to say. I think that normative decision and game theory is an important field of study. It is by no means obvious what ideal rationality should be. There are conflicting tendencies in the thinking about this, and a long process of deep analysis and intense discussion is needed to arrive at a balanced view of ideal rationality. In the course of this process, mankind learns something valuable about itself.

Empirical arguments are irrelevant for normative decision and game theory. What counts is the appeal to underlying tendencies in the thinking about what fully rational man is like. The situation is similar to theology, which is concerned about

303

what we should think about God. The questions about God asked by theology are important, simply because they seek to clarify an idea of great importance for mankind regardless of whether God exists or not. In view of the analogy to theology, the study of fully rational man may be called "rationology."

Descriptive decision and game theory is concerned with what people really do. Only empirical arguments are important here. Of course, descriptive theories also involve some idealization. A balance must be struck between precision, accuracy, and scope of applicability, on the one hand, and simplicity, on the other hand. However, it is not important what we think about what should be done by a fully rational decisionmaker in the situations under consideration.

Arguments valid for normative theory are irrelevant for descriptive theory, and vice versa. This is the essence of methodological dualism. However, I do not want to say that there is no relationship between normative and descriptive theory. In sufficiently simple decision situations, normative theory may correctly predict experimentally observed behavior. Moreover, predictions provided by normative decision and game theory are of great heuristic value as benchmarks for experimental research. If one wants to explore behavior in situations for which an adequate descriptive theory has not yet been developed, it is useful to look at predictions derived from normative theory, even if one can be pretty sure that they will be off the mark. The way in which behavior deviates from normative predictions can provide insight that leads to better descriptive theory.

There is another way in which normative theory may prepare the way to descriptive theory. In many situations, evolution or learning may result in a tendency toward optimization. This is the reason why noncooperative game theory became important in evolutionary biology. In this field, game equilibrium is understood as the result of a process of natural selection. Rationality does not even enter the picture. Nevertheless, structural knowledge that has its origin in normative game theory turns out to be useful. We may talk of descriptive relevance by reinterpretation.

Processes of evolution and learning have become fashionable in game theory and its applications to economics. This is partially due to the success of noncooperative game theory in biology, but it is also due to the fact that the inadequacy of the strong rationality assumptions of neoclassical economics has become more and more clear. However, whereas evolutionary game theory in biology is always under a strong pressure to establish a close connection between theoretical analysis and phenomena observed in nature, the relationship to empirical observations is much weaker in evolutionary mathematical modeling of economic behavior. It is not yet sufficiently well understood that theoretical economic research in this area needs an empirical background. I hope that in the future the research community will more firmly insist on the requirement that assumptions about human behavior are justified by experimental findings or other empirical evidence rather than by the mere analytical convenience and fruitfulness of proving theorems.

Experimental research indicates that in some repeated games with incomplete information game equilibrium has descriptive relevance by reinterpretation. Curiously enough, it is not the equilibrium of the game with incomplete information that is descriptively relevant, but that of an associated game with complete information. Thus, a repeated oligopoly game in which each competitor knows only its own cost function may converge to the equilibrium of the game with complete information that would be played if the demand function and all cost functions were known to everybody.

Just before I left Germany to give a talk in Boston and to participate in this meeting, I had to write a report on a theoretical and experimental Ph.D. thesis by a student of mine, Karim Sadrieh (1998), in which he explores the "alternating double auction." This version of the double auction is similar to others played in computerized laboratories, but unlike most of them, it has a clear sequential structure, such that its rules, completed by beliefs about costs and the redemption values of others, define a game with incomplete information. In the alternating double auction, too, behavior tends to converge to competitive equilibrium. Karim Sadrieh investigated the associated game with complete information. In spite of the complexity of this game, he succeeded in showing that a class of subgame perfect equilibria delineated by some additional plausible selection criteria predicts prices at a competitive equilibrium, or very near to it. In my view, this result is an important contribution to the descriptive theory of the double auction.

As we have seen, normative game theory, applied in an oblique way, is sometimes very useful for descriptive purposes. It may also happen that experimental research with a descriptive aim helps to achieve progress in normative theory. Let me tell you a story about my own scientific development that illustrates this point.

After I received my master's degree in mathematics, I began to do research on economics under the supervision of the economic theorist Heinz Sauermann. He encouraged my idea to perform oligopoly experiments, and he himself became involved in it. My first published paper, written together with him, had the title "Ein Oligopolexperiment" (1959) (An oligopoly experiment). This was not my first scientific work, since before that I had written a master's thesis on a topic in cooperative game theory. This research also has been published, but somewhat later.

In the late 1950s and early 1960s much of my scientific work was concentrated on oligopoly experiments. I looked at some dynamic oligopoly situations that seemed to be interesting as simplified models of economic reality, for which, however, a theoretical solution was not known. In particular, my colleague Reinhard Tietz and I intensively explored one of these dynamic games, an oligopoly model with price variation, investment, and demand inertia.

In our little group of young experimental economists, we sometimes talked about the lack of a theoretical solution for this oligopoly game. Eventually I decided to attack the problem with a highly simplified model. I cut out all indivisibilities, the difference between the interest rates for debts and positive accounts, and sunk costs of investment. I succeeded in finding an equilibrium of the dynamic game by backward induction, but my game-theoretic training very soon made me aware of the fact that the game had many other equilibria. Nevertheless, the one I had found by backward induction seemed to be the most natural one. Thinking about the reasons for this intuition, I came up with the concept of subgame perfectness (Selten 1965).

My early oligopoly experiments are not much known internationally, since this work was almost exclusively published in German. At that time it was neither customary nor good for the career of a young German economist to publish in English. This is very different nowadays. My theoretical paper on the dynamic oligopoly model with demand inertia was written in German too. Nevertheless, at least its title became very well known eventually.

The aim of my oligopoly experiments was descriptive from the outset, even if in the beginning I probably had not yet completely shed the eggshells of naive rationalism. A naive rationalist is somebody who thinks that what is real is rational and what is rational is real, as Hegel said. Of course, here the word *rational* must be understood in the sense of modern Bayesian decision and game theory, not in the sense of Hegel.

A naive rationalist thinks that behavior can be deduced from principles of rationality. According to him, there is no need for experiments wherever a rationalistic deduction is available. However, when I began to do experiments, I was inspired by the experimental investigation of characteristic function games by G. Kalish, J. W. Milnor, J. F. Nash and E. D. Nering (1954). The meaning of rationality was much disputed in cooperative game theory, and many different solution concepts competed for attention. The idea suggested itself that experiments might help to find which was the right one. The situation of oligopoly theory was a similar one.

It was somewhat surprising to me that the experiments described in the paper with Sauermann to some extent supported Cournot's theory but no other oligopoly theory. At that time Cournot's theory was not very popular. It was attacked as a "double idiocy." The oligopolists should become aware of the fact that the total supply of the other oligopolists does not stay constant, if everybody's beliefs are as described by Cournot. However, in our experiments this kind of behavior seemed to be the most rational one observed.

I do not know exactly when I read the two pioneering papers by Herbert Simon on bounded rationality in his book *Models of Man* (1957), but I remember that I was immediately convinced by his arguments. I tried to find principles of bounded rationality in the results of my experiments, and I think that I succeeded to some extent. Thus, in my second paper on oligopoly experiments, I described the qualitative reasoning by subject groups representing firms with the help of a graph structure that I called a "causal diagram." By the way, these graph structures have a connection to political science, since they are similar to those introduced later by Robert Axelrod in his book *Structures of Decision* (1976) under the name "cognitive maps."

In 1962 Heinz Sauermann and I published the paper "Anspruchsanpassungstheorie der Unternehmung" (Aspiration adaptation theory of the firm). This was a heroic attempt to create an integrated picture of boundedly rational behavior. The theory has its deficiencies, but it seems to me that even today, after thirty-five years, it is not without interest.

The more experiments I made, the more cautious I became in my theorizing on bounded rationality. I learned to be suspicious of bold ideas of sweeping generality. Today I aim at descriptive theories of limited scope that fit experimental data. I made the remarks on my early work in order to argue against the idea that I joined the forces of behavioral economics only late in my life. In fact, before I saw the necessity of a noncooperative reorientation of game theory, I already was involved in two other revolutions—the introduction of experimental methods to economics, and the bounded rationality movement initiated by Simon.

I would also like to make a remark on my attempts to make some direct contributions to political science. In the late 1960s I had the opportunity to work with a group of famous game theorists and mathematical economists on a research project financed by the Arms Control and Disarmament Agency. At this time I developed a strong interest in the theory of international relations.

My first contribution in this area took its point of departure from a model of nuclear deterrence proposed by Herbert Scarf. Together with Reinhard Tietz (Selten and Tietz 1972), I developed a theory of "security equilibria" for a cooperative game structure for which we introduced the name "irreversible game." This structure combines elements of a characteristic function game and an extensive game with perfect information. From one position a new one may be reached by the joint action of a coalition, but no coalition can be sure to be the one to act first. A security equilibrium assigns a security level for each player to every position. The security level is the maximum that can be guaranteed by the player's behavior under the condition that nobody else does anything that lowers his or her security level.

Later I collaborated with Amos Perlmutter, who is an area specialist for the Middle East. We tried to apply game theory to the conflicts in this area. At first I thought of constructing a game model with nation-states as players, in the spirit of Hans Morgentau. In this model, it would be the aim of each player to maximize its power. However, I soon found out that Amos Perlmutter had a completely different way of thinking about international relations in the Middle East. Nation-states do not have an abstract aim of maximizing power but are motivated by historically evolved goals and fears deeply rooted in the thinking of those with influence on foreign policy. Thus, it may be felt to be of utmost importance to regain a nearly valueless piece of land while there is no interest in acquiring a much richer piece of territory that could be conquered easily without any serious international repercussions.

On the basis of this picture of international relations, we developed a method of constructing simple game models called "scenario bundles" on the basis of expert judgments. In 1976 funding by the Volkswagen Foundation provided us with the opportunity to apply this "scenario bundle method" at a small conference of area specialists. The subject matter was the situation in the Persian Gulf. Unfortunately, our experts reached the consensus that a revolution in Iran was highly improbable. Therefore, we did not construct a scenario bundle with this initial event as its starting point, and we missed the most important political development in the next few years. This is maybe one of the reasons the results of the conference were never formally published. However, my systematic explanation of the method will be included in one of two volumes of collected papers of mine to be published next year (Selten 1999).

In the 1980s Peter Bernholz, an economist who has written a book on power relations between nation-states, asked me to join him in teaching a course on this subject in the framework of the Austrian College, which regularly organizes adult education summer courses at Alpach. It was my primary task to supply some background in game theory, but I felt that I should do something more; therefore I developed a parlor game for the illustration of the balance of power theory. With my analysis of a simplified version of this game I aimed at a game-theoretically precise version of the balance of power theory (Selten 1991).

It is maybe not appropriate to say more about my feeble attempts to qualify as a political scientist, but I thought that the occasion requires that I not remain silent about my substantive interests in the field. I would like to be seen as somebody who is genuinely interested in the subject matter, not only in aspects of formal analysis and behavioral foundations.

I must beg your pardon for these very personal and maybe somewhat immodest remarks about my own work. It is hard to avoid the impression of advertising in a curious mixture of methodological statements and autobiographical reminiscences. In fact, I freely admit that I yielded to the urge to propagandize the experimental method and its use for the construction of a theory of boundedly rational economic and political behavior.

REFERENCES

Axelrod, Robert. 1976. *Structure of Decision: The Cognitive Maps of Political Elite.* Princeton, N.J.: Princeton University Press.

Kalish, G., J. W. Milnor, J. F. Nash, and E. D. Nering. 1954. "Some Experimental n-Person Games." In *Decision Processes*, edited by R. M. Thrall, C. H. Coombs, and R. L. Davis (eds.) (New York: Wiley).

Sadrieh, Abdolkarim. 1998. *The Alternating Double Auction Market—A Game Theorotetic and Experimental Investigation.* Lecture notes in Economics and Mathematical Systems, no. 466. New York: Springer-Verlag.

Sauermann, Heinz, and Reinhard Selten. 1959. "Ein Oligopolexperiment." *Zeitschrift für die gesamte Staatswissenschaft* 118: 577–97.

———. 1962. "Anspruchsanpassungtheorie der Unternehmung." (Aspiration adaptation theory of the firm). *Zeitschrift für die gesamte Staatswissenschaft* 118:577–97.

Selten, Reinhard. 1965. "Spieltheoretische Behandlung eines Oligopolmodells mit Nachfrage-tragheit." *Zeitschrift für die gesamte Staatswissenschaft* 121: 301–24, 667–89.

———. 1976a. "Investitionsverhalten im Oligopolexperiment." In *Beiträge zur experimentellen Wirtschaftsforschung*, edited by H. Sauermann (Tübingen, Germany: J. C. B. Mohr [Paul Siebeck]), 103–35.

———. 1976b. "Ein Oligopolexperiment mit Preisvariation und Investition." In *Beiträge zur experimentellen Wirtschaftsforschung*, edited by H. Sauermann (Tübingen, Germany: J. C. B. Mohr [Paul Siebeck]), 103–35.

———. 1991. "Balance of Power in a Parlor Game." In *Game Equilibrium Models IV*, edited by R. Selten. New York: Springer-Verlag.

———. 1999. Game Theory and Economic Behavior: Selected Essays. Chaltenham, U. K.: Edward Elgar.

Selten, Reinhard, and Reihard Tietz. 1972a. "Security Equilibria." In *The Future of the International Strategic System*, edited by Richard Rosencrance (London: Chandler Publishing), 103–22.

———. 1972b. "A Formal Theory of Security Equilibria." In *The Future of the International Strategic System*, edited by Richard Rosencrance (London: Chandler Publishing), 185–202.

Simon, Herbert. 1957. *Models of Man.* New York: Wiley & Sons.

Tietz, Reinhard. 1967. "Simulation eingeschränkt rationaler Investitionsstrategien in einer dynamischen Oligopolsituation." In *Beiträge zur experimentellen Wirtschaftsforschung*, edited by H. Sauermann, (Tübingen, Germany: J. C. B. Mohr [Paul Siebeck]), 169–225.

Chapter 7

DISCUSSION OF POLITICAL SCIENCE AND ECONOMICS: THREE RESEARCH PROGRAMS IN CONSTITUTIONAL POLITICAL ECONOMY

James M. Buchanan

I do not propose to follow the instructions implied in the announced title for this panel session. I shall not make what would surely be an arrogant effort to tell you what I think about political science, either as an academic discipline or as a continuing source of explanation of the institutions of modern politics that we observe. I shall, instead, use this occasion to summarize three separate research programs that have commanded some of my attention and effort, in varying degrees, over the half-decade of the mid-1990s: generality as a constitutional constraint, constitutional geometry, and federalism and communitarianism.

Each of these programs could be classified under the inclusive rubric "political science," or more narrowly, "constitutional political economy," or perhaps even "political philosophy." As you know, I have never paid much heed to disciplinary boundaries. My purpose is to stimulate your potential interest in these programs, both in the narrow sense of encouraging you to examine some of my analyses and in the wider sense of challenging you to examine more fundamentally the existing structures of political order.

I hope that my summaries of these programs will provide at least some flavor of an economist's approach to political subject matter.

GENERALITY AS A CONSTITUTIONAL CONSTRAINT

In early 1998 Cambridge University Press published a book, which I have written jointly with Roger Congleton, titled *Politics by Principle, Not Interest: Toward Non-discriminatory Democracy*. In summary, this book extends the generality principle or norm to democratic politics from its more familiar application in law and legal structures.

In *The Calculus of Consent*, which I wrote jointly with Gordon Tullock and published in 1962, we challenged the dominant normative status of majority rule in both academic and public attitudes. That book was strongly influenced by Knut Wicksell (1896), who had suggested that more inclusive decision rules might ensure greater efficiency in collective action. Moving the Wicksellian vision to the constitutional level, we suggested that, for some categories of collective action, supramajorities might be required for implementation.

Over the several decades since the publication of that book, I have come to realize that the association between "democracy" and "majority rule," in a positive evaluative sense, is much more deeply embedded in public and scientific attitudes than I might have imagined to be possible. This realization has forced me to acknowledge, perhaps reluctantly, that if constitutional constraints are to be imposed on political processes, these must be applied to the choice set itself rather than directly to the decision rule.

In *Politics by Principle, Not Interest*, Congleton and I examine the effects of applying a generality constraint on the set of constitutionally permissible political outcomes. This constraint requires that political action, when taken, be general rather than discriminatory in applicability, as among persons and groups within the polity. In a quite abstract representation, we may think of political space as n-dimensional, with the collectively imposed impact on each person being a single dimension. The generality constraint then requires that all feasible solutions lie along the n-dimensional diagonal through n-space. Majority voting may be retained as the means of selecting among the subset of feasible or permissible solutions on the diagonal, but all positions off the diagonal are ruled out of bounds, because each such position would embody differential or discriminatory treatment of persons by the collectivity.

The most familiar defense of generality is grounded in precepts of fairness or equity. But this defense, perhaps dominant in application to the rule of law, is not at all central to our argument. Our emphasis, instead, is on the *political efficiency* of such a constraint. The logic is straightforward. If discriminatory treatment of persons and groups is constitutionally impermissible, incentives for investment of effort toward securing differentially favorable treatment or avoiding differentially unfavorable treatment are removed. Majoritarian rent-seeking, as we observe it, would very substantially disappear. And prospects for majoritarian cycling would be eliminated under many settings.

As with other analytical constructions, it is much easier to discuss the generality constraint in application to stylized models than it is to be specific in defining just what generality would mean in practical circumstances. It is always easier to use the generality principle as a criterion for evaluating specific collective actions than it is to define precisely the set of actions that would qualify as meeting some ideal. Nonetheless, there are several applications with more or less direct policy relevance.

The construction provides a normative analytical defense for general taxation that, under one interpretation, becomes flat-rate or proportional taxation of incomes. And on the payments or transfer side of the account, the implication is that transfers should take the form of equal-per-head demogrants. But perhaps the argument against collective fiscal actions that introduce or expand discrimination in treatment is more important. The argument strongly condemns means testing or targeting as ways to rescue general or quasi-general welfare-transfer programs in fiscal crises.

As applied to politicized efforts to interfere in markets through such instruments as tariffs, subsidies, or quotas, the implication is that, if one industry is protected, the same treatment must be extended over all industries. Such a constraint, if enforced, would, of course, remove much of the support for interferences in the first place.

The analysis does not address the question of how much government should do. The normative argument is limited to the proposition that, whatever government does, it should be constitutionally required to do it generally in a nondiscriminatory fashion.

CONSTITUTIONAL GEOMETRY

A second research program, which we call constitutional geometry, is in a much more preliminary or formative stage than the generality program. It is quite distinct in several respects from the first program, although in one sense it is a direct follow-on. This inquiry, which I am now undertaking with Yong Yoon, is more positive, more inclusive, more exploratory, and more formal than the generality program. We are, again, examining the effects of imposing constitutional constraints on the set of admissible political outcomes rather than on the rules through which the collectivity selects among the outcomes. But we extend the analysis to possible constraints different from those dictated by the generality principle. Although our central focus remains on the predicted operation of majority rule within defined constraints, we also examine the results under alternative rules.

The stylized constructions are intrinsically fascinating, and the central interpretation of constitutional rules as reducing the dimensionality of the collective choice space leads directly to the spatial metaphor, as introduced by the use of "geometry" in our title. If constitutionalism is about boundaries or limits on political action, the appropriate mathematics is surely geometry, which originated in ancient Egypt through efforts to draw new boundaries on flooded lands. As noted, work in this research program remains incomplete, but we have been able to transfer and translate some constructions from both game theory and Paretian welfare economics; these constructions allow us to classify subsets of positions attainable under alternative decision rules and alternative constraints.

One important element in this research program, and one that I have developed in a preliminary version (Buchanan 1995), is perhaps more conventional in orthodox political science than it has been in the social choice-public choice literature. I refer here to the necessary interdependence between the decision rule itself and the alternatives that are to be presented for choice under that rule. Early social-choice and public-choice models more or less presumed that the alternatives among which choices are to be made exist exogenously and are simply presented to the choosing body, as if by some external agent. There was a failure to recognize the simple point that alternatives themselves must emerge from somewhere; they are not "out there." And members of potential majority coalitions will never present alternatives that are dominated for all members by alternatives that might be brought forward.

I cannot predict just how this research program in constitutional geometry will develop. I can only say "stay tuned."

FEDERALISM AND COMMUNITARIANISM

The third research program that I want to discuss briefly describes, not a projected book-length project upon which I have been engaged, but an encompassing program, with many variants, within which I have variously worked throughout my research career.

"Federalism," "devolution," "decentralization," "subsidiarity," "denationalism," "privatization"—these are political terms of the 1990s. The current relevance of these terms stems from widespread acknowledgment that, either directly or indirectly, regulatory authority has been too much concentrated in central governmental units, with the result that bureaucratic inefficiencies have become omnipresent. The argument from organizational efficiency alone dictates institutional reform in the direction of decentralization.

My own interest has never been in organizational efficiency as such. I have long supported federalized structures of politics on what are essentially classical liberal principles, that is, as a means of limiting or restricting the exercise of central government authority. For me, the ideal political structure, especially in large polities, is one described by competitive federalism: the central government remains strong but severely limited in its range of powers, and the separate but integrated lower-level units compete with one another in providing for most of the collectively supplied services as demanded by the citizenry.

The most exciting potential application of genuinely federalist principles seemed to me to be present in the European thrust toward effective political and economic integration. In 1990 I presented a paper in Paris, "Europe's Constitutional Opportunity," in which I outlined what seemed to be a once-in-history chance for Europe to establish a strong, and limited, central authority with competing national units and open internal markets. That paper, and others that I have written, has been quite severely criticized, and equally so from both the left and the right. Those on the left, reflecting what I have called the Brussels mentality, object strenuously to my call for political competition among the separate nation-states; this group supports, instead, extensive regularization and harmonization across all of Europe, as laid down from Brussels. The criticisms from the right, mostly from British sources, stem from those who object, even violently, to any suggestion that the nation-states should give up even so much as one whit of sovereignty to the central European authority—or to any federalized order.

My assessment now is mixed; Europe may well have missed out on its constitutional opportunity. But offsetting this is the force of history itself. I have the sense that Europe, as an idea, must exert itself, while at the same time the separate nation-states will surely retain considerable authority to shape their own internal affairs.

In the more general sense that motivated me to add communitarianism to the name of this third program, let me repeat the point I made in my review (Buchanan 1997) of Michael Sandel's book *Democracy's Discontent* (1996). There seems to me now to be a unique opportunity for those who have traditionally supported federalism on essentially classical liberal grounds to join forces with modern communitarians who emphasize the alienation sensed by persons who are organized politically in units that are simply too large to command personal allegiance and cannot convey any sense of personalized participation. As I argued some years ago (Buchanan 1978), our moral capacities for politicized compassion, as required by the demands of the welfare-transfer state, simply cannot extend over memberships of many millions. Devolution of political authority to units of such sizes that will at least command more personalized loyalties almost becomes a necessary reform if the excesses of the "churning state" (De Jasay 1985) are to be avoided.

Care must be taken, however, to ensure that devolution of political authority does not, at the same time, allow for retrogression toward the "natural" chaos of tribal anarchy, in which groups are classified along racial, ethnic, or religious lines. Competition among units within an integrated polity, with a strong but limited central authority—this is a pattern to be desired. But as among the separate units themselves, the membership should ideally be classified orthogonally to tribal boundaries. In our country, the separate states, as they exist, might meet this requirement. But is it too much to hope that the American states can come to command sufficient personalized loyalties as to make viable federalism possible?

REFERENCES

Buchanan, James M. 1978. "Markets, States, and the Extent of Morals." *American Economic Review* 68 (May): 364–68.

———. 1990. "Europe's Constitutional Opportunity." In *Europe's Constitutional Future*. (London: Institute of Economic Affairs), 1–20.

———. 1995. "Foundational Concerns: A Criticism of Public Choice Theory." In *Current Issues in Public Choice*, edited by José Casas Pardo and Friedrich Schneider (Cheltenham, Eng.: Edward Elgar), 3–20.

———. 1997. "Divided We Stand" (originally titled "Democracy Without Community"; review of Michael J. Sandel's *Democracy's Discontent*). *Reason* 28(9, February): 59–60.

Buchanan, James M., and Roger D. Congleton. 1998. *Politics by Principle, Not Interest: Toward Nondiscriminatory Democracy*. Cambridge: Cambridge University Press.

Buchanan, James M., and Gordon Tullock. 1962. *The Calculus of Consent: Logical Foundations of Constitutional Democracy*. Ann Arbor: University of Michigan Press.

De Jasay, Anthony. 1985. *The State*. Oxford: Basil Blackwell.

Sandel, Michael J. 1996. *Democracy's Discontent: America in Search of a Public Philosophy*. Cambridge, Mass.: Belknap/Harvard University Press.

Wicksell, Knut. 1896. *Finanztheoretische Untersuchungen*. Jena: Fischer.

IN ANTICIPATION OF THE MARRIAGE
OF POLITICAL AND ECONOMIC THEORY

Douglass C. North

The charge that I got from Margaret Levi when she asked me to participate was threefold: We were to talk about, one, the strengths and limits of economics in understanding political questions; two, the influence of political science on economics; and three, the way in which some of the most important work in both disciplines reflects a marriage between the two. Now Jim Buchanan, in all his modesty, has said that it would be hubristic to undertake such an assignment, but no such limitation is going to stop me.

Let me first of all talk about the strengths of economics. The most obvious strength is a straightforward one, and it is a very powerful one. Economics is about scarcity. I recommend to you Paul Heyne's *The Economic Way of Thinking* (1991). I think the economic way of reasoning and the approach to looking at a world in terms of the constraint of scarcity has provided a very powerful way to think about problems—not just economic problems, but political, social, all kinds of problems. The enormous contribution that I believe economics has made to political science has been to apply the economic way of reasoning to political science. The classics on that are straightforward, and the most important is the one by Jim Buchanan and Gordon Tullock, *The Calculus of Consent* (1962). This book opened the door to suggesting and making clear to political scientists what a powerful set of tools we had in an economic way of reasoning and in using opportunity costs, scarcity, and the marginal calculus to look at problems. I think it was a great contribution. Anthony Downs's *An Economic Theory of Democracy* (1957) and Mancur Olson's *The Logic of Collective Action* (1965), if perhaps not quite equal to *The Calculus of Consent*, are still major works dealing with the same issue. They set off a revolution in political theory that is still going on and that augurs a promising future, which I hope we will realize.

Now that is a big contribution, but the weaknesses of neoclassical economic theory are equally glaring. They come to three things: One, there are no institutions; two, we have an inadequate behavioral assumption underlying the theory; and three, there is no consideration of time. Let me talk about each in turn.

In 1937 Ronald Coase, who won the Nobel Prize in 1991, wrote a deceptively simple essay called "The Nature of the Firm." In this essay, he asked why do firms exist? Now, if you were not hidebound by a discipline and a paradigm that prevented you from seeing things, you would say, what a silly question. But economists really had got themselves caught up in a model of the world in which markets were always more efficient than any other alternative way of doing things, and so Coase's question was very straightforward: If markets are so efficient at doing things, why do firms exist? And the answer, also straightforward, and still revolutionizing economics, and political science as well, I hope—is that there are costs associated with human organization of any kind, political, social, or economic, and those costs, which we call transaction costs, make it so that frequently one way of organizing activity, whether through markets or through organizations, can produce more efficiency than another way. Coase's essay, which took the economics profession some forty-odd years to appreciate, is still, in my view, the opening wedge to an important revolution that I hope is going to have more influence on political theory in the future. A transaction cost approach to economics is, I think, the key to unraveling a lot of our problems in economics, and a transaction approach to politics, or a transaction cost theory of politics, also promises to make a lot of sense out of politics. What Coase started with the transaction cost approach, I think, is well on its way to being a foundation for restructuring social science theory generally, not just political theory or economic theory.

I want to call your attention to another essay that I think belongs in the category of revolutionary contributions but that so far has had only modest influence in economics and probably even less influence in political theory. That is an essay, published in the 1983 *American Economic Review,* by Ronald Heiner called "The Origins of Predictable Behavior." What makes Heiner's essay so important is that Heiner asked himself what I believe is the fundamental question that we are all concerned with in social sciences: What is the fundamental, underlying basis for human motivation and for the way in which we structure human interaction? What Heiner pointed to runs counter to some fundamental implications of economics: the desire of human beings to be able to structure the world in ways that reduce the uncertainty of human interaction. In "The Origins of Predictable Behavior," Heiner said that the rules and structures we impose on society reduce this uncertainty. He went on to suggest all kinds of implications for looking at human organization in this fashion, both in economics and in political and social theory. It is surely not a new idea; after all, it is what Hobbes was talking about. But of all the articles we have, Heiner's probably provides the best foundation for structuring a new social science concerned with human interaction.

Second, I want to talk about the rationality assumption. The rationality assumption as economists traditionally used it was simply empty. It was empty in the sense that you could define rationality any way you wanted to and with that definition you could then make yourself a model. But the rationality assumption in its simplest form said that human beings know what they are doing and act accordingly. Well, for somebody like myself who studies economic history over ten millennia, thinking that human beings have known what they are doing all that time and acted accordingly is ridiculous. They have operated on the basis of ideologies, beliefs, prejudices, and half-witted truths all through history, and they still do. We are interested therefore in how human beings think, how they arrive at the choices they make.

Herbert Simon here deserves our endless appreciation and applause for the fact that he forced economists, and I hope political scientists, to ask the question of exactly what is going on when we say that human beings act in a way that deals with maximizing their expected utility. What Simon is forcing us into is cognitive science, which I think has the promise of becoming one of the most important disciplines of all the social sciences in the future. How does the mind work? How do beliefs evolve? Why do beliefs take the form and shape that they do? What makes them successful, what makes them accepted, and what causes them to be rejected? After all, could economics or political science in its original form explain the rise and decline of communism in the twentieth century? This was surely the single most interesting and important issue for society in this century. You cannot make sense out of it without taking into account the power of beliefs, the way they have shaped and influenced institutions, and indeed the way in which beliefs evolve and, as communism did in 1989, decline. All of that, I think, Simon opened up, but I do have one critical comment. His initial view, which is carried over into the modification of the rationality assumption, is expressed in the term "bounded rationality." I do not like the term. It implies a very limited view of how we want to think rationality is constrained; that is, it implies that the constraint is simply on the computational ability of the players. That is not the limitation; that is only one limitation, and it is just saying that the players operate like computers but like lousy computers. There are all kinds of other limitations on the ability of human beings to be rational, in the sense of being completely informed and able to make decisions on that basis, other than the complexity of the problem in terms of the computational ability of the players. It is not just an issue between "Deep Blue" and Kasparov; it is a much more complicated issue in terms of the degree to which there is good feedback on the results of our choices, on the way we therefore modify them over time, on the way in which prejudices and all kinds of irrational activities influence choices. The way human beings think and believe and the way preferences and beliefs evolve are at the very frontier of the issues that I think we must concern ourselves with.

Third, I want to talk about time. For an economic historian, time has always been something that is fundamentally disturbing, because there is *no time* in neoclassical theory. The neoclassical model is a model of an instant of time, and it does not therefore take into account what time does. Yet time is a dimension in which human learning occurs, and human learning, in the way it is cumulative and occurs not only in an individual's lifetime but across generations, is one of the most important things that constrains and shapes the world we are evolving in. Hayek (1952) probably more than anybody else was responsible for our beginning to think of the way in which time and collective learning—which he viewed as the learning of past generations, embodied in the institutions and ideas that we have today—constrain and influence how we determine and make choices today. Of all the things that are powerful in constraining the choice set, in shaping the way we think, time and the way learning is embodied in history are certainly among the most powerful. There is some very exciting work that overlaps with cognitive science and the kinds of things that Hayek was talking about. Ed Hutchins, in *Cognition in the Wild* (1994), attempts to incorporate into how we arrive at decisions today the multitudinous forces from the past that have constrained and shaped the way we live. I will be blunt: Without a deep understanding of time, you will be lousy political scientists, because time is the dimension in which ideas and institutions and beliefs evolve.

So much for what has happened. Second, I was asked to talk about the influence of political science on economics. The influence on traditional, neoclassical economics has been—and I use the word politely—slight, to put it mildly. Political scientists were not influential at all in developing standard, neoclassical economic theory, and indeed, if you follow the economic paradigm as it evolved in the most elegant, mathematical structures of modern neoclassical theory—which has become more and more precise about less and less—they still have no influence whatsoever. But political theory as it is evolving today in interaction with a lot of the exciting things that I have just been talking about is having a very powerful influence on where we are going. Indeed, I would argue that a marriage between the two is something that I see happening down the road.

Let me just give you a personal anecdote. I spent thirty-three years at the University of Washington in Seattle, and my colleagues there were certainly not interested in politics. For a number of years Margaret Levi and I together taught a program in political economy, without much enthusiasm on the part of either her colleagues or my colleagues. And so I left. I wanted to go to a place where we would try to provide for a theoretical merger of political and economic theory, and at that time at Washington University in St. Louis there was a very bright group of young people, Ken Shepsle, Randy Calvert, Jim Alt, Barry Weingast, all of whom were doing such work. So I went to Washington University. I might add that they promptly left. Nevertheless, we did create a center in political economy, which my colleague Norman Schofield runs now, and we are attempting to pull together and run models of political economic processes that are serious and realistic and can deal with problems that I think are at the very forefront of issues. I say this advisedly, because without an ability to model the way the polities evolve and the way they in turn both specify and enforce the rules of the game of a society, we are at a loss to deal with the fundamental problems that I think we are concerned with, both historically and within polities and economies today. Modeling political economy, therefore, is still, in my view, a central concern that we should be concerned about within our work.

Now let me conclude with the marriage. I think it is happening. If somebody had asked me the questions that were proposed to me today ten years ago, I would have been very pessimistic, but economics is being forced gradually to alter, to incorporate ideas from allied fields in the social sciences. Indeed, if I had to make my guess, I would say that fields like political science, anthropology, may be more exciting fields in the future than economics; it is very hard for economics to shed enough of its traditional paradigm and to be open enough to focus on what I consider to be the very fundamental and exciting issues that are in prospect for us and that I hope we will address in the near future. But I think the marriage is happening. I see it in Elinor Ostrom's work, concerned with both theory and applied work. I see it in a variety of studies by people in this volume who are doing exciting work on politics and political economy, on norms, on a variety of issues that I think are the very focus of what we want to do if we are going to arrive at a social science body of theory that can help us solve problems in the future that we have not solved in the past.

REFERENCES

Buchanan, James M., and Gordon Tullock. 1965. *The Calculus of Consent: Logical Foundations of Constitutional Democracy*. Ann Arbor: University of Michigan Press.

Coase, Ronald. 1937. "The Nature of the Firm." *Economics and Politics* (November): 386–407.

Downs, Anthony. 1957. *An Economic Theory of Democracy*. New York: Harper.

Hayek, Fredrick. 1952. The Sensory Order. London: Routledge & Kegan Paul

Heiner, Ronald A. 1983. "The Origin of Predictable Behavior." *American Economic Review* 73 (September): 560–95.

Hutchins, Ed. 1994. *Cognition in the Wild*. Cambridge, Mass.: MIT Press.

Heyne, Paul. 1991. *The Economic Way of Thinking*. New York: Macmillan.

Olson, Mancur. 1965. *The Logic of Collective Action*. Cambridge, Mass.: Harvard University Press.

COMMENTS ON REMARKS OF
JAMES M. BUCHANAN AND DOUGLASS C. NORTH

Herbert A. Simon

Jim Buchanan addresses himself primarily to normative questions, but with strong empirical assumptions implicit in his justification of his values. For example, he advocates generality as a fundamental constitutional constraint. Now, generality for generality's sake needs no further justification, nor can it find one. However, Jim argues also that generality is a condition for fairness because it removes the motivation for individuals to invest effort toward securing differentially favorable treatment—a politicized version of Adam Smith's ubiquitous invisible hand. This, of course, is an empirical assertion, which rests on (among others) an equally empirical (and, I believe, flawed) assumption that all political actors are wholly selfish. Elsewhere I have given reasons for doubting this last premise, because it ignores the extensive altruism that arises from the identification of individuals with groups.

But as several members of the audience pointed out, generality is also highly ambiguous. It becomes definite only when we specify what principles of classification are acceptable, and as the questioners pointed out, this reopens the whole question of fairness. Communism in its purist form meets one criterion of generality (to each according to need, from each according to ability); so does neoclassical competitive market capitalism; so does the flat tax (for example, a 80 percent flat tax on all income, half used to support governmental services, the other half paid out on a fixed per capita basis to the entire population). Requiring generality of the constitution does not seem to settle much; certainly it does not define fairness.

Exercise: Analyze the arguments of both sides of any of the current large-scale political donnybrooks that plague our planet (Bosnia, Ireland, Burundi, Sri Lanka), and decide which side adheres to generality and fairness. Somehow the real issues lie at a more concrete level and are not just value questions but also involve beliefs about how human beings are motivated and behave—empirical questions familiar to political science and psychology.

Not surprisingly, I find Doug North's views much more simpatico. Moreover, I am very grateful for his kind words about my work and embarrassed that I have to correct his reading of the meaning of "bounded rationality." The term has always embraced multiple limits on human rationality, among which limits on calculation (erroneously regarded by Doug as spanning its whole scope) are usually not the most important. The others include: the incommensurability of individual goals; goal conflicts between individuals; the fact that alternatives are not given but must be searched for; radical incompleteness of the knowledge needed to evaluate alternatives; and the consequent uncertainty about the consequences of action. The roles that these have played in bounded rationality from the beginning can be seen from my 1955 paper "Behavioral Model of Rational Choice" or my 1959 paper "Theories of Decisionmaking in Economics and Behavioral Science," both reprinted in volume 2 of *Models of Bounded Rationality* (1982).

Doug's picture of the future of political inquiry is right on target. The cognitive models of human thought, unlike the equilibrium models of neoclassical economic theory, are theories of process and change. Within psychology they have been mainly kept to the level of individual thinking (for example, problem solving) and to a modest time scale. Fields like sociology, history, and anthropology have studied social processes up to whole societies and even beyond, and through time periods that sometimes extend over centuries.

Of course, no one person can master this whole range of facts and ideas. But just as virtually all physicists share a common core of knowledge, however esoteric their specialties, so the post–World War II era of behavioralism, encouraged by Ford Foundation largesse, demonstrated that social scientists (including historians and those economists who wished to) could share a common core of knowledge about the bases of individual and social behavior. Center for Advanced Study in the Behavioral Sciences (CASBS) at Stanford is a living monument to the viability of a core social science. Ideas and facts (above all, facts) can indeed move across the boundaries of our specialties. Methodologies can move too.

Innovation in methods is a major driving force in every science. The post–World War II history of economics can be written mainly in terms of its rapid conversion to formal mathematical models tied to equilibrium and combined with the empirical methodology of regression analysis of noisy aggregated numerical data. Both its theoretical strengths and its empirical weaknesses (and the huge gaps between them) can be traced in large part to these methodological innovations.

The post–World War II history of psychology records the gradual rejection of behaviorism (not to be confused with "behavioralism," mentioned earlier) in favor of a search for the processes of thought, using such novel methods as computer simulation of mental processes and thinking-aloud protocols of persons performing difficult tasks. The price that the new methodologies exacted was attention primarily to individual behavior studied dynamically but over relatively short time periods. Two decades ago this began to change with new research on the behavior of experts (behavior that is at least a decade in gestation because of the knowledge and skill the expert must acquire) and on the processes that scientists use to discover new laws. These new directions required an extension of time horizons and close attention to the interaction of the individual with the social environment and context.

Somewhat more recently, anthropology and sociology have also been moving strongly in new directions. Their methodological innovation is focused on the idea of "deep description"—always studying behavior in its social and historical context (for example, the work of Ed Hutchins that Doug North refers to).

That methodological trend has had three aspects that I personally find rather regrettable: a demand that all research deal explicitly with its social context; acceptance of highly subjective standards of data interpretation; and sometimes extreme claims of the social relativity of scientific "truth." I think these deviations from usual scientific practice can be greatly mitigated without loss of the ability to study behavior in context, but the issues are far too complex to be dealt with in these brief comments.

More important—and positive—cognitive research on expertise and scientific discovery is demonstrating that the social context of thought can be captured by paying due attention to knowledge and skill stored in memory and to the modeling of social interaction. We are beginning to see convergence, in research if not in debates about methodology, between cognition in the laboratory and "cognition in the wild." As one example, the careful historical account by the historian of science Frederic L. Holmes (1991) of the biochemical discoveries of Hans Krebs has been modeled successfully by Kulkarni and Simon (1988)—and in a second effort, by the team of Grasshoff and May (1995)—as a cognitive discovery process. As a second example I would mention Kevin Dunbar's (1995) intensive, yearlong field studies of three biochemistry laboratories.

Thus, I concur with Doug North that we are today free from the bonds of static equilibrium analysis. This is a promising time to bring all of the social sciences to bear on understanding our economic, political, and social institutions and understanding them in historical perspective. The methods are there; all we need is the will to sharpen and use them.

REFERENCES

Dunbar, Kevin. 1995. "How Scientists Really Reason: Scientific Reasoning in Real-world Laboratories." In *The Nature of Insight,* edited by Robert J. Sternberg and Janet E. Davidson (Cambridge, Mass.: The MIT Press) 365–96.

Grasshoff, Gerd, and Michael May. 1995. "From Historical Case Studies to Systematic Methods of Discovery." *Proceedings of the AAAI Spring Symposium of Systematic Methods of Scientific Discovery:* 46–57.

Holmes, Frederic L. 1991. *Hans Krebs: The Formation of a Scientific Life: 1900–1933.* New York: Oxford University Press.

Kulkarni, Deepak, and Herbert Simon. 1988. "The Processes of Scientific Discovery." *Cognitive Science* 12: 139–76.

Simon, Herbert A. 1955. "A Behavioral Theory of Rational Choice." In *Models of Bounded Rationality,* edited by Herbert Simon (Cambridge, Mass.: MIT Press, 1982), 2:239–58.

———. 1959. "Theories of Decisionmaking in Economics and Behavioral Science." In Simon, *Models of Bounded Rationality* (Cambridge, Mass.: MIT Press, 1982), 2: 253–83.

REFLECTIONS ON POLITICAL SCIENCE

Kenneth J. Arrow

I speak of political science from the viewpoint of an interested and indeed concerned outsider. That is, I am acquainted with only a small and selected part of the vast literature of political science. My own interests arose from the intersection of the two, the implementation of economic policy through the political system. Part of this interest was what is called political philosophy, the normative justification of policies. Part is descriptive: which economic decisions does a state make, and how do they depend on different factors, such as the electoral system or the economic interests of different individuals and groups in the society?

I will confine my remarks to two ways in which the viewpoint of an economic analyst can be brought to bear on political science. I am not offering any answers or suggesting that they can be obtained with ease by transfer from standard economic theory. On the contrary, I am raising questions for possible research.

One of the two suggestions from the economist's viewpoint is the grounding of the analysis in the motives of individuals. The other is the habit of looking at the economy as an interacting system and asking if the polity can be looked at similarly. This perspective suggests in particular that the rules of the game are important determinants of outcomes—for example, in economics, state monopoly versus private enterprise with free entry—and raises the possibility that electoral systems and systems of parliamentary procedure may be variables of similar importance in the explanation of political outcomes.

Economic analysis tends to be based on individual behavior; in modern parlance, economic analysis is a form of agent-based modeling. One possible assumption in an agent-based model for politics is that the individual motives for political action are the same as those for action on the market, though the range of actions may be different. This is the kind of assumption that has been basic to economic thinking since the 1870s, and it draws on a legal and political tradition going back to Condorcet and Jeremy Bentham beginning in the late eighteenth century. More specifically, the motives are regarded as rational, which, in this context, means only that they satisfy certain consistency conditions (preferences are transitive and complete).

In various ways of differing rigor and completeness, the hypothesis of the unity of motives, as we may term it, has not been absent from political and social analyses—for example, the economic interpretation of politics, as in Karl Marx or Charles Beard (1935), or the study of interest groups, as in Arthur Bentley (1935). Indeed, that some legislation and other political actions were and are intended to help private economic interests is "too evident for detection," to use a phrase of Samuel Johnson.

In fact, the hypothesis that a common set of preferences underlies political and economic action does not imply the simple-minded notion of economic determinism. Some dimensions of action cannot be expressed on the market, just as others are not expressible in political terms. The first are what usually are termed "externalities," although, candidly, that term is so broad that it is ceasing to be analytically useful. In the narrow sense, it refers to goods whose consumption, for technical or physical reasons, cannot be determined in the market, for example, air or water pollution or, more generally, the presence of "fugitive" resources of which the ownership cannot be conveniently ascribed. More broadly, externalities might include expressions of altruism whereby one individual gains from another's giving; though altruism can be supplied privately, the supply should, according to standard economic theory, be too low relative to some norm, such as Pareto efficiency. Many years ago, James Q. Wilson and Edward Banfield (1964) showed by analysis of voting on local bond issues the extent of what they called "other-regardingness." On the other hand, decisions reflecting individual tastes or localized knowledge that cannot easily be disseminated can be made on the market but not easily by a political or legal system with a tendency toward rules of uniform application.

The hypothesis of common economic-political preferences is therefore consistent with the observation that the economic system and the political system deal with separate (though overlapping) decision areas and that their modes of operation are different. Still, there is an alternative theory, which has found strong support among cognitive psychologists, that there is no single set of preferences or beliefs but that they are constructed to meet a particular decision situation and they can differ according to the perceived frame of reference.

One concrete area of public decisionmaking in which the issues have been joined is that of environmental controls. Economists have succeeded in establishing the principle (more honored in the breach than in the observance) that large public works, especially those having to do with water, should be judged by benefit-cost analysis. However, since the benefits (and some of the costs) are derived from externalities (such as abatement of smog or biodiversity), they cannot be estimated from market transactions. A technique for deriving benefits called "contingent valuation" has been developed: in questionnaires, a sample of the population is asked what they would be willing to pay for the benefits. This approach has been used especially with regard to oil spills, clean water, and wilderness preservation, not only for policy formation but also, and perhaps more important, as the basis for claims for environmental damages. In some ways, contingent valuation is a novel form of voting. It turns out that in many cases the results contradict the normal tenets of consistency; for example, the willingness to pay is remarkably insensitive to the degree of environmental damage averted. The conjecture has been made that the responses are preferences constructed for the occasion and therefore not necessarily consistent with responses on other occasions.

More generally, an individual in a political situation—in the ballot booth, for example—may put on a different *persona* and act in an expressive way, for example, by taking on the role of Adam Smith's (1759) "impartial spectator." James Buchanan, whose important work has been based largely on the unity of political and economic motives, has nevertheless also explored (jointly with Geoffrey Brennan) the view that votes may be cast for expressive reasons rather than for achieving the same ends as in daily economic life (1984).

Let me turn to a different lesson that might be drawn from the methods of economic analysis for the political system. It is the concept that outcomes result from an interacting system. In economics we are accustomed to the view that changes in the system of resource allocation will be accompanied by changes in the outcomes. The economist usually concentrates on one such change, the efficiency of the allocation, but others are certainly relevant, such as the vertical or horizontal equity of the outcomes, the effects on different specified groups, or the degree to which negative externalities are controlled and positive externalities encouraged. Economists argue typically that water resources are inefficiently utilized because the property rights are assigned in a special fashion (water is drawn from wells without regard to the fact that the underground supply to others is reduced; rights to the use of stream water are not transferable, so that a farmer cannot be compensated for reducing his or her use for the benefit of others; and irrigation water is usually supplied by the government below cost). Some industrial countries permit large-scale cartelization; others prohibit it. Larger changes, such as socialization of the economy or the granting of monopolies to favored friends and relatives, have presumably even larger effects.

What is the political analogue? It is a long-held argument that the electoral system has an important effect on the outcome. Of course, by itself, this is not exactly a novelty to political thinking. The members of the Constitutional Convention and the authors of *The Federalist* were obviously concerned with this issue, though such an intelligent observer as the eighteenth-century poet Alexander Pope in *An Essay On Man* did not agree: "For forms of government let fools contend." Harold Hotelling (1929) and Joseph Schumpeter (1942) drew inferences about political outcomes from electoral competition, and in this they were followed by Howard Bowen, Duncan Black, Anthony Downs, James Buchanan, Gordon Tullock, Richard McKelvey, myself, and many others. In this development, noncooperative game theory has been a basic tool.

Still, despite all this analysis, there are unresolved issues of the greatest practical importance. For example, what is the relation between democracy and economic development? The favorable economic experience of several Asian countries under authoritarian or even totalitarian regimes (the Republic of Korea, Hong Kong, Taiwan, Singapore, Indonesia, and, more recently, China) has been something of a shock to those who think of democracy as best representing the interests of the people. (Of course, there is no shortage of dictatorships that manage to achieve economic chaos.) Indeed, the view that democracy is, so to speak, a luxury good, a consequence rather than a cause of economic growth, has also received support. The political choice analysts have been hard at work on the causes and implications of redistributive policies in advanced countries.

A number of countries have debated in one form or another the exact form of their voting methods. Israel has made a significant change in having the prime minister directly elected. Others have discussed multi-member constituencies, various forms of proportional representation, or other systems based on voters' submitting preference orderings of candidates or, on the contrary, moving toward "first past the post" methods. The arguments are in terms of outcomes, both substantive (for example, benefits for small elements of the population) and procedural (the stability of governmental coalitions, for instance, or the multiplicity of parties represented in the legislature). What is striking are the difficulties both of modeling the process and of finding relevant data.

One class of implications that my research direction has made me emphasize is the role of intransitivity of preferences as revealed by outcomes. In my own work, I have put emphasis on the normative aspects. If there is any meaning to a social preference that aggregates individual preferences, it ought to be an ordering and therefore transitive. But I also feel (and indeed indicated briefly in my monograph) that intransitivity is an empirical phenomenon. One form it takes is that votes on separate occasions (usually on legislation rather than on candidates) exhibit intransitivity. In recent years there have been analyses of Supreme Court decisions by Frank Easterbrook (1982), Maxwell Stearns (1995), and others that have identified such cycles. Similarly, under the usual rules for drafting legislation, both in committees and in the legislatures themselves, intransitivity takes the form of path dependence; the order in which alternatives are considered affects the outcome. This in turn leads to a struggle over agenda control. William Riker (1958) and Kenneth Shepsle (1979) have studied various aspects of these questions. The theoretical implications of intransitivity under majority rule for electoral competition have been studied by Richard McKelvey, Gerald Kramer, and Norman Schofield, among others. I believe that the ambiguity due to intransitivity is not merely an interesting curiosus but a deep fact about democratic politics.

Finally, I mention another aspect of electoral behavior, the interaction of different dimensions of political choice. Political choices, like economic choices, are made over a variety of issues. These issues may be linked directly, in that outcomes in some dimensions may substitute for others (full employment will reduce the need for welfare), while others are complementary (an activist foreign policy increases the value of increased military expenditures). They may be linked through resource constraints: an expensive policy in any one area—say, medical care—will increase the pressure to reduce expenditures everywhere. They may be linked simply through political bargaining: a group wanting support on one issue may agree to support another issue it only mildly disapproves of in return for support on the issue it cares about. When I was a high school student, "log rolling" was considered a social vice. But the logic of preference tells us that the opposite may be true. Almost all of us coming out of the tradition of modern economics, James Buchanan as much as myself, consider that the objects of choice should be statements of position on every issue under consideration, vectors that define the whole social state, just as individuals choose their commodity bundles.

The problem with this position is its implementation. Decisions on different issues are in fact made one at a time (with exceptions). Indeed, the rule of parliamentary procedure requires that amendments be germane. Of course, these rules are sometimes violated in practice through the practice of inserting riders. But there are limits. One reason for this particular failure of rational-choice theory is the need for deliberation. A piece of legislation is shaped by exchange of information (including information about political power), and this process takes time. The importance of deliberation is not well represented in social-choice or political-choice theory. Certainly, considerations of time have played an important part in political tactics and may possibly be of importance even over a longer run. The implications of sequential rather than simultaneous choice for agent-based models of political choice seems a problem that needs to be studied, both empirically and theoretically.

The second half of my remarks has assumed that the political actors (voters, candidates, officials, and so forth) make their individual choices within given electoral and procedural forms. A different view is that an underlying distribution of power will determine outcomes regardless of institutional forms. This determination will operate by bargaining to determine the strategic moves that lead to the desired outcomes under the rules of the political game. This is the point of view expressed in modern terms by cooperative game theory, as illustrated by Ronald Coase's (1960) argument that unlimited bargaining, even over public goods, will lead to efficient outcomes. Another illustration of this viewpoint is George Stigler's (1971) contention that regulatory commissions are captured by the industry regulated. The importance of money in politics—always there but even greater today—shows how economic power can indeed influence the polity, independent of the particular electoral form.

I throw out this last hypothesis as an alternative to stressing the importance of electoral systems. Of course, as Coase pointed out, in the real world there are transaction costs that prevent, for example, full efficiency with unlimited bargaining. Here, too, transaction costs—for example, those of coordinating a very large number of voters—may cause electoral systems and other social decision procedures to still be consequential and affect the way power structures can influence outcomes.

I have tried to discuss genuinely political problems from some perspectives opened up or illuminated by developments in economic analysis. Whether these are interesting questions, I will have to leave to those more knowledgeable.

REFERENCES

Beard, Charles. 1935. *An Economic Interpretation of the Constitution of the United States.* New York: MacMillan.

Bentley, Arthur. 1935. *The Process of Government.* Bloomington, Ind.: The Principia Press.

Buchanan, James, and Geoffrey Brennan. 1984. "Voter Choice: Evaluating Political Alternatives." *American Behavioral Scientist* 28(2): 185–210.

Coase, Ronald. 1960. "The Problem of Social Cost." *Journal of Law and Economics* 3: 1–44.

Easterbrook, Frank. 1982. "Ways of Criticizing the Court." *Harvard Law Review* 95: 802–32.

Hotelling, Harold. 1929. "Stability in Competition." *Economic Journal* 39(1): 41–57.

Riker, William. 1958. "The Paradox of Voting and Congressional Rules for Voting on Amendments." *American Political Science Review* 52: 349–66.

Schumpeter, Joseph. 1942. *Capitalism, Socialism, and Democracy.* New York: Harper.

Shepsle, Kenneth. 1979. "Institutional Arrangements and Equilibrium on Multidimensional Voting Models." *American Journal of Political Science* 23: 27–59.

Smith, Adam. 1759. *Theory of Moral Sentiments.* Reprinted in 1982. Indianapolis: Liberty Fund.

Stearns, Maxwell. 1995. "Standing Back from the Forest: Justiciability and Social Choice." *California Law Review* 83: 1309–31.

Stigler, George. 1971. "The Theory of Economic Regulation." *Bell Journal of Economics and Management Science* 2: 3–21.

Wilson, James Q., and Edward Banfield. 1964. "Public-Regardingness as a Value Premise in Voting Behavior." *American Political Science Review* 58: 876–87.

REMARKS ON THE METHODOLOGY OF SCIENCE: DISCOVERY AND VERIFICATION

Herbert A. Simon

In discussions of scientific methodology in the literature of the philosophy, history, sociology, and psychology of science, and in statistics, two interrelated components of scientific activity are commonly distinguished: the *discovery* of new phenomena and of hypotheses and laws to describe and explain these phenomena, and the *verification* (or, more often, falsification) of hypotheses or laws by observation and experiment. To this list we should add at least two other kinds of activities, which, as their importance becomes increasingly recognized, are receiving much attention: the invention of new instruments for *observing* and *measuring* symbolically and pictorially. I will limit this discussion to the first two kinds of activity: discovery and verification, which have been, until recently, the focus of most discussion of method.

One is struck by two features of the literature on these topics. First, both philosophy of science and statistics have been preoccupied almost exclusively during the past half-century with verification and falsification and have almost ignored the processes of discovery. This neglect can be attributed in considerable part to Karl Popper, who, in his influential *The Logic of Scientific Discovery* (1959), announced (in spite of his book's title) that there could be no logic of discovery, but only a logic of falsification. Consistent with this view, the statistical literature on the design of experiments and on tests of statistical significance has been concerned almost exclusively with methods for testing hypotheses to the exclusion of methods for discovering them. This is curious in that the same literature tells us that we must have hypotheses before we can design, much less carry out, experiments, leading us to wonder where the hypotheses come from, and by what magic ("intuition"? "inspiration"? "creative genius"?) they are produced.

The second striking feature in the literature—this time including the literature on the history of science—is that, between the discovery of phenomena (by observation and experiment) and the invention of theory, the greater attention is generally and increasingly given to theory rather than to phenomena. This tendency is not without notable exceptions, but it marks even writing about the great observers and experimenters (Michael Faraday, for example), in whose work, however important their theoretical contributions, empirical observation led the way to theory, rather than theory largely guiding observation.

THE TRADITIONAL PRACTICE OF POLITICAL SCIENCE

Let me turn now from philosophy of science to the actual practice of research in political science (excluding normative political theory). The "classical" tradition of empiricism in political science has been observational rather than experimental. Observing the phenomena is taken as the first task, even in an advice-laden (hence theory-laden) book like Machiavelli's *The Prince* (1513/1935). More modern, and more striking, examples would include Tocqueville's *Democracy in America* (1835/1942) and James Bryce's *The American Commonwealth* (1893). Bryce (1893, vol. 1, 4) finds even Tocqueville too theoretical for his taste. According to Bryce, Tocqueville's "conclusions are illustrated from America, but are founded, not so much on an analysis of American phenomena, as on general and somewhat speculative views of democracy which the circumstances of France had suggested." In contrast, Bryce says, "I have striven to avoid the temptations of the deductive method, and to present simply the facts of the case, arranging and connecting them as best I can, but letting them speak for themselves." Of course (Bryce's protestations notwithstanding), both of these observers and others who have followed them generated hypotheses (laws) from the pattern of phenomena they saw.

Traditionally, political scientists did not test their hypotheses experimentally and made rather little use of statistical theory for the tests. The social scientists of the behavioral persuasion, beginning after World War I and flourishing after World War II, worked mainly in this observational tradition (although Gosnell, in 1927, carried out one controlled experiment on voting and did use statistical tests). Among these behavioralists were the members of the "Chicago School" of political science and urban sociology, Paul Lazarsfeld, Samual Stouffer, and the organizations at Michigan and Chicago that were formed to conduct voting and other opinion polls. These empirical scientists observed systematically but ran few experiments. When they used significance tests, their hypotheses arose from the same data, or the same kinds of data, as those they were testing.

"Standard" methodology, from econometrics and statistics, arrived in political science mostly after World War II, partly as a result of trends toward quantification and mathematization in the social sciences that were stimulated, in turn, by the Committee on Mathematics in the Social Sciences of the Social Science Research Council. We will consider these developments in the broader context of what economics brought to political science.

WHAT ECONOMICS BROUGHT TO POLITICAL SCIENCE

In brief, econometrics brought to political science regression analysis of observational data and hypothesis testing, and public-choice theory brought maximization of subjective expected utility—that is, neoclassical economic theory.

Econometrics introduced political science to the methodological rules for experimentation, that is, for validating hypotheses that had somehow already been generated. Generating hypotheses by observing data was denigrated as "counting the bricks in a wall," and no alternative methods were proposed for discovering new hypotheses. The methodological training of political scientists in statistical methods derived from econometrics made it increasingly difficult for them to justify observational studies of "interesting" phenomena, guided only by very general ideas of what they might find. Nor were they generally exposed to the cognitive science research of the last decade or two on the processes of scientific discovery (Langley and others 1987), which could have suggested hypothesis-finding methods to them.

With respect to the contributions of neoclassical economic theory, old-timers like myself may perhaps be forgiven for believing (perhaps even remembering) that many of the "new" discoveries brought to political science by public-choice theory were familiar old ideas: for example, the generalization, formalized in Hotelling's theorem, that under a two-party system the policy positions of the parties will converge toward the median of public opinion; or the idea that the party in power will suffer in an election held during economically bad times. The idea that economic interests governed the geographical pattern of voting on adoption of the Constitution was introduced by Charles Beard (1913) long before public choice appeared on the scene.

To the extent that the hypotheses proposed by the public-choice approach were already familiar from observational research, its gift was to dress them in the judicial robes of statistical hypothesis testing, with emphasis on verification and little attention to empirical processes for discovering new phenomena, thence new hypotheses. After examining the articles in the *International Encyclopedia of the Social Sciences* (Sills 1968) under the headings "Political" and "Parties," which largely reflect the behavioral tradition, one might regret the subsequent decline of the tradition of careful observation and description of institutions and processes, represented by the work of Maurice Duverger (1951) and many others, that had already provided a rich body of data against which public-choice (or other) theories of the phenomena could be tested.

But these are impressions, not the results of historical inquiry. A careful history of the impact of public-choice theory on research in political science remains, as far as I know, to be written. Even less appears to be known about the possible reverse import into economics of ideas that originated in political science. One anecdote about this commerce: My own ideas about bounded rationality and organizational organization had their origin, as recounted in my autobiography (1996), in direct observations of municipal budget practices that stubbornly refused to fit economics' recipe for equating marginal costs with marginal revenues. Robert Axelrod's (1980) empirical observations of human behavior in the prisoners' dilemma game provide another striking example of this reverse commerce in its impact on game theory in economics.

SOME SPECIFIC PROBLEMS WITH PUBLIC-CHOICE THEORY

These reservations about the contributions of economics to political science can be summarized in two main claims. First, econometrics addresses only the hypothesis-testing part of science and provides no guidance for research aimed at generating hypotheses from observations and experiments. Second, neoclassical theory brought its hypotheses of utility maximization ready-made but did not bring the empirical knowledge needed for their application to particular phenomena. A few explanatory words are needed about the latter claim.

The empty utility function has to be provided with content before it can be applied. In public-choice theory, the "filling," which is usually selected a priori, generally takes the form of vote (or power) maximization, or of maximization of income or wealth. The former is usually the assumed goal of professional politicians, the latter the goal of voters. Even assuming the empirical correctness of these goals, the theory provides no basis for predicting the nontrivial processes needed to translate them into practical political decisions about party position or voting.

Moreover, it is extremely dubious that these goals are in fact the actual guidelines for behavior. Utility theory provides no empirical basis for dealing with the phenomena of altruism, and the phenomena of organizational identification linked to altruism, both of which are essential for explaining the behavior of employees and administrators in governmental and other organizations. Although in recent years bounded rationality assumptions have become popular, they have generally been introduced ad hoc and unsystematically, without empirical rationale from observation. This is especially true of theorizing within the framework of game theory, where myriads of definitions of rationality have been introduced to deal with "outguessing" phenomena, all leading to different predictions of outcomes. Bounded rationality assumptions that lack empirical foundation provide no better path to sound theory than utility-maximizing assumptions with the same deficiency.

At the same time, aspects of bounded rationality, in addition to organizational identification, have been largely ignored that do have a strong basis in empirical observation. One of these is the well-documented fact that limits on the span of human attention force seriality in behavior, and in particular limit the number of major issues that can be on the active political agenda at any time. Another aspect, already alluded to, is the fact that the attempts of political actors to achieve their goals (for example, economic welfare) are strongly mediated by the measuring rods they know and use to assess goal attainment (for example, unemployment rates, inflation, and income distribution). Again, it is impossible to push theory forward without strong foundations of empirical knowledge about these relevant phenomena.

WHAT IS TO BE DONE?

Political science needs to return to the phenomenon-finding and hypothesis-finding component of science, not limiting itself to hypothesis-testing in experiments. It needs to be alert to interesting and possibly significant phenomena. At times it needs to count bricks in a wall in order to look for patterns. It must liberalize its attitude toward experimentation. You do not need a hypothesis to run an experiment; you only need a setting that is likely to produce some new patterns, and you must watch for them.

There are sound methodological foundations today for this broader approach to discovery and verification. Under the general label of "data analysis," statisticians have begun to describe ways of examining data derived from observation as well as experiment, aimed at pattern discovery rather than law verification. With the huge new data banks available today on the World Wide Web and elsewhere, new ideas are developing about effective data-mining processes. The discovery processes disclosed by the researches of historians of science and cognitive modelers are available for application to the sciences, and we are already seeing the development and use of a variety of expert systems that have been proved capable of aiding discovery processes in particular sciences.

A recent example of work in the history of science that reveals the processes leading to important discoveries is Frederic L. Holmes's (1991) study of the research path of the biochemist Hans Krebs regarding the synthesis of urea—and the model of the processes creating this path in the computer program KEKADA (Kulkarni and Simon 1988). There is a computer model, BACON (Langley and others 1987), of the processes for discovering patterns (laws) in data, and a number of expert computer systems are in actual use for carrying out similar processes. We have extensive knowledge of the observational strategies used by Faraday, and of the successful exploitation of surprising phenomena that was at the heart of the discoveries of the Curies (radium) and Fleming (penicillin). In short, we have today a large body of knowledge about the processes of discovery, and we need no longer attribute these processes to the mysterious forces of intuition, inspiration, and creativity.

I am proposing a return, in a sense, to Tocqueville and Bryce, but with a much larger repertory of methodological tools: polls, search engines, protocol analysis, and symbolic models, among others. I am not suggesting that we abandon the methodologies of verification, but that we pay adequate attention to the methodologies of discovery. If we look hard at the actual phenomena of politics, then new and better theories will emerge.

REFERENCES

Axelrod, Robert. 1980. "Effective Choice in the Prisoner's Dilemma." *Journal of Conflict Resolution* 24: 13–25, 379–403.

Beard, Charles A. 1913. *An Economic Interpretation of the Constitution of the United States.* New York: Macmillan.

Bryce, James. 1893. *The American Commonwealth.* 3rd ed. New York: Macmillan.

Duverger, Maurice. 1951. *Political Parties.* 2nd ed. New York: Wiley.

Gosnell, Harold F. 1927. *Getting Out the Vote.* Chicago: University of Chicago Press.

Holmes, Frederic L. 1991. *Hans Krebs: The Formation of a Scientific Life, 1900–1933.* New York: Oxford University Press.

Kulkarni, Deepak, and Herbert A. Simon. 1988. "The Processes of Scientific Discovery." *Cognitive Science* 12: 139–76.

Langley, Pat, Herbert A. Simon, Gary Bradshaw, and Jan Zytkow. 1987. *Models of Scientific Discovery.* Cambridge, Mass.: MIT Press.

Machiavelli, Niccolò. 1513/1935. *The Prince.* London: Oxford University Press.

Popper, Karl. 1959. *The Logic of Scientific Discovery.* London: Hutchinson.

Sills, David L. (ed.). 1968. *International Encyclopedia of the Social Sciences.* New York: Macmillan/Free Press.

Simon, Herbert A. 1996. *Models of My Life.* Cambridge, Mass.: MIT Press.

Tocqueville, Alexis de. 1942. *Democracy in America.* New York: Knopf. (Originally published in 1835)

~~ Chapter 8 ~~

CONCLUSION

Margaret Levi, Elinor Ostrom, and James E. Alt

We began this project by thinking about how we, as political scientists, do and should take economics seriously. We conclude by realizing how much the Nobelist economists, at least the ones in this volume, do and should take politics seriously. In one sense, this is hardly surprising; it simply reflects the selection bias in our project. After all, we chose economists already in a conversation with political scientists. What we have discovered, however, is the process by which these economists came to their views about politics and how these insights influenced economics as well as political science. Nearly all of the economists discussed in this book have come to more fully appreciate the importance of the agenda of the one political scientist who has won the Nobel Prize in Economic Science: Herbert Simon. By confronting the world investigated by political scientists, economists have transformed their theories and research in significant ways.

The advances in political science and economics that have resulted from the interaction of these Nobelists, other economists, and political scientists include at least the following:

1. An evolving set of assumptions about human behavior that are not as sparse as those of the neoclassical model of the individual but far more explicit than many behaviorally oriented political scientists were earlier in this century (although no more explicit than the assumptions made by Hobbes, Locke, the Federalists, and Tocqueville).

2. A more rigorous approach to values and to political and social choices.

3. A revival and transformation of the interest in institutions within both economics and political science as a result of applying economic tools to the classic questions of political science such as: what differences do institutions make in the outcomes of social interactions?

4. A stronger emphasis on doing empirical studies and rejecting theories that are not supported by evidence found in mainstream economics or in mathematical political economy.

5. A growing recognition of the importance of theoretical equilibria in predicting and explaining behavior and a simultaneous awareness of how multiple equilibria and chaotic outcomes may be a part of social life.

6. A rethinking of the relationships among the social sciences and the important contributions of each.

EXPLICIT AND RICHER MODELS OF THE INDIVIDUAL

Although the sparse but hyperrational model of the individual continues to be used in mainstream economics, extensive work in cognitive science, social psychology, and political economy has led to a recognition by many scholars that more complex assumptions about human behavior would be appropriate to many action situations. Few economists believe that humans actually behave in the myopic, but fully informed and maximizing mode characterized by homo economicus. In an open, competitive market for private goods without externalities, however, the institutional setting produces the relevant information needed to make maximizing choices, and those individuals who do not maximize profits are eventually selected out of the system. Paradoxically, within strong, competitive institutions even the interaction of dumb robots produces macrolevel behavior that strongly resembles the macrobehavior predicted for hyperrational, all-knowing individuals. Thus, the model works in this institutional setting—in the sense that aggregate behavior is predicted, and policy interventions based on this model in this environment tend to produce predicted results.

Long ago, however, Simon found that decisionmakers within organizations, such as public agencies, that do not face such stringent competition rarely know all of the alternatives available to them, do not rank even those that are known along a single value function, and use heuristics rather than maximization to decide what actions to take. Further, individuals may identify with the organizations they work in and adopt goals and objectives that are consistent with the expectations of their co-workers and supervisors. Extensive research by cognitive scientists has given us a much better understanding of the types of heuristics used by decisionmakers in a wide diversity of organizational settings. To a striking extent, Arrow, North, and Selten, among others, have appealed to developments in cognitive science and attempted to incorporate them into their own work. This is evident in North's investigation of "mental models" as a means to get at a theory of ideology and culture, Arrow's long-term interest in incomplete and asymmetric information, and Selten's experimental research on the limits of rationality.

The implications of Simon's research program for economics remain controversial, however. The debate between Goodin and Simon (this volume) highlights the prevailing tension between wanting to make a minimal change in the neoclassical model of the individual and taking the work in cognitive science more seriously. The fact that economists and political economists are increasingly incorporating models of asymmetric information, signaling, and the like into their work does not represent an embrace of bounded rationality. Such models are an advance on standard neoclassical models and may well transform the paradigm. They nonetheless retain the basic assumptions of maximizing and rationality. It is not, therefore, surprising that Simon criticizes these approaches as inadequate. On the other hand, such models complicate the simple world of neoclassical economics and provide significant new insights into political behavior and processes.

VALUES AND CHOICES

There is also the important question of what values are included in any particular person's utility function. A fundamental tenet underlying rational-choice theory is that individuals pursue a variety of ends. Sometimes those ends are focused entirely on material outcomes, such as profits. If an individual is in a setting where he or she is not able to survive without paying primary attention to such ends, it is not unreasonable to assume that in that setting he or she does exactly that. Whether under conditions of considerable uncertainty and innovation it is actually possible to maximize is indeed a major puzzle, but the utility function itself is likely to focus more specifically on profits than on other people's welfare in such highly competitive environments. Political economists have long recognized that it is possible to undertake a rational-choice analysis of a complete altruist as well as a complete hedonist. The variables affecting utility for a more socially oriented individual are derived from his or her view of how outcomes affect others. Thus, the specific variables on which utility is based are left open to the analyst. Many political economists focusing on political rather than market questions have had to broaden their assumptions about what is in individual utility functions. It is not at all unusual to see assumptions made in rigorous mathematical formulations that individuals obtain a "warm glow" from seeing their actions generate benefits for others, or that individuals adopt norms that affect which values they pursue or which actions they consider to be appropriate. All of the Nobelists discussed in this volume have made assumptions in their work that broaden the model of the individual used both in economics and in political science while retaining the rigor of specific assumptions about human behavior. Even Gary Becker, known for his efforts to extend the standard neoclassical assumptions into non-economic spheres, is currently trying to develop the concept of social capital as a means of bringing norms, values, and the origin of preferences into the neoclassical model.

Scholars are now coping with deep puzzles at the heart of political science—such as those related to achieving collective action. Theories based on assumptions of hyperrationality and narrow self-interest are not empirically supported. Nor are theories that posit individuals who always seek social instead of personal goals. Consequently, more recent theories of these political situations tend to posit individuals who have incomplete information about the types of people with whom they are interacting, about individuals who share norms of reciprocity, and about individuals who develop reputations for following norms of behavior. There is no single model of the individual that has achieved universal acceptance by political scientists and economists alike. Instead, there is growing consensus that the appropriate theoretical model of the individual is situation-dependent rather than universal. Situations need to be conceptualized as broadly as possible so as to avoid positing different assumptions for closely related processes. The usefulness of one overarching model of the individual for explaining behavior in a competitive market as well as in social dilemmas, however, has been challenged. Further, individuals may also have preferences regarding the processes by which decisions are reached—their legitimacy, for example—as well as regarding the value of outcomes.

One important consequence of the increased attention to values and to social and political choices is a more rigorous set of theories related to constitutional choices, legislatures, bureaucracies and organizational behavior, the provision of public goods, and the development of social capital than existed prior to the work of the Nobelists discussed in this volume.

THE REDISCOVERY THAT INSTITUTIONS MATTER

Reevaluation of behavioral assumptions is linked to the revival of scholarly interest in institutions. Institutions—defined as the rules of the game and the norms used by participants in pursuing objectives within a particular structure—affect what outcomes can be achieved and the strategies that can be used to achieve them. The type of institution also affects incentives and behavior and can transform the rational choices of individuals into irrational outcomes, or vice versa.

Both economists and political scientists now draw more on their classic roots. The experimental tradition among economists has led to a clear recognition that small changes in the structure of an action make dramatic changes in the efficiency and distribution of the outcomes achieved. Political scientists have been stimulated by the work of Kenneth Arrow to examine how specific institutional structures reduce the likelihood of endless cycles in legislative and electoral processes. In doing so, they have also established that particular procedural rules strongly affect which outcomes are most likely. Thus, political scientists' long-term fascination with process is now equipped with much more rigorous theories to study process, but economists have also learned that ignoring process can lead to erroneous predictions.

Interest in institutions also leads to a recognition that there is no simple connection between levels of analysis. The reductionist hope that all political and economic phenomena could be explained by a common set of assumptions at the individual level has been challenged as much as the holistic dream that culture or organizations were the primary source of behavior. The same individuals coming from a similar culture and background will produce highly efficient or equitable outcomes within one set of rules and highly inefficient or inequitable outcomes within another.

The fascination with the prisoners' dilemma game and with the Arrow impossibility theorem stems precisely from this disconnect between rationality at the individual level and irrationality at the collective level. One cannot blame outcomes in many situations on the irrationality of individual decisions. Whether brilliant or stupid, personal strategies are likely to lead to particular sets of outcomes. As Gary Miller said at our Carnegie meeting, "Some bad outcomes are robust to smartness in the same way that some good outcomes are robust to dumbness in other institutions." Further, as Herbert Simon stressed in the same discussion, the preferences of individuals are frequently influenced by the institutional arrangements in which they find themselves. "This fuzzes the line between individual and institution, which makes the problem doubly endogenous," Simon argued. Another complication is that individuals can change institutions over time in an effort to produce results closer to their preferences. Thus, collective-choice institutions themselves result from constitutional processes. And public policies made within collective-choice institutions affect the rules of everyday life that we all face. Thus, it is essential to study both individual choice and nested sets of institutional rules to understand behavior. Determining which institutional contexts produce the same results irrespective of individual characteristics is a rich research area being pursued by both political scientists and economists.

Consequently, another result of the challenge presented by these six Nobelists is a greatly expanded interest in institutions at a global, national, or local level. The first attack on a rigorous study of an institutional arrangement will frequently assume fully rational individuals and ask what they would do in this type of setting. Only when anomalous results are obtained does it make sense to start moving toward more complex settings with different assumptions about individual knowledge, preferences, and decision calculi. The study of institutions has thus broadened out from the core of economics (markets) and political science (elections) to the study of how various institutions affect the capacity of boundedly rational individuals who gain information and learn how to do better as they try to solve a variety of problems. The problems being addressed by institutional analysts have gone beyond simple market or electoral outcomes and now include a range of difficult externality problems, including pollution, conserving natural resources, and global warming.

FACTS MATTER

Work in political science and economics is now proceeding in a fashion that is closer to that of the physical and biological sciences than it was before the work of the Nobelists included in this volume. Political scientists have never been satisfied with beautiful theories that have little empirical support. Economists have never been satisfied with learning about facts without a theory to explain them. Both disciplines are now relating theories and data more closely together. The experimental economists influenced by the work of Reinhard Selten, Vernon Smith, and Charles Plott have now accrued an impressive record that strongly supports the empirical validity of price theory when applied to private goods without externalities in competitive markets. The record here is as strong as that supporting the hard sciences where they can predict single, rather than multiple, equilibria. Experimentalists in both disciplines, however, have challenged other theories as not explaining observed behavior, and they are broadening their reach to politics.

Economic historians, influenced by Douglass North and Robert Fogel, have brought statistical analysis to bear on long-term secular processes—in politics as well as economics. The work of North and, equally important, that of William Riker and Mancur Olson encouraged and compelled scholars of legislatures, parties, and movements to search for compelling evidence and tests of their provocative hypotheses and claims. And most of this empirical research came from political scientists struggling, often successfully, to synthesize theory and fact. The result was to push the theoretical program even further.

Contrary to the hopes of some economists, the core of economic theory, when applied to many political settings, does not work as well as it does when applied to highly competitive institutions, including two-party competition. The empirical study of the provision of public goods has repeatedly presented anomalies, and political economists are working hard to modify theories so as to explain these anomalies (without losing the power to explain empirical regularities that are already well explained by theory). A similar challenge has resulted from the study of ultimatum and dictator games, where the predicted theoretical results have infrequently been observed in empirical studies. A third area of considerable empirical and theoretical work relates to coalitions among small groups of individuals because of the weakness of game theory to predict observed results. In many of these efforts, political scientists are using transcripts or other forms of recording the perceptions of individuals, their goals and aspirations, their reasons for choosing initial strategies, and their processes of learning and changing behavior. As more is learned about the lack of common knowledge in some settings, theorists have devised powerful models to explain anomalous behavior by dropping the very strong assumption of common knowledge that underpins most of modern noncooperative game theory. Thus, the presence of some individuals who adopt norms of behavior contrary to those posited by a narrow, hyperrational model of the individual may induce other individuals, who could be best described by traditional models of rationality, to adopt for themselves "nonrational" strategies.

BEHAVIOR OUTSIDE EQUILIBRIA

Empirical research is essential in those areas of politics where current theory does not predict the existence of a single equilibrium. Arrow's discovery that welfare functions meeting a simple list of normatively attractive criteria could not be constructed started a deep rethinking of behavior in settings where a single equilibrium result is not likely. Earlier economic theory had presumed that the core academic challenge was to determine the centers of gravitation for an economic or social system. The scholarly task was to discover the laws that created these resting points and predict where the system would come to rest. If the "natural" resting places were not normatively attractive, one could then use the laws themselves to change the predicted equilibrium. This approach has worked extremely well in the central areas of modern economics—as Arrow himself has helped to establish—and been one of the main attractions of economic theory to many social sciences.

As Norman Schofield argues (this volume), one of the major distinctions between politics and economics is that "the conditions sufficient for the existence of a core . . . are only likely to occur in pure private good economics." This means that the study of political phenomena, where there could be an empty core, compels political economists to adopt approaches distinct from those of neoclassical economics. In many important realms of political life, current theories predict either the absence of an equilibrium or multiple equilibria. In indefinitely, repeated n-person prisoners' dilemma games, for example, the equilibria include everyone cooperating at all opportunities, everyone defecting at all opportunities, and all combinations of these two strategies. Given this array of equilibria, no useful prediction can be made using well-established tools.

Once again, rigorous consideration of political phenomena has pushed economists, political economists, and political scientists to consider the importance of institutions and to search for a parsimonious nonmaximizing model that works with what we already know about institutions.

THE RELATIONSHIPS AMONG THE SOCIAL SCIENCES

All of the economists among the Nobelists in this project began their work on politics with a similar instinct: economic theory could illuminate political processes. They were right *and* wrong. On the one hand, applying the tools of their trade to our subject matter did produce some extremely interesting insights and research programs. On the other hand, the theories, assumptions, and models that explain market behavior transport less than perfectly into political interactions. Confronting the institutions that are regularly studied by political scientists generated an awareness of the limitations of economic theory. The effort to use economic theory to account for political behavior and institutions has led to significant revisions of the neoclassical paradigm. Social choice, the theories of clubs, coalitions and constitutions, and the new institutionalism all represent significant challenges to the neoclassical view of the world. What represents an even greater challenge is the reconsideration of the standard neoclassical assumption of rationality. Outside of applications to strongly competitive environments, theories based on assumptions of hyperrationality tend to fail to predict and explain behavior. This was always part of Simon's program. Now Arrow, North, and Selten are also exploring and applying the insights of cognitive science in their own research. Becker is beginning to theorize about the role of values and preference change. Buchanan is exploring how alternative rules are placed on the agenda for collective choice rather than being just out there to be considered.

The revelation of this project was the extent to which political and other social science analysis has touched economics, but we have also been made more sensitive to the considerable influence of these Nobelists on both the normative and positive programs of political science and political economy. All six of these Nobelists have normative agendas that have significantly affected the study of politics. The commitment of Buchanan and Arrow to improving democratic institutions has animated their explorations into the institutional arrangements that strengthen or weaken democracy. The commitment of Selten and Simon to uncovering a more powerful model of human motivation and choice has led them to engage in empirical research on how individuals really act. The commitment of Becker and North to improving public policy has spurred them to develop better models of the relationship between economic and political decisions.

The essays in this volume also reveal the important influence of these Nobelists on the way political scientists go about their research. All six have reinforced and encouraged rigor, powerful theory, and a more deeply scientific approach. Each in his own way has inspired a positive research program that has, in turn, transformed what we mean by political economy and what we do as political economists and political scientists.

All six of the Nobelists visited the house of politics and found some of their own tools in need of revision. All six have enriched the house of politics, as well as the house of economics, as a result of their efforts. Political scientists and economists— as well as many other social scientists—are beginning again to take each other's work seriously. They are building theories that are powerful explanatory tools in multiple settings and rejecting theories that do not have good empirical support. Research findings from one research program are successfully applied to puzzles addressed in other programs. Social scientists from multiple disciplines are involved in the current ferment around the study of heuristics, the framing of problems, asymmetric information, presence or lack of common knowledge, multiple beliefs and valuations held by individuals, norms, and processes of institutional choice. Consequently, social scientists who pay attention to individual choices, institutions, and behavior are building a cumulative body of theories.

We expect the next century to witness a major flowering of scientific achievement across the social sciences similar to the neo-Darwinian synthesis of this past century in biology. Such progress will require all the social sciences to participate and to learn from each other. By demonstrating how much economists have gained from their interactions with political scientists while themselves contributing to political science, this book represents a modest step in this great venture.

⁓ Index ⁓

Boldface numbers refer to figures and tables.

Acción Democrática (AD), 215
AD (Acción Democrática). *See* Acción
  Democrática
Adams, John, 123
Administrative Behavior (Simon), 57–58, 71–72, 86
agency problem, 205–6
Aldrich, John, 148
Alt, James, 198, 317
Ames, Barry, 224*n*13
Amrekulov, Nurlan, 286
anchoring heuristic, 290–91
appropriateness, logic of, 72–77
Argentina, privatization in, 213, 215–16
Aristotle, 7–8, 51
Arrow, Kenneth: biographical material, 1–3; choice
  function, 176; cognitive science, 332; contingent
  contracts, 2–3; elections and political outcomes,
  323, 334; equilibrium and dynamic systems,
  51–54; game theory, 113; impossibility theorem,
  5–7, 33, 35, 263–64, 336; majority cycles, xvi;
  markets, 41–42; preferences, 12–16, 18–19,
  21–23, 41, 54–55; public choice/formal theory,
  4–5, 144; social choice and the problem of aggregation, 8, 10, 27–28*n*29; social disorder, 43, 45;
  social welfare functions, 1–2
asymmetry heuristic, 291
Auden, W. H., 75
Aumann, Robert, 41, 43
availability heuristic, 282–90
Axelrod, Robert, 37, 258, 267, 299, 306, 328

Bagehot, Walter, 125
Banerjee, Abhijit, 293
Banfield, Edward, 322
Barry, Brian, 165
Bates, Robert, 229, 284
Baumgartner, Frank, 103
Bayes, Thomas, 176
Beard, Charles, 51, 321, 328
Becker, Gary: biographical material, 155–57; discrimination, 159–60, 192; human capital,
  161–62, 177; normative v. positive approaches to
  science, 191–92; political science and, 158–59,
  162–65; pressure groups, xviii, 160–61, 192–96;
  rational choice approach, 158; social capital, 170,
  172–73, 185–87, 333; utility function, 173–75,
  177–82
behavioral approach: decision theory, 96; public
  organizations, 87–89
benefit–cost analysis, 322

Bentham, Jeremy, 128, 173–74, 321
Bentley, Arthur, 160, 321
Berezhkova, Nataliia, 290
Bernholz, Peter, 307
Bikhchandani, Sushil, 293
Black, Duncan, 5, 39, 52, 144, 323
Blount, Sally, 18
bounded rationality: appropriateness, logic of,
  73–74; distributions, non–Gaussian, 93–94;
  empirical grounding, need for, 114, 118, 329;
  evolution of the concept, xvii, 57–58, 61; formal
  theorists v. experimentalists, 68–71; information
  and limited attention, 67–68; institutions/
  organizations, 86–89, 116–17; nonlinear deci-
  sionmaking, 97; rational/public choice theory,
  61–66, 85, 90, 118; rationality, v., 92–94, **98**,
  104–7; Selten's embrace of, 254–55, 303, 306;
  term, critique and defense of, 316, 318
Boutros–Ghali, Boutros, 238
Bowen, Howard, 52, 323
Boyd, Robert, 275, 292–95
Bradshaw, Gary, 115
Brams, Steven, 143
Brazil, electoral corruption in, 209
Brehm, John, 157, 170–72
Brennan, Geoffrey, 132, 322
Bretton Woods monetary regime, 233
bribes. *See* corruption
Bromiley, Phil, 116
Brouwer, Luitzen, 33
Bryce, James, 327, 330
Buchanan, James: biographical material, 120–21;
  Calculus of Consent, The, 123, 126–28, 137–39,
  145–50, 314; collective decisions, endogeneity of
  choices, 152–53; constitutional political economy, 126, 131–34; contractarianism, 141–44;
  elections and political outcomes, 323–24; expressive reasons, voting for, 322; externalities,
  xvi–xix; generality and constitutional design, 318;
  majority rule, 144–48; methodological individualism, 127–28; pork barrel legislation, 148–50;
  public choice theory, 113; public economics,
  137–39; public goods, 129; rationality assumption, 143; rent–seeking, 153
budget, U.S.: distributions of data, 103–4; percentage changes of authority, **105**
Burger, Edwald, 253
Burks, Arthur, 36
Calculus of Consent, The (Buchanan/Tullock), 123,
  126–28, 137–39, 145–50, 314
Caldera, Rafael, 252

Calvert, Randy, 317
Canada–U.S. Free Trade Agreement, 240–41
Cantillon, Richard, 39
capital: forms of, 177–79; human (*see* human capital); interpersonal, 183–87; social (*see* social capital)
Cárdenas, Cuauhtémoc, 217
Cardoso, Fernando Henrique, 215
Carnap, Rudolf, 57
Center for Advanced Study in the Behavioral Sciences, 319
chaos, v. equilibrium, 33–36
Chile, privatization in, 213, 216
Chiluba, Frederick, 215
choice. *See* individuals; preferences
CITES (Convention on International Trade in Endangered Species). *See* Convention on International Trade in Endangered Species
Clark, John, 134
Coase, Ronald: contributor to political science, xvi; firm, theory of the, 76, 314–15; and the new institutional economics, 248; North, influence on, 197; transaction costs, 228, 249; unlimited bargaining and efficient outcomes, 325
cognition: and heuristics, 96; information and limited attention, 67–68; pattern recognition, 95; and preference formation, 19. *See also* framing heuristics; heuristic theory
cognitive science: future significance of, 315–16, 319–20; individual, models of, 332; North, work on, 197–98; rationality postulates and, xix, 70–71; Simon and rationality, 78
Coleman, James, 144, 156–57, 170–73, 177–78, 185–86, 191
collective action: choice alternatives, endogeneity of, 152–53; cost calculus for decisions, 128; necessity of, 7; prisoner's dilemma, 139–40, 145–46
Collor, Fernando, 215
communitarianism, 312
Condillac, Étienne, 39
Condorcet, Nicolas, Marquis de, 39–41, 43, 53, 55, 321
Condorcet (voters') paradox, 6, 10, 26n11
Congleton, Roger, 153, 309–10
Congress, U.S., and game theory, 264–66
conservatism, in decisionmaking, 95
constitutional political economy: American Founders and, 123–24; constitutional geometry, 310–11; contractarianism, 139–44; cost calculus for collective decisions, 128; individualism and rules of assembly, 129–31; majority rule and the generality principle, 309–10, 318; methodological individualism and constitutional choice, 127–28; and public choice theory, 121; public goods, 129; puzzles and promises of, 131–34; turn away from in the twentieth century, 124–26
contingent valuation, 322
contractarianism, 139–44
contracts: base–point bias in a two–person social, **140**; contingent, 2–3

contractualism, and institutions, 243n3
Convention on International Trade in Endangered Species (CITES), 234
Cooper, Richard, 230
corruption, 201, 207–10, 221–22, 251
Cournot, Antoine–Augustin, 306
Cox, Gary, 208
Cremer, Jacques, 268
cues and preference formation, 17–19. *See also* framing heuristics
cultural hedging, 295–97
Cyert, Richard, 71, 74, 116

Dave, Bhavna, 285–86, 288, 291, 295
Debreu, Gerard, 2, 35
decisionmaking: Buchanan, individual decision calculus, 147; choice alternatives, endogeneity of, 152–53; cognitive capacities, 94–96; information flows, 97–99; innovation, need to account for, 115; institutions and bounded rationality, 86–87, 332; nonlinear and bounded rationality, 97; rationality v. bounded rationality, 85, 92–94, 106–7; response distributions, hypotheses and empirical testing, 99–106. *See also* cognition; individuals; preferences
Deering, Bill, 103
democracy: aggregating preferences and social welfare, 4–8, 23–25; Hobbes on, 131. *See also* elections; voting
Demsetz, Harold, 224n17
Dennett, Daniel, 33
Descartes, René, 39
Deutsch, Karl, 71
developing countries: corruption in, 207–10, 221–22; democracy and economic development, 323; institutional change, North's theory of, 200–201, 222, 251; political supporters, need to reward, 206–7; privatization in, 212–23. *See also* economic development
development, economic. *See* economic development
Diatlova, Marina, 283
Director, Aaron, 190
discrimination, Becker on, 159–60, 163, 192
Djilas, Milovan, 125–26
Dokuchaeva, A., 285–86
Douglass, Mary, 191
Downs, Anthony, xvi, 63, 113, 144, 314, 323
Dunbar, Kevin, 320
Dusenberry, James, 191
Duverger, Maurice, 328

Easterbrook, Frank, 324
economic development: import–substitution industrialization, 201; politicians, motives to support, 204–6. *See also* developing countries
economic history, use of by North, 197

economic theory: neoclassical (*see* neoclassical economic theory); new economic institutionalism (*see* new institutionalism)

economics: experimental, 114, 335; innovation, need to account for in decision making, 115; organizations, need to account for, 116–17; political science, contributions from, 331–37; political science, influence of, 316–17; political science, lessons for, 321–25, 327–28; political science, limits of contributions to, 328–29; preferences, model relating choice to, **20**; public, 137–39; rationality, reluctance to admit limits of, 68–70; strength of, 314

Edgeworth, F. Y., 183

Edwards, Ward, 95

efficient market thesis, 90–92

elections: belief convergence and, 39–42; bounded rationality, 89; corruption, 207–10; cumulative negative changes in margins, **104**; mobilization of the vote and supply of public goods, 206; output distributions, 102–3; pork barrel legislation, 149–50; questions regarding, 323–25; results and Gaussian distributions, 91–92; rulership for North, 203–4; voting systems and outcomes, 323–24. *See also* democracy; voting

Elster, Jon, 78, 180

empirical research: field work and formal theory, advantages of combining, 298–99; need for, xviii–xix, 335–36; Selten on human behavior, 254; Simon on the need for, 114, 118–19

enforcement: in international regimes, 234–35, 249–50; as transaction cost, 247–49

entrepreneurs, compared to rulers, 202–4

equilibrium: belief convergence and, 39–42; dynamic systems and, 51–54; points (Nash), 260–61, 263; political life and, 336; selection, Harsanyi/Selten collaboration, 254; social disorder and, 42–45; social mathematics, possibility of in, 33–36; society, views of and, 36–38; temporality and, 267–68. *See also* subgame perfection

Estonia, linguistic identity in, 285, 287–89, 290–91

ethnography, 274–75

Eucken, Walter, 131

European Union, 238, 240–41

evolutionary game theory: described, 273–74; Selten and human behavior, 254–55, 304

evolutionary theory: biases, 292–93; cultural hedging, 295–97; frequency-dependent bias, 294–95; game theorists, attraction for, 291–92; indirect/runaway/herding bias, 293–94

executives: privatization in developing countries, 212–22; privatization and interests of, **213–14**

experimental research: in economics, 114, 335; preferences regarding principles of justice, 22–23

externalities, xvi–xix, 146, 322

Fama, Eugene, 91

Fechner, G. T., 90

federalism, 311–12

Figueiredo, Rui de, 284

Filmer, Robert, 38

fiscal illusion, 121, 138–39

Fogel, Robert, 197, 335

Ford Foundation, 319

Foucault, Michel, 75

framing heuristics, 17–18, 24–25, 69–70, 74, 77, 96. *See also* cognition; selective attention

Franco, Francisco, 215

free riding: global climate change, 239; North and ideology, 236–37

frequency-dependent evolutionary bias, 294–95

Friedman, Milton, 155, 190

Frohlich, Norman, 54–55

Fujimori, Alberto, 215

Fukuyama, Francis, 157, 170–72, 184, 186

Galileo, 36

game theory: development of, xvii–xviii, 256–57; equilibrium selection (*see* equilibrium); evolutionary (*see* evolutionary game theory); field research and, 298–99; international relations and, 306–7; noncooperative (*see* noncooperative game theory); normative (*see* normative game theory); outcomes, relative frequency of, **19**; political institutions and, 263–64; prisoner's dilemma, 139–40, 145–46, 334; Selten, contribution to, 268–69; Simon on, 113–14; temporality and, 267–68; the ultimatum game, **261**; uncertainty, 280–81. *See also* equilibrium; strategic interaction

garbage can theory of organizational choice, 71

GATT (General Agreement on Tariffs and Trade. *See* General Agreement on Tariffs and Trade

Gauss, Johann, 258

Gauthier, David, 38, 141

Geddes, Barbara, 251

General Agreement on Tariffs and Trade (GATT), 233–34, 238, 240–41

generality principle, and constitutional design, 309–10, 318

German School of Experimental Economics, 253

Giere, Ronald, 19

global climate change, 239–40

Gödel, Kurt, 35, 45

Gödel–Turing theorem, 33–34

Goldstein, Judith, 229

González, Felipe, 215–16

Goodin, Robert, xvi, 92, 332

Gosnell, Harold, 57

Gould, Stephen Jay, 44

Grasshoff, Gerd, 320

Gray, John, 38

Green, Donald, 5

Greif, Avner, 46*n*7

Habermas, Jurgen, 29*n*49
Haggard, Stephan, 229
Hallik, Klara, 289
Hamilton, Alexander, 123–25, 129–30, 186
Hammerstein, Peter, 273–74, 292, 298
Hansen, Wendy, 163, 194
Hardin, Russell, 37, 61, 190–91
Harsanyi, John, 253–54, 257, 280–81
Hayek, Friedrich von, 33, 38, 42, 44, 51, 316
hedging, cultural, 295–97
Heiner, Ronald, 315
herding evolutionary bias, 293–94
Herring, Pendleton, 113
heuristic theory: anchoring, 290–91; asymmetry,
    291; availability, 283–90; critique of normative
    game theory, relationship to, 282–83. *See also*
    cognition; framing heuristics
Heyne, Paul, 314
Hicks, John, 45
Hilbert, David, 35
Hinich, Melvin, 90
Hirshleifer, David, 293
Hobbes, Thomas, 36–38, 130–31, 140–41, 143, 184
Hollis, Martin, 79*n*7
Holmes, Frederic, 320, 329
Hotelling, Harold, 1, 52, 323, 328
human capital: Becker on, 156, 161–63; distin-
    guished from other forms of capital, 177–
    79; social capital and, 173
Hutchins, Ed, 316

identity choice: cultural hedging, 295–97; Russian
    speakers in non–Russian republics,
    275–77, 279–80, 283–89, 290–91; tipping game,
    analysis through, 277–80, 289–90
ideology: defined by North, 236; free riders and
    North, 236–37; importance of, 252;
    international regimes and, 230–31, 237; knowl-
    edge and, 241–42; role of belief systems, 250–51;
    transgovernmental networks and, 239–41
import–substitution industrialization (ISI), 201
impossibility theorem, Arrow's, 5–7, 33, 35, 263–64,
    336
incrementalism, 88–89
indirect evolutionary bias, 293–94
individuals: aggregating choices, problem of, 7–8;
    behavior, 321; choice and social
    welfare, 4–7; indeterminate preferences, likeli-
    hood of, 19–21; methodological
    individualism, 127–28; models of, 332–33; as
    unit of analysis, xv. *See also*
    decisionmaking; preferences
institutions: bounded rationality and, 86–87; con-
    tractarianism, 139–44; contractualism, 243*n*3;
    defined by North, 228–29; efficiency of, 93; equi-
    libria, defined as, 34; game theory and, 263–66;
    importance of, xviii, 334–35; individual prefer-

ences and, 8–10, 23–25; information flows,
    97–99; non–Gaussian distributions, 93–94; prop-
    erty rights and, 200; transaction costs and, 230,
    315. *See also* organizational behavior
interest groups, Becker on, xviii, 160–63, 192–96
interests, and consumptions, 176
Intergovernmental Panel on Climate Change
    (IPCC), 239, 241
international organizations. *See* international
    regimes
international political economy: international
    regimes (*see* international regimes); North and,
    229–31; transgovernmental networks (*see* trans-
    governmental networks). *See also* world politics
international regimes: emergence and problems of,
    231–33; ideology and, 237, 242–43; transaction
    costs in, 233–36, 242–43; transgovernmental net-
    works (*see* transgovernmental networks)
international relations and game theory, 306–7
International Society for the New Institutional Eco-
    nomics, 197–98
interpersonal capital: enabling and constraining,
    185–87; trust, 183–85
IPCC (Intergovernmental Panel on Climate
    Change). *See* Intergovernmental Panel on
    Climate Change
ISI (import-substitution industrialization). *See*
    import–substitution industrialization

Jay, John, 123
Jefferson, Thomas, 40, 123
Johnson, Samuel, 321
Jones, Bryan, xix, 95

Kahneman, Daniel: experimental research, xix, 54,
    69, 275, 280, 282–83, 288, 290–93;
    framing heuristics, 19; prospect theory, 16–17, 96
Kaldor, Nicholas, 45
Kalisch, Gerhard, 254, 306
Kaminski, Antoni, 134
Kaunda, Kenneth, 215
Kawabata, Yasunari, 176
Kazakhstan, linguistic identity in, 285–88, 291, 294
Kent, James, 123
Keohane, Robert, international institutions and
    ideology, 249–51
Kerwin, Jerry, 112
Keynes, John Maynard, 43–44, 191
Knight, Frank, 120, 190
Kramer, Gerald, 324
Krebs, Hans, 320, 329
Kuchma, Leonid, 289–90
Kulkarni, Deepak, 320

Labov, William, 293
Lange, Dorothea, 197

Langley, Pat, 115
Laplace, Pierre–Simon, 34
Larrick, Richard, 18
Laslett, Peter, 38
Lasswell, Harold, 57, 125
Lazarsfeld, Paul, 113, 327
Leff, Nathaniel, 223*n*3
legislative politics: explanations through game
    theory, 263–66; pork barrel, 148–50;
    privatization and, 219–21. *See also* elections;
    majority rule
Levi, Margaret, 223*n*1, 229, 247, 317
Lindblom, Charles, 71
Lippmann, Walter, 133
Locke, John, 38, 141, 143–44, 147
logic of appropriateness, 72–77, 118
Lorenz, Edward, 52
Loury, Glenn, 191
Loveman, Brian, 134
Lowi, Theodore, 80*n*15
Luce, Duncan, 256, 267
Lusinchi, Jaime, 215

Machiavelli, Niccolo, 327
McKelvey, Richard, 53, 264, 323, 324
MacPherson, Crawford B., 36
Madison, James, 40–41, 123, 125, 143, 186
majority rule: Buchanan on, 144–47; constraints on
    outcomes through constitutional
    geometry, 310–11; external costs of, **145**; game
    theory, institutions and explanations through,
    265–66; game theory, origins of explanations
    through, 263–64; generality principle, 309–10,
    318; political parties and, 147–48; pork barrel
    legislation, 148–50; strategic explanations,
    264–65
Malthus, Thomas, 39
managers, North's comparison of firm and political,
    203–4
Mandeville, Bernard, 39
Mantel, Rolf, 35
March, James, 61, 71, 73–75, 116, 281–82
Margolis, Howard, 95
Markov, Andrey, 258
Marshall, Bill, 249
Marx, Karl, 51, 174, 321
Masanov, Nurbulat, 286
May, Kenneth, 16, 18, 147
May, Michael, 320
May, Samuel, 57
measurement, as transaction cost, 247–49
Menem, Carlos, 214–15
Merriam, Charles, 57, 113
methodology: aggregation, problem of measuring,
    7–8; discovery and verification, 326–30; emer-
    gence of formal theory, 4–5; ethnography,
    274–75; hierarchy of models, **43**; methodological

individualism, 127–28, 130; new trends in social
    science, 319–20; Selten's dualist, 273–74,
    298–99, 303–6
Mexico, privatization in, 213, 216–17
Michael, Robert, 174
Miller, Gary, xvi, 334
Miller, Merton, 90
Miller, Nicholas, 11
Milnor, John, 34, 254, 306
mimicking behavior, 96
Mitchell, William, 162
Mitzkewitz, Michael, 254
models: "billiard–ball" of world politics, 237–38;
    garbage can of organizational behavior, 71;
    hierarchy of, **43**
money in politics, 325
Morgenstern, Oskar, 5, 36, 52, 113, 260–62
Morgenthau, Hans, 307
Morrow, James, 258
Morse, Marston, 34
Mueller, Dennis, 26*n*7, 144
Mulligan, Casey, 193–94
Munger, Michael, 90, 162

Nachbar, John, 41, 45
NAFTA (North American Free Trade Agreement).
    See North American Free Trade Agreement
Nagel, Thomas, 182
Nardulli, Peter, 103
Nash equilibria, 37, 44, 260–61, 263, 298
Nash, John, 44, 253, 254, 257, 260, 306
neoclassical economic theory: assumptions and dis-
    satisfaction, xv; limitations of, xviii, 228, 314–16,
    328–29; modification by North, 197; time and,
    316; value bias of, 117
Nering, Evar, 254, 306
new institutionalism: Coase on the firm, 76; institu-
    tions and majority rule, 264–66; logic
    of appropriateness, 72–77; origins, 71, 197, 264;
    polity and the, 248–49; Selten's contribution to,
    257; strategic perspectives and, 262
Newcomb, Simon, 196
Newell, Allen, 58, 90
Newton, Isaac, 34, 39, 42
Nicklass, Alexander, 279
noncooperative game theory: development of,
    256–57, 261–62; politics and, 269; Selten's
    contribution to, 254
normative game theory: critique of, 281–83; heuris-
    tic theory and, 283–91; Selten and rational
    behavior, 254–55
North American Tree Trade Agreement (NAFTA),
    238
North, Douglass: biographical material, 197–98,
    228–29; bounded rationality, 318; cognitive sci-
    ence, 332; equilibrium and institutions, 34; ideol-
    ogy, xix, 230–31, 236–37, 241–42, 250–51;

North, Douglass: biographical material, (*cont:*) institutions and institutional change, 200–201, 209, 228; international political economy, 229–31; neoclassical economics, criticism of, 228; rulers and entrepreneurs, theory of, 202–4; the state, 229, 231–33; statistical analysis, 335; transaction costs, xvii, xix, 222, 228, 230, 242

Nozick, Robert, 37–38, 141

Nye, Joseph, 239

Obolonsky, Alexander, 134

oligopoly games, 253

Olowu, Dele, 134

Olsen, Johan, 61, 71, 73–75

Olson, Mancur, xvi, 129, 144, 236, 314, 335

Oppenheimer, Joe, 54–55

opportunism: in the absence of common values, 241; global climate change and, 239; international regimes and, 235, 240–41

organizational behavior: economics, need to account for in, 116–17; rationality, limits of, 87–89. *See also* institutions

organizational theory: garbage can model, 71; logic of appropriateness, 74–75

Ostrom, Elinor, 132, 273, 317

Ostrom, Vincent, 139, 152

ownership, state, 201, 210–12, 251. *See also* privatization

Padgett, John, 94

Paine, Thomas, 40

Panhellenic Socialist Movement (PASOK), 215

Papandreou, Andreas, 215

Pareto optimality: majority rule and, **10**; outcomes and, **11**; principle of, 9–10

Pareto, Vilfredo, 12

Parsons, Talcott, 155

Partido Justicialista (PJ), 215

Partido Revolucionario Institucional (PRI), 212, 216–17

Partido Socialista de Obrero Español (PSOE), 216

PASOK (Panhellenic Socialist Movement). *See* Panhellenic Socialist Movement

pattern recognition, 95

Peltzman, Sam, 193

Penrose, Roger, 33–34, 45

Perlmutter, Amos, 307

Petersen, Roger, 279

Pettai, Vello, 287, 289

Piketty, Thomas, 64

Pinochet, Augusto, 215–16

PJ (Partido Justicialista). *See* Partido Justicialista

Plato, 4

Plott, Charles, 16, 87, 114, 335

Poincaré, Henri, 34, 42

political parties, 147–48

political science: Becker's lack of impact on, 158–59; contributions from Becker, 162–63; contributions from economics, 321–25, 327–28, 331–37; contributions from economics, limitations of, 328–29; emergence of formal theory, 4–5; future directions, 329–30; influence on economics, 316–17; innovation, study of, 115; learning from Becker, reasons for not, 163–65; methodology, traditional, 326–27; public economics and, 137–39; social choice theory and, 7; what should have been learned from Becker, 159–62

politicians: corruption and, 206–10, 221–22; dictators, length of term in office, 224*n*12; public goods and citizen support, 204–6; state ownership and privatization, 206–7, 210–12. *See also* executives

politics: defined, 7; society, views of and, 36–38

Politics by Principle, Not Interest (Buchanan/Congleton), 309–10

Pool, Jonathan, 299*n*3

Pope, Alexander, 323

Popper, Karl, 33, 42–44, 51, 74, 326

pork barrel legislation: logic of, 148–50; porcine incentive of local agents, **149**. *See also* elections; legislative politics

preferences: Arrow on, 54–55; Becker, capital and utility functions, 179–82; belief convergence and, 39–42; choices and traditional economics model, **20**; cognitive processes and the formation of, 17–19; common political and economic, 321–25; context-dependent, 16–17; expanding the domain of, 12–14; generating different through cues, **21**; indeterminacy, likelihood of, 19–21; ordinal voting and, 10–12; rational v. boundedly rational decisionmakers, 106; social disorder and, 42–45; social welfare and satisfying individual, 4, 8–10, 23–25; society, views of and, 36–38; universal set, problems identifying the, 15–16, 21–23. *See also* decisionmaking; individual choice

pressure groups, Becker on, xviii, 160–61, 162–63, 192–96

PRI (Partido Revolucionario Institucional). *See* Partido Revolucionario Institucional

Prigogine, Ilya, 42

prisoner's dilemma, 139–40, 145–46, 334

privatization: in developing countries, 212–23; executive's interests and, **213–14**; ideology and, 252; incumbents v. newcomers, 221–22; political support, mobilization of and, 210–12; presidential interest and legislative support, **220**; property rights and enforcement, 251–52; shared party affiliation and, **218–19**. *See also* state ownership

property rights: economic development and, 200; international political economy and, 229; rulers and entrepreneurs, North's theory of, 202–3

PSOE (Partido Socialista de Obrero Español). *See* Partido Socialista de Obrero Español

psychophysics, experimental, 94–95

public choice theory: bounded rationality and, 85, 89–90; constitutional political economy and, 121; political science, contributions to, 327–28; political science, limitation of contributions to, 328–29; public economics, Buchanan's interest in, 137–39; Simon on, 113. *See also* rational choice theory; social choice theory
public goods, 129, 204–6
Publius Syrus, 13
Putnam, Robert, 157, 170–73, 178, 184–86

Quattrone, George, 16

Rahn, Wendy, 157, 170–72
Raiffa, Howard, 256, 267
Rashevsky, Nicolas, 57
rational choice theory: Becker, contributions by, 158; bounded rationality and, 61–66; formal theorists v. experimentalists, 68–71; meta–rationality, 132; origins within political science, 264; temporality and, 267–68; utility and values, 332–33. *See also* game theory; public choice theory; social choice theory
rationality: assumptions by Buchanan, 143; bounded (*see* bounded rationality); cognitive psychology, altered by, 78; cognitive science and (*see* cognitive science); economic, 63–64; efficient market thesis, 90–92; full, 303; individuals as situation dependent, 333; logic of appropriateness, 72–77; naive, 254, 305–6; normative game theory, critique of, 281–83; normative ideal, choice, and framing, 77–78; organizational behavior and, 87–89; organizational sociology, altered by, 78; in public choice theory, 89–90; public choice v. bounded, 85; realms of, 75; roles of, 75–76; situated logics, 74–75; social relations and, 76–77. *See also* public choice theory; rational choice theory; social choice theory
Raun, Toivo, 300n4
Rawlings, Jerry, 215
Rawls, John, 13, 15, 22, 38, 141, 143–44
reciprocity, in international regimes, 234, 250
regimes, international. *See* international regimes
rent–seeking, 153
reputation, in international regimes, 234–35, 240–41, 250
resource allocation, 322–23
revenue: maximization by rulers, 202–4; regimes and taxation, 223n1
Richerson, Peter, 275, 292–95
Ridley, Clarence, 57, 89
Riker, William, 90, 106, 139, 144, 324, 335
risk, rational behavior and incrementalism, 106
Roeder, Philip, 134
Rogowski, Ronald, 192–96, 229
Romer, Thomas, 265–66

Rosenthal, Howard, 265–66
Rousseau, Jean–Jacques, 141, 144, 236
Rubinstein, Ariel, 266
Ruggie, John, 229
rulers: compared to entrepreneurs, 202–4. *See also* executives; politicians
Russian speakers: identity problem in non–Russian republics, 275–80, 283–91, 295–97; linguistic tipping game, **279**
Ryle, Gilbert, 75

Saari, Donald, 35
Sadrieh, Karim, 305
Salinas, Carlos, 215, 217
Samuelson, Paul, 51, 155, 268
Sandel, Michael, 312
Sargent, Thomas, 114, 195
satisficing, 61–71
Sauermann, Heinz, 253, 305–6
Sawyer, Amos, 134
Scarf, Herbert, 35, 306
Schama, Simon, 40
Schelling, Thomas, 261, 275, 277–78, 289
Schofield, Norman, 51–54, 264, 317, 324, 336
Schultz, Theodore, 177
Schumpeter, Joseph, 33, 43–44, 51, 155, 190, 323
Schutz, Alfred, 75
science, international networks and transaction costs, 239–40
Schwartz, Thomas, 152–53
selective attention, 95, 115. *See also* framing heuristics
Selten, Reinhard: backward induction, xvii–xviii; biographical material, 253–55, 257–58; cognitive science, 332; experimental economics, 114, 335; methodological dualism, 273–75, 291–92, 298–99, 303–6; noncooperative game theory, 261; political science, contributions to, 257–59, 269, 306–7; subgame perfection, 263, 266; as theorist and empiricist, 268
Sen, Amartya, 13, 26n12, 29n45
Sepp, Nina, 284, 287
Shapiro, Ian, 5
Shaw, Cliff, 58
Shepsle, Kenneth, 317, 324
Shliminov, L., 287
Shorter, Richard, 95
Shultz, R. W., 57
Simon, Herbert: biographical material, 57–58, 331; bounded rationality, xvii, 61–72, 112–13; cognitive discovery process, modelling of, 320; decisionmakers and bounded rationality, 86–87, 94, 107, 332; game theory, 113–14, 281–82; heuristics, 96; institutions, 334; intellectual progeny, **72**; logic of appropriateness, 72–77; measurement products of municipal service agencies, 89; political science, contributions to, 60–61, 71–72;

Simon, Herbert: biographical material, (*cont:*) public choice, 113, 118; rationality, xix, 78, 315–16; Selten and bounded rationality, 254–55, 303, 306

Simons, Henry, 57, 112

Slaughter, Anne–Marie, 239, 241

Slovic, Paul, 54

Smale, Stephen, 34, 42

Smith, Adam, 39–40, 173, 322

Smith, John Maynard, 292

Smith, Vernon, 114, 335

Smithburg, Don, 58

social capital: Becker's utility function and, 174–75, 333; conceptions of, 170–73, 191; distinguished from other forms of capital, 177–79; human capital and, 173; preferences and Becker's inclusion in his utility function, 180–83

Social Choice and Individual Values (Arrow), 4–7, 10, 43

social choice theory: Arrow's early interest in, 1; defining, 26n12; impossibility theorem, 5–7; indeterminate preferences, likelihood of, 19–21; political science and, 7; preferences (*see* preferences). *See also* public choice theory; rational choice theory

social relations, contracting and the logic of appropriateness, 76–77

Social Science Research Council, 327

social welfare functions, 1–2

society, views of, 36–38

Solow, Robert, 52

Sonnenschein, Hugo, 35

Spain, privatization in, 214–15

Sproule–Jones, Mark, 134

state ownership, 201, 210–12, 251. *See also* privatization

state, the: Buchanan on, 121; defined by North, 231; developing countries and reward of supporters, 206–7; international regimes and, 231–33; North on, 229; property rights and, 200

Stearns, Maxwell, 324

Stegner, Wallace, 51

Stevens, S. S., 90, 94–95, 97

Stigler, George, 156, 174, 325

stock market performance, **100–103**

Stockman, David, 148

Stouffer, Samual, 327

strategic interaction: extensive form, 259–61; normal form, 260–62; subgame perfection, 262–63. *See also* game theory

Suárez, Adolfo, 215

subgame perfection, xvii–xviii, 253, 262–63, 266, 305

Sugden, Robert, 37

Swidler, Anne, 276, 297

taxation, 194–95, 202–4, 223n1

Taylor, Alan, 143

Taylor, Michael, 37

Taylor, Paul, 197

Taylor, Shelley, 282

Thomas, Robert, 200, 231

Thompson, Victor, 58

Tiebout, Charles, 126

Tietz, Reinhard, 305–6

Tilly, Charles, 231

time, necessity of understanding, 316

tipping model: cultural hedging and, 297; linguistic identity and, 277–80, 289–90, 295; Russian speakers' children and schools, **279**

Tobin, James, 75

Tocqueville, Alexis de, 123, 125, 132–33, 327, 330

transaction costs: as analytical approach, xvii, xix, 247–49; in developing countries, 222; ideology and, 237, 242–43; institutional analysis and, 228, 230, 315; in international regimes, 233–36; international scientific networks and, 239–40; rational v. boundedly rational decisionmakers, 105

transgovernmental networks: bureaucratic and legal professionalism, 240–41; ideology and knowledge, 241–42; in international rule–making, 238–39; science as an example, 239–40

True, James, 89, 103

trust, and interpersonal capital, 183–85

Tsymbaliuk, V., 284

Tullock, Gordon: bureaucracy and neoclassical economic theory, 126; coauthor, *The Calculus of Consent*, 123, 127–28, 137, 144, 309, 314; elections and political outcomes, 323; philosophical differences with Buchanan, 152; rent–seeking, 153

Turgot, Anne–Robert–Jacques, 39

Turing, Alan, 35–36

Tversky, Amos: experimental research, 54, 69, 275, 280, 282–83, 288, 290–93; framing heuristics, 19; prospect theory, 16–17, 96

UCD (Unión del Centro Democrático). *See* Unión del Centro Democrático

Uhlich, Gerald, 254

Ulam, Stanislaw, 36

uncertainty: in game theory, 280–81; human interaction and, 315

Unión del Centro Democrático (UCD), 215–16

UNIP (United National Independence Party). *See* United National Independence Party

United National Independence Party (UNIP), 215

United Nations, 238–39

Uruguay, state–owned enterprises in, 210

utility functions: Becker's conception of, 173–75; capital in Becker's conception of, 177–79; instant v. reasoned, 183; interests, consumptions, and welfare, 176; momentary v. lifetime, 180–83; values and choices, 332–33